ANOTHER SUCH VICTORY

DATE DUE

DEC 1 5 2006	
FEB 1 8 2010	

D1211279

ANOTHER SUCH VICTORY

President Truman and the Cold War,
1945–1953

ARNOLD A. OFFNER

Stanford University Press, Stanford, California

Stanford University Press, Stanford, California

© 2002 by the Board of Trustees of the Leland Stanford Junior University
Printed in the United States of America on acid-free, archival-quality paper.

Cover photograph of Harry S. Truman: National Park Service Photograph—Abbie Rowe,
courtesy of the Harry S. Truman Library. Cover photograph of the atomic explosion over
Nagasaki: photo by U.S. Army Air Corps, courtesy of the Harry S. Truman Library.

Library of Congress Cataloging-in-Publication Data

Offner, Arnold A.
    Another such victory: President Truman and the Cold War, 1945–1953 / Arnold A.
    Offner.
        p. cm. — (Stanford nuclear age series)
    Includes bibliographical references and index.
    ISBN 0-8047-4254-5
    ISBN 0-8047-4774-1
        1. Truman, Harry S., 1884–1972.   2. United States—Foreign relations—
1945–1953.   3. Cold War.   4. United States—Politics and government—1945–
1953.   I. Title.   II. Series.

E813.036 2002
973.918′092—dc21   2001049130

Typeset by G & S Typesetters, Inc., in 10/12.5 Times

Original Printing 2002

Last figure below indicates year of this printing:
11   10   09   08   07   06   05   04   03   02

For Ellen, with love

Contents

Preface

At the start of the twenty-first century, President Harry S. Truman's reputation stands high. This is especially true regarding his stewardship of foreign policy although, ironically, he entered the Oval Office in 1945 untutored in world affairs. Moreover, during his last year in the White House the Republicans accused his administration of having surrendered fifteen countries and 500 million people to Communism and of having sent twenty thousand Americans to their "burial ground" in Korea. Near the end of his term, Truman's public "favorable" rating had plummeted to 23 percent.[1]

Within a decade, however, historians rated Truman a "near great" president, crediting his administration with reconstructing Western Europe and Japan, resisting Soviet or Communist aggression from Greece to Korea, and forging collective security through the North Atlantic Treaty Organization (NATO). In the 1970s the "plain speaking" Truman became a hero in popular culture. In 1986 Britain's Roy Jenkins hailed Truman as a "backwoods politician who became a world statesman." Recently, biographers have depicted him as the allegory of American life, an ordinary man whose extraordinary character led him to triumph over adversity from childhood through the presidency. Some writers, such as David McCullough, have even posited a symbiotic relationship between "His Odyssey" from Independence to the White House and America's rise to triumphant superpower status. Melvyn Leffler, in his prize-winning *A Preponderance of Power,* has judged Truman to have been neither a naif nor an idealist but a realist who understood the uses of power, and whose administration, despite serious, costly errors, prudently preserved America's national security against real or perceived Soviet threats. And for the last quarter of a century, nearly every Democratic or Republican candidate for president has claimed to be a latter-day Truman.[2]

Collapse of the Soviet Union and Europe's other Communist states, whose archives have confirmed Truman's belief in 1945 that their regimes governed largely by "clubs, pistols and concentration camps," has further raised the former president's standing. This has encouraged John Lewis Gaddis and other historians to focus on Stalin's murderous domestic rule as the key determinant of Soviet foreign policy and the Cold War. As Gaddis has contended, Stalin was heir to Ivan the Terrible and Peter the Great, as well as to Karl Marx and V. I. Lenin. The Soviet leader was responsible for more state-sanctioned murders than Adolf Hitler and treated world politics as an extension of domestic politics: a zero-sum game in which his gaining security meant depriving all others of it. For Gaddis and others, that is basically the answer to the question of who caused the Cold War.[3]

But as Walter LaFeber has said, to dismiss Stalin's policies as the work of a paranoid is to greatly oversimplify the complex origins of the Cold War. Indeed, recent revelations from many sources—including Soviet, German, Eastern European, Chinese, and Korean archives, published government documents, memoirs, and oral histories—have provided an extremely complex picture of relations between and among nations and the interplay between foreign and domestic policies and ideology and geopolitical issues during the formative Cold War years of 1945–1953. Recent scholarship has put forward new information, insights, and lines of argument, but, as Leffler has pointed out, the conclusions that have emerged are highly diverse and no "single master narrative" suffices to explain the Cold War.[4]

Further, despite recent emphasis on Stalin as one who combined the worst traits of tsarist imperialism and Communist ideology, historians drawing on newly available materials seem to be of the preponderant view that the Soviet leader pursued a cautious but brutal realpolitik in world affairs. He aimed to restore Russia's 1941 boundaries, establish a sphere of influence in border states, provide security against a recovered Germany or Japan or hostile capitalist states, and gain compensation—notably German reparations—for the ravages of war. Stalin calculated forces, put Soviet state interests ahead of Marxist-Leninist ideology, recognized the superior industrial and military power of the United States, and pursued pragmatic or opportunistic policies in critical areas such as Germany, China, and Korea.[5]

There is no evidence that Stalin intended to march his Red Army westward beyond its assigned European occupation zones. He did not intend to attack Iran or Turkey, and he afforded little support to Communist revolution in Greece and China. He also seriously miscalculated when he let Kim Il Sung persuade him that North Korea could win a swift victory over South Korea before the U.S. could or would intervene.

So too have new sources and new assessments provided vital insights into the foreign policy of Mao Zedong and his Chinese Communist Party (CCP). As historian Michael Hunt has shown, Mao was a Chinese populist and patriot bent on throwing off foreign domination and imperial control of his nation and restoring it—the Middle Kingdom—to its rightful place in Asia and the world. From the start of his revolution in the 1920s until the 1940s, he pursued pragmatic alliances at home and abroad, and he was prepared to accept U.S. assistance consistent with his principles. He welcomed both the first official American visitors, the "Dixie Mission," to his headquarters in 1944 and the mediating mission of General George C. Marshall in 1946. Mao felt betrayed by Marshall's failure to effect the coalition government to which the CCP had agreed, and by U.S. military support for Jiang Jieshi's Guomindang (GMD) regime to wage civil war against the CCP.[6]

Still, Mao was amenable in 1949 to relations with the U.S. provided it broke relations with the GMD and accepted the CCP revolution. But Truman refused to deal with the emergent People's Republic of China (PRC) and supported the GMD's counterrevolutionary war from its new base on Taiwan. This only hastened Mao's seeking an alliance with the USSR, but the Chinese leader proved far less subservient than Stalin expected and Truman presumed. In fact, the Sino-Soviet treaty of 1950 forced Stalin to divest his recently regained imperial port and railroad concessions in Manchuria, and limited the two nations' defensive agreement to matters of mutual interest, thus freeing the PRC from the need to take part in any American-Soviet conflict in Europe.[7]

It is also evident from new documents that Mao would have preferred to focus on domestic reconstruction rather than enter the Korean War in 1950. But the U.S. decision to permit General Douglas MacArthur's forces to cross the 38th parallel and march unconstrained toward the PRC border posed too great a threat. Nonetheless, newly available Russian documents indicate that even as late as October 2, 1950, Mao, who faced strong Politburo opposition to China's entering the war, cabled Stalin that the PRC lacked the necessary troops and equipment to fight. But goaded by Stalin and fearful that opponents at home and abroad would be "swollen with arrogance" if enemy troops reached the Yalu, Mao committed the PRC to a war that, for many reasons, would have dire consequences for the Chinese, American, and Korean people. Still, it is clear that prior to October 1950 the CCP leadership had never shown the intention to use military force to conspire with the Kremlin to upset the status quo in Asia or drive the U.S. from the area.[8]

Thus the time seems propitious, given our increased knowledge of Soviet,

European, Chinese, and Korean policies, to reconsider President Truman's role in the Cold War. As Thomas G. Paterson has written, the president stands at the pinnacle of the diplomatic and military establishment, he has great capacity to set the foreign policy agenda and to mold public opinion, and his importance—especially in Truman's case—cannot be denied. Contrary to prevailing views, however, I believe that Truman's policy making was shaped by his parochial and nationalistic heritage. This was reflected in his uncritical belief in the superiority of American values and political-economic interests, his conviction that the Soviet Union and Communism were the root cause of international strife, and his inability to comprehend Asian politics and nationalism. Truman's parochialism also caused him to disregard contrary views, to engage in simplistic analogizing, to show little ability to comprehend the basis for other nations' policies, and to demonize those leaders or nations who would not bend to the will of the U.S. Consequently, his foreign policy leadership intensified Soviet-American conflict, hastened division of Europe, and brought tragic intervention in Asian civil wars and a generation of Sino-American enmity.[9]

In short, Truman lacked the qualities of the creative or great leader who, as James MacGregor Burns has written, must broaden the environment in which he and his citizenry operate and widen the channels in which choices are made and events flow. Truman, to the contrary, narrowed Americans' perception of the world political environment and the channels for policy choices, and created a rigid framework in which the United States waged long-term, extremely costly global Cold War. Indeed, before we celebrate America's victory in this contest, we might recall that after King Pyrrhus' Greek forces defeated the Romans at the battle of Asculum in 280 B.C., he reflected that "another such victory, and we are undone."[10]

Acknowledgments

I have worked on this book for a long time and have relied on many institutions and, above all, individuals who have facilitated my work and sustained and encouraged me in all of my scholarly endeavors. I am pleased to acknowledge them and to offer public thanks to all who have so generously afforded me their wise counsel, support, and friendship.

At the Harry S. Truman Library in Independence, Missouri, archivists Dennis Bilger, Harry Clark, Jr., Philip Lagerquist, and Erwin Mueller were extremely helpful in putting the voluminous records in their charge at my disposal. Similarly, Pauline Testerman, audiovisual archivist at the Truman Library, provided invaluable assistance in gathering photographs for this book. The staffs at the Robert M. Cooper Library at Clemson University, the Houghton Library at Harvard University, the Manuscript Division at the Library of Congress, the Public Record Office in London, and the Seeley G. Mudd Library at Princeton University were also highly accommodating.

Similarly, Neil McElroy, director of Lafayette College's Skillman Library, and his librarian colleagues have been unfailingly quick to purchase new scholarly books and journals and to locate and bring to campus many out-of-print books and documentary volumes important for my research. And my Lafayette College undergraduate research assistants (EXCEL Scholars), especially Greg Domber, Graham Byers, and Daniel Arnold, have been of great help in searching out and assessing materials and serving as highly interactive sounding boards for my ideas.

Robert Beisner, Fred Greenstein, Jussi Hanhimaki, Hope Harrison, Lawrence Kaplan, Walter LaFeber, Norman Naimark, Edmund Wehrle, and Ran-

dall Woods have all read portions of this manuscript in one form or another, listened to my oral arguments, and provided critical insights and constant encouragement. For more than three decades, Theodore Wilson has been a remarkably
supportive friend, as well as scholarly critic, conference collaborator, and co-
editor, who has helped to sustain my research and writing of this book from
my first days at the Truman Library to the conclusion. Garry Clifford and
Thomas Paterson, whose New England Foreign Policy Seminar at the University of Connecticut provided an intellectual and spiritual home for me over
many years, have read, listened to, and critiqued more versions of this book
than I had a right to impose on them. But they have always generously taken
time from their own work to advance mine, and from the first to the most recent reading, they have never seemed to tire of providing critical advice and ex-
horting me to carry on.

Melvyn Leffler has been a consistently constructive supporter. Most significant, at a crucial juncture he provided a searching and intellectually honest
critique that bore the hallmarks of an exemplar scholar and devoted friend
whose single goal was to inspire me to write the best book I could. I could not
have asked for any greater favor. Similarly, Martin Sherwin, general editor
of Stanford University Press' Nuclear Age series, has taken an unwaveringly
strong interest in my work from the beginning. He has shared with me all of his
documents and exceptional knowledge pertaining both to "atomic diplomacy"
and U.S. foreign policy, and his vigorous editing of my writing has served to
increase my trust in my ideas. He has also constantly buoyed my spirits through
long confidence-building lunches at one of our favorite ethnic haunts.

Last but not least among scholar-friends stands Robert H. Ferrell. He took
me, as he has countless other aspiring historians, under his wing four decades
ago, and ever since has looked after my academic and personal welfare. He
has also shared with me his extraordinary knowledge of American diplomacy
and has, in his incomparable style, read and edited every book or article I
have written. Moreover, although some of my views may have given pause to
this eminent and prolific scholar, his editing has always been intended only to
help me articulate my ideas as clearly as possible. My debt to Bob Ferrell is
incalculable.

I am also delighted to acknowledge my gratitude to Lafayette College,
which since 1991 has provided me with an unusually collegial and supportive
academic home in which to teach and to engage in scholarly enterprise. I wish
to thank former Lafayette College president Robert Rotberg for welcoming me
to this community and encouraging my work, and former Provost Gillian Cell
for providing academic support, as well as friendship that endures. I owe special thanks to Nina and Charley Hugel, who have been great benefactors of

Lafayette. Their generosity and interest in history made it possible for me to join this faculty, and they have continued to demonstrate enthusiasm for my work. My past and present History Department colleagues, Jack Cell, Andy Fix, D. C. Jackson, Deborah Rosen, Donald Miller, Richard Sharpless, and Robert Weiner, all bear responsibility for having taken me in (as they like to say) ten years ago, for accepting my peripatetic lifestyle, and for encouraging new colleagues, Paul Barclay and Joshua Sanborn, to be equally forbearing.

I also owe great thanks to Lafayette's provost, June Schlueter, an outstanding scholar in her field of English, who truly understands the search for documents and an elusive truth. She has been a patient and strong supporter of all my endeavors, as well as a very good friend. Similarly, President Arthur Rothkopf has consistently encouraged my scholarly pursuits and my participation in Lafayette's exceptional system of shared governance, and he has been remarkably tolerant of my sometimes contrarian ideas in both realms. I have learned a great deal from his style of leadership and feel privileged to have him as a friend.

Finally, I wish to acknowledge my immeasurable gratitude to my family. My two older brothers, the late Charles, and Elliot, have always exercised the privilege of their seniority to be demanding of their younger sibling, but they have also stood firmly and devotedly behind me throughout every venture. My daughter Deborah (and her husband, Sam Roth) and son Michael have been the most loving and inspiring boosters and critics that a scholar or father could ever imagine. No matter how dark the day of writing, their smiles have always brought sunshine. Above all my wife, Ellen, has been at the center of my life, family, and work for more than forty years. She has guided and vastly enriched one and all by her perceptive criticisms and editorial skill, by the example she has set in her own career (far removed from academe), and by the fullness of her love and devotion.

I remain solely responsible for all errors of fact or interpretation in this book.

Arnold A. Offner
Easton, Pennsylvania, and Newton, Massachusetts

ANOTHER SUCH VICTORY

Independence to Washington

Harry S. Truman was born on May 8, 1884—when Chester A. Arthur was president, having succeeded the assassinated James A. Garfield—in a five-room house without plumbing in Lamar, Missouri, a village of seven hundred inhabitants 120 miles south of Kansas City. Sixty-one years later, upon the death of President Franklin D. Roosevelt on April 12, 1945, Vice President Truman became president. For nearly eight years he profoundly influenced American foreign policy in an era when the United States, more than ever before or after in its history, affected the course of world politics.

Truman liked to say that he had learned early in his life that "it takes men to make history. . . . History does not make the man." Nonetheless, whereas Roosevelt aspired to the presidency from early manhood and fashioned his life accordingly, Truman entered the White House because of history, or fortuitous events rather than by plan or personality. Once there, however, he determined to leave his mark. Indeed, both admirers and critics have contended that his administration transformed U.S. foreign policy and significantly determined the course of world politics during the next half century. Admirers have credited Truman's administration with moving the U.S. onto a permanent new path of internationalism, reconstructing Western Europe and Japan, resisting Soviet or Communist aggression from Greece to Korea, and forging collective security through NATO. Critics have contended that Truman's uncritical belief in the supremacy of American values and political-economic interests and his tendency to ascribe only dark motives to nations and leaders whose plans conflicted with U.S. policies—combined with his aggressive and occasionally "atomic" diplomacy—intensified Soviet-American conflict, hastened division of Germany and Europe, and brought tragic intervention in Asian civil wars. In ways that have not been fully assessed, Truman's early life and career profoundly and significantly shaped his approach to the presidency and foreign policy.[1]

I

Harry Truman's grandparents on both sides of his family were Kentucky pioneers who migrated to western Missouri in the 1840s. His parents, Martha Ellen Young and John Truman, married in 1881 and settled in Lamar. John Truman farmed and speculated in land, livestock, and grain futures without long-run success. Short of stature, occasionally truculent in demeanor, defensive and thin-skinned with regard to any criticism of his honor or family, he was also a Baptist, an ardent Democrat, and a dabbler in local politics. Martha Ellen came from comfortable circumstances and studied art, literature, and music at Baptist Female College in Lexington, Missouri. She was an ardent Democrat, and a devout Christian given to biblical strictures.[2]

Harry Truman's brother, John Vivian, was born in 1886, and his sister, Mary Jane, in 1889. The Truman family moved twice in young Harry's life before settling in 1887 on his grandfather Solomon Young's 600-acre farm near Grandview, eighteen miles south of Kansas City. They moved again in 1890 to Independence—where Harry went to school—a small town east of Kansas City with a genteel Southern ambiance. John Truman lost all his money speculating in grain futures in 1901, and eventually he and his family returned to the Grandview property where he farmed and served as a township road overseer. In 1914 he strained himself while moving a boulder, underwent an operation, and soon died.[3]

Harry Truman later conjured images of a bucolic life on the farm and in Independence that included an extended, loving family and friends, Baptist religiosity, tasty foods, and time for chores and pranks. He once said it was the "happiest childhood that could ever be imagined." Reality was more complex. After his mother learned that he suffered from hyperopia (extreme farsightedness), from about age eight, Harry had to wear thick and expensive glasses, which precluded sports and roughhouse activities with other boys. He was further cut off from his peers by a diphtheria attack that caused months of paralysis of his arms and legs, and later by his self-consciousness about his "sissy" piano playing.[4]

Further, his feisty father appeared to favor the more robust Vivian, whom he gave a checkbook and incorporated into his business ventures. Although Truman recalled his father as an honorable man who did a day's work for a day's pay and whose guarantee of a horse in a trade was as "good as a bond," he also recalled that his father's scolding hurt more than his mother's spanking and that when Harry fell off a pony, his father made him walk home, crying all the way.[5]

Harry would emulate aspects of his father's way of life, including searching for money, keeping one's word, and venturing into politics. But disapproval from his father and distance from peers also fostered ambivalence toward powerful men. Thus Truman would eventually defer greatly to strong leaders, such as his political benefactor, "Boss" Thomas G. Pendergast, or secretaries of state George C. Marshall and Dean G. Acheson, whose manner and firm views he found reassuring. But he would denounce leaders whose styles or ways of thinking were unfamiliar. This included political "fakirs" [sic] such as Theodore and Franklin Roosevelt, "professional liberals," and the State Department's "striped pants" boys, while Charles de Gaulle, Joseph Stalin, Ernest Bevin, and Douglas MacArthur were each, at one time or another, a "son of a bitch." Truman's need to demonstrate his authority would also underlie his upbraiding of officials such as Soviet foreign minister Vyacheslav Molotov and Secretary of State James F. Byrnes in 1945.[6]

Martha Truman nurtured young Harry. She taught him his "letters" before he was five. The boy with thick glasses read many books, including the Bible (with its large print) three times through before he was twelve. Later he would admonish people and nations by referring to the "system of morals" taught by Moses in the twentieth chapter of Exodus—the Ten Commandments—and to the Sermon on the Mount as reported in the Gospel according to St. Matthew. But Truman seems to have derived less a code of behavior or religiosity from his biblical readings than belief that "punishment always followed transgression," a maxim that he would later apply to North Korea and the People's Republic of China.[7]

Truman also remembered that his mother and an aunt had left a church because of "liars and hypocrites," and that as a fourteen-year-old, he had seen his boss in a drugstore dispense whiskey from unmarked bottles stored under the prescription counter to "amen-corner-praying" churchmen and Anti-Saloon Leaguers who lacked courage to drink publicly. Later he was quick to apply the hypocrite label to critics of "Boss" Pendergast and of himself as president.[8]

Reading provided young Truman with a sense of history. When he was about ten his mother gave him Charles F. Horne's newly published (1894) *Great Men and Famous Women,* four massive tomes titled *Soldiers and Sailors; Statesmen and Sages; Workmen and Heroes; Artists and Authors.* Truman remembered mainly the soldiers and statesmen, his "great captains of history"; the others he largely forgot. His *Memoirs* relate that he "pored over" Plutarch's *Lives* and that he exhausted the Independence public library before he was thirteen.[9]

Truman's self-tutelage in history enhanced his vision of the globe but provided little sense of ambiguity or complexity, and instilled exaggerated belief that history was cyclical, that the "true facts" could resolve any dispute, and that current events had exact analogues that provided the key to contemporary policy. As president, Truman would uncritically apply analogues and "lessons of history" about appeasement of Nazi Germany and Japan in the 1930s to diplomacy with the Soviet Union and crises over Iran, Greece, Turkey, and Korea.[10]

During his senior year in high school, Harry helped to found the school's magazine, *The Gleam,* after Tennyson's "Merlin and the Gleam." From then on he carried in his wallet a copy of that poet's poem "Locksley Hall," which envisioned a "Parliament of Man, the Federation of the World." After graduation in 1901, Truman sought to enter West Point, but an army recruiter persuaded him that poor eyesight precluded passing the physical examination. He enrolled in a commercial college in Kansas City, but his family's financial reverses forced him to withdraw.[11]

Truman held several jobs in the next years: timekeeper for a contractor laying track for the Santa Fe Railroad; mail clerk for the *Kansas City Star;* then bookkeeper for the National Bank of Commerce and the Union National Bank in Kansas City. By 1905 he was earning a "magnificent" salary by Kansas City standards—one hundred dollars monthly—and enjoying its theater and musical advantages. He also joined the newly formed Battery B of the Missouri National Guard, which drilled weekly and went on summer maneuvers. But since his uncle Harrison was retiring from farming, Truman quit his job in 1906 and returned to Grandview to help his father, who had gone there after a recent business failure.[12]

For the next eleven years, Harry Truman tilled the soil and raised livestock, including purebred cattle. He helped to found, and became president of, the Jackson County Farm Bureau; joined the Belton Lodge of the Masons; and started the Grandview Lodge of the Masons, later becoming state grand master. He took over his father's road overseer job after his death but lost the position, he said, because the presiding judge (administrator) of the county court concluded that "I gave the county too much for the money." He also managed to become Grandview postmaster, but gave his salary of fifty dollars per month to an assistant, a widow with children.[13]

Truman later insisted that farming, along with financial and military experience, was essential preparation for the presidency. But during his farm years he wrote repeatedly that life was tedious and tiring, and he dreamed that a miracle would turn the farmer into a political leader, "like Cincinnatus," his Roman hero. He also said that if "debts give a man energy—I ought to be a shining example of that quality." He had to sell his prize cattle to pay his father's funeral costs. Moreover, when Louisa Young, his maternal grandmother, died in 1909 and left her farm to Martha Ellen and Harrison—Truman's mother and uncle—five other siblings contested the will. Only after years of litigation was Martha Truman able to buy them out by assuming a mortgage, which Harry could never reduce. The farm remained a burden, and Harry shared brother Vivian's sentiment about the settlement: "The lawyers got most of it. All we got was debts." [14]

Truman's Missouri heritage also included parochial nationalism and racism, albeit of relatively benign character. Preparing for a trip to South Dakota in 1911, he jested that there were more "bohunks" and "Rooshans" up there than white men. He believed that the United States should have halted the flow of immigrants before the arrival of Asians and Eastern Europeans, allowing "good Americans" to preserve their land and virtuous agrarian society rather than become an industrial nation plagued by "large cities" and "classes." Truman's casual language included "nigger," "coon," "Chink doctor" (to whom he faithfully took his sick father), "Dago," "Jew clerk," and "Kike town." He insisted that each race belonged on a separate continent. Experience would help him to outdistance his admitted "hate" and "race prejudice," but his private comments included an occasional ethnic slur. His cultural perspective remained nationalist and parochial. [15]

In 1914 Harry Truman purchased a used Stafford touring car. This lessened the isolation of farm life and made it easier to court Elizabeth Virginia Wallace. "Bess," daughter of David Willock Wallace and Madge Gates Wallace, came from two prominent Independence families, with her maternal grandfather a founder of the Waggoner-Gates Milling Company. Truman first saw Bess as a five-year-old in Sunday school, later alleged that it took him five years to muster courage to speak to her, and at middle age wrote that from the moment they met "I thought (and still think) she was the most beautiful girl I ever saw." They attended high school together, and sometimes studied at the house of his cousins Ethel and Nellie Noland, who lived across the street from Bess' house at 219 North Delaware. After high school, Harry went to work and Bess went to Barstow's School for Girls in Kansas City. Her father, an alcoholic, and despondent about his health and finances, committed suicide in 1903. Thereafter Bess lived under the watchful eye of her mother, who judged no suitor worthy of her daughter. [16]

Truman renewed his friendship with Bess in 1910, proposed marriage the next year, and seemed relieved when she said no to this farmer of scant means. He persisted, however, and a few years later may have considered them to be engaged. He also felt inspired to raise his financial status. He borrowed money from his mother, and then had her cosign a bank note, to invest first in a lead and zinc mine in Oklahoma and then in a company that drilled for oil and sold rights to wildcatters on leased lands in the Southwest. The mine venture foundered, and his company discovered no oil. The coming of the World War led Truman and his partners to sell their oil rights to another company, which later struck the immense Teter oil pool in Kansas. If he had stayed home to run his company, he would have become a millionaire, Truman later wrote, "but I always did let ethics beat me out of my money and I suppose I always will."[17]

President Woodrow Wilson's message urging American entry into the World War in April 1917 led the thirty-three-year-old farmer to enlist. He was moved by patriotism, desire for adventure, and hope that Bess would marry him, although he dared not ask. "I'll never forget how my love cried on my shoulder when I told her I was going," he wrote. "I was a Galahad after the Grail."[18]

Military life provided surprising success. Truman hoped to become a sergeant, but the enlisted men elected him a first lieutenant. The guardsmen then became the 129th Field Artillery of the 135th Division and moved to Camp Doniphan at Fort Sill, Oklahoma. Truman was given charge of the regimental canteen. He chose for his assistant Sergeant Edward Jacobson, a friend from National Bank of Commerce days before "Eddie," son of a Jewish shoemaker, left to work in a clothing shop. The partners raised twenty-two hundred dollars from the troops to stock the canteen, bought a cash register, and in six months made a profit of fifteen thousand dollars by clever marketing.[19]

Shrewdness accounted for Truman's canteen success; grit helped him in other endeavors. He recalled that high-ranking officers made a "mystery" out of artillery firing by emphasizing higher mathematics. He struggled, until Colonel (later Brigadier General) Robert M. Danford, an authority on firing and a demanding but excellent leader, reminded the troops that the goal was to hit the target, which these "good old squirrel rifle shots" rapidly learned to do. Truman claimed that he learned more about commanding men and artillery in six weeks from Danford than in six months of school and drills, and he emulated Danford when he became an artillery instructor. Danford also recommended him for promotion to captain in February 1918. Truman had to stand outside in zero-degree temperature for an hour and a half before facing a panel of senior officers, including a general who liked to berate young officers. He came away convinced that he would not be promoted. He sailed to France in March 1919, in advance of the 129th Field Artillery, for special training in firing of French artillery and learned of his captain's commission from a newspaper report.[20]

Captain Truman said he was too smart to earn a Croix de Guerre by "stopping bullets," but the front provided opportunity for leadership. He was "badly frightened" when given command of the 129th's raucous Battery D, composed largely of Irish and German Catholics from Rockhurst Academy in Kansas City. His troops promptly tested his limits, but he warned the corporals and sergeants that they had to maintain discipline or they would be busted. "We hit it off," he wrote. Shortly Captain Harry, as he became known, took his men into the Vosges Mountains in Alsace. In late August they fired their first shots at the Germans, whose devastating return of shells caused a sergeant to sound a frantic retreat. Truman unleashed mule-skinner's language to turn panic into regrouping and earned his reputation for bravery under fire at the "Battle of Who Run." He also recommended transfer, rather than court-martial, for the sergeant.[21]

During the last bitter weeks of the war, Truman never hesitated to reconnoiter in advance of his men. He also saved American troops from being shelled by German artillery by ordering his gunners to fire outside their authorized section. For this he braved a colonel's wrath and threat of court-martial. By armistice time, Truman had lost his "wild desire" for a West Point education or to be a Napoleon. He had seen enough of the land of "*vin rouge* and frogeater victuals" and wanted only to return to Bess and to his farm. But demobilization took months. Truman played almost continuous poker—"probabilities"—and traveled in the south of France and then to Paris for a glimpse of President Wilson and performances of opera and the Folies Bergère, which he deemed "disgusting." Having returned to the U.S. in April 1919, he was discharged in May with the rank of major in the reserves. For years afterwards he enjoyed the camaraderie of reserve camp in the summer.[22]

From the vantage point of the White House, Truman held that his "whole political career" was based on his war service and army associates. He had been a brave commander and won his troops' lasting respect. But Truman's wartime experiences did not broaden his perspective. New York City remained "Kike town," he deplored France's "narrowly dirty streets and malodorous atmosphere," and he believed that the kaiser aimed to despoil America and its "beautiful women." Fighting for principle was "tiresome," and he did not care about the League of Nations, peace terms (save that "the Hun" deserved a "bayonet peace"), or whether the Russian government was "Red . . . or Purple." Upon reaching the shores of "God's country," he vowed never to return to Europe: "I've nearly promised old Miss Liberty that she'll have to turn around to see me again."[23]

Harry and Bess married in June 1919 and settled in, with her domineering mother, at her house in Independence. Truman's chance encounter with Eddie Jacobson led to their opening a men's furnishings store in Kansas City. They turned a handsome profit the first year, but recession and deflation in 1921 forced them to close in 1922. They tried to pay their debts, but Jacobson had to declare bankruptcy. Truman averted this, but in 1929 a bank won a judgment for $8,944 plus a 160-acre farm he owned, although his brother Vivian bought back the bank note for $1,000 during the Great Depression. Harry Truman remained in financial straits until 1945.[24]

Defeat in the haberdashery at age thirty-eight hurt badly, but Truman made a quick and fortuitous entry into politics in 1922. Tom Pendergast's Democratic machine sought a malleable candidate for judge, an administrative post charged with financing and managing county roads and public buildings, of the Eastern District (Independence and environs) of Jackson County. Jim Pendergast, nephew of Tom and son of his brother and political lieutenant, Mike, knew Truman from wartime service. Jim and Mike proposed Truman, whose political profile was correct: Baptist, Mason, farmer, and veteran with a clean record. Truman also got help from the editor of the *Independence Examiner,* Colonel William Southern, who was anti-Pendergast but the father-in-law of one of Bess Truman's brothers. Truman won narrowly over four other candidates in the primary, during which race he offered the politician's homage—a ten-dollar membership fee—to the rising Ku Klux Klan. But they returned the money when he would not pledge to deny jobs to Catholics, including his Battery D boys. Truman won the November general election handily.[25]

For two years he performed creditably as one of three judges administering county affairs, but an intraparty Democratic dispute cost him reelection. He then sold automobile club memberships, resumed evening courses begun earlier at Kansas City Law School, and solicited deposits for two savings and loan associations, one of which he left after learning that it was ridden with financial irregularities. In 1926 he hoped to run for county collector, which could offer high compensation since pay was based on fees collected. But Tom Pendergast gave the job to someone else. Instead, Truman won the first of two four-year terms, at six thousand dollars annually, as presiding judge of Jackson County.[26]

Judge Truman earned considerable success. He got local bankers to reduce interest rates for buying the county's tax-anticipatory notes by inviting bids from banks in St. Louis and Chicago. He appointed two engineers to draft a plan to redo the county's roads, and against political advice gained public approval of a $6.5 million bond issue in 1928 and of another $8 million issue in 1931. He told Pendergast that contracts would be bid competitively and payment made only for jobs properly completed. The Boss' concrete company paved just one-half mile of the county's 225 miles of redone roads. Still, Truman confessed privately that politics forced him to expend about a million dollars putting "sons of bitches" on the payroll or overpaying them for supplies.

But he took not a penny for himself, and in 1931 went on a long architectural study trek by car, at his own expense, to ensure that the new Kansas City courthouse, to be completed in 1934, would be a showpiece. Truman also became president of the Greater Kansas City Planning Association and director of the National Conference on City Planning.[27]

He was only a spectator at the Democratic National Convention in 1932, but Pendergast's well-timed delivery of votes to Franklin Roosevelt led to Truman's appointment as federal reemployment director for Missouri in 1933. That fall he and other Kansas City officials met with FDR's relief administrator, Harry Hopkins, before they created the Civil Works Administration, which funded more than 110,000 jobs in the Kansas City area that the Pendergast machine controlled. In Truman's view, America was redistributing its wealth "but, thank heaven, we are going about it more peacefully than was done in Russia, Germany, and Italy."[28]

Despite success in local politics, Truman was disconsolate: "Tomorrow I'll be forty-nine," he wrote in May 1933, but "for all the good I have done the forty might as well be left off." He was unhappy that his honest public service brought only modest compensation, whereas corrupt officials, such as a West Point associate who was as unfaithful to his office as he was to his wife, grew rich. Truman once noted that he could have had a million and a half dollars in graft, but since childhood he had believed in "honor, ethics, and right living as its own reward." Meanwhile, Tom Pendergast, angry that his "crooked contractors got no contracts," chided him that his honor would not be worth "a pinch of snuff." Still, after the Boss' brother, Mike, died in 1929, Pendergast named Truman to Mike's job as head of the county organization.[29]

Truman admired Pendergast, even if he owned "a bawdy house, a saloon and gambling establishment," because he was a "man of his word"—on the few occasions he gave it—and not a hypocrite like the "sniveling church members" who played with whores, drank, and sold out to the Big Boss on weekdays, and then repented on Sunday. Truman lamented that "I am only a small duck in a very large puddle" who would leave office poorer than when he entered. He hoped to finish his second term without any more bond issues or troubles, then "run a filling station or something," and go to "a quiet grave."[30]

Truman seemed to have run out of luck and jobs by 1934. Limited by precedent to two terms as presiding judge, he had sought the nomination for governor in 1932 and more recently for a House seat, or even for collector. But Pendergast chose other people. He also had at least four different candidates in mind to run for senator in 1934, but each declined. Once again his nephew Jim, and James Aylward, the state chairman from Kansas City, proposed Truman. The Boss resisted an "ordinary county judge" unknown outside of Jackson

County. But Truman's backers insisted that the machine's statewide contacts would make up for this. The two men offered Truman the Pendergast machine's support.[31]

Truman seized the moment. Arising at 4 A.M. the next day, May 14, in a hotel room in Kansas City where he would announce his candidacy, he wrote that whereas two weeks earlier he foresaw retiring on a small pension from a minor county office, now he was about to make the "most momentous announcement" of his life. He had reached the place "all men strive to be at my age." He recalled the books he had read as a youth, and his belief that great men never thought of themselves as such but strove to attain self-discipline and to overcome their "carnal urges." He admired only those who fought for what they thought was "right and for their countries." If God willed that he become senator, he would pray for wisdom to do the job.[32]

It is uncertain whether Pendergast chose Truman to be rid of him or thought that he would make an able candidate untainted by Kansas City's corrupt and violent politics. His machine had long moved beyond stuffing ballot boxes to turning politics, prohibition, prostitution, and gambling into commercial enterprises. One of his "chief lieutenants," Johnny Lazia, dominated the police department in Kansas City, now a haven for organized crime, and in 1933 helped nationally known gunman Charles "Pretty Boy" Floyd flee the city after he took part in the murder of four police officers. Federal officials were able to convict Lazia for income tax evasion only, and he was soon free on bail. In March 1934 his thugs led the Pendergast machine to a riotous victory in Kansas City elections, which included mayhem in the streets and four murders. In June an unknown assailant gunned down Lazia.[33]

Truman knew that the Pendergast machine was corrupt, but "I owe my political life to the machine." He was confident that the Boss would not ask him to act illegally, and he drew a convenient line between his behavior and that of the machine. And soon pressed by his opponents to explain Pendergast's backing, he dissembled: "I live in Independence. . . . I've never voted in Kansas City."[34]

Truman faced two veteran congressmen in the Senate primary: Jacob "Tuck" Milligan from nearby Richmond, who had strong support in rural regions and from Pendergast's rival for power in Missouri, Senator Bennett Clark of St. Louis; and John C. Cochran from St. Louis, the candidate of the *St. Louis Post-Dispatch*. All three candidates supported Roosevelt and the New Deal. Each candidate alleged that his rivals were agents of power brokers, with Milligan charging that Truman would get "calluses on his ears" taking orders over the telephone from Pendergast.[35]

Truman relied on his record as presiding judge and statewide ties to county judges, which meant friends at every polling place; his "dirt-farmer" status in the hinterlands; his work as federal reemployment director; and his unflagging campaign into nearly every county. But the key to victory was the Pendergast machine's delivery to him of 35,000 more votes from Kansas City than Cochran gained in St. Louis, although Kansas City's population of 400,000 was less than half that of St. Louis. Milligan ran last. There was truth to the *St. Louis Post-Dispatch* lament that Tom Pendergast had willed an "obscure man" to victory as the Democratic nominee for senator.[36]

In the general election, Truman easily defeated Republican senator Roscoe C. Patterson, an undistinguished arch-conservative. Truman assailed the Smoot-Hawley protective tariff of 1930 as a new high in "national stupidity" that promoted economic warfare, and lauded the Roosevelt administration's Reciprocal Trade Agreements Act of 1934 as providing lower tariffs and increased trade. He defended New Deal expenditures, especially public works, as far less costly than that "orgy of slaughter," the World War. His efforts and the rising national Democratic tide won him nearly 60 percent of the vote in November. Shortly, Truman set off for Washington elated, yet sobered by sharp campaign criticism that he was the senator from Pendergast.[37]

II

Truman was sworn in as a senator on January 3, 1935. He suffered from the Pendergast label, poor speaking ability, and a serious sense of inadequacy. He recalled that liberal colleagues shunned him as a "hick politician," that it took him six months to see Roosevelt—for seven minutes—and that few New Dealers, except Hopkins, were kind to him. This fueled his defensiveness and bitter comments about "professional liberals" and Roosevelt as a "fakir."[38]

Truman took a colleague's advice to be a workhorse rather than show horse. He made the most of his assignments to the Appropriations and the Interstate Commerce Committees. He also formed important friendships with the insurgent progressive and chair of the Interstate Commerce Commission (ICC), Burton K. Wheeler of Montana, and moderate conservatives, including Alben Barkley of Kentucky, Carl Hayden of Arizona, and Tom Connally and Vice President John Nance Garner of Texas.[39]

Truman blended Midwestern populism and interest-group politics. From his "backbench seat" he supported the major New Deal programs, including social security, collective bargaining, regulation of public utilities holding companies, farm parity payments, federal housing, and a federal minimum wage. He went along with FDR's court-packing plan in 1937, saying that the court was already packed anyway. He helped to gain passage of the 1938 Civil Aeronautics Act, which created the Civil Aviation Authority and stressed the military role of civil aviation, and the compromise 1940 Transportation Act, which codified regulation of land and water carriers.[40]

During ICC hearings on railroad financing in 1937, he took a reflexive populist approach to attacking Wall Street banks, insurance companies, and the "tricks" of law firms. He was reluctantly ready to vote to make lynching a federal crime in 1938 and took an antidiscrimination stance regarding economic opportunity, legal rights, and military enlistment. But he was careful to note that blacks wanted "justice, not social relations," and sidestepped controversies in Missouri over eviction of black sharecroppers and establishment of a patently unequal law school. Truman made a "good New Deal Senator," as Secretary of the Interior Harold Ickes noted in 1940, although he—and FDR— had favored another candidate in Missouri's Senate primary.[41]

Much to his ire, Truman remained outside the New Deal circle. The patrician Roosevelt never accepted him, and the senator openly refused the president's request in 1937 to switch his vote for majority leader from arch-conservative Pat Harrison of Mississippi to Barkley. In 1938, after Roosevelt renominated Maurice Milligan as U.S. attorney for western Missouri, who was at the time investigating the Pendergast machine for election fraud, Truman assailed Milligan's alleged "Hitler-Stalin tactics" and cast the sole vote against confirmation. In 1939 the senator risked a bad-weather flight back to Washington to vote for the president's executive reorganization bill and then called the White House to say he was tired of the "office boy" treatment. Roosevelt invited him for a talk the next day, but offered only a dutiful thanks and said he wanted to see Kansas City politics cleaned up.[42]

A few weeks later Milligan had Pendergast indicted for taking a $750,000 bribe to fix state-regulated insurance rates and concealing another $1 million of income. The Boss pleaded guilty and was sentenced to fifteen months in Leavenworth penitentiary and five years' probation. Milligan secured more than 200 other convictions, and the Pendergast machine was destroyed.[43]

At Pendergast's indictment, Truman said he would not desert a sinking ship but insisted that "our association has been only political." Scandal never touched him, although he considered resigning and spent a lonely year seeking friends and funds for his seemingly doomed reelection in 1940. The major challenge came from Governor Lloyd C. Stark, an Annapolis graduate and wealthy apple grower who had split with Pendergast and who had FDR's tacit support. U.S. Attorney Milligan was also a candidate, although a Truman friend seems to have lured him into the race to drain Stark votes. Roosevelt did try to entice Truman to withdraw by offering a seat on the ICC, but Truman said he would run even if he got only his own vote.[44]

"I'm whipped. This is the end of me," Truman told a Cabinet official in January 1940. Still, he managed through the powerful senator James (Jimmy) F. Byrnes of South Carolina to secure vital campaign funds from Wall Street speculator Bernard Baruch. Other Senate friends, including Barkley, also lent support. Once again Truman campaigned ceaselessly, while Stark seemed to court bids for vice president and a Cabinet post and also fought with the legislature. Late in the campaign, Senator Clark switched his support to Truman; and Robert Hannegan, the Democratic chairman in St. Louis, held together a foundering deal to get out the Truman vote there in return for Jackson County Democrats backing the St. Louis machine's gubernatorial candidate. Truman edged Stark by 8,000 votes, his margin in St. Louis, and returned to Washington to cheers from his Senate friends. He then ran as a New Dealer and military preparedness advocate to defeat his Republican opponent, Manvel Davis, in November.[45]

Meanwhile, Missouri constituents complained that they were not getting a fair share of burgeoning defense contracts or fair government reimbursement for their services or property, to which Truman sometimes replied, "Yes, let's give 'em hell." Then a Kansas City journalist moved him to propose an investigating committee in February 1941. The White House was wary, but after Truman made assurances that he would not hurt the defense effort, he got a modest $15,000 appropriation to chair the seven-member Special Committee to Investigate the National Defense Program. He set out to get "the facts," avoid conflict with the chief executive, and submit only nondivisive unanimous reports.[46]

Between March 1941 and August 1944, the Truman Committee held countless hearings and issued thirty-two reports on the war economy, except for the $2 billion Manhattan Project, which Truman avoided at the behest of Secretary of War Henry L. Stimson. Despite his caution, Truman naively let his name be signed to a ghostwritten article, "We Can Lose the War in Washington," that appeared in *American Magazine* one week before the congressional elections in 1942. Roosevelt was angered, but Truman earned praise for candor. The committee's findings encouraged FDR to replace the Office of Production Management with the War Production Board in 1942. They also revealed, for example, ALCOA's contract with I. G. Farben to restrict production of magnesium—vital to build airplanes—and that wartime Washington's "dollar-a-year men" assigned most contracts to their former large companies.[47]

The Truman Committee pointed mainly to flagrant production abuses or failures and tried to assure the public that the war's costs were reasonable, although it did not save nearly the $15 billion that Truman claimed it did. Still, he got national publicity in 1943 as a "Billion-Dollar Watch Dog," and a 1944 poll of Washington journalists named him one of the ten civilians who had done most for the war effort. The tarnished image of the senator from Pendergast had brightened enough to earn mention as a vice presidential candidate.[48]

Truman seemed to have no reason to seek that "fifth wheel office." Nine years of hard work as a senator had brought the status and security he craved. He scoffed that the vice president merely presides over the Senate and "sits around hoping for a funeral." Strained relations precluded working with Roosevelt, and despite speculation about FDR's health, Truman did not want to move into the White House "through the back door—or any other door at sixty." He also worried about disclosure that since 1941 he had kept Bess on his office payroll (another aide did most of the work), while his sister, Mary Jane, worked in his Kansas City office. Bess feared revelation about her father's suicide.[49]

The chief contenders for vice president were the incumbent, Henry A. Wallace, and Jimmy Byrnes, now director of the Office of War Mobilization and Reconversion (OWMR). Wallace came from an illustrious Iowa farming family, had been an excellent secretary of agriculture in the 1930s, and was FDR's dictated choice for running mate in 1940. Wallace was the administration's most advanced liberal, a spokesman for social justice at home and abroad in a "century of the common man." But he had poor relations with the senators, over whose chamber he presided. Byrnes, a political ally of Roosevelt since 1912, had won seven terms in the House and two in the Senate, where he was de facto majority leader in the 1930s. FDR named him to the Supreme Court in 1941 but then asked him to direct war mobilization from a White House office, leading to his label of "assistant president."[50]

Cautious Democratic officials set out to find a new consensus candidate. They held that Wallace was too liberal and that Byrnes, a Catholic turned Episcopalian and conservative Southerner, was unacceptable to critical elements of the New Deal coalition, especially labor and blacks. The conspirators were led by Edwin Pauley, party treasurer and wealthy oilman, who told White House visitors that they were choosing not a vice president but a president. Pauley was abetted by, among others, Major General Edwin "Pa" Watson, Roosevelt's appointments secretary; Robert Hannegan, now Democratic national chairman; and postmaster Frank C. Walker.[51]

Roosevelt could have named his running mate, but his Byzantine political style, wartime preoccupations, and fatigue made him unwilling to choose. At a secret White House meeting on July 11, 1944, he acceded to the politicians that Truman, and liberal Supreme Court justice William O. Douglas (who lacked organizational backing), would be acceptable running mates. Hannegan later claimed that FDR then wrote this down. But when Byrnes soon complained to

Roosevelt that party leaders had told him that the president preferred "Truman first and Douglas second," FDR reassured Byrnes that Byrnes was the one closest to him, with Wallace next, and "I hardly know Truman." At the same time, Roosevelt also promised Wallace a public letter stating his support for him.[52]

Truman probably knew of these machinations but ignored them. Just before he departed for the Democratic convention on July 14, he agreed to Byrnes' request that Truman nominate him and then lobbied for him. Meanwhile Hannegan, worried that Roosevelt was reneging on his commitment, got the president, en route to the Pacific coast for military talks in Hawaii, to stop his train in Chicago on July 15. Hannegan then persuaded FDR to tone down his support for Wallace and to reaffirm, in a note postdated to the convention opening on July 19, that "Harry Truman and Bill Douglas" were acceptable running mates. The president also told Hannegan that Byrnes was agreeable to this but to "clear it with Sidney" Hillman—the influential president of the Amalgamated Clothing Workers Union and head of the CIO's Political Action Committee—who FDR knew opposed Byrnes. Hillman confirmed his opposition when he met with Truman on the day before the convention began.[53]

Hannegan, meanwhile, floated rumors that FDR supported Truman, causing Byrnes to withdraw in a fury. Truman still resisted declaring his candidacy, perhaps determined to have FDR anoint him. On July 20 Hannegan called the senator to his hotel room where, Truman recounted, he heard Roosevelt exclaim to the party chieftain over the telephone from San Diego that if Truman wanted "to break up the Democratic party in the middle of a war, that's his responsibility." The president then slammed down the phone. Truman claimed to be incredulous but could not resist the call to duty. The next day, Hannegan and his friends outmaneuvered Wallace's forces on the convention floor to gain Truman's nomination, which he accepted with a terse pledge to help shorten the war and win the peace.[54]

"I've really arrived," Truman exulted, although he knew that his selection was expedient and that he had not been FDR's first choice, as Hopkins admitted after FDR's death. But Hopkins added that Roosevelt had chosen the senator because he "wanted somebody that would help him when he went up there and asked them to ratify the peace."[55]

III

From the perspective of politics and foreign policy, Truman appeared to be a relatively safe choice. He identified with Wilsonian internationalism, favored low tariffs, and backed the Reciprocal Trade Agreements Act of 1934 and Export-Import Bank credits to foster foreign purchases of American goods. He never regretted American intervention in 1917 and said that the British and French had undermined Wilson by adopting a "conqueror theory" that made the vanquished pay for the war. He believed strongly in a League of Nations, voted in 1935 for Roosevelt's modest but failed proposal to have the U.S. join the League-sanctioned World Court, and persisted in believing that the nation could no longer pursue an "ostrich-like" foreign policy.[56]

Truman acceded to the majority in voting for the Neutrality Acts of 1935–1937 but was an early supporter of their revision—blocked until 1939—to provide "cash and carry" war materials to Britain and France. He was a staunch proponent of increased military spending and continued to insist that it was necessary to "be prepared for war" to preserve peace. He deplored German, Italian, and Japanese action, and in 1937 proposed that the U.S. join with other democracies to warn the "savage" nations that they would be punished. He voted for Selective Service in 1940 and then sought active service as an artillery officer, but Chief of Staff General Marshall told him he was too old. In 1941 he voted for Lend-Lease aid for Britain and then for the Soviet Union. Truman could rightfully say, as he did in March 1939, "I am no appeaser."[57]

His worldview, however, reflected unquestioned faith in American moral superiority and his cultural nationalism, and his foreign policy proposals dealt mainly with military preparedness. He deplored disarmament and pacifists, called outlawing of war a "silly" phrase, and was quick to blame international conflict on "outlaws," "thugs," and "totalitarians." He was indifferent to General Francisco Franco's reactionary assault on the government of Republican Spain. In 1939 he asked Roosevelt to meet with the head of Moral Rearmament (MRA), a conservative Christian movement whose leader had declared Hitler a bulwark against Bolshevism, and to take part in an MRA world broadcast for peace. FDR sidestepped the invitation. But Truman enthusiastically supported MRA, even seeking draft deferments for its members, and he did not cut his ties until warned in 1944 of its profascist and anti-Semitic leanings.[58]

Following the fall of France in June 1940, Truman called for global preparedness to protect America's democracy and access to resources against any contingency in the Atlantic or Pacific: "[W]e have Russia and Japan at Alaska's doorway." He also said that America should crack down on "fifth column activities" and deport "disloyal inhabitants" to the countries that they admired. Later on President Truman would question the "loyalty" of "hyphenate" Americans, charge that the "Crazy American Communist" was "loyal to Stalin and not to the President" and should be sent to Russia, and sign off on an unprecedented peacetime loyalty program.[59]

Germany's attack on the Soviet Union on June 22, 1941, prompted Truman's oft-quoted remark that "if we see that Germany is winning we ought to help the Russians and if Russia is winning we ought to help Germany and that way let them kill as many as possible, although I don't want to see Hitler victorious under any circumstances. Neither of them think anything of their pledged word." To be sure, Truman spoke hastily, and his words reflected widespread hostility toward both sides for their cynical division of Europe in their 1939 Nazi-Soviet Pact. He also opposed a German victory in any case, and he favored wartime aid, as he said in 1943, to that "brave ally" who was killing Germans.[60]

Nonetheless, Truman's antipathy toward the Soviet Union and Communism was deep-seated. He never departed from his view, as expressed in 1941, that the Russians were as untrustworthy as "Hitler and Al Capone," and he deplored "those twin blights—atheism and communism." As president he would also be quick to conclude that Stalin broke every agreement he made, and to insist that the Soviet Union was as aggressive and expansionist as Nazi Germany.[61]

During the war, Truman and three defense committee colleagues—Republicans Joseph Ball of Minnesota and Harold Burton of Ohio, and Democrat Carl Hatch of New Mexico—discussed a postwar security organization. Then in early 1943, perhaps with a nod from the White House, Truman—who deferred to Senator Lister Hill of Alabama because of defense inquiry obligations—helped to plan the bipartisan Ball-Burton-Hatch-Hill resolution, known as B_2H_2, which urged U.S. membership in a postwar organization that would maintain a military force to oppose aggression. That summer, Truman and Republican congressman Walter Judd of Minnesota toured the Midwest to promote this idea.[62]

When the Senate took up B_2H_2 in October, Foreign Relations chairman Connally substituted a vaguer resolution that omitted mention of military power for an international body. Truman then joined with twelve colleagues to cosponsor Senator Claude Pepper's amendment providing for U.S. membership in an organization with a military force. The Roosevelt administration then gained a compromise when the Senate backed the recent Moscow declaration that committed the Big Four powers to create a body to consult about "joint action" to preserve peace. Connally incorporated this into his resolution, and the Senate approved overwhelmingly. Thus Truman helped to reverse the "mistake" of 1919, as the *New York Times* reported. In spring 1944 he also supported a Senate resolution to create the Foreign Economic Commission to assist China and other underdeveloped nations vault from "oxcart to airplane stage."[63]

The postwar world that Truman envisioned rested on traditional American liberal political, economic, and moral pillars. He saw the U.S. as essentially a benign and selfless arbiter of world affairs. His means to preserve peace depended on the nearly automatic invocation of international military force to deter or suppress "aggression," a charge difficult to define. Truman presumed the gravest threats to peace would come from "outlaw" nations rather than from conflicts among the Big Four. To some extent, by mid-1944 his evolving foreign policy views were consonant with those of the Roosevelt administration, although he had almost none of FDR's patience or fondness for diplomacy and its inevitable ambiguities. As Truman told one constituent in 1943, "[D]iplomacy has always been too much for me." Truman was also far more inclined than FDR to presume the worst with respect to the claims or intentions of other nations who resisted American policies, and he had little of FDR's sense of the deep currents of nationalism and anticolonialism that the war had unleashed. In that regard, many liberal internationalists had reason to feel that Roosevelt had betrayed them by abandoning as his running mate the far more liberal Wallace for Truman.[64]

After his nomination, Truman did not meet with Roosevelt until they had lunch outdoors at the White House on August 18. Truman reflected that FDR mainly offered "hooey" about what the senator could contribute to the campaign. Still, party leaders developed an extensive schedule for Truman, who knew that Roosevelt's wartime leadership was the overriding issue, and that newspaper coverage would focus mainly on the bitter battles of the final year of war in Europe and Asia.[65]

Throughout the campaign, Truman applauded Roosevelt as a statesman who had the confidence of both British prime minister Winston Churchill and Soviet premier Joseph Stalin and would get the "best deal" for Americans. Proclaiming that foreign policy was the most important campaign issue, Truman alleged that the Republican presidential nominee, Governor Thomas E. Dewey of New York, was a fence-straddler who flirted with isolationists. Truman also charged that Dewey's refusal to assert that he would allow a U.S. representative to the emergent United Nations (UN) to vote to allow use of force—including American troops—without first gaining Congress' approval would condemn that body to the same fate as the League of Nations.[66]

Roosevelt and Truman won thirty-six states in November 1944, although the president's popular margin was the smallest by far of his four elections, and his greatest support came from big-city voters concerned more about New Deal programs than foreign policy. But defeat of isolationists in both parties and election of several new senators of internationalist outlook led to the view, as reported in the *New York Times,* that FDR had gotten the "great and solemn referendum" that had been denied to President Wilson. On election night a weary but elated Truman cabled Roosevelt: "Isolationism is dead. Hope to see you soon."[67]

Truman saw little of Roosevelt thereafter. Two days after their inauguration on January 20, 1945, the president embarked for Yalta, icily instructing Truman to send him only *"absolutely urgent"* messages, with the White House Map Room communications officer to determine transmission mode. FDR returned to Washington on February 27 and addressed a joint session of Congress on March 1. With his failing health painfully evident, he delivered a long and sometimes rambling speech attesting that the Yalta agreements marked the end of unilateral actions, exclusive alliances, and spheres of influence. He asked public approval of the conference results and the new "universal organization" that would be open to all peace-loving nations. When reporters asked Truman for his response, he said that it was "one of the greatest speeches ever given," and laughed.[68]

The new vice president, meanwhile, set about to do his duty. He had created a flap in late January by commandeering an army bomber to fly to Kansas City for Tom Pendergast's funeral, insistent that they had always been friends. Thereafter Truman presided with spirited resignation over his former colleagues in the Senate, "where it's my job to get 'em prayed for and goodness knows they need it," he wrote. "I am trying to make a job out of the Vice Presidency and it's quite a chore." He labored to become "a politician's Vice President" and to help Roosevelt. When FDR angered Senate conservatives by ousting Secretary of Commerce Jesse Jones—no political ally of FDR—Truman worked hard to secure Henry Wallace's confirmation in the post. Truman also helped overcome congressional resistance to renewing Lend-Lease on April 10. Although the bill prohibited use of Lend-Lease for postwar aid, Republican senator Robert Taft sought to extend the ban to postwar shipments of goods already under contract. His amendment failed, in a 39–39 tie vote; Truman happily added his extra nay vote.[69]

Truman also planned a series of speeches on the "winning of the peace and the dangers of disunity at home." In late February he warned on national radio that Americans could no longer "sit smugly behind a Maginot Line," that their choice was to repel aggression alone or in concert, and that partisan politics could not be allowed to undermine the UN at the coming San Francisco Conference. Truman's focus was mainly anti-isolationist, but he feared that senators were making the same speeches that had been made in 1919.[70]

Public anxiety increased in late March when Stalin insisted that Foreign Minister Vyacheslav Molotov was too busy to attend the San Francisco meeting, and then when Roosevelt revealed that at Yalta he had agreed to three votes for the Soviet Union (and six for the British Commonwealth) in the UN General Assembly. Truman was "completely flabbergasted," and said that Roo-

sevelt had told him that American delegates were to be free agents on this issue. But the vice president was even more distressed, he wrote on April 6, that
the "sabotage press" was doing all it could to ruin the San Francisco meeting.[71]

Further, FDR never briefed Truman about difficult matters that were less
public. Since early March the president had been engaged in sharp, even bitter,
exchanges with Churchill and Stalin over Soviet imposition of a Communist-
led government in Rumania and insistence on control over which Polish leaders would be allowed to join a "new" or "reorganized" government in Warsaw.
Stalin, in turn, charged that exclusive Anglo-American negotiations led by
Allen Dulles—head of the Office of Secret Services in Switzerland—with
German *Schutzstaffeln* (S.S.) officers in Bern about surrender of all German
forces in northern Italy were intended to gain political advantage and violated
the principle of unconditional surrender.[72]

Roosevelt told Churchill that Russian military control and security concerns in Rumania meant that it was not a good place for a "test case," but cautioned Stalin that a "thinly disguised" continuation of a Communist government in Poland would cause the American people to regard Yalta as having
failed and end prospects for postwar allied unity. FDR also told Stalin that he
bitterly resented the "vile misrepresentations" of those who had informed him
about the Bern talks. The president then cabled Churchill on April 6 that in
a few days "[o]ur Armies" will be in a position to "permit us to become
'tougher'" with the Russians. But in his last dispatch, written from Warm
Springs on April 11, Roosevelt told Churchill that they should minimize their
problems with the Soviets because most issues would be straightened out. "We
must be firm, however, and our course thus far is correct." Most likely FDR intended to continue his "Yalta system" rather than get "tougher" with the Russians. Regardless, the next day he suffered a massive cerebral hemorrhage and
died shortly before 4 P.M.[73]

Meanwhile, that fateful afternoon, listening to a "windy Senator" ramble
about a proposed Mexican-American water rights treaty, Truman wrote to his
mother and sister that the next night they could tune in his Jefferson Day speech
on national radio, after which he would introduce the president. When the Senate adjourned a few hours later, Truman headed for the Capitol building "hide-
away" of Sam Rayburn, Speaker of the House, for drinks with congressional
cronies and arrived about 5 P.M. Truman poured a bourbon and responded to a
message to call FDR's press secretary, Stephen Early, who told him to come to
the White House, through the main gate.[74]

The vice president was greatly anxious over the summons. In November
1944 he had confided to a friend that when he visited with Roosevelt in August,
he had seen the "pallor of death" on his face, and Truman expressed similar

concern to friends numerous times thereafter. Now on April 12 he asked his colleagues in Rayburn's office to say nothing about Early's call. Truman eluded his Secret Service agent, ran through a narrow Capitol basement corridor to his Senate office, grabbed his hat, and had his chauffeur drive him to the White House. He reached the second floor about 5:30 P.M. and entered the sitting room of Eleanor Roosevelt. "Harry," she said, "the President is dead."[75]

The vice president was stunned that the "full weight of government" had fallen on him. The machinery of state grinds on, however. Cabinet and congressional officials, and Truman's wife, Bess, and daughter, Margaret, soon gathered. By 7:09 P.M., Chief Justice Harlan Stone had sworn in Truman as the thirty-third president of the United States. During the next hour he authorized Secretary of State Edward R. Stettinius to say that the San Francisco Conference would begin on schedule, and the new president tersely commented that the Allies would continue to prosecute the war in Europe and Asia with full vigor.

Throughout the improvised proceedings, Stettinius noted, Truman seemed "shocked and startled," "bewildered." He handled himself well, however, and left "no feeling of weakness whatsoever." Still, Senator Arthur Vandenberg, ranking Republican on the Senate Foreign Relations Committee and a key delegate to the San Francisco meeting, wrote that "the gravest question-mark in every American heart is about Truman." The president, meanwhile, returned to his small apartment on Connecticut Avenue about 9:30 P.M., had a sandwich and a glass of milk and, he wrote, "went to bed, went to sleep, and did not worry anymore."[76]

First Encounters

Harry Truman worried far more in April 1945 and thereafter than he liked to admit. He confronted the near-herculean tasks of establishing himself as president and charting American foreign policy during the conclusion and aftermath of a global war. No one, especially in this circumstance, could have succeeded Roosevelt and not suffered by comparison. Moreover, Truman was an outsider in his administration. Ardent New Dealers would lament that "the country and the world doesn't [*sic*] deserve to be left this way" and excoriate "that Throttlebottom, Truman," or insist that "I just can't call that man President."[1]

Truman manifested his anxieties. He was so self-deprecating and given to asking people to "pray" for him that Senator Barkley cautioned him that this could erode his executive authority. Assistant Press Secretary Eben A. Ayers noted in late May that "the President still finds it hard to realize he is President," and months later Truman wrote that "I never think of anyone as the President but Mr. Roosevelt."[2]

The new president commented caustically about White House visitors who had "an ax to grind" or who came to "tell me how to run the State Department and Supreme Court" and "settle world peace." He denigrated the "Prima Donnas" in Washington who had helped to "drive the Boss to his grave" and now surrounded the new president, and he alleged that numerous Cabinet officers were afflicted with "Potomac fever."[3]

"Loyalty" was paramount in Truman's mind. After deciding to retain Roosevelt's chief of staff, Admiral William D. Leahy—a gruff conservative hostile to the Soviet Union—and to letting him speak his mind, Truman quickly added that "after a decision is made, I will expect you to be loyal." A few weeks later the president gave his Cabinet officers a "vigorous, decisive and hard boiled" talk about avoiding public disagreements and soon told them that they were "simply a Board of Directors" appointed by the president to carry out his orders and government policy. He insisted that he would run his administration in the manner of President Lincoln, who once cast the only yes vote at a Cabinet meeting and declared that "the ayes have it." Truman doubted that a presidential aide could be "a loyal Roosevelt man and an equally loyal Truman man," reviled foreign policy critics as "parlor pinks" and "crackpots," and questioned the loyalty of the "Polish-Americans, Irish-Americans, Swedish-Americans or any other sort of hyphenate."[4]

Truman did not grasp the difference between Cabinet officers, often powerful figures with large constituencies, and staffers whose sole function was to serve the president. Most important, his insecurity and excessive suspicions about government officials and private spokespeople would eventually narrow the range of views or policy options to be placed before him, infuse policy debates with bitter charges about loyalty, and lead to unfortunate dismissal or resignation of senior officials.

The pace of the presidency and constant flow of paper seemed to overwhelm Truman. To compensate, he sought to speak and act quickly and decisively. Speaker Rayburn worried that the new president might make decisions without adequate information. Wallace noted that Truman seemed almost "to decide in advance of thinking." Moreover, while Truman insisted that he would base each decision on "the facts" and "then forget that one and take the next," this style of discrete decision making emphasized the present without due concern for complex backgrounds and long-term objectives.[5]

Diplomacy and foreign policy proved especially vexing. Poring over minutes of the Yalta Conference, Truman found "very hazy" agreements and new meanings with every reading. "They didn't tell me anything about what was going on," he lamented to Wallace in mid-May, and then told Secretary of the Treasury Henry Morgenthau, Jr., that he could not imagine how difficult matters were: "Everyone around here that should know something about foreign affairs is out."[6]

Truman reached for political support. On his first full day in office he broke tradition by eating lunch on Capitol Hill with leading Democrats and Republicans in an effort to defuse long-standing executive-legislative tensions. He insisted on addressing a joint session of Congress on April 16, the day after Roosevelt's burial, to stress continuity with FDR's policies, especially the demand for unconditional surrender and the need for postwar cooperation. On the train ride back from Hyde Park, Truman offered Byrnes appointment as secretary of state, but to avoid undercutting the incumbent Stettinius, this would not be announced until the San Francisco Conference, due to start in late April, finished its work on the new United Nations.[7]

Byrnes had recently resigned as OWMR director and returned to South Carolina, but immediately after FDR's death had sent "Dear Harry" a telegram offering his help. Truman decided to see him "first thing in the morning," and they began to confer about "everything under the sun." Truman might have sought to learn about Yalta from Byrnes, who had accompanied Roosevelt and taken shorthand notes of the plenary sessions that he was allowed to attend, although he knew far less, especially about the Far East accord, than he let on. Still, Truman intended Byrnes' appointment to "balance things up" for 1944 and to buttress himself with a powerful political operative who would also be next in line of presidential succession.[8]

Byrnes, like Truman, regretted American refusal to join the League of Nations and had managed Roosevelt's preparedness and aid-to-the-allies legislation during 1939–1941. FDR had sent him back early from Yalta to foster a positive public consensus about the agreements. With a politician's respect for Byrnes' skills, Truman referred to him as a "fixer" and "able and conniving," and wanted him to deal with "Mr. Russia and Mr. Great Britain," congressional critics, and the "Sabotage Press." In a revealing episode in August 1945 after the Potsdam meeting, Truman insisted that Byrnes tell the Cabinet that Stalin had saluted the secretary as the most honest horse thief he had ever met.[9]

Truman, initially at least, viewed the Russians and Stalin with similar grudging regard. He analogized the Russians to bad-mannered people from across the tracks who lived under a frightful totalitarian regime, but evidently they liked it "or they wouldn't fight and die for it." They were also "touchy and suspicious of us" and, he would later tell an impatient friend, they were "tough bargainers, and always ask for the whole earth, expecting maybe to get an acre."[10]

Truman similarly worried that Stalin might run out of control or would give in to pressure from Napoleonic generals. But the new president regarded the Soviet leader as dependable, if only because he took consistent positions. After their first encounter in July 1945, Truman wrote—with a sense of relief—"I can deal with Stalin. He is honest—but smart as hell." Shortly after this, Ayers noted that the president had found Stalin impressive and likeable, and four years later Truman would say that Stalin was as much like Tom Pendergast as anyone he had ever known. After leaving office, Truman, despite charging that Stalin had broken every agreement made at Potsdam, would insist that in the summer of 1945 "I liked the little son-of-a-bitch."[11]

Finally, in April 1945 Truman assured Stettinius that he would honor any commitment Roosevelt had made, regardless of consequence. He also told

Wallace that the United Nations and world peace depended upon American-Soviet cooperation and that war between the two powers was unthinkable. As Ayers noted, Truman's "sincerity and his desire to do what is right is continually evident." [12]

I

Truman inherited an expedient wartime alliance, symbolized by the Big Three leaders, that stood on shaky ground in 1945. Roosevelt was heir to Wilsonian internationalism but was also a highly pragmatic statesman given to personal diplomacy and deals that he cloaked in Wilsonian rhetoric to assuage public opinion. He had recognized the Soviet Union in 1933 but little came of this, while Stalin's brutal purges of 1936–1938 intensified American fear and loathing of Communist Russia. FDR deplored the Nazi-Soviet Pact of August 1939 and subsequent division of Poland, which he worried were prelude to a greater division of the world from the Atlantic to India. Still, in late 1939 FDR contrasted Germany's bourgeois culture with Russia's "brutality" and then deplored the latter's assault, or "dreadful rape," of Finland. But after Germany invaded Western Europe in spring 1940, he concluded that the Nazi state was bent on global conquest and that the U.S. had to provide all possible aid to Germany's opponents. [13]

These opponents included the Soviet Union after it was attacked by Germany in 1941. In fact, FDR viewed the assault as auguring Europe's liberation if the Russians could tie down German armies long enough for the U.S. to mobilize for the conflict that he saw as inevitable. Thus, FDR made as the "centerpiece" of his world strategy, especially after the U.S. entered the war, keeping Russia in the extremely costly struggle against Germany, and ultimately Japan. Meanwhile, he sought to forge agreements that were consonant with American principles and interests but that also accommodated legitimate Soviet historic and security interests, which implied allowing the Soviets to regain European and Asian territory or concessions that were part of pre-1917 Russia. Roosevelt also envisioned that his Big Four Policemen—including a restored China—would have to cooperate under a UN umbrella to preserve postwar order, with each great power taking primary responsibility for its region or sphere of influence. [14]

His British counterpart, Churchill, was a shrewd realist of imperial Victorian bent who was determined, despite Britain's long-term financial and industrial decline, to preserve his nation's remaining empire and status as a great power through close collaboration with Roosevelt and the U.S. Churchill had a long record of anticommunism that dated to his support for Western intervention in the Russian civil war in 1918, and even in May 1940 he held to his belief that harmony was impossible between "Bolshevism and present civiliza-tion." But the German attack on Russia led him to agree with Roosevelt that "Hitler is the foe we have to beat" and that Nazism exceeded "all forms of hu-man wickedness." By March 1942 Churchill proposed to restore Russia's 1941 borders and thought that he could deal with Stalin on a quid pro quo basis, de-spite worry that the Soviets might try to impose their will or ideology beyond their territory, notably in strategic areas vital to Britain.[15]

Stalin was a ruthless domestic dictator who presided over a police state and did not hesitate to imprison or execute political opponents. Nonetheless, he pursued a cautious, if brutal, realpolitik abroad and was always ready to jetti-son ideology in favor of diplomatic gain. During the 1920s he resented Wilson-ian internationalism and perceived the U.S. as a new economic colossus that could subordinate Europe. But he admired America's industrial prowess and considered it the least warlike of the imperialist states. He respected Roose-velt's New Deal leadership but surely agreed with Foreign Minister Molotov in August 1940 that "nothing good" could be said about Soviet-American rela-tions. Stalin also repeatedly complained about the West's failure to effect FDR's commitment to a Second Front in Europe in 1942, but may have done so less to show that he considered the promise realistic than to assure the flow of sup-plies and perhaps to soften the West regarding territorial negotiations. Regard-less, by 1944 Stalin was at least willing to admit that he preferred FDR's focus on "bigger coins" to Churchill's penchant to steal even as little as a kopeck. Stalin believed as well that "whoever occupies a territory also imposes on it his own social system. . . . It cannot be otherwise."[16]

From start to finish of wartime negotiations, Stalin argued for restoration of Russia's expanded 1941 borders. This included territory gained from the Winter War with Finland in 1940, the Baltic States, and territory lost to Poland and Rumania after World War I. In talks with British foreign secretary An-thony Eden in December 1941, Stalin dismissed the Atlantic Charter—which emphasized national self-determination—as "algebra" and stated his pref-erence for a firm treaty: "practical arithmetic." He also told Eden that even though Hitler was very able, he did not know where to stop, but "I do know." Eden concluded that Stalin was motivated more by the ideas of Peter the Great than Marxist ideology and thought that the Russian would be reasonable. Roo-sevelt would probably have agreed to negotiate a treaty but State Department officials insisted that any deal would rekindle memories of the Munich Con-ference, violate the Atlantic Charter, advance Communism, and spur Stalin to greater demands.[17]

Stalin also sought to gain compensation, especially German reparations, for the ravages of war, and to guarantee security against a restored Germany or

Japan or hostile capitalist states. He sought a sphere of influence in bordering states but did not plan to impose Communist governments there (except in Rumania, a German ally that had attacked Russia in June 1941). Nor did he intend to march the Red Army westward beyond its assigned occupation zones in Europe. In short, in crafting foreign policy, Stalin put the interests of the Soviet state before desire to spread Marxist-Leninist ideology, pursued pragmatic or opportunistic agreements, recognized America's vast military and industrial power, and always calculated what he called the "correlation of forces."[18]

Senior Soviet officials charged with postwar planning were of similar realpolitik outlook. This was especially evident in papers drawn at Molotov's behest during late 1994–early 1945 by the Soviet Union's three most experienced experts on the West: Ivan Maisky, ambassador to Great Britain; Maxim Litvinov, foreign minister and collective security advocate during 1933–1939 and now Molotov's deputy in charge of postwar planning; and Andrei Gromyko, ambassador to the United States. These diplomats' planning reports assumed that postwar cooperation with the United States and Great Britain was possible and desirable; that the U.S. would like to expand its markets to include resource-rich Russia; that Germany (and Japan) should pay heavy reparations and be kept weak; and that Soviet security required Western acceptance of its 1941 borders. These officials did not rule out prospective Big Three conflicts arising in Europe, the Near and Middle East, or Asia. But their emphasis was on postwar cooperation and spheres-of-influence diplomacy, albeit with Soviet security—or territorial—concerns uppermost in mind.[19]

During wartime negotiations, Roosevelt and Churchill privately acceded to restoring Russia's 1941 borders but were unable to effect accord between the mutually hostile prewar Polish government-in-exile in London and the Russians. Polish-Soviet relations worsened in April 1943 after the Germans exposed the Katyn Forest mass graves of some 5,000 Polish army officers presumably killed by the Russians after their 1939 invasion. Polish demand for an international inquiry led only to Stalin's breaking relations. Meanwhile at Teheran in November 1943, FDR and Churchill agreed to redraw the Russo-Polish border to approximate the Curzon Line of 1919 and to compensate Poland by moving its border with Germany westward to the Oder and Neisse Rivers. But from winter through summer 1944 neither Churchill nor Roosevelt could persuade the London Polish government, which was not told of the Teheran agreement with Stalin, to accept such a settlement.[20]

Meanwhile, Russian armies entered Poland in January 1944 and began to hand over control of liberated areas to Boleslaw Bierut's puppet Communist regime based in Lublin. Then as the Red Army halted at the Vistula River near Warsaw on August 1, the London Poles ordered their Underground Army to rise up against the Germans, both to show its willingness to fight Nazi forces and to try to take Warsaw and compel the Russians, when they entered, to recognize the Poles' official control in the name of the London regime. Stalin, however, halted the Red Army and delayed aid from Anglo-American airborne units flying from Russian bases until mid-September, thus allowing the Germans to crush the insurgents in early October.[21]

Churchill, who was then in Moscow to negotiate his "percentages" deal over Anglo-Soviet spheres of control in Greece and the Balkan States, got Stalin to invite a reluctant Stanislaw Mikolajczyk, the Polish prime minister and head of the Peasant Party, for talks. Stalin was adamant that the Lublin regime have majority control in the Polish government and that the Curzon Line serve as the Russo-Polish border. (If the Curzon Line were used as the border, the city of Lwow, which had a Polish majority, would be within Russia.) Mikolajczyk insisted, despite sharp criticism from Churchill, that his regime retain 50 percent control of any Polish government and that the border be settled on the basis of self-determination at a postwar conference. Churchill continued, in Moscow and upon his return home, to press the London Poles to accept a minority role in the government—with Mikolajczyk as prime minister—and the Curzon Line, and held out prospect of a guarantee of independence. But the London Poles refused and then appealed to Roosevelt, who balked at any commitment. Mikolajczyk resigned in November, and on January 5, 1945, Stalin recognized the Lublin Communists, now based in Warsaw, as Poland's Provisional Government (PPG).[22]

By the time of the Yalta meeting in early February, the Red Army predominated in Poland and Eastern Europe and stood forty miles from Berlin, while American forces were recovering from the Battle of the Bulge in the Ardennes Forest in Belgium. FDR and Churchill now sought to negotiate a "new" or "fully representative" Polish government, but Stalin would agree only that the Provisional Government should be "reorganized" to include democratic leaders from within Poland and from abroad. Molotov and the American and British ambassadors to Moscow, Averell Harriman and Sir Archibald Kerr, were constituted a Commission of Three to consult Polish leaders, who would reorganize their government. The Americans and British would then recognize this "new" Polish Provisional Government of National Unity, which would hold free elections. And with Poland in mind, Roosevelt proffered a Declaration on Liberated Europe that pledged the Big Three to help establish democratically elected governments. But Stalin refused FDR's proposed "appropriate machinery" to effect this, limiting the agreement to consultations, which he was confident—Molotov later recalled—would allow him to control events. Still, as FDR would tell an aide who complained that Stalin could stretch these Yalta accords to his liking, "It's the best I can do for Poland at this time."[23]

The Big Three also affirmed their accord on a modified Curzon Line as the Russo-Polish border. Roosevelt did make a last effort to gain Lwow for Poland, but Stalin refused. The Soviet leader also urged setting Poland's western boundary with Germany at the Oder and western Neisse Rivers, which would have given Poland control of all of German Upper Silesia. But FDR and Churchill balked at this transfer of territory and would not agree to set the border beyond the eastern Neisse. Thus the Big Three settled on a promise to Poland of "substantial accessions of territory in the north and west."[24]

The Yalta agreements, presaged at Teheran, reflected Russia's preponderant power in Eastern Europe, where their armies predominated, just as Anglo-American forces gave their governments control in Greece, Italy, and Western Europe. FDR would put the best public face on matters when he reported to Congress on the accords on March 1 that the "new-reorganized" Polish government would be "temporary" and that Yalta signaled the end of unilateral action and spheres of influence. The Russians, meanwhile, insisted that the Commission of Three consult first with the Communist PPG about acceptable representatives, that the PPG be given approval right over the London nominees, and that it form the "nucleus" or "base" of a reorganized government.[25]

Churchill, who now faced political attack in Britain that he was appeasing Russia over Poland just as Neville Chamberlain had appeased Germany over Czechoslovakia at Munich, proposed to Roosevelt that they make Poland a "test case between us and the Russians." But FDR said that while he opposed a "whitewash" of the Lublin regime, he still hoped to bring Stalin into line through negotiations.[26]

By late March, however, Roosevelt was concerned that Stalin was violating the Yalta accords although, he reminded Churchill, the Big Three had put "somewhat more emphasis" on the Lublin—now Warsaw—Poles than on the other groups. But FDR thought it time to intervene, and on April 1 he rejected Russian control over the selection of Polish representatives and warned Stalin that a "thinly disguised" continuation of the Warsaw regime would cause Americans to regard Yalta as having failed. The Warsaw Poles had been assured a "prominent" role in the government, FDR said, but reorganization meant "a new government." On April 7 Stalin was persistent that the Warsaw regime had to be the "kernel" of any government and proposed the formula recently used in Yugoslavia: an approximate 4:1 ratio of Communist to non-Communist ministers. At the same time, the Americans learned that sixteen Polish underground officials, loyal to the London Poles but accepting of the Yalta agreements, had been invited to talks with the Russian military but were now missing.[27]

Deadlock over Poland continued, but Roosevelt cautioned Churchill not to excoriate the Russians publicly, insisting that the problems usually straightened out, as evidenced by the brief controversy over the Bern negotiations. FDR also said that advancing American and British armies would allow them to be "tougher" than before, and on April 11 he insisted that "we must be firm, and thus far our course is correct." He died the next day, leaving no further word. There is no reason to think, however, that he intended to challenge Stalin over Poland or to forge an anti-Soviet coalition.[28]

II

President Truman initially sought to hew to Roosevelt's positions as these were explicated to him by advisers who were often strongly anticommunist and now had more chance to press for a harder line with the Soviets. Still, at first Truman warned Churchill that a public attack would dash Polish negotiations and military collaboration with the Russians, and insisted that they jointly have "another go" at Stalin. Based on State Department advice that Yalta had provided for a "new" Polish government, the president then proposed to Stalin on April 16 that they invite three Polish leaders from London and five from within Poland—who could arrive first—to consult in Warsaw with the Commission of Three. But while granting that Yalta allowed for the Warsaw Poles (now PPG) to play a "prominent" role in a new government, there could be no prior agreement with them, no Soviet veto over selection of delegates, and no Yugoslav formula. Meanwhile, Stalin took Harriman's suggestion that Molotov, who earlier had claimed to be too busy, should attend the San Francisco Conference, stopping first in Washington. There he could pay tribute to Roosevelt, meet Truman—the Russians were concerned that they knew little about him—and discuss Poland. At the same time, the Soviets announced that the Warsaw government wanted a mutual security pact.[29]

Harriman now raced for Washington, intent to brief the new president before Molotov arrived. Heir to a railroad and banking fortune, Harriman served as expediter of Lend-Lease to Britain and Russia from 1941 until he assumed control of the Moscow embassy in 1943. His approach to diplomacy was governed by his cosmopolitan businessman's belief—and his own conceit about his abilities—in high-level negotiations and tough quid pro quo bargaining, with the diplomat's word as his bond. Like Truman, Harriman held that Stalin and the Russians needed to be taught how to behave in the civilized world. When they acted like the "world bully," he said, the United States should be patient but firm, especially since the Soviets usually took their toughest stance just before making concessions. The ambassador also thought that FDR had not been tough enough with Stalin, and he worried, as he told Secretary of the Navy James Forrestal on April 19, that Communism's "outward thrust" was not dead and "we might have to face an ideological warfare just as vigorous and dangerous as Fascism or Nazism." He also believed that Yalta provided for a "new" Polish government but advised compromise.[30]

At the White House on April 20, Harriman provided Truman with a grim overview: the Russians were cooperating with the U.S. to secure postwar aid but also extending their control over bordering states through secret police and extinction of liberties—a "barbarian invasion of Europe." He insisted that the Russians always mistook generosity for weakness and did not follow accepted principles of international affairs. But they preferred aid to confrontation, and the U.S. could establish workable relations by being firm but making concessions.

The language appealed to Truman's instincts. He responded that he was not afraid of the Russians and that they "needed us more than we needed them." He would be "firm but fair" and seek "give and take" relations, but he would "make no concessions from American principles or traditions." He did not think he could get 100 percent of what he wanted but should be able to get 85 percent on important matters. He would tell Molotov "in words of one syllable" that if the Russians refused to compromise on Poland, the Senate would not ratify the UN Charter, but he doubted that there was much prospect for the UN without the Russians, and he wanted the Big Three foreign ministers to continue negotiating about Poland at San Francisco.[31]

When word came two days later that the Russian-Polish mutual security pact had been concluded, Truman told Stettinius and Harriman that he would not raise the issue with Molotov—and if the Russian did, the president would say only that this had not been helpful. After Eden joined the conversation—the British were vexed by the Russian-Polish pact—Truman reiterated his intent to speak plainly, if briefly, to Molotov about Poland.[32]

At his first encounter with a Russian diplomat on April 22, Truman affirmed FDR's commitments and desire to resolve difficulties, especially over Poland, which the American people regarded as the symbol of international relations. Molotov replied that Poland bordered on the Soviet Union and was vital to it but that Yalta had provided a solution. Both men agreed that questions about the San Francisco Conference could be resolved, and in reply to Molotov's query, Truman affirmed the American commitment to Yalta's secret agreements on the Far East. The meeting ended shortly thereafter, with no other scheduled.[33]

When the foreign ministers met that night, however, Eden sharply criticized the Soviet security pact with the Warsaw regime and pressed the Truman-Churchill proposals of April 16 to Stalin to open talks with Polish representatives about a new government. Molotov testily rejoined that Poland did not border the United States or Great Britain and was not a gateway to either country for aggressors. He insisted that the Warsaw Poles had to predominate in the government and that they should be invited to the San Francisco Conference. The meeting got *"nowhere,"* a British diplomat noted, and there was no progress the next morning, April 23. At Eden's behest, Stettinius "mobilized" Truman to call in Molotov for a "Dutch Uncle" talk late that afternoon; meanwhile, the president hastily assembled his advisers.[34]

Stettinius sought to set the tone of the meeting by insisting that the Soviets were trying to impose a "puppet" government on Poland and that Molotov had been warned that failure to fulfill Yalta would shake the American people. Truman gave quick accord. American agreements with the Soviet Union had been a "one way street," he said, and it was "now or never" regarding the San Francisco Conference. The Russians could go along or "they could go to hell."

Secretary of War Stimson, taken aback by this rhetoric, urged caution. He, too, thought that occasionally the Russians needed to be taught "manners," although they had been reliable on big military matters. It would be dangerous not to know what they were driving at in Poland, given their different view of independence and democracy. He also held that the Russians were probably more realistic about their vital security areas and would not yield over Poland. Similarly, Chief of Staff General Marshall warned against breaking with the Russians, whose military assistance was needed in the Far East.

Forrestal took the harshest view: Russian behavior in Poland was indicative of their effort to dominate Eastern Europe, and if they persisted, "we had better have a showdown with them now than later." Harriman thought that the Russians were trying to prop up a "shaky" regime in Warsaw and that the issue was whether the U.S. would be party to Soviet domination. Refusal might lead to a "real break" with the Russians, but proper handling could avoid that. Admiral Leahy said he had left Yalta convinced that the Russians would not permit a free government in Poland, but a break was a "serious matter." He proposed to tell the Russians only that America stood for a free government in Poland. But his admission that Yalta was susceptible to two interpretations caused Stettinius to snap that there could be only one. Major General John R. Deane, chief of the American military mission in Russia, counseled firmness and said that the Russians would enter the war in the Pacific regardless of developments elsewhere.

Stimson was the only official to concede the Soviet Union a sphere of influence in Poland. All the others—save Leahy—pressed the American view of Yalta but also believed that firmness would facilitate a bargain and reassure the public. Only Forrestal wanted a "real break." When Harriman first raised that prospect, Truman interjected his intent to clarify the position of the U.S., not deliver an ultimatum to Molotov.[35]

Later that afternoon Truman firmly told Molotov that the United States had gone as far as it could to meet Russian demands over Poland. The president insisted on a government that represented all democratic elements. He recounted Roosevelt's earlier concern about the need for public support for postwar collaboration, including—Truman added—economic assistance. He brushed aside Molotov's interjections about Soviet security and the Yugoslav formula, and said that it remained for Stalin to carry out the Yalta agreement. Truman warned that American adherence to agreements could not continue to be a "one way street." Later Truman wrote that Molotov finally said, "I have never been talked to like that in my life," to which he retorted, "Carry out your agreements and you won't get talked to like that." Some historians have cited this exchange as indicative of Truman's new and more confrontational policy toward the Soviets, although his sharp words do not appear in the minutes of the meeting, only in his *Memoirs,* which he likely embellished.[36]

Unquestionably, Truman spoke in his brusque style, the more so because he was personally anxious. He was also speaking to Molotov, who Americans believed engaged in a "war of nerves" to wear people down and deliberately gave Stalin inaccurate reports about the United States. In addition, the State Department had just briefed Truman that Molotov was given to bluntness but that he might be more inclined to make concessions than Stalin—Truman's ultimate audience—whom Hopkins had told the president was a "forthright, rough, tough Russian" who likewise might be spoken to "frankly."[37]

Likely Truman hoped that his bluntness would help gain Soviet adherence to the Anglo-American view of Yalta and facilitate the San Francisco Conference. He did not want a "break," and on this same day he also rejected Churchill's proposal to delay withdrawal of American forces in Germany to previously agreed-upon occupation zones in order to bargain with the Russians. Further, diplomat Charles E. Bohlen, who interpreted for FDR and Truman, later asserted that except for diplomatic style, Truman spoke exactly as FDR would have. But this view ignores that Truman did wish to make Poland a test case of sorts, that for the first time he asserted America's direct interest in Poland, and that he did believe he could get 85 percent from the Russians on important matters. In that sense, the confrontation over Poland marked a Cold War milestone, at least in terms of outlook. Not surprisingly, when Stettinius soon recounted the Truman-Molotov talk to Vandenberg in San Francisco, the senator crowed that "FDR's appeasement of Russia is over."[38]

Truman's firmness gained little result. Years later Molotov said that he resented the president's "imperious tone" and thought his approach, even if intended only to show "who was boss," was "rather stupid" and reflected a "very anti-Soviet mindset." Further, the only response from Stalin was a brisk lecture about Poland bordering the Soviet Union, Russian security concerns, and "unbearable" Anglo-American efforts to dictate to the Russians, who had never questioned how democratic were the British-backed regimes in Belgium and Greece. The Yugoslav formula was the "one way out" of the Polish impasse, he concluded. But this argument inspired Churchill to a long defense of Britain's policy, to insist that its people would never believe that the Second World War had "ended rightly" unless Poland was given a "fair deal," and to warn that Soviet violations of Yalta augured a larger quarrel between the English-speaking and Communist nations that would "tear the world to pieces."[39]

Truman feared this prospect, as he told Joseph E. Davies on April 30. Davies was a wealthy lawyer and prominent Democrat, whose dinner parties and card games Truman frequented. Davies was also ambassador to the Soviet Union during 1937–1939 and author of the wartime best-seller *Mission to Moscow*. He acted as occasional wartime liaison for FDR, but foreign service officials disdained him for not being critical enough of Soviet leaders. Still, Truman enjoyed Davies' company, and in relating his recent talk with Molotov, the president said, "I gave it to him straight. I let him have it. It was the straight one-two to the jaw." Truman added, however, that his purpose was to make the Russians understand that cooperation had to be two-sided—that the United States would carry out its agreements. He had just rejected a German offer to surrender only to the Americans and British, and he would honor the Soviets' request for three votes in the General Assembly. Now the Russians had to live up to their commitments. "Did I do right?"

Davies tactfully said that the president had commanded Russian respect but he needed to earn their confidence. The Russians had accepted American and British "vital interests" in Italy, Greece, and North Africa, took a dim view of the "hostile" Polish regime in exile in London, and would insist on "freedom from fear" of attack through Poland. Moreover, it was impossible to use economic aid to "get tough" with the Russians, who had managed on their own for a generation. Davies urged Truman to emulate Roosevelt by balancing between the British and the Russians, who had won the right to respectful treatment. Davies left the meeting convinced that Truman had heard him out and was seeking to learn both sides, and in his "honest, practical minded, and fair" way would seek peace in victory. But the deadlock over Poland still remained.[40]

III

Truman sought an expedient peace, or to resolve rapidly converging issues before they became a seamless web. On the evening that Truman became president, Stimson told him that an explosive of "almost unbelievable destructive power" was under development, but Truman, undoubtedly exhausted and always deferential to the venerable secretary, asked no questions. The next day Byrnes told the president about the ultrasecret Manhattan Project and a prospective atomic bomb "great enough to destroy the whole world." Byrnes also said that the bomb "might well put us in a position to dictate our own terms at the end of the war," Truman recalled, but he never indicated the terms or country to which Byrnes allegedly referred.[41]

It is clear that Truman inherited an ambiguous atomic policy marked by great power rivalry. Although Roosevelt had frequently said that the Four Policemen would maintain postwar peace through an unassailable "reservoir of force," in August 1943 at Quebec, he and Churchill agreed secretly to require Anglo-American mutual consent before sharing atomic information with other nations or using atomic weapons. They also gave the president discretion to determine a fair basis for postwar scientific exchange and industrial and commercial collaboration. This agreement signified American predominance in atomic matters, and that regardless of FDR's views of postwar relations with the Russians—who did not give priority to atomic development until late 1943—he did not wish to inform them of the existence of the Manhattan Project, despite reports from various agencies, including army intelligence and the Federal Bureau of Investigation, that they were spying on it.[42]

During 1944 Roosevelt evinced interest in the views of scientists affiliated with the Manhattan Project, such as Niels Bohr, a Nobel Laureate physicist who had escaped from Nazi-occupied Denmark in 1943. Bohr did not question the development or wartime use of an atomic bomb, but he believed that scientific information could not be contained within national borders. Thus, in separate meetings with Churchill and Roosevelt in June and August 1944, he urged preliminary planning with the Soviets for postwar control. FDR appeared amenable, but at Hyde Park in September 1944 Churchill prevailed upon him to sign a secret aide-mémoire reaffirming Anglo-American atomic development in "utmost secrecy" in postwar collaboration, and to take steps to ensure that Bohr leaked no information, "particularly to the Russians." Roosevelt and Churchill further agreed that after a bomb was available, it "might, perhaps, after mature consideration" be used against the Japanese, who were to be warned that it would be repeatedly used until they surrendered. Thereafter, despite urgings similar to Bohr's from Manhattan Project senior administrators and scientists, Roosevelt never lifted the veil of atomic secrecy, and neither he nor Stimson—who would oppose sharing with Russians without "a real *quid pro quo*"—expressed reservations about using the atomic bomb.[43]

Stimson purported not to have burdened Truman immediately with atomic policy. But after the confrontation with Molotov on April 23, the secretary said he had to discuss a secret matter that affected all of his thinking about foreign policy. Truman promptly met with him and Major General Leslie R. Groves, administrator of the Manhattan Project, on April 25. Stimson provided a summary of prior Anglo-American atomic policy. He then said that in the next few years only the Soviet Union was capable of atomic production but that thereafter it was extremely probable that smaller nations might secretly build a bomb and deliver it devastatingly against larger nations. He concluded that finding the "proper use" of the weapon would determine whether world peace and civilization might be preserved. He proposed, however, only that a committee be established to recommend executive and legislative policy after full secrecy was removed. General Groves assured Truman that a deliverable atomic bomb would be ready in the summer, that the Americans and British had a near corner on fissionable materials, and that the Soviets were spying. One week later Truman accepted Stimson's recommendation to establish a new Interim Committee to determine atomic policy. Stimson would chair this body, and Byrnes—"who could keep his mouth shut"—would be the president's personal representative. Thus, in spring 1945 the Americans emphasized caution regarding postwar relations and international atomic control. Nothing was said, as yet, about delaying negotiations with the Soviets until an atomic bomb was ready. Meanwhile Truman tried to dispatch nettlesome issues.[44]

For example, at the outset of the UN Conference in San Francisco on April 25, Molotov rejected the tradition that the head of the host delegation—Stettinius—should preside, and insisted that the Big Four rotate the conference chairmanship. The Americans worried that the Russians wanted to set a precedent they could use later to delay Security Council action. Truman dismissed the Russian proposal as "absurd" and told Stettinius to "stick to your guns." But the president and the delegation quickly acceded, with some misgiving, to a British compromise to rotate the plenary session chairmanship, while Stettinius would retain effective control by chairing the conference's Steering and Executive Committees. Molotov conceded, although he assailed Mexico's foreign minister, Exequiel Padilla, for backing Stettinius. Truman also ordered the U.S. delegation to honor FDR's pledge to admit the Ukraine and Byelorussia to the General Assembly; when the Russians pressed to seat their republics at the conference—Roosevelt had averted this at Yalta—Truman asked only that the invitation be delayed briefly. But he heartily backed Stettinius' rejection of Molotov's request to seat the Communist regime of Poland.[45]

Truman also opposed admitting Argentina, which had maintained close relations with Germany until 1944 and had not declared war on the Nazi state until March 27, 1945, three weeks after the deadline set at Yalta to gain admission to the UN conference. The Argentines had also been excluded from the Inter-American Conference held February 21–March 8, 1945, at Chapultepec

Castle in Mexico City. There the U.S., spurred by the Latin American nations, signed the Act of Chapultepec, which established a nominal wartime alliance, with a view to its extension into the postwar era, that declared an attack on one power to be an attack on all the signatories. U.S. officials said the act made the Monroe Doctrine applicable to the entire hemisphere; the Latin Americans held that Chapultepec meant that the U.S. could no longer use the Monroe Doctrine to act unilaterally but would be subject to collective review. The assembled nations also agreed to resume diplomatic relations with Argentina and to press for its membership in the UN provided that it restricted Axis power activities, declared war on Germany, and signed the Act of Chapultepec, which the Argentines did in early April.[46]

Truman disdained Argentina's "band wagon" politics but after Stettinius told him that Roosevelt had agreed to Argentine membership in the UN if they "cleaned house," the president acceded yet hoped that the U.S. might get around the issue. But at the San Francisco meeting the Latin American delegations, strongly encouraged by Assistant Secretary of State Nelson Rockefeller, insisted on seating Argentina as a quid pro quo for White Russia and the Ukraine. Truman consented "to make a deal." Thus, on April 30, after the Russian republics were admitted, Stettinius helped "steamroller"—as Walter Lippmann wrote—the Argentine invitation over the bitter objections of Molotov, who again raised the futile issue of seating the Warsaw Poles. Still, Stettinius had to mobilize Vandenberg to persuade Truman's former Senate allies and B_2H_2 spokesmen, Carl Hatch and Lister Hill, that the Argentine vote had been essential to placate Latin America and to preserve the new UN. At the same time, Senator Vandenberg exulted that Molotov had done "more to put the two Americas into a solid bloc" against Russia than anything that ever happened heretofore.[47]

Yet, even Harriman thought that Stettinius and Rockefeller had gone too far with Argentina, although the ambassador was not concerned about its Axis ties so much as determined not to give the Russians precedent for demanding a seat for the Warsaw Poles. In fact, despite Harriman's advocacy of bargaining with the Russians, he now lectured the American delegation about traditional Russian efforts to achieve their goals by "chisel, by bluff, pressures and other unscrupulous methods," and their use of the Red Army to build a tier of friendly states in Eastern Europe. He also gave bitterly anti-Soviet off-the-record interviews that made their way into the newspapers under the journalists' names.[48]

Acrimony did not preclude accommodation at San Francisco, although delegations sometimes reached accord for different, even conflicting, reasons. For example, during the war the Big Three had agreed that the UN should assume authority for global security, even though each of the Four Policemen would respond to aggression in its respective region of special interest. The Big Three never reconciled, however, the potential conflict between the global versus regional authority. The proposed UN Charter, drafted by the Big Three at the Dumbarton Oaks meeting in the summer of 1944, permitted bilateral or regional pacts consistent with its purposes but gave the Security Council predominant jurisdiction over security matters. Thus, nations that acted under bilateral or regional treaties would need prior permission of the Security Council, whereas permanent members such as the United States and the Soviet Union had veto power, an arrangement that smaller powers, including those of Latin America, viewed with distrust.[49]

Then at San Francisco on May 3, 1945, the Russians proposed that their security pacts drawn up in 1942 with Britain and during 1943–1945 with Czechoslovakia, France, Yugoslavia, and Poland should be exempt from Security Council jurisdiction in order to allow them to deal with attacks by current "aggressor states." The Russians, citing two decades of German aggression, refused to subordinate their regional system to an untested UN. The British, hinting at a future treaty with France, supported their proposal, although they hoped that ultimately the UN would assume sole responsibility for security.[50]

The technicalities of the global versus regional security issue perplexed the Truman administration. Officials suspected that the Russians sought to use their pacts to dominate bordering states or even all of Europe. But after considerable debate, the U.S. delegation, which understood Russian fears about Germany, reluctantly agreed to the Soviet proposal, providing that action be directed only at current "enemy states" and, as the British insisted, that action cease after the Security Council was given authority. Molotov quickly accepted the first proviso and soon agreed to the second on May 7.[51]

The decision to exempt the Soviet treaties from the Security Council's paramount authority ignited demands from the Latin American delegations, backed by Vandenberg and Rockefeller, to provide the same exemption for their regional system proposed by the Act of Chapultepec. Vandenberg, urged on by Rockefeller, argued that the U.S. could neither abandon its inter-American obligations under Chapultepec or the Monroe Doctrine, nor make "our Allies" in Latin America depend on an "untested" UN. He proposed to exempt "Western Hemisphere self-defense" from a Security Council veto and contended that this would not promote other regional blocs or harm the UN.[52]

Meanwhile, incensed Latin American delegations, supported by Arab states and Australia, argued that an inter-American system was essential to curb either a renewed Axis threat or Soviet encroachments. If the UN were allowed to manage Latin American affairs, the delegates said, that would spell the end of the Monroe Doctrine and the inter-American system and cause Latin Americans to seek favor with one or another of the permanent members of the Security Council. The Latin Americans insisted they would not vote to exempt the Russian treaties without a similar exemption for Chapultepec, which they also hoped—but did not say—would constrain the U.S. in the Western Hemisphere through collective decision making and preclude its use of the veto in the Security Council to block UN review of Washington's conduct or even sanctions against it.[53]

Protracted discussion among U.S. delegates revealed that they had differing goals. Some opposed an inter-American exemption because they wished to preserve the UN's predominant authority, and others favored the exemption to advance Latin America as an anti-Soviet bloc. Other delegates were ready to support both Latin American and Soviet regional claims. Numerous officials argued that regional systems undermined the UN and might create armed blocs, but they resisted reneging on the Russian security exemption. Consequently, the Americans proposed a compromise: to expand a nation's right to self-defense to include a group of nations acting under an agreement. They also acceded to Rockefeller's claims about the "sales value" in Latin America of citing Chapultepec specifically. But officials in Washington and San Francisco continued to insist that their intent was to promote self-defense, not regionalism, and after Stettinius gave Truman a hasty summary on the telephone on May 12, the president approved.[54]

It was Eden, however—not the Russians—who dismissed the proposal as "clearly of Latin American origin" and "regionalism of the worst sort," and he vetoed specific mention of Chapultepec. The British did not object to all alliances, however, and wished to allow self-defense against indirect attacks such as a (presumably Soviet-inspired) Bulgarian assault upon Turkey, which might be perceived as a threat to their empire. Thus, the British backed a French proposal to allow UN members the "inherent right of individual or collective self-defense" against attack, with the Security Council retaining its authority to act. Later that day the Russians, Chinese, and Americans tentatively approved.[55]

The Latin Americans, however, persisted in their efforts to have the UN Charter recognize joint action under Chapultepec. U.S. officials opposed this specificity but feared that the Latin Americans might otherwise block the Soviet security exemption or the whole charter. Stettinius again called Truman, who sanctioned private assurances that the U.S. would negotiate a mutual defense pact to implement Chapultepec in the autumn, with the delay intended to forestall Soviet complaints at San Francisco. But the Latin Americans demanded immediate and public assurance. Stettinius called Truman, and on May 15 the president announced that the U.S. would negotiate hemispheric defense. Within a week the delegations at San Francisco approved the arrangement that became Article 51 of the UN Charter, allowing member nations the right of "individual or collective self-defense" against an armed attack until the UN took measures to maintain peace and security.[56]

This provision legitimized the later development of armed blocs, although this was not exactly what Truman or the American delegation intended in 1945. In fact, on May 14 the president had emphatically opposed a Chinese proposal for a Pacific security pact because such a regional, or power politics, agreement would undermine the UN. Rather, the Soviet request for an exemption from UN predominance over their security pacts had touched off debate over the long-unresolved global-versus-regional security conflict. The matter was further complicated by British, French, and Latin American desires to protect their special interests. Thus, collective defense, as Vandenberg noted in May 1945, seemed to satisfy practically everybody by providing for "legitimate regionalism" and the "over-all authority" of the UN, although it obscured rather than resolved the jurisdictional conflict between the UN and regional associations.[57]

To be sure, Truman wished to move toward establishment of the UN, and later use of Article 51 to justify armed camps was as much a reflection as a cause of the Cold War. Still, this does not negate the fact that the Article 51 solution approached spheres-of-influence diplomacy and allowed the United States to maintain its claim to act unilaterally under the presumed authority of the Monroe Doctrine, while the Latin Americans would find that despite their greater numbers, they still lacked the collective force to restrain their northern neighbor when it chose to exercise its overwhelming power.[58]

IV

While the diplomats debated in San Francisco, the war in Europe had been grinding toward its troublesome end. The Soviet Union on April 27 unilaterally recognized the compliant Austrian regime of the aged Social Democrat, Karl Renner, and marched their troops deeper into the proposed British occupation zone of Styria. The Yugoslavian forces of Marshal Joseph Tito moved into northeastern Italy—the region of Venezia Giulia, including Trieste—with announced, albeit halfhearted, Soviet backing. The Russians captured Berlin on May 2 while the British barely outraced them to Lubeck, cutting off the Red Army's access to Denmark.[59]

That same day Stalin offered a small compromise over Poland: the Warsaw regime would name only one of the three negotiators to be sent by the government in exile in London, and Mikolajczyk, the former prime minister, could begin preliminary talks in Moscow. But on May 4 the Russians announced that the sixteen Polish Underground officials missing since March had been arrested and would be tried for "diversionary activities." The Russians also brushed off American complaints about the Warsaw regime's incorporation of territory in eastern Germany—Danzig and Upper Silesia—that was technically under Soviet military occupation. The American chargé in Moscow, George F. Kennan, said Russian actions in Poland were "common knowledge to every sparrow in Eastern Europe," and he advised that the U.S. "teach the Russians an overdue lesson" by similarly carving western Germany among its allies.[60]

At the same time Truman received ominous warnings from returning U.S. representatives on the tripartite Allied Control Commissions (ACC) in Eastern Europe and from the special State Department summaries that he had requested. The strong consensus was that the Russians sought to dominate every country within reach through unilateral action, political repression, high reparations, and confiscation of property. As Under Secretary of State Joseph C. Grew told Truman in early May, even in Austria and Czechoslovakia, where "real Soviet cooperation" had been expected, the Russians seized every advantage and there would inevitably be a struggle throughout southeastern Europe. Grew proposed that American armies advance as far as they could along the Danube and Moldau Rivers for purposes of "hard bargaining."[61]

Similarly, Major General William J. Donovan, head of the Office of Strategic Services (OSS), provided Truman with a lengthy military assessment that epitomized the growing consensus about the "Problems and Objectives of United States Policy." The report presumed that the U.S. military was currently superior and that the Russians would likely seek to avoid a major conflict for ten to fifteen years, content with a "sphere of control" in Eastern Europe and China's northern borderlands. But ultimately the Soviets might outstrip the U.S. militarily; revert to either the "predatory tradition" of the tsars or the "dynamism of the Communist international"; and seek to control all of Europe and Asia. Further, although Stalin might prove the "soul of moderation," his successor might be a "military conqueror." American "national security" could not wait upon events while the Soviets sought a "belt of states" on its frontier and entrenched its armies in Germany.

But rather than a showdown, the OSS strategists advocated a firm, non-provocative policy that included initiating timely and acceptable compromises to prevent any clash between Russia and Western European powers; encouraging development of progressive and prosperous regimes in Western and Central Europe and the Mediterranean; and seeking to establish a "democratic-socialist Germany balanced between the Eastern and Western blocs but aligned with neither." Donovan noted for Truman that this policy was intended to show the West's readiness to consider Russia's problems while safeguarding its own interests.[62]

The predominant advice that Truman received in late April and early May 1945 from career diplomatic and military officials accorded with his view, as well as that of Harriman and even of Stimson, that the Russians did not follow traditional great-power norms and were engaged in a barbarian invasion of Europe, or at least of bordering states. But the Americans also believed that they might bargain the Russians out of a showdown. Thus, when Churchill urged on April 30 that U.S. forces, moving chiefly into southern Germany and westernmost Austria, instead liberate Prague and as much as possible of Czechoslovakia because this "might make the whole difference to the post-war situation" in east-central Europe, Truman replied that he had already approved General Dwight D. Eisenhower's assertion that he would make no "militarily unwise" move. In fact, a few days later the Russians rejected Eisenhower's request to move his troops east of the previously agreed-upon Pilsen-Karlsbad line to Prague. Next, Churchill pressed for Anglo-American forces to maintain their positions "obtained or being obtained" while they decided "how much we have to offer or withhold" from the Russians. But Truman still refrained from trying to gain political advantage by extending U.S. lines. He knew as well that Stalin would not deal over Berlin or Vienna until the occupation lines were cleared.[63]

During the first week of May the president rejected German efforts to surrender only on the western front while continuing to fight in the east. He also declined Churchill's proposal on May 7 that they break their accord on a tripartite announcement of Germany's unconditional surrender and instead broadcast one day early the capitulation of the Third Reich at Eisenhower's headquarters at Reims (where a Russian general had countersigned the document) because the news was already public. Truman sought Stalin's approval, but when no reply came, the Americans held back for twenty-four hours.[64]

Truman awoke cheerfully on May 8, his sixty-first birthday, and wrote his family that Churchill had been "mad as a wet hen" over his refusal to break ranks with the Russians, and that so far "luck" had been with him and he hoped that when a mistake inevitably was made, it would not be hard to rectify. The president then officially proclaimed Germany's surrender: "The flags of freedom fly all over Europe." Meanwhile the Russians sought delays and then a repeat surrender ceremony on May 9 at their headquarters near Berlin. Perhaps the Soviets sought to delay the war's end in order to continue to move their armor into Prague; they may also have wished to stage a "super-Hollywood" ceremony to celebrate their victory over Nazi Germany, as an American officer present in Berlin noted. Regardless, Eisenhower himself deplored skillful German propaganda seeking to promote an anti-Soviet coalition and shortly arrested German high command officials for prolonging the fighting on the eastern front.[65]

Meanwhile, Truman told Churchill that he agreed with the prime minister's recent assessment that only a Big Three meeting could resolve differences with the Soviets, especially over Poland, but that he could not leave Washington before June 30, the end of the fiscal year. He proposed that Churchill prepare an agenda, although he preferred that Stalin, who no longer had excuses not to "come west toward us," be the one to request a meeting. The president added that he would stick to the Anglo-American interpretation of Yalta.[66]

Truman's desire to delay a meeting at this time reflected the caution of a diplomatically inexperienced president who hesitated to deal with momentous issues directly across the table with two of the most experienced and shrewdest statesmen of the century. He also hoped that the professional diplomats might resolve the thorniest issues prior to a heads-of-state meeting. In a letter on May 10 to Eleanor Roosevelt seeking to set the record straight on Germany's surrender, he evinced interest in averting conflict with the Soviets: "I have been trying very carefully to keep all my engagements with Russians because they are touchy and suspicious of us. The difficulties with Churchill are very nearly as exasperating as they are with the Russians. But patience I think must be our watchword if we are to have World Peace. To have it we must have the whole-hearted support of Russia, Great Britain, and the United States."[67]

Nonetheless, once again Truman and Churchill tersely rejected the Soviet-proposed Yugoslav formula both to reorganize the Polish government and to provide a seat for the Warsaw Poles at the San Francisco meeting, where American diplomats also conveyed Truman's distress at the Russians' arrest of Polish Underground officials. But on May 10 Stalin was persistent that the American attitude precluded solving the Polish problem; while Churchill urged Truman to meet with him before confronting "U.J." outside Russian-occupied territory and to maintain U.S. forces in their advanced positions until they were satisfied with Soviet occupation policy in Germany and every country from the Baltic to the Balkans.[68]

Meanwhile, Under Secretary Grew reported that the continued advance of Marshal Tito's forces into Venezia Giulia in northeastern Italy, and especially their occupation of Trieste—which vital Adriatic port the Russians were eyeing, Grew added—was "strictly reminiscent" of the methods Japan used in Manchuria and Hitler copied in 1938–1939 to plunge the world into war. Moreover, if Tito succeeded, he would press claims on Austria, Hungary, and Greece. Grew's report ignored, however, that for nearly a century Slovenian, Croatian, and Italian nationalities had claimed the ethnically mixed region, which Italy had annexed after World War I and Tito was determined to regain regardless of great-power interest in the area.[69]

Nonetheless, the analogy moved Truman. On May 10 he snapped to Grew that the only way to deal with Tito's forces was to "throw them out," and the next day the president told Churchill that the overarching issue was whether territorial settlement would proceed by orderly process or by "force, intimidation, or blackmail," and that "our Allies" could not use the tactics of "Hitler and Japan." Diplomatic protests to Tito, and similarly to Stalin as provided under Yalta, were the first step; thereafter, troops under the ready command of Field Marshal Sir Harold Alexander might be used to expel Tito from Trieste. Truman was convinced that the only way to avoid further encroachments was to be firm here as over the issue of Poland.[70]

Churchill did not care much about what Tito did in Venezia Giulia, but he was bent on preserving Trieste for Italy, a Mediterranean ally. Thus the prime minister could scarcely wait for the protests to be delivered. He now argued in grandly crafted, ominous cables on May 11 and May 12, that the Russians had drawn an "iron curtain" down upon their front and withdrawal of Anglo-American power from the Continent would open the way to one of the "most melancholy" events in history: Russian ability to engulf "all the great capitals of middle Europe" and to press through a "ruined and prostrate Germany" to the North Sea and Atlantic Ocean. Nothing was more urgent than a "speedy showdown and settlement" with the Soviet Union before there were "no prospects of a satisfactory solution and very little of preventing a third world war."[71]

At the same time, the Truman administration precipitated a brief, bitter dispute with the Russians over Lend-Lease aid. Since 1941 the U.S. had provided Lend-Lease—ultimately $50 billion in military and industrial equipment and foodstuffs—to the Allies. But from 1943 onward, politicians, business groups, and the armed services—concerned about tax dollars, foreign trade, or military priorities—sought cutbacks. Beginning in 1944 only the Soviet Union was accorded unconditional aid (no justifications) and during March and early April 1945, while then vice president Truman presided over sharp Senate debate, Congress renewed Lend-Lease but prohibited its use for postwar reconstruction. Further, the Roosevelt administration barely defeated Senator Taft's "ironclad" amendment to prevent postwar shipment of goods already under contract and had to break negotiations with the Russians about financing transitional postwar aid. Long-term aid to the Allies remained highly uncertain.[72]

In late April 1945 Truman told his budget director that he feared that acrimony over Lend-Lease appropriations would intensify the "isolationist spirit" recently manifest in various guises, and that use of Lend-Lease for postwar reconstruction would "open ourselves to a lot of trouble." Meanwhile, Harriman's belief that economic aid provided a powerful lever to influence foreign political behavior spurred on American diplomats, who agreed with Foreign Economic Administration (FEA) officials to end the Soviet Union's unique unconditional aid status and to satisfy only war-related, justified requests at minimum levels. The diplomats reasoned that this would comply with Congress' recent legislation and make the Russians more responsive to American concerns. But they would take these steps, Stettinius instructed Grew, immediately after VE Day and without threat or political bargaining.[73]

After Harriman explicated the issue to Truman on May 10, the president supported "getting tough" with the Russians on Lend-Lease. For reassurance, Grew, Leo Crowley, head of the FEA, and Assistant Secretary of State William Clayton again briefed Truman on May 11. That night the president authorized restricting Lend-Lease to materials under contract to complete industrial plants or necessary for Far Eastern operations. Crowley also included excessively legalistic language—whose significance went unnoticed—to cut off at once all other supplies, and the next day zealous FEA officials even unloaded ships in port and called back others at sea headed for the Soviet Union.[74]

"The storm broke almost at once," Truman recalled, with protests from every ally—the British were "hardest hit"—but most significantly from the Russians. Harriman and Clayton were shocked, at least by the sweeping execution of the president's order, and within twenty-four hours they got Truman to countermand the unloadings and recall of ships and to limit the Lend-Lease "readjustment" as originally intended. Later Truman faulted chiefly himself for executive inexperience: signing the order without reading it once Grew and the "anti-Russian" Crowley told him that Roosevelt had previously approved, after which the two officials—Truman implied—overstepped their delegated authority.[75]

Despite Truman's effort to share or shift the blame for this episode, it is clear that he and his advisers purposely did not consult or warn their allies about the legislatively mandated Lend-Lease cutbacks because they intended to send the Russians a subtle but firm message, as nearly everyone had been advising in the last weeks. In that sense this "fiasco" resulted less from bureaucratic incompetence than from a self-inflicted wound. Not long afterwards Stalin would label the manner of cutbacks "unfortunate and even brutal," a "scornful and abrupt" termination of an agreement between two governments. He also said that it was a "fundamental mistake" to think that this would "soften them up." More questionable, however, were Stalin's assertions that the Russians had based their economic plans on Lend-Lease, that they would not have been angry if warned about the cutbacks, and that they regretted not being able to show their gratitude.[76]

Thirty days into his presidency Truman was dismayed. Triumph in Europe had brought not peace but diplomatic swords, never more apparent than in the May 10–12 wrangling over Poland, Yugoslavia, Lend-Lease; Churchill's foreboding, and desire for an early "showdown"; and the reports of American officials that failure to resolve current problems quickly and conclusively would lead to future crises. With his usual levity that disguised his discouragement, Truman would write a family friend in Independence on May 13 that having been "forced" to become president, he would "face the music" and do his best. That same night, however, confiding in a diplomat, Truman described far more somberly the crises he confronted as president, and his concern that perhaps he was "the last man fitted to handle it."[77]

Preparing for Peacemaking

Truman was not alone in worrying about Soviet-American relations in May 1945. Returning from the San Francisco Conference to Washington, Bohlen and Harriman agreed that perhaps the president might send Harry Hopkins, Roosevelt's personal wartime emissary to Stalin, to talk to the Soviet leader. They sounded out Hopkins who, even though he had been seriously ill and about to retire from government service, was now game for this mission. Harriman put the question to Truman, who said he had to think it over.[1]

Then on Sunday afternoon, May 13, Davies telephoned Truman to register alarm about Soviet-American relations. The president asked him to come at once to the White House, where Davies found him—barely moved into his quarters, books piled in hallways—in shirtsleeves at his desk in his second-floor study where they talked frankly for several hours. Davies was adamant that America's "tough" policy would produce only sharper rejoinders from the Russians, who probably believed that Hitler's defeat meant that once again their capitalistic enemies would seek to encircle them. The Russians were always hard-boiled about security and no longer feared "going it alone"; now their isolationists or military—or a Soviet Napoleon—might impose a *cordon sanitaire* of "friendly" states in Europe and Asia. Soviet isolation would prolong the war against Japan, and ultimately cause the U.S. to become an arsenal whose democratic institutions would erode. The president had to avert this tragedy through negotiating and a meeting of heads of state, a meeting that, Davies said, Molotov had just endorsed in a personal letter.

Truman confided his distress at the confrontations: no one seemed able to help him, and the newspapers—"these damned sheets"—only made matters worse. But the Russians were apparently backing Tito, Stalin was already "out of control," and "the Generals" were in charge. Davies said that it was more likely that the Russians were preparing to confront a hostile coalition, but rather than debate the matter, he proposed a summary of wartime diplomacy so that Truman, now an enthusiastic listener, might better find his course.

Davies afforded a perspective and information notably different from what others had provided Truman. When the ambassador recounted that in 1942 the Russians—"out of respect for President Roosevelt"—dropped their demand for a treaty to revise their frontiers, Truman interjected, "They did that?" Similarly, Davies reviewed the complex, bitter relations between the Soviets and the "Polish Reactionary Government"; the way in which he had facilitated FDR's first meeting with Stalin at Teheran by conveying Roosevelt's acquiescence in Russia's regaining its former Baltic provinces and Polish territory; and the way that FDR had won Stalin's confidence by playing the "Good Broker" between the Soviet Union and Britain. Davies contended that the fragile coalition was threatened by State Department animus toward the Russians, disputes over Argentina, and even Truman's brusque statements about Poland to Molotov, which had caused him to go "white." In short, if the Russians concluded that the West was ganging up on them again, Davies said, the worst was yet to come.

Truman was impressed, although he persisted that budget matters constrained him until July. But he asked Davies to go to Moscow to prepare a summit meeting, in Siberia if necessary. Davies declined because of poor health but agreed to take up the task by cable, while Truman, worried that Stalin might refuse, lamented the "terrible responsibility" of the presidency—and questioned his own ability to handle it. Yet with a flash of optimism, he added:

> Here lies Joe Williams, he did his best
> Man can do no more
> But he was too slow on the draw.

The president proposed a "little libation," insisted that Davies stay for "supper" with Truman's ninety-three-year-old mother, and regaled him with Calvin Coolidge lore. Davies left the White House buoyed by Truman's "horse sense," while the president sought a way to enhance American interests but accommodate the Soviets—or at least not provoke antagonism.[2]

I

Truman realized that the advice he had taken to be "hard" with the Russians had failed, as a visitor noted on May 16. The president would continue to resist pressure for an early summit from Churchill, who was bent on meeting before allied armies "melt away," and from Grew and Harriman, who believed that it was essential to take up the issues of Poland and Germany. At the same time, however, Truman determined to act on the Bohlen-Harriman advice and dispatched Hopkins to Moscow, despite objections from the State Department and from Jimmy Byrnes. "No need for anyone else to get the credit," Truman noted.[3]

The president's parochial outlook and his interest in accommodation with the Russians were revealed in his reflections a few days after his May 19 meeting with Hopkins. Truman seemed to need to reassure himself about Hopkins' "integrity" and "horse sense" liberalism, feared that Churchill and Stalin were trying to make him "THE PAW OF THE CAT" to pull their chestnuts out of the fire, and indicated that he had "no faith in any totalitarian government" because they were premised on "lies." But he also thought that the ninety years of world peace he sought depended on great power "trust," and he wanted Hopkins to convey that he sought a "fair understanding" with the Russians regarding the "purported" Yalta accords. Thus, he asked his envoy to tell Stalin that the U.S. always honored its agreements "to the letter" and "we intended to see that he did." Hopkins could make this point with diplomatic language or a "baseball bat."[4]

Truman appeared to accept the Yalta accords. He wanted Hopkins to indicate that American interest in the Baltic and Eastern European states was limited to "World Peace" concerns, that "Poland ought to have 'free' elections at least as free as [Frank] Hague and Tom Pendergast" and other politicians permitted in their bailiwicks, and that Stalin should restrain Tito and "make some sort of gesture"—even if he did not mean it—to show Americans that he would keep his word. "Any smart political boss will do that." Above all, Truman told Stettinius, Hopkins' mission—which Stalin accepted immediately—would "unravel" most of the issues, and by the time the Big Three met, "most of our troubles would be out of the way." At this same time, the president also commissioned Davies, with his "Order of Lenin—just conferred," to go to London to make Churchill "see the light."[5]

This Yalta-style diplomacy seemed to gain benefits even before Hopkins departed for Moscow in late May. Although Truman remained adamant that Tito's forces should not annex the Austrian province of Carinthia or Italy's Venezia Giulia, including Trieste, he moved cautiously. Need to redeploy U.S. troops to the Far East was one concern, but the president was also far less eager than Churchill, always a lion about British interests in the Mediterranean, to battle the Yugoslavs, or "Muscovite tentacle," as the prime minister called them. Truman now revised his recent "throw them out" directive and during the period May 14 to May 16 told Churchill that he did not want war with Yugoslavia. Four days later the president agreed that Field Marshal Alexander and General Eisenhower (who had submitted plans to move several U.S. divisions to southern Austria, just above the Italo-Yugoslav border) could use a show of force to "bring Tito to his senses," but they were to take maximum precautions not to have to fire the first shot.[6]

Truman also invited Stalin's help by invoking the "spirit" of Yalta and stating that at a peace conference the U.S. would recognize Yugoslavia's legitimate claims and its contributions to defeating Germany. Stalin, who had already pressed Tito to evacuate Carinthia, promptly proposed a military demarcation line that followed British preferences in Venezia Giulia and left Trieste in the hands of the Allied Military Government (AMG). Tito protested sharply in public on May 27, but a few days later Stalin told him that he had to withdraw his forces within forty-eight hours "because I do not wish to begin the Third World War over the Trieste question."[7]

Tito soon agreed in principle to a military demarcation line in Venezia Giulia, although the U.S. had to exert strong diplomatic pressure to gain his signed accord on June 8, with some arguments continuing another two weeks. But the agreement provided for exclusive AMG control over western Venezia Giulia, including Trieste, with the Yugoslavs administering the province's eastern area. Truman then overrode British and Italian pressures to impose strict administrative-territorial constraints on the Yugoslavs. Notably, the settlement he gained resembled FDR's Four Policemen model more than Wilsonian idealism or zealous anticommunism. Stalin in turn displayed his emphasis on realpolitik and concern to weigh each crisis in terms of its significance to Soviet interests rather than to act as a Communist ideologue bent on unlimited conquest.[8]

Truman was also determined to prevent General Charles de Gaulle, president of the Provisional French Government, from using military advance to gain political advantage. The French were aggrieved by their exclusion from wartime Big Three conferences, especially Yalta, where Stalin—despite the recent Franco-Soviet alliance—opposed their claim to an occupation zone in Germany and membership on the Allied Control Council (A.C.C.) that would govern the defeated nation. But strong pressure from Churchill, and then Roosevelt, caused Stalin to agree that the U.S. and Britain could carve a French zone out of their occupation area in Germany and that France could also join the Big Three—now Four—on the A.C.C. Nonetheless, when in late April, de Gaulle refused Eisenhower's request to withdraw French forces from Stuttgart so that he could incorporate the city into the U.S. zone, Truman threatened to reorganize the military command in Germany and to cut off French supplies even before the war ended. De Gaulle gave way but warned that U.S. policy might cause him to work with the Russians, despite their intent to "gobble" the continent. "I don't like the son-of-a-bitch," Truman snapped, and soon said that he was psychopathic.[9]

Relations with the French assumed crisis proportions in mid-May, when the French began to reinforce their garrisons in their former mandates of Syria and Lebanon (independent since 1941) and to seek special privileges, including control over their former local armies and military bases. The French also ignored Eisenhower's request to withdraw their forces from the Val D'Aosta in northwestern Italy in favor of Field Marshal Alexander's AMG, prompting concern about French annexationist tendencies. Foreign Minister Georges Bidault, in Washington from May 17 to May 21, further upset U.S. officials when he said that the French sought to take only a few villages for reasons of "amour propre," or recompense for Italy's 1940 invasion. Truman insisted that even among friends it was "best to place one's cards face up," and replied that French behavior in Italy threatened peaceful settlements as much as Tito's did. Grew added that French action in Syria and Lebanon greatly distressed the smaller nations at the UN Conference and might jeopardize Allied redeployment through the Mediterranean to the Pacific theater.[10]

French maneuvers in Lebanon and Syria soon precipitated armed resistance, and France, in turn, bombed Damascus. The French should be "castrated," Truman fumed, but appealed only for peaceful resolution. Churchill, however, determined to assert British primacy in the Mediterranean as well as preclude the inevitable Soviet note calling for great-power consultation. On May 31 British forces swiftly contained the French and restored order, opening the way to a negotiated settlement. Truman concurred in the action and dispatched a warship to Beirut, not to shoot, he said, but "simply to have the American flag in that part of the world."[11]

De Gaulle, bent on not suffering "another humiliation," promptly ordered his commander in the Val D'Aosta to maintain control by all means necessary, while Field Marshal Alexander sought permission to establish AMG authority, even by force. Truman was ready to agree, but took Stimson's advice to reiterate privately to de Gaulle his objection to military advance for political ends and disbelief at the prospect of American-French conflict. The president also threatened again to cut off France's supplies. On June 8 Grew reported that Truman's "masterly letter"—or "sledge hammer," as the president interjected—had caused de Gaulle to "climb down." This fact, plus containment of Tito and recent reports from Hopkins in Moscow, made the world scene look brighter.[12]

The Hopkins-Stalin talks had opened on May 26 and soon elated Truman. Poland would prove a vexing issue, but other matters were swiftly resolved. There was quick accord on Stalin's choice of Berlin for a conference site and

Truman's preferred late meeting date of July 15, which he chose in order to await results of the atomic test that was scheduled for July. Still, Stalin was not available until after June 28, and he also concurred that the meeting would be only preliminary to a full peace conference. Truman then denied Churchill's final pleas to meet earlier and to delay troop withdrawals to forestall the Soviets from drawing down their "iron curtain" in Europe. The president's only concessions to the prime minister were to abandon his intention to meet first with Stalin, to agree that Eisenhower should ensure that they were able to encamp on equal footing with Stalin in Russian-occupied Berlin, and to accept Churchill's name for the conference, "TERMINAL," whose dark symbolism was unintended.[13]

Hopkins also secured Stalin's reassurances about the Far East on May 28, namely that Russia, as agreed at Yalta, would enter the war by August 8, pending Chinese agreement to the Yalta concessions. The Soviet leader also endorsed China's unity and its sovereignty over Manchuria, under Jiang Jieshi's Guomindang government, and said that only the U. S. had the capital and personnel to underwrite China's reconstruction. Stalin sanctioned a trusteeship for Korea and expressed preference for unconditional surrender for Japan, while Hopkins probably went further than Truman would have in assenting to Stalin's allusion to a Soviet occupation zone in Japan. Still, Truman thought that Stalin "would come along all right now," as Wallace noted on May 29, and the president promptly told Hopkins that he would press the Chinese to meet Yalta's terms.[14]

The foremost issue remained: Poland. Initially, Hopkins tried to soften Stalin by insisting that Truman wished to continue Roosevelt's policy, whose "cardinal basis" was that the U.S. and Russia had worldwide, but reconcilable, interests. But failure to effect the Yalta accords, Hopkins said, had shaken public faith in Soviet-American amity and made Poland a symbol of whether the two great powers could cooperate. Hopkins delicately posited that although the U.S. claimed no special interest in Poland, except that its people should be free to choose their government, and that government had to be friendly to the Soviet Union. But the Truman administration believed that the Russians and the PPG, or Warsaw regime, had begun to exclude the U.S.

Stalin was unmoved. The Soviet public had been equally disheartened by America's "brutal" Lend-Lease cutbacks, support for Argentina, and refusal to share surrendered German ships. Stalin acquiesced in Hopkins' explanations of these incidents but persisted that Yalta provided for the Warsaw regime to be the basis of a new government. Stalin, however, was unyielding about Soviet security concerns and in his opposition to alleged British efforts to use Poland to erect a *cordon sanitaire,* and he held that the Soviets had taken less drastic measures—except for wartime exigencies—in Poland than the British had in Greece. But he proposed to resolve the Polish issue by agreeing to permit non-Communists, including former prime minister Mikolajczyk, to occupy four or five of the eighteen-to-twenty Cabinet posts.[15]

Hopkins accepted Stalin's "Yugoslav formula" but needed a week's tedious dealings to gain accord over which Polish representatives from London and Poland would negotiate with Warsaw regime officials to form a government. Stalin was insistent that he could veto elected London Poles, while Truman pressed Churchill to accede to the overall list. Truman and Churchill also sought to gain release of the sixteen arrested Polish Underground officials—the president feared that bad trial publicity would overshadow agreement on a government—but acceded to Stalin's pledge of leniency for lesser offenders to allow Hopkins to conclude his mission on June 6.[16]

Simultaneously, Truman gained a small concession that helped smooth public acceptance of the Polish accord. For the past two weeks the UN Conference had been snarled over Soviet insistence that Yalta had provided that permanent members of the Security Council, in addition to their veto power over decisions involving sanctions, could also veto placing on the agenda any dispute to which they were not a party. Truman deplored this veto over "free speech," as did Vandenberg, who assailed carrying Yalta to this "final, absurd extreme." Nevertheless, when the Yalta notes of both the State Department and Byrnes confirmed the Russian position, Truman prepared to acquiesce. But his sense that the issue was not merely "facts" but "politics" led him to take Stettinius' suggestion to appeal through Hopkins, who had just won Stalin's thanks for helping to resolve the Polish issue. Stalin promptly brushed aside Molotov's objections and agreed to forgo the veto over discussion. "America Wins!" Vandenberg exclaimed, and the way was now opened to rapid completion of the UN Charter.[17]

"We may get a peace yet," Truman exulted about Hopkins' work on June 7. The president now told Churchill that the Polish agreement was the best under the circumstances and rebuffed his repeated plea that Hopkins stop in London. Truman was also convinced that Davies, having returned from his May 25–28 talks with Churchill, "did a good one" calming the prime minister, who was enraged at the Russians—as well as Tito and de Gaulle—and at the prospect of withdrawal of U.S. troops from Europe to Asia. But Davies pressed the president's view that the U.S. and Britain would neither gang up on the Russians nor use troops for political leverage. Instead, they would "carry out Yalta" and seek a "balanced tripod of power." Meanwhile, even the crusty Harriman confirmed for Truman that whereas Stalin, "a realist in all his actions," would never understand the Americans' faith in abstract principles or principled interest in a "free Poland," the Soviet leader recognized his need to accommodate Anglo-American views. The Hopkins mission had succeeded beyond Harriman's hopes and shown the usefulness of dealing directly with Stalin. The special envoys had done good work, Truman concluded after meeting with them on June 13, and had fostered prospects for a "peaceful conference."[18]

Truman also noted that whereas the Soviet "dictatorship of the proletariat" was no different from that of the tsar or Hitler, he still hoped to "get along" with the Russians because they had been friendly toward the U.S. and willing to die for their own government. He worried that "every time we get things going halfway right with the Soviets some smart aleck attacks them," and he anxiously assailed former isolationists and conservatives who had "wanted to appease Germany but just can't see any good in Russia." He worried as well that "hyphenates" and "crackpots"—whether "Polish-Americans" or "Communist-Americans"—might harm rapprochement with the Russians.[19]

Thus, Truman told journalists on June 13 that Hopkins and Davies had cleared the way for a successful Big Three meeting and for resolution of the Polish issue "with no change in American policy." There had been a "very pleasant yielding" by the Russians, which showed "conclusively" that they wished to get along with the U.S. He refused to say anything to embarrass the Russians, criticized the London Poles for foot-dragging over final accord on a coalition government, and implored reporters not to go "muddying it all up." The State Department meanwhile concluded that the "weapons" that the London Poles proposed the Americans use to pressure the Russians would lead only to war.[20]

Ironically, both the trial of the sixteen Polish underground officials and negotiations over a Polish government proceeded in Moscow from June 17 to June 21. In the former case, all sixteen defendants were found guilty. A few key leaders were sentenced to eight-to-ten years in jail, with the others given, by Soviet standards, much milder punishment. Meanwhile, the Communists and their allies received seventeen Cabinet posts—including foreign affairs, defense, justice, and security—in the new Polish government, while Mikolajczyk took his seat as deputy prime minister along with three other non-Communist Cabinet members. Truman promptly recognized the new government—which was committed to hold early, free elections—on July 5, with the British reluctantly in tow.[21]

The president and most U.S. officials believed that they had achieved a pragmatic solution even if they deplored the "blackout" in Poland, and they hoped that free elections and "reasonably generous" economic assistance would prevent Poland from becoming a "Soviet satellite." Still, the U.S. seemed prepared to acquiesce, as the State Department put it, in "a political configuration in Eastern Europe which gives the Soviet Union a predominant influence in Poland," an inevitable development from the summer of 1944, when the Polish government-in-exile in London failed to reach political or territorial accord with Stalin and Nazi forces crushed the Warsaw uprising. Truman's announcement that he would take Davies and Hopkins to Berlin (the ailing Hopkins declined, partly to avoid upstaging incoming Secretary of State Byrnes) appeared to indicate that the president hoped to "get along" with the Russians.[22]

II

No issue was more important to getting along with the Russians than determining how to deal with defeated Germany. Roosevelt's wartime planning was often ambiguous, but he believed that the German nation and people had to bear responsibility, or guilt, for their "lawless conspiracy." FDR was adamant that surrender be unconditional and that Germany be rid of Hitler, the Nazis, and the "Prussian military clique." FDR commented viscerally about curbing Germany's "war-breeding gangs" through castration and thin daily diets from army soup kitchens and was readily amenable to breaking the nation into smaller pieces to curb its power.[23]

Similarly, Stalin believed that the Germans had to pay heavily for the devastation that they had imposed on the Soviet Union and be rendered incapable of waging such a war again. He proposed to extirpate Nazism and militarism, and during wartime would also press breaking the German state into smaller bodies, although Soviet vision of a future settlement was "hazy" and political goals were less important than economics and security.[24]

At Teheran in November 1943 Roosevelt proposed that Germany be dismembered into at least five states. Churchill balked, and suggested two states: Prussia and the rest of Germany, which would be tied to Austria and Hungary. Stalin flatly rejected Churchill's idea and expressed preference for FDR's proposal, but also wanted Allied occupation at military strongholds to protect against Germany's inevitable revival within twenty years. Teheran thus led only to preliminary agreement in principle that Germany would be dismembered and pay large reparations, as well as cede eastern territory to compensate Poland for its expected acceptance of the Curzon Line. All questions about Germany, however, were to be referred to the Big Three's recently created European Advisory Commission (EAC).[25]

The EAC made little progress over the next year. Then in September 1944 FDR supported Secretary Morgenthau's "Program to Prevent Germany from Starting a World War III." This Morgenthau Plan proposed to divide Germany into northern and southern states, dismantle heavy industry, and extract large reparations from existing German resources. FDR and Churchill endorsed this program to "convert Germany into a country primarily agricultural and pastoral," but FDR retreated in fall 1944 after the State and War Departments and British Cabinet argued that the Morgenthau Plan was too vengeful and that European prosperity depended on German productivity.[26]

At Yalta in February 1945 Stalin again pressed for agreement on German dismemberment—his policy of choice until then—but Churchill strongly resisted. FDR then effectively compromised the issue into abeyance: Germany's surrender terms would include dismemberment, but the steps to achieve this—along with disarmament—would be determined later, as the Allies deemed requisite for Europe's peace and security. FDR and Stalin also agreed that an Allied Reparations Commission would use $20 billion as a "basis for discussion" in determining how much the Germans would pay to compensate for damages done. The Soviets, who had suffered the most, would receive 50 percent of the reparations ($10 billion being a figure frequently mentioned), which were to be drawn from all of Germany and composed of existing resources, national treasure, current production, and labor. The British agreed to the Reparations Commission recommendations but stipulated objection to prior mention of any fixed sum. And at British and U.S. insistence, Stalin acceded to an occupation zone for France—to be carved from the British and American areas—and a seat for France on the governing A.C.C. Germany would also cede Königsberg to the Soviets and "substantial accessions" of its eastern territory to Poland in exchange for the now-imposed Curzon Line.[27]

In early March 1945 the State Department persuaded Roosevelt to sign a revised version of the War Department's directive, originally issued in September 1944 and known as Joint Chiefs of Staff (JCS) 1067, intended to help the military commander in the American occupation zone implement a harsh peace. Instead, the new JCS 1067 authorized the military commander to create centralized financial and economic institutions and to reduce reparations payments (to be limited to ten years) if these precluded a minimum standard of living for the Germans or required foreign loans. Morgenthau branded this document "damnable, an outrage," and after two weeks of lobbying got FDR to sign another revised JCS 1067 on March 23. The directive satisfied the War Department that the U.S. commander had governance discretion in his own zone and enough authority over German productivity to prevent inflation. But the German economy was not to be rehabilitated, the Germans were to be responsible for their reparations obligations, and their standard of living was not to exceed that in neighboring countries. The four-power A.C.C. would have "paramount" authority for occupation policy and promote political and economic decentralization, denazification, demilitarization, and democratization.[28]

Roosevelt's German policy was neither naive nor purely vindictive. He may have underestimated the need for German reconstruction to rehabilitate Europe. But he sought to effect retributive justice for Germany and to respond to legitimate claims of the Russians: their country had been devastated, but they now occupied eastern Germany. FDR intended that German and Polish territorial transfers redress Russian historical and national security claims; that German reparations compensate the Russians and others for war damages and preclude German war potential; and that the British revive their economy by taking over Germany's former export trade. Further, the president would not have to ask Congress, already reluctant over Lend-Lease, for postwar loans to Europe.

President Truman issued JCS 1067 on May 11, 1945, three days after Germany surrendered. An exultant Morgenthau hoped that "somebody doesn't recognize it as the Morgenthau Plan." Truman and others did, however, and there were complaints. General Lucius D. Clay, who had been deputy director under Byrnes of the Office of War Mobilization and then named by FDR in early April as Eisenhower's deputy for military government in Germany, disliked the directive. But he determined that it was subject to enough interpretation to be workable. However, his orthodox financial adviser (and FDR's first budget director), Lewis Douglas, declared the directive to be the work of "economic idiots!" and shortly resigned.[29]

Truman had issued JCS 1067 to provide an order for the initial "rough and tumble" period without deciding on postwar policy. In late April during an interdepartmental meeting on Germany, Truman told Morgenthau that he had read a "million words" since becoming president and that he was ready to read another million words. Then on May 4, after studying Treasury Department policy books for Germany, the president, rather nervously, told Morgenthau that he had been up all night worrying about the Yalta accords and it was clear that "Churchill, Stalin and I have to agree on a plan. . . . It's up to me. . . . You have to give me time."[30]

Truman balked for several reasons. He was never comfortable with Morgenthau and resolved to keep him at the fringe of policy making after he was known to oppose Byrnes' impending appointment as secretary of state. Truman had also long rejected the "old conqueror theory" of making the vanquished pay for the war and believed that Germany always confronted powerful tension between its "population and economics." He claimed never to have liked the Morgenthau Plan and was more disposed than the secretary or FDR to view German reconstruction as essential for Europe.[31]

Equally significant, Truman believed that he could drive a better, or harder, bargain over Germany than he thought Yalta had provided. On April 20 he ordered Isador Lubin, the White House economist whom FDR had designated to negotiate the final reparations agreement with the Russians, to delay departing for Moscow. Truman then named Edwin Pauley as his ambassador, reporting directly to the president, to head reparations negotiations. Truman chose Pauley, the extremely conservative California oil entrepreneur and Democratic party treasurer who had pushed him for vice president in 1944, because he wanted a bargainer "as tough as Molotov." Pauley paid little attention to anyone. He promptly told even the cautious State Department, anxious to coordinate policy, to "go to hell." And he set about to strike a bargain that would prove tougher and more divisive than Truman had imagined when he gave him so much authority.[32]

The president, meanwhile, listened to State-War-Treasury Informal Policy Committee on Germany (IPCOG) discussions. On May 5 William J. Donovan presented him with a lengthy OSS memorandum contending that amid uncertainty over whether the Russians were pursuing tough spheres-of-influence diplomacy or seeking unbridled expansion, Germany was the most critical region. "The Russia that dominates Germany will dominate Europe," Donovan's paper warned, and the Soviets would fight to prevent Western domination of Germany. The choice was partition between Western and Eastern blocs or, better, "a democratic-socialist Germany balanced between the Eastern and Western blocs but aligned with neither," albeit an extremely difficult compromise to effect.[33]

Truman told Morgenthau on May 9 not to publish anything about Germany. The president, an inveterate poker player who increasingly likened diplomacy to this game, insisted that "I have got to see Stalin and Churchill, and when I do I want all the bargaining power—all the cards in my hands, and the plan on Germany is one of them. I don't want to play my hand before I see them. . . . I am studying this myself." The next day Truman overruled Morgenthau's proposal that the U.S. military commander destroy Germany's synthetic oil plants.[34]

A week later Stimson presented his views. Long opposed to the Morgenthau Plan, he had argued powerfully to Roosevelt in 1944 that every European country, including Russia, depended on Germany's exports, imports, and raw materials, and that it was inconceivable that this "gift of nature," populated by people of "energy, vigor, and progressiveness" could be turned into a "ghost territory," a "dust heap." He was prepared to allow major territorial transfers (East Prussia, Upper Silesia, Alsace, and Lorraine), even north-south partition and internationalization of the Ruhr. But if the Allies kept Germany's economy at too low a "subsistence" level, this would only turn the German people's anger against them and "obscure the guilt of the Nazis and the viciousness of their doctrines and their acts."[35]

Stimson pressed these views to Truman during his first weeks in office and, at the president's urging, brought him a summary memorandum on May 16. The secretary supported punishing Germany's war criminals, disarming Germany permanently, and guarding "her government action until the Nazi-educated generation has passed from the stage." But occupation policy had to deal with reconstruction, including some reindustrialization. Germany had thirty million more people than agriculture could support, and together with Austria determined the balance of power in Europe. World peace depended on pursuing a policy that would not drive these people into a "nondemocratic and predatory habit of life." Stimson also insisted that because the U.S. and Britain would occupy the industrial regions and the Russians the agricultural areas, "we must find some way of persuading Russia to play ball." Truman found this viewpoint "very sound."[36]

The State Department provided similar briefing papers for Truman and Byrnes to use at Potsdam. The diplomats opposed dismemberment, which had been discarded at Yalta, as Stalin had acknowledged to Hopkins on May 28. They also opposed heavy reparations but were prepared to agree to $12–$14 billion as the basis for talks. State Department papers stressed the "lessons" of recent history, warning against repeating "the history of the Treaty of Versailles" and fixing harsh policies that would require German "Quislings and Vichyites" to carry out. They insisted that the German people would accept only national unity and that a "poor house" standard of living for Germany meant the same for Europe. U.S. officials also opposed a British proposal to merge the three western zones. They said this would prejudice chances for agreement with the Russians on economic matters and tend toward establishment of an economic wall between Eastern and Western Germany, and probably Eastern and Western Europe. The diplomats further warned against France's "obsession," as per its failed policy after World War I, with detaching Germany's bordering coal and industrial regions, the Ruhr and the Rhineland.[37]

Truman found the emerging State–War Department consensus compelling. When in mid-June Morgenthau asked if he might testify before the Senate about his plan for Germany, and also accept an invitation from France to travel there in July, the president, "much distracted and fidgety," put him off. Then on June 18 Truman rejected both proposals. He insisted, "I have got to work out a plan with Stalin and Churchill for Germany," and he was determined that neither Morgenthau, nor his ideas, would count for much anymore. The treasury secretary finally faced up to this three weeks later. He then sought reassurance from the president, about to leave for Europe, that he wished him to remain in the Cabinet until the war with Japan was over. Truman refused this, and Morgenthau had to resign.[38]

Meanwhile, the president ordered maximum coal production in Germany, although this did not signify reconstruction. Despite German hardships and protests, the coal was to be exported to avert a European crisis. The British and French approved this decision, which would require that more, and costly, foodstuffs and equipment be imported into Germany to increase coal production, while State Department reintegrationist views would predominate in formulating policy toward that country. This aid to Germany did not preclude reaching a reparations accord with the Soviet Union, although Pauley had already begun to question whether it was "premature" to agree to any specific sum that the Russians or others might expect from Germany, and Byrnes would ask whether even the State Department was not proposing too many constraints on Germany's economy. Truman would insist on leaving the details to experts, but by early July 1945 he clearly regarded Germany as a critical card in the "high stakes" diplomacy he was about to undertake at Potsdam. The other card was the atomic bomb.[39]

III

There was little strategizing about the bomb and diplomacy after Stimson and Groves briefed Truman about the weapon on April 25. But Stimson did talk at length on May 8 with the president's representative on the Interim Committee, Byrnes. This may have reinforced his view, as Truman recalled Byrnes saying to him that the bomb was so powerful that it "might well put us in a position to dictate our own terms at the end of the war," but Truman did not indicate whether the statement referred to Japan or the Soviet Union.[40]

Stimson first tied the bomb directly to war and diplomacy at the initial Interim Committee meeting on May 9 when he asked General Marshall whether the U.S. might reduce its casualties if it did not invade Japan until after the bomb had been tested, and learned that "we could get the trial before the locking of arms and much bloodshed." Later that day Stimson talked to Harriman, who persisted in saying that despite the Russians' fear of U.S. power, they would try to "ride roughshod" over their neighbors. Stimson noted that "S-1" was tied to this issue. Then on May 12 the State Department asked Stimson whether Russian entry into the war against Japan was so valuable that it precluded reconsidering the Far Eastern concessions granted at Yalta, and if Russia's claim to share in Japan's occupation might harm long-term U.S. interests. The State Department proposed that before fulfilling Yalta, the U.S. should seek Russian reassurance about their commitment to China's unity under Jiang's regime, restoration of Manchuria, and a trusteeship for Korea.[41]

"These questions cut very deep, and are powerfully connected with our success with S-1," Stimson noted on May 13. The next day he added that America's industrial power, combined with its forthcoming "unique" weapon, constituted a "royal straight flush and we mustn't be a fool about the way we play it." Still, he thought it premature to take up Far East matters—better not to argue with the Russians than to "let our actions speak for themselves." On May 15 he said as much to Grew and Forrestal. After the meeting, Stimson, in mistaken belief that Truman had scheduled a summit conference for July 1, despaired that this would occur so far in advance of the atomic test because it might be necessary to "have it out" with the Russians over Manchuria and North China, and S-1 would be "dominant" in these problems. It would be unwise to meet without knowing whether the bomb was "a weapon in our hands," he wrote, and it would be "a terrible mistake to gamble with such big stakes in diplomacy without having your master card in your hand." But he needed to "think over these things a little bit harder."[42]

Stimson met with Truman May 16 and was pleased to learn that the president intended to delay any summit meeting. "We shall probably hold more cards in our hands later than now," the secretary thought, although matters could be sorted out with the Russians, and he was anxious to differentiate his approach from that of "our hasty friends" in the State Department. Thus, he spoke to the president primarily about having the Chinese, not Americans, fight the Japanese in China; securing sufficient rations so that liberated Western European nations would not turn to "revolution or communism"; and designing German occupation policy to achieve reconstruction, which implied Allied "coordination" and persuading Russia to "play ball."[43]

Truman found this advice "very sound." He now believed that he had good reason, as he told Davies shortly, to postpone a conference until July, when the atomic bomb would be ready. The president intended to use his "ace in the hole," as he soon glibly referred to the bomb, against Japan for military purposes, but it might also bolster his negotiating hand or provide a hedge against undesirable concessions.[44]

The next week Stimson, responding to the State Department's queries, said that the Russians alone would determine whether they entered the Pacific war, but if they did "it will materially shorten the war and thus save American lives." He added that it was no use to seek Russian reassurances about the Far East because they could do as they pleased militarily in the northern Pacific. Further, Russian occupation of Japan might be helpful but was politically unwise, as the German case indicated. Thus, Stimson, who had counseled Truman not to confront the Russians over Poland, opposed reneging or a showdown in the Far

East. He believed that Soviet entry into the war would hasten Japan's surrender and save American lives but equally that America's unique weapon would be a "master card" in negotiating with the Russians.[45]

During the next weeks Stimson had little time to think about the relationship between S-1 and U.S. diplomacy. Meanwhile, Leo Szilard, eminent chief physicist of the "Metallurgical Laboratory" (code name for nuclear chain reaction project) at the University of Chicago, sought an interview with Truman to express his long-held concerns about an atomic arms race. Using a letter of introduction from Albert Einstein and an intermediary from Kansas City, Szilard got to the White House on May 27. But the president, anticipating the subject matter, had him referred to Byrnes, then in South Carolina, where the disappointed but undeterred physicist went the next day. In a prepared memorandum, Szilard insisted that either the demonstration of the atomic bomb or its use on Japan would precipitate an arms race with the Soviet Union. The U.S. would quickly lose its initial lead, and both nations would face mutual destruction. He recommended that the U.S. continue atomic development in secret for several years and build a highly advantageous position from which to negotiate international controls. As were most U.S. officials, Szilard was suspicious of Soviet behavior but convinced that the bomb would provide only short-term advantage and that its current use would not alter Soviet behavior favorably. His concern was to avert an arms race.

Byrnes was unmoved. He said that Groves had told him there was no uranium in Russia; Szilard doubted this, saying that the Soviets had access to rich uranium ore in Czechoslovakia. Byrnes apparently convinced Szilard that Congress might not continue to appropriate money for the atomic bomb unless its "success" was demonstrated, and that no government would formulate an arms control policy without an informed public to demand this. Szilard was distressed, however, that Byrnes thought it necessary to use the bomb to persuade the Russians to remove their troops from Eastern Europe. Or as the physicist recollected fifteen years later, he was "completely flabbergasted" by Byrnes' assumption that "rattling the bomb might make Russia more manageable." Szilard left the interview "depressed" but determined to petition Truman against use of the bomb on moral grounds.[46]

That same day Grew used his status as acting secretary (Stettinius was in San Francisco) to gain a meeting with Truman. Ambassador to Japan during 1931–1941 and an advocate of close relations with that nation—rather than China—to influence Asian affairs, Grew now proposed that the president use his Memorial Day speech to induce the Japanese into a face-saving version of unconditional surrender by declaring that after their defeat they could determine their own political structure, namely, retain the emperor, and maintain a functioning economy. This would allow for a stable constitutional monarchy.

Truman replied that he had been thinking along these lines, but asked Grew to discuss the matter with the senior military officials before setting a White House meeting. Grew met with Stimson, Marshall, Forrestal, and Chief of Naval Operations Admiral Ernest J. King, as well as various departmental aides who, along with Grew, were not apprised of the atomic bomb. For this reason Stimson weighed canceling the meeting. Instead, he got the group to agree that a negotiated settlement was desirable but for military reasons that Stimson could not divulge, the president should not make the proposed statement. "Timing remained the nub of the matter," Stimson concluded. When Grew reported this outcome to Truman, he immediately postponed any decision to modify unconditional surrender.[47]

Meanwhile Byrnes had returned to Washington to meet on May 31 with the Interim Committee, its Scientific Panel, and invited military officials. The agenda Stimson had prepared did not include the question of whether to use the bomb chiefly because everyone assumed its use to shorten the war, although the issue would arise and be discussed at lunch. Stimson's opening remarks that the bomb was not merely a new weapon but a "revolutionary change in the relations of man to the universe," and that the bomb would prove to be either a "Frankenstein which would eat us up" or a means to secure world peace, were intended to convince the assembled scientists that the policy makers grasped the implications of atomic weapons and to focus discussion on how to use the bomb. Comments that followed indicated consensus that vastly more destructive weapons would be produced in the next few years; that fundamental scientific principles were known in many countries and could not be "nationalized"; that the U.S. might share atomic information and retain its construction lead and that it would take a "competitor" five to ten years to catch up; and that the preferred course would be to establish an international system for inspection, controls, and sharing information. That led physicist J. Robert Oppenheimer, director of the Los Alamos Scientific Laboratory, where the bomb was being developed, to stress the possibility of preliminary talks with the Russians, who he said should not be prejudged on this matter. Marshall agreed. Prior Soviet-American differences usually evaporated, he said, and Russian uncooperativeness derived from security concerns. He suggested that the U.S. might build a coalition of "like-minded powers" to "force" Soviet agreement. To this end he proposed to invite two prominent Russian scientists to witness the first atomic test.

Byrnes immediately interjected that if Stalin were given any information, he would request full partnership. The president's spokesman quickly persuaded the committee that the U.S. should push ahead in secret with atomic research and "make certain to stay ahead" while also seeking better relations with the Soviets. No one asked if these goals were contradictory or whether maintaining an atomic monopoly would inhibit Soviet-American relations. During lunch either Byrnes or Stimson initiated talk about an atomic demonstration to induce Japan's surrender. But statements that there were technical difficulties, that there would be fanatical Japanese resistance, and that the Tokyo firebombings in March had killed as many people as would the atomic bombs caused the idea to be shelved. In the afternoon, Stimson guided the committee toward consensus that Japan should be subjected to successive (two) bombings, without warning, which would be restricted to noncivilian areas but intended to have profound psychological impact. The next day Byrnes got formal committee accord that "the bomb should be used against Japan as soon as possible; that it be used on a war plant surrounded by workers' homes; and that it be used without prior warning."[48]

Stimson and Byrnes chiefly were responsible for the critical Interim Committee decision reached May 31–June 1 to move swiftly to drop two atomic bombs on Japan without warning. Their primary goal was to gain Japan's prompt surrender. But as Byrnes' rapid negative response to the Oppenheimer and Marshall ideas about taking the Russians into camp on the bomb indicated, he and the secretary of war hoped that sudden use of the atomic bomb and atomic superiority would allow the U.S. to limit Soviet influence in the Pacific and negotiate arms control and scientific exchange on favorable American terms.[49]

Truman fully accorded with this "atomic diplomacy." He raised no questions when a "highly pleased" Byrnes brought first word of the Interim Committee recommendation, nor when Stimson presented his report on June 6. When the secretary of war stressed that S-1 should not be revealed until the "first bomb had been successfully laid on Japan" and that he worried about what might inadvertently be said before this at a Big Three meeting, Truman reiterated that he had delayed Potsdam until July 15 "on purpose to give us more time." Stimson continued that if the bomb were further delayed and the Russians got word of the project and asked to be taken in as a partner, the president should "do just what the Russians had done to us, namely to make the simple statement that as yet we were not quite ready to do it." When the secretary added that granting "partnership" implied gaining "quid pro quos," Truman immediately listed his priorities: "settlement of the Polish, Rumanian, Yugoslavian, and Manchurian problems."

Truman also seemed pleased to inform Stimson of Hopkins' having recently gotten Stalin to affirm that Manchuria would remain "fully Chinese"; Stalin wanted only Yalta's agreed concessions at Lushun (Port Arthur) and Dalian (Dairen) and joint operation of the Manchurian railways. Stimson cautioned that the Soviets would have more "actual power" in Manchuria than Jiang's government did, but the president reiterated that he had Stalin's "promise." Stimson then indicated that he had restrained the Air Force in order to leave targets in Japan that would allow the new weapon to "show its strength." The president "laughed and said he understood."[50]

Three days later Truman gave the Chinese their first notice of Yalta's terms. They balked at reestablishing special leases for the Russians. But he said firmly that his "chief interest" was to secure Soviet entry into the war, to save American and Chinese lives, and to settle postwar questions in order to eliminate future "tinderboxes." When the Chinese proposed that the U.S. become a third party to a Sino-Soviet treaty, the president said he was committed to Yalta and could not reinterpret it. Then on June 18 he had Grew tell Ambassador Patrick Hurley, with Jiang's government in China, that the Russians would never agree to a multilateral pact intended to regulate Sino-Soviet relations. The Chinese were to give the Russians their due within Yalta's terms, but no more. He hoped this would facilitate a timely but limited Soviet advance in Manchuria.[51]

The president, meanwhile, sought final plans to subdue Japan. At the same time there emerged the one group that knew of the bomb and unalterably opposed its use. This was a committee of scientists that had recently been created by Arthur Compton, head of atomic research at the University of Chicago, to weigh political and social implications of the bomb in response to Szilard's efforts to prevent its use and General Groves' complaint that scientists—especially Szilard—were not adhering to the chain of command. Chaired by Nobel physicist James Franck, this committee concluded on June 11 that surprise use of the atomic bomb was inadvisable from every viewpoint. It would be morally equivalent to Germany's indiscriminate rocket bombings, precipitate an arms race, and undercut U.S. credibility in negotiating postwar atomic arms control. Most important, the Franck Committee believed that the greater the "shock" value of the atomic bomb, the less likely (not the more likely, as Byrnes believed) were the Russians to be cooperative in helping to avert an arms race. But if the bomb had to be used eventually, the scientists proposed that it be demonstrated at an uninhabited area and only later be dropped on Japan if it still refused to surrender. Franck and Compton tried to see Stimson the next day, but he apparently evaded them. Thus, Compton left the report for Secretary Stimson with his own cover letter, which undermined the scientists' position by saying they had failed to note that use of the bomb would ultimately save lives and warn against future wars.[52]

Then on June 16 the Scientific Panel of the Interim Committee met to weigh the Franck Report and the issue of immediate use of the bomb. In its report to Stimson, the panel said that although opinion was divided over whether to use the bomb, the scientists could not propose any technical demonstration of the atomic bomb—except direct military use—likely to make Japan surrender. The panel recommended, however, that the U.S. should forewarn all of its allies of its impending atomic action, although it disclaimed special knowledge about the political problems atomic power created. Then on June 21 the Interim Committee reconfirmed its recommendation to use the bomb, but with the important added proviso that the president should give the Russians advance notice of the bomb's use at his forthcoming meeting with them, albeit without further information save that of U.S. interest in its future control.[53]

Meanwhile, Grew met with Truman several times between June 15 and June 18. The under secretary implicitly questioned the tactics, although not the objectives, of U.S. policy. With victory at hand on Okinawa, and bolstered by his department's Japan experts and former president Herbert Hoover, Grew reiterated his view that the Japanese could be persuaded to surrender if the president publicly guaranteed their "irreducible demands": the safety and preservation of the imperial dynasty. Grew's avowed purpose was to save American lives, but he also believed that the best means to regenerate Japan along constitutional lines and promote U.S. interests in the Pacific was to maintain the imperial household. Moreover, having led the State Department effort to question the need for Russian entry into the war and adhering to Yalta, Grew thought that successful implementation of his proposal might forestall Russian advances in the Pacific.[54]

Truman deferred the proposal to the Potsdam agenda for two reasons: Grew admitted that its effectiveness was "guesswork," and it contravened the doctrine of unconditional surrender. Further, officials strongly believed that even after the atomic bomb was dropped, there would be a protracted struggle to subdue Japan, which may explain Truman's diary notation on June 17 that his "hardest decision" to date was whether to "invade Japan" proper or to "bomb and blockade."[55]

The president called a special meeting on June 18 at the White House to take up this issue with the JCS. Marshall spoke first and authoritatively from a JCS memorandum that likened the scheduled invasion of Kyushu—Operation Olympic—on November 1 to the Normandy invasion. By then, however, he expected that air action would have smashed "practically every industrial target worth hitting in Japan" and the Japanese navy—"if it still exists"—would be powerless. Still, there was "no bloodless way" to end the war, "irresolution" among leaders could prove costly, and Russian entry into the war might be the "decisive action" that would force Japan to surrender, thus eliminating need for invasion of Honshu—Operation Coronet—in March 1946. Meanwhile the military estimated that casualties (dead, wounded, and missing) in the first month of the Kyushu attack would not exceed thirty-one thousand, the price paid for Luzon but less than for Okinawa. Marshall added his personal view that the invasion was the only course to pursue and that air power alone would not succeed, as the German case proved. The JCS agreed, as did Stimson, although he added that there was a "submerged class" in Japan who did not favor the current war—but would fight fiercely if attacked on their own ground—and he still hoped that something might be done to increase their influence.

Truman was especially worried that invasion by "white men" would further unite the Japanese (Stimson agreed), and he feared "an Okinawa from one end of Japan to the other." But the military had persuaded the president, who approved Olympic and reserved decision about Coronet. He also said he would do all he could at Potsdam to secure Russian aid in the war against Japan, and wanted to know what he had to do to occupy the strongest negotiating position.

However, when Admiral Leahy responded that he did not think it was necessary to insist on unconditional surrender—which would only increase Japanese resistance and U.S. casualties—Truman exhibited no leadership. He replied that this was up to Congress. But that body, of course, had no knowledge of the impending invasion, the atomic bomb, or current diplomacy. Perhaps the president meant to sidestep Leahy's point to assure that the bomb would be used, which presumably would strengthen his hand at Potsdam and shorten the war. As the meeting was breaking up, Assistant Secretary of War John McCloy, making reference to Japan's "submerged class," suggested that although use of an atomic bomb might avert an invasion and casualties, perhaps the president should first propose to the Japanese that they could retain the emperor and their own form of government and, at least for moral reasons, also warn them of the atomic bomb, or a "terrifyingly destructive" weapon. Truman agreed that this could be explored, perhaps with Byrnes. But the president said that the meeting had clarified for him the need for the JCS to proceed with the Kyushu invasion, although everyone in the room knew that a successful atomic test in the next month might eliminate need for the attack.[56]

Truman promptly departed for a week for the San Francisco meeting and promulgation of the UN Charter, while Stimson, working chiefly with Grew, Forrestal, and McCloy, took primary responsibility for drafting what would become the Potsdam Declaration. The secretary of war concluded that the JCS meeting had reached consensus on military plans although he and his associates now were moved to seek a way to induce Japan to "yield without a fight to the finish." But after Grew reported that Truman had already rejected the idea of assuring the Japanese of the safety of their imperial household, Stimson held that this must have conflicted with the president's plan regarding his meeting with Churchill and Stalin. Still, Stimson was determined, as he noted on June 19, to give the Japanese a "last chance warning" before a ground attack, perhaps in conjunction with "sanctions" such as heavy conventional bombing and "and an attack of S-1." A few hours later Marshall added that Russian entry into the war would be an additional sanction.[57]

Stimson continued to search for a way to avert or minimize an invasion even as he presumed use of the atomic bomb. He hesitated only slightly after discovery on June 25 of the Roosevelt-Churchill Hyde Park aide-mémoire of September l944—mislaid since then—which stated that the bomb "might, perhaps, after mature consideration" be used against the Japanese, who were to be warned that the bombardment would continue if they did not surrender. Despite the tentative language about the use of the bomb and lack of clarity about whether the warning was to precede or follow its use, Stimson said the memorandum was not a "bombshell." He noted the next day that in order to induce a swift surrender, Japan had to be "sufficiently pounded," although only "possibly with S-1." But he remained certain that "the country will not be satisfied unless every effort is made to shorten the war," which suggested use of the bomb. A couple of days later, Under Secretary of the Navy Ralph Bard, a member of the Interim Committee who had reversed himself about use of the bomb, proposed in a "thinking out loud" memorandum that the U.S. should negotiate with Japanese representatives and give them a few days notice of intent to use an atomic bomb, an offer to retain the emperor, and a warning of Russia's entry into the war. But Stimson, and then Truman—who apparently did not give Bard much weight—replied only that the issue was under study.[58]

Stimson brought Truman the proposed declaration on July 2 that he, Grew, and most officials in their departments thought should be drawn to permit the U.S. to maintain unconditional surrender but state more precisely the treatment that the Japanese would be accorded, especially regarding the "fate of their throne." The declaration called for unconditional surrender of Japan's military forces and "stern justice" for "war criminals," but otherwise pledged civil liberties and a "sustaining" economy and integration into the world trade order, and a post-occupation representative form of government, which could include a "constitutional monarchy under the present dynasty."

The declaration, however, did not mention Russian entry into the war or the atomic bomb. But Stimson's covering notes to Truman proposed that if the Russians were about to enter the war, they should be asked to sign (as an additional "warning") the declaration, which could be easily revamped to include the "efficacy" of the bomb if the warning was to be delivered in conjunction with the bomb's use. Most important for Stimson was that the declaration's terms be stated unalterably—no deviation, no alternatives—so that the Japanese, who were susceptible both to "fanatical resistance" and "reason," would see no choice but to surrender prior to the American invasion. Hence the declaration's success depended on its "potency," and it was not to be issued until Japan's "impending destruction" was "clear beyond peradventure" but "had not yet reduced her to fanatical despair." He concluded that if the Russians were part of the warning, the declaration and bomb's use had to come before their attack on Manchuria had "progressed too far."[59]

In effect, Stimson believed that the bomb, combined with modified unconditional surrender, and perhaps the additive of a Russian attack, provided the "potency" to induce Japan's quick surrender. This would save victor and vanquished the agony of an invasion and expedite future reconciliation. Early release of the declaration and bomb were also intended to limit the Soviet advance into Manchuria to Yalta's terms. Finally, Stimson and Truman had agreed so often that the bomb would be a "master card" in diplomacy that this was now an article of faith.[60]

Truman read Stimson's papers carefully on July 2, was markedly impressed, and invited the secretary for a lengthy talk the next day. The secretary used this "fireside chat" to press the Interim Committee's recommendation that the Russians be informed about the atomic bomb. He urged that if relations with Stalin seemed good enough at Potsdam, the president should "look sharp" for the proper moment to tell him that the Americans were "working like the dickens" on the atomic bomb and were near ready to use it on Japan. But he should offer no further details except U.S. interest in later discussions about how to use the bomb for world security. Truman replied that this was the best way to do it—and also agreed to Stimson's request that he and McCloy be allowed to attend the Potsdam meeting. On July 3 Stimson told British members of the Combined Policy Committee, created in 1943 by FDR and Churchill to deal with the atomic bomb, that although the weapon might not be ready for use until a few weeks after the Potsdam meeting, failure to mention it to the Soviets there would seriously affect Big Three relations.[61]

Truman now appeared to have a coordinated military-diplomatic policy to end the Pacific war. He also appeared to have made progress toward having his diplomats resolve, or establish strong negotiating positions for, his toughest problems before he departed for Potsdam. He preferred to leave the details to his "experts," who seemed to have gotten him through crises over Poland and Yugoslavia, decided to use German coal to provide for Europe's immediate needs, and put off the Russians on a German reparations settlement while weighing how to deal with this defeated nation. Further, as several of the president's "kitchen cabinet" advised on July 6, the day before he would depart, "We think that as a well-known Missouri horse trader, the American people expect you to bring something home." The president—"blue as indigo," he would tell his wife—gathered his "negro preacher coat and striped pants, tails, tux, winter clothes and spring ones, high hat, soft hat, and derby," and set sail for Europe. "It'll be a circus sure enough," he wrote. "But we will get it done I hope." He would, but at greater cost than anyone imagined at the time.[62]

A Stony Place: Potsdam

Harry Truman returned to Europe for the first time since World War I on July 15, 1945. The president's ship anchored in Antwerp and then he flew from Brussels to Berlin to take up residence in suburban Potsdam in the "Little White House," a commandeered stucco mansion filled with hastily gathered and mismatched furniture, overlooking Lake Griebnitz. Churchill and Stalin would be housed in the neighborhood of Babelsberg, and Big Three formal meetings would be in the nearby Cecilienhof Palace, an ornate Tudor structure completed for Crown Prince Wilhelm in 1917.

The war's carnage revolted Truman: Berlin reduced to rubble, pathetic refugees dragging belongings to nowhere, and Russian soldiers brutalizing and looting—just as the Germans had done to them, he noted, "retribution to the nth degree" brought on by Hitler and the German people. And grim reminder that machines were centuries ahead of mankind's morals.[1]

Truman was not the idealist or innocent at Potsdam he alleged to be, nor a statesman. He went there to work solely for American interests, "win, lose or draw—and we must win." He would not give away American assets. "Santa Claus is dead," he said, and even Europe's starving millions had to learn to help themselves. Never again would the United States "pay reparations, feed the world, and get nothing for it but a nose thumbing." The president would rely chiefly on Byrnes, his "conniving" secretary of state, for tough negotiating. Even the State Department stood, "as usual," against American interests, while Churchill, Truman noted after meeting him for the first time on July 16, was too clever and given to "hooey" and "soft soap" about Anglo-American affection. The president seemed almost to prefer Stalin, who at their introductory meeting the next day responded warmly to Truman's assertion that he was not a diplomat but a "yes or no" man. The president seemed unperturbed at the Soviet leader's proposed broad agenda. "I can deal with Stalin. He is honest—but smart as hell," Truman recorded, perhaps to reassure himself. He would note repeatedly that Stalin liked his blunt talk, or "hammer," and was ready to compromise when unable to get his way.[2]

At the outset of the Potsdam meeting, however, Truman's chief concern seemed to be to gain the swiftest, least costly end to the Pacific war by securing Russian entry as agreed at Yalta, which Stalin confirmed at their first meeting would occur by August 15. "Fini Japs when that comes about," Truman exulted on July 17, although he also thought the Japanese would fold up even sooner: "when Manhattan appears over their homeland." Quick end to the war thus seemed assured, and despite Stalin's "dynamite" agenda, Truman believed that the "dynamite" he would soon explode guaranteed that he could shape, or "win," peace on his terms.[3]

I

The atomic bomb did not change basic American foreign policy at Potsdam. But its presence was immediate, its influence pervasive. Truman and Byrnes quickly became confident that they could achieve their goals in the Pacific and in Europe with little or no yielding to Russian claims, and despite Yalta. "Atomic diplomacy" thus constituted efforts to revise or "contain" prior accords, and to press American negotiating positions to the limit, or "impasse," as Truman would soon say. As Stimson reflected shortly after leaving Potsdam in late July, even he had been unaware of the bomb's great psychological effect on his thinking.[4]

Stimson had consistently advised Truman to use the bomb on Japan without warning to end the war expeditiously and to contain Russian advances in Manchuria. But the declaration the secretary had proposed on July 2 sought to lessen Japan's will to fight by holding out prospect of a post-occupation constitutional monarchy, an idea probably borrowed from Under Secretary Grew, who did not know about the bomb. Grew gave his own draft declaration, containing an offer to retain the emperor, to Byrnes as he departed for Potsdam. But other State Department officials, including assistant secretaries Dean Acheson and Archibald MacLeish, and former secretary of state Cordell Hull, disagreed, and Grew dutifully forwarded their views to Byrnes. In sum, these officials opposed modifying unconditional surrender because they linked the emperor to Japanese militarism, and also feared that Japan's military would thwart Grew's proposal or that Americans would construe it as "appeasement."[5]

Truman and Byrnes reserved decision during their Atlantic crossing, but by July 16 officials in Washington and Potsdam had learned from diplomatic intercepts that Foreign Minister Togo Shigenori had just asked Ambassador Sato Naotake in Moscow to see if the Soviet leaders, after their return from Potsdam, would receive a special envoy, former prime minister Prince Konoye Fuminaro. He would be under instruction from Emperor Hirohito to negotiate a rapprochement with the Russians (this would forestall their attack on Japan) and seek Moscow's good offices in brokering a peace with the U.S. and Britain with the understanding that the primary obstacle to ending the war was unconditional surrender.[6]

The "psychological moment" was at hand, Stimson concluded on July 16. He no longer thought that Japan had to be "pounded" with S-1, given the marshaling of U.S. forces, the threat of Russia's entry, and "recent news" of Japan's attempted approaches to Moscow. He urged Truman to issue a "prompt" surrender warning, "rather earlier than later," and a commitment to retain the emperor as a constitutional monarch. The Russians, however, were not to be notified unless there was full agreement on the terms of their entry into the war. Meanwhile, conventional bombing and Russian war preparations would continue, providing more reason for Japan to surrender; but if it did not, then "the full force of our newer weapons should be brought to bear."[7]

Stimson's sense of urgency heightened that night upon receipt of first word of the successful test of S-1, and he rushed to the Little White House to inform Truman and Byrnes. The conversation was brief. The president and secretary of state were "delighted" with the atomic news, and afterwards Truman casually commented that he felt "greatly relieved." But when Stimson returned the next morning to discuss his proposed early warning, Byrnes ruled this out and outlined a timetable, Stimson concluded, to which Truman had already agreed. The secretary of war abandoned his proposal without demur. Meanwhile, Byrnes instructed the State Department that there would be neither an early warning for Japan nor a guarantee for the emperor. The final moment, and no longer than that, for atomic restraint had passed.[8]

Assured that the bomb worked, Truman and Byrnes were now determined to use it not only to subdue Japan but to advance their political objectives. This became evident at Potsdam first with respect to the Far East. The Yalta accords had conceded that the Russians would regain use of Lushun (Port Arthur) as a naval base and Dalian (Dairen) as a commercial port, joint operation of the Chinese Eastern Railroad and South Manchurian Railroad, and the right to safeguard their preeminent interests. During July 14–17, however, Stimson and Harriman insisted that the Russians intended to monopolize Manchuria's railroads and trade, jeopardizing the Open Door policy. There was also concern that the Soviets wanted to extend their military zone in Lushun to Dalian, although State Department analysts conceded that this "threat" to U.S. interests in China was not in the Russians' proposals, only their future violation.[9]

When Stalin assured Truman on July 17 of Russian entry into the Pacific war, the Soviet leader complained that the Chinese were snarling the Sino-Soviet treaty requisite to implement Yalta by thwarting the Russian effort to protect their preeminent interests through appointment of a Russian director of railroads and a majority on the governing board. But when the president asked how Russian control might affect U.S. interests, Stalin affirmed that Dalian would remain a free port—the Open Door, Truman interjected—while Byrnes cautioned that a treaty had to stay within Yalta's limits. Stalin insisted that Soviet terms were more liberal than those of Yalta, which, he said, would have allowed Russian troops in Manchuria as under the tsars. But the Chinese, he complained, neither saw the big picture nor understood horse trading. The Americans merely reasserted their interest that Dalian be a free port.[10]

Truman left the meeting in high spirits. He had just "clinched" the Open Door in Manchuria, he told Stimson, and the next day wrote that "I've got what I came for," namely, Russian entry into the war "with no strings on it" and a pending Sino-Soviet treaty in "better form" than expected. The president's enthusiasm, however, was limited to his belief, or relief, that the combination of atomic and Soviet attacks guaranteed Japan's quick defeat, a year sooner than expected. "Think of all the kids who won't get killed!" he wrote. He was also more determined than ever to use the atomic bomb to further his diplomacy.[11]

Indeed, Truman seemed "greatly reenforced," Stimson noted on July 18 after relaying a second, detailed report of the atomic test. Further, when at midday Churchill suggested modifying unconditional surrender to allow the Japanese to quit the war with honor, the president sharply rejoined that they had abandoned honor at Pearl Harbor. Moreover, he would not tell the Soviets about the bomb until the end of the conference, although he soon acceded to the prime minister's expedient advice, which accorded with the earlier views of Stimson and the Interim Committee, that they avoid Russian recrimination by giving notice, but no detail, of the atomic experiment. Later that day, when Stalin ostensibly solicited the president's opinion about whether to reply to Japan's proposal to send a diplomatic mission to Moscow and a message from the emperor indicating that unconditional surrender left "no way out" of the war, Truman again disparaged Japan's good faith, leaving Stalin to say that he would "lull" the Japanese with a vague answer. In fact, the Russians believed that they had more to gain by entering the war than by dealing with Japan, and Stalin had already asked his military to try to advance their attack by ten days.[12]

The Americans were equally intent to try to lull Stalin. As Truman wrote, "Manhattan" would cause Japan to fold up "before Russia comes in," while

Byrnes indicated on July 20 that he thought he could "out maneuver Stalin on China" by having the Chinese stall negotiations. This would assure use of the bomb and the war's end before Stalin could "take over" in Manchuria, from which the Russians would be hard to dislodge, and this would "save China." When Stimson the next day brought General Groves' complete and "eloquent" report on the atomic blast, which had proved far more destructive than anticipated, Truman and Byrnes were "immensely pleased." The president was "tremendously pepped up," Stimson observed, talked about it repeatedly, and said that it "gave him an entirely new feeling of confidence"—as it did Churchill, who now concluded that telling Stalin about the bomb was a way "to use it as an argument in our favor in negotiations."[13]

Truman grew even more confident when Stimson brought him an "accelerated timetable" for the bomb on July 22. He also supported the secretary in his debate with General Groves and the atomic bomb Target Committee in Los Alamos. In May this group had proposed Kyoto as an atomic target, but Stimson flatly rejected destroying Japan's ancient capital and site of its major religious shrines and palaces. Now the Target Committee again proposed to hit Kyoto, only to have Stimson say he would not change his decision and would take his case to the president.[14]

Even if the "Japs" were "savages," Truman noted, the U.S. as the world's leader had to restrict this "most terrible" weapon in history to military targets, which provided even more reason to be thankful that neither "Hitler's crowd [n]or Stalin's" had discovered it. Thus the president again backed Stimson, although expediency played a significant role in their decision. As the secretary recorded, "wanton" bombing of Kyoto might preclude Japan's reconciling in the postwar era with the U.S. rather than the Soviet Union, and undermine American policy in event of future Russian aggression in Manchuria. Ironically, however, there still remained in force the Interim's Committee's conclusion on June 1 that the atomic bomb should be used to produce as great a psychological impact as possible upon the Japanese people, namely, it should be dropped without warning on an area that included factories and workers' homes.[15]

Readiness of the bomb also led Truman to conclude, as Churchill observed, that he no longer wanted the Russians in the Pacific war. On July 23 the president asked Stimson to obtain General Marshall's opinion on this matter. Marshall indicated that the Soviets had already served U.S. purposes by drawing Japan's forces toward Russian troops massed on the border of Manchuria, but the latter could not be prevented from entering and plundering the province. He proposed, however, that Truman might inform Moscow that the American and British chiefs of staff had finished their business at Potsdam and were going home, which might encourage the Soviets to indicate their military plans. Stimson concluded from this that Marshall shared his view that "with our new weapon we would not need Russian assistance to conquer Japan." The next morning Stimson conveyed this information to Truman, who said that he would follow up on the idea that afternoon. He also saw no choice other than to urge the Chinese to continue, rather than break off, their treaty negotiations with Moscow. But he insisted that they were to offer no more than Yalta's concessions, although the negotiations were now intended less to meet the terms intended to bring the Russians into the war than to forestall a preemptive strike in Manchuria.[16]

Byrnes, however, indicated on July 24 that he still hoped to play for time to be able to defeat Japan with the atomic bomb, and thus Russia would "not get in so much on the kill" nor be able to press its claims on China. Nor would the Russians have a claim to an occupation zone in Japan, which the Americans were determined to preclude, especially given recent experience in Germany. Not surprisingly, Stimson recorded that "the program for S-1 is tying in what we are doing in all fields." At the same time, officials in Potsdam pressed the Interim Committee for a definite atomic schedule, and learned on July 24 that the bomb would be ready about August 4 or August 5, and not later than August 10.[17]

Stimson informed Truman, who said that he now had exactly what he wanted and was "highly delighted." The British had just approved the proposed Potsdam Declaration, which Byrnes had redrafted so that it demanded that Japan surrender unconditionally or face prompt and utter destruction. The Japanese were not to be destroyed as a people or a nation, and they would be allowed to maintain an economy to sustain themselves and pay reparations. But the Allies made clear their intent to disarm Japan, mete out "stern justice" to war criminals, and occupy the nation. The declaration contained no references, however, to the atomic bomb or impending Soviet attack, nor to the emperor or his fate. There was only a vague proviso that the Japanese might freely choose a peaceful government after Allied objectives were achieved. At the behest of Stimson, who had swung back to slight hope of averting an atomic blast, Truman agreed to give verbal assurances to the Japanese about the emperor's status if that alone barred surrender, but the president thought this development unlikely. Meanwhile, he had the Potsdam Declaration rushed to Jiang Jieshi for his signature, but when there was no immediate response, he said he would wait only twenty-four hours before acting. Most important, the president would not ask the Russians to sign, although this would have added a compelling new threat to Japan.[18]

Nor did Truman follow Stimson's or the Interim Committee's recommendation to inform the Russians about the atomic bomb. Instead, the president engaged in a small charade intended to maintain the image of a faithful ally. After the Big Three meeting on July 24, Truman told his interpreter, Charles E. Bohlen, not to accompany him as he deliberately approached Stalin and nonchalantly remarked that the U.S. had a new weapon of unusual destructive power. The Russian leader may have offered only a perfunctory thanks for the information, although Truman later recalled his having said that he hoped it would be put to good use against Japan. But at the time the president naively exulted that his little deception had worked, while Byrnes, as calculating as Churchill, guessed that Stalin would grasp the significance of Truman's words by the next day.[19]

Probably Stalin already had, even if he did not recognize the full import of the bomb at that moment. Still, he agreed with Molotov's view of Truman's cryptic message that the Americans sought to surprise the Russians and to "raise the price." Stalin indicated no willingness to pay, however. He had already asked his military to move up their attack on Japan, and now he ordered Soviet atomic research to be speeded up. In the meantime on July 25, Stimson and Marshall approved the directive for General Carl Spaatz, head of the Strategic Air Force, to drop an atomic bomb on one of four designated targets (Hiroshima, Kokura, Niigata, and Nagasaki) about August 3, and "additional bombs" as soon as they were ready. This single order for the bombs would stand, Truman said, unless Japan accepted America's surrender terms.[20]

The U.S. issued the Potsdam Declaration on July 26. The Russians protested that they had not been asked to sign. Byrnes rejoined that the president did not wish to embarrass them because they were not yet in the war, although on July 28 the secretary told Navy Secretary Forrestal that he was "most anxious to get the Japanese affair over with before the Russians got in." Whether Soviet adherence to the declaration would have induced immediate Japanese surrender is moot. But significantly, at just this time Foreign Minister Togo (who was interested in ending the war) had authorized Ambassador Sato in Moscow to approach the Foreign Ministry again to reiterate Japan's interest in having Prince Konoye travel to Moscow with the emperor's sanction in an effort to solidify Russo-Japanese relations and have Moscow mediate an end to the war. To be sure, as Sato told Togo, Japanese failure to formulate "concrete" terms for a settlement virtually precluded a positive result. But on July 28 Togo said that he would not even try to deal with the Potsdam Declaration until he had a reply from the Russians. Of course, if Stalin had been signatory to that document, there would have been nothing to await. In fact, that same day the Soviet leader told Truman that he intended to give an even more emphatic no to Japan's overtures than previously. Still, when Stalin requested an invitation to join the Pacific war, the president skirted this through his advisers' legalism that the Soviet Union could invoke the 1943 Moscow Declaration and the UN Charter to collaborate for peace.[21]

The Japanese government, meanwhile, never weighed surrender on the basis of the Potsdam Declaration, whose public communication via broadcast and leaflets, rather than through diplomatic channels, led them to regard it as propaganda. Further, even Togo rejected unconditional surrender as offering "no solution other than for us to hold out until complete collapse because of this one point alone." But the Japanese, especially the military, had additional conditions, including that there be no occupation, or a very limited one, of the home islands, and that they disarm themselves and hold their own "war crimes" tribunals. Thus, during Cabinet deliberations Prime Minister Suzuki Kantaro proposed to respond to the Potsdam Declaration with a policy of *mokusatsu,* meaning "to take no notice of," but also carrying a connotation of "to treat with silent contempt." On July 28 the government made this policy public.[22]

The Americans made no effort to explore Japan's *mokusatsu* response. There was neither intention nor time to do so, because the schedule for rapid use of the atomic bombs was already in play. On July 30 Stimson, who had returned to the U.S., informed Truman that progress on S-1 was so swift that officials wanted immediate approval for its use. The president scrawled his reply the next day across the back of the cable: "Release when ready but not sooner than August 2. HST," by which time, Truman knew, he and his delegation would have departed from Potsdam, convinced that use of the atomic bomb would assure that they had outmaneuvered the Russians in China and secured control over Japan's defeat and occupation. Further, as Stimson had said a week earlier, the bomb was "tying in" with everything they were doing, including in Europe, especially in Germany. In fact, Truman's diplomacy of the past two weeks suggested that he thought that the bomb empowered him to press maximal negotiating positions and that eventually the Russians would prove manageable, as Byrnes had said in May.[23]

II

Truman went to Potsdam convinced that he had to negotiate with Stalin over Europe if only because the Red Army stood astride half the continent. Germany was foremost on the agenda, Eastern Europe next. Truman remained steadfast about retaining every bargaining card regarding Germany. He fully supported the predominant State–War Department consensus of mid-July that there were only three choices for Germany: to destroy the nation, which was "unthinkable"; to occupy and police it permanently, which was "inconceivable"; or to reeducate the Germans to live freely and, ultimately, with access to modern science and industry, which were basic for making weapons but did not cause militarism. The soul of man abhors a vacuum, the analysts said, and it was necessary to create a new German state and mind in place of the old. And just as Russia feared Germany and would substitute Communism for Nazism, the U.S. had to play its historic role and propagate liberty.[24]

Specifically, Germany should be denazified and temporarily demilitarized. But the government had to be given economic means and responsibility to sustain a reasonable national living standard and to pay moderate ($12–$14 billion) reparations, and to do so without heavy foreign borrowing to avert post–World War I mistakes and to assure the U.S. that it would not have to fund German rehabilitation or reparations. The Americans and British agreed that politics and economics required that Germany should be reconstituted along its 1937 frontiers, while recognizing that Yalta provided that Poland should receive substantial accessions of territory in the north and west from Germany, presumably the region in East Prussia that Poland already occupied up to the Oder River. But the French were not to annex the Ruhr or Rhineland, nor were the Russians to be allowed to use internationalization to gain direct access to the region's industry and coal or to intrude in Western Europe. Indeed, the Russians had already exceeded Yalta and created economic problems by permitting the Poles to push their border with Germany beyond the Oder–eastern Neisse River to the western Neisse to incorporate Silesia, with its coal mines.[25]

Then in early July Truman and Byrnes approved reparations negotiator Ed Pauley's firm statement to the Russians of the Americans' new "first charge" principle: there would be no annual reparations from current German production until payment was first made, presumably from a "large" export revenue balance, for occupation costs, foodstuffs, and essential imports. Pauley insisted that it was necessary to feed the cow to get milk, even if the cow was to be kept slim and without horns. Finally, on July 16 Stimson reiterated his arguments to Truman that European and world recovery depended upon Germany's productivity and reintegration into world trade. Stimson and Byrnes also rejected a last-minute State Department proposal to internationalize the Ruhr and Rhineland.[26]

Truman accepted as well the prevailing view that the Declaration on Liberated Europe required the Big Three to facilitate representative governments and stable economies in Eastern Europe. Although Soviet seizures of property as war booty, and pressure for reparations agreements (as with Rumania in 1944), joint stock companies, and bilateral trade treaties threatened Americans with uncompensated property losses and closed economic doors, this concern was not determinative. The U.S. had only 4 percent of its overseas investments in Eastern Europe and sent only 2 percent of its annual prewar exports there. But steady reports from the field about how the Russians dominated the tripartite ACCs and facilitated the rise to power of local Communists appeared to confirm Harriman's dire April warning that Russia was engaged in a barbarian invasion of bordering states, and concern that "unconditional appeasement" of the Soviet Union meant the inevitable advance of its tyranny from "agrarian Europe" to the industrial heartland and across the globe.[27]

Despite scant prospect of changing the reality in Eastern Europe, American diplomats insisted that before the U.S. recognized the new regimes there, the Russians should agree to power sharing on the ACCs and to Big Three–supervised elections, after which peace treaties and reparations could be negotiated. But as the JCS cautioned in late June regarding Poland's incorporation of German Silesia, there could be no military response to Soviet violations of Yalta in its occupation zone, although the issue might be used to bargain.[28]

Soviet policy in Germany in spring 1945 remained uncertain and opportunistic, as well as contradictory given that the Red Army's raping, pillaging, and property removals alienated the population from its occupiers. Stalin, speaking to leaders of the German Communist Party (KPD) in Moscow in early June, urged them to resist the idea of a nation divided between the Western Allies and Russia. Rather, the KPD should establish a unified working-class party whose influence would spread across the whole nation and ultimately bring about its unification. Historian John Gaddis has cited this conversation as evidence that the Soviet leader ultimately intended a Communist takeover in all of Germany. But this ignores the more obvious deduction that it was good politics for Stalin—as it was for Truman—to speak in favor of German unity when addressing German politicians because with few exceptions, that is what they favored. Moreover, as Stalin had emphasized to the KPD leaders, Germany did not need a socialist but rather a bourgeois-democratic revolution, which would also permit cooperation with the Western Allies, who had control of the industrial Ruhr.[29]

Indeed, by summer 1945 the Russians were determined to exact Yalta's proposed $10 billion in reparations, to gain access to Ruhr industry if possible, and to prevent Germany from ever being able to wage war against them. Still, Soviet ravaging in Germany heightened American anxiety. Nearly everyone at Potsdam agreed with Harriman that Russia was becoming "a vacuum into which all movable goods would be sucked," although Ambassador Davies noted that the French, and some Americans, were carting off almost everything. Truman viewed the "hell of a mess" stoically: the Russians were "looters" by nature who were exacting retribution. But if they continued to strip the country and kidnap the population, there would be "no reparations." And as Stimson told him, the Russians' "rather oriental" approach to war booty provided more reason to preserve western Germany's economy.[30]

Although Soviet police-state tactics soon led Stimson and Byrnes to state that ideology precluded long-term cooperation with Russia, Truman was persistent that he could do business with the ruthless but realistic Stalin, who threatened Europe less than would a "demagogue on horseback" at the head of the Russian military machine. Still, victory in Europe appeared fraught with tragedy. As Byrnes said, the British had failed to prevent Hitler's rise and to recognize that a democratic Germany made a far superior ally than Russia. Now "somebody" had made an "awful mistake" by creating a situation that had allowed the Soviet Union to emerge from the war with so much power, which Truman and others hoped to contain.[31]

The president revealed the U.S. program at the first Big Three plenary session on July 17. After Stalin moved that Truman chair the conference, the "scared" but eager president quickly introduced five position papers: to create a Council of Foreign Ministers (CFM), including France and China; to prepare a final peace conference; to decentralize Germany's political and economic structure and accept the "first charge" principle for reparations; to implement the Declaration on Liberated Europe; and to moderate the stern 1943 Anglo-American surrender terms imposed on Italy and admit it to the UN, ostensibly for having helped to defeat Germany and declaring war on Japan.

Cross fire was immediate. Churchill and Stalin scoffed at involving China in Europe's affairs, and neither leader had yet studied the German paper. Churchill wanted retribution for Italy's 1940 attack that had cost Britain so heavily in the Mediterranean and North Africa. The prime minister also wanted to talk about Poland, especially free elections, and Rumania and Bulgaria. (The latter two had "already been taken care of," Molotov interjected.) Then Stalin stated issues: division of the captured German merchant fleet and navy; "Franco Spain," where Hitler and Mussolini had imposed a regime that endangered the UN; the émigré Polish government in London; Syria, Lebanon, and Tangier; and trusteeships everywhere, perhaps.

The agenda was so full, Churchill said, that the foreign ministers would have to refine the issues and select agreeable ones for discussion. But the disagreeable ones were inescapable, Stalin retorted, while Truman, impatient throughout the conference, insisted that he did not want to discuss but to decide: an issue a day. Then as they moved to adjourn, Stalin posed a final question: Why had the prime minister refused to share captured German ships? Because he was uncertain, Churchill replied, whether to share or destroy these horrible weapons. Then divide them, Stalin retorted, and sink your share.[32]

Truman found presiding "nerve-wracking"—by comparison, Senate debate seemed tame—because Churchill talked all the time and Stalin "just grunts but you know what he means." The worst was yet to come. But the president was confident of the results, he wrote on July 18 with veiled reference to the bomb, because "I have several aces in the hole." But the next two Big Three meetings saw limited progress. To avert repeating the hectic diplomacy of 1919, the new CFM would prepare peace treaties for Finland, Italy, and the Eastern European states, but China would be excluded from European negotiations and France would be included only in negotiations regarding Italy. Truman agreed that the Russians would get one-third of the German navy and merchant ships when the Pacific war ended, and Stalin acceded that the "starting point" for reconstituting Germany would be its 1937 frontiers. But Truman brushed aside his proposal that they also fix Poland's western frontier, including Polish-occupied East Prussia and Silesia.[33]

The bitterest exchanges were between Churchill, often given to a "wild rampage," aides noted, and Stalin, a deft debater. The Soviet leader pressed the Americans and British to break relations with Franco's regime, this "cancer" on Europe, and to assist the Spanish people to restore democracy. Churchill rejoined that the British did not meddle with nations that had not molested them, and to do so would cause the Spanish to rally to Franco. Truman had "no love" for Franco but no wish to get involved in another civil war. Churchill then raged that Marshal Tito had built a police state and should be impelled to broaden his government and hold elections within three months. Then invite the Yugoslavs to Potsdam to respond to the accusations, Stalin rebutted, while Truman, to Churchill's ire, insisted that the Big Three could not hear every dispute and had to drop the matter.[34]

On July 20 at their fourth meeting, Truman brushed aside British concerns to press his moderate peace for Italy. The wily Stalin agreed: revenge and retribution were poor advisers in politics. The best guide was the "calculation of forces." But if Italy had to be detached from Germany's orbit, so did the other satellites: Rumania, Bulgaria, and Hungary. It was time to ease conditions there, and to begin by resuming diplomatic relations even if their governments were not democratically elected, as they were not in Italy, France, or Belgium. Stalin's linkage did not escape Truman, who insisted that their proposals be sent separately to the foreign ministers. Or as Churchill liked to say, "When you come to a stony place, you adjourn."[35]

Big Three debates were not all theater. The powers were each establishing positions, the spheres in which they wanted their influence to prevail. Further, as Churchill noted, the "big question" was Germany, and the foreign ministers were stymied. They agreed in principle to establish a four-power (France included) A.C.C. to assume paramount authority for Germany's political and economic programs and, per Yalta, to treat Germany as an economic whole in exacting reparations, with the Russians to get 56 percent and the British and Americans, 22 percent each. But the U.S. held that the Russians' stripping their zone of industrial equipment virtually precluded assessing what remained (or its current value) for reparations. Further U.S. insistence on its first-charge principle for occupation costs, foodstuffs, and imports gave no assurance that significant German goods or revenue would remain to pay reparations, which the Russians insisted should take priority over all else. Moreover, the Americans likened occupied Germany to a corporation in receivership, with creditors having first claim on revenue, while the Russians argued that capitalists always wanted the profits from foreign trade but cared nothing about reparations for the (Russian) people who had suffered from the war. As Molotov remembered, Stalin was determined not to be "cheated" at Potsdam, and the Soviets were highly worried about reparations and the critical German-Polish boundary issue.[36]

Deadlock neared. Truman was "sick of the whole business" but determined not to pay reparations and get nothing but a nose-thumbing, he wrote. Then on July 21 Stimson brought General Groves' full report on the atomic bomb, and less than an hour later at the fifth plenary session, the president displayed his "entirely new feeling of confidence." He insisted that Italy and the Eastern European states had to be considered separately, and he would not recognize the latter governments until they were properly organized; nor would he recognize the Polish-German border, or accede to Poland's becoming an unauthorized fifth occupying power in Germany by taking control of East Prussia and Silesia. He warned that this "carving up" of Germany and loss of food and coal lands jeopardized any reparations accord. Stalin gave no ground, however. If Italy and Eastern Europe were not to be considered together, they could be postponed together. Poland's administration of German territory, he argued, derived from Yalta, economic necessity, and Red Army security needs. And he added fatuously, if this harmed Germany, it also diminished a major American and British competitor. Truman would have none of it. Germany would not be given away "piecemeal," and they had reached "impasse."[37]

"The President's best day so far," Foreign Secretary Eden exulted. Meanwhile, Churchill, upon reading Groves' report, told Stimson he now understood why Truman was "a changed man": he had stood up to the Russians emphatically, and told them "just where they got on and off and generally bossed the whole meeting." The prime minister was so delighted that he proposed they use disclosure about the atomic bomb to leverage negotiations.[38]

Truman sought similar objectives with a different tactic. The program for the bomb was tying in with what the Americans were doing in every field, Stimson noted; the atomic news had cheered the entire delegation, and Truman confirmed that he was relying upon it "greatly," especially to stand firm with the Russians. U.S. officials had not changed their basic objectives in Europe. But now they now believed that the bomb enabled them to achieve their goals without compromise.[39]

Potsdam meetings ground ahead slowly. Having returned on July 22 to days of debate over Poland's pushing its border westward into East Prussia and Silesia, Stalin insisted that not one of nine million former German residents remained in the area. ("Of course not, the Bolshevics have killed them all," Truman purported Admiral Leahy to have whispered.) An enraged Churchill nonetheless sought, without success, an expedient Big Three demarcation line to prevent the Poles from consolidating their hold, while Truman insisted— "yesterday . . . today, and . . . tomorrow"—that the Poles had no authority to be there, and that an agreement had to await a peace conference. And Truman was persistent that he would not recognize Eastern European governments until they were organized democratically. Stalin argued that they were as democratic as Italy's regime, and that reports of lack of free access were "all fairy tales."[40]

Reparations talks went no better. Initially, Molotov pressed the Yalta terms: $20 billion in German reparations equally divided between capital equipment and current production, with the Russians to get 50 percent of the total. Byrnes insisted that battlefield destruction since Yalta and Russian removals made this unrealistic, and that first Germany had to pay those who were supplying it before paying reparations. Further, he suggested that each power could get what it needed by taking reparations from its own zone, and exchange food or coal from the east for machinery from western Germany. Molotov countered that Stalin strongly favored an overall treatment of Germany for reparations (otherwise the Soviets would be denied access to the Ruhr's heavy industry) and that the Russians would consider lowering their claims. Molotov proposed that the Allies agree on a fixed sum of reparations—the Russians would accept a billion or two less than Yalta's proposed $10 billion—or that they give equal priority to occupation/import costs and reparations and pay for both by imposing a first charge on German production. Byrnes refused; he insisted that "not a dollar will be paid on reparations until imports are paid for."[41]

Resolving peripheral issues did not lessen discord. Russian pullback of forces in Austria and pledge of foodstuffs eased U.S. and British entry into their occupation zones, where they accepted the authority of Socialist Karl Renner's Provisional Government. The Big Three also agreed to immediate withdrawal of forces from Iran, and Stalin assured Truman that Russia would not act against the Teheran government. Truman and Churchill agreed in principle to transfer of the ice-free port of Königsberg in East Prussia to the Soviets, and to revision of the 1936 Montreux Convention, which gave Turkey sole right to fortify the Dardanelles and to close them at threat of war. Thus, Stalin argued, a small nation had "a hand on Russia's throat," a state of affairs that neither the British (who backed the Turks, he said) nor the Americans would tolerate at the Suez or Panama Canal.[42]

Stalin's national security points seemed well taken. Britain and France had forged the Straits in 1918 to intervene in the Russian civil war, and in 1944 the Germans got Turkey to allow eight warships through the Straits into the Black Sea. At Yalta, Churchill agreed to support multilateral revision of Montreux, while in the spring of 1945 Stalin pressed the Turks for joint control of the Straits and a Russian base there. He also refused to renew their treaty of friendship without prior return of the districts of Kars and Ardahan, which the Russians had ceded in 1921. The Turks would not budge on any issue, and in June the Americans, convinced that the Russians were making claims but not threats, declined a British-proposed joint *demarche* to Moscow. This left the British to mild protest on their own. Then at Potsdam on July 22, Stalin renewed his claims on Turkey and pressed the British over Italy's former colonies, rousing Churchill's fury. The Russians also expressed their interest in Libya and in sharing in administration of Tangier, and briefly proposed Big Four talks about Syria and Lebanon, which the British were policing.[43]

U.S. officials feared that the Soviets no longer sought to be just a continental power but to branch out everywhere. But Truman labeled Stalin's claims "bluff" and determined to press a proposal intended both to assuage and to contain the Soviets, who he was always quick to assume were ready to seize the Straits. But he also saw their concern and, as he said on July 23, he long believed that constraints on trade and its vital arteries had spurred two centuries of war in Europe's heartland from the Baltic to the Black Sea and from France to Russia. Thus, while he skirted Russo-Turkish debate over bases and borders as bilateral matters, he proposed that the Big Four and Europe's riparian powers jointly maintain free passage on the Continent's waterways, the Rhine and the Danube, and that they internationalize the Straits.

Churchill warmed to the proposal: it was "remarkable" that the U.S. would extend a guarantee (and its influence, even if Truman precluded fortifications) to the Eastern Mediterranean. Stalin saw that, too—and that neither his base in the Straits, nor Kars and Ardahan, were in the offing, nor would there be Big Four control at Panama or Suez. The Soviet leader concluded that Russia should talk separately to the Turks and shelve Truman's proposal.[44]

Truman remained steadfast, from Germany to the Straits. "Watch the president," Chief of Naval Operations Admiral Ernest King whispered to the British. "This is all new to him, but he can take it. He is a more typical American than Roosevelt, and he will do a good job, not only for the United States but for the whole world." The British noticed. Lord Moran, Churchill's doctor, wrote on July 24 that the president would not feed from anyone's hand, and when

Stalin gets tough, "Truman makes it plain that he, too, can hand out the rough stuff." The prime minister agreed: "If only this had happened at Yalta." Now it seemed too late. The Red Army was everywhere. The next morning the Big Three met only briefly, again at a "stony place," and then adjourned to permit Churchill and Eden to return to London to await the election returns that would see Labor's Clement Attlee and Ernest Bevin replace them.[45]

III

Truman was undaunted. The Big Three had been at it "hammer and tongs," he wrote on July 25, but they had done a great deal, and a reparations accord seemed near. But he would neither accede to Russia and Poland having "gobbled" Germany nor recognize "police governments" in Eastern Europe.[46]

Nor was Churchill's political defeat distressing. "It is too bad about Churchill," Truman wrote, "but it may turn out to be all right for the world." Indeed, cautious politics and ambivalence toward the British led Truman to resist their overtures nearly as firmly as he did Russian claims. Grateful that England—alone—had "held the fort" against Germany in 1940, and sympathetic to Churchill's review of his nation's "melancholy" finances, the president feared that the prime minister was too clever. His "soft soap" would burn "to beat hell" in the eyes, but Truman would make no commitment about further Lend-Lease or postwar aid. The JCS would not share their exclusive command in the Pacific with the British, allow them to join the American-Soviet exchange of information about operations against Japan, or discuss postwar continuation of the Combined Chiefs of Staff.[47]

Truman was highly sensitive about a postwar Anglo-American military connection. When he indicated concern about access to British air and communications bases in Africa and elsewhere that had been built with American money, Churchill, too cleverly, leapt to offer British bases globally for joint defense. The president insisted that would be proper only if applied to all of the UN. Churchill disdained such a common right as no more alluring than would be a young lady's reply to a man who proposed marriage that she would always be a sister to him. Truman, however, rejected a "crude" military alliance. As Admiral Leahy said, at Potsdam the British "did most of the proposing, and the Americans did most of the disposing." And that relationship prevailed even in Big Three meetings, and became even more marked after Attlee assumed Churchill's position at Potsdam on July 28 and began to attend what the British now called meetings of the "Big Two and a Half."[48]

Truman viewed Attlee as an Oxford man who talked in the same way as the "much overrated" Eden. The president also likened the blustery Bevin, former head of the huge Transport and General Worker's Union and general strike leader in 1926 but a staunch anticommunist, to an "English John L. Lewis," who was hardly an imaginable secretary of state. Further, while England's new government seemed more resistant than its predecessor to expedient deals with the Russians and Poles over German territory and reparations, the Americans doubted that they would be able to get along with the Laborites, who they concluded misperceived issues and strategy. Even Stalin seemed wary of Britain's new leaders, and Truman surmised that the Russian longed for his old but familiar rival, Churchill. The Americans determined, however, to wind up matters swiftly and with slight regard for British presence or accord.[49]

Potsdam now hinged on its two hardest issues, Truman wrote in late July: German reparations, which Davies told him had "poisoned" the conference, and Poland's western border. Byrnes was ready to do "a little horseback trading" and to end talks in a few days if agreement was not in sight. The American view rested on realism and atomic power. As Truman now wrote, "I like Stalin. He is straightforward. Knows what he wants and will compromise when he can't get it." The president recognized as well that the Poles had moved into East Prussia and Silesia and "unless we are willing to go to war again they can stay and they will stay with Bolsheviki backing."[50]

So too did Byrnes recognize certain limits of power. On July 27 he withdrew the U.S. proposal to admit Italy to the UN because raising this "Italian baby" served only to allow Stalin to hang on it "Franco britches" and a "Rumanian and Hungarian coat." But the secretary was also confident, especially regarding the critical reparations issue, that the atomic bomb would induce the Russians to see things the U.S. way. As Davies recorded on July 29, Byrnes had suggested that "the New Mexico situation had given us great power, and in the final analysis it would control."[51]

Possession of the land and atomic power would determine Potsdam's outcome. The Americans realized that, at least for the time being, the Poles could not be moved from Germany, and the Russians recognized that the Americans were unlikely to be moved on reparations. When Molotov queried Byrnes on July 27 about the secretary's earlier suggestion that each country take reparations from its own zone, the Russian also noted that failure to reach an agreement on Germany overall would produce the same results. "Yes," Byrnes said, as he formally withdrew the Yalta accord. Dramatically changed conditions in Germany made it "impractical" to determine how much Germany could pay, he said, and mere agreement to discuss $20 billion "does not mean that I will write a check for it." That ruled out a fixed sum of reparations, despite Molotov's insistence that the Russians deserved better for having suffered the most in the war.[52]

The Soviets shortly proposed a total reparations settlement of just $8 billion. But Truman and Byrnes were now ready to proffer their own deal to Molotov on July 29, while Stalin was indisposed, perhaps having had a heart attack, and the British were left uninformed. Byrnes made the initial bid: Polish administration of German Silesia up to the eastern Neisse if the Russians agreed to his plan for zonal reparations, which could include exchange of industrial equipment from the Ruhr (in the British zone) for coal and foodstuffs from the Russian zone. Molotov said Stalin would insist on Poland's border reaching to the western Neisse, and Russian reparations had to include at least $2 billion in Ruhr machinery. Byrnes refused even this partial fixed sum, offering instead to give 25 percent of whatever equipment might prove available for reparations. Molotov retorted that 25 percent of an unknown amount meant very little.[53]

The next day Byrnes, without a word to the British, acceded to Polish control up to the western Neisse, and offered to the Russians an additional 15 percent of "available" Ruhr machinery free of exchange. But rather than have the A.C.C., as previously agreed, exact reparations and treat Germany as a single economic unit, now the military commanders in each zone would have final authority—a virtual veto—over reparations removals. Molotov, who insisted that the Western powers controlled more than half of Germany's wealth and its best industrial capacity, resisted this de facto economic division of Germany. He invoked past Allied talks dating to Teheran about internationalizing the Ruhr and pressed for a fixed sum to be taken from all three Western zones.[54]

It was time to strike a deal or to go home, the Americans concluded. Truman left the hard bargaining to Byrnes, who bluntly spelled out the final package, largely of his design, at the foreign ministers' meeting on July 30 and privately the next morning. Byrnes insisted that there were now three—not two—remaining issues: German reparations, Poland's western border, and, reintroduced, Italy's admission to the UN, which he linked to the status of Eastern Europe's governments. Two problems would be relatively easy. The U.S. had already conceded Poland's control to the western Neisse. Now Byrnes proposed that after the Big Three concluded a peace treaty with Italy, which all the powers had recognized, they would support its admission to the UN. The same would apply to Finland and to the Eastern European states if in the near future each of the Big Three could examine conditions in the former Axis satellites with a view to diplomatic recognition. That left the toughest issue: German reparations. Byrnes proposed to resolve this through his plan for zonal reparations, including certain exchanges, and with the West having exclusive control of the Ruhr. But then came the secretary's ultimatum: the three issues were inseparable and had to be resolved all together and at once. Otherwise the president and he would depart for the U.S. the next day.[55]

"Mr. Stalin is stallin'," Truman wrote hours before the climactic Big Three plenary session on July 31. But that would be of no use to the Russian leader, because "he doesn't know it but I have an ace in the hole and another one showing—so unless he has threes or two pair (and I know he has not) we are sitting all right." Stalin, of course, was unmoved by the aces—which would soon be dropped on Japan—but he understood the "calculation of forces," especially on the German issue. He would contend that Byrnes had linked unrelated issues and that the Russians would vote on them separately. But bargaining over Germany now moved swiftly, to American liking.[56]

At the Big Three plenary session on the afternoon of July 31, Byrnes successfully pressed the U.S. program. Each power would take reparations from its occupation zone. The Russians would also receive 25 percent of the capital equipment, unnecessary for peacetime use, from the western zones: 15 percent in exchange for foodstuffs and raw materials from the east, and 10 percent free of exchange. Total equipment removals would be determined within six months and completed within two years. But there was no specific sum for reparations, nor would they be taken from current production until Germany had a balanced subsistence economy. Most important, the zonal military commanders, not the A.C.C., had final authority over reparations. This would allow the U.S. to drop its first-charge principle and agree to a Soviet proposal for the A.C.C. to create central economic and political agencies, but not a central government. The A.C.C. was also instructed to establish within six months a level of industry for Germany's economy.[57]

Byrnes' zonal reparations plan augured de facto economic division of Germany, and perhaps of Europe, as U.S.—and British—officials recognized. Further, the zonal reparations and central economic agencies were contradictory concepts, an illogical settlement, albeit one that allowed the U.S. and the USSR to act as they wished in their own zones and also claim to be cooperating and working toward a unified German state. Most important, Truman and his advisers were convinced that U.S. and Western European prosperity and stability depended upon western Germany's economic-industrial vitality, and they were determined not only to avoid, as Truman wrote on July 30, having to "pay reparations" as after World War I, but to preclude Russian influence in western Germany, especially the Ruhr. They also believed that ultimately their military and economic "master cards" would induce the Russians to cooperate on American terms in Germany and elsewhere.[58]

Recently, historian Marc Trachtenberg has contended that at Potsdam the Americans gave up on the idea of four-power rule in occupied Germany and that Byrnes' tripartite deal was intended to establish nonconfrontational spheres-of-influence governance. Under Byrnes' system, the U.S. gained the economic control and stability it sought in western Germany—the most valuable part of the country—but assuaged the Russians with two concessions: industrial exchanges and the Oder–western Neisse boundary. Trachtenberg says Byrnes put a "premium" on relatively friendly relations with the Russians, and by dividing American and Soviet areas of control, he hoped to avert endless quarrels that would inevitably derive from efforts at trying to govern all of Germany in concert with the Soviets. In effect, Byrnes opted to pull the two powers apart and allow each to have its own way in its own zone, Trachtenberg says, and the Russians warmed to this idea once they got their concessions.[59]

Trachtenberg's argument ignores critical factors, however, not least the significance of the atomic bomb for American diplomacy. The record is clear that the readiness of the atomic bomb inspired Byrnes and Truman to take an aggressive negotiating stance with the Russians and to believe that they could impose their will. This was highly evident when Byrnes pressed his tripartite ultimatum between July 29 and July 31—the atomic bomb would "control," he said—and Truman's belief that his "aces" would beat any cards Stalin had. Moreover, Trachtenberg misleadingly implies that negotiation over German reparations was amicable. In fact, the diplomatic debates were tenacious, and the Russians acceded only because they recognized that the "calculation of forces" ran against them in Germany, at least with respect to control of the industrial Ruhr. Thus the Russians "compromised," but remained angered by U.S. failure to give them what they believed was their reparations due. As Stalin biographer Dmitri Volkogonov has written, throughout the negotiations the Soviet leader repeatedly wrote in his notepad "reparations," "contributions," and "shares of reparations." He resented America's abandonment of the Yalta formula as seriously disadvantaging his country and giving the lie to Truman's claim of desiring friendship. Neither the U.S. nor Britain had suffered the wartime devastation that Russia had, Stalin believed, but the Western powers just turned a deaf ear to his claims.[60]

Most important, while economic division of Germany did not make political division inevitable, the Potsdam decisions made this outcome more likely, along with ensuing East-West tensions. Thus, if Yalta had symbolized U.S.-Soviet detente and common belief that peace depended on a moderately punitive policy toward a defeated Germany, Potsdam represented a bitter chill in American-Soviet relations and an initial step toward integrating the occupied halves of Germany into separate political-economic systems.

Nonetheless, accord over Germany underlay compromise over Poland's Oder–western Neisse border, Italy and Eastern Europe, and many minor or technical issues. "That's the way most conferences go," a British diplomat wrote. Once a major issue loosens, "the whole thing breaks free." But discord, real and symbolic, continued. Stalin acceded to referring Truman's European waterways proposal to the foreign ministers, and to its mention in the conference's unpublished Protocol. The president was piqued inordinately, however, that Stalin opposed mention of the waterways proposal in the public Communiqué as strongly as he resisted inviting U.S. influence in the Straits area. And when the president repeated his waterways request on the last day of Big Three meetings, one observer has said that Stalin interrupted his interpreter: "*Nyet.* No, I say no."[61]

Perhaps the most symbolic colloquy occurred that same day regarding reparations details. Stalin withdrew Russia's claim to 30 percent of German investments, assets, or gold west of the line that divided the Soviet occupation zone from that of "the Allies," but asserted Soviet control of everything to the east of that line. Then when Truman asked if that line ran from the Baltic to the Adriatic, and Byrnes inquired further if the Soviet zone meant the area occupied by the Red Army, Stalin answered yes to both questions. In sum, what the "Allies" and the Russians could not jointly govern or share they agreed to divide. And the divide was marked by their armies.[62]

IV

Truman departed his first, and last, summit with the Russians the next day, August 2, reasonably confident. The Russians were "pig-headed" and Stalin was a "son-of-a-bitch," Truman commented, but—he said almost proudly—the Soviet leader probably felt the same way about him. The Russian leader had also proved to be a realist who saw "straight through" issues, took a position, and then held to it. This inspired in Truman nearly the same ambivalent admiration for Stalin that he had for his mentor and ultimate American political boss, Tom Pendergast, and the president likened the two men. He also noticed that during the closing pleasantries at Potsdam, Stalin, "from my heart," singled out Byrnes as having worked harder than anyone else to assure the conference's success, and the president delighted to have his secretary recall for the Cabinet Stalin's grudging accolade for him: "the most honest horse thief he had ever met."[63]

The president also put a good public face on the agreements. He said that by eliminating a fixed high reparations sum, the Potsdam settlement was more realistic than that of Yalta or Versailles, and he contended that shipping capital equipment to the Russians would serve to redress economic imbalance between western and eastern Germany, and Poland's economic, strategic, and ethnographic necessities justified the Oder–western Neisse line. Every international agreement depended on give and take, he said, and willingness to meet a neighbor halfway.[64]

Even as Truman spoke, however, the grim politics of war in the Far East persisted. At Potsdam he had ordered that the atomic bomb be used only after his departure on August 2. But during the first days of his return voyage on the battleship *Augusta,* he and his senior aides worried that Japan's continued effort at a settlement through the Soviet Union rather than a neutral such as Sweden might not only diminish America's four years of hard-earned military predominance in the Pacific but allow the Russians to increase their postwar claims on Manchuria and influence in Japan. Thus, on August 5 Truman ordered Harriman to inform Stalin that the Chinese, who had resumed treaty negotiations in Moscow, had already met Yalta's terms and should not be asked for further concessions, especially extension of the Soviet military zone around Lushun to Dalian. He also approved Harriman's proposal to seek written assurance from Stalin about the Open Door in Manchuria, which would be published simultaneously with a Sino-Soviet treaty. That evening Truman also emphatically, but incorrectly, told his dinner companions that no "deal" had been made to bring the Russians into the war, and that development of a new weapon meant that the U.S. did not need Russia or any other nation to defeat Japan.

Then as the *Augusta* approached the New Jersey coast on August 6, Map Room watch officer Captain Frank Graham brought first word that the atomic bomb had been dropped on Hiroshima. Ten minutes later a cable from Stimson reported that the bombing had been even more "conspicuous" than at New Mexico. "This is the greatest thing in history," Truman exclaimed to Graham, and then raced about the ship to spread the news, insisting that he had never made a happier announcement. "We have won the gamble," he told the assembled and cheering crew. He also released a statement that the Japanese had to surrender or face a "rain of ruin" from the air.[65]

The president's behavior lacked remorse, compassion, or humility in the wake of nearly incomprehensible destruction—about 80,000 dead at once, and tens of thousands dying of radiation—wrought by that "most terrible" weapon in history. Surely, Truman felt relief from Potsdam's tensions and delight that Japan's surrender now loomed imminent. This would obviate need for a costly U.S. invasion in November, although by that time air and naval assault could have subdued Japan. But personally Truman tended toward Old Testament retribution—"punishment always followed transgression," he believed—and he would insist publicly that use of atomic weapons against the Japanese had to be balanced against their Pearl Harbor attack and execution of American prisoners. He also said privately to someone who criticized use of the atomic bomb that regrettably "when you deal with a beast, you have to treat him as beast."[66]

It is equally clear from a political perspective that Truman was elated on August 6 because he believed not only that the atomic bomb ensured Japan's swift surrender but that the Russians would scarcely get in on "the kill" (as Byrnes had said) or be able to continue pressing claims in excess of those agreed upon at Yalta. Truman was also convinced—reasonably so—that the atomic bomb had spurred Stalin to bring Russia into the war on August 8, a week sooner than he had pledged at Potsdam (but within Yalta's time frame of ninety days after the end of the European war), and without having secured the desired Sino-Soviet treaty. Further, Harriman reported that the Russians were rapidly penetrating Manchuria and pressing a definition of "war trophies" that was pretext to seize Japanese property—much as they had stripped Germany—and to dominate Manchuria industrially. And he warned that Soviet management style and secret police made Stalin's verbal Open Door pledge worthless.[67]

Thus, when Stimson showed Truman pictures and reports of postatomic Hiroshima on August 8 and urged that Japan be persuaded to surrender quickly, the president, who said all the destruction had brought terrible responsibility, did not consider delay of the second atomic bomb. Admittedly, the original July 25 order to General Spaatz had called for use of atomic "bombs" as soon as they were ready. But the second atomic assault—advanced by two days to August 9 by the military due to impending bad weather—on Nagasaki was also perceived as a way to end the war before the Soviets could push further into Manchuria or step up claims on China or Japan, as Truman anticipated they would.[68]

Ironically, it was more the Russian entry into the war on August 8 than the next day's Nagasaki blast (which killed 35,000 at once, and thousands more slowly by radiation) that spurred Japan's surrender. Until this time Japan's war-weary and bitterly divided government was unable to agree whether, or on what terms, to surrender. Numerous civilian leaders favored capitulation, as did the emperor after he read reports of the Hiroshima bombings—it was time to "bear the unbearable" he remarked—although the military prevented wide dissemination of information about the blast. Most significant, there was a stalemate in Japan's Supreme Council for Direction of the War, which was led by the "Big Six" Cabinet members: Prime Minister Suzuki, Foreign Minister Togo, and Navy Minister Mitsumasa Yonai favored surrender, while War Minister Korechika Anami, Army Chief of Staff Umezu Yoshijiro, and Navy Chief of Staff Toyoda Seomu refused to capitulate, at least not until Japan had fought one more great battle that would prove extremely costly to the Americans and cause them to offer favorable peace terms.[69]

Then came the Russian attack and collapse of Japan's Manchurian army. This exposed the nation's military vulnerability and caused Suzuki to say that "the game is up" and the military leaders to abandon their veto over efforts to negotiate a surrender. Meanwhile, Emperor Hirohito, at a long meeting on the night of August 9 to August 10, formally implored his ministers to "bear the unbearable" and to accept surrender on the basis of the Potsdam Declaration, provided that one condition was met, namely, preservation of the imperial household, or the national polity, or *kokutai*. On this basis Japan's government made its initial offer to the U.S., through Swiss officials, to surrender provided that they were given "explicit indication" that the emperor's prerogatives as sovereign ruler would be preserved.[70]

Early on the morning of August 10 Truman met with his advisers in the Oval office. Leahy, Forrestal, and Stimson favored accepting Japan's proposal, and Truman agreed. The "horse sense" reasoning, Stimson noted, was clear: the emperor's authority would save the Americans from "a score of bloody Iwo Jimas and Okinawas" and allow them to get into Japan "before the Russians could put in any substantial claim to occupy and help rule it." Byrnes was of like mind but strongly objected that anything less than strict unconditional surrender might lead to "crucifixion" of the president given strong public sentiment (which included 153 of 170 telegrams to the White House) for harsh terms only. Forrestal then pressed to accept Japan's offer with language that would preserve the intent of the Potsdam Declaration. Truman instructed Byrnes to draft the eventual compromise: from the time of surrender, the authority of the emperor and government to rule would be "subject to the Supreme Commander of the Allied Powers" (SCAPJ), and ultimately the Japanese would choose their own form of government, a fair assurance about the emperor, albeit less explicit than the Japanese sought.[71]

Truman sent the draft proposal to America's allies. That afternoon he told his Cabinet ("fiercely," Wallace noted) that he did not expect to hear from the Russians, but he would act without them. Stimson said that they would probably try to delay the war's end to push into Manchuria. Truman added that this was not in America's interest and then—once again—denied that there was any agreement with the Soviets about Manchuria. Further, Truman and Byrnes emphasized that the "top dog," or Supreme Commander (and not Command) would be an American: the U.S. would not be "plagued" by joint responsibility, as in Germany. Finally, in response to Stimson and Forrestal having urged an end to all bombing of Japan, the president halted further use of atomic bombs, a small concession because the next one would not be ready for use for about two weeks. But conventional bombing would continue and be stepped up. Truman evidently wished to keep pressure on Japan, but atomic warfare had chastened him: it was too horrible, he said, to kill another 100,000 people, especially "all those kids."[72]

The Russians, in fact, gave quick accord to the modified surrender terms.

They also suggested that the U.S. should reach agreement with its allies over choice of a Supreme Commander, or that perhaps there should be a U.S. and a Soviet commander. Harriman rejected these proposals in Moscow as summarily as Truman would have in Washington. But at the last minute Stalin interceded: there had been a "misunderstanding." He wished only to be consulted. At the same time Stalin also withdrew his request for a military zone around Dalian and quickly concluded Sino-Soviet treaty negotiations, within the Yalta framework, on August 14. If Stalin was not intimidated by America's use of atomic bombs, they did move him to act with deliberate speed and expeditiously as the Pacific war neared its climax.[73]

The U.S. sent its revised terms to Japan on August 11. Debate and political intrigue raged in Tokyo for the next three days. Junior officers plotted a coup and refused to surrender until given explicit assurances about the emperor. Most of the Cabinet inclined to surrender, but the critical Big Six remained deadlocked at 3–3, with the military leaders adamant that lack of an absolute guarantee for the emperor threatened the life of the nation. Finally, Lord Keeper of the Privy Seal Kido Koicho (who had favored surrendering since 1944), aided by Prime Minister Suzuki, spurred Emperor Hirohito to call an imperial conference on August 14. The military leaders again demanded firm assurances for the emperor. But he said that it was pointless to continue the war, that he accepted the Allies' commitment to him, and—once again—that it was necessary to bear the unbearable. The emperor had never before intervened so openly or spoken so directly in politics, and this swayed War Minister Anami to agree to surrender, with the Cabinet following suit. The Foreign Ministry promptly communicated Japan's surrender offer based on the Potsdam Declaration, although the diplomats added a separate note requesting that the Allies give notice of where their forces would land, keep their occupation points to a minimum, and allow the military to disarm itself under the emperor's direction. Meanwhile, Anami and Army Chief of Staff Umezu resisted strong pressures to join a coup and worked to keep other senior officers loyal and to prevent insubordination among troops in the field ordered to surrender.[74]

Japan's surrender proposal reached Washington at 6 P.M. on August 14. Within an hour the president broadcast that Japan had surrendered unconditionally, notwithstanding that the U.S. had made a commitment to the emperor. There was also no mention of the other "requests," which the U.S. rejected three days later. Meanwhile, on October 15 Truman issued General Order #1 to the SCAPJ, General MacArthur. The Japanese were to be ordered by their emperor to surrender to the Russians in Manchuria, in Korea north of the 38th parallel, and in Karafuto (southern Sakhalin); to the Americans in Japan, the Bonin, Ryukyu, and other Pacific islands, and in Korea south of the 38th parallel; to the Guomindang regime in China (with U.S. marines transporting Jiang Jieshi's troops north from Chungking); and to British and Australian forces elsewhere in Southeast Asia.[75]

Stalin immediately requested a Soviet occupation zone in the northern half of Hokkaido and Russian authority in the Kurile Islands, which had been pledged to them at Yalta to atone for Japan's occupation of Siberia during 1919–1921. Truman flatly refused Soviet entry into Japan, while he acceded to the Kuriles and asked for a U.S. military and commercial air base there. Stalin angrily replied that such a request was usually put to a defeated nation or an ally incapable of self-defense, neither of which applied to the Soviet Union. Truman backed off. He said landing rights were for "emergency use" during the occupation, and Stalin acceded on that limited basis. Three days later, on September 2, General MacArthur received Japan's formal surrender on the battleship *Missouri* in Tokyo Bay.[76]

The Second World War was over and "retribution" had been won, Truman announced. He might also have reflected that in the Pacific, as in Europe, the dividing line between the Russian occupation zone and that of "the allies" was marked by their respective armies.[77]

V

The Grand Alliance was born of necessity among nations that were united by their desperate need to defeat Germany and Japan. After this was accomplished, struggles among the great powers to secure their respective interests and visions of a new world order were inevitable. In war-torn Europe, Americans and Russians confronted one another most directly in Germany. The president and his chief advisers deemed German stability and resources vital to U.S. and European prosperity and, for practical and ideological reasons, quickly moved away from the Yalta accords to minimize Soviet reparations claims and influence on western industrial Germany. The Russians held fast to a Yalta-style settlement, but once Stalin recognized the calculation of forces in Germany, he acceded to the tripartite Truman-Byrnes deal, or ultimatum, on zonal reparations, Polish control of Silesia, and the Italy–Eastern Europe trade-off. Tough negotiations on these issues would continue at CFM meetings for the next few years, although Potsdam may have presaged the economic-political division of Germany and Europe.

The Americans and Soviets also sought to end the Pacific war on terms favorable to their postwar interests. At Yalta, Roosevelt had reason to want the Soviets to join the war against Japan, and he acceded to restoration of the status quo in the People's Republic of Outer Mongolia, return of southern Sakhalin and of former tsarist concessions (bases in Lushun, Dalian, and joint control of railroads) in Manchuria, and cession of the Kuriles. Stalin probably hoped to gain an occupation zone in Japan, but he did not raise the issue until August, when Harriman summarily rejected the idea.

Still, Truman and key officials, including Stimson, Byrnes, and Harriman, quickly concluded that the Soviets sought to dominate or annex Manchuria and other Chinese provinces in North China and perhaps subordinate the whole country. Soviet designs on Japan were also highly suspect. In short, the president and others doubted that the Soviets would carry out their Far Eastern agreements, especially the Open Door in Manchuria. Hence they used General Order #1 to move U.S. forces into southern Korea to take the Japanese surrender there, while U.S. marines backed up Jiang's troops in North China, with Communist forces excluded from the surrender process.[78]

It is also clear that possession of the atomic bomb infused American thinking about diplomacy and the end of the war. Undeniably, the poker-playing Truman, Byrnes, and Stimson believed that their "royal straight flush," "master card," or "ace in the hole" so strengthened their hands that they could induce the Russians to accede to U.S. terms in Germany and contain Soviet gains in Asia. The president delayed Potsdam partly because he wanted to have the bomb at the ready during negotiations. He also said that Stalin's dynamite agenda did not faze him because he had his own dynamite to explode, and atomic reports encouraged him to stiffen his bargaining posture until by July 31 he was confident that his "aces" meant that Stalin had to accept the Truman-Byrnes tripartite ultimatum.

This is not to say that Truman and others determined to use the bomb solely for diplomatic purposes—to "out maneuver" the Russians in Europe and Asia. There were many reasons that impelled the Americans to use the bomb, including long-standing presumption that it would be used. Further, Byrnes especially feared domestic political criticism for having spent $2.2 billion for no particular reason or for having failed to do everything necessary to gain unconditional surrender from a hated enemy. Moreover, years of brutal warfare hardened human sensibilities and made it seem that the atomic bomb was not qualitatively different from other weapons or means of mass destruction, including firebombings of cities such as Dresden and Tokyo, where 135,000 and 83,000, respectively, were killed. There was also reason to think that the bomb might preclude need for an invasion of Japan or shorten the duration of an invasion, and thereby save lives. But the number of American deaths prevented would have been at most 20,000 (not an insignificant number), and probably far fewer, but nowhere near Truman's postwar claim to have saved 500,000 lives or Stimson's extrapolation in 1947 of having averted 1,000,000 American casualties if the war had continued into late 1946, which no one expected to be the case.[79]

Japan's government must also be blamed for prolonging the war and thereby inviting use of the atomic bomb, as numerous scholars have written. Too many Japanese officials, including the chief military leaders as well as Emperor Hirohito—the latter did not join the peace faction until June 1945—refused to recognize that their nation was defeated and were persistent that one last battle might restore Japan's position or allow it to bargain for better terms. They also failed to recognize the futility of negotiations with the Russians, who had far more to gain as a victor than mediator, and probably would have had little influence on U.S. policy.[80]

Most important, as Ikira Iriye has written, the Japanese should have surrendered rapidly on the basis of the Potsdam Declaration and negotiated its vague or oblique offer to retain the emperor, which the Americans quickly saw would serve their occupation interests. Instead, Japanese officials did nothing to move toward surrender for the next ten days, until the atomic bombing of Hiroshima on August 6, after which military officials minimized dissemination of the news. Not until the Soviet attack two days later did they recognize or own up to their nation's total vulnerability. The first atomic blast on Hiroshima and then the Soviet attack also provided the context for the emperor's long-overdue initial intervention, but the incontrovertible atomic "rain of ruin" was also brought to bear on Nagasaki and conventional bombing on Tokyo and other cities continued for another five days. Even at that, however, military chieftains like Anami and Umezu had to labor to restrain their younger officers still bent on a last battle and diplomatic bargaining.[81]

This does not gainsay, however, that at the start of the Potsdam Conference Truman believed that although Russian entry into the war meant that the Japanese were "Fini," use of "Manhattan" would cause them to "fold up" even sooner. In short, Truman and Byrnes believed that quick atomic defeat of Japan might allow them to "out maneuver" the Russians in Manchuria and preclude the need to share power during the postwar occupation of Japan. The American leaders displayed little interest in exploring ways to induce Japan's surrender by proposing to retain the emperor, as Grew, McCloy, and Bard had suggested, and as Stimson proposed shortly before and then at Potsdam. Truman and Byrnes did not seek to "coerce" Japan by giving truly dire warnings about the atomic bomb or Russian entry into the war. Only after they had used their unique weapon on Hiroshima and Nagasaki, which presumably would impress the Soviets, did the Americans give the critical assurance about the emperor that, combined with the Soviet assault, spurred Japan's capitulation.

To be sure, no single reason suffices to explain the "decision" to use atomic bombs against Japan. But the answer to the question of whether the bombs were used for diplomatic or military purposes (historians generally agree that the second bomb used on Nagasaki was not militarily necessary) is evident. In short, the prospect, or temptation, of diplomatic-political gain precluded serious thought, or "mature consideration" (as stipulated in the Roosevelt-Churchill aide-mémoire of September 1944), about *not* using atomic bombs. In this sense, the political gains to be made were more than just a "bonus" derived from military action. Rather, they were a prize worth winning in their own right. This all but assured that Truman and Byrnes would not seriously weigh the ideas of those who proposed to try to gain Japan's quick surrender on the basis of offering to retain the emperor, whether the reason was to prevent a costly invasion, ease postwar reconciliation, or even minimize Soviet advance in the Far East.[82]

This does not mean, however, that Truman and Byrnes were sinners; nor were they saints. They were American politicians of limited international experience and vision suddenly thrust into positions of global leadership. Their souls, or sensibilities, were undoubtedly hardened by witnessing a global war of unparalleled devastation and atrocities. They were appalled and frightened by Soviet advances in Europe and Asia and readily equated Communists with "Nazis and Fascists" or other imperial or "Tsarist" aggressors. They quickly persuaded themselves that if they got "tough," they could make the Russians more "manageable" and willing to accede to American principles and interests, which Truman had said were the only ones he intended to work for at Potsdam. Thus it is not surprising that at the dawn of the atomic age, whose power and horror were not yet fully revealed, Truman and Byrnes were inclined or readily tempted to use atomic bombs not merely to end the Second World War expeditiously but to "win" the peace on U.S. terms. Their action may not have foreordained Cold War, but it did increase Soviet-American discord, while the people of Hiroshima and Nagasaki were left to bear the unique burden of atomic death and suffering.

A Personal Declaration of Cold War

In autumn 1945 Truman sought to be realistic about world affairs. After the first CFM meeting deadlocked in October, he insisted that airing Soviet-American disputes was a step toward resolution. When Senator Kenneth McKellar objected to a proposed loan to the British, the president's draft reply noted his gratitude to "Russia and Britain" for their wartime sacrifices and America's obligation to aid reconstruction, although his special counsel excised the reference to Russia. Senior officials noted that Truman remained "passionately desirous" of peace with the Russians and concerned that Stalin, who he believed moderated Soviet policy, remain healthy.[1]

The president's parochial nationalism undercut possible accord, however. He appeared to listen to officials who said that atomic energy had brought a sudden sea change in international relations, especially with the Russians, yet he believed that the U.S. had to be world's "trustee" for this new power, and he aligned with advisers who resisted atomic sharing. Truman also backed Byrnes' initial "bomb in his pocket" diplomacy toward the Russians, never questioned American primacy in Italy or Japan, and soon insisted that the Soviets' "police state" tactics in Eastern Europe and pressures in the Near East meant that they understood only "force."[2]

Finally, Truman derailed Byrnes' major initiative at the CFM in Moscow in December 1945. During the fall Truman seemed to prefer that Byrnes be a "Super" secretary. The president brushed off queries about a heads-of-state meeting and laughed at reports that while the State Department fiddled, "Byrnes roams." Byrnes relished his role. He kept Truman informed, but much less so White House staff and State Department officials, whom he distrusted. Unfortunately, while Truman approved foreign policy in general, he often mis-perceived substantive implications or significant detail and did not follow closely Byrnes' tactical or strategic shifts. Thus, when the secretary moved away from confrontational toward quid pro quo diplomacy, Truman, stirred by his insecurity and Byrnes' critics, reproached the secretary and set the stage for confrontation.[3]

I

Atomic power posed great questions in 1945, although the British, not the Russians, were the first to raise them. The Americans, with their British and Canadian allies, had developed the bomb in secret and negotiated secret, exclusive control over uranium in the Belgian Congo and thorium in Brazil and the Dutch East Indies. But postwar military and industrial atomic collaboration, which many Britons saw as a panacea to maintain great-power status, was uncertain. The Roosevelt-Churchill Quebec Agreement of August 1943 provided that the president would determine on what basis the U.S. might share any industrial or commercial advantage that derived from wartime development of atomic power, and the Hyde Park aide-mémoire of September 1944 called for postwar military and industrial collaboration but did not specify how this was to be done. Truman was not bound by FDR's executive agreements. Thus, shortly after Potsdam, Prime Minister Attlee, anxious about British interests and concerned that atomic power demanded "immediate" readjustment of international relations, proposed an Anglo-American declaration not to use atomic power selfishly but solely by the U.S. and Britain as "trustees" for humanity to promote peace.[4]

Truman expressed interest but acted alone and with different emphasis. On August 9 he declared that the atomic bomb could not be let loose in a "lawless" world and that the nations who had its "secret" had to constitute themselves its "trustees" and would not reveal "the secret of its production" until they could ensure its peaceful use only. Truman also released Princeton University physicist Henry D. Smyth's general account of atomic military power. The president did so chiefly to assuage those who said this was necessary to permit informed public discussion, while the report revealed no information that other nations could not acquire within a few months and omitted mention of the prospect of thermonuclear weapons. On August 15 Truman directed Cabinet, military, and scientific officials not to release information related to bomb design or production without his approval. He also put off for further administrative study Attlee's proposal jointly to authorize Anglo-American collaboration. Meanwhile, Byrnes told George Harrison, Stimson's aide for atomic matters, that contrary

to the views of many concerned scientists and their director J. Robert Oppenheimer at the Los Alamos laboratory, international atomic agreement was impractical at present. Atomic weapons research and efforts at exclusive rights to
materials were to continue "full force."[5]

As the British government's high-level Advisory Committee on Atomic
Energy concluded, Truman's call to preserve the atomic "secret" was "categoric" and controlling for them, although most of their senior officials already
believed that the Russians would view any offer to share as weakness and evade
safeguards. Thus the British precluded even preliminary discussion of atomic
energy at the forthcoming London CFM. Meanwhile, on September 2 Byrnes
gave Assistant Secretary of War McCloy the impression that he thought the
Russians were aware of the power of the bomb and that he could do much better at the CFM if he "went with it [the bomb] in his hip pocket" even if he did
not make express threats. The next day Byrnes, who was "quite radically opposed" to any approach to Stalin and denounced his "acts of perfidy" at Potsdam, similarly impressed Stimson that he looked to go to London with the
"bomb in his pocket, so to speak, as a great weapon" to help him work through
his problems with the Russians. A distraught secretary of war immediately
sought to engage Truman but was able to see him only briefly on September 4
to warn that this "power politics" threatened an "international world." Byrnes
sailed for London the next day.[6]

Truman in fact saw eye to eye with Byrnes' "atomic diplomacy" and gave
him a free hand at the CFM meeting, which began on September 11. The secretary kept Truman informed but sent only press releases to the State Department, and he took as an adviser John Foster Dulles, his unofficial Republican
counterpart. The specter of the atomic bomb was also present, although it was
confined to diplomatic banter. Thus, when early on Byrnes chided Molotov at
a reception that he seemed to prefer sightseeing to negotiating, the Russian
asked if the secretary had an atomic bomb in his side pocket. Byrnes retorted
that Southerners carried their artillery there and that he would let Molotov
"have it" if he did not get down to business. The foreign minister laughed, and
at a banquet a few nights later he toasted Byrnes' eloquence, and possession of
the atomic bomb. Later on, appearing slightly inebriated, he blurted, "We've
got it." Molotov was feigning but also signaling that the Russians would not be
intimidated.[7]

In fact, in autumn 1945 both Stalin, who determined Soviet strategy, and
Molotov, who executed it with ever so rare individual initiatives, anticipated
hard bargaining with the West that would require extra resolve in the face of
America's atomic advantage. As Stalin had said in mid-August, "Hiroshima has
shaken the whole world. The balance has been destroyed." But at the same time

both men viewed with some optimism the prospect of reaching accord with the Alllies.[8]

At the start of the CFM, therefore, Molotov deliberately acceded to the Anglo-American interpretation that the Potsdam agreement allowed France and China to discuss all proposed peace treaties for defeated nations, although they could vote on them only in cases where they had been signatory to the surrender. In this way France would at least be allowed to discuss the Balkan treaties, and China would not be excluded from every European issue. But substantive talks about the treaties quickly reverted to a Potsdam-style standoff.

Byrnes proposed a lenient treaty for Italy: low reparations; control of predominantly Italian Trieste; and great power collective trusteeships under UN auspices over Italy's former colonies, notably Libya. Molotov pushed high reparations: Yugoslav control of Trieste; and individual trusteeships, with Russia taking Tripolitania in western Libya and the British, the eastern region of Cyrenaica. The British military, concerned over defense of Egypt and Suez, were tempted. But neither Byrnes nor Bevin would allow a Russian base on the Mediterranean, or near the Belgian Congo where, Byrnes remarked, Anglo-American uranium contracts were only as safe as the battleship that guarded them. Further, Molotov knew — as he said later — that it would be difficult to make the argument for a Soviet trusteeship (and naval base) in Libya. But when he correctly argued that the U.S. had agreed in June at the San Francisco Conference to Russian eligibility for a trusteeship, Byrnes snapped that this did not mean the "moon and the sun."[9]

The sharpest exchanges came over Bulgaria and Rumania. The Soviets proposed treaties for Finland, Hungary, Bulgaria, and Rumania that approximated their 1944 armistice terms. Byrnes acceded to Soviet policy in Finland and Hungary. But roused by bitter reports from foreign service officers returned from Eastern Europe, he took the State Department hard line (urged at Potsdam) that precluded recognizing, or negotiating peace treaties for, the Bulgarian and Rumanian governments until they were more broadly constituted and allowed Western journalists freer access. He insisted, however, that the U.S. sought governments that were both "friendly" to the Soviet Union and more representative of democratic elements and cited the Polish precedent.

Molotov would have none of it. Russia had been more flexible with Poland because it had been a wartime ally, and its coalition derived from having had two governments. Further, the Russians had not demanded a new regime in British-controlled Greece, whose government had less public support than Rumania's. Byrnes' reply that journalists had greater freedom in Greece than in Rumania only opened him to Molotov's riposte that "apparently in Greece the correspondents were happy but the people were not; whereas in Rumania, the people were happy but the correspondents were not." Simply put, the Russians would not compromise on their vital sphere of influence even at risk of breaking up the conference.[10]

Byrnes despaired quickly: two days after talks began he was certain that the Russians were "welching" on every Yalta and Potsdam accord and then insisted that they were preparing for war with the U.S. The London Conference was futile. The only hope was to deal directly with Stalin in Moscow. But on September 20 the secretary appealed privately to Molotov, saying that he and Truman favored augmenting Russian security with a four-power, twenty-five-year treaty to demilitarize Germany. Molotov expressed interest but persisted in saying that America's Rumanian policy challenged Russia. Byrnes left in a huff, convinced that Molotov was a "semi-colon figure" who aimed to do in a "slick dip way" what Hitler had done in Europe, although this would lead Russia to the same fate as Germany.[11]

Truman provided no advice to break the standoff. A year later he would insist that the proposed German treaty had been a "test case" of Soviet-American relations ("calling their bluff"), which Molotov rebuffed although it might have appealed to Stalin. But at the time Truman did not urge Byrnes to follow up on the proposal, which contained no specifics. The president merely instructed his secretary, with familiar loyalty, to "stick to your guns" on Italy and Bulgaria, and "Give Em Hell."[12]

In fact, Stalin apparently had little or no interest in the German proposal at this time if only because he did not want to further enhance the U.S. role in Europe and also thought that the pact would divert attention from the Far East, where the U.S. exercised virtually exclusive control over Japan. At the same time, under instruction from Stalin, Molotov stalemated negotiations on September 22 by declaring that the foreign ministers had to revise their initial decision that allowed the French and Chinese to discuss treaties where they had not signed the surrender because this violated Potsdam. The Soviets now reverted to insisting that deliberations had to be limited mainly to the Big Three. Truman appealed twice to Stalin not to undercut the conference with this "strict," although correct, interpretation. But Stalin was unmoved. The Russians would oppose any proposal that affected their predominance in their "zone of influence," as Bevin told his Cabinet; later he also told Byrnes that in Eastern Europe one had to "to be prepared to exchange one set of crooks for another."[13]

Truman was equally protective of American zones. The same day that Molotov had stymied talks, the president proclaimed that if the occupying powers in Japan disagreed, "the policies of the United States will govern." Then on September 24 he declared that General MacArthur's authority with respect to the Japanese was "supreme," and at his press conference two days later he reiterated the primacy of U.S. policy in Japan. When asked about a mechanism to effect concerted allied policy in Japan, Truman replied that MacArthur had been designated to act for all the powers and that the Russians could be in touch with him through their representative on his staff.[14]

Even Byrnes noted that Truman's statements offended every U.S. ally and gave the appearance that in Japan the Americans were "going off in a unilateral way as the Russians were going off in the Balkans." Still, the president and secretary refused to add to the London agenda Soviet proposals to create an Allied Control Council in Japan, despite Ambassador Harriman's advice that this "brush off" would fuel Soviet suspicions and that it would be advisable to establish an A.C.C. comparable to Balkan ones, provided MacArthur had "final voice." Byrnes refused to link Japan and Eastern Europe, however, and insisted that the U.S. confronted a "new Russia" taking "aggressive" positions.[15]

"I agree with your stand," the president reinforced Byrnes on September 25. "Do everything you can to continue, but in the final analysis do whatever you think is right and tell them to go to hell if you have to." The secretary briefly reconsidered. He had pushed the Russians as far as he could, he told Dulles on September 30; it was time to compromise. But Dulles threatened to attack him publicly as an appeaser. Thus, Byrnes asked Molotov to agree that ultimately more than just the Big Three would fix the Balkan treaties. Meanwhile, "some change" in the Rumanian and Bulgarian regimes would allow review of nonrecognition. Molotov insisted, however, that recognition had to precede treaty negotiation, lest there appear to be agreement where none existed. Two days later, on October 2, the conference ended without an agreed communiqué.[16]

Byrnes' personal, or atomic, diplomacy had failed. He would seek to compromise over Rumania and Bulgaria, but he was convinced that the Russians had designs on both Greece and Libya to gain a hold on the Mediterranean and on Belgian Congo uranium. From the Soviet perspective, Stalin and Molotov had no intention of making any deal so long as the U.S. refused substantive concessions on either the Balkans or Japan. They believed that the failure of the CFM meant that Byrnes' diplomacy had failed, and that provided no reason to grieve. At the same time, Stalin viewed the London CFM as a "combat reconnaissance" operation, and he was willing to continue hard bargaining at a later date.[17]

Truman also seemed to take matters in stride. He repeatedly brushed off the London failure as a necessary exercise and told his Cabinet not to tell the public how much the Russians had tried American patience. Meanwhile, he faced perhaps his "most momentous" decision, he wrote to his wife Bess. His anxiety reflected in his bravado that the "ayes" would have it even if his was the only one.[18]

II

Truman's view that America and its atomic partners should be the world's trustees of the "secret" of the atomic bomb hardly resolved the profound problem of atomic weapons and encouraged the "power politics" that failed at London. Stimson was certain of that, and after spending three weeks away from Washington reassessing atomic power in international perspective, he took his case to the president on September 12. The secretary insisted that the atomic bomb dominated Soviet-American relations and that it was impossible to maintain an Anglo-American atomic bloc or continue to negotiate with the bomb "rather ostentatiously on our hip" without precipitating "a secret armament race of a rather desperate character," which he feared had already begun. Worse, "secrecy and nationalistic military superiority" applicable to conventional weapons did not apply to atomic weapons, which signified a revolutionary change in man's control over nature, the climax of the race between his capacity for destruction or survival. Further, there were no "secrets" of the bomb, or none the Soviets would not obtain, and it did not matter whether they did so in four, or twenty, years, only that they did so through peaceful collaboration.

Stimson implored that there was no logical alternative to a direct American approach "to Russia" to proscribe use of the bomb (perhaps impounding American bombs and halting further manufacture) and to foster scientific exchanges and peaceful use of atomic energy. He did not propose immediate sharing of "secret ordnance procedures" related to bomb production, but he minimized America's "momentary superiority" and said that only direct dealing with the Russians (bypassing the UN to preclude debate by countries without atomic potential) would persuade them of American seriousness. Civilization had to be saved not just for a period of years but forever, and if this agreement required trust, the "only way to make a man trustworthy is to trust him," even if the Russians got the bomb "a little earlier" than otherwise.

Truman read and approved every paragraph of Stimson's memorandum, agreed that "we must take Russia into our confidence," and pledged to devote an entire Cabinet session to the atomic issue. But the president probably never accepted or assimilated Stimson's approach. Within a week he would insist, in his vernacular, that no great power would ever give up the "locks and bolts" necessary to protect its "house" against "outlaw attack" and then remarked in Cabinet that the U.S. should inform the UN about atomic energy but had to preserve the bomb's "secret," or "know-how," a phrase soon adopted from Manhattan Project administrator, General Leslie Groves.[19]

Truman, his Cabinet, and other senior administration officials took up atomic power on September 21. Years later Acheson would state, and historians would repeat, that "the discussion was unworthy of the subject" if only because no one had a chance to weigh the complexities of the issue. In fact, much of the commentary was highly thoughtful. It also revealed the growing divide between those officials who seemed to be more conversant with the scientific issues and dissemination of information, and who thought it necessary to try to cooperate with the Soviets on a range of issues, and those who saw the atomic power issue in the more narrow frame of preserving what they held to be a long-term advantage that they did not wish to share with anyone, especially not the Russians.[20]

Stimson, who would retire from office at the end of the day, opened the Cabinet discussion by insisting that world peace depended on establishing a pattern of Soviet-American understanding and then reiterating his call for a direct approach to the Russians to proscribe atomic weapons and to encourage scientific collaboration. There was no atomic secret to give away, he said; "the secret will give itself away." Acheson (then under secretary of state) propounded a Stimson-like program, including the growing consensus that there was no "secret" to contain and that the Russians would rival American knowledge and industrial-engineering applications within five years. Further, America's self-declared "trustee" role would only promote Soviet hostility and an arms race in which current advantage would prove worthless since there was no defense against atomic war, especially after atomic weapons were joined to rockets.

Strong support for this position came from a majority of those present, including Robert Patterson, the under secretary of war about to succeed Stimson; Vannevar Bush, the president's scientific adviser and head of the Office of Scientific Research and Development (OSRD), who affirmed Russian ability to achieve atomic bomb parity within five years; Secretary of Commerce Wallace, who sought to focus Cabinet argument by having Truman state that the issue was not the immediate sharing of "factory techniques or know-how" and who derided the idea that America could achieve security behind a "scientific Maginot line"; and Acting Secretary of the Interior Abe Fortas, who warned that "ultranationalism" could not contain scientific information and that America's challenge was not to devise a quid pro quo but an international course of conduct to avert mutual destruction.

But ultranationalism, and mistaken historical analogies, persuaded a minority to resist dealing with the Russians, or anyone else. With Byrnes at the CFM in London, Navy Secretary Forrestal led the way. The Russians were "Oriental" in their thinking, as unlikely as the Japanese—allies in World War I—to remain friendly or to honor arms agreements. Further, there were "no returns on appeasement," as Hitler had shown. Forrestal proposed American trusteeship, under UN auspices, over atomic power; or at least Security Council control, with annual inspection of every nation. Even more exclusive, almost chauvinist, arguments came from Secretary of the Treasury Fred Vinson, Secretary of Agriculture Clinton Anderson, and Senator Kenneth McKellar of Tennessee. They insisted that the American public's "property rights" in atomic energy precluded the government's sharing commercial or military information and further, that the genius of American technology that had brought world leadership in production of automobiles and airplanes now guaranteed America's permanent lead and security in an atomic arms race. Other nations could copy all that they wanted, Anderson paraphrased Rudyard Kipling, but none could copy the American mind.

Truman did not reveal a fixed position. He seemed to favor exchange of scientific, but not industrial, knowledge, although the distinction was somewhat artificial and not of enduring military value. He invited those present to put their views to him in writing and said he would inform them of his conclusion.[21]

To some extent, the president was unnerved by the "stormy" Cabinet debate, by leaks (generated by Forrestal) that exaggerated Wallace's views, and by complaints that the executive branch sought to preclude Congress' role in atomic policy. Prime Minister Attlee's renewed request on September 25 for Anglo-American talks, and his view that their atomic lead was temporary, also concerned Truman. Moreover, British Ambassador Lord Halifax noted that the president was "frankly fogged" by Russian bitterness at the London Conference.[22]

Truman sought to attain consensus and to buy time. His special message (largely the work of an assistant to Acheson) to Congress on October 3 stated that atomic principles were well known and that foreign research would soon match American. He proposed initial talks about international control with the British and Canadians and pledged to reveal nothing about bomb manufacture. He also asked Congress to create a body to control atomic power and resources in America.[23]

Despite the edge toward international collaboration, Truman's proposal to deal first with the British was a step back from the Stimson-Acheson direct approach to the Russians, notably unmentioned in the address, and his emphasis on preserving applied information suggested limited "trust" and desire to preserve commercial advantage. Two days later he shelved meeting with Attlee and remarked in private that while he doubted that the atomic bomb could ever be used, the Russians seemed to understand only "divisions."[24]

Then at a press conference on October 8 in Tiptonville, Tennessee, Truman, taking pains to be "on the record," not only reiterated his refusal to share atomic know-how but explicated the nationalist Vinson-Anderson-McKellar view that America's unique ability to apply science assured world leadership in producing cars and long-distance bombers and that no other nation—despite consensus about Soviet (and British) atomic capability—had the industry, engineering ability, or perhaps resources to use the technical data. Nations that sought to catch up with the U.S., he said, would have to do it "on their own hook, just as we did." He also said that U.S.-Soviet disagreements derived from their lack of understanding due to different languages, not America's atomic monopoly. Newspapers trumpeted Truman's decision not to share atomic secrets, and when shortly an old friend stopped at the White House and asked whether the "armaments race is on," the president said yes and that "we would stay ahead."[25]

At the same time the Joint Chiefs of Staff, as Truman already knew, opposed atomic sharing. They insisted that urban-industrial America was highly vulnerable to atomic attack and opposed any accord that would give other nations, especially the Soviets, access to atomic weapons information. So too did Byrnes, returned from London, resist sharing, which he said depended on inspection; Russian behavior in Eastern Europe made it "childish" to think that they would allow oversight or honor their agreements.[26]

But Attlee persisted about an atomic meeting, while White House aides, chafing at liberal criticism of the administration's "nakedly nationalistic" policy—but assured by Groves that they could safeguard the bomb's secret—proposed an "exploratory" Big Three meeting. Truman bent, slightly. In a rousing Navy Day speech on October 27, in which he omitted mention of the Russians except to stress that he would not recognize governments imposed by a foreign power and would not compromise with "evil," he announced that he would meet with the British and Canadians but accented America's control of atomic power as a "sacred trust."[27]

Truman hoped to occupy Attlee and Canada's prime minister, Mackenzie King, with ceremony. Meanwhile, Byrnes advised that the Quebec accord did not call for sharing information about bomb manufacture. Hasty conference planning fell to Vannevar Bush, the president's scientific adviser, who wanted minimal sharing but American access to British-controlled resources. More important, however, Bush shared the Stimson-Acheson outlook: the Russians could produce a bomb within five years and the "great question" was how to approach them before the UN took up the issue. He sought to avert an arms race/war through agreements that the "secretive and suspicious" Russians would find worth keeping and to proceed by "partial payments," or sequential steps, telling the Russians at the outset that the U.S. intended to "go the whole distance."

Bush proposed three steps: first, an Anglo-American approach to the Russians to create a UN agency to disseminate basic information, with scientists traveling and reporting freely, which required "no policing" and "costs us nothing"; second, exchange of industrial data, with the quid pro quo of ensured inspections; and third, all nations pooling, and allowing inspection of, their fissionable materials to ensure peaceful use. The steps would take "many years"; meanwhile the U.S. could produce, but need not assemble, atomic explosives.[28]

Truman and Byrnes approved on November 7. They had no other plan, while going to the UN provided a means to move forward without making hard decisions with respect to the Russians. At the same time, Molotov announced in a Kremlin speech that the Russians would soon have "atomic energy, and much else," and that no nation or Anglo-American bloc could monopolize atomic energy or use it to intimidate. In sum, the foreign minister stated his nation's two major goals: to break the U.S. atomic monopoly and to let the U.S. know that it would not profit from its temporary advantage.[29]

The British, too, were determined to have independent nuclear capacity, hence their early October decision to build a research plant at Harwell. But they also sought U.S. collaboration. Initially, Attlee and Bevin as well favored international cooperation, being moved by idealism, the belief that U.S. atomic diplomacy spurred Russian intransigence, and the sense that there was no atomic secret. Similarly, Ambassador Halifax pressed atomic sharing even at "one chance in ten" of success, while numerous Cabinet ministers urged, upon Attlee's departure for America, that he "take risks" for peace, including atomic disclosure.[30]

But senior officials, including the government's Advisory Committee on Atomic Energy and the highly select Cabinet committee "General 75," persisted in saying that the Russians respected only strength, that inspection would prove unacceptable or unworkable, and that Britain could not get out in front of America. Further, Conservative leaders like Churchill (and Eden) eschewed "acts of faith" with the Russians, which were likely to raise "immediate suspicion in American breasts." They also lauded the Anglo-American "special relationship" on atomic matters as virtually a military treaty. By late October Attlee, and more so Bevin, who complained that Soviet policy never varied, were more reserved about international collaboration, differentiated scientific and applied knowledge, and concluded, as Attlee told his Cabinet on November 5, that the U.S. would not yet renounce development or use of atomic weapons.

Attlee thus proposed a national program that would become international. Each nation would develop—and control—atomic power to deter aggression by threat of atomic retaliation, exchange scientific information, and help to create a United Nations that ultimately might foster advanced atomic cooperation. Meanwhile, national programs would forestall discord with the Russians over inspections, veto power, and pooling of resources. But Attlee sought to continue Anglo-U.S. cooperation, albeit without the Quebec proviso that the president would control postwar commercial exchanges in return for U.S. access to British-controlled ores.[31]

During initial Washington talks on November 10 and November 11, however, Truman pressed for UN control of atomic energy but not before it could be "absolutely certain" of every nation's good faith, which would take considerable time and require Russian cooperation to be "proven in practice." The Americans further stressed that technical exchange was impossible without prior "effective, reciprocal, and enforceable safeguards," meaning physical inspections that would provide "a useful hold over the Russians." The British, in turn, were filled with "gloom" at what they perceived to be America's program to preserve exclusive atomic control.[32]

The president's aides held firm during two more days of intense talks while he cracked the deadline whip, and then announced an accord to be signed November 15. The Truman-Attlee-King Joint Declaration was largely an American document that agreed in principle to exchange of scientific data but deemed that industrial data were subject to military use and required strictest safeguards. The three leaders thus proposed that a UN commission effect a program for scientific exchange, peaceful use of atomic energy, elimination of atomic weapons, and inspections to protect complying nations. The commission's work would proceed by stages, with completion of each a requisite for the next. Truman took no questions from the press, while Republican senator Arthur Vandenberg of Michigan and Democrat Tom Connally of Texas, the ranking members of the Senate Foreign Relations Committee, were hastily summoned to the signing and left before the picture-taking to protest the administration's failure to consult Congress. The British, distraught at U.S. refusal to renegotiate the Quebec Agreement to provide for industrial exchange, sought benefit in two unannounced agreements, signed the next day, that preserved two wartime committees to foster atomic cooperation—with American access to British resources—but relegated exchanges about atomic plant development-operation to future ad hoc agreements.[33]

Truman and his Cabinet were delighted. They had tied Britain and Canada to their atomic policy at no cost but great gain in resources. They also presented a seemingly palatable *fait accompli* to the Soviet Union and won public acclaim. Even the crusty Forrestal exulted that the vital role of the UN might turn it into a "living thing." The liberal Wallace approved too, but with two insights: that to preclude industrial exchange—ostensibly subject to military use—prior to full safeguards was a deceptive way to forestall initial, safe sharing for industrial use; and that to proceed by stages suggested that the Russians had to "pass the first grade in moral aptitude," although Truman rejoined that it was best to go step by step with them. Most important, perhaps, Truman's policy fostered misguided public belief in an enduring atomic "secret" and a permanent American lead and security in an arms race. Further, and ironically, current atomic policy may have spurred conflict between Truman, growing more reluctant to compromise with the Russians, and Byrnes, who had long opposed atomic accord but now thought he had a vital bargaining chip with which to induce Soviet cooperation. The Russians, meanwhile, denounced the Anglo-American-Canadian accord as Western "atomic diplomacy."[34]

III

During the fall of 1945 Truman grew increasingly wary of the Soviets around the globe. At Potsdam he had agreed in principle to revision of the 1936 Montreux Convention that gave Turkey sole control of the Straits. But then he pressed his idea to internationalize European waterways, which Stalin rebuffed. U.S. officials then resisted even minor modification of Montreux and, above all, the prospect of Soviet bases in the Dardanelles area, despite what army officers called the "logical illogicality" of U.S. and British control over Panama and the Suez, respectively, and U.S. claims to bases from Iceland to Pacific islands. American diplomats and military planners also recognized that despite the presence of large numbers of Soviet troops in Bulgaria and Rumania, they were too weak to undertake action over the Straits and risk general war. The Russians intended only to intimidate the Turks.[35]

Still it remained an article of faith for Truman, as he wrote to Byrnes in mid-October 1945, that the Russians intended to take the Straits as well as the bordering Turkish provinces of Kars and Ardahan by "direct action." Thus the president persisted with his proposal to internationalize the Straits until his secretary tactfully told him in late October that Turkey would not give up its fortifications (however outmoded) without a U.S. guarantee, which Congress would not permit. Truman shelved his idea, although he told Byrnes that "we should keep pushing our program so as to prevent Russia from taking the Straits over."[36]

The president grew anxious soon again when the Russians, who had doubled their divisions in the Transcaucasus and had 200,000 troops in Bulgaria, stepped up their "war of nerves," including maneuvers on the Bulgar-Turkish frontier. But Molotov insisted to Harriman that war was "unthinkable," while the Americans now proposed to revise Montreux so that the Straits would always remain open to warships of Black Sea nations. Thus, Turkey could not deny passage to Soviet ships but the Soviets would not need bases. They replied, however, that the Turks would be unable or unwilling to prevent an attack through the Straits. There matters rested, with the Turks conceding in early November that Soviet troop withdrawals made an attack unlikely. But Truman remained convinced, as he told a White House aide, that the Russians would "grab" the Straits and present an "accomplished fact." They understood only "divisions," he said in mid-December, and he lamented that he had none to send.[37]

The president also feared Russian troops in northern Iran, based there since the (British-inspired) Anglo-Soviet occupation of August 1941 that was intended to preclude a German takeover of that nation's rich oil fields or an attack on Russia, whose Baku oil fields were just one hundred miles north of Iran. Shortly thereafter, Reza Shah Pahlavi, long friendly to the Germans, was forced to abdicate in favor of his young son, twenty-two-year-old Mohammed Reza. Then in late January 1942 the British, whose forces controlled the south, and the Soviets, who controlled five northern provinces, signed a treaty with Iran agreeing to remove their troops within six months of the end of the war. The U.S. then sent two noncombat military missions of 5,000 men to advise Iran's army and the police, and numerous civilian experts to advise the government, especially about oil. By late 1942 Wallace Murray, head of the State Department's Near Eastern and African Affairs (NEA) division, said that the U.S. would soon be "running" Iran through "an impressive body of American advisers." Meanwhile, the British continued to maintain their oil monopoly through the Anglo-Iranian Oil Company, although in 1944 U.S. firms began to press hard for concessions. Then in autumn of that year Stalin demanded an oil concession in northern Iran, while the Iranian Parliament, or Majlis, passed a law forbidding the government to negotiate or grant an oil lease without its permission.[38]

By spring 1945 the Iranians were pressing both the British and Russians to remove their troops from the country, and at the Potsdam Conference the British urged the Russians to agree to an accelerated timetable for mutual withdrawal. Truman supported the British proposal and said that he expected U.S. troops to depart Iran within sixty days. Stalin agreed only to evacuation of Teheran, and at the CFM in London in September, the British and Soviets agreed that they would respect their treaty obligation and withdraw their troops by March 2, 1946. But Stalin also renewed his demand for an oil concession in northern Iran, and Russian troops there gave support to revolts for autonomy by Kurds and Armenians and for self-determination, or autonomy, by the new Democratic-led (Communist) party in the bordering province of Azerbaijan. U.S. officials feared that the "ruling class" in Teheran had neither the will nor ability to improve the "deplorable" conditions in northern Iran. Byrnes and others also believed that the Russians had fomented the uprisings and might annex Azerbaijan or use it to turn the whole country into a satellite. This they feared would block a U.S. oil concession and threaten other holdings in the Middle East, especially in Saudi Arabia, where the U.S. also planned an airfield. Thus in November Byrnes proposed early withdrawal of all foreign troops from Iran by January 1946 and urged domestic reform on Teheran. But the Soviets cited their 1942 treaty and in mid-December heralded a new "national government" in Azerbaijan, although Moscow did not seek either to annex the province or foster separation from Iran. But in private Truman rebuffed the view that the Russians' main goal in Iran was an oil concession or that they had security concerns in a region once part of their imperial sphere of influence. Soviet unilateral action belied "peaceful intent," he said, and was also further proof of their aim at the Straits.[39]

Truman also worried anew about the Russian role in China. At the war's end the U.S. continued to supply Jiang Jiehsi's GMD with military equipment, helped to transport 500,000 of its troops from southern to northern China, and engaged some 60,000 U.S. Marines to assist in securing reoccupied territory. Truman judged this policy to be consistent with Roosevelt's and "in the middle" between the GMD and Mao's CCP. He admitted that if the U.S. pulled out, the GMD could not continue, but he felt some loyalty because they had fought "side by side" with Americans, and he alleged that the "so-called Commies" had often "helped the Japs." He also brushed off concern about America's role in a renewed civil war by stating that "we can't walk out and leave a million armed Japs in China."[40]

Crisis loomed by November, however. The Communists moved into Manchuria as the Russians began to depart, stripping the industry to their benefit. Meanwhile, Jiang's troops moved forward, and the fighting began. U.S. officials in China cabled alarming reports about GMD political-military corruption and incompetence, and by late November Cabinet officers weighed whether to abandon America's active but indirect role in China or to intervene directly against the Chinese Communists, which implied conflict with the Soviets. At first the Forrestal-Patterson interventionist view prevailed, but at second thought Byrnes and Acheson, concluding that Communist strength derived from more than just Russian aid, proposed return to the wartime policy of seeking a coalition, even cutting aid if Jiang resisted.[41]

Then Ambassador Patrick J. Hurley resigned on November 27. Hurley was a flamboyant former Republican secretary of war whom Roosevelt had appointed in summer 1944 to effect a GMD-CCP coalition. But he could not do so and then blamed allegedly disloyal U.S. diplomats and Russian conspiracy. Recently returned to Washington for consultation, he had repeatedly threatened to resign, but Truman and others dissuaded him. But now, perhaps fearing blame if China were "lost," he quit and released his letter to the president excoriating foreign service officers and British and Soviet imperialism.[42]

"Look what a son-of-a-bitch did to me," Truman railed to his Cabinet that afternoon, anticipating congressional inquiry and partisan criticism. But he adroitly seized the suggestion to appoint General Marshall, retiring chief of staff, as his special emissary. Truman did not question or resolve contradictions in America's China policy, however. He said that the U.S. should "stand pat" and refuse aid to Jiang until he came to terms with the Communists. But he also insisted that Britain and Russia were seeking a weak and divided China and that unless the U.S. took a strong stand there, "the Russians would take the place of Japan in the Far East." Then on December 11 the president, Marshall, and Byrnes agreed that no matter how badly Jiang behaved, they could not abandon him because that meant Russian control of Manchuria, division of China, and negation of America's wartime goals. Truman shortly instructed Marshall to seek a coalition regime in China but agreed secretly to continue to support Jiang even if he did not cooperate.[43]

More important, from Truman's perspective in autumn 1945 the Soviets seemed bent on a course of aggrandizement in Europe, the Middle East, and Asia that threatened America's vital interests. He did not think war inevitable, but he was uncertain how to proceed, and he always shied from summit diplomacy. Responsibility for negotiating a reduction in conflict thus fell to Byrnes, on whose diplomacy Truman relied. The secretary had concluded as far back as the CFM in September that the best, and perhaps only, route to agreement was to deal directly with Stalin. But first the secretary sought to resolve the Balkan impasse by appointing Mark Ethridge, liberal publisher of the *Louisville Courier-Journal,* to head a commission to Bulgaria and Rumania, presumably to report that conditions there were less oppressive than charged by the anti-Soviet diplomats in the field. Then in a speech in New York on October 31, Byrnes acknowledged Russia's "special security interests" in Eastern Europe.[44]

Byrnes had also sent Harriman to Stalin in mid-October with a letter from Truman stating that the U.S. policy of nonrecognition was not motivated by an "unfriendly attitude" toward the Soviet Union, and imploring settlement. Stalin, on vacation at his dacha in the Crimea, had the ambassador flown there. Stalin proposed another foreign ministers' meeting but was persistent that only the Big Three could write the peace treaties. The most significant aspect of the message, however, was Stalin's expressed anger at U.S. refusal to consult about Japan, which he likened to treating the Soviet Union as a Pacific "satellite" or a "piece of furniture." Stalin's rhetoric aside, an "astonished" Harriman urged a face-saving compromise over Japan so long as MacArthur retained his final authority. He also lectured the State Department about Japan's threat to Russian security over two generations. Byrnes was equally astonished that Stalin gave priority to the Far East over the Balkans and attributed Russia's recent intransigence to disparity between its proud role in the war and being "left out in the cold" over Japan. He decided to go to Moscow, where Stalin would be close by, to gain a settlement that would satisfy Russian "pride and prejudice" and preserve U.S. primacy.[45]

Byrnes found a means to his goal when he remembered that the Yalta accords had provided for periodic meetings of the Big Three foreign ministers, as distinct from the five-member CFM that included France and China and had led to conflict over including them in the treaty writing. On his own initiative on November 23, he proposed to Molotov a Big Three meeting in Moscow, and Molotov quickly acceded. The British, mainly Bevin, balked. He was piqued at not being consulted and feared lack of preparation. He also thought that the Russians had overreached themselves at London. But after two weeks he gave way to his advisers and to Byrnes' threat to go it alone.[46]

Meantime, Byrnes concluded that he had a second, compelling reason to negotiate. He had recently received two remarkably similar cables, one from Harriman, the other a copy of a cable from Sir Archibald Clark-Kerr, Britain's ambassador in Moscow, to Bevin. Both cables argued that the Soviet leaders had been engaged in a desperate struggle for survival, from the era of their revolution through years of fear of capitalist encirclement and then Nazi invasion. But finally the Red Army had turned the tide and brought a sense of national security. "Then plump came the Atomic Bomb," threatening all at one blow, fueling old suspicions, and giving rise to aggressive behavior at the London CFM and Molotov's fiery speeches. It also jeopardized the coming UN meeting at which the Truman-Attlee atomic plan would be presented. Harriman claimed only to be explaining Russia's recent "strange" behavior, not proposing policy. But his view fit with growing political and scientific advice about need to consult the Russians, and gain their sponsorship, for a UN atomic energy program.[47]

Byrnes was persuaded. He put atomic energy first on his proposed Moscow agenda, although the Soviets feigned indifference and placed the issue last. Meanwhile, his advisers' draft accord followed the Truman-Attlee-King Declaration to establish a UN commission to oversee atomic developments and added Russian cosponsorship. Rather than rest atomic exchange on successive stages, however, they proposed "affirmative action," where likely to be fruitful, and immediate exchange of scientists and basic data, while technical data would require establishment of safeguards. Forrestal resisted Soviet sponsorship, and scientific exchange without reciprocity. But the British were delighted that Byrnes finally recognized that the Russians would not let international surveyors roam the Urals and Siberia before discussing exchange of atomic "know-how."[48]

Truman, however, confessed to being "baffled" by recent events and tended to blame Byrnes for the unsettled state of affairs. Then on November 29 the president, unaware of Byrnes' recent initiative, publicly denied prospect of a Big Three meeting and said that the UN was the best forum for great powers to resolve conflicts. This confused the British and others, and after announcement of Byrnes' mission, required a transparent public explanation that the president had referred only to a heads-of-state meeting. Truman now called Byrnes a "conniver," and questioned the secretary's judgment and loyalty. The president, former Ambassador Davies wrote, had been "poisoned and his mind was quite set. Jim is through, and it is a great pity." Shortly Truman snapped, after a Byrnes speech about Germany, that he was tired of learning about U.S. policy in the newspapers.[49]

Worse, Byrnes only belatedly briefed senators on the Foreign Relations and new Atomic Energy Committees about his Moscow plans on December 10, just two days before his departure. The senators assailed, and misread, the State Department program. Vandenberg charged it was "giving . . . away" atomic secrets without safeguards, that is, before the Soviets were willing to be "policed." He opposed any exchange of scientists and information as "sheer appeasement." The Russians had nothing to exchange, the Senator said, despite his own admission that the Russians, and others, could build a bomb in about two years.[50]

The next day the senators met with Truman, who was torn between seeking atomic accord but doubtful that Russian habits had changed "so far as honoring contracts is concerned." He shared the senators' concerns but was certain they misunderstood Byrnes' proposal. When Vandenberg insisted that to release even basic data meant giving away half of America's "trading stock," however, the president agreed to instruct Byrnes, en route to Moscow, to put an agreement on safeguards first, before any exchanges. The senators were appeased and unanimous that "the Byrnes formula must be "stopped." Meanwhile, Acheson sent Byrnes a Truman-approved summary of the talk, noting that any atomic agreement would require prior White House approval. Further, the president had "no intention of agreeing to disclose any information regarding the bomb at this time or unless and until arrangements for inspections and safeguards could be worked out." Byrnes replied, obliquely, that any proposal he made would stay within the framework of the Truman-Attlee Declaration.[51]

Suspicion and politics had taken a toll on U.S. policy and the Truman-Byrnes relationship even before the Moscow Conference began on December 15. Truman, however, had given Byrnes a letter for Stalin stating that the primary issues were Japan, the European peace treaties, and atomic energy, essentially Byrnes' agenda. Byrnes also brought with him the recent report from Ethridge, his Balkan emissary. The Ethridge Report declared that the Russians had established and directed "front" governments in Bulgaria and Rumania and dominated them politically and economically. The Soviets had also destroyed civil liberties and made coercion the hallmark of Bulgaria's recent November 18 elections. Ethridge concluded that while Russian behavior might be attributed to wartime bitterness and security concerns, the U.S. now had to demand adherence to Yalta's principles of representative government and free elections. More important—at least from Truman's perspective, as events would show—was Ethridge's view that even if the Soviets sought only security in Eastern Europe, they would undoubtedly use their position there to put pressure on Greece and Turkey and to be a springboard to aggression in the Eastern Mediterranean. But rather than publish the report, Byrnes hoped to use it privately to wrest concessions.[52]

The Moscow meeting quickly revealed sharply divergent Big Three perspectives. Bevin claimed that the Russians undercut the British Empire wherever they "rubbed" it—in Greece, Turkey, and Iran—and that they acquired land as zealously as British admirals once seized islands. He charged that the world was being divided into "three Monroes," with the U.S. dominating its continent and expanding to the Pacific, and the Russians creating a "Monroe" area from the Baltic to the Adriatic and in Manchuria. Byrnes rejoined that many of the Pacific islands that the U.S. was demanding for "security" were uninhabited. He said nothing about Japan or China where, Stalin would note, the U.S. had a "sphere of interest," while the British had India, but Russia had "nothing." Except, Bevin rejoined, a sphere from "Lubeck to Port Arthur."[53]

Recognizing spheres of interest may have spurred flexible, if hard, bargaining, and accord. First the negotiators resolved the European peace treaty procedure. The Russians insisted, as at London, that only signatories of the surrender agreements ("those who had shed the blood," Stalin said) could draft the treaties. But Byrnes got the Soviets to agree to admit France to the Italian treaty talks and then to have all the agreements made subject to review by a broad twenty-one-nation conference that would meet in Paris by May 1946. Truman then wired his approval of the draft treaty formula. He preferred to make the recommendations of the conference binding but acceded to Byrnes' view that the U.S. could gain a similar result by refusing to sign any final treaty that unwarrantably disregarded the recommendations.[54]

Byrnes also sustained American primacy in the Far East. Stalin scarcely objected to the U.S. proposal to establish a twelve-nation (to placate Britain and the Dominions) Far Eastern Commission, to be located in Washington, to formulate occupation policy in Japan. Power to implement policy, however, would be lodged in a Tokyo-based, four-power Allied Council, chaired by Supreme Commander General MacArthur, who would have sole executive authority and whose decisions would be "controlling." He would presumably await Commission consensus before acting on basic issues, but in fact MacArthur would remain America's proconsul for Japan.[55]

Byrnes also gained sanction for America's unique role in China. He insisted, despite Molotov's queries about U.S. troops and pressure for simultaneous Soviet-American withdrawals, that U.S. forces were in China solely to disarm the Japanese. Stalin finally acceded to their presence, with the barb that he would merely "like to be told about them" and that Jiang might have more influence with the Chinese people if he did not depend on foreign troops. The foreign ministers then reaffirmed need for a unified, GMD-led government and noninterference in China's affairs. The Marshall mission would remain free to "mediate." The Americans and Russians also agreed to a Joint Commission to set up a provisional government in Korea, looking toward trusteeship and then independence.[56]

Most significant, Byrnes secured the American position on atomic energy, "by far" his most important agenda item, he said. On December 18 he submitted the U.S. proposal to create a UN commission to develop a program for scientific exchange, peaceful use of atomic energy, atomic disarmament, and safeguards. At first he omitted reference to proceeding by stages, but Bevin pressed this and also proposed that the commission report to the Security Council, not—as the U.S. preferred—to the General Assembly. Byrnes agreed to add the stages but not the Security Council proviso, fearing public debate about allowing the Russians a veto. Then Molotov amazed the Americans by quickly affirming the plan, although he too insisted on Security Council control over the commission and later said that to agree to proceed by stages meant endorsing the Truman-Attlee statement, to which Russia was not party. Byrnes appealed to Stalin, who said he had taken "nine-tenths" of the American program; his "one-tenth" was the Security Council. Thus Byrnes acceded to the Russians and British and, ironically, to Vandenberg, who wanted to assure a U.S. veto over Russian proposals. Most important, Byrnes had gained Soviet commitment to deal on Truman-Attlee terms, which included moving ahead by stages with atomic power, with each stage to be completed before moving to the next one.[57]

Shortly afterwards, at a Christmas Eve dinner in the Kremlin, Molotov proposed a toast to Byrnes' scientific adviser, James Conant, and suggested that perhaps "after a few drinks we could explore the secrets I had and if I had a bit of the atomic bomb in my pocket, to bring it out." Stalin angrily interrupted:

"Here's to science and American scientists and what they accomplished. This is too serious a matter to joke about," and it was now time to work to see that atomic power was used for peaceful purposes. Interpreter Charles Bohlen later wrote that Stalin had obviously reversed Molotov and his bravado and indicated that from then on the Russians would take the atomic bomb seriously. Stalin, of course, had taken the bomb seriously since Hiroshima even if he would not bend Soviet policy to U.S. atomic diplomacy.[58]

The Russians exacted their price at Moscow, including control in their Eastern European sphere. Neither Molotov nor Stalin were moved by Byrnes' "threat" to publish the Ethridge Report. Nor would they bend much to meet his proposals to reorganize the Bulgarian and Rumanian governments, to "do something" about the Ministries of Interior and Justice, or to permit free elections. Molotov remained adamant that both governments were superior to that of Greece, that the Red Army did not impair internal affairs, and that Bulgaria already had free elections. Byrnes made a last appeal to Stalin, who granted that he would "advise" the Bulgarian government to take in two members of the "loyal opposition," while the Big Three could send a tripartite commission (as per Yalta on Poland) to counsel the Rumanian regime to include two non-Communist party leaders and then hold elections. Afterwards the U.S. and Britain would recognize Bulgaria and Rumania. Byrnes had little choice but to agree. Bevin was unequivocal about going along.[59]

Byrnes also pressed Russian withdrawal from Iran, warning that the issue might come to the UN in January. Stalin replied that no one would need "to blush" about Soviet troops. He denied territorial ambition in Iran, berated the "hostile" Teheran government, and insisted on Russia's treaty rights and its alleged need to protect its Baku oil fields. At last on December 24 Bevin proposed a tripartite commission to accelerate Allied troop withdrawals and to advise Teheran about domestic reform. Molotov seemed amenable (even as he took note of U.S. Marines in China), but as the conference wound down, he insisted that the matter be dropped. Byrnes acquiesced because he was determined to conclude all prior accords, although he evidently made last-minute efforts, and also proposed that Bevin seek out Stalin. But Stalin would not agree to Bevin's proposal for a tripartite commission. Thus, Iran went unmentioned in the conference Communiqué, but there remained the March 2, 1946, deadline for troop withdrawal agreed upon at the London CFM. Turkey also was not mentioned or much discussed, although Stalin persisted about a base in the Straits and a revised Kars-Ardahan border. But he dismissed talk of war as "rubbish." Finally the foreign ministers signed the conference accords at 3:30 A.M. on December 27. Harriman sent the Communiqué to Washington for release late that night.[60]

The Moscow Conference was marked by a Yalta-style blend of great-power accord and tacit spheres of influence. Byrnes gained acknowledgment of U.S. primacy in Japan and in China. There was accord on the Truman-Attlee atomic program, the European peace treaty process (at no cost), and a credible compromise in Korea. The Russians prevailed in their vital spheres of influence, Bulgaria and Rumania, while their claims on Iran and Turkey waited on events. Even the hard-bitten Molotov wrote that the agreement on important European and Far East issues indicated "development of cooperation" among the Big Three. Acheson approvingly referred to Byrnes as "St. Nickolas."[61]

But even before the Communiqué reached Washington, Byrnes and the Moscow results came under attack. Kennan, chargé in the Moscow Embassy, opposed virtually any accord with the Russians. He wrote that the secretary knew nothing about Koreans, Rumanians, and Iranians and sought agreement solely for "political effect at home." Kennan claimed that Byrnes' atomic proposal divided the Americans and British, and he penned a classic description of Molotov, cigarette dangling from his lips, eyes flashing confidently, capitalizing on Anglo-American uncertainty: "He had the look of a passionate poker player who knows that he has a royal straight flush and is about to call the last of his opponents." Kennan was wrong. Byrnes had succeeded on atomic energy, did well enough with Korea, and did what little he could for Bulgaria and Rumania. Similarly, Harriman charged that Byrnes' having delayed agreement over Japan for months had made it easier for Stalin to gain his way over Bulgaria and Rumania. That was not so; regardless, Truman was equally responsible, although no one (then or later) would say this.[62]

Meanwhile, Truman's White House chief of staff, Admiral Leahy, who was bitterly anti-Soviet and who alleged during the Hurley affair that Byrnes was not immune to "communistically-inclined" advisers, now fumed that the secretary's concessions violated the president's "righteous policy" and that the Moscow Communiqué was an "appeasement document." Influential journalists and politicians said Byrnes had not restrained the Russians on Iran and Turkey. And Vandenberg rushed to the State Department to charge that listing safeguards last in the atomic accord meant that the U.S. had to reveal atomic secrets without protection. Acheson knew the senator had misread matters but deftly telephoned Truman in Missouri, who agreed with him that Byrnes was right. The president authorized a White House statement, issued by Vandenberg, that the four stages were to be read as one and that complete "security" was to be part of each stage.[63]

Truman's mood was darkening. He was beset by advice to take a firmer grip on foreign policy, in effect, to become his own secretary of state. He was also distressed by White House pressure. His Christmas trip home to Independence had brought only sharp rebuke from his revered Bess about the brevity of his visit, which rekindled anxiety that he lacked ability to be the "No. 1 man in the world." Then came the Moscow Conference criticism, and word—brought by Acheson to defuse presidential anger—that Byrnes had already planned a national address upon his return. Truman acceded, but told his secretary to report to him first on the *Williamsburg,* already cruising down the Potomac. Disconsolate and exhausted from his long journey, Byrnes hastened to catch up.[64]

Truman and Byrnes met privately for an hour and a half on December 29. They talked amicably, but the president complained that the Moscow Communiqué was released before he had seen it. Byrnes attributed this to poor telephone and cable communications. Truman was "satisfied," Leahy would note, and the two men emerged in good humor for drinks and a friendly dinner, at which Leahy needled Byrnes, chiefly about Bulgaria and Rumania. Truman invited Byrnes to remain overnight, but he declined in order to work on his speech. Despite Truman's later claims, there is no evidence that he had "reversed Byrnes" or told him that "his appeasement policy was not mine." The next night in a national radio broadcast, the secretary praised the president and said that modern events required swift diplomacy and that the Moscow accords and compromises had promoted Big Three understanding. Truman, Byrnes, and friends spent New Year's eve on the *Williamsburg.* But four days later Truman complained that no one had informed him about U.S. recognition of Yugoslavia and that while he loved Byrnes "like a brother," he was "too disposed to compromise things."[65]

On the next morning, January 5, 1946, Truman received from Byrnes a copy of Mark Ethridge's December 8 letter about Bulgaria and Rumania and conceivable Soviet aggression in the Eastern Mediterranean. Truman was enraged, by the letter and by Byrnes' delay of it. The president promptly poured out his grievances in a quasi-formal (signed) letter to "My Dear Jim." Truman spoke first about procedure. He wished to delegate authority but not all of it, and not his prerogative to make "final decisions." He charged that Byrnes had spent only thirty minutes with him before going to Moscow and had not sent interim messages or cleared the Communiqué. Until he summoned Byrnes to the *Williamsburg,* Truman said, "I was completely in the dark on the whole conference."

Then came the political divide. The president said that he had not seen the Ethridge letter until that morning and that he would not recognize Bulgaria and Rumania, "two police states," until they radically reorganized their governments. He likened Soviet behavior in Iran to its "program" in the Baltic states, and bitterly recalled that at Potsdam he was forced to accept Russian occupation of Eastern Poland and Polish occupation of German Silesia, "a high handed outrage," because he wanted the Russians in the Pacific war.

Now the U.S. faced "another outrage": Iran. Further, the Russians intended to attack Turkey and seize the Straits. But Truman would no longer "play compromise": the Russians understood only an "iron fist" and "How many divisions have you?" Thus, Truman would not recognize Bulgaria and Rumania, and he would state America's position on Iran in "no uncertain terms." He would also persist in trying to internationalize Europe's waterways and the Straits, "maintain complete control" of Japan and the Pacific, rehabilitate China and Korea, and demand Lend-Lease repayment. "I'm tired [of] babying the Soviets," he concluded.[66]

Whether Truman read the letter to Byrnes—as the president later claimed—or only used it to guide himself in his talk does not matter. More important, the letter reveals Truman's jaundiced perception, then and later, of events and how he sought to direct U.S. foreign policy. Truman had reason to be annoyed with his "Super" secretary's condescending ways, almost proprietary control of foreign policy, and minimal reports from Moscow. Harriman ascribed this to Byrnes' claim that the president had given him "complete authority" and that the White House "leaks." But Truman was not kept "completely in the dark" before or after Moscow. He and Byrnes usually met twice weekly, not just for thirty minutes before the secretary left for Moscow. Truman had already reviewed the atomic issue, and his letter to Stalin stipulated that atomic policy, Japan, and the peace treaties were the main agenda items, which the secretary negotiated with great success. Unfortunately, Truman did not attach the same significance that Byrnes (and Acheson and others) did to atomic accord as a means to ameliorate Soviet-American relations and preclude an arms race. The president also ran scared of criticism, often misguided, from politicians like Vandenberg. Moreover, Byrnes had also filed twenty-seven dispatches from Moscow; and Truman saw many of them and approved the peace treaty formula. Byrnes also clarified the Communiqué matter when he first saw Truman on the *Williamsburg,* a week before the January 5 letter.[67]

Truman's memory of Potsdam was also faulty. He did not accede to Russian-Polish border revisions with Germany to bring the Soviets into the Pacific war. By then he and Byrnes had sought to preclude Soviet entry, while the border changes, terms for German reparations, and Italy's UN entry were part of Byrnes' deal that broke the Potsdam impasse. Similarly, while Byrnes did little about Eastern Europe's "police states," Truman hardly grasped that region's complex, antidemocratic politics, Ethridge's reference to Soviet security interest, or U.S. control of Japan as a part of the Eastern European trade-off. Truman could criticize Russian pressures on Iran and Turkey, but he seemed to ignore their foreign and domestic political contexts, while his certainty about imminent Russian attack on the Straits derived mainly from simple historical notions about imperial nations seizing strategic waterways. His "threats" to internationalize Europe's rivers and the Straits (but never Suez or Panama) or to "rehabilitate" China were unrealistic.[68]

Almost exactly five years later, however, when the U.S. was locked in even more bitter cold war with the Russians and hot war in Korea, Truman would say that he had initiated his administration's "firm" foreign policy when he had "reversed Byrnes" and that current policy derived from decisions taken in 1946. As usual, Truman exaggerated. His private letter was not a policy directive, although it provided a significant backdrop for crystallizing resistance in 1946 to "appeasement" of Russia and for Byrnes' public warning against any form of "aggression." The U.S. would also take a much harder line over atomic energy, Iran, Germany, and Korea. In one sense, six weeks before Kennan would send to Washington his famous "long telegram" with its scathing analysis of Soviet behavior, and two months before Churchill would deliver his "Iron Curtain" speech in Missouri, Truman had made his personal declaration of Cold War.[69]

The Year of Decisions

The world was "bewildered, baffled, and breathless," Churchill wrote to Truman in January 1946. Similarly, the president seemed at bay on every front. Twice that month he proclaimed "1946 our year of decision," but his efforts to exhort rapid economic reconversion could not avert the largest wave of industrial strikes in American history. Truman and his senior officials also fretted that rioting soldiers in Europe and Asia and "over-rapid" demobilization would harm U.S. foreign policy. At the same time, his Fair Deal program, including his universal military training, which he thought vital to America's world leadership, remained mired in Congress.[1]

Meanwhile the president's nomination of reparations negotiator Edwin Pauley to be under secretary of the navy (also FDR's choice for the post) ran afoul of Secretary of the Interior Harold Ickes. Truman hoped that the hard-bitten Pauley would "put the admirals in their place," prevent "sabotage" of military unification, and become the first secretary of defense. But Ickes, an "Old Curmudgeon" and former Progressive Republican protector of the public interest, was incensed that this California oil man who opposed federal control of the tidelands would now have control of naval oil reserves. Ickes testified to the Senate's Naval Affairs Committee that in 1944 Pauley, then Democratic Party treasurer, had suggested to him that if the federal government withdrew its claim to offshore oil, significant campaign contributions would flow to the party. Truman continued to back Pauley, and Ickes had to resign. But after the Naval Affairs Committee affirmed Pauley's integrity, Truman had to withdraw the nomination.[2]

The president also stumbled on foreign policy issues. On January 8 he said he was "satisfied" with the Moscow Conference, but when a reporter said that to recognize Bulgaria and Rumania meant to abrogate Yalta's commitment to free elections, Truman snapped that he still had "final say" about those two countries and that Yugoslavia's recognition was "conditional." He was also edgy about atomic energy negotiations with the Russians. He insisted that only Congress, not the Moscow Conference's proposed international commission, could decide what data the U.S. must reveal. He also secretly asked Byrnes to explore elimination of the Security Council veto, only to learn the Senate would not have ratified the UN Charter without it.[3]

Then amid Senate hearings on atomic energy came radio news commentator Drew Pearson's claim on February 3 of a Russian atomic spy ring in Canada. Byrnes denied that U.S. security had been breached. But continuing publicity and leaks by General Groves, intended to promote military control over atomic policy, caused the Canadian government—which had not yet completed its months-long investigation into Soviet spying—to arrest twenty-two suspected Soviet agents being directed from their Ottawa embassy. That same day, February 16, Washington reporter Frank McNaughton alleged that the State Department had restrained FBI intercession against Soviet spies in the U.S. to preserve stable relations with Russia. Then the British arrested physicist Alan Nunn May, the so-called master spy who was working on the Canadian-American atomic bomb project and who had also visited U.S. laboratories. The disclosures led to allegations about "atom spies," who may have saved the Soviets a year or so with respect to design and development of an implosion-type (plutonium) atomic bomb, although they would have been able to develop their own gun-assembly (uranium 235) bomb by 1951. The key issue for the Russians' bomb program remained the need to find sufficient quantities of uranium, which the U.S. sought to deny to them by continuing its secret effort to gain exclusive rights to all fissionable materials outside the Soviet Union.[4]

Meanwhile, in late January a reporter asked Acting Secretary Acheson whether the Russians would turn over the Kurile Islands to international trusteeship as the U.S. proposed to do with some captured Japanese islands. Acheson replied that the Yalta accords provided for Soviet occupation, with a peace conference to determine their final status. The Russians promptly announced that the Yalta accords had ceded the Kuriles and southern Sakhalin to them. On January 29 Byrnes admitted that the Russians were right but that the secret agreement required treaty ratification. He then sought to distance himself by saying that he had learned of the agreement only after Japan's surrender. Truman had to explain the next day that he had read the accord—which he now minimized as a "wartime understanding"—while preparing for Potsdam. He said that the text had always been in the White House files and would be released as soon as the British and Soviets agreed to this. The text was published on February 11. But now the Kuriles seemed to matter far less than evident Soviet-American and Truman-Byrnes discord, as well as growing criticism of Yalta-style diplomacy and the administration's failure to inform the public.[5]

Further, Ambassador Lord Halifax wrote that many judged the president "pretty lost with it all," and there were even whispers of "resignation." Truman would complain that he had to read thirty thousand words of memoranda a night and felt overwhelmed by an "avalanche of things." But he told his press secretary, "I am going to be the president for the next three and a half years and by God I am going to make it stick," while his mother advised it was time to "get tough with someone." That meant the Russians, on every issue and on every front. In short, in early 1946 the president and his aides began to reformulate U.S. foreign policy from the top down. They now regarded the Soviet Union not as a difficult ally but as a potential enemy who threatened America's vital interests and world peace. The president's decision to "get tough" provided vital receptivity and impetus for newly emergent Cold War policies.[6]

I

Truman now believed that the Russians had deceived Roosevelt at Yalta and had presented too many *faits accomplis* (or "outrages") at Potsdam, which he worried history would judge a bad conference. The president doubted that the Soviets would risk another world war but would instead wage "local aggression" until they were halted by "world opinion," namely a U.S.-led UN. As Admiral Leahy noted on February 20, Truman sharply disapproved of recent "appeasement" of the Russians and wished to take a "strong attitude" without delay. He had not abandoned diplomacy but saw little hope for it without brandishing a big stick, and he nurtured the new Cold War consensus.[7]

The initial major consensus markers are well known. In late 1945 Forrestal, convinced that Russia was driven by a "religion" devoted to world revolution and use of force to gain its ends, commissioned a study by a Smith College economics professor, Edward F. Willett, then working for the navy secretary. Willett, who was out of his depth on this assignment, produced a report—"The Philosophy of Communism"—in mid-January 1946 stating that Communism aimed to destroy private property and the capitalist state, that the fanatic commitment of Soviet leaders to global revolution made a violent clash between the U.S. and USSR virtually "inevitable," and that the only safeguard for the U.S. was to build an "invincible" defense force. Forrestal at once sent copies to Truman and to many government and other leaders, including the Pope. Knowledgeable officials who received Willett's report found it to be a superficial assessment of conditions in the Soviet Union and its leaders' policies and aims.

But Forrestal held to his view that the Communist zealots in the Kremlin might initiate war against the U.S.[8]

Then came Stalin's speech on February 9 on the eve of "elections" to the Supreme Soviet. The Soviet leader asserted that the same economic contradictions among capitalist nations that had incited "encirclement" of Russia and the Second World War were still operative. This meant that after Germany and Japan had recovered in fifteen to twenty years, the imperialist states would war among themselves and then turn on the Soviet Union. Thus he exhorted the Russian people to commit themselves to reindustrialization, meaning three more Five-Year Plans, to insure the Soviet Union "against any eventuality." Stalin had reasserted Marxist-Leninist theory of imperialism as the basis for analyzing international relations. But he did not expect war in the near term, or else he would not have stressed industrial reconversion as well as demobilization; the latter had begun in May 1945 and continued to 1947, during which time the armed forces were cut from 11.3 million to 2.8 million troops, and the defense budget fell from 128 billion to 55 billion rubles. Stalin also believed, as he told Molotov, that Russia was now far more secure with the recent restoration of its historic borders, which included a new boundary with an independent Poland in Europe and return of southern Sakhalin and the Kurile Islands in Asia. These changes, combined with Western war weariness and relatively short supply (about eight) of U.S. atomic bombs in 1946, indicated that war was unlikely for at least another fifteen or twenty years. Of course, Stalin still regarded America's atomic monopoly as marking a great symbolic power differential, and he would seek to end this as soon as possible. But the primary purpose of his speech was to promote postwar industrial reconstruction, not war making.[9]

American views divided sharply. Many diplomats, including the usually critical Harriman, asserted that the speech was aimed at the Russian people, who were being urged to commit to heavy industry over consumer goods. Another sharp critic, Elbridge Durbrow, chief of the Division of East European Affairs, similarly said that the speech reflected the serious problems confronting the Soviet regime with regard to "reconstruction, reconversion, and rehabilitation" and that it did not foreclose international collaboration where this would serve Russian interests. But a greater number of analysts saw only an ominous blueprint: "the Communist and fellow-traveler Bible throughout the world," a State Department official said, or, as liberal Supreme Court Justice William O. Douglas told Forrestal, "The Declaration of World War III." The navy secretary himself was certain that the U.S. could not resolve its differences with Russia peacefully. And the JCS soon weighed in with their judgment that U.S. policy should firmly resist Soviet expansion and that world security depended on the "absolute military security of the United States."[10]

In public, however, Truman casually recalled a fellow senator's comment,

"Well, you know we always have to demagogue a little before elections," although Wallace noted that privately Truman was "very critical." Most revealing, perhaps, was his insistence that "Russia couldn't turn a wheel in the next ten years without our aid" and his current, markedly different responses to British and Soviet requests for postwar aid.[11]

As soon as the fighting in the Pacific had ceased in mid-August 1945, the president ordered Russian Lend-Lease ended, and shortly that of the British and others. Truman (like Roosevelt) insisted that the law allowed only wartime aid. But British protest led him to extend it until Japan's formal surrender in September, and reluctantly he did the same for the Soviets. Later the president and his aides regretted his ill-advised, highly nationalistic decision, and Truman called the *British* cutoff the greatest mistake of his presidency. But no one ever regretted the Russian cutoff, which was intended—like that of May 1945—to be coercive.[12]

The British soon sought to recoup from their economic Dunkirk, as John Maynard Keynes termed it, by having the economist lead a delegation to Washington in September to secure a large postwar credit. They wanted $6 billion interest-free, but after hard bargaining they settled in early December for a fifty-year, $3.75 billion loan at 2 percent interest, which was further reduced by payments deferred, or waived, when Britain had a trade imbalance. The U.S. also canceled Britain's $20 billion Lend-Lease debit and exchanged $6 billion in surplus property for $532 million. In return the British agreed to make sterling convertible within a year, to dismantle restrictions on U.S. trade, and to join the American-led incipient multilateral world trading system. This meant ratifying the 1944 Bretton Woods Agreements that had created the International Monetary Fund (IMF), intended to stabilize currencies and their exchange, and the International Bank for Reconstruction and Development (IBRD, or World Bank), intended to promote long-term development projects. The U.S. would predominate in both institutions—to be located permanently in Washington—through its voting power, derived from providing one-third of the capital for the IMF and World Bank lending funds.[13]

America's relatively generous British loan terms still drew fire on both sides of the Atlantic. The British, distraught at no longer being "top dog," as Bevin said, recoiled at a "financial Munich." Conservatives railed that loan terms assaulted British industry and imperial preferences, and Labor officials said that they undercut their capacity to run a socialist economy. But Attlee's government finally gained parliamentary approval in mid-December 1945. Meanwhile, the loan came under attack in the U.S. from critics of foreign lending, traditional Anglophobes, and critics of British imperialism or socialism and policies in Ireland and Palestine. And Vandenberg and others worried that the British loan would spur a Russian request.[14]

Truman defended the loan by recalling Britain's huge contribution to the war and insisting that its rehabilitation served American moral and financial interests. In January 1946 the president asked Congress for a special appropriation and emphasized that Britain was a major trading partner who absorbed raw material and foodstuff surpluses and was vital to establishing the Bretton Woods system. Truman reiterated the "good business" aspects of the loan in a second message on March 4 in which he transmitted support of his National Council on International Monetary and Financial Problems. Administration officials also showered Congress and the public with statistics showing that a revived British economy was essential to Anglo-American and world trade. By June Truman believed that "I have pulled every possible string I can" to secure loan approval, which finally came in July, spurred by widespread sentiment that Britain was a vital bulwark against Soviet expansion.[15]

By contrast, Truman never sought to pull strings for a Soviet loan, which had been talked about since nearly the end of the war. Some officials favored a generous loan to foster amicable relations and to open doors to Russian trade and raw materials. Other officials opposed a loan, and others proposed to use a loan to leverage Russian cooperation. In January 1945 the Soviets had requested a $6 billion loan at 2.25 percent for heavy industrial and transportation equipment, but Roosevelt never discussed this matter—nor did Stalin raise it—at Yalta. FDR probably feared Congress' adverse response and hoped instead to assuage the Soviets with high German reparations.[16]

In the spring of 1945 Truman thought that economic and atomic power would prove to be "master cards" in dealing with the Russians. He was briefed to talk about aid at Potsdam, but neither he nor Stalin brought up the issue. Shortly the administration got Congress to raise the Export-Import Bank's loan ceiling from $100 million to $3.5 billion, with prior approval for a $1 billion loan for the Russians. They applied for this on August 21 at 2.375 percent interest. The Bank agreed in principle but deferred action because its minimum interest rate was 3 percent. Truman approved continued negotiation.[17]

Little happened. In mid-September Stalin told Representative William Colmer of Mississippi, head of a visiting House Select Committee on Postwar Economic Planning and Policy, that there had been no reply to Russia's request in January 1945 for a $6 billion loan and that interest rates could be adjusted if prices were right. Stalin then specified Russia's need to purchase capital equipment and foodstuffs, alluded to its "boundless" import market, and assured that it would be "suicidal" not to convert to a peacetime economy. He also made similar comments at this time to Senator Claude Pepper, who favored a loan.[18]

Kennan apparently thought that Stalin's remarks were sincere, but neither Harriman nor Byrnes believed that a loan would help to alter Soviet policy. In

November the Colmer Committee's report insisted that the U.S. would not grant a loan unless the Russians provided verifiable statistics on vital industrial and armament production, withdrew their troops from Eastern Europe, and subscribed to U.S. trade principles. In sum, as John Gaddis once wrote, the Soviets would have to reform their internal system and foreign policy. Meanwhile, Byrnes deferred State Department action, and Truman did nothing to clarify matters. At his December 7 press conference, the day after accord on a British loan at 2 percent, he denied that the Russians had formally sought a $6 billion loan during his presidency (he was probably poorly briefed about the pre-Yalta request and Stalin's references to it in September) and gave no indication of opening talks.[19]

In late January 1946 Stalin, noting U.S. news stories that cited Russian failure to request postwar credits, asked Harriman whether the Americans "would meet them half way," although he made clear that the Colmer Committee conditions were "offensive." Harriman later wrote that this confirmed his belief that the Russians had not yet decided whether to press for a large loan. But this view ignores their prior $6 billion and $1 billion requests, the "offensive" Colmer conditions, and Harriman's own reply to Stalin that little could be done until the British loan, then under fire, was settled.[20]

This context also reinforces viewing Stalin's February 9 "election" speech as an exhortation on Soviet need to go it alone on reconstruction. Moreover, Truman may have confirmed this outlook on February 21 when he told a reporter that he had no plans to ask Congress for a Russian loan. Similarly, the State Department, embarrassed at news stories that it had never responded to Russia's $1 billion request in August 1945, now said that it would discuss this loan request "among a number of outstanding economic questions." This included a Lend-Lease settlement, Russia's trade policies in Eastern Europe, and its willingness to join the initial IMF and World Bank meetings in early March in Savannah, Georgia. The Department also soon offered an improbable excuse for its belated response to the Russians' loan request, claiming that it had been lost in the postwar transfer of papers from the Foreign Economic Administration.[21]

In mid-March the Russians agreed to discuss Lend-Lease and a trade treaty. But they would not take up Eastern Europe or their refusal to join the IMF and World Bank—a decision Stalin apparently made—which required extensive reporting on member nations' gold, industrial production, imports and exports, and conformance to their financial standards. The loan issue was dead, or reduced to charade. For example, when on March 14 Secretary Wallace asked Truman to send an expert committee to Moscow to open comprehensive economic talks as an essential complement to a political initiative, the president "ignored" the letter, although Wallace finally persuaded him to give a copy to his newly appointed ambassador to Moscow, General Walter Bedell Smith. Then in late April Byrnes specifically tied a prospective loan to Russia's willingness to liberalize economic policy in Eastern Europe and to join the IMF and World Bank. Meanwhile the State Department removed its hold on $1 billion in Export-Import Bank funds for the Russians and in early May pushed through a $650 million credit for France, leaving less than $200 million in uncommitted Bank funds.[22]

Byrnes virtually ended loan talk in June by stipulating Russian need to agree to U.S. principles and practices on a broad array of economic issues. Then on July 18 Truman, three days after he signed the British loan, reiterated that he would not ask Congress for funds for Russia. And when Wallace, in a letter that Truman's aides termed highly thoughtful, proposed economic negotiations without demand for "unrelated" concessions, the president offered only a perfunctory response. Thereafter, aid to Russia did not arise, except fleetingly, until the administration, in an entirely different context, took up European recovery in mid-1947.[23]

It would have been politically difficult to manage a major Russian loan in 1946, and there is no way to demonstrate that it would have resolved other major Soviet-American conflicts. But even Harriman conceded as early as November 1945 that America's loan policy had caused the Russians to "tighten their belts" at home and contributed to their "avaricious" policies in countries the Red Army liberated or occupied. Surely U.S. loan policy did not lessen Russia's quest for German reparations, which—as Truman's negotiator, Ed Pauley, would say—intensified Soviet-American division of that country. Meanwhile the U.S. provided generous aid to Britain, while Churchill publicly proposed creation of an Anglo-American bloc, which the Russians could argue was intended to deny them a coveted oil concession in Iran and access to atomic power. In short, a loan to the Soviet Union was no panacea, but withholding it probably heightened Cold War tension and reflected Truman's shortsighted judgment (or tactic) of March 1946 that without American aid the Russians could not "turn a wheel."[24]

II

Truman's "get tough" policy in 1946 was augmented in late February–March by diplomatic gestures, notably statements by Kennan, Vandenberg, Byrnes, and Churchill, and by hard-line policy over Iran. The president inspired and condoned the new Cold War consensus and gave it the stamp of national policy.

Early in February the Americans reluctantly recognized Rumania, but not Bulgaria. Then on February 25, after reviewing a series of cables in which his commander in Korea, General John. R. Hodge, bitterly charged that the Russians were not only imposing "Communist stooges" in the North but trying to do the same in the South, Truman exclaimed to his White House staff that "we were going to war with Russia" and that Korea would be one of two fronts. Three days later he approved a proposal, brainchild of Forrestal and Byrnes, to send a formidable task force into the Sea of Marmara with the battleship *Missouri* when it returned the ashes of Turkey's deceased wartime ambassador, Mehemet Ertegun, although American military analysts and Turkish officials agreed that Turkey was not under threat of attack. As a Truman aide recorded, however, the president sought "'to honor a dead Turk.' (And impress Russia?)." Churchill, currently in the U.S. and privately informed by the administration, cheered this "very important act of State" calculated to make the Soviets deal reasonably with the West. The *Missouri* voyage was announced on March 6, the day after Churchill's heralded address, although the task force could not be mobilized until the summer.[25]

But mobilization of public opinion could continue. Forrestal had begun with the Willett Report in January. Stalin's election speech, and responses to it, sped matters. Then the State Department, inspired by a Treasury Department inquiry about what underlay Soviet refusal to join the IMF and World Bank, asked Kennan to provide an interpretive analysis of Soviet policies in light of Stalin's speech and recent Soviet actions. The chargé, miserably ill in Moscow, and feeling that his earlier admonitions about Stalinist Russia had been ignored, poured out his "whole truth" in an eight-thousand-word dispatch on February 22. The Kremlin's "neurotic" view of world affairs, he posited, derived from traditional Russian society, which never knew a friendly neighbor or tolerant internal or international balance of power. Russian rulers, knowing that their system could not stand contact with advanced Western societies, sought security only by totally destroying rival power, never by compact or compromise. Soviet leaders then grafted to their Russian heritage their even more truculent Marxist-Leninist dogma, the intellectual "fig leaf" with which they covered, or justified, the dictatorship, cruelties, and militarism necessary to preserve their internally weak regimes. Further, Soviet leaders were fanatically committed to destroying America's way of life and its international authority. In sum, the Soviet party line was not based on objective analysis of the world beyond Russia's borders but was driven by "inner-Russian necessities." Soviet power was impervious to the "logic of reason" but could be deterred by American readiness to use the "logic of force."[26]

Kennan and his "Long Telegram" became famous instantly. Byrnes commended his analysis, and Forrestal circulated it to the Cabinet, nearly every high government and military official, and embassies around the globe. Harriman and Kennan believed that Truman read it (the president's circle surely discussed it), but there is no direct evidence, only White House aide George Elsey's later comment that the cable "didn't tell us anything we didn't already know."[27]

That is the vital point, however. As Kennan and historians have noted, the cable's extraordinary influence derived from its exquisite, if fortuitous, timing and official Washington's profound psychological receptivity. In that sense, the cable squared precisely with Truman's immediate mood and his long-held, if less elegantly articulated, views about the near-identical expansionist traits of tsarist and Soviet Russia, the West's moral and technological superiority, the necessity of preparedness, and need to deal with international outlaws not by reason or quid pro quo diplomacy but by the "logic of force." Thus Kennan's dispatch gained him, with Forrestal's sponsorship, appointment as deputy commander of the National War College in Washington—where he taught geopolitics and strategy to senior military and foreign service officers—and then as head of the State Department's newly organized Policy Planning Staff (PPS) in early 1947. Truman got absolution for his "get tough" diplomacy.[28]

At the same time, Truman also chafed at the strongly implied criticism of his administration when Vandenberg, in a dramatic Senate speech on February 27, asked rhetorically, "What is Russia up to now?" He then charged it with perfidious activities in Poland, the Balkans, and Manchuria and urged that the U.S. speak and act firmly in defending its interest and that it assume the moral leadership of the world. Truman was in accord with Vandenberg's position. What the president disliked was the senator's hasty effort to steal the political thunder of the speech that Byrnes was scheduled to give the next day at the Overseas Press Club in New York in which the secretary would for the first time publicly articulate the new "get tough" policy.[29]

Here Truman was explicit. Byrnes, who was now being highly solicitous of his president, gave him an advance copy of the speech. Truman underlined the passages "I particularly like." This included the need for "frank discussion" to deal with certain justified suspicions among great powers; that "we intend to act to prevent aggression"; and—obviously referring to Iran and Turkey—that "we cannot allow aggression to be accomplished by coercion or pressure or subterfuge such as political infiltration" nor permit "a war of nerves to achieve strategic ends." Byrnes would also declare that no state had a right to station troops on another's soil without consent, that the U.S. had to be ready "to provide armed contingents on short notice" and, anticipating Churchill, that it was not enough to deny wanting war: "Hitler said that" but sought world domination "without war if possible" and "with war if necessary."

Truman now boasted to an aide that he had "told Byrnes to stiffen up and try for the next three months not to make any compromises." Meanwhile, journalists viewed the speech, called by some a second Vandenberg concerto, as a "warning" to Russia and a signal that U.S. foreign policy was nearing a turning point.[30]

The president sought to hasten this through former prime minister Churchill's address on March 5 in Fulton, Missouri, although Truman may not have grasped fully the implications of his, or Churchill's, undertaking. The episode began innocently in early October 1945 when the president of Westminster College, Frank L. McCluer, learning that Churchill would be on a winter vacation in Florida, decided to proffer a lecture invitation through his former Westminster classmate, and now Truman aide, Brigadier General Harry Vaughan. Truman then added a genial postscript to Churchill, offering to introduce him if he would speak at this "wonderful school in my home state." Churchill agreed (he had hoped for Congress). His intention was to promote a British loan and, above all, Anglo-American military collaboration that would win "realistic" Russia's respect and provide "salvation for ourselves and . . . the world."[31]

No one knows exactly how closely Churchill described his "fraternal association" speech to Truman and Leahy at their White House meeting on February 10. But Leahy understood the subject would be "the necessity of full military collaboration between Great Britain and the United States" to preserve world peace — and that the Russians would forcefully object to this bilateral alliance. Similarly, after having talked with Leahy and Churchill later that night, Ambassador Lord Halifax wrote that Churchill's proposal would start "a very violent argument here" and preempt "forceful" Soviet objections to Anglo-American military association. But the ambassador also wrote that Churchill reported that Truman was "quite happy, and more than happy" about the speech, and Churchill soon told Bevin that the president "welcomed the outline I gave him."[32]

Thus, Truman gave presidential seal, almost license, to an unprecedented proposal for a peacetime Anglo-American alliance (to "contain" Russia?) and brushed aside friendly cautions from Democratic Party Chairman Robert Hannegan and Ambassador Davies by assuring that Churchill intended only the usual "hands across the sea" speech. On February 21 the president publicly disavowed knowledge of the speech. He also implied that Byrnes knew nothing, although the secretary had flown to Florida for a briefing four days earlier and approved the idea of an Anglo-American "special friendship" within the UN framework. Further, the White House asked British Information Services to provide press liaison for the speech, thereby assuring widest distribution but allowing Truman to distance himself in event of adverse public response.[33]

Byrnes and Leahy were "excited" and "enthusiastic" after reading the full text at the British Embassy on March 3. Churchill then briefed Truman again. The president also got a summary the next day from Byrnes but naively said that he would not read the speech so that no one could accuse him of "ganging up" on the Russians. Then on the train to Missouri, with Truman and his card-playing aides teaching Churchill the "study of probabilities" at a cost to him of seventy-five dollars, the president read the speech and remarked that it was "admirable" but sure to "cause a stir."[34]

Churchill made two major points in his "iron curtain" (his first public use of that fearsome phrase) address on March 5. The "crux" of his message, he said, was that neither the prevention of war nor growth of the UN would be possible without an Anglo-American "fraternal association." This required continuation of "intimate" military relations, namely, common study of potential dangers, similar weapons systems, and joint facilities, which would double U.S. air and naval mobility. He also noted that "God has willed" American control of the atomic bomb and inveighed against sharing its "secret."

His second major point was that the Soviet Union and its agents had darkened the world scene. "From Stettin in the Baltic to Trieste in the Adriatic an iron curtain has descended across the Continent," he said, and put behind it all of the ancient capitals of Central and Eastern Europe. The Russians had also pressed claims on Turkey and Iran and fostered Communist rule in Soviet-occupied Germany and in France and Italy. The Soviets did not desire war, he intoned, but they desired the "fruits of war and the indefinite expansion of their power and doctrines." Churchill's conclusion, the connection between his two points, was obvious. The Russians admired strength above all and disdained weakness, especially military. Hence, if the U.S. and the English-speaking Commonwealth joined together, "in the air, on the sea, all over the globe, and in science and in industry, and in moral force," their balance of power would preclude adventurism and guarantee security.[35]

Truman was unprepared for the public reaction. Churchill's dark view of Soviet behavior gradually gained favor, despite notable criticism of his traditional imperialist, anti-Soviet views. But his proposed Anglo-American alliance drew sharp fire. Thus the president again denied advance knowledge of the speech and refused comment, except to affirm continued Combined Chiefs of Staff planning until the war ended officially. Privately, Truman even complained to have been "sucked in" and "insulted" by the proposal of an alliance while he was on the platform. But he also said that the speech had done "some good" even if he was not ready to endorse it. Three years later Truman still denied prior reading but exulted that Churchill had said what "I wanted him to say," and that if he had known more about the Russians sooner, he would have taken the former prime minister's advice in spring 1945 and "gone to the eastern [western?] boundaries of Russia."[36]

The latter claim was probably hyperbolic. But it might suggest why the Russians, seeing Churchill's anti-Soviet posture gain approval, would charge that he sought to inspire an "atomic Anglo-Saxon bloc." Or as Stalin said in *Pravda* on March 14, Churchill's claim to the English-speaking nations' moral superiority was akin to Hitler's "racial theory" and intended to promote "war against the Soviet Union." Kennan rebutted this as a "polemic" to incite Russian fear of Western attack to justify aggressive steps, notably in Iran, as defensive. But at least one high Soviet official, who had been with Stalin and Molotov at the time of Churchill's address, indicated that they saw it as an effort to re-create a *cordon sanitaire* to contain Russia.[37]

Truman sought to minimize controversy by refusing comment on Stalin's remarks. Acheson canceled plans to attend another Churchill speech in New York on March 15, in which he again challenged Russia's global ambitions and restated his near chauvinistic belief in an Anglo-American mission to preserve peace. The next night Byrnes urged U.S. preparedness and readiness to deter aggression by force but disavowed interest in any alliance.[38]

Growing concern, however, about Churchill debating Stalin from the U.S. and demise of Big Three diplomacy led Truman to invite Stalin to America despite the president's disinclination and his doubt that Stalin would accept. But Truman sent the invitation via his new ambassador, General Smith, with instruction to convey U.S. apprehension about Soviet support for UN principles and concern that Stalin, who Truman held to be "a man to keep his word," had not withdrawn Russia's troops from Iran despite the March 2 deadline.[39]

Truman was right that Stalin would not want to visit the U.S. He told Smith on April 4 that "age" precluded this. More to the point, the Russian ruler also assailed Churchill's speech as an unwarranted attack on him and the Soviet Union and as indicative of an Anglo-American alliance to thwart Russia, perhaps aiming to repeat the Churchill-inspired Western intervention of 1919. Molotov similarly told Byrnes that Churchill had sought to create a coalition to "contain" Russia, and years later Soviet leader Nikita Khrushchev would allege that Stalin viewed the Fulton speech as the start of the Cold War.[40]

That was exaggeration. But clearly Truman and Byrnes, seeking public support for their "get tough" policy, had sanctioned Churchill's extraordinary call for alliance against the allegedly aggressive Russians, who were not so "stupid," Stalin said, as to be unable to distinguish friends from potential enemies. Nor to miss the point—even if it happened to be a coincidence—that on the day of Churchill's clarion call, Byrnes sent a protest note to the Soviets over Iran that tied policy to rhetoric and proved to be a signal Cold War development.

III

Continued Soviet political and military pressure on Iran in 1946 provided occasion for the Truman administration to test its "get tough" policy and to expand U.S. influence over a vital area and resource—oil—in a country where the Russians and British had long held sway. Truman, of course, had already decried Soviet behavior in Iran as "an outrage" and intuited it as part of an imperial design on Turkey and the Eastern Mediterranean. He would also claim in his *Memoirs* to have been concerned that any Soviet control over Iranian oil meant a serious change in the world balance of raw materials, although U.S. officials deliberately did not publicly mention oil in 1946. But Byrnes, as FDR's wartime "Assistant President," had inspired U.S. firms in 1944 to seek oil concessions in Iran, where the government, which disliked the British and feared the Russians, employed countless U.S. advisers to reform its administration, finances, army, and state-run enterprises. In 1945 Secretary Byrnes had sought to avoid a clash with the Russians, but at the Moscow Conference he warned Stalin that Iran would raise Russia's intervention in Azerbaijan at the UN. Stalin rejoined that the Soviets would not need to "blush" about troops in Iran. There matters rested, although Byrnes was soon mindful of Truman's criticism of him for "appeasing" the Russians.[41]

Stalin's ambitions in Iran cannot be stated precisely. But recently accessible records and analyses provide important revelations. The German threat during the Second World War and the British-inspired Anglo-Soviet occupation of Iran led him to seek to reassert traditional Russian influence there and to think in terms of state security, i.e., to protect the Soviet Union and its Baku oil reserves from attack. British and American oil activities in Iran also fueled his demand for a comparable oil concession. Further, Stalin supported groups in northern Iran, especially in bordering Azerbaijan, seeking autonomy or separation. Thus in July 1945 the Politburo authorized formation of the Communist-led Democratic Party in Azerbaijan, and used Mir Bagirov, head of the Communist Party in Soviet Azerbaijan, to organize support for the new Separatist Party. Meanwhile, Stalin did not hesitate to make political or military threats against the Iranian government. His purpose, however, was neither to annex Iranian territory nor to encourage violent separation; rather he sought to wrest concessions, especially an oil one, from the Teheran government. Whether officials in Washington and London could have been certain of Stalin's limited intentions in 1945–1946 may be questionable. But as the crisis developed, even Ambassador Wallace Murray and British Foreign Secretary Bevin thought that the Soviets' primary goal was not to annex Azerbaijan or advance on the Mediterranean but to gain an oil concession in the north, outside the American and British spheres of influence, that would put the Soviets on equal great-power footing.[42]

Indeed, when the Iranians requested on January 19, 1946, that the Security Council investigate Soviet interference in their internal affairs, the U.S. and Britain resisted burdening the newly organized Council with the issue. After a talk with Andrei Vishinsky, assistant foreign minister and head of Russia's UN delegation, Byrnes was "convinced that the problem will not be on us." He also disregarded one State Department view that it was a "test case" of a "small state victim of large state aggression," declined public comment that might indicate American bias, and was satisfied that the Security Council, while reserving the right to request information, endorsed Soviet-Iranian negotiations.[43]

Then Ahmad Qavam became prime minister of Iran in late January. He came from one of Iran's most powerful aristocratic families, had presided over Cabinets in 1922–1923 and in 1942, and was long at odds with the family of the young shah, Mohammed Reza Pahlavi. Qavam was also an old-school Persian politician who knew how to balance foreign and domestic rivals and who sought to preserve Iran's independence as well as his power. In mid-February he went to Moscow to insist on Soviet troop withdrawal but was willing to edge toward a settlement on oil and some autonomy for Azerbaijan, despite the Majlis' 1944 ban on oil negotiations with any nation whose troops remained there. Stalin, however, rejected Qavam's call for troop withdrawal without an oil concession, which the prime minister would not discuss. Then in late February Stalin demanded a majority share in a Soviet-Iranian oil company and proffered limited troop withdrawal. He also cited for the first time a 1921 treaty that allowed Russian troops in Iran when there was threat of foreign invasion and said that Russian forces would remain until security was established. The Soviets also continued to encourage Azerbaijani autonomy demands. Qavam, about to return to Teheran on March 4, finally replied to Stalin that if he removed his troops and ended the pressure on Azerbaijan, the prime minister would have enough time to formulate terms for a Soviet-Iranian oil company to present to the Majlis.[44]

Meanwhile, rhetoric about Russia heated, from Truman's complaints about appeasement to Kennan's Long Telegram, Churchill's talks with officials, and the speeches by Vandenberg and Byrnes. By late February the secretary was moved to say that "we're going to take a stand" on Iran. Yet all he told Qavam was that if the Moscow talks threatened Iran's integrity, he could revert the matter to the Security Council. But soon Iranian ambassador Hossein Ala (known to act on his own), and then Qavam, sought a U.S. protest to Moscow in anticipation of its failure to meet its March 2 withdrawal deadline.[45]

Not until three days after the deadline, however, and only after receiving reports of "exceptionally heavy" movement of Soviet troops, tanks, and trucks from Tabriz in the north toward Teheran, did Byrnes protest to the Russians their violation of the 1942 Tripartite Treaty and 1943 Teheran Declaration, and call for withdrawal. It was also by coincidence, not design, that this protest came only hours after Churchill's heralded March 5 address. Regardless, Stalin did not reply, while further reports of troop movements fired up State Department officials. They prepared a large map for Byrnes with arrows showing the Russians marching toward the Turkish and Iraqi borders and Teheran. This caused the secretary (as an official recalled nineteen years afterwards) to say that the Russians were adding military invasion to political subversion and that "now we'll give it to them with both barrels."[46]

Still, Byrnes' request to the Soviets on March 8 that they explain their movements—the troops were in fact headed home, not in the direction of the State Department arrows—was, as Acheson said, designed to "leave a graceful way out" and to avoid a showdown. But Moscow again did not reply. Meanwhile, Truman refused to speculate publicly about the Russians' failure to withdraw and said that they were unlikely to "go down a one way street." Newspaper reports about the military maneuvers created a brief "war scare" on March 12 and March 13 and perhaps explain Harriman's later claim that Truman told him that the Iranian problem "may lead to war." But the president again declined to comment about the Russians' tactics and about Harriman's assertion that they were "bluffing." The Russians did not reply to any charge about their troops but assailed Churchill for seeking to stir a war. The Truman administration encouraged Iranian resistance and an appeal, which came on March 19, to the Security Council in New York.[47]

Truman and Byrnes sought the glare of publicity to force Soviet retreat. The secretary took charge of the U.S. delegation at the UN to argue Iran's case, and perhaps he also hoped to bolster his own status. The president refused Russia's request to postpone the initial Security Council session from March 25 to April 10, although Qavam and even the usually hostile shah were amenable to the delay. Truman also rejected having the Big Three take up the issue. Meanwhile, Byrnes told Bevin he insisted on "disposition now," and shortly exclaimed that he had "nursed" the Russians before, and that now they could make their motion—on the radio and before the world—and he would answer them before the world.[48]

The Russians signaled interest in defusing tension in general by ending their occupation of the Danish island of Bornholm, agreeing to a level-of-industry plan for Germany, and announcing withdrawal from Manchuria. They also sent a new ambassador to Teheran on March 18 with a proposal to withdraw from Iran in exchange for a joint ownership of a Soviet-Iranian oil company. Ambassador Murray thought this would be a good way to end the crisis without having the Russians smarting for revenge. But the White House apparently took up Kennan's concern that to offer concessions now might cause the Russians to miscalculate how far they might go later, and Bevin insisted that any "weakening" would put the UN future on a "slippery slope." Then on March 24 the Russians announced that their troop withdrawal had begun and would be completed within six weeks. Stalin also replied to a United Press query about Churchill's statement that Russia had to leave Iran quickly and that there was already an "understanding," which, it gradually emerged, included Russian troop withdrawal, 51 percent control of a joint oil operation, and Moscow's mediation in the Azerbaijan crisis. But the understanding was not yet complete.[49]

Byrnes promptly called Stalin's "gigantic bluff," as one historian has labeled it, insisting that Iran confirm the understanding and unconditional Russian withdrawal. The Security Council then rejected Russian motions to remove Iran's complaint from its agenda or to postpone debate, which led the Soviet ambassador to the UN, Andrei Gromyko, and his advisers to stalk dramatically from the chamber. Byrnes then pushed for a Soviet-Iranian report on negotiations within a week. Then on April 4 he agreed to Ambassador Ala's proposal that if the Russians gave assurance of troop withdrawal by May 6, Iran would not press its case further, although Byrnes insisted that it remain on the UN agenda.[50]

Late that same night General Walter Bedell Smith, having just taken up his post as ambassador to Moscow, had an interview with Stalin. Smith, who had gone over his presentation with Truman, told Stalin that the president considered him a man of his word but that Russian troops in Iran "upset that theory." Smith also said that the U.S. worried about what the Russians wanted and how far they intended to go, and that while Truman and Byrnes believed they would hold to their commitment, this should not be seen as a sign of American weakness.

Stalin in turn complained "somewhat bitterly" about Anglo-American efforts to deny Russia an oil concession in Iran and refusal to delay Security Council debate. He also insisted that the Soviets could not tolerate a hostile regime in Iran, a principle that the U.S. and Britain—he cited examples—followed in their international relations. He was also particularly resentful of Churchill's attitudes, citing the Allied intervention in 1919 and his recent "iron curtain" speech. But in reply to Smith's query about how far Russia intended to go, the Soviet leader said, "We're not going to go much further." He also said that a deal had been struck with Iran. Indeed, in the early morning of April 5 (but with a date of April 4) the Russians and Iranians issued a joint Communiqué announcing agreement on the terms that the Soviet ambassador had brought to Teheran on March 18: unconditional Russian withdrawal within six weeks and 51 percent control of a joint oil company, with the Majlis to ratify the deal within seven months and Iran to handle Azerbaijan as a domestic matter.[51]

The next day Truman, in an Army Day speech in Chicago devoted to calling for extending Selective Service and establishing universal military training, said that the U.S. would strengthen the nations of the Near East by helping them develop their resources and institutions and would use its military might to bolster the UN. Two weeks later, however, Truman sought to allay concern about a conflict by declaring that he had only the "friendliest" feelings for Russia and that the U.S. and USSR were akin to "horse traders," given to "pretty rough" bargaining but unlikely to end up in a "fist fight." Still, the president revealed his global impulse by insisting that the U.S. had to be the "umpire in the world situation" and his nationalist view by his persistence that U.S. interests came before all others.[52]

Byrnes, meanwhile, pressed the Security Council to keep the issue of Iran on its agenda until certain of Russian withdrawal. He persisted in this, to Russian anger and Iranian surprise, even after Qavam affirmed Russian troop withdrawal in late May. Finally the Security Council adjourned discussion permanently. Clearly, Byrnes' actions were motivated largely by domestic politics. Having been sharply criticized for "appeasing" the Russians, he said, now he enjoyed praise for standing firm. Moreover, he told French foreign minister Georges Bidault in May that the U.S. had sought to cooperate with the Soviets, but they had dissipated their popularity in America, where opinion "was no longer disposed to make concessions on important questions."[53]

Publicly Truman denied that U.S. policy had changed—"and *I* make the policy," he told reporters, almost defensively. But events underscored the difference. In June 1946 the new ambassador to Teheran, George V. Allen, wrote that the Iranians knew how to counteract one foreign influence only by inviting another. He also told Qavam, then seeking to conciliate Azerbaijan, that the U.S. could not interfere in Iran's affairs. Yet Allen also warned the prime minister that his "warm expressions" toward the Russians and attacks on right-wing critics might make the U.S. think that it would have gained more by urging a revolt against his regime. Thereafter the ambassador schemed with the shah to depose Qavam, although the shah did not know of anyone else he could entrust to run the government. By mid-October, however, the shah forced Qavam to dismiss recently appointed Tudeh Party members from his Cabinet and get rid of other officials deemed unreliable.[54]

At the same time the JCS, taking recent State Department queries to mean that war with Russia "is a possibility," concluded that Iran's oil made that nation a "major strategic interest" and vital to U.S. interests throughout the Middle East. This justified "token" military assistance. Then in October Allen and the State Department sought to bolster the shah by supporting a $10 million military credit to help Iran's army maintain "law and order." The State Department and Byrnes acceded to this in mid-November.[55]

Qavam, meanwhile, was also under pressure from the Soviets to hold national elections and then submit their April oil agreement to the Majlis for ratification. In early November he finally set elections for December 7 but also announced that he would send government troops to Azerbaijan to maintain order. After learning of U.S. military aid, he decided to send security forces as well. This drew sharp criticism from the Soviets, who said that this action created a problem on their frontier, and from Democratic Party officials, who vowed armed resistance. The government then put off elections until January 1947. Then with strong support from the State Department, Qavam sent thousands of Iranian army forces into Azerbaijan on December 9, and within six days the Democratic regime in Tabriz and separatist movements had collapsed. The shah then offered such "fulsome" tribute to the U.S.—he called Azerbaijan "the Stalingrad of the western democracies"—that even Allen was embarrassed, while Byrnes reiterated the need for reform in Iran.[56]

Nonetheless, collapse of the Azerbaijani "house of cards," as Ambassador Smith in Moscow called it, was a major and profitable victory for a "firm policy" toward Russia. The Anglo-Iranian Oil company now gave two U.S. companies, Standard Oil of New Jersey and Socony Vacuum, a 20 percent marketing share in its annual production. The elections to the Majlis in January 1947 brought blocs of delegates favorable to the shah, Qavam, and the British, but not to the Russians. The prime minister then delayed submission of the proposed Soviet-Iranian oil agreement of April 1946 until October 1947, when the Majlis rejected it overwhelmingly. The Soviets, who had removed their troops from Iran and apparently banked on ratification of the oil agreement, had been outmaneuvered, chiefly by the wily Qavam. Nonetheless, the shah, with strong U.S. support, soon forced him from office.[57]

Truman and his aides were certain of the moral that the Iran case provided, despite Byrnes' caveat to Allen in late 1946 that it should not be viewed as a victory or defeat for any outside power but a successful UN defense of a nation's independence. Throughout the crisis the Americans insisted that they sought to defend principle and the UN Charter. But they were equally concerned not to mention that "hot subject," as Forrestal dubbed foreign oil in 1946, nor their geostrategic concern for a new area of vital interest that brought them into a much older, and bordering, Russian sphere of interest. Further, the president and his aides took Iran as a vital reference when they crafted the Truman Doctrine in March 1947. Then in April 1952 Truman would boast to the press that he had driven the Russians out of Persia with an "ultimatum," although no such document existed, and a White House spokesman was quick to say that the president had spoken nontechnically. In fact, Stalin had withdrawn his forces—and also abandoned the Democratic separatists—in exchange for a presumed oil concession. Still, Truman privately was persistent that he had "forced Stalin out of Iran" just as he would later exaggerate that "Trumanism" had saved Greece, Turkey, and Western Europe from Soviet invasion.[58]

IV

Renewed debate over international control of atomic energy in 1946 bore out Byrnes' assertion amid the Iran crisis that the U.S. was "no longer disposed to make concessions on important issues" and also underscored the limits of Truman's leadership and political acumen. In January Acheson indicated to David Lilienthal, head of the Tennessee Valley Authority, that neither the president nor the secretary of state knew the facts or understood atomic energy and that commitments had been made and communiqués signed without knowledge of "what the hell it is all about—literally." Further, General Groves had a virtual veto on any action by claiming "military security," and he was "almost running foreign policy." Thus Acheson induced Truman and Byrnes to create a committee, which was headed by the under secretary and included Groves, Vannevar Bush, John McCloy, and James Conant. Acheson in turn named Lilienthal to chair a scientific Board of Consultants, which included the forceful and imaginative physicist Robert Oppenheimer, now resigned as head of the Los Alamos laboratory. Byrnes, meanwhile, secured a UN resolution, identical to that of the December 1945 Moscow Conference, establishing an Atomic Energy Commission (UNAEC) to develop a program, in stages, for scientific exchanges, peaceful uses of atomic energy, atomic disarmament, and safeguards, including inspections.[59]

During February–March 1946 the Acheson-Lilienthal groups hammered out a plan, largely of Oppenheimer's design, to create an international Atomic Development Authority (ADA) that would own, extract, refine, and use all uranium and thorium deposits, and operate all atomic plants engaged in dangerous activities. Individual nations would be licensed to use "denatured" (harmless) materials for peaceful (medical or commercial) research. ADA plants would be located strategically so that no one nation could seize them and gain preponderant atomic power. Further, the plants would be constructed to prevent their conversion to military use in less than a year, thereby providing other nations with ample warning to determine appropriate action. Little was said about inspections, and sanctions were left to UNAEC negotiations. Lilienthal wanted to consider all elements of the plan "integral," i.e., to be effected as a group. But the atomic planners agreed instead, as Acheson said, to assure that all nations were "playing pool" by implementing the program in stages (from basic exchange and a geological survey through plant construction) that would last five or six years. The U.S. would retain its atomic monopoly during this transition, although personally Acheson thought that the U.S. could not win the trust of other nations until it stopped producing atomic bombs.[60]

The Acheson-Lilienthal plan went far beyond traditional national arms control, inspections, sanctions proposals, or proposals to "outlaw" war. Instead the plan sought, as Lilienthal said, "security through cooperative development" by means of international (ADA) ownership and control of materials and plants adaptable to military use. This averted need for inspections, which Acheson said "made no sense at all" because they could not alter Russian behavior (only "civilization" could do that) nor detect plant conversion to military use before it was "too late." Similarly, sanctions were ineffective because there was no American "sheriff" who could enforce the law automatically nor any such thing as automatic sanctions. But by not prescribing sanctions the U.S. would avoid conflict with the Russians, who were bound to insist on retaining their Security Council veto. The sanctions-veto issue was also academic, Acheson said, because only the great powers could act against an aggressor, and they would do as they saw fit regardless of treaty obligation. Thus international security depended not on sanctions or punishment but on Soviet-American accord and on having the world's best atomic scientists collaborate on peaceful enterprises.[61]

Admittedly, prospects for international control lessened with news in February about Russia's atomic spying in Canada. The Soviets then admitted, for the first and only time, having received only insignificant secret data, which they lamely sought to excuse as justified by Allied wartime duplicity. Then came Congress' debate over control of atomic energy, during which Truman provided little clarity. In autumn 1945 he had supported the conservative proposal of Democratic Representative Andrew May of Kentucky and Senator Edwin Johnson of Colorado to give control over atomic energy to a part-time commission authorized to appoint a military man as chief administrator. But the president retreated from the May-Johnson bill when a broad political-scientific coalition disputed the legislative jurisdiction of the House and Senate military affairs committees and also strongly opposed military control. Then Democratic Senator Brian McMahon of Connecticut fostered a special Senate Committee on Atomic Energy and in December proposed that the president appoint a full-time Atomic Energy Commission (AEC). Truman now fully supported civilian control and government ownership of fissionable materials but not the McMahon Committee's requests for atomic data, which General Groves and the War Department controlled.[62]

Truman also vacillated about the McMahon Bill when the atomic spy stories broke. He remained aloof in March 1946 when Senator Vandenberg had the bill amended to create a Military Liaison Board empowered to review all AEC actions that affected "defense and security" and to appeal all decisions directly to the president, a procedure that McMahon complained was tantamount to veto power. Eventually the board was restricted to review of military matters only, with appeals to the secretaries of war and navy, Cabinet officers who could go directly to the president. Thus the McMahon Act, which was finally voted in July 1946, provided considerable military oversight. It also sharply limited prospects for international sharing, including with the British, by eliminating all distinction between basic and technical information and prohibiting exchange of "all data" concerning atomic weapons and fissionable materials.[63]

Regardless, Truman shied from even Anglo-American exchange. For example, when in April 1946 Prime Minister Attlee, looking to build an atomic plant, invoked the unpublished November 1945 Anglo-American atomic agreements (the so-called Groves-Anderson Memorandum stipulating full and effective basic exchange and ad hoc agreements to share technical data), the president replied that he had never intended to share technical data. He also said that current UNAEC efforts at a general accord precluded bilateral collaboration, although the U.S. still demanded, and got, full access to Canadian developments. In effect, Truman shut off the British before the McMahon Act did, and then after the alleged constraint of UNAEC talks had passed, he showed no interest in Anglo-American exchange.[64]

Similarly in March 1946 the president undermined the Acheson-Lilienthal Report (although he called it "a great state paper" in his *Memoirs*) by appointing Bernard Baruch as chief delegate to the UNAEC negotiations. The seventy-five-year-old Baruch was a prominent financier, former head of the War Industries Board in World War I, and industrial adviser during World War II. He also had extensive political ties to influential senators as well as to fellow South Carolinian, Byrnes, who recommended his appointment. The president noted after his initial talk with Baruch on March 16 that he "wants to run the world, the moon and maybe Jupiter—but we'll see." Later on, however, Truman claimed that he chose this self-promoting "adviser to presidents" to foster public support for international control amid the spy scandals and McMahon Bill debate.[65]

But Baruch's commitment to international exchange was already suspect. Acheson, in fact, had tried to dissuade Byrnes from the appointment, and Bush told Baruch directly that he was hopelessly unqualified for the job. Lilienthal said the choice of Baruch made him "sick," that he was far too vain, unwilling or unable to work hard or sort out scientific complexities. Moreover, he would make the Russians think that he was "simply out to put them in a hole, not caring about international cooperation." In fact, Baruch had already written to Byrnes that he would insist on introducing inspections into the negotiations, and that if the Russians balked, this would "immediately stop the discussion" about atomic energy.[66]

The Acheson-Lilienthal supporters tried to rally public support by leaking their plan. But after Baruch disclaimed it and threatened to resign on March 26, Truman assured him of a strong policy role. As Baruch recalled, he asked who was to draft the American proposal, and the president replied, "Hell, you are!" Two days later Truman publicly refused to endorse the Acheson-Lilienthal Report. In mid-April Byrnes reassured Baruch and said that he would be allowed to announce atomic policy, although this was normally the president's prerogative. By mid-June, however, Byrnes would concede to Acheson that Baruch was "the worst mistake I have ever made. But we can't fire him now, not with all the other troubles."[67]

During April through June, Baruch and his highly conservative advisers significantly altered the Acheson-Lilienthal Report, despite strong resistance from Acheson and others. The "essential difference," Baruch told Truman in early June, was his plan's new emphasis on sanctions, or what he called "swift and sure punishment." He held that "penalization" had to be the "sine qua non" of U.S. policy. But since the ultimate sanction might be (atomic) war, the veto over this had to be eliminated. Further, Baruch insisted that "capitalistic nations" would oppose ADA ownership and management of all uranium and thorium mines because this would destroy or seriously limit private enterprise, although he settled for Acheson's vague compromise that the ADA would instead exercise "dominion" through licenses and inspections. Baruch also pressed a preliminary survey of raw materials but not as extensive as when first conceived to probe Russia. Finally, the plan would be effected in stages of indefinite length, during which the U.S. would retain its atomic monopoly, or "winning weapons," as Baruch would say in June. In sum, the Baruch Plan's emphasis on inspections, swift sanctions, no veto, and limited ADA role differed sharply from the Acheson-Lilienthal focus on security through international cooperative development. Lilienthal feared that Baruch's proposals would be put forward "in a spirit that would insure Russian refusal." At the least, the Baruch Plan was a maximal position but one from which the chief negotiator would not budge. He also drew strong support from White House Chief of Staff Leahy, Army Chief of Staff Eisenhower, and other military officials who viewed the prospect of atomic retaliation as a deterrent to any aggressor. They were reluctant to yield this advantage before gaining a treaty system or world order to their liking.[68]

Truman agreed with this strategy. He was convinced of America's technological-industrial superiority and ability to stay ahead in an arms race and considered the bomb to be a "sacred trust." In March he supported the military's demand for an atomic test on Bikini Island despite Byrnes' objection that this would hinder all negotiations with the Russians, although the first test was delayed—unfortunately, as it turned out—until July 1. In May the president supported Baruch's plan to eliminate a veto on UN sanction despite the arguments of Acheson and others that the Russians would construe this as a means to use the UN to threaten war because only the U.S. could deliver "swift and sure" punishment. But Baruch "told the president that if that didn't stay in he would resign," Lilienthal recalled, "so it stayed."[69]

Then on June 7 Baruch went to the White House, where Truman approved his proposal. He put a check mark at each paragraph, including those on "penalization" and no veto, and recalled a favorite analogy, namely, that "if Harry Stimson had been backed up in Manchuria there would have been no war." Further, the president's negotiation guidelines reemphasized "penalties and concerted action," enumerated ADA functions (including "tight control," or inspections, of raw materials), and deemed as "most important" the Plan's stages, which would preserve America's atomic monopoly indefinitely.[70]

Baruch proffered his Plan with dramatic flourish at the UN on June 14. He insisted that the world had to "make a choice between the quick and the dead." He carefully described his plan for atomic development and control, including a lengthier list of violations than had been stipulated previously that would draw swift punishment. He was equally firm that "there must be no veto to protect those who violate their solemn agreements." And he made clear that "before a country is ready to relinquish any winning weapons," it had to be assured that all weapons of mass destruction, not just atomic ones, were eliminated, with perhaps war itself outlawed. This was a noble aim but far beyond the scope of current negotiations or policy.[71]

Five days later the Soviet delegate, Andrei Gromyko, countered with a proposal that called for an international convention prohibiting production, stockpiling, and use of atomic weapons. All existing atomic weapons were to be destroyed within three months of a treaty, and penalties were to be established within six months. But the veto over sanctions had to remain.[72]

The Baruch Plan and the Soviet proposal rested on wholly different premises. The U.S. had conceived creation of a powerful international agency to control military uses of atomic power. But the Americans hedged their commitment by emphasizing punishment and no veto as well as preservation of the U.S. atomic monopoly, at least until the U.S. had gained a comprehensive treaty. The Soviet proposal was modeled on interwar disarmament agreements that relied on national governments for enforcement and lacked provisions for inspection and control. The Soviets believed, not incorrectly, that the U.S. wished to preserve its atomic monopoly as long as possible and to pressure them on the diplomatic front. At the same time, the Soviets were moving ahead rapidly on their atomic project and most likely Stalin was determined to gain his own atomic bomb, which would strengthen his hand in any negotiation.[73]

Deadlock, or "show down" with Russia loomed, as Vandenberg noted on June 19. Still, the UNAEC's twelve member nations set about to examine the U.S. and Soviet proposals. Meanwhile the U.S. exploded an atomic bomb over Bikini Atoll in the Marshall Islands on July 1, and a second bomb underwater on July 24, with each UNAEC nation, including the USSR, sending two invited observers. These tests, delayed from March, derived from the military's desire to measure the effectiveness of an advanced Nagasaki-type bomb, not intent to influence atomic negotiations. But the unfortunate timing provided basis for the Soviet press to challenge U.S. sincerity to be rid of atomic weapons.[74]

In fact, Baruch wrote Truman on July 2 that the U.S. could not give up its atomic weapons before it secured a comprehensive treaty on its terms. There could be "no compromise" on this position. Three days later he rejected the Soviet proposal and its request that the U.S. halt manufacture of atomic bombs. "Stand pat on our program," the poker-playing president reinforced to Baruch on July 10. "We should not under any circumstance throw away our gun until we are sure that the rest of the world can't arm against us. I think we understand each other on this subject."[75]

Two weeks later Gromyko rejected the Baruch Plan and on July 26 again proposed a treaty to outlaw production and use of atomic weapons. Thereupon the French, perhaps to avert a break, got the UNAEC delegations to agree to have their scientific advisers study the possibility of controlling atomic production. American officials feared that the U.S. might then be blamed for blocking progress by withholding technical information. Baruch, however, told his staff that it was necessary to draw the Russians out, but he was adamant that there was no alternative to the "American Plan" and that "we had the right as well as the power on our side" and the Russians would be brought around.[76]

Thereafter Baruch resisted change, whether on the veto, sanctions, or calling a halt to U.S. manufacture of atomic bombs, which the administration increasingly saw as a counter to the Red Army, although Truman always seemed uninformed about how few atomic bombs and bomb assembly teams were available. Meanwhile, General Groves worked on a proposed nine-stage, four-to-six-year plan for the ADA to take control of dangerous atomic materials and production, after which the U.S. would hand over its atomic weapons. Meanwhile, in late August Gromyko called for a UN investigation of the presence of U.S. troops in countries that were not used as bases of operations against the Axis powers during the Second World War. By then Baruch's delegation was convinced that "Russia is the stumbling block" to an agreement and that delay would cause nations "to shift away from the us." [77]

Hence Baruch informed Truman on September 17 that he saw "no possibility" of reconciling the U.S. and Soviet positions and that he wished to reach closure on atomic negotiations by the year's end. He became even more adamant that same day when, amid a more general dispute over foreign policy between Wallace and Byrnes, the president's press secretary, Charles Ross, released a letter from Wallace to Truman of July 23 that contained the statement that the Baruch Plan's "fatal defect" was its demand that the Russians suspend their atomic research and reveal their uranium and thorium holdings prior to any scientific exchange. Baruch immediately threatened to resign unless Truman repudiated Wallace's views. So too did Byrnes, who was then at a CFM meeting in Paris, threaten resignation. But after two days of awkward public statements, Wallace "resigned," although he and Baruch would continue to bicker into early October. [78]

At the same time, the UNAEC's Scientific and Technical Committee agreed unanimously that control of atomic power was technically feasible and soon reached accord on other issues, including safeguards regarding misuse and raw materials surveys. But privately, on October 12 the Soviet scientists on the committee wrote Molotov that the Baruch Plan would mean permitting an international organization, likely U.S.-dominated, to control or inspect all aspects of Russian atomic production and resources. The Russian scientists rejected this in favor of first catching up to America's atomic productive capacity before allowing inspection and control. At the UN General Assembly in New York on October 29, Molotov attacked the Baruch Plan as seeking to preserve America's "monopolistic possession" of the atomic bomb. He proposed instead a resolution for general disarmament that would include atomic energy. [79]

Baruch now pressed for a vote on his plan. In early November he won the support of Byrnes, and then of Truman, who regarded the Molotov proposal as a propaganda initiative. Acheson still resisted Baruch's emphasis on inspections and sanctions with no veto and thought that the U.S. had to find a way to cooperate with the Russians or the U.S. would have to "lick the hell out of them in ten or fifteen years." But in late November Byrnes said it was time for a "showdown." Shortly thereafter, Baruch's chief delegate rebuffed Russian concessions as well as British, Canadian, and French entreaties to compromise on the veto. As Baruch told Lilienthal, now chairman of the AEC, on December 22, "America can get what she wants if she insists on it. After all, we've got it and they haven't and won't for a long time to come; I don't know how long, but it will be some time."[80]

The Security Council endorsed the Baruch Plan 10–0, with Russia and Poland abstaining, on December 31, 1946. One week later Baruch resigned, to acclaim. He advised Truman to increase production of atomic bombs, which he insisted, "keeps Russia from overrunning Europe." The diplomatic "victory" at the UN, however, proved to be of propaganda value only. During the next two years of UNAEC talks, both the Americans and Russians held to their positions with little prospect of a treaty, especially as Soviet-American conflict worsened.[81]

Surely Russian insistence on immediate destruction and outlawry of all atomic weapons was self-serving because it ended their atomic disadvantage at once and at no cost. At the same time, they sought to preserve their veto and a large, if overestimated, conventional force. More important, as David Holloway has said, neither Stalin nor Truman saw the bomb as a common danger to the human race, although Stalin saw the U.S. monopoly as a threat that could be countered only by building a Soviet bomb. The Soviets also had reason to oppose the Baruch Plan, which underscored their atomic disadvantage and vulnerability to sanctions and denied them a veto in the UN, which they believed the U.S. controlled. They were also unlikely to agree to the extensive inspection of their resources and facilities that the Baruch plan portended. Nonetheless, as Dean Rusk, then a junior member of the Truman administration—and secretary of state in the 1960s—reflected four decades later, if the U.S. and Soviet positions had been reversed in 1946 with respect to atomic power, it is doubtful that the Americans would have agreed to a Soviet-style Baruch Plan. Thus it is not surprising, to use Truman's words at Tiptonville in October 1945, that the Russians elected to "catch up on their own hook."[82]

It is equally evident that Truman never truly supported the 1945–1946 consensus of Stimson-Acheson-Lilienthal-Wallace that there were no atomic secrets, that America's atomic monopoly was ephemeral, and that security through cooperation was the best way to avert an arms race and its attendant problems, even if this meant taking a calculated risk for peace. Instead, Truman set the diplomatic posture, with Baruch as chief negotiator, that presumed the U.S. to be the world's "sheriff" who would not "throw away our gun" and sought to preserve every atomic advantage—technical information, weapons, and raw materials—even over its Allies, as witness negotiations with the British and the McMahon Act.

Further, while Acheson criticized the inspections–sanctions–no veto proposals and insisted that the U.S. could not earn the trust of other nations before it halted bomb production, others like Interior Secretary Ickes detected a tendency in 1946 to "flaunt our stockpile of atomic bombs, explode them with intimidating effect, and arrogantly display our naval strength." Similarly, Wallace told Truman in July that America's atomic bombs and tests, long-range bombers, and bases within one thousand miles of Russia gave the appearance of "preparing to win an inevitable war" or trying to establish intimidating preponderance of power. Truman would have denied this. But his decision to "stand pat" on the Baruch Plan, and likewise his decisions to "get tough" with the Russians over a loan and the issue of Iran, and to approve Churchillian rhetoric about need for an Anglo-American "fraternal association" to counter Russia's quest for the "fruits of war" indicated that in 1946 the president was less interested in gaining Soviet accord by compromise than in implementing Baruch's dictum that the U.S. could get what it wanted by insisting upon it.[83]

The Die Is Cast

During 1946 Truman often glossed over matters. In April he said that Soviet-American relations were cordial as ever, and in May he denied that Byrnes' hard line at the CFM meeting in Paris signaled sharp change in American policy. In September he told a Cabinet officer that there was no "get tough" policy (troops and equipment were lacking, he added) and then wrote that there was too much "loose talk" about "shooting troubles" with the Russians, who usually asked for the "whole earth" but expected "maybe . . . an acre." Peace was possible, Truman contended, if Stalin would come to a summit in the U.S.[1]

Neither genial rhetoric nor self-deception could gainsay grim reality. The Americans felt stymied that they could not divine Soviet goals. After Ambassador Smith had asked how far the Russians intended to go, Stalin had said not much further. But when next Byrnes asked Georges Bidault in May whether the Russians sought security or expansion, France's foreign minister replied "security through expansion probably." Shortly confronted by coal mine and railway strikes, and propaganda war at the CFM, Truman imagined court-martialing the labor leaders and dropping an atomic bomb on Stalin.[2]

Most significant, as historian Daniel Yergin has written, by spring 1946 U.S. policy makers not only assumed as an axiom that the Soviet Union was aggressively expansionist, but they perceived every Russian claim, or any conflict, as a threat to national security. This newly fashionable term, or "Commanding Idea," was broadly construed and inspired by four perceptions. First was the view that the Eurocentric system of international relations had ended and that America and Russia now dominated the global order, with the world looking to the U.S. to preserve peace. Second were history's "lessons": failure to respond forcefully to prior Asian and European crises had only spurred the aggressors and led to world war. Third was belief in the necessity of permanent military preparedness, and fourth was need to integrate industrial capacity to maintain an arsenal for democracy.[3]

Truman fostered these emergent national security state precepts. "The Lord" had bestowed world leadership on the U.S. a generation ago, he said in March 1946, but whereas Americans had shirked their duty earlier, now they would play their rightful role. In April Truman called for unification of the armed services, temporary extension of Selective Service, and creation of universal military training. He insisted publicly that the U.S. had to be concerned about every nation and every region in the world, no matter how remote. "Remember that the First World War began in Serbia," that the Versailles peace was first breached in Manchuria, and that the Second World War began in Poland. "Our foreign policy must be universal," he concluded.[4]

Shortly, former president Hoover advised Truman that he had to confront the Russians with a "truculent spirit." Meanwhile, a published State Department report, blending the Willett-Kennan-Churchill theses, argued that the Kremlin understood only "power backed by reason and right" and that the U.S. had to maintain a strong military establishment and not hesitate to aid "friends" in order to deter Russia's "adventurous . . . aggrandizement." Then amid a Cabinet crisis over foreign policy in September, Truman, in an autobiographical note, analogized the two postwar eras. He feared that just as after World War I, Americans had turned from the discipline of wartime efforts to personal aggrandizement and disarmament and refused to participate in world crises, now selfishness and greed were raising their ugly heads and the "same old pacifists" were talking disarmament. But this time that "serviceman" who had overcome adversity in the Argonne Forest in 1918, and many times since, was ready to meet awesome new responsibility and to "outface" demagogues at home and abroad.[5]

The new American attitude was evident. In June a prominent journalist remarked that Truman seemed "awfully cocky" about U.S. ability to "lick" Russia. In August Ambassador Lord Inverchapel noted that the Americans viewed Russia's claim to joint defense of the Straits as aimed at turning Turkey into a "satellite" and controlling the Middle East, while Yugoslavia's downing of two U.S. planes for overflying its airspace had led to talk of "the possibility, and even the desirability of an early war" with Russia. Meanwhile in Paris, the Americans were locked in the "battle of Europe," particularly a "dangerous struggle for the body and soul of Germany." Further, the president did not fear to press America's position. He did not want war, he wrote in November, but the Russian regime was a "totalitarian state" no different from that of the tsars or Hitler. Thus better to learn sooner, not later, whether they wanted peace.[6]

I

On April 4, the day the Iran crisis was "resolved" but with Churchill's iron curtain message still reverberating, Byrnes proposed that the foreign ministers join with their deputies, who since the Moscow Conference in December 1945 had been trying to draft treaties for Germany's former allies (Finland, Italy, Rumania, Bulgaria, and Hungary) that were to be ratified at a peace conference in May. But the recent hardening of ideological lines precluded progress. The chief U.S. negotiator, Assistant Secretary James Dunn, insisted that the Russians sought either no agreement in order to maintain their troops and "puppet stooge governments" in Eastern Europe or to impose dreadful last-minute compromises. Dunn also said that the Soviets were currying Eastern Europe's favor by pressing even harsher terms on Italy. But he concluded realistically that no Balkan treaty was possible that did not confirm the "special Soviet position there."[7]

Byrnes acquiesced about Eastern Europe. The "serious" problems, he told the Cabinet in mid-April, were Russian desire for a Mediterranean base (Tripolitania in Libya) and reparations from Italy. The secretary had strongly opposed a Soviet base in Libya at the London CFM in September 1945 and argued that high reparations from Italy would siphon reconstruction aid from a country that the U.S. (and Britain, reluctantly) currently treated not as a former enemy but friendly power. Byrnes predicted that there would be an "impasse" at the CFM talks and that the Western powers would sign a separate treaty with Italy. Truman agreed. He reverted to his exaggerated view that the Potsdam Conference had made clear that "we will not under any circumstances pay reparations to Russia" and was content to have Byrnes, now attuned to staying in close touch with him, run matters.[8]

The CFM met in Paris in two extended sessions: April 25–May 16 and June 15–July 12. The Russians at once dropped their long-held objection to France's participating in drafting all the peace treaties, but then the foreign ministers were given to speech making and "throwing commas and colons at each other," as Vandenberg noted. But as Truman liked to say, the secretary had brought the "right attitude" to Paris and had learned his history "lessons." There would be *"no more appeasement,"* and the U.S. had to act like the *"Number One World Power."*[9]

The Americans and British rejected the Russians' claims for $100 million in Italian reparations (plus $200 million for the Balkan States) and trusteeship over Tripolitania, and efforts to gain Trieste and most of the province of Venezia Giulia for Yugoslavia. (Vandenberg said no to Byrnes' brief interest in "trading" Trieste.) Molotov in turn refused to discuss Austria and branded as "capitalist enslavement" Byrnes' efforts to add "open door" clauses to the Balkan treaties and to open the Danube to all nations. And when Byrnes asked why there had been no response to the draft treaty he had sent to Moscow in early February proposing four-power demilitarization of Germany for twenty-five years, Molotov retorted that this postponed real German disarmament. Undoubtedly the Soviets preferred to bargain first over reparations and access to the Ruhr, although they also minimized Byrnes' proposal.[10]

The diplomats managed the Finnish treaty, and the Russians eventually dropped their Tripolitan claim and agreed that Italy might administer its former colonies. Then came some progress on reparations and the Balkans. But with deadlock certain over Trieste and a peace conference date, Byrnes got Truman to approve a "breakdown, presumably to teach the Russians international conduct," as Bevin's private secretary noted. Then after a few sharp exchanges over Germany preliminary to later battle, the delegates adjourned on May 16.[11]

"Paris was Munich in reverse," Vandenberg rejoiced, and "appeasement" was over. Meanwhile, a French diplomat worried that neither Byrnes nor Bevin aimed to compromise with the Russians but to put the onus on them for deadlock. At the least Truman and Byrnes sought a tough public posture. Thus the president quickly approved his secretary's May 20 radio report that blamed the "disappointingly small" progress on the American-Soviet conflict (ignoring Western discord). Byrnes warned that the Soviet quest for security might diminish world security and stated for the first time that if the CFM did not agree on peace treaties, the U.S. would turn to the UN. Bevin cautioned this would produce "a first class row" with the Russians, and Molotov rejoined that the Soviet Union would not be intimidated nor deprived of its rightful international role.[12]

The CFM resumed wrangling in mid-June. After two weeks the Russians made minor Balkan concessions and then surprisingly acceded to a Franco-Italian frontier, to Greece retaining the Dodecanese Islands, and to Byrnes' prior proposal that the Big Four control Italy's colonies for a year (the British insisted on their military administration) and seek a final solution. The foreign ministers then accepted France's proposal to internationalize Trieste, with a UN governor, and the French demarcation of the Italo-Yugoslav frontier. Byrnes agreed to $100 million in Italian reparations for Russia, and Molotov accepted the start of a peace conference on July 29, with the Big Four to suggest, but not fix, as the fearful Russians wanted, conference rules. Thus the

CFM agreed on the framework for Europe's minor treaties and ratification procedures. More significant, just before concluding on July 12, the foreign ministers resumed their war of words over Germany, "the core of the whole European problem," Vandenberg wrote.[13]

II

Truman's German policy was marked by increasing discord and ambivalence during 1945–1946. To recall, Truman sympathized with Germany's historic tension between its "population and economics," and he rejected the "conqueror theory" that the loser pays for the war. In May 1945 the new president signed the revised War Department directive JCS 1067, which gave the U.S. occupation commander broad authority and looked toward a harsh peace. But Truman soon affirmed the Stimson–State Department view that a reconstructed and reintegrated Germany was necessary to prevent reversion to antidemocratic politics and irredentist foreign policy, and vital to Western political-economic stability. At Potsdam Truman backed Byrnes' zonal reparations deal, which denied Russia a fixed sum and access to Ruhr industry and gave the military commanders in each zone final authority over reparations. Truman in turn acceded to Poland's de facto control of Silesia, a "Bolsheviki land-grab," he said. The Potsdam accord also called for the four-power A.C.C. to treat Germany as a single economic unit and to create central agencies for finance, transport, trade, and industry.

In sum, although Truman and his aides recognized that their zonal reparations policy might imply political-economic division of Germany, in 1945 they presumed that their military and economic "master cards" would induce Soviet cooperation on American principles. At the same time, Truman and the State Department opposed both Britain's interest in merging the three Western zones, because that would create an "economic wall" between East and West, and France's heavy reparations claims and "obsession" with detaching the Saar, Ruhr, and Rhineland, policy they likened to France's post–World War I militaristic diplomacy.[14]

From fall 1945 to late 1946 nearly every report Truman received from officials about policy and administration in Germany insisted that France was the chief barrier to implementing the Potsdam accords. In November 1945 the president's special emissary, Byron Price, stated that the French, bent on "dismemberment," had "deadlocked" the A.C.C., preventing creation of central agencies or treating Germany as an economic unit, and perpetuating chaos. Truman, greatly impressed, circulated this long report to his principal Cabinet officers, who pushed its release on November 28. The next week Byrnes stated that the Big Three, but not France, were ready to begin work on various German central agencies.[15]

Thereafter, Secretary of War Robert Patterson; Assistant Secretary for Occupied Territories John McCloy; political adviser for Germany, Robert Murphy; and Deputy Military Governor General Lucius Clay argued that French "obstructionism" and "sabotage" of Potsdam's provisions and efforts to detach the Saar, Ruhr, and Rhineland jeopardized quadripartite governance, caused higher occupation costs and U.S. need to finance reparations, and impended economic disaster in Germany and the world. The French insisted that creation of central agencies would preclude their ability to detach Germany's western areas to serve as bulwarks against German or Russian aggression. American officials countered that French policy would only foster German anger and Soviet consolidation in the East. And when in March journalist Cyrus Sulzberger faulted the administration for failure to establish central agencies, Acheson told Truman that France's "stubborn opposition" was to blame, but he would not say this publicly because of "unstable political conditions" there.[16]

Soviet behavior in Germany was also difficult for the Americans, although not without prospect for accord. Moscow's policy makers were divided. Some favored a Sovietized eastern zone that anticipated the division of all of Europe between capitalist and socialist states. Others sought to maintain maximum flexibility to accommodate four-power agreement on German unification, demilitarization, and neutrality that would open the way to their gaining a desperately desired share of western German coal, mineral resources, and reparations and also keep western Germany's industrial power from being integrated into a U.S.-led Western condominium. The chief Soviet policy maker, Stalin, thought that a divided Germany would prove to be militaristic and vengeful. Thus he was content to keep his options open and to move slowly and cautiously while also encouraging development of "anti-fascist democratic forces."[17]

Thus between late 1945 and spring 1946 the Soviet Military Government in Germany (SVAG) took the lead in pressing the Social Democrats (SPD) and Communists (KPD) in their zone to form one Socialist Unity Party (SED) that would be led by Otto Grotewohl of the SPD and Wilhelm Pieck of the KPD. Although there was strong opposition to this forced merger from SPD members in eastern and western Germany, there was also considerable sentiment for reunion of these two Marxist parties whose separate existence dated from a split in the SPD ranks during World War I. Finally, in late April 1946 the SPD leadership gave in to the merger.[18]

General Clay and Byrnes said that the U.S. would not recognize the merger unless it was supported by SPD rank and file, not just party leaders, but little else could be done except to deny the SED standing in Berlin and in the U.S. zone in western Germany. Thus Moscow gained a party that would follow its line closely. But when the Soviets sponsored district and provincial assembly elections on October 20, the SED gained less than a majority (47.5 percent) of the votes cast in the eastern zone, while in Greater Berlin (all four zones) the SED finished an embarrassing third with 19.8 percent, while the traditional SPD got 48.7 percent and the conservative Christian Democratic Union (CDU) got 22.2 percent.[19]

Other Russian policies in Germany were of equally dubious success, at least in terms of winning public support. Soviet armies, moved by battle hardship and revenge, looted and raped massively, while "trophy" battalions sought out military machines, scientific laboratories, and communications equipment, as well as coal, iron ore, and steel for removal to Russia. Most significant, as Norman Naimark has written, because the Potsdam agreement did not provide for collection and distribution of reparations, "the Russians were left with little choice but to take reparations from their own zone." This they did by dismantling factories for transshipment to the USSR, and as the Foreign Ministry made clear in July 1946, they viewed $10 billion as "minimum compensation" for their devastating wartime losses.[20]

Despite unsettling Soviet behavior, in January 1946 Clay and his aides brokered a compromise on the level of German steel production. The British (in control of the Ruhr) had wanted to set it high enough to sustain an unsubsidized German economy; the Russians had wished to keep it low enough, at about 4.6 million tons annually, to permit reparations. But they agreed to have production raised to 5.8 million tons annually plus another 1.7 million tons of retained capacity. This steel accord then provided the basis for Big Four agreement in March on Germany's level of industry, which would be approximately 55 percent of prewar capacity, about a 30 percent reduction in standard of living, and would include elimination of important war industries. An effusive Clay wrote Eisenhower on March 21 that the agreement "proves . . . conclusively that cooperation and understanding are possible between our country and the Soviets" if Americans would be more patient and more willing to understand "the tremendous problems which the Soviets face internally." The British conceded that the Russians had made "substantially greater" concessions than anyone else.[21]

Then on May 3 Clay, largely on his own initiative, halted dismantling of industrial plants in the U.S. zone for reparations delivery (the British reluctantly did so too), but this action was aimed mainly at the French, not the Russians, although they would bear the main burden. Clay now proposed major policy changes, including merger of zones, to effect administrative and economic unity in Germany. He presumed that the British would accept, that so too would the Russians (whom he called "tough horse-traders") after a battle over details, and that the French would strongly resist. Still, even in late July he foresaw agreement with the Russians, as Assistant Secretary of War Stuart Symington told the White House after visiting Clay in Berlin. Indeed, the deputy military governor ascribed much Soviet-American antipathy to the U.S. decision to close its zone to the Russians in December 1945 and to "old school diplomats" who were offended by Russian rudeness and Marxist rhetoric. Clay thought U.S. officials should spend less time thinking about what might occur in fifteen or twenty years—that tended to make war seem "inevitable"—and more time getting to know the Russians.[22]

Nonetheless, the growing Cold War consensus soon overtook German policy. In early March, not long after he had sent his Long Telegram, Kennan challenged the views of U.S. officials in Berlin. He said that Moscow's goal was to dominate all of Germany. The first step was insistence in 1945 on the Oder–western Neisse boundary, which took Silesia from Germany, weakened the country, and kept it at odds with Poland, which would be militarily dependent on Russia. Now the Soviets, in order to dominate their own occupation zone, were hiding behind French opposition to central agencies and backing "the sole authoritarian party" (the SED) in a country used to authoritarianism. But at the right opportunity the Soviets would push central agencies to penetrate the rest of Germany and champion creation of an "anti-Fascist Republic" that would serve as a road paver for a Soviet Socialist state. Kennan thus proposed "walling off" the western zones of Germany, integrating them into Western Europe, and abandoning the call for a united Germany. Ambassador Smith in Moscow endorsed Kennan's views, especially the idea of uniting the western zones and orienting them toward Western Europe.[23]

From Berlin, Murphy cabled that Clay was "pretty violent" against the Kennan line, while the political adviser himself insisted that the Russians had been "meticulous" in observing Potsdam and friendly toward the Americans. He wished "to make it quite clear that in our local innocence, we have never and still do not believe for a minute in imminent Soviet aggression." But Kennan was unmoved. He was persistent that the Soviets sought to dominate Germany through "puppet agencies" and that it was time for the U.S. to abandon the Potsdam agreement, call for German unity within its old borders (except for East Prussia), and if the Russians refused this, proceed with unifying western Germany without them. For the most part State Department officials agreed with the Kennan-Smith dark view of Soviet aims. But they hesitated to advocate partition or division of Germany because they doubted that the western zones could be integrated with Western Europe fast enough to avert an economic crisis, and they feared that leaving the Russians and KPD as sole advocates of a unified nation might cause many Germans to turn to Communism.[24]

Amid the wrangling over German policy, and just as the U.S. was winning its way over Russia in Iran and Baruch was taking a tough stance on atomic negotiations, Byrnes called for a CFM meeting to begin in Paris in late April. The secretary intended to take up German problems as well as negotiate peace treaties for Italy and the Balkan States. But he intended to maintain a very firm stance. Even before Byrnes departed, he predicted to the Cabinet that the meeting would end in impasse. And a week into negotiations he told Foreign Minister Bidault that he—the secretary—had been criticized for appeasing the Russians at Moscow and that now the public was in no mood for concessions on major issues.[25]

As for Germany, although both Truman and Byrnes appeared to accord with Clay's gritty optimism, the president persisted in his view that Potsdam had made clear that the U.S. would not underwrite reparations payments to the Russians. The Americans would proclaim their commitment to Germany unity, but Byrnes did not intend to articulate a program to achieve this. Instead, he apparently hoped to offer security and an end to German militarism to the Soviets (and French) by proposing a four-power, twenty-five-year treaty that guaranteed German disarmament. Vandenberg had first suggested this in a speech in January 1945, and Byrnes had raised the idea briefly and unsuccessfully with Molotov at the London CFM that September. The secretary later claimed that Stalin had agreed informally to such an agreement at the Moscow Conference that December and that Truman had "heartily approved" and was so certain of the proposal's acceptance that he called it "Byrnes' treaty." The secretary had a draft prepared secretly and sent to Moscow in February 1946, but the Russians replied only that it raised "serious objections."[26]

Then at the CFM on April 28 Byrnes said that the Russian response to this treaty would reveal whether they sought "security or expansionism." Molotov affirmed the treaty in principle but argued sharply that German disarmament had already been agreed upon in June 1945 when the four powers assumed authority and that this new treaty would slow reduction of Germany's "war potential." The Soviets preferred a commission to verify whether disarmament was being effected in each zone. The next day Byrnes tried to assuage Molotov by insisting that, unlike in 1918, the U.S. was "not going to leave Europe" and was ready to assume obligations. But the foreign minister retorted that the Russians were still uninformed about disarmament in the other zones. Two weeks later, twelve days after Clay's reparations halt, Byrnes pressed a November deadline for discussing his proposal and a full German peace treaty. But Molotov stood fast, with provocative blasts that the Russians knew nothing about British controls in the Ruhr, the "center" of Germany's heavy industry and war-making capacity.[27]

Byrnes was so angered by Russian rejection of his treaty that shortly he confided that he had "about given up hope for a unified Germany," and he began to think of making the three western zones a viable entity. The Russians, meanwhile, continued to define disarmament, or "security," to include reparations and elimination of German industrial qua military capacity. They revealed their sensitivity about exclusion from the Ruhr and surely were ambivalent about the long-term U.S. presence in Europe that Byrnes had assured. The British were surprised that Byrnes had introduced his treaty to the CFM and gave it only lukewarm support. The French wished to talk chiefly about regaining the Saar coal mines and securing political-military control of the area; putting the Ruhr and its industrial capacity under "international control," with French influence predominant and the Russians excluded; and placing French and other Western European forces along the left bank of an autonomous Rhineland. The British preferred to unify Germany but to socialize the Ruhr's industries. Truman and Byrnes opposed French separatism and British socialization.[28]

The CFM also made little progress on other matters, including peace treaties for Italy and the Balkan States. Byrnes insisted that the Russians take their $100 million claim in reparations from Italy from its assets in the Balkans, and he deflected Russian claims for $200 million in Italian reparations for Yugoslavia, Greece, and Albania. With Bevin's help Byrnes also blocked a Russian joint trusteeship proposal (aimed at Libya) for Italian colonies and, to Molotov's consternation, he was persistent that Trieste be placed under UN aegis rather than ceded to Yugoslavia. Anglo-American insistence on equal-trade-opportunity clauses also blocked agreement on Balkan treaties.[29]

While the diplomats were throwing commas and colons at each other, as Vandenberg wrote, Truman offered only his stock advice to Byrnes: "Do everything you can to continue but in the final analysis do whatever you think is right and tell them to go to hell if you have to." The secretary continued to negotiate until May 10, by which time, as Bevin's private secretary noted, he seemed "bent on a breakdown, presumably to teach the Russians international conduct." Four days later Byrnes pressed to adjourn the CFM until June 15, with a peace conference to follow shortly. The Russians agreed to adjourn, with the Big Four's deputies to remain in Paris to work on peace treaties, but the conference date was left in abeyance. Byrnes returned to the U.S., briefed Truman, and stated in a national address on May 20 that while the U.S. should not attempt to impose its will on others, the reverse was equally true. He warned that the Soviet quest for security "might lead to less rather than more security" in the world.[30]

Paris was Munich in reverse, Vandenberg wrote with his propensity for hyperbole. But a French diplomat confirmed for him that neither Bevin nor Byrnes had sought to find out how far the Russians would go toward compromise and instead spent their time trying to blame Soviets for the deadlock. Byrnes especially seemed to want to let the Russians know that the "sucker season had ended and that henceforth the Americans would be tough." [31]

The CFM reconvened on June 15, with both sides playing tough for two weeks. Then during the first week of July they compromised on a draft of the Balkan treaties, and the Russians accepted, to the great surprise of Byrnes and Bevin, a French-drawn Italo-Yugoslav border, with Trieste placed under UN supervision. Byrnes then acceded to the Russians' claim of $100 million in Italian current production reparations if they provided the raw materials and assented to a peace conference in late July. Procedural niceties were then agreed upon so that it would not appear that Byrnes had bought a peace conference. [32]

With the minor treaties out of the way, the Soviets appeared to steal a march near the end of this second CFM session. On July 9 Molotov assailed Byrnes' proposed treaty to guarantee German disarmament for twenty-five years. The foreign minister said that the treaty should run at least forty years and that it had to deal not just with disbanding troops but industrial demilitarization, decartelization, and denazification. He also scored its failure to take up Yalta's $10 billion in reparations and Clay's "unlawful" reparations halt in May that reneged on Potsdam. The next day Molotov astonished his colleagues when he declared that the Soviet Union eschewed revenge as policy toward Germany. Instead, he proposed a democratic, unified Germany, with no dismemberment in the west, that would be politically and economically reconstructed with central agencies and peaceful industries but with "inter-allied control" in the Ruhr and a commitment to deliver reparations, presumably from current production. A peace treaty would follow. [33]

Byrnes immediately agreed to a longer term for a German treaty and said that his proposal had purposely dealt with disarmament only as defined by the Big Four's generals in June 1945. But the Russians' lenient terms clearly stunned Byrnes. At first he blamed the delay in setting German policy on difficulties in implementing Potsdam and drafting Balkan treaties. Then he wrote Truman that Molotov's speech was "a long harangue" that criticized everything and "showed no willingness to agree upon or take up any proposal other than his own." Later on, with more acumen, he termed Molotov's "performance" the first round in "a battle for the minds of the German people." [34]

Regardless, after consulting Clay and Murphy on July 11, Byrnes proposed that the Big Four establish central agencies to forge German economic unity. Failing that, he offered a "last resort suggestion," namely that the U.S. would merge its zone economically with that of any other ally. The next night Byrnes asked Molotov what was really in his "heart and mind" regarding Germany. The Russian replied: $10 billion in reparations and a share in four-power control of the Ruhr. Byrnes was sure that was the truth, he would write the next year. But it was also precisely what neither he nor Truman would ever allow.[35]

Further, while Byrnes' public report on the CFM on July 15 ascribed Russian intransigence to poor diplomacy, he asked whether German militarism was "to be used as a pawn in a struggle between East and West." Most Americans thought yes, Ambassador Lord Inverchapel wrote. They now looked most suspiciously upon the Russians, who had forced the KPD-SPD merger into the SED "unity" party, begun to halt industrial dismantling in order to take reparations from current production, and stopped supporting French tactics. This could only mean that the Soviets were determined to dominate their zone, penetrate the western zones through central agencies, and then ally with a united, centralized, and Soviet-dominated Reich.[36]

Thus the Truman administration's zonal merger proposal was intended less to gain German economic unity than to effect the merger of the western zones and gain control over the British-held Ruhr industries, which the State and War Departments insisted were vital to U.S. national security. But western zonal unity was also a means to try to compel Russian acceptance of U.S. policy in Germany even at the risk, or perhaps hope, of dividing that country. Hence the British worried in July 1946 that to accept the U.S. proposal would "increase the tendency to split Europe into two parts," although they hoped that their action might have a "salutary effect" on the Soviets. But the British Cabinet, deeply worried over occupation costs and anxious for access to U.S. foodstuffs and capital, quickly acceded on July 30 to merge their zone with the American one (to be called Bizonia), which would become effective at the start of the new year.[37]

Similarly, Clay noted that "we have cast the die here in economic integration with the British zone," which he hoped would expedite quadripartite action. But he also recognized that it "may just have the reverse effect." Thus to foster quadripartite unity and appeal to the populace, the military commander drafted a new summary of U.S. policy objectives in Germany. He proposed holding early national elections, forming a national provisional government and central agencies, and ending the "air-tight" zones through free exchange of goods, people, and ideas. He also sought to assuage the French by conceding the Saar to them and the Russians by proposing to recognize the Oder–western Neisse boundary, and to accept any "rational plan" for internationalization of the Ruhr and Rhineland industries as long as they were integrated into the German economy. He further suggested reduction of occupation forces to smaller security groups.[38]

But the State Department refused to allow Clay to publish his document. Officials there did not want to upset the French over the Ruhr and Rhineland and prospect of a German national government, but they were even more opposed to Clay's concessions to the Soviets. Disappointed and angry, in mid-August he called Byrnes, then in Paris negotiating peace treaties, and asked him to come to Germany to make a positive U.S. policy statement that would reassure the Germans, especially those who had cooperated with the U.S., about the future and get the French to comply with the Potsdam agreements.[39]

The result was Byrnes' speech on September 6 at the Stuttgart Opera House. As the secretary told Truman a few days earlier, Molotov's July 10 "performance" had garnered German public support, and visiting American reporters and others were seeking comment to offset the view that the U.S. was so disgusted with European problems that it would leave Germany. Byrnes had his aides draft a speech that drew heavily on Clay's unpublished policy statement, although the general was more flexible than Truman or Byrnes about reparations, some internationalizing of Ruhr coal and steel, and the Oder–western Neisse line. Truman then approved the speech.[40]

Byrnes declared that the U.S. sought to extirpate militarism but opposed a vengeful peace, and did not want Germany to become a "pawn or a partner" in an East-West military struggle. He proposed that the Germans begin to build democratic political structures "from the ground up," insisted that German and European economic rehabilitation were interdependent, and declared that it was time to establish central administrative agencies. He recognized French claims to the Saar, but was adamant that no foreign power could encroach on the Rhineland or Ruhr, whose industries could be subjected to controls only for security reasons. And he looked ultimately to German membership in the UN.

But in addition to seeking to gain French compliance with Potsdam, Byrnes also issued warnings to the Russians. The German provisional government, a major step toward self-governance, was not to be "hand picked by other governments." The U.S. would try to create central agencies and economic unity but failing that, would secure "maximum possible unification." The U.S. opposed any more reparations than agreed at Potsdam, the established levels of production did not allow for reparations from current production, and clearly implied, the Russians would not get direct access to the Ruhr. Moreover, the U.S. was not tied to the Oder–western Neisse boundary: Silesia had not been ceded to Poland, and final settlement awaited a peace conference. (Byrnes evidently thought that this would force the Soviets to choose between supporting their Polish allies or German Communists.) And in a last-minute addition pushed by Clay that Byrnes was unable to clear with Truman—but the president was of like mind—the secretary declared that as long as occupation troops were in Germany, "American armed forces" would remain. "I want no misunderstanding. We will not shirk our duty. We are not withdrawing. We are staying here."[41]

Small wonder that Byrnes left the Opera House to a standing ovation from his chiefly German audience. He had reassured them of their future and indicated that they would not be left alone to contend with the Soviets and their Communist allies. He had sought to mollify the French and did not openly blame them for A.C.C. failure to agree on central agencies. He had also taken a tough stance with the Soviets regarding German reparations, unity, and the Oder–western Neisse line. And by creating Bizonia, as Charles Maier has said, the U.S. had underscored that its "pre-eminent concern" was a "Western economic and geopolitical entity."[42]

The president loved Byrnes' speech. He remarked jocularly to one Cabinet official that it must have been "pretty good" because neither the British, French, Germans, nor Russians liked it. But in a serious vein he linked it to Byrnes' disarmament treaty: the Russians' "bluff" had been called, and he did not think that they would go along. But "if not, there was nothing left to do. Britain and the United States would have to go along without them." Similarly, Cabinet officials (but notably not Wallace), Vandenberg, Clay, Churchill, and others sang Byrnes' praises. Predictably, the Soviets and Polish officials assailed the U.S. stance on the Oder–western Neisse, while the French, piqued that Byrnes had "kissed Germania" on both cheeks, continued to press their Rhineland and Ruhr claims. They also opposed zonal merger and Byrnes' four-power treaty, despite his argument that the latter gave them all that Clemenceau had sought from Wilson a generation before.[43]

The British pushed on with merger accords. Yet they remained uneasy, as Lord Inverchapel wrote, about the American-Soviet struggle over Germany's "body and soul." So too was Clay uneasy. He was still persistent, without encouragement from Washington, that it was possible to reach agreement on current production reparations with the Russians that would lead to further political accord. In fact, by mid-October the Russians had made an offer, close to U.S. terms, to have recipient nations of current production reparations provide raw materials for the goods, and after the A.C.C. set a current production level the Russians would agree to raise the German level of industry.[44]

Political adviser Murphy contended that the "concessions" the U.S. wanted were nothing more than an "honest implementation" of the Potsdam agreements, to which the Russians were already committed. Thus it was no accident that the recent elections in the Soviet zone and in Berlin that had proved a "heavy blow" to the Soviets had been "free and orderly," for they were the result of months of difficult negotiations. Further, if the Soviets reneged on the deal, the U.S. could cut off the reparations flow. In effect, Clay and Murphy distinguished the U.S. position in Germany from its far more limited presence in Eastern Europe, and they were determined to negotiate to unify Germany economically and politically rather than settle for western zone unity.[45]

By late fall Clay believed that he had figured out a deal to provide the Russians with current production reparations in return for raw materials that would allow a 15 percent increase in the level of industry and provide for a vast increase in production to support Western Europe and the Soviets, inspire German public opinion, avert the need for partition, and lead to "full political unification of Germany." To be sure, the plan rested on the untested results of a positive production balance over that needed for Germany's internal economy and Russian agreement on an export-import program for Germany and willingness to allow free elections.[46]

But no one in the State Department supported this deal, and Byrnes evinced no interest in taking it up at the CFM. Further, Truman had recently threatened war with the Soviets in a crisis over the Turkish Straits and in September had suffered an embarrassing open split in his Cabinet between Byrnes and Wallace over foreign policy. The president had also received a top-level report from his White House aides and national security advisers that it was pointless to negotiate with the Russians because they understood only military force and sought world domination. Finally, in early December Clay personally took his proposal to Byrnes—just as the U.S. and Britain were concluding their deal on Bizonia. The secretary promised only that it would be brought up at the next CFM in March 1947, by which time Byrnes would be gone from office, political-economic conditions in Europe would be extremely dire, and Soviet-American conflict would be raised to increasingly bitter heights.[47]

III

On August 7 the Soviets at last put forward to Turkey their proposal, awaited since the Potsdam meeting, to revise the Montreux Convention regarding control of the Straits. Copies of the note were also delivered to Washington and London. According to Molotov's recollection decades later, Stalin had wanted to accomplish his aims peacefully, through the UN, but failing that he now ordered Molotov to "demand" joint possession of the Straits despite the foreign minister's warning that the Western powers would not allow it. Regardless, the first three points of the note—opening the Straits to commercial ships of all nations and to all Black Sea powers' warships, but not to non–Black Sea powers' warships except in special cases—were similar to those in the U.S. proposal of November 1945. But points four and five called for a new regime comprising only Black Sea powers to govern the Straits, and Russia and Turkey to establish joint defense, which meant Soviet bases in Turkey.[48]

The Soviet note was presented following a year of harsh language, with their ambassador reportedly having told the Turks that Russia had waited a long time for its arrangement with Poland and "we can wait regarding Turkey." There were several hundred thousand Russian troops in Bulgaria and Rumania, periodic Russian troop movements—a war of nerves—along the Turkish frontier, and provocative statements made by Russian generals in the area. All of this was reported by American intelligence to Washington. So too, in March, did Ambassador Edwin C. Wilson in Ankara say that Soviet tactics, including the request for bases, were intended to "break" the Turkish regime and allow the Russians to dominate Turkey and expel Western influence. He did not rule out, "illogical as it may seem," Russian use of force against Turkey. Similarly, British intelligence reported that Soviet forces might possibly "present the world with local *faits accomplis.*"[49]

Nonetheless, by late June Russian forces began to withdraw from the Balkans. Both U.S. and British intelligence took the view that Turkey was "no longer an immediate target for Soviet aggressive action." Moreover, the Russian note of August 7 met Montreux's required deadline and Potsdam procedures for proposing revision of Straits governance. It also emphasized Russian security needs by citing numerous times that Axis warships had penetrated the Black Sea via the Straits. Further, the Russians softened their stance by omitting their prior territorial claims on the provinces of Kars and Ardahan. Ambassador Wilson reported that the Turks were not alarmed but even encouraged that the note had been sent to the U.S. and Britain. Elbridge Durbrow, the charge in Moscow, reported that on three occasions Stalin had told the visiting Czech foreign minister, Jan Masaryk, and others (much as he had also told Ambassador Smith in April) that Russia did not intend to attack Turkey. Nor did the Turks think that was likely. Finally, Loy Henderson, who was head of NEA in the State Department and very hostile to the Soviets, had advised months earlier against protesting their request for bases. He said this would not only cause comparisons to Suez and Panama but draw attention to U.S. efforts to negotiate permanent military bases where the British held sway, from Iceland to the Azores and Cape Verde Islands, India, and the central and western Pacific.[50]

U.S. officials brushed aside these concerns. Truman had long presumed that the Soviets would "grab" the Straits, although in 1945 policy makers thought that the Soviet leaders regarded themselves as too weak to prompt a war over Turkey, and in March 1946 the JCS saw the Soviet request for bases as intended to protect oil and industrial facilities in the vital Ploesti, Kharkov, and Baku areas. The president had hoped to avert a Soviet call to revise Montreux through his vague proposal at Potsdam to internationalize the Straits and provide a Big Four guarantee. But Stalin had rebuffed this—he had no reason to invite a U.S. presence in the area—and shortly Byrnes insisted to Truman that Congress would not give Turkey a requisite security guarantee. When the U.S. sent the *Missouri* to Turkey in March 1946, the Ankara government arranged large public receptions in order to encourage greater U.S. presence, despite lack of a Soviet threat. Further, on August 24—two-and-a-half weeks after the Soviet note and nine days after the U.S. formulated its response—General Hoyt S. Vandenberg, director of the Central Intelligence Group (CIG), assured Truman that there were no unusual Russian troop movements or concentrations or supply buildups.[51]

In fact, the issue at hand was not a Soviet military threat to Turkey but broad U.S. political-strategic concerns. In April the JCS had completed their first basic plan, code-named Pincher, for global war with the Soviets and then set about devising its regional components. In so doing, military and civilian planners agreed that the likeliest scenario was a Soviet attack on Europe. This meant that highest priority had to be given to preserving Turkey and the Straits as a buffer necessary to allow the U.S. to control the vital Cairo-Suez area and contain Soviet submarines in the Black Sea, and then launch from Turkish bases counteroffensive air attacks on Russian and Rumanian vital oil and industrial sites. Secretary of War Patterson explained this strategy, code-named Griddle, to Truman on July 27. Soon there was consensus on need to preserve Turkey for reasons of Middle East strategy. Military planners completed Griddle by August 15, the day that Truman would meet with his top advisers to respond to the Soviet note to Turkey.[52]

Under Secretary Acheson set the tone for that meeting one day earlier at a gathering with the State-War-Navy Coordinating Committee (SWNCC). Acheson, who had been given to a more accommodating style with the Russians until spring 1946, had moved to a "tough" posture because of the Iran crisis, troubles in Germany and Greece, and perhaps the criticism he had suffered from Baruch's proponents during negotiations over atomic power. Now he took the lead in telling the SWNCC that "for *global reasons*" Turkey had to be preserved from the Soviets; if not, other "bulwarks" in Europe and the Far East would "begin crumbling at a fast rate." The "only real deterrent to Soviet plans for engulfing Turkey and the Middle East," Acheson said, "would be the conviction that the pursuance of such a policy will result in war with the United States." SWNCC officials agreed and accepted his draft policy proposal.[53]

Then came Truman's critical White House session with his civilian and military advisers on August 15. Once again Acheson held sway. He put before the group a memorandum stating that the Soviet goal was to obtain control of Turkey, eliminate Western influence, and then take Greece and the Middle East, which would allow it to achieve its objectives in India and China. Although Acheson's policy paper conceded that it was first necessary to discuss the Soviet note frankly with all the nations involved and to seek support for Turkey in the UN, the key point was that it was in America's "vital interest" to deter the Soviets and that this could not be done unless they were persuaded that the U.S. was prepared to meet their aggression with "force of arms."

Truman at once said that he would pursue this policy "to the end." He took the view, as Forrestal noted, that "we might as well find out whether the Russians were bent on world conquest now as in five or ten years." Indeed, the president responded so fast, Acheson vividly recounted, that one of the JCS asked if he understood all the implications of his decision. Truman thereupon pulled a large, worn map from his desk and lectured about the historic-strategic significance of the Middle East.[54]

American and British diplomats now encouraged Turkish officials in their resistance to Russian claims. Then on August 19 the U.S. informed the Soviets that while it was amenable to discussing passage of commercial ships and warships through the Straits, it could not accept the Soviet proposal to limit Straits governance to Black Sea powers—thus excluding the U.S.—nor agree to the Soviets joining in defense of the Straits, a matter best left to Turkey. Further, any threat or attack on the Straits would be subject to Security Council action. That same day Henderson told British embassy officials in Washington of the contents of the message and apparently said that the U.S. was prepared to see this matter "through to the end." This led Lord Inverchapel to inquire if the U.S. was prepared to go to war. Acheson responded that this was ultimately a matter for Congress but that the president and other officials fully realized the seriousness of the issue raised and were prepared to act accordingly. Two days later Britain and Turkey sent similar messages to Moscow, with the Ankara government stating firmly that Soviet bases in the Straits were incompatible with Turkish sovereignty. Shortly the JCS reiterated their view of Soviet intent to make a "satellite" of Turkey, "strategically" the most important factor in the Eastern Mediterranean and Middle East. They recommended that Turkey be allowed to buy U.S. arms and planes and that Washington send U.S. technicians, including officers, there.[55]

The Straits controversy was suddenly overshadowed on August 19 by news that for the second time in ten days Yugoslav planes had downed an unarmed U.S. Army C-47 transport—with the crew killed—for overflying their territory, which U.S. planes often did on flights between Italy and Austria. U.S. officials were extremely angry, especially because they viewed Marshal Tito, despite his having set his own course, as a stalking horse for Soviet expansion in the Balkans. They were also greatly antipathetic toward Yugoslavia because of its (Soviet-backed) claims on Trieste and Venezia Giulia, where tension was high between occupying American and Yugoslav forces. From CFM talks in Paris, Byrnes urged sharp protests and fighter escorts for the C-47s. The JCS, however, opted for armed bombers for transport because their flight patterns were steady and their air actions had to be seen as defensive. The secretary then proposed to cut off Yugoslavia's considerable aid from the United Nations Relief and Rehabilitation Administration (UNRRA), but Acheson advised that this was inappropriate for an international organization and that the U.S. lacked the votes. Truman reinforced U.S. troops along the demarcation lines, but by September mutual assurances and Yugoslavia's paying an indemnity for the dead crew ended the crisis. As General Eisenhower told a slightly surprised navy secretary Forrestal, neither the shooting down of a few planes nor Russian occupation of the Straits was cause for war.[56]

At the same time, the Truman administration maintained its diplomatic stance over Turkey and in late August sent the aircraft carrier *Franklin D. Roosevelt* and other ships to the Mediterranean. "It is nobody's damn business where we go," Admiral William "Bull" Halsey blurted to the press. Meanwhile there were mixed reports about Russian activities. General Vandenberg again told Truman that Soviet demobilization continued and that there were no unusual troop movements or military buildups. Soon, however, there were reports that the Soviets had halted demobilization, were increasing their forces and supplies in the Balkans, and—British intelligence warned—had just moved a new armored corps into Bulgaria that perhaps was the vanguard of an armored army.[57]

Despite the flurry, Turkish officials persisted in saying that they did not expect the Russians to attack or even to call a conference to revise Montreux. Rather, the Russians would sustain the status quo and press their claims later. Then came the Soviet response on September 24, a tedious twelve-page note reiterating—in language "softer" than in their August note—their position on Straits governance and bases there and proposing bilateral talks. Ankara officials concluded that since the Russians had taken a month to answer Turkey's August 22 note, there was no need to hurry a reply. They waited until mid-October to send an equally tedious, but "nonprovocative," reiteration of their position and to contend that preliminary, or bilateral, talks were now completed. Further negotiation, they said, was possible only at a conference that included both the U.S. and Britain. The Turks knew that was of no interest to Moscow and they expected, and got, no response. Shortly U.S. officials learned that the September 20 report from British intelligence on new Russian armored forces entering Bulgaria was incorrect; these forces had already been there, then gone back to the Soviet Union to be reequipped, and were now returning. In effect, the Turkish crisis was ended by November, while Soviet troop withdrawal continued throughout Europe, with all forces removed from Bulgaria by December 1947.[58]

But expansion of U.S. power into the Mediterranean had just begun. In late September 1946 Byrnes and Bevin agreed that it was Britain's duty to supply military aid to Turkey (and Greece and Iran) but, Byrnes cabled Washington, "if he [Bevin] fails to act then we can." The State Department's NEA division promptly wrote, echoing the JCS, that Turkey was the "stopper in the neck of the bottle" that prevented Soviet political-military influence from overflowing the Mediterranean and Middle East and that the U.S. should supply military aid through the British, or directly if need be. The same applied to Greece, the division wrote separately that same day, while Iran's aid had recently been agreed upon. Meantime, the White House cleared Forrestal's October 1 announcement of creation of a Mediterranean command that by year's end comprised twelve ships and made the U.S. the dominant sea power there.[59]

Several questions remain to be answered about the Turkish Straits crisis. Did the Truman administration overreact to the Soviet note of August 7, and would the U.S. have gone to war if the Russians had attacked Turkey? And did the Russians ever intend to do so but, for some reason, change their minds? In his study of this "war scare" of 1946, historian Eduard Mark argues that the Truman administration had "ample grounds" to fear a Soviet invasion of Turkey. These included Russian behavior in Iran, constant political-military threats against Turkey, large numbers of Soviet troops near Turkish borders, and constant maneuvers, especially of armored forces in Rumania, although the British intelligence report on them proved to be inaccurate. Mark further contends that Truman's willingness to fight the Russians in event they attacked Turkey was not only proper in the context but proved useful. According to Mark, Donald Maclean, one of the so-called "Magnificent Five" British diplomatic-intelligence officials who spied for the Soviet Union, was then assigned to the British Embassy in Washington and likely informed Moscow of both Henderson's August 19 remarks that Truman intended to see the matter "through to the end" and Acheson's similar response to Lord Inverchapel on August 20. The result, Mark says, was that "Stalin back-pedaled" and thus war may have been averted.[60]

Mark's thesis is questionable, save for the fact that the president and his senior advisers probably would have fought if Russia had attacked Turkey. Certainly senior officials talked on August 14 and 15 as if they would when they discussed a response to the Soviet note of August 7, and Acheson did tell Lord

Inverchapel that U.S. officials were prepared to act in keeping with the serious-ness of the matter at hand. During August and September the War Department began to study rapid mobilization and drew plans for an air war against Russia, and by December U.S. Air Force officials had concluded a plan for atomic at-tacks. Only General Eisenhower, it seems, did not think that Soviet occupation of the Straits was cause for war.[61]

The U.S. reaction to Soviet pressure on Turkey was marked by significant overreaction, however. Neither in August nor September to October did Turk-ish officials expect an attack, and on September 21 Truman wrote that he did not anticipate any "shooting trouble" with Russians, who were tough bargain-ers. But from the outset of the "crisis," the president, Acheson, and other sen-ior advisers focused almost exclusively on "worst case" assumptions, namely a Soviet assault on Turkey as prelude to an advance upon the Middle East, India, and China. There was, however, little evidence to support this analysis, which, it must be noted, was drawn more than six weeks before the ominous if incor-rect report about Russian armored troop movements in Rumania.

Moreover, U.S. officials seemed to take no account of the Soviets' usual blustery diplomatic style or that they had already backed down in Iran. Little importance was attached to traditional Russian misgivings about Turkish reli-ability, or strength, in defending the Straits, and the fact that by spring 1946 the JCS and British intelligence had recognized that Soviet pressure in the region derived from concern to protect vital industry and oil resources in southeastern Russia.[62]

Nor did the Americans mention, or consider the impact of, their own global search for bases and developing strategic interests in the Near and Middle East, as underscored by the plans they developed so quickly to use Turkey as a base of military operations against Russia and their effort to establish a naval pres-ence that would transform the Mediterranean into an American lake. (The U.S. surely would not have allowed the Russians similar status in the Caribbean.) Perhaps, then, Acheson did not mean to exaggerate three years later when he told Turkey's foreign minister, Necmeddin Sadak, that Truman considered his opposition to Soviet "demands" in August 1946 to have been "the most impor-tant decision he had made subsequent to the bombing of Hiroshima." What was left unstated, and unexamined, was how the Russians might have viewed U.S. actions.[63]

IV

Truman faced another crisis in September 1946. He was largely to blame for his immediate problem, but it was Commerce Secretary Henry Wallace who sought the public policy debate. Wallace was the most prominent and advanced, and now last, New Dealer in the Cabinet. There was distrust between this former vice president, who the Democratic politicos (including Truman ally Robert Hannegan) drove from that office in 1944, and his successor, now the president. Truman, and Wallace of Iowa, were both Midwesterners, but Wallace was a plant geneticist and agronomist who also understood atomic science. In comparison, Truman seemed more a country farmer given to homespun. They managed mutual respect amid ambivalence. Truman thought that Wallace, a "dreamer," had been America's best secretary of agriculture but questioned his suitability for the position of commerce secretary. Truman also called him a "cat bastard" (whatever that meant) in June 1945. Wallace believed that Truman was well intentioned but a "small" man given to altering his views to suit his audience. "I suspect there has never been a President who could move in two different directions with less time intervening," Wallace wrote after a Cabinet meeting in July 1946. Worse, Truman seemed undisturbed that his mind went in different directions "almost simultaneously."[64]

Wallace and Truman shared Democratic foreign policy positions, but with profound differences. While both were avid wartime internationalists, Wallace held far more advanced views about need for making social change abroad and melding American power into multilateral institutions. He also staunchly favored the Acheson-Lilienthal atomic proposals over the Baruch Plan. Both men displayed mild Anglophobia, although Truman's derived from personal insecurity and Midwestern distrust of the British, whereas Wallace's stemmed from his deep anti-imperialism and sense that the British, masters at "intrigue," sought to bolster their declining empire by fostering American-Soviet conflict. And where Truman increasingly viewed the Russians' aggressive behavior as an extension of tsarism and bolshevism, Wallace attributed it to insecurity from centuries of foreign encirclement and invasion, and now U.S. economic primacy and nuclear monopoly.

Moreover, while a proponent of an "open" world, Wallace also evinced a "spheres of influence" approach. He told Truman that the "Russian attitude in the Balkan States was not so greatly different from our attitude with regard to Mexico and Cuba." Finally, from spring 1945 Wallace worried that too many U.S. officials dealt with Russia as if war were inevitable. He also thought that Truman's universal-military-training address in October seemed "almost like the prelude to the Declaration of World War III," while in March 1946 the president viewed as "sabotage" Wallace's reported comment that Russia would feel less threatened and peace would be better served if the U.S. did not seek an air base in Iceland.[65]

Churchill's "iron curtain" speech spurred their critical divide. Wallace heard it as a call to rally anti-Soviet officials to an Anglo-American military alliance. Two weeks later he rejoined publicly (privately noting Truman's approval) that the world's common people would not tolerate any "recrudescence of imperialism even under enlightened Anglo-Saxon atomic bomb auspices." Meanwhile, on March 14 Wallace also urged Truman to create a commission, which the secretary hoped to head, to initiate broad trade and economic talks with the Russians to "disabuse" them of their fears of Western hostility and capitalist encirclement. He then pressed the president to initial his approval of this letter and give it to newly appointed Ambassador Smith. When Truman balked, Wallace challenged him to explicate his foreign trade policy.[66]

Wallace then sent Truman on July 23 a carefully crafted twelve-page, single-spaced letter stating that heavy military spending, atomic tests, search for air bases, and production of B-29s made the U.S. appear to be readying for an "inevitable war." He assailed the Baruch Plan in particular (its "fatal defect" was to insist on sharing by stages, and the veto issue was "bogus"); deplored the general acceptance of isolationism masquerading as "tough realism"; and proposed instead, even at risk of "epithets of appeasement," that the U.S. agree to reasonable security guarantees for Russia, and then a loan, broad economic negotiations, and joint projects on the Danube, all without prior "unrelated" political and economic concessions.[67]

The president asked his special counsel, Clark Clifford, for analysis, admonishing that Wallace was "going to pull an Ickes" and quit. Clifford thought that the letter was intended for publication and sent Byrnes a copy. Only White House aide George Elsey, despite his wanting to "indoctrinate" Wallace with the "facts of life" about Russia, saw a "very earnest plea by an intellectual for a program in which he ardently believes." But Truman's only reply to Wallace's letter was a cursory thank you. Later the president disparaged the letter as covering everything from "Genesis to Revelation."[68]

Wallace next met with Truman on September 10 to gain clearance for a speech to be given two days later in New York's Madison Square Garden under auspices of the CIO's political action committee. "The Way to Peace" warned that those who lived by atomic bombs would perish by them. He eschewed forming an Anglo-American alliance or leaving policy to those who wanted to "get tough" with the Russians, to make war, or to revive German military power against them. Wallace insisted that he was neither pro nor anti the British or the Russians. He urged Americans to view the world through their own eyes, not those who sought to preserve the British Empire or purchase Middle East oil with lives; to recognize Russian concerns about foreign invasion and security; and to agree that the U.S. had no more business in Eastern Europe's political affairs than the Soviets had in Western European or Latin American politics.

The peace treaty the world needed most, he said, was between the U.S. and USSR, whose peaceful competition would make them more alike.[69]

According to Wallace, Truman went over the speech "page by page" and approved repeatedly. But the secretary also told an aide that the speech would "probably make everybody sore," and he seemed surprised that Truman "apparently saw no inconsistency between my speech and what Byrnes was doing; if he did he didn't indicate it in any way." Truman first noted that "it took 30 minutes to read the speech" and that one or two things were "a little wild," but "I didn't interpret them as contrary to the general policy." Next he wrote that he had barely skimmed the speech because Wallace did not show it to him until just three minutes of meeting time remained. Later the president told aides he had seen only "parts" of the text and in his *Memoirs* claimed to have read none of it.[70]

Truman's difficulties began even before Wallace spoke on the night of September 12. Pressed by a reporter at his afternoon press conference, the president said that he had approved not only the paragraph about being neither pro nor anti Britain or Russia but "the whole speech." He then answered that Wallace's and Byrnes' Russian policies were "exactly in line." Hours later the president refused a request from Acting Secretary of State Will Clayton and Navy Under Secretary John L. Sullivan, who had just seen Wallace's text, to "head off" the address. Truman said it was too late. The speech might "ruffle" Byrnes but would not do permanent damage. Besides, Truman had approved it for its "political effect" in New York.[71]

The moment Wallace spoke, the president caught "hell." At first he tried to ride it out in silence and asked Byrnes, at the Paris peace treaty talks, to do likewise. But Senators Vandenberg and Connally declared that they could support only one secretary of state at a time. Soon the "drum fire of criticism" led to Truman's lame September 14 statement that he had meant to indicate approval only of Wallace's right to make a speech, not its content. But Wallace reaffirmed his views and intent to speak again soon and then informed the White House on September 17 that Drew Pearson had gotten a copy of his July 23 letter to the president and would publish it the next day. Truman and Clifford feared this would reveal that the president long knew Wallace's positions and either approved (or perhaps did not comprehend them) or was currying votes in New York. They urged trying to halt publication. But they discovered that Truman's press secretary, Charles Ross, bent on denying Pearson a scoop, had already agreed that Wallace should give copies to other journalists. Consequently, on September 18 Truman faced resignation threats from Byrnes and Baruch, while the White House released a joint statement from war and navy chiefs Patterson and Forrestal rebutting Wallace's claim that they sought war.

The president assured everyone that he would reach accord with Wallace that afternoon. Truman also suspected that Wallace had "arranged" the controversy from July forward but would quit now—and "I won't shed any tears."[72]

At his lengthy session with Wallace, Truman took major blame for the crisis, stressed Byrnes' sense of being undercut, and declared the need for a "united front"—and hinted that Wallace "must quit talking foreign affairs" or resign. Eventually Wallace agreed to remain silent until the Paris negotiations ended, with the proviso that he could then speak freely. Truman summoned Ross, amazed to become the mediator, who said that the "truce" was unacceptable because after it ended, the same problem would recur. But Ross also grasped Truman's desire to retain his commerce secretary through the November elections. This led to the final compromise: Wallace's pledge not to speak during the Paris talks; the future was unmentioned.[73]

American and foreign observers at once saw through the transparent accord. Byrnes informed a State Department aide that he would resign if the president had nothing new to say. Truman, however, had been initially pleased with the accord and had sought to telephone Byrnes but could not get through (except by teletype) until the next morning, September 19. Byrnes then said he would resign if Wallace were allowed to resume criticism. Truman said there was no agreement that Wallace would resume speaking and that everybody's speeches would have to be cleared. He casually exhorted Byrnes to "feel good" and to have a drink.[74]

But public critics and accounts of the Truman-Wallace exchanges caused the president's spirits to plummet, and rage replaced reason. In a classic personal memorandum a few hours later he damned Wallace as a "pacifist 100%" who sought to disband America's military and give Russia its atomic secrets and who was more dangerous than Fritz Kuhn and the German-American Bund had been. "All the 'Artists' with a capital A, the parlor pinks and the soprano voiced men," the president wrote, had become a "national danger," a "sabotage front" for Stalin that always criticized America's aid to its friends but not Russia's occupation and "loot" of the Balkans and Manchuria. Later that night Truman fired off a "low level" letter demanding Wallace's resignation. The secretary graciously returned the missive to a highly grateful president and then resigned. Truman promptly announced this with no comment, except to tell Ross: "Well, the die is cast."[75]

"L'Affaire Wallace," as a White House aide dubbed it, revealed critical Truman failings. Surely his amiability, regard for Wallace, and effort to preserve a Democratic coalition led the president to go to tortuous lengths not to break with that Cabinet officer who was an eloquent political spokesman for peace and progressivism. But more significant, Truman knew in detail Wallace's serious objections to current U.S. foreign policy but never sought to come to grips with these, if only to discuss their implications. Instead, Truman barely acknowledged Wallace's "position papers" from March to September, was deceptively agreeable at personal talks, and afterwards disparaged Wallace's motives. Further, whether Truman reviewed the September speech "page by page," for thirty minutes, or thirty seconds, even a cursory glance ought to have signaled that it contravened current policy, especially coming just six days after Byrnes' Stuttgart address and amid the bitter Turkish and Yugoslav episodes. The speech could only publicly highlight deep substantive and jurisdictional disputes between the secretaries of state and commerce, and leave Byrnes no choice but to insist that he or Wallace must resign. It was Byrnes, White House aides, and public furor that forced an indecisive president to "fire" Wallace—with no grace—and to affirm his administration's own policy. Moreover, Truman's "low level" attack on Wallace and "parlor pinks" was not the first nor last time the president expressed such views. Finally, his current response to a recent report on Russian policy showed how readily he accepted the darkest, and sometimes spurious, estimates of the threat to America at home and abroad.[76]

V

During the course of the Turkish crisis and Wallace affair, the president's special counsel, Clark Clifford, and White House aide Elsey, were readying a new report on Soviet-American relations. The origins of the report are traceable to March 1946, when Truman told Adolf A. Berle, former assistant secretary of state and recently resigned ambassador to Brazil, that he thought Stalin had deceived FDR at Yalta and that at present he was at loss about how to deal with the Russians, except "to keep every agreement we make and expect them to keep every agreement they make." Berle, who was convinced that the Soviets were "approximating" Nazi policy, replied that Truman should have his best intelligence people estimate Russian aims and capabilities, which was what he thought Roosevelt had lacked at Yalta.[77]

Truman waited until July, and as the CFM meeting in Paris moved toward its bitter close, he told Clifford that "Now's the time to take [a] stand on Russia." As Elsey recorded, the president was "tired of being pushed around—here a little, there a little, they are chiseling from us," and he would not back down even if the Paris talks failed. Then he would go on the air to tell the world the "facts." Then Truman, who was "awfully vague" on every conference except Potsdam, as Elsey noted, directed Clifford to prepare a report on Soviet adherence to every agreement made since 1941 and on how Russian policy affected American security.[78]

Clifford circularized the senior civilian and military officials. But he had already decided that the memorandum should "point out what appeasement had led to" and show that the Russians sought "aggrandizement" from the outset. Remarkably, nearly uniform "worst case" assessments rolled in from Leahy, Patterson, Forrestal, Chief of Naval Operations Admiral Chester Nimitz, the JCS, and key diplomatic and intelligence officials. All assumed, as per Kennan's Long Telegram, that Soviet policy was motivated by Russian imperialism, fear and loathing of the West, and Communist belief in inevitable war with the capitalist states. Thus the Russians sought to maintain permanent war footing, to build an air force and atomic weapons to be able to "carry aggression" anywhere in the world, and to extend their power and influence around the globe. The Russians' claim to $10 billion in German reparations (and taking of current production) repudiated the spirit of Potsdam and kept Germany economically divided. Their aggression in Iran and effort to make Turkey a "satellite" jeopardized U.S. influence and oil throughout the Middle East. And the Soviets also aimed to discredit America's China policy and its "national security" rationale for seeking Atlantic and Pacific air bases.[79]

Acheson and the State Department, listing every post-1941 accord, said that the Soviets did not violate their letter but transgressed their "spirit" and interpreted them differently to gain their global ends. Further, the JCS said that the Russians, or their agents, sought to "capture" the U.S. labor movement, to promote unrest in the military by agitating for desegregation, and to prepare for industrial sabotage in event of war—and revolutionary upheaval in the long run. Thus, as Leahy concluded, the U.S. had to continue to develop new weapons, establish "outlying" bases and military agreements with every Western Hemisphere nation, strengthen countries it wished to keep out of the Soviet sphere, prevent Communist infiltration of American institutions, and assume that the only deterrent the "Soviet mentality" understood was "force." This meant that the U.S. had to be ready to use bacteriological and atomic warfare.[80]

Clifford and Elsey (the latter wrote most of the report) combined these dire assessments with the Kennan cable emphasis on the Kremlin's "neurotic" worldview to produce the eighty-two-page "Russian Report" that Clifford gave to the president on September 24. Although Clifford's cover letter said that U.S. officials' grave view of Soviet-American relations augured well for an effort to improve them, the report virtually foreclosed every prospect. Kremlin leaders were "ignorant" of the rest of the world, "blinded" by Marxist dogma, and made only strategic accommodations—without abandoning their long-run commitment to revolution. The Russians sought to expand Communist influence in France and Italy, establish "puppet" regimes in Greece and Turkey, and ultimately dominate a centralized regime in Germany. They would also develop a strategic air force and atomic weapons to wage offensive war, undermine America's military, and capture its labor movement. Consequently, the U.S. had to recognize that the Soviets understood only military power and to devise a unified and global foreign policy, reject every disarmament or arms limitation proposal, and develop atomic and bacteriological warfare capability.[81]

As Melvyn Leffler has written, the Clifford Report made no effort to be objective or balanced. Despite Truman's being vague on every conference but Potsdam, the report provided no sketch of the complex diplomacy from 1942 through Yalta that might have provided some basis to attribute current conflicts to causes other than just Soviet aggression. There was no mention of Byrnes' contentious diplomacy at the Potsdam Conference that led the Soviets to charge that the U.S. had reneged on its Yalta commitment to $10 billion in reparations. Nor was there reference to Clay's belief that the Russians had honored their agreements in Germany and could be negotiated with, or that the Russians had allowed free elections in Hungary and Czechoslovakia and withdrawn their troops from northern Norway and Bornholm Island. There was no indication that Moscow had reason to fear a revived Germany or Japan and perhaps reason to seek assurances about control of the Straits to protect their vital regions, much as Britain held sway at Suez and the U.S. at Panama, and that they now intended to patrol the Mediterranean. Moreover, Moscow had allowed U.S. forces into Korea, hardly protested U.S. predominance in China, and acceded to it in Japan. Further, the report stressed, as had Kennan, that it was useless to negotiate with the Russians. They understood only "military" power and could be moved only when they were persuaded it would be to their detriment not to act according to the U.S. conception of a proper world order. In sum, Truman had told his aides that the Russians understood only an iron fist and that he was tired of "being pushed." In turn, as Clifford recalled, they prepared a report calling for a new policy in the kind of language that Truman liked: "black and white."[82]

At this same time Leahy, looking to root the report's apocalyptic views in history, gave both Truman and Clifford copies of the alleged "political testament," or "will," of Peter the Great, in which the tsar exhorted the Russian nation to maintain constant war footing; to insinuate itself into the affairs of the Baltic, German, and Polish states; to vanquish Persia and Turkey and press on India; and finally, to use its Baltic and Black Sea bases—and "Asiatic hordes"—to conquer Europe.[83]

Not surprisingly, Truman found the Russian Report so "hot" that he immediately ordered Clifford to lock all twenty copies in the president's office safe. This was done presumably to prevent leaks, such as that the U.S. saw no reason to negotiate with the Soviets and thought it necessary to prepare for atomic and biological warfare, that might embarrass the U.S. or worsen American-Soviet relations. But merely because the report remained under lock and key did not mean that it did not express a powerful consensus in the administration as well as confirm Truman's belief that the Russians responded only to divisions. Equally important, if not astonishing, was the acceptance, without one question, of the veracity of Peter the Great's "will." In fact, the document was an historic eighteenth-century forgery drawn by anti-Russian French officials and Polish émigrés. But Truman took the will at face value and shortly wrote that he saw no difference between Molotov's government and that of the tsars (or Hitler's, he added). Then in 1948 Truman would rejoin a mild criticism of U.S. policy that Russian leaders "have fixed ideas and these ideas were set out by Peter the Great in his will—I suggest that you read it." Soon informed of the forgery, Truman denied that the will had influenced policy, although his beliefs about the will and Russian policy remained fixed.[84]

Ironically, at the same time Clifford was readying his report, Nikolai Novikov, the charge in the Soviet Embassy in Washington, was preparing an analysis—perhaps custom ordered by Molotov—of U.S. foreign policy for the Kremlin. Novikov's long cable of September 27 cited Truman and Byrnes as representing the triumph of the "most reactionary circles" in the Democratic Party over the more liberal FDR-Wallace wing. The Russian emissary called attention to increased U.S. military spending, the global search for bases, the movement of the battleship *Missouri* to Turkey, U.S. failure to demilitarize Germany, and its efforts to gain allies along Soviet borders and to dominate China and Japan. This was all part of a new "hard line"—including numerous calls for atomic war—intended to contain the Soviet Union and gain world supremacy.[85]

Novikov's analysis was clearly exaggerated. It misstated U.S. policy, much as the Clifford Report did with respect to the USSR, and it may well have been deliberately designed to provide Molotov and others with a document that they could use to press for increased toughness on the part of the Soviets. But it also provides insight into the way in which Soviet leaders, for all of their bravado and ostensible belief that the Marxist dialectic, or history, was on their side, may have felt threatened by the unrivaled atomic, air, and naval power of the

U.S. So too may the Russians have balked at the manner in which American officials tended to state that their military and economic master cards, and need to protect U.S. national security, allowed them to establish their interests and shape the outcome of every conflict around the globe, often without much deference to Russian historical or security concerns. In effect, by fall 1946 both American and Soviet leaders viewed one another and the world scene through a glass darkly.[86]

VI

Much as the Truman administration might have preferred not to negotiate with the Russians in 1946, Byrnes and the CFM had returned to Paris in late July to facilitate the twenty-one-nation peace conference's drafting of treaties for Germany's former satellites. During the next two months Yugoslavia's downing of two American planes, the Turkish "war scare," Byrnes' Stuttgart speech, and the Wallace affair overshadowed proceedings. But the diplomats' public sparring still made headlines, with Byrnes convinced that only by rousing the small nations and the press might he pry "jury room" agreement from the Russians. The secretary gained an initial procedural victory that allowed conference recommendations to pass by a simple majority instead of a two-thirds vote, despite Molotov's bitter insistence that earlier the CFM had agreed on two-thirds. Each side now accused the other of bloc voting, and when shortly Byrnes referred to the wartime generosity of Lend-Lease, Russian delegate Andrei Vishinsky retorted that the U.S. sought to dominate the world by "hand-outs." This drew applause from two Czech delegates. Byrnes in turn had the State Department cancel the remaining $40 million of a projected $50 million surplus property credit for Czechoslovakia and suspended its application for a $50 million Export-Import Bank loan.[87]

Despite the verbal warfare, the delegates finished their treaty work in early October, passing fifty-four recommendations by two-thirds and forty-one by a majority vote. Trieste would become a Free City; Italy would pay reparations to Russia and Yugoslavia in the amount of $100 million each, and to Greece, $105 million. Every treaty would contain a nominal clause about nondiscriminatory trade and equal commercial opportunity, and another conference would consider an agency for Danube traffic. Byrnes' radio report minimized American-Soviet differences, and Truman's October 23 address at the opening session of the UN stressed the obligation of the Big Five Security Council members to reach agreements that would preserve peace for a war-weary world. Stalin and Molotov made similar moderate public statements.[88]

But when the CFM convened on November 4 to prepare the final draft

treaties, Molotov retaliated for Byrnes' procedural victory by pressing countless amendments to the Trieste and Italo-Yugoslav settlements. Afterwards
Byrnes claimed that he ended the deadlock in late November by threatening a
publicized break in negotiations, but the diplomatic records suggest that accord
came from minor trade-offs on the Italo-Yugoslav reparations and boundary
settlements. By December 6 the CFM concluded the Finnish, Italian, and Balkan treaties, which the signatory states ratified in early 1947.[89]

The Americans and Russians had compromised. Each power dominated its
sphere. The Balkan treaties ended the tripartite Control Councils, with Russian
troops to remain in that region until conclusion of the German and Austrian
treaties. Russia also regained Bessarabia from Rumania and reestablished its
more secure 1940 boundary with Finland, and kept its troops there. In short,
Soviet borders now approximated those of 1917 imperial Russia, while the U.S.
asserted its predominance over Italy, whose reparations payments and territorial losses were minimal, and denied the Russians a Mediterranean base. But as
the prescient journalist Walter Lippmann wrote in December 1946, the Truman
administration's unprecedented decision to begin the treaty making with the
satellites of the former principal enemy was "a gigantic blunder" because the
Russians felt most challenged in Eastern Europe, yet their position of strength
there allowed them to be most tenacious and brutal. Further, the year's bitter
diplomacy brought no treaty for Germany, which was the core of the European
problem and where the West was strongest.[90]

Nonetheless, Truman could claim some diplomatic advance, and Byrnes
could resign with honor. The president and secretary were always an uneasy
pair, the more so since Truman's reproaches after the Moscow Conference.
Then in April 1946 Byrnes got a medical report indicating heart damage, and
he resigned privately as of July 1, by when he hoped to finish the peace treaties.
A second medical opinion gave him a new lease on his job, although he threatened to resign during the Wallace imbroglio. On December 19 Byrnes again offered to resign, perhaps with slight hope that Truman would ask him to stay.
But the wily president offered regrets only and then feigned seeking advice
about a successor. In fact, six months earlier he had arranged to appoint General George C. Marshall at first opportunity. Byrnes would leave in early January 1947.[91]

Truman's charge two years later that Byrnes "ran out on me . . . when I
needed him worst" did not derive from their division over foreign policy but
from their post-1946 split over domestic politics. Nonetheless, the president
had never acknowledged that Byrnes had served him well, although only weeks
after Byrnes left office Truman proposed that he should rebut Republican critics with a "hard-boiled" foreign policy speech at a "little school" in Fulton,

Missouri. But this reflected less the president's desire to afford Churchillian stature to Byrnes than recognition of the ironic fact that as the secretary departed office to accolades—*Time*'s "Man of the Year" for 1946—Truman's public esteem was at a new low.[92]

The president had presided, not very skillfully, over an extraordinarily difficult year of demobilization and reconversion marked by historic labor-management confrontations and fierce wage–price control battles. In the spring, Truman had fantasized about court-martialing American labor leaders and dropping an atomic bomb on Stalin. In October, after livestock raisers had created a meat "famine" and forced Truman to end all controls, the president penned another of his acerbic, and undelivered, addresses castigating the citizenry for abandoning both American principles and their president for "a mess of pottage, a piece of beef"—and he said that he "quit."[93]

Then came the bitter congressional campaigns and November elections. The president shied from making a speech while the Republicans assailed Democratic liberalism and failure to stem Communism at home or abroad, and made "To err is Truman" a catchphrase. The Republicans' smashing victory— they gained control of both houses of Congress for the first time since 1928— reflected current discontents as well as the ongoing decline of FDR's New Deal coalition. But Truman bore the brunt of criticism for lackluster leadership. Indeed, on election day Democratic senator J. William Fulbright of Arkansas proposed that if the Democrats lost, Truman should appoint a Republican secretary of state and then resign the presidency in his favor. Truman, of course, was never given to resigning, except in undelivered addresses, but he had long since committed to a new secretary of state who had greater public stature than he did but harbored no political ambition. His appointment signaled a near end to diplomacy with the Russians.[94]

In Behalf of Europe

The Truman Doctrine, 1947–1952

The events of 1947, especially the Truman Doctrine and Marshall Plan—"two halves of the same walnut," the president said—heralded a new American foreign policy. For some historians, this policy represented aggressive global containment of the Soviet Union and Communism and direct intervention in other nations' internal politics. Others have insisted that the administration chiefly sought to protect U.S. national interests against real or perceived threats from the Soviet Union, while still others have contended that the U.S. sought only to reestablish a traditional balance of power in Europe as a basis to negotiate with the Russians. Regardless of judgment, from the president's perspective, the Truman Doctrine in particular marked "the beginning of his own foreign policy," and in his *Memoirs* he called it "the turning point in America's foreign policy, which now declared that wherever aggression threatened the peace, the security of the United States was involved."[1]

The president seemed on the defensive in early 1947. Returned to the White House after a New Year's Eve cruise on the Potomac, he felt more "lonesome" than ever. He promptly telephoned his family in Missouri and sixteen past and present Cabinet officers and politicians, including Republicans Arthur Vandenberg, now president pro tempore of the Senate and chairman of the Foreign Relations Committee, and Joseph Martin, Jr., of Massachusetts, the new Speaker of the House. From the latter two Truman sought, to no avail, prior assurance about his forthcoming State of the Union address, which blandly noted his acceptance of the Eastern European treaties and American-Soviet mutual interest in peace. Shortly, the president's proposed fiscal year 1948 budget of $37.5 billion, including $11.2 billion for national defense, drew congressional criticism for failure to reduce spending enough. Meanwhile, Cabinet and military officials remained mired in their long ongoing debate over military unification.[2]

At the same time, the British government began to make public its desperate financial straits, while the nation confronted drastic food and fuel shortages, factory shutdowns, escalating unemployment, and bitter blizzards. Conditions on the Continent were more bleak.[3]

Winds of change were blowing, especially since the Russian Report of September 1946 had affirmed the Truman administration's consensus that the Kremlin's foreign policy was aggressive, expansionistic, and unlimited. As Lord Inverchapel wrote from Washington in early 1947, the Americans had abandoned their "one-world" outlook. Now they judged all events by their effect on U.S. and Soviet policies and were ready to assert world power. Further, with Wallace gone from the Cabinet, and General Marshall replacing Byrnes as secretary of state, there would be little dispute over policy. And once Truman made a decision, there would be "no deviation."[4]

The president was ecstatic at his appointment of Marshall, an austere man of Victorian morals who harbored no political ambition. He was born and raised in Uniontown, Pennsylvania, but had Virginia family roots that ran back to Chief Justice John Marshall. George Marshall attended Virginia Military Academy and served as an aide in World War I to General John J. "Blackjack" Pershing, Truman's hero. As chief of staff of the army in World War II, Marshall had earned from Winston Churchill the accolade "the true organizer of victory." When the general retired from his post in November 1945, Truman proclaimed him "the greatest military man" in American history. The president became even more enamored when Marshall, who had barely returned to his Virginia home, immediately agreed to his request—upon Patrick J. Hurley's politically charged resignation as ambassador to China in November 1945—to undertake a mission to attempt to reconcile the ruling Guomindang regime and the Communists. "What I like about Marshall," Truman said, "is he's a man."[5]

The general's thirteen-month mission to China ultimately failed, but his joining Truman's Cabinet in January 1947 overshadowed Byrnes' departure. A grateful president announced that Marshall would have a "free hand" at the State Department, where his formal staff organization and procedures—distinct from Byrnes' freelancing—gave senior subordinates, especially Under Secretary Acheson, greater responsibility and influence through their committee structures, position papers, and briefings. Moreover, Marshall's near legendary reputation and nonpolitical status meant that he would neither rival Truman for the presidential nomination in 1948 nor be a target for Republican partisan attack. "The more I see and talk to him the more certain I am he's the great one of the age," Truman wrote even before Marshall had acted; "I am surely lucky to have his friendship and support."[6]

I

The president's luck seemed to be improving. Initially the Republican-controlled Eightieth Congress sought to slash his $37.5 billion budget by $6 billion, but strong statements by Marshall, Secretary of War Patterson, and Secretary of the Navy Forrestal that the cuts would wreak havoc with defense and occupation policies in Europe helped to effect a $3 billion compromise reduction. Then came the battle over military unification.[7]

From the formation of the United States until 1947, the secretaries of war and of the navy were Cabinet officials who reported to the president in his capacity as chief executive and commander in chief. But otherwise the war and navy secretaries and their departments and respective army and navy service branches had no common superior, operated independently of one another, curried powerful allies in Congress, and were fierce rivals for appropriations and resources. In 1903 the war and navy secretaries established the Joint Army and Navy Board to effect cooperation between the services and added a Joint Planning Committee in 1919. Both the war and navy secretaries traditionally opposed unification of the services, however, and little was done to achieve this except for a failed congressional effort in 1932.[8]

In 1939 President Roosevelt took direct control of the Joint Board, which evolved into the Joint Chiefs of Staff in late 1941. During the war the JCS served as the U.S. representative to the Anglo-American Combined Chiefs of Staff and as the supreme command and planning body for all U.S. forces. But the JCS operated on the principle of unanimity, which meant that each of the five member generals and admirals had a veto. Moreover, while FDR's military chief of staff, Admiral Leahy, presided over the JCS, he did so as the senior military officer, not as adviser to the president. Further, when FDR discussed grand strategy with the JCS, the war and navy secretaries were rarely included, nor did they receive JCS papers. In effect, except for the president's oversight, the JCS operated without civilian control.[9]

Marshall broke with the War Department's long-standing opposition to military unification in 1943 when he submitted to the JCS a proposal for a "Single Department of Defense in the Post-War Period." But that led only to creation of another committee in May 1944 under retired admiral James O. Richardson, former commander of the Pacific Fleet, to study this complex problem. At the same time, a House Select Committee on Postwar Military Policy held hearings on unification but concluded in June 1944 that the time was inappropriate to reach any decision. Then on April 11, 1945—the day before the death of Roosevelt, who had offered no advice on unification—the Richardson Committee called for establishment of a secretary of the armed forces to preside over a single military department. But the secretary would deal with political-economic issues while a technically subordinate commander of the armed forces, who would also be chief of staff to the president, would command the military heads of the service branches.[10]

President Truman was quick to identify military unification as a major political issue. Ever since his wartime Senate committee investigation of military expenditures, he had favored unifying the armed forces under a single defense department with one administrative head. This would not only make planning, procurement, and operations more effective, he told Forrestal in June 1945, but foster universal military training, the president's somewhat idyllic version of a citizen-soldier-officer reserve that he believed would eliminate the "political cliques" that ran the army and navy and lessen the influence of those "finishing schools" for specialists, West Point and Annapolis. At Potsdam in July Truman told Forrestal that he intended to present legislation to Congress that would "wrap the entire question . . . into one package."[11]

Similarly, General Marshall still sought to unify the armed services. He supported a War Department plan—a composite of his 1943 initiative and the Richardson Committee plan—to have one civilian Cabinet-level secretary of the armed forces preside over a Department of the Armed Forces. The secretary would have his own chief of staff who would be his principal military adviser and command the military heads of the army, navy, and a separate air force. There would also be a Combined Chiefs of Staff (formerly JCS) who would make recommendations to the president through the secretary. This plan preserved the separate status of the army and navy, enlarged the JCS, and let the navy keep its air wing and marines. The Truman-Marshall approach presumed to be more economical and efficient than the current system of independent and extremely competitive services.[12]

But the Navy Department and the admirals balked. Forrestal insisted that the job envisioned for a single defense secretary was too big and that the service chiefs' autonomy would be too restricted. He also strongly preferred to expand the political and military influence of his office and the navy, perhaps by creating the equivalent of the British War Cabinet. Thus he used Truman's expressed interest in Cabinet efficiency in July 1945 to commission Ferdinand Eberstadt, a friend, former Wall Street associate, and vice chairman of the War Production Board, to draft an organization to protect U.S. "national security."[13]

The Eberstadt Report of September 1945 proposed to retain the War and Navy Departments and add a Cabinet-level Department of Air. Most significant, the report called for a new National Security Council (or Council of Defense) to formulate and coordinate political and military policies. The president would preside over that body, which would include the secretaries of state, war, navy, and air. The report also advanced a new National Security Resources Board to oversee industrial preparedness, an updated version of the wartime munitions board, a new Central Intelligence Agency, and retention by law of the JCS. The Eberstadt-Forrestal approach differed critically from that of Truman and Marshall. It sought to promote a permanent program of preparedness by mobilizing the nation's resources and every branch of civil and military government to protect or expand America's global interests. Hence, while there would be no single defense secretary or defense department, nor a unified military, the politico-military roles of the army, navy, and air force and their secretaries would be expanded to include coordination of defense policy. Further, the president would have to sit and formulate policy and make decisions with a National Security Council composed mainly of military chieftains, who would wield great influence. The military would also dominate the resources and munitions boards. In effect, the Eberstadt Report gave enormous power to the military departments and emphasized total organization for total war.[14]

Truman was reluctant about this design, and his White House staff, including Clifford (then his naval aide) and Elsey, were concerned that the president's constitutional authority, and the principle of civilian leadership, would be eroded by his collective deliberations—tantamount to decision making—in the presence of so many military chiefs on the National Security Council and the resources and munitions boards. Still, Clifford and Elsey, both navy people, were sympathetic to Forrestal's concerns and urged Samuel Rosenman, the president's speech writer, to include a national security body in the draft message he was preparing for Truman, who was determined to press military unification. But at a White House meeting on November 21 with Forrestal; Senator David Walsh of Massachusetts, chairman of the Senate Naval Affairs Committee; and Congressman Carl Vinson of Georgia, the extremely powerful chairman of the House Naval Affairs Committee and known as "Admiral," Truman could not win their support for a bill to unify the armed services. He also allowed Forrestal and the navy to continue to state their views.[15]

Consequently, the president decided to move forward on the basis of a plan drawn by Secretary of War Robert Patterson. On December 19 Truman proposed to Congress to establish an executive branch department of national defense with a Cabinet-level secretary and three assistant secretaries to head army, navy, and air force; and one chief of staff who, along with the commanders of the three service branches, would advise the president and the secretary. Truman also conceded that the navy could retain its own aviation wing and maintain the Marine Corps. He talked about correlating manpower and raw materials with military needs, peacetime industrial mobilization planning, scientific research for military purposes, and dissemination of Intelligence Service information. But he did not mention a National Security Council or resources or munitions boards.[16]

Clifford later said that Truman's recommendations "never had a chance" because the navy and Vinson were dead set against them. Vinson likened centralization to German and Japanese militarism. Forrestal said that the proposals were "completely unworkable" and neither he nor navy officials would testify in their favor. Navy officers were publicly critical of Truman's plan, and Forrestal and his aides successfully testified to the Naval Affairs Committee against an alleged army takeover of the navy. Opponents of unification also skillfully contended that centralization through a powerful defense secretary and military chief of staff would not bring efficiency but would threaten democratic principles and civilian leadership, especially the president's. At a White House meeting in mid-May with civilian and military leaders Admiral Leahy said he viewed a single military chief as "dangerous" and that during the war, when he was FDR's chief of staff, he could have augmented his power had he so desired. The president promptly gave way on the chief-of-staff concept as "dangerous" and suffering from too much "man on horseback" philosophy. But despite this concession and his having opened the meeting by bluntly stating that interservice rivalry was preventing an integrated military budget and balanced defense system, Truman was reduced to a supplicant pleading with the War and Navy Departments to reach agreement by the end of the month.[17]

No accord was forthcoming, although in a letter of May 31 Patterson and Forrestal outlined their eight points of agreement. This included security and resources boards and an intelligence agency. But Patterson remained adamant about a Cabinet-level secretary heading a defense department, while Forrestal persisted on strong service secretaries with Cabinet rank and clearly defined roles for them and their service branches, with defense downsized to a presidential deputy presiding over an office. Truman tried to gain a strong defense secretary by conceding that the services could retain their autonomy subject to defense's overall control. He agreed as well to support a National Security Council and resources board that, by definition, would be dominated by officials from the military establishment. This despite the fact that White House staff, Budget Director Harold Smith, and Treasury Department officials warned that the military and their thinking were coming to predominate over civilian government and democratic traditions. Then on June 15 Truman publicly restated his position to the chairmen of the House and Senate Naval Affairs Committees and to Patterson and Forrestal. Patterson was amenable to the president's compromise. But Forrestal reiterated the navy's misgivings over the army's "mass play–steam roller tactics" and hinted that major disagreement would bring his resignation. The deadlock continued, and even General Douglas MacArthur opined that perhaps Truman should fire a high-ranking official to halt the "sabotage" of his policies.[18]

At another White House meeting with key aides and military officials on September 10, Truman said it was a "fact of life" that the army and navy had agreed on eight points, that he intended to have a bill drawn that would become "the doctrine of his administration," and he expected everyone to support it. Forrestal balked again at testifying in favor of the legislation the president favored, and he offered to resign. Truman again said this was unnecessary. Then over the next three months Forrestal and his aides lobbied against unification while interservice bitterness greatly intensified. Finally, after a Cabinet meeting in early January 1947, Patterson and Forrestal concluded that it was necessary to reach accord and halt the escalating acrimony. Truman offered more compromises to the navy and soon announced that the armed services had agreed on a unification plan.[19]

The president sent his draft legislation to Congress in late February. After five months of hearings Congress passed the National Security Act on July 26, 1947, modeled closely on the Eberstadt Report. Truman had gained his way with regard to a secretary of defense. But unlike other Cabinet officers, the secretary would not preside over a department, only an office, or "National Military Establishment" (NME), and would exercise only general authority or control over the service departments and other defense establishment agencies. The legislation also created a statutory Joint Chiefs of Staff—without a single head—and the Departments of the Army, the Navy, and the Air Force. The navy retained its full aviation functions and the Marine Corps, with few limits on its size or operations, despite the real desire of Truman, Marshall, and Eisenhower to eliminate or constrict it. As Senator Millard Tydings of Maryland told Clifford, the marines were "the boys who took Mt. Suribachi," while Truman would later complain—when the marines were seeking, and eventually would gain, a seat on the JCS—that they had a propaganda machine "almost equal to Stalin's."[20]

The National Security Act also created the National Security Council (NSC), a smaller War Council, the National Security Resources Board (NSRB), and the Central Intelligence Agency (CIA)—all of which Marshall had urged Truman to scrap even before he submitted his draft legislation because these agencies gave the military excessive influence over foreign policy matters and infringed the constitutional authority of the president and secretary of state. Moreover, the State Department was barely consulted regarding the NSC, owing partly to Truman's low regard for the "striped pants boys." Meanwhile, Congress made the president, against Truman's will, a statutory member of the NSC, although it allowed him to choose its executive director. Truman elected Admiral Sidney Souers—a prominent Missouri businessman known to him and Clifford—who had worked in wartime naval intelligence and then headed the newly created Central Intelligence Group in 1946.[21]

At his first NSC meeting in September 1947, Truman stated that the NSC was to be *"his"* council—i.e., advisory only—and that he would not tolerate "prima donna" behavior. Thereafter, he met with the NSC at only twelve of its next fifty-seven meetings, keeping it at arm's length until the Korean War. As for the CIA, the memory of Pearl Harbor made its creation almost inevitable. But over strong objection, including Truman's public concern about creating "a Gestapo" or "military dictatorship," the agency was allowed both to collect and evaluate information, to obtain—with written permission—records from the AEC and FBI, and to have a military person as its director. Finally, Truman never made progress with his universal military training, which he naively hoped would be a hedge against the pitfalls of America's new military-national security establishment.[22]

The National Security Act of 1947 established the modern mechanisms of the national security state, as Michael Hogan has written. If there were compromises, they were on Forrestal's terms, and it was he who Truman soon appointed the first secretary of defense. The legislation provided neither unification nor economy. Creation of an independent air force, in Hogan's words, meant "triplification, not unification" of services and increased expenditures. The legislation also gave autonomy to the armed services and institutionalized the NME, and later both the NSC and CIA, as rivals to the secretary of state and his department. To be sure, the NSC and CIA did not create Truman's feared "Gestapo" or military dictatorship. But together they gave the military pervasive and profound influence from preparation to execution of foreign policy, for both overt and covert activities. As Clifford would later reflect, "covert activities became a self-sustaining part of American foreign operations," and the CIA "became a government within a government, which could evade oversight of its activities by drawing the cloak of secrecy around itself.[23]

Finally, as one British diplomat noted in February 1947, even those who favored the toughest policy toward Russia felt embarrassed that movement of the State Department at this time into the old War Department building at Foggy Bottom (War Department having vacated to the Pentagon) meant that henceforth Secretary of State General Marshall would receive Russian diplomats amid a "massive panorama" of murals of "soldiers, bald eagles, four-engine bombers, and oversized cannon." Perhaps this was fitting symbolism for the national-security-state consensus that was now firmly in place and the increasing need Truman and others saw to intervene in conflicts around the globe.[24]

II

Neither the president nor his advisers expected military confrontation with the Russians in 1947 or for years to come. Reports from many officials, including General Eisenhower, said that the state of their nation and economy were appalling and they lacked the necessary long-range or powerful weapons to fight effectively against the U.S. But Truman believed that since Potsdam he had made repeated concessions to the Russians, only to discover that "there is no way to please them." They negotiated from day to day, always bringing new demands, and then broke every agreement. By early 1947 Truman was anxious to declare that diplomacy was at an end and that the Soviet-American contest would determine whether freedom or totalitarianism would prevail throughout the world. Britain's decision to halt aid to Greece and Turkey provided the necessary "crisis."[25]

As Greece was liberated from German occupation in October 1944, the British restored the extremely conservative monarchist government-in-exile in Egypt of Prime Minister George Papandreou. Meanwhile, Churchill went to Moscow and entered into his famous Balkan "percentages" agreement with Stalin that recognized Britain's sphere of control in Greece and Russia's control in Rumania. Wartime resistance to the Nazis in Greece, however, had come chiefly from the National Liberation Front (EAM) and its National Popular Liberation Army (ELAS). The Communists (KKE) had been the original organizers of EAM and predominated in its leadership. But by 1944 EAM had developed into a broadly based leftist-republican coalition (it claimed a membership of 1.5 million people, about 20 percent of the population) with a radical populist program. ELAS was a strong guerilla army that controlled most of the country, including the areas around Athens and Salonika. EAM-ELAS also adamantly resisted reversion to the prewar social order governed by General John Metaxas' fascist dictatorship of 1936–1941, in which urban elites had dominated the nation's political machinery and economic resources. The other resistance force in Greece was the small and conservative National Republican League (EDES), which the British supported. Beginning in 1943, however, EDES and EAM-ELAS began to fight one another over postwar control, although a truce ended this "first round" of civil war in February 1944.[26]

Churchill then pressed Papandreou's National Unity government to give EAM a role in its coalition. EAM leaders, divided over whether to choose a revolutionary course or conventional politics, ultimately accepted a government role in August 1944. EAM refused to disarm ELAS, however, unless royalist forces returning from abroad (which the British intended to make the core of a new national army) put down their guns. This led to political confrontation in Athens in early December 1944 and a brief but bitter "second round" of civil war. Churchill pledged "no peace without victory" and ordered British troops from Italy to crush ELAS. The British then imposed an armistice and disarmament upon EAM-ELAS in February 1945 in exchange for promises of political liberties. But the so-called Varkiza Agreement brought no peace.[27]

The primary responsibility for bloodshed through 1945 belonged to right-wing forces, who alleged prior left-wing atrocities. But as ELAS forces withdrew from Athens in February, they dragged along several thousand hostages; some died, and others were severely mistreated. There was also discovery of a mass grave outside Athens where ELAS had executed several hundred prisoners during the winter fighting. This led the government and rightist-royalist factions to inflict increasing terror upon EAM-ELAS and its sympathizers across the country. Then in March 1946 the government, under strong Anglo-American pressure, held parliamentary elections despite the protests of many—including several government ministers—that conditions were too chaotic. Leftists and republicans boycotted the voting. This led to installation of an even more rightist regime under Prime Minister Constantine Tsaldaris and increased terror. Then a government plebiscite in September recalled King George II—symbol of Metaxas' repressive ancien régime—to the Greek throne from his exile in London.[28]

Greek politics had reached a new divide. Most historians now believe that until this time the KKE had opted for a program of legality and national unity and might have stayed with this course, as did the Communists in Italy and France. But many KKE members now felt excluded from the electoral system and increasingly repressed. Thus they demanded more militant action. Hence, as Communists and other EAM members took to the mountains in spring and summer 1946, they sought to secure weapons, supplies, training, staging areas, and sanctuaries in neighboring Balkan states, chiefly Yugoslavia but also Albania and Bulgaria. By fall the rebels had also created a Democratic Army led by a Communist, Markos Vafiades, that was initially intended to pressure the government rather than effect a revolution.[29]

Significantly, Stalin held to his policy and his 1944 accord with Churchill to leave Greece to British control. The Soviet leader provided neither direction nor material aid for the Greek rebels. Ambassador Lincoln MacVeagh—who kept tabs on these matters—reported to Washington in March 1945 that the Greek Left "had waited in vain for Russia to support them in their revolt" of that winter. Further, Russian records now reveal that EAM and KKE leaders who went to Moscow in January 1945 could not even get an audience with Stalin or Molotov.[30]

So too did the Russians balk at a meeting in January 1946, while they also made clear that they wanted the KKE to participate in the 1946 elections. Moreover, while the Soviets proposed to provide the rebel forces with some money and light weapons, they gave no assurance about large-scale aid from Moscow or the Balkan States. Even in late December 1946 the Soviets indicated that the gathering Democratic Army would not be able to count on aid from Yugoslavia. Thus it was not until late May 1947—after the U.S. had formally committed to Greek military aid—that Stalin received Nikos Zacharaides, head of the KKE, and agreed to provide war material. Then in June, Moscow negotiated terms with Belgrade to provide heavy weapons and ammunition for the Democratic Army, although the Russians questioned whether Yugoslavia would be able to supply this from their own stocks. In effect, Stalin was not moved to supply aid to the KKE until after passage of the Truman Doctrine, which threatened Russia in the south. Perhaps the Soviet leader also felt need to show that he was as good a revolutionary as Tito. But even at that, the Soviet commitment would not last long.[31]

Nonetheless, by mid-1946 the "third round" of the Greek civil war had already gotten under way. From the onset of civil war in Greece, U.S. officials were persistent—regardless of lack of evidence—that EAM-ELAS was directed by Communists directed by Moscow. These officials feared that either British heavy-handedness or total withdrawal, or the Greek government's refusal to reform its repressive domestic policies, would further polarize Greece's political-economic life. They worried as well that the government's "Greater Greece" territorial claims against Albania and Bulgaria, and disputes with Yugoslavia, might precipitate a Balkan war. The resulting chaos would lead the Greek people to seek stability, Ambassador MacVeagh warned in January 1946, through an authoritarian regime backed by a "violent police and pliant army." But such a government would inevitably bow to a "dictatorship of the left" and subject Greece, standing at the "historical cross-roads of empire," to Russian domination.[32]

In the aftermath of World War II, however, U.S. officials had provided Greece with little more than advice. They viewed its request in August 1945 for a $250 million loan as excessive, and in January 1946 arranged only a $25 million Export-Import Bank credit that came with a Truman-approved note urging extensive reform. As MacVeagh reported from Athens seven months later, the government's "extremist policy" of branding everyone except royalists as Communists, and consorting with former Metaxists and Nazi collaborators, only made more enemies than friends. At the same time, Truman said no to a

Greek mission's request for a large credit. He told his visitors that aid and reform were "a two-way proposition."[33]

Truman's cautious policy shifted dramatically when he and his advisers
firmly opposed Moscow's August 1946 note to Turkey proposing to share in
governance and defense of the Straits. The Americans, as noted earlier, viewed
this as a Soviet pretext to make Turkey a "satellite" and to dominate the Eastern Mediterranean. Now Greece was raised to the same level of strategic importance as Turkey. But whereas previously Churchill and then Bevin had
maintained a strong British military and financial presence in Greece, now
Prime Minister Attlee and the treasury were insistent that economic constraints
compelled disengagement. Shortly thereafter, one-half of Britain's thirty thousand troops were withdrawn. Then in late September Byrnes insisted that
U.S. aid had to replace that of the British, and Forrestal and Patterson strongly
backed this view.[34]

In October Byrnes approved a Loy Henderson memorandum that articulated the new policy perspective that Greece had become the "focal point" of
strained international relations that would determine the fate of the Near and
Middle East. In short, the Soviet Union sought to use its Balkan "satellites" to
destroy the Greek government and establish hegemony there, encircle Turkey,
and dominate the Eastern Mediterranean, which was strategically and economically vital to U.S. security. Despite the Greek regime's failings, therefore,
the U.S. had to sell it weapons to maintain internal order as well as defense,
provide economic aid, and counsel reform. Byrnes soon approved sale of
weapons to Britain for transfer to Greece and asked MacVeagh for a "full list"
of Greek needs. As the secretary told Forrestal and Patterson, Greece and Turkey are "our outposts."[35]

When Prime Minister Tsaldaris visited Washington in January 1947, however, he enraged Byrnes by hinting publicly that a $6 billion loan was pending,
while Acheson judged Tsaldaris to be "obsessed" about resolving Greece's
problems by gaining Albanian and Bulgarian territory. When the prime minister complained that he had done all he could to reform Greek finances, Marshall, now secretary of state, retorted that Greek leaders lacked the "vision,
restraint, and patriotism" to form a "leftist, liberal, and center" coalition. Tsaldaris soon left office, but U.S. officials reported that Greece was about to
dissolve.[36]

In mid-February, Paul Porter, former head of the wartime Office of Price
Administration and now chief of a special economic mission to Greece, reported that Greece was virtually bankrupt. The government had spent half the
national income on nonproductive uses; corruption was rampant and the civil
service a "farce"; the wealthy escaped taxes; and the new prime minister, Dimi-

trios Maximos, was "inept," and his coalition was strictly rightist-conservative. "There really is no State here in the Western concept," Porter said, only a "loose hierarchy" of politicians who cared only about their own power struggles. Greece could be saved economically and politically, he hoped, but this would require the presence of Americans to provide "day by day guidance."[37]

Similarly, Mark Ethridge, now head of a UN Special Commission on the Balkans (UNSCOB) investigating Greece's charges of subversion by its Balkan neighbors, said that the Soviets were encouraging their satellites to foment "anarchy" in Greece, which the Russians saw as a "ripe plum ready to fall into their hands." "If Greece goes," so would the Middle East and Italy and France. Ethridge soon added "China and the Far East" to the "plums"—or dominoes—and urged a dramatic gesture, perhaps a Marshall visit. Meanwhile, MacVeagh confirmed that only the U.S. could prevent Greece's "imminent" collapse. Shortly Acheson's composite report to Marshall on February 21 insisted that Greece's "capitulation" to the Soviets meant loss of the Middle East and North Africa. He urged economic and military aid. The secretary immediately instructed him to "prepare the necessary steps" for economic and military aid.[38]

Later that same Friday afternoon, the Attlee government published its White Paper with its exceptionally bleak economic forecast for 1947, the "most disturbing statement ever made by a British government," the *Times* said. At the same time the British Embassy in Washington delivered two notes to the State Department (formal notice would be given to Marshall on February 24, after he had returned from his long weekend of travel), which cited the strategic importance of Greece and Turkey, stated that British aid would end on March 31, and asked the U.S. to step into the breach. Although Acheson later declared that the British notes were "shockers," U.S. officials were well aware of Britain's economic woes and recent announcements that it would be granting independence to Burma and India and referring its costly mandate over Palestine to the UN. Moreover, in the fall of 1946 former secretary Byrnes had begun the policy of supplying military aid to Iran and expressed interest in doing the same for Turkey.[39]

Further, Marshall had already asked Acheson to draw up plans for economic-military aid for Greece. Now the under secretary informed him and the president by telephone of the British notes and then put the State Department to work over the weekend to ready the necessary reports under the direction of Henderson, whose hostility toward the Soviets and Communism and advocacy of strong intervention in Greece and Turkey were well known. And when he asked Acheson whether they were working on the "making" or "execution" of a decision, the latter retorted "execution."[40]

State Department officials, as one recalled, were "openly elated" at the prospect of broad-scale U.S. action in the Middle East despite some concern that the British were exaggerating their plight. The State Department quickly resolved that the choice was to send aid to Greece and Turkey (although there was no crisis in the latter) or to face Soviet domination of the Middle East and "large parts" of Western Europe. Thus the Greeks were to be instructed to request aid. Meanwhile, as many arms as possible would be shipped under current law. There was also sentiment to address financial aid globally and to state the case to Congress in order to "electrify" the public.[41]

Acheson handed the recommendations to Marshall on February 24 with the comment that they represented "the most important major decision with which we have been faced since the war." The secretary then met with Lord Inverchapel to receive formal notice of Britain's decision. Marshall viewed this as "tantamount to British abdication from the Middle East, with obvious implications as to their successor." Two days later he met with SWNCC to secure Patterson's and Forrestal's support for the State Department's program for aid to Greece and Turkey. Marshall then took the papers to the president, who readily agreed but, fearful of the Republican Congress' budget cutting, insisted on privately informing House and Senate leaders.[42]

The president met "secretly" with leading members of Congress at the White House on February 27. Those present included Senator Vandenberg, chairman of the Foreign Relations Committee; ranking Democrat Tom Connally of Texas, the Speaker of the House; Joseph Martin of Massachusetts; and minority leader Sam Rayburn of Texas. Truman said little, although he later wrote that he made clear at the meeting's outset that he had decided to aid Greece and Turkey. His designated speaker was Marshall, who spoke almost apocalyptically: if the U.S. did not assume British burdens in Greece, that nation would dissolve in civil war. This would lead to Soviet domination there and in Turkey, and perhaps in "Europe, the Middle East, and Asia." But the secretary's dry style did not move the congressmen, who resisted increased spending and pulling "British chestnuts" from the fire.

Thus an eager Acheson, who recalled that "I knew we were met at Armageddon," quietly sought permission to speak. He made an impassioned recital that closely resembled the position he had taken in August 1946 over the Soviet note to Turkey. He argued that the last barrier to a Soviet breakthrough was Greece, and if it fell, "like apples in a barrel infected by a rotten one, the corruption of Greece would infect Iran and all the East." The infection would then spread to Africa, Asia Minor, and through France and Italy to all of Europe. Britain's power was gone, and only the U.S. could contest the Soviet Union. The world faced the greatest polarization of power since Athens and Sparta, and the choice was between American democracy and individual liberty or Soviet dictatorship and absolute conformity. Upon conclusion, Vandenberg said that if the president would say that to Congress and to the public, he—and probably most of his colleagues—would support him, although allegedly Henderson later recalled that the senator had told Truman that he had to address Congress personally and "scare hell out of the country."[43]

III

Truman left Acheson and Clifford to draft his speech. There was immediate and near unanimous agreement to emphasize global-ideological confrontation. At a SWNCC meeting the next day, Acheson reported on the accord just reached at the White House to supply money and arms to Greece, and said that Marshall believed that it was necessary to do everything possible to sustain the U.S. position in the Near East regardless of its consequences on the forthcoming CFM meeting in Moscow. Acheson also alluded to Vandenberg's advice to Truman to put the matter forcefully and apparently told his staff that Greek-Turkish aid was not "do-goodism" but "protecting our whole way of life." Meanwhile the U.S. persuaded the British to keep their troops in Greece past their stated March 31 deadline and provided the Greek government—which Acheson later referred to as a "semiconscious patient"—with draft copies of the request that it was expected to make for military and economic aid.[44]

Francis H. Russell, director of the State Department's Public Affairs Office, quickly drafted a "United States Policy Statement" that SWNCC approved on March 3. This public information statement emphasized "communism vs. democracy" and stated that there was a current world conflict between "two ways of life," one based on free institutions and the other based on oppression and imposition of the minority will on the majority. Accordingly, it was America's duty to support "free peoples who were resisting subjugation from armed minorities or outside forces" (a passage that would be repeated almost verbatim in Truman's speech). Russell gave the statement to Acheson, who discussed it with Marshall, and then asked Joseph Jones, a special assistant to the assistant secretary for public affairs, to put the text in the form of a speech to Congress. At the same time, Clifford and Forrestal agreed on the need to focus on the "central problem" of "which of the two systems currently offered the world is to survive." Vandenberg presumed that the Greek crisis was "symbolic of the world-wide ideological clash between Eastern Communism and Western Democracy."[45]

George Kennan, then assigned to the National War College but soon to head the State Department's Policy Planning Staff, reviewed Jones' first draft. Ken-

nan thought Greek economic aid was fine, but he opposed the "sweeping" language that might open the U.S. to endless requests from other nations. He disputed need for Turkish military aid, given that Russia's challenge was political.
He also doubted that the Soviets, even if Greece collapsed, could dominate the
Moslem Middle East. Acheson brushed aside these reservations.[46]

Similarly, White House aide Elsey said that no recent Russian action
justified such an "'All-out' speech"—the Greek situation was relatively "abstract"—and that it would destroy the CFM meeting. But Clifford rejoined that
the speech was intended to be "the opening gun" in a campaign to make the
American people realize that "the war isn't over by any means." Hence, even
when Marshall and his adviser, Charles Bohlen—then en route to Moscow—
criticized the speech's "flamboyant anti-Communism," they were told that the
president felt that this was essential to gain Congress' approval. Meanwhile,
Truman went off to give speeches in Mexico City on March 3 and at Baylor
University in Waco on March 6, in which he promoted the good-neighbor policy and fewer trade restrictions. He also stressed that political and economic relations were indivisible and that two world wars had shown that the U.S. could
never again be indifferent to events beyond its borders nor allow the "lawless-
ness" of any nation to threaten others. The British viewed this as the president's
way of rousing the public to conclude that the U.S. had to pluck the "torch of
world leadership from Britain's ailing hands."[47]

Truman reinforced the "All-out" approach on Greece at a Cabinet meeting
on March 7. He said that he confronted the most serious presidential "decision"
in history and had Acheson reiterate his view of Greece as the "key" to Soviet
efforts to encircle and dominate Europe and the Middle East. The president
then emphasized the profound implications of his action: "This is only the beginning. It means [the] U.S. going into European politics. It means the greatest
selling job ever facing a president."

Cabinet officials agreed unanimously that only one decision was possible.
They also conceded that $250 million in Greek aid was only a "finger in the
dike." According to Averell Harriman, now secretary of commerce, their real
task now would be to "rebuild the dike," i.e., take economic control of Greece.
Truman dismissed concern about the "conflict" between Greek aid and disen-
gaging in China: "Chiang-Kai shek will not fight it out," he said, but the Communists would. Hence aid to China would be "pouring sand in a rat hole." The
president's chief interest now was to have Secretary of the Treasury John Snyder head a Cabinet committee to mobilize business and labor leaders to get the
"facts" to the public about Greece."[48]

Three days later Truman promised his Cabinet and congressional leaders a
"very explicit" statement. In readying the final text, Clifford contrived the line

that the Greek government had requested American administrators in order to ensure efficient use of the money. He also reduced reference to the UN to a brief note that it was not yet able to provide major assistance. More important, Acheson excised three revealing references that may have spoken more to U.S. interest than the public focus on Communism and Greek society. Thus there was no mention of Greece's strategic relation to the Middle East or to that region's resources, nor was anything said about the administration's concern that there was in many nations a recent trend away from free enterprise toward state-directed economies. Finally, Jones asked Acheson whether the request to Congress was to be limited to money for Greece and Turkey or be left open to include other nations deemed at risk. The under secretary replied that "if FDR were alive" he would probably make a statement of "global policy" but limit his request for funds to Greece and Turkey. Acheson's draft legislation, however, was carefully framed to cover other countries if analogous situations developed.[49]

Significantly, Truman's speech said little or nothing about the complexity of the Greek civil war and the nature of the Greek and Turkish governments, and it did not state that more than two-thirds of the proposed aid would be for military purposes. There was no mention of the Soviet Union, lest it react violently, although it was the unspoken enemy. Clearly, the purpose of the speech was not to explicate national interest or security issues but to rouse the public to support "freedom" against "totalitarianism," which meant Communism. Thus a "frankly anti-Soviet policy," the British ambassador wrote, would be "metamorphosed" into a "crusade for democracy." He might also have said that the text and style fit the man who would deliver the speech.[50]

In his epoch-making address before a joint session of Congress on March 12, 1947, Truman said that Greece, ravaged by war, occupation, and "internal strife," had urgently appealed to the U.S. for financial and economic aid necessary to survive. The British could no longer help, and the UN was not ready. Only the U.S. could assist "democratic Greece," whose government was "not perfect," and where Right and Left had engaged in "extremist measures." Similarly, only the U.S. could provide Turkey with aid necessary to preserve its integrity, as well as "order" in the Middle East.

Truman acknowledged that supplying aid had great implications. But he insisted that just as the U.S. had fought to prevent Germany and Japan from coercing other nations, now America could not meet its long-term world peace and national security goals if it did not help free peoples resist the imposition of totalitarianism. "At the present moment in world history, nearly every nation must choose between alternative ways of life," he said, between majority will and free institutions, or forcibly imposed minority will, terror, and oppression.

America's duty was clear: "[I]t must be the policy of the United States to support free peoples who are resisting attempted subjugation by armed minorities or by outside pressures." Greece could not be allowed to fall to an "armed minority," for this would gravely affect Turkey, the Middle East, and probably Europe. He asked for $400 million in aid for Greece and Turkey and the right to detail civilian and military personnel to these countries. This was only a tiny fraction of America's World War II expenditures, he said, but equally essential to halt totalitarianism. "If we falter in our leadership," he concluded, the U.S. and world peace would be endangered.[51]

Congress' response was moderate, despite Acheson's recollection of a standing ovation, albeit for a "brave man" rather than the policy. Mainstream public response was generally supportive, but serious questions were raised about acting unilaterally and failing to consult the UN. Critics on the political Right bridled at a costly intervention or bailing out the British. Critics on the Left—including Wallace, now editor of *New Republic*—challenged giving aid to repressive governments or undertaking an anticommunist crusade. Truman, who left immediately after his speech for a Key West vacation, was greatly relieved to have made this "terrible decision," which he felt had been hanging over his head for six weeks. Perhaps fatigue added to his tendency to malign liberal critics of his speech. As he wrote to his daughter, Margaret, the next day, "[T]he attempt of Lenin, Trotsky, Stalin, et al., to fool the world and the American Crackpots Association, represented by Jos. Davies, Henry Wallace, and Claude Pepper and all the actors and artists in immoral Greenwich Village, is just like Hitler's and Mussolini's so-called socialist states." Two weeks later Truman would assail resistant congressmen as "ignorant demagogues."[52]

Just nine days after his speech Truman also signed Executive Order 9835. This order established the federal civilian Employee Loyalty Program and made "reasonable grounds" for belief that a person was "disloyal" the standard for refusal to hire individuals, or to dismiss current employees, in executive departments and agencies. The Civil Service Commission, which was to establish a Loyalty Review Board, would investigate all prospective employees, and each department or agency would create review boards to investigate its own current employees. Field investigations of employees suspected of disloyalty would be done by the Federal Bureau of Investigation, headed by its longtime and powerful director, J. Edgar Hoover, a virulent anticommunist who, as Clifford later said, "was very close to being an American fascist." Truman worried that if Hoover and the FBI got all that they wanted, they "will become an American Gestapo." But the FBI had more investigative resources and experience than any other agency, and Congress appropriated to it more than two-thirds of the investigatory funds. Finally, suspect employees would be subject to an administrative hearing (with final appeal to the Loyalty Review Board) but not have the right to know all the charges against them or to confront hostile witnesses.[53]

Truman's loyalty program derived from many sources. There was traditional American disdain for Communism and alleged subversives, as evidenced by the so-called Red Scare after World War I. There was considerable congressional investigation of "un-American" activities before World War II, and many claims afterwards—including by Hoover, who also leaked documents—about "Red Fascism" having invaded vital American institutions, including schools, churches, colleges, and the media. There was increasing concern about Soviet spying, especially after revelation of their atomic spy ring in Canada in February 1946, and the growing tension—real and rhetorical—of the Cold War. Finally, there was the Republican victory at the polls in November 1946, which led Truman to appoint Attorney General Tom Clark to head a Temporary Commission on Employee Loyalty with a view to preempting legislative action.[54]

Clark himself told his commission that even one disloyal person constituted a threat to U.S. national security. Similarly, the president—who had proposed to deport "disloyal inhabitants" in 1940—tended to dwell on issues of "loyalty," personal and political, and to assail liberal critics as a "sabotage front" for Stalin. Moreover, senior officials in the administration were not averse to seizing the anticommunist banner from the Republicans for political purposes. The consequence was expedient acceptance of the Clark commission's highly flawed program in March 1947 at the height of Truman Doctrine rhetoric about the struggle between free and Communist societies.[55]

Most significant, the Truman administration's unprecedented program confused the separate issues of security (a legitimate concern) and loyalty (a vague term that was left undefined and subject to highly diverse interpretations). The program also jettisoned basic legal procedural safeguards, virtually included a presumption of guilt, and did not distinguish between sensitive federal jobs, such as atomic scientist, and clerk or janitor in the Agriculture Department. Most unfortunate, many states emulated the federal loyalty program and ultimately denied jobs to countless numbers of people, such as professors whose work had nothing to do with national security and whose only crime was to hold views that did not conform to the reigning political orthodoxy. In sum, Executive Order 9835 opened the way to purges of large numbers of federal employees—including highly knowledgeable foreign service officers, especially Asian affairs specialists—that helped to set the stage for the later nihilistic anticommunist crusade of the likes of Joseph R. McCarthy, just elected to the Senate in November 1946. Not surprisingly, in March 1947 Britain's ambassador noted that the loyalty program was "further striking evidence" of how far American fear of Communism at home and abroad had progressed.[56]

Meanwhile, White House aides sought to blame "Communist sympathizers" for inspiring opposition to Greek-Turkish aid. They soon realized, however, that criticism came from a broad liberal-conservative spectrum concerned that the U.S. was bypassing the UN, setting a precedent for universal aid requests, playing a "reactionary" role in Europe by supporting the Greek and Turkish regimes, and solidifying East-West blocs. Even Vandenberg, now a firm supporter of the administration's program, complained that Truman had used the presidential tactic of not presenting the "crisis" until Congress' discretion was "pathetically limited" and it could only "declare war."[57]

Nonetheless, the power and prestige of Truman's office served his purposes. This became clear during the Senate Foreign Relations Committee hearings from March 13 to April 3. As Vandenberg said, "[W]e are confronted with the fundamental fact that if we desert the President of the United States at [this] moment we cease to have any influence in the world forever." To which Ambassador MacVeagh replied, "I am afraid that is true." Similarly, Senator Henry Cabot Lodge declared that the choice is "whether we are going to repudiate the President and throw the flag on the ground and stamp on it. . . ." And after the House voted the legislation in May, Republican Francis Case of South Dakota would tell Truman that he and at least seventy-five other representatives would have voted "no" except that they did not wish to pull the rug from under the president.[58]

In pressing for the aid bill, Truman and his aides also stressed strategic interests and the threat of unlimited Soviet expansion. When Eleanor Roosevelt complained that the U.S. should not assume Britain's imperial role in the name of democracy, the president replied, "I would argue that if the Greek-Turkish land bridge between the continents is one point at which our democratic forces can stop the advance of communism that has flowed through the Baltic countries, Poland, Yugoslavia, Rumania, and to some extent Hungary, then this is the place to do it, regardless of the terrain." Similarly, Acheson insisted to the Senate Foreign Relations Committee that the Russians could not be allowed to control the Straits and that it would be a "mistake" to believe it was possible to negotiate with them: "You cannot sit down with them." Forrestal insisted that the "demolition" of Greece and Russian control of the Straits would mean that "you have cut the world in half." Ambassador MacVeagh warned that along the entire "critical crescent" from Finland to Afghanistan the "expansionist" Soviet state had "bulged, and bulged, and bulged," and that "the appetite grows with the eating." And ambassador to Turkey, Edwin C. Wilson, said that country was the only free one along the Soviet border from the Baltic to the Black Sea. Unless the Russians were resisted, he said, "there is nothing between them, then, and the Persian Gulf, Suez Canal, on out to the East—Afghanistan, India, and China."[59]

Acheson insisted that the U.S. did not intend to do battle everywhere in the world, certainly not in "the Russian sphere of physical force" in Eastern Europe nor, he told House members lobbying support for Jiang Jieshi, was further China aid required. But the U.S. would intercede where it could be "effective," as in Korea, where the line was "clearly drawn" between Americans and Russians. The administration also finessed criticism that it was acting unilaterally and undermining UN authority by acceding to a friendly amendment by Vandenberg (who thought that Greece could collapse "fifty times" before the UN acted) that the U.S. aid would end if the Security Council or General Assembly said that it was no longer necessary. But this was "window dressing," Acheson recalled. The U.S. controlled enough UN votes to preclude a call for withdrawal.[60]

The president readily gained his way on Greek-Turkish aid despite some initial resistance to his policy. Ten days after his speech, newspapers were regularly referring to the "Truman Doctrine," Lord Inverchapel wrote, and by early April it was "dogma" among majority opinion. Congressional opposition soon became nominal, and the legislation carried easily: the Senate passed it 67–23 on April 22, and the House, 287–107 on May 8. Truman signed the bill into law on May 22. He remained insistent that the U.S. was advancing the goals of the UN.[61]

The next day UNSCOB released a report—which Marshall and the State Department had done all they could to influence—that held Yugoslavia, and to a lesser extent Albania and Bulgaria, responsible for aiding Greek guerillas. But the report also stated that the Greek government's persecution of minorities and political opponents had helped to start the conflict. In effect, the findings confirmed that Balkan national rivalries exacerbated Greece's civil war. But there was no support for the major premise of the Truman Doctrine that the Soviet Union had incited Communist insurgency to impose totalitarianism and to dominate the Mediterranean. Nonetheless, the Truman administration persisted in this view.[62]

Truman would now insist that the purpose of his doctrine was to restore "free government." But the Greek Communists saw it as an "undisguised declaration of American imperialism," and predicted new levels of conflict. In fact, injection of U.S. aid in the summer of 1947 seemed only to spur the Greek regime to greater terror—more executions and concentration camps—led by the minister of public order, Colonel Napoleon Zervas, who formerly headed EDES and had collaborated with the Nazis. Truman stated that he had "no attitude" toward the "political arrests," and Marshall repeatedly said that the U.S. could not interfere with Greece's administration of "justice" and need for a "firm policy" with Communists. Not until 1949, when the civil war was winding down—and UN pressure rising—did the U.S. abandon its "benign neglect" toward the Greek regime's terrorism and encourage a more moderate policy of surrender and amnesty. But there was to be no political compromise. In effect, Cold War diplomacy abetted authoritarianism.[63]

The Truman administration took increasing hold of Greek political-economic and military affairs. Fearful at the outset of pouring money into a "rat hole," the Treasury Department sought "control" of the Greek government. But Acheson said this was "completely unrealistic." The Greeks acceded, however, to an advisory American Mission for Aid to Greece (AMAG), headed by Dwight Griswold, a World War I friend of Truman, former Republican governor of Nebraska, and currently a U.S. military government official in Germany. But as Robert Lovett, successor to Acheson as under secretary, said in August 1947, Greek officials were so selfish that there was "no Greek government to deal with." Hence AMAG took virtual control over governmental functions, with Griswold soon publicly labeled the "Most Powerful Man in Greece." The State Department denied this, but the blunter AMAG chief insisted that Congress and the public expected "forthright" (but not dictatorial) action to rehabilitate Greece and to check Communism. "This means involvement in internal affairs and I see no advantage in pretending it is something else," he said in fall 1947.[64]

The Americans also took military command. As Lovett said, U.S. officials were perplexed that more than 100,000 Greek forces could not deal with "a few score or a few hundred" rebels. Thus when the British announced in July 1947 that they intended to withdraw their remaining 5,000 forces, MacVeagh and Griswold called for U.S. troops. Truman considered calling a special session of Congress. But Marshall reminded him that passage of the Truman Doctrine had been predicated on a strictly advisory military role. When pressure grew again in early 1948 for introduction of U.S. forces—Henderson pressed for their use and the Greek government encouraged the idea—Marshall resisted again, and Truman concurred. The secretary's concerns were largely pragmatic. He held that there was a shortage of combat-ready troops and that they would be too vulnerable on Greece's difficult terrain. He also worried about political backlash, and that if the Soviets were to exert pressure, the forces would either have to be "backed up" or withdrawn "ignominiously." Later in spring 1948, State Department officials inclined toward use of U.S. troops, but the JCS was persistent that this would be "militarily unsound."[65]

Consequently, Truman held to his decision made in the summer of 1947 to "deal roughly"—use economic leverage—with the British to keep their troops in Greece. They remained there until 1954. Meanwhile, Washington was disappointed with the military results gained by General William L. Livesay, first head of the United States Army Group in Greece (USAGG). Then in January 1948 Marshall named General James A. Van Fleet, an aggressive commander, to head USAGG. He and 450 military advisers rapidly took charge of the Greek army, providing organizational and operational advice from the highest level through the divisions, as well as on-the-spot advice in combat. By 1949 the U.S. and Van Fleet had built the Greek army to more than 263,000 forces—as against 23,000 rebels—at a cost of almost $500 million. Overall, U.S. aid to the Greek regime "dwarfed" Balkan nation support for the Greek rebels.[66]

The president and his associates always held that U.S. aid saved Greece, and perhaps Europe, from both Communism and Soviet domination. As journalist Mark Ethridge recalled, when in March 1947 his Russian counterpart on UNSCOB, Alexander Lavrischev, asked the meaning of Truman's speech, the American replied, "It means you can't do it," to which the Russian replied: "I quite understand." That November the president stated that "if Russia gets Greece and Turkey, then they would get Italy and France and the iron curtain would extend all the way to western Ireland. In that event, we would have to come home and prepare for war." Marshall likewise justified increased military aid in 1948 by insisting that the Greek conflict was "but a piece or a portion . . . of the general Soviet effort."[67]

Undoubtedly, U.S. support enabled the Greek regime to prevail over the rebels. But victory was significantly advanced because Stalin "never once said a word," as Churchill said, when the British assaulted Greek Communists in 1944–1945 and, as noted earlier, the Soviet leader refused to send aid or grant exile to Greek Communists in 1945–1946. He also reacted mildly to the Truman Doctrine and its military implementation. As William Taubman, a sharp critic of Stalin's diplomacy, has written, the Soviet leader was prepared to continue "detente," to treat Truman's anticommunism as propaganda, and to cede Greece and Turkey to Western influence. To be sure, Stalin finally approved limited military aid for the Greek Communists in June 1947, and the Soviet Union and Yugoslavia broke relations with the Greek government in August 1947. Notably, however, Stalin did not invite the Greek Communists to the first Communist Information Bureau (Cominform) meeting in September, nor did the Soviet Union or any Communist state—to the chagrin and dismay of the KKE—recognize the Communist-led "Free Greece" regime that was formed in December. Most important, by early 1948, just six months after agreeing to provide aid, Stalin decided to halt support for the Greek rebels.[68]

Stalin was most blunt with Yugoslav and Bulgarian leaders in early February 1948. Always hostile to Tito's independent ways and a Balkan State confederation that might delimit Soviet influence in Albania, the Soviet leader demanded that aid to the Greek rebels be terminated. "The uprising is to fold up," he said. When Yugoslavia's vice premier, Eduard Kadelj, hinted that the rebels might win if foreign intervention did not increase and political-military mistakes were avoided, Stalin was adamant: "If, if! No, they have no prospect of success at all. What do you think that Great Britain and the United States—the United States the most powerful nation in the world—will permit you to break their line of communication in the Mediterranean Sea! Nonsense. And we have no navy. The uprising in Greece must be stopped, and as quickly as possible." Moreover, Greece was "an entirely different situation" from China, and they must not hesitate to "put an end to the Greek uprising."[69]

When Tito persisted with Greek aid, Stalin promptly announced withdrawal of all Russian military and civilian advisers from Yugoslavia. He also determined to punish Tito's regime for what he considered the demands of a small state to have the Soviet Union take a position that was to its own detriment. Thus in a meeting in late June 1948 in Bucharest, Communist representatives from the Soviet Union, Eastern Europe, France, and Italy expelled Yugoslavia from the Cominform and called on the Yugoslavs to elect new leaders. To be sure, in the first half of 1948 U.S. officials could only dimly grasp the implications of the Tito-Stalin conflict. But they also showed no interest in differentiating between Communist states or assuming other than that the Soviet Union controlled its "satellites" and used them to achieve its goals directly or through subversion.[70]

U.S. officials disdained any negotiated settlement with Greek Communists, who now divided into rival Stalinist and Titoist factions, although both showed interest in a compromise settlement. But Americans in the field in Greece and in Washington agreed that the war should not be ended by "appeasement or conciliation." There could be only "crushing defeat" of the rebels. As Marshall instructed in August 1948, he hoped to see the "cycle of killing" end, but he opposed compromise with "International Communism" and affirmed the Greek government's demand for "unconditional surrender."[71]

The Greek rebels sustained themselves for another year with limited support from Yugoslavia. But Stalin increased political and economic pressure on Tito and—cynically—also abetted the Greek Communist call for an independent Macedonia that posed a threat not only to the Greek government but to Yugoslavia's control of its southern republic. The Americans and British, meanwhile, refused badly needed economic assistance to Yugoslavia. By January 1949 Yugoslav aid to the Greek guerillas had slowed to barely a trickle. Finally in July 1949 Tito announced closure of the Greek-Yugoslav frontier, cessation of all aid to the rebels, and dismantlement of their camps. At the same time, Stalin's massive purge of "Titoist" Communists in Eastern Europe halted even the extremely limited Albanian and Bulgarian aid. Finally, in October 1949 the Greek rebels had to lay down their arms. The civil war was over. But 108,000 people had been killed (including 5,000 executed), and tens of thousands were wounded or worse. There were also 800,000 refugees, including 100,000 who fled to the Communist north, and 28,000 children were taken abroad. Greece's economy and social structure were devastated.[72]

In addition to bolstering the Greek government during 1947–1949, the U.S. also expended several hundred million dollars in Truman Doctrine assistance to modernize Turkey's army, navy, and air force. Initial aid was given to enhance Turkish ability to resist any Soviet assault—although none was foreseen—through the Straits or Black Sea. Later assistance was given to halt a prospective Russian attack on Iran or the Persian Gulf; and finally, aid was given to develop air capacity, including U.S. use of its own B-29s, to bomb vital Soviet oil resources in the Caucasus and in Rumania. In 1952, Greece and Turkey would be admitted to the fledgling North Atlantic Treaty Organization (NATO).[73]

IV

In April 1949 Bevin thanked Truman for the decision he had made two years earlier "in behalf of Europe." The Truman Doctrine had saved Greece—"a bastion of civilization"—and Turkey and had preserved the independence of the Middle East. "The importance of your decision cannot be underestimated," the foreign secretary concluded. The president's reply acknowledged only modest achievement. By 1952, however, he reflected that his decision to intervene in Greece marked "the beginning of his own foreign policy." In his *Memoirs* he called his decision "the turning point in America's foreign policy."[74]

Unfortunately, assessment of U.S. policy in Greece is more complex than Truman or Bevin would have it, especially because both sides in this civil war not only fought fiercely but committed atrocities. This included summary executions, torture, and movement of children—EAM began this policy in January 1948—to safe havens. Presumably this was done to protect the children from war and starvation, but charges flew of darker political motivations. In addition, CBS reporter George K. Polk was murdered in Salonika in May 1948. EAM accused the government of the murder because of Polk's critical reports. The Athens regime hardly investigated, claiming that the Communists did it to discredit the government, and eventually accused and convicted three Communists. But the bitter truth about this murder remains uncertain.[75]

Not surprisingly, historians remain sharply divided over the Truman Doctrine. Those favorably disposed have said that the administration reasonably held that it was in the U.S. national interest to assume Britain's role of sustaining non-Communist regimes in the strategically vital Eastern Mediterranean. They have also held that the U.S. pursued a flexible and restrained policy. Moreover, even historians critical of U.S. policy—such as Daniel Yergin and Melvyn Leffler—have allowed that U.S. national security managers had reason to fear that an EAM victory and a broad leftist government in Greece might have given way later to a Stalinist-style Communist regime and tempted the Soviet leader to try to predominate in the Eastern Mediterranean and Middle East. This, they say, might have had grave implications for European politics.[76]

Truman's defenders have also argued that his doctrine was not a new departure: the U.S. had already begun to "get tough" with Russia in 1946 with Churchill's iron curtain speech and action over Iran and the Turkish Straits. Further, although Truman's rhetoric was exaggerated and created an "ideological straitjacket" for later policy, his immediate purpose was to jolt a fiscally conservative Republican Congress and to rouse a reluctant public to greater concern about international affairs. Finally, defenders of U.S. policy have said that the administration did not intend to police the world or to militarize American foreign policy in 1947. This came only with the Korean War.[77]

Historians more critical of U.S. policy have argued that the Truman administration took the Greek "crisis" as the "fitting moment" to seize the anticommunist banner at home and abroad from its Republican opponents—the president's popularity rose sharply in spring 1947—and used Greece and Turkey as pawns on the international chessboard to advance a political-economic-military policy that fostered authoritarian regimes in the name of helping "free" people resist allegedly Soviet-inspired Communist subjugation. These writers further contend that Truman's policy never addressed the basic causes of the Greek civil war. Instead, it made the Soviet Union the villain of every crisis or conflict, heightened East-West bloc confrontation, and established the model "aid" program for later disasters, most notably assistance to the French in 1950 to wage war in Indochina. Equally significant, but often overlooked, is the fact that the president's rapid response to the start of war in Korea in 1950 would be marked by his view that "this is the Greece of the Far East. If we are tough enough now there won't be another step." In addition, Congress set a bad precedent by giving the president authority to wage Cold War as he saw fit.[78]

Finally, historians have challenged the national security argument by contending that EAM and the Greek Communists did not derive their strength from Soviet support. Rather, they had deep roots in Greek society and in the long struggle against reactionary rulers. The prospective triumph of the Greek Left did not necessarily portend a Stalinist state that would have marched to the Soviet leader's drumbeat any more than did Tito's Yugoslavia or Mao's China, whatever the failings of these societies. Prospects for legitimate parliamentary politics in Greece and coexistence with Western societies were real. But the U.S. chose instead to intervene to contain the Greek Left no less than the Soviets by supporting authoritarian regimes that would keep Greece in the U.S. orbit. The legacy of this action was that for about three decades, successive Greek governments used the state apparatus—decrees, the police, the military, and a Central Service of Information modeled on the CIA—to systematically persecute their former enemies and deny them their basic rights and livelihood. In that sense, U.S. policy with respect to Greece resembled that of the Soviet Union toward its Eastern European satellites.[79]

The debate may never end, although the critics would appear to have had the better of it. Perhaps it would seem too harsh to conclude with Senator William Fulbright's judgment, rendered at the height of America's war in Vietnam, that "all American mistakes committed abroad since 1947 stem from the Truman Doctrine." But it is imperative to recall, as has the eminent historian William H. McNeill—who served as military attaché in Greece from 1944 to 1946—that even if the U.S. set out with good intentions to check "communist aggression," ultimately U.S. intervention in Greece proved as high-handed as that of Britain in 1944, and that Anglo-American officials played roles similar to those of the German wartime occupation forces. Or as Robert A. Pollard, an historian who has inclined to view the Truman administration's policies as successful, has conceded, "[I]n effect, the United States adopted a military solution to the Greek problem, substituting the annihilation of the enemy for the reform of the social and economic conditions that had fostered the insurgency in the first place." Further, not only did U.S. intervention in Greece and collaboration with repressive right-wing regimes run until 1963, but in 1967 the U.S. assisted a military coup against a democratically elected government that led to another seven years of military dictatorship.[80]

Equally significant, Truman's rhetorical division of the world into "free" versus "totalitarian" states signaled his abandonment of diplomacy as a means to deal with the Soviets. Always given to sweeping analogy rather than fine distinction, now more than ever—as he said repeatedly in March, April, and May 1947—he saw no difference between "totalitarian or police states, call them what you will, Nazi, Fascist, Communist, or Argentine Republic." "The police state is a police state," he said; "I don't care what you call it." The time had come "to state our case to the world."[81]

Truman also convinced himself that from the Potsdam Conference to the spring of 1947 he had done his "level best" to conciliate the Russians, but that they dealt from day to day and always asked for more. Further, the president told radio news analysts in May that he had labored to make "straight out and out agreements" with the Russians, but "not a single one . . . is carried out. I have got to use other methods. They understand one language, and that is the language they are going to get from me from this point." [82]

Two years later, replying to Bevin's accolade that the Truman Doctrine was action taken in behalf of Europe, the president would reiterate his conviction that from 1945 to 1947 he had done his best to reach agreement with the Russians, but that he had at last been forced to conclude this was "an impossibility unless the Russians know they can't run over the rest of the world." He was now confident, however, that the Truman Doctrine had put the U.S. "well on the road" to attaining that necessary position of strength. [83]

Greta Kempton portrait of President Harry S. Truman, 1948 and 1970. Courtesy of the National Portrait Gallery, Smithsonian Institution: gift of Dean Acheson, Thomas C. Clark, John W. Snyder, Robert A. Lovett, Clinton P. Anderson, Charles F. Brannan, Charles Sawyer, W. Averell Harriman, David K. E. Bruce, Edward H. Foley, Stuart Symington, William McChesney Martin, Clark Clifford, Charles S. Murphy, Ward M. Canaday, and Joseph Stack.

Harry Truman at age thirteen, with the thick glasses he had to wear from about age eight to compensate for his extreme far-sightedness. Photo courtesy of the Harry S. Truman Library.

Harry S. Truman riding on a cultivator on his Grandview farm. He found the work tiring and financially unrewarding. Photo courtesy of the Harry S. Truman Library.

Harry S. Truman (third from right) and men of Battery D in France after World War I. Truman proved to be a brave and respected commander, but he vowed in 1919 never to return to Europe. Photo courtesy of the Harry S. Truman Library.

Harry Truman in the Truman and Jacobson Haberdashery in Kansas City, Missouri. After one profitable year, economic recession forced closure in 1922, and Truman remained financially strapped until 1945. Photo courtesy of the Harry S. Truman Library.

American and Russian troops meet for the first time on April 25, 1945, at the Elbe River near the town of Strehla, Germany. Photo by U.S. Army Signal Corps., courtesy of the National Archives, photo no. 111-SC-181990.

Allied troops in Berlin: first members of Women's Air Corps walking along Potsdamer Strasse. British Combine Photos, courtesy of the Harry S. Truman Library.

Premier Joseph Stalin, President Harry Truman, and Prime Minister Winston Churchill at Potsdam, July 1945. Truman initially claimed to like Stalin and thought he could deal with him, but that view changed quickly. Churchill, voted out of office while at Potsdam, did not return to power until 1951. Photo by U.S. Army Signal Corps, courtesy of the Harry S. Truman Library.

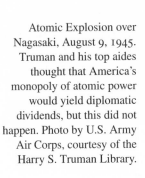

Atomic Explosion over Nagasaki, August 9, 1945. Truman and his top aides thought that America's monopoly of atomic power would yield diplomatic dividends, but this did not happen. Photo by U.S. Army Air Corps, courtesy of the Harry S. Truman Library.

President Truman and General
Charles de Gaulle on the White
House lawn, August 1945. Truman
was wary of General de Gaulle and
resisted France's postwar efforts to
gain high reparations and control
over the Ruhr from Germany.
National Park Service Photograph–
Abbie Rowe, courtesy of the
Harry S. Truman Library.

Banners of Allied Nations. President Truman gives Navy Day Address in Central Park,
New York City, October 27, 1945, in which he heralds America's atomic power as
a "sacred trust" and opposes compromise with "evil." Photo courtesy of the Harry S.
Truman Library.

President Truman and Soviet Foreign Minister Vyacheslav Molotov, 1946. Truman's first meeting in April 1945 with the foreign minister was a stormy one, and U.S. officials continued to regard Molotov as Stalin's hard line negotiator. Photo courtesy of the Harry S. Truman Library; permission granted by Stock Montage Gallery.

Battleship Missouri, sent by U.S. officials to Turkey in March 1946 to encourage that nation to resist Soviet claims on the Straits. Photo courtesy of the Harry S. Truman Library.

President Truman with (clockwise) George Marshall, secretary of state, Paul G. Hoffman, administrator of the Marshall Plan, and Averell Harriman, U.S. special representative in Europe for the Marshall Plan. The Marshall Plan provided a cornerstone for over a half century of Western European economic and political cooperation. National Park Service Photograph-Abbie Rowe, courtesy of the Harry S. Truman Library.

General Lucius D. Clay, U.S. deputy military governor in Germany, 1945–47, and military governor, 1947–49. Clay took a critical lead role in organizing resistance to the Russians' blockade of West Berlin. Photo courtesy of the Harry S. Truman Library.

A C-47 being loaded with food and supplies at Wiesbaden in August 1948 during the Berlin air lift. U.S. officials surprised even themselves by airlifting about 4,500 tons of supplies daily to support 2.2 million people in West Berlin. Photo courtesy of the Harry S. Truman Library.

President Truman receives a Torah from Dr. Chaim Weizmann, first President of Israel, May 25, 1948. The two men got on well together, and Weizmann apparently persuaded Truman in 1947 to support including the strategically important Negev in the new Jewish state. Brown-Suarez photo from Bettmann/Corbis, courtesy of the Harry S. Truman Library.

General Marshall (President Truman's special representative to China, 1945–46) reviews Chinese Communist honor guard with (on left) Chairman Mao Zedong and General Chu Teh. Marshall wanted the Chinese to forge a coalition government but Jiang's Nationalists resisted. Photo courtesy of the Harry S. Truman Library.

Attorney General Howard McGrath (on left), President Truman, and Defense Secretary Louis Johnson walking from Blair House to White House after conferring on Korean War, June 27, 1950. Truman was about to inform congressional leaders that he had already committed U.S. ground, as well as air and naval, forces to fight in Korea. Photo courtesy of the Harry S. Truman Library.

President Truman and General Douglas MacArthur during their meeting at Wake Island on October 15, 1950. Truman flew half way around the world to gain credit prior to the congressional elections from MacArthur's military advance, but also to signal control over MacArthur in wake of recent U.S. overflights of Soviet borders. Photo by U.S. Department of State, courtesy of the Harry S. Truman Library.

General Matthew B. Ridgway (with binoculars and hand grenades), commander of the Eighth Army in Korea, and staff officers check front line positions north of Anyang-mi, February 2, 1951. After Truman fired MacArthur in April 1951, Ridgway became commander of United Nations forces in Korea. Photo by U.S. Army, courtesy of the Harry S. Truman Library.

Official U.S. Navy photograph of President Truman, December 14, 1952. Photo by U.S. Navy, courtesy of the Harry S. Truman Library.

The World Split in Two

The Marshall Plan and the Division of Europe

One year after the president's dramatic call for aid to Greece and Turkey, a reporter asked him if he intended to expand the Truman Doctrine. He said no. The doctrine had been successful but was preliminary to and consistent with the recently established European Recovery Program (ERP), or Marshall Plan, which would accomplish the same goals. Similarly, White House aide Elsey had noted in fall 1947 that the Marshall Plan would be the "Truman Doctrine in Action." And forty years later one historian of American economic diplomacy would concur that the Truman Doctrine, despite its rhetorical excesses that led to unintended consequences, had forced a reluctant Congress and public to focus on international economic problems and thereby provided the president with a mandate for European reconstruction.[1]

Unfortunately, this belief that the Truman Doctrine and Marshall Plan were "two halves of the same walnut," as the president stated, does not square with the views of key officials in 1947–1948 who drew sharp distinctions between their program for European recovery and the Truman Doctrine. Further, linking the two programs obscures the Marshall Plan's more sophisticated purposes and undervalues Truman's enthusiasm for European reconstruction, which he thought would also serve to "raise the Iron Curtain."[2]

Judgments of the Marshall Plan have varied dramatically. Some scholars have celebrated it as a unique act of international idealism that rescued a politically and economically beleaguered Europe. Others have perceived it as Cold War diplomacy intended to bolster a U.S. economy dependent on exports, contain the Soviet Union economically, and promote U.S. geostrategic supremacy. Still others have seen it as part of a U.S. long-term liberal corporatist effort to reshape Western Europe in America's image. Regardless of view, historians have judged that the Marshall Plan was far more constructive than the Truman Doctrine and that ERP became a cornerstone of a half century of Western European democratic stability and increasing political and economic cooperation, if not integration. The Marshall Plan has also endured, if only symbolically, as a prototype for galvanizing underdeveloped, or newly liberated, economies around the globe.[3]

I

In early 1947 Europe appeared to be in desperate financial and economic straits, which the previous summer's drought and then a Siberian-like winter had worsened. Great Britain's White Papers in January and February had detailed the nation's economic plight, including its rapidly dwindling dollar and gold reserves and diminished coal and industrial production. On the Continent the wartime devastation of productive facilities and transportation networks was evident. Equally crippling, if less visible, were the disrupted trade patterns, obsolete machinery, and collapse of workforce morale induced by food shortages and inflation that eroded wages. Most significant, industrial production in Western Europe fell in the first quarter of 1947 from 83 percent to 78 percent of 1938 levels and barely reached one-third of prewar levels in the three western zones of Germany. Winston Churchill's depiction in mid-May 1947 of Europe as "a rubble heap, a charnel house, a breeding ground for pestilence and hate" was not wide of the mark.[4]

The Truman Doctrine was irrelevant to these problems. As one State Department official recalled, there was general dislike of the doctrine's "negative, retaliatory, counter-punching features" and its implications for "economic and ultimately military warfare." The country had "gagged" when it had to swallow a slapped-together, anti-Russian policy of replacing Britain as policeman in Greece. Further, as Kennan and his newly created PPS quickly concluded in May 1947, the administration had to correct two damaging Truman Doctrine impressions: that U.S. policy was a defensive reaction to Communist pressure, with economic assistance only a byproduct of that reaction; and that the doctrine was a "blank check" for military and economic aid to oppose Communists. Above all, the primary challenge for the U.S. in Western Europe was to advance political and economic well-being, with economic reconstruction the basis for political stability.[5]

Money alone was no solution. Since the war's end in 1945 the Truman administration had provided, chiefly through the UN Relief and Rehabilitation Administration (UNRRA), nearly $10 billion in foreign aid, including a hard-won $350 million European loan in February 1947. But as the State Department warned in 1947, U.S. exports ($16.2 billion) would exceed imports ($8.7 billion) by $7.5 billion, with the U.S. having to lend or spend about $5 billion in occupied areas to help finance foreign purchase of American goods. But the outflow of governmental, or taxpayer, dollars would taper off rapidly in late 1948 and 1949, and private lending would also decline. Worse, the rest of the world, especially Europe—America's primary trading partner—now had to spend heavily to import foodstuffs and coal and could not continue to buy U.S. goods at current levels for more than another twelve to eighteen months. Already, Europe's payment deficit to the U.S. in 1946 was $4.2 billion. In short, Europe's increasing lack of funds, or "dollar gap," stemming from limited production and export revenues, seemed to preclude restoration of international trade. This augured greater European political instability and might allow Communist parties to make great political gains, perhaps to win or seize power, and then align their nations with the Soviet Union, to the detriment of the U.S. economy and national security.[6]

U.S. officials now concluded that rapid European reindustrialization was imperative and was dependent upon revived western German production. This had been implicit policy in former secretary of state Byrnes' Stuttgart speech in September 1946 and the creation of Bizonia. It had become an article of faith in the State Department, as well as among influential former government officials and private-sector leaders, by January 1947, when planning began for the forthcoming CFM meeting in Moscow. Meanwhile, in mid-March 1947 former president Herbert Hoover, who had gained Truman's permission to turn a late 1946 War Department request to assess Germany's food supplies into a broad study of the economy, delivered his lengthy report. The Hoover Report sharply criticized the Potsdam policy of dismantling German industry to pay reparations, as well as decartelization and denazification policies. Most important, the report insisted that the only way to revitalize the intertwined German and European economies was to abandon the level-of-industry agreement of March 1946 and to end restrictions on German heavy industrial production—steel, chemicals, and machine tools. The report warned that to keep Germany in "economic chains" meant to keep Europe in "economic rags."[7]

At the same time, the Hoover Report and other proposals for German reconstruction augured problems in dealing with the Soviet Union, which since 1945 had sought to constrain Germany economically while staking its claim to current production reparations. But the U.S. now sought to use these to benefit Western Europe. In effect, Hoover-style reconstruction of Germany implied continued division of that country.[8]

The Hoover Report gained broad public approval and support from Forrestal, then secretary of the navy, and Harriman, then secretary of commerce. State Department officials insisted, however, that its emphasis on unconstrained German economic growth ignored British and French economic and security interests. Truman was clearly disposed to German recovery, although he shared State Department concerns. Thus he sent the Hoover Report to his former reparations negotiator, Ed Pauley, who had resisted Russian claims in 1945. But now Pauley warned that an economically unbridled Germany would be even more powerful and dangerous—especially compared to its weakened neighbors—than it had been in the 1930s. He contended that U.S. policy, including industrial dismantling and transfer and reparations payments, had been intended to ensure European peace both by slowing German recovery and by bolstering European states—including Russia—that had been victims of German aggression. This would cost fewer tax dollars than another war, he said. And the best answer to dealing with Germany would be a unified nation overseen by some sort of "Peace Production Board." The president sent the divergent Hoover-Pauley analyses to White House adviser John Steelman, who concluded that Pauley's view better reflected European political and economic realities, despite Hoover's concern about Germany's daily rations. Thus while the U.S. had to speed European recovery—which it might start to do by lifting its 1946 ban on reparations shipments from its zone—it was also necessary, Steelman said, to avoid re-creating another 1930s-style "German colossus."[9]

Debate over Germany was now also center stage at the CFM meeting in Moscow from March 10 to April 24, but prospects for agreement were not good. First, Secretary Marshall, recently returned from his China mission, was tired and not well informed on the issues, and his tedious statements about need to restore democracy in Germany were unlikely to move the Russians. Second, the U.S. delegation was chiefly concerned with restoring western Germany economically to benefit Western Europe; only General Clay emphasized need to reach accord with the Russians on reparations and a unified Germany. Finally, the Truman Doctrine speech on March 12 clouded matters. Acheson later recalled that Marshall had instructed that the president's speech should be written without regard for the Moscow talks, a decision Acheson likened to that of a courageous field commander calling down fire on his own position to defeat the enemy. In 1947, however, Foreign Secretary Bevin's final conference report to his Cabinet held that the president's speech had ended chances for a German settlement, although the Soviets made no reference to Truman's provocative statements and at the outset of the meeting British officials detected signs of Russian desire for agreement.[10]

Both U.S. and British negotiators pressed formation of a provisional federal, or decentralized, form of government in Germany, with significant power vested in the states (Länder), which were more numerous in the west. Presumably this structure would preclude a Hitler-like seizure of power, but it was also intended to avert Communist control of centralized government. In addition, the Anglo-Americans sought to raise Germany's level of industry to become self-supporting at the average European standard of living and to meet Europe's need for German products and trade. This was a sharp departure from the Potsdam accord that Germany would produce only enough to meet its own needs. Marshall also proposed to join the French and Soviet zones to Bizonia, and to revive the Truman-Byrnes four-power pact to keep Germany demilitarized.[11]

The French, however, wanted security through industrial-economic primacy. They sought to annex the Saar, to detach the Rhineland and the Ruhr—whose coal and industries they wanted to control—and to form an alliance to defend against Germany. The Russians advocated a centralized government in Germany, presumably to delimit corporate and reactionary political interests in separate states, but also because only a strong regime could effect industrial production controls to meet reparations demands. The Soviets, like the French, had little interest in the four-power pact, which resembled too much the failed interwar agreements. But the Russians resisted detaching the Rhineland and the Ruhr; they sought access to the vital industry there along with a final reparations settlement. They also rejected Marshall's provocative proposal to restudy the German-Polish, or Oder–western Neisse, frontier. They deemed this settled at Potsdam.[12]

The key issue, and sine qua non of a German agreement, was reparations, especially from current production. The Soviets proposed to raise Germany's level of industry and to abandon capital removals from their zone if they got Yalta's estimated $10 billion in reparations, especially from current production. They held this to be their right based on their wartime contributions and immense losses. As historian Carolyn Eisenberg has written, security, national pride, and material necessity demanded that the Yalta terms be fulfilled. But Marshall persisted in the standard Anglo-American argument that this would depress Germany's economy and burden their taxpayers. He said that moreover the Russians had already removed $7 billion (a high estimate). The Americans also worried that the Russians sought reparations to breed social unrest and Communist advances.[13]

Then in late March General Clay, perhaps the only U.S. official at the CFM who still believed it was possible and desirable to reach a comprehensive agreement with the Russians, persuaded Marshall to weigh offering current production reparations to induce Soviet accord on German unification, revision of Germany's Polish border to include more land for foodstuffs, and a four-power pact to keep Germany disarmed. In Clay's view, "[W]e should not take an adamant stand against current production reparations," which he confidently saw as the basis for an agreement that would allow the U.S. to extend its influence throughout all of Germany.[14]

Marshall put the proposal to the president, who reverted to his most unyielding position. There would be no current production reparations until all German imports were paid for, including reimbursements for Anglo-American occupation costs and back payments to balance Soviet removals. Nor would there be diversion of vital coal or raw materials from the German economy. Even the usually unquestioning Marshall replied that this was "too restrictive" and denied him "elbow room" to negotiate, and he did not bother to initiate his proposal. Clay, angry and convinced that he could serve no useful purpose in Moscow, returned to his post in Berlin. Meanwhile, in Cabinet discussion Truman remained "solidly against" current production reparations and hinted that there would be no more foreign ministers' talks, only a peace conference in Washington.[15]

Serious diplomacy at the CFM meeting was ended, although on April 15 Marshall, seeking to bring matters to a conclusion, accepted Stalin's long-standing invitation to each of the foreign ministers for a personal talk. After an initial exchange of pleasantries, the secretary warned Stalin that U.S. public regard for the Russians was declining owing to their apparent intractability on every issue, from opening consulates and settling Lend-Lease accounts to the form of the German government and the proposed four-power pact. Marshall said that the U.S., like the Soviets, favored a centralized German government, but not one that would dominate industry, finance, and education. The U.S. also wanted an economically unified Germany and was disappointed at Soviet resistance to a four-power treaty. The U.S. had no desire to convert the Soviet Union to its form of government but would do what was necessary to help deteriorating economies, with no intent to dominate any part of the world.

Stalin was equally polite but firm. He resented the two-year delay—"sloppiness"—by the U.S. in responding to Russia's $6 billion loan request in 1945, and he regarded German economic unity as impossible without political unity. Above all, he wanted the Yalta reparations, which might not be popular in the U.S. but were "very popular in the Soviet Union" and were not hard to pay over twenty years. The situation was not tragic, however, Stalin said. These were only the "first skirmishes and brushes of reconnaissance forces" on these issues, and patience would produce compromise.[16]

The CFM meeting was dead, although it lingered ten more days. But Marshall took Stalin's emphasis on patience as a ploy to foster European economic collapse and Communist predominance. The secretary had decided, he later confirmed, that it was impossible to negotiate with the Russians. Thus as Robert Murphy, General Clay's diplomatic adviser, later said, the Americans held that the Moscow Conference "really rang down the Iron Curtain," although who had pulled the ropes is debatable.[17]

In fact, by the time of the CFM meeting virtually no U.S. official, except Clay, was interested in effecting a unified and neutralized Germany. Perhaps, as Marc Trachtenberg has written, officials doubted that the Soviets would abide by any agreement. They were also concerned that a unified but weak Germany would be subject to Soviet pressure, whereas a unified but strong Germany might play East against West. But most important, the Americans were determined to make western German economic rehabilitation the basis for Western European reconstruction. Consequently, they took an uncompromising, almost nonnegotiable, position, especially with respect to current production reparations, Russian access to Ruhr industry, and the form of the German government. In so doing, the Truman administration was opting for a separate western German political-economic entity and the division of Germany.[18]

Whether Stalin would have been willing to agree to a politically unified and neutralized Germany, thus abandoning Soviet control of East Germany, in exchange for $10 billion in reparations, four-power supervision of the Ruhr, and accord on the de facto (and perhaps remodified) German-Polish border, remains a question. But during CFM talks the Russians did show flexibility regarding willingness to raise Germany's level of industry and forgo capital dismantling, and they might well have compromised in the direction of a federal form of government if assured of Germany's demilitarization and denazification. In fact, for many years historians—including those most sharply critical of Stalin—have held that it was a distinct possibility he would have compromised over Germany and that this would have been a good bargain for the West.[19]

Most significant, and most recent, Norman Naimark's thorough and highly critical study of Russian policy in Germany has concluded that "in the Eastern zone, the Soviet Union had different intents and purposes than it did in Poland, Rumania, or even Czechoslovakia and Hungary. In Germany, the Soviets were interested in maintaining maximum flexibility to accommodate to a four-power agreement on the unification, demilitarization, and neutralization of the country. The Soviets were too desperate for a share of West German coal and mineral resources and too worried about the integration of West German industrial power into an American-dominated Western condominium to give up easily on hopes for a neutral Germany." Or as historian Wilfried Loth has recently written, Stalin did not regard the CFM in spring 1947 as a preliminary discussion about partition of Germany, and he continued to believe that he would have greater success regarding German economic and political unity at the next CFM later in the year.[20]

Nonetheless, in 1947 Marshall returned from the CFM meeting to proclaim, in Truman-like style in a national broadcast on April 28, that the Russians had obstructed every American proposal from Potsdam to the present: they wanted a centralized German government in order to seize the country, which lacked adequate land to feed its people, and they wanted Germany to turn over too much of its production as Soviet reparations. The secretary concluded that Germany and Austria were the "vital center" of Europe, where recovery had gone far slower than expected, disintegrating forces were evident, and the patient was sinking while the doctors deliberated. The U.S. could not await "compromise through exhaustion"—it had to act at once. The next day Marshall told Kennan to form the PPS and to prepare a program for Europe.[21]

II

By spring 1947 Truman had begun to edge toward a major European reconstruction initiative, the Marshall Plan, of diverse but intertwined origins and purposes. In mid-April Truman approved a SWNCC subcommittee report that detailed the impending trade and dollar-gap crisis and insisted that America's long-term foreign commerce depended on European recovery. The SWNCC report also posited that U.S. "national security" required collaboration with nations that possessed or controlled substantial industrial and military facilities and personnel, vital raw materials, and strategic areas. U.S. aid had to promote orderly political processes and economic stability, and resist the spread of Communism.[22]

These tasks required a comprehensive program. Thus Truman, having asked Acheson to speak in his stead at a Delta Council meeting of farmers and businesspeople in Cleveland, Mississippi (the president wished to stay aloof from a state Democratic Party fight), agreed that the under secretary's speech about European aid should "shock" the public. The Council of Economic Advisers (CEA), however, worried that these dollars, which would be spent on American goods, would fuel inflation. But Truman was willing to bear this political cost. He also wished to fight the conditions that his administration believed spurred Communism.[23]

The president, as CFM talks in Moscow showed, also opposed concessions to the Soviets over Germany, whose reconstruction he knew underlay European recovery. But German reconstruction meant more than just saying no to the Russians. The administration now believed it necessary to dissuade the British, who had agreed to raise German industrial levels, from socializing Ruhr industry. Similarly, it was necessary to press the French on two fronts: to agree to allow an increase in German production and to cease their efforts to detach the Ruhr and Rhineland, whose coal and industrial capacity they wished to use for their own modernization program—drawn by the well-known lawyer-businessman, Jean Monnet—that the Paris government had recently approved. At the same time, as the Hoover-Pauley-Steelman debate now swirling about the White House indicated, the U.S. had to avert re-creating a 1930s "German colossus." [24]

Thus U.S. aid—or the Marshall Plan—confronted complex tasks. Its primary purpose would be to spur the reconstruction and integration of Britain and Western Europe, whose stable political economy would favor America's political, economic, and military-strategic interests. U.S. aid would also serve to minimize Communism in Europe and "contain" the Soviet Union. But first Britain and France would have to be appeased into abandoning their socialist and separatist plans for western Germany, which would be reintegrated, but also contained, within the new European order, whose strength and appeal might loosen the Soviet Union's hold on Eastern Europe. [25]

Events moved swiftly. On May 8 Acheson's Delta Council speech, which Truman later called the "prologue to the Marshall Plan," stressed that world recovery depended on reconstructing Germany and Japan, the "workshops" of Europe and Asia. The immediate concern of the U.S., Acheson said, had to be the "free world": German-European recovery would proceed even without four-power accord and would require unprecedented foreign aid. Truman soon confirmed publicly that Acheson's remarks were "policy." [26]

Four days later the JCS, having studied the SWNCC report, weighed in with their report (JCS 1769/1) on "United States Assistance to Other Countries from the Standpoint of National Security." They concluded that Britain and France—or Western Europe—were the areas most vital to U.S. national security and most in need of aid. They also said that the decisive diplomatic contest between totalitarian Russia and the Western democracies was taking place in Germany, whose people were the "natural enemies" of the Soviet Union and Communism. Hence the U.S. had to persuade the resistant French to agree to the complete industrial resurgence and economic revival of Germany, potentially the strongest military power in the area. In sum, a strong Germany was critical to U.S. and Western European security. Further, the U.S. should not give aid to the Soviet Union or the Eastern European countries it controlled. [27]

In mid-May Kennan's PPS proffered short- and long-term aid proposals aimed at balancing Germany's reconstruction with its neighbors' security by integrating Germany into an "intramural economic collaboration" and a "regional political association." The PPS, however, emphasized "national security" far less than did SWNCC or the JCS. The planners said that American aid should not be aimed to combat Communists—who exploited rather than created Europe's crisis—but to restore Europe's war-torn socioeconomic structures. Further, Europe should develop its own recovery program, perhaps using the UN's recently established Economic Commission for Europe (ECE). Moreover, the Soviet Union and Eastern Europe might be allowed to participate if they abandoned their exclusive economic orientation.[28]

Marshall doubted that Europe could act on its own, with or without the Soviets. But Kennan advised against drawing a line through Europe. The U.S. should "play it straight," he said, and invite "constructive" Soviet involvement. The secretary was noncommittal. The Truman administration had just offered aid to France and Italy to encourage them to oust Communists from their governments, and the World Bank had loaned France $500 million.[29]

Then Will Clayton, under secretary for economic affairs, who had just returned from tariff and trade talks, reported on May 27 that the U.S. had "grossly underestimated" Europe's economic disintegration, which ultimately threatened the U.S. economy and world peace. He urged a "strong spiritual appeal" from Truman or Marshall for a three-year aid program including $6–$7 billion annually. The Europeans should initiate their own program, or "economic federation," Clayton said, but he resisted UN involvement: *"The United States must run this show."*[30]

Clayton also urged taking over Ruhr coal production ("at which the U.K. has failed") and excluding Soviet–Eastern European participation and UN management. But the State Department declined to rule out either the UN or Eastern Europe, if it gave up its "near-exclusive" Soviet economic orientation. Then Marshall, scheduled to speak briefly at Harvard University's commencement on June 5, instructed his aides to draft a major address.[31]

Marshall did not show the text to Truman, who had left Washington to be with his dying mother. But the two men were in accord on need for European aid. The secretary feared, however, adverse public response to a "Santa Claus offer," so he kept the text closely guarded to minimize publicity. Reporters would not immediately grasp the speech's significance, and the British Embassy sent its advance copy to London by surface mail, although British journalist Leonard Miall recognized the similarity between a recent Acheson policy briefing and the text, and would transmit it via telephone over the BBC. Meanwhile the president deflected publicity by calling a press conference for the morning of June 5. He denounced as "an outrage" events in Hungary, where the Red Army's arrest in February of the former head of the conservative Smallholders party, Bela Kovacs, now led to his "confession," allegedly implicating Prime Minister Ferenc Nagy in an anti-Soviet conspiracy. This caused Nagy to resign on June 1 and to go into exile.[32]

Then came Marshall's speech at Harvard. The secretary said that the wartime destruction of Europe's cities, factories, mines, and railways was plainly evident but that the dislocation of the entire fabric of its economy was less visible. Consequently, the time needed for European reconstruction had been underestimated. He then blended Clayton's warnings about Europe's economic plight with the Kennan-PPS concept of a European-directed recovery program presumably open to Russia and Eastern Europe. Marshall warned that Europe's economic deterioration threatened not just the U.S. economy but world peace. He proposed that the U.S. provide three or four years of foodstuffs and essential products, and insisted that U.S. policy was "not directed against any country or doctrine" but only against hunger, poverty, and chaos. Its purpose was to foster conditions that would spur free institutions. Nations that cooperated would get U.S. aid; nations that obstructed would get nothing. But Europe had to take the initiative, and the program had to be the work of a number of "if not all European nations."[33]

Truman's blast at Soviet behavior in Hungary drew more headlines than Marshall's speech, but Bevin immediately grasped the latter's "historic significance." He proposed a meeting to the French in mid-June. They in turn invited the Soviets to join in talks at the end of the month in Paris, although Ambassador Jefferson Caffery reported from there that neither Bevin nor Foreign Minister Georges Bidault wanted Russian participation. Nor did they want to use the UN's ECE, to which the Russians belonged.[34]

Neither did the Truman administration want or expect Soviet acceptance. Marshall stated on June 13 that he included both Britain and the Soviet Union in the definition of Europe, and State Department Counselor Benjamin V. Cohen said that the U.S. intended to help Eastern Europe "insofar as was possible." Clayton opposed Soviet or Eastern European involvement, and Forrestal lamented that "there was no chance of Russia's *not* joining in this effort" but that it would be "disastrous" if they did. British officials doubted that Congress would vote aid for the Soviets.[35]

Truman kept a low profile for weeks. He worried about public-congressional support for major European aid, especially after Truman Doctrine debate, and happily attached his revered secretary of state's name to the new program. The president's commencement address at Princeton University on June 17 focused on Universal Military Training (UMT). Five days later he announced formation of three committees, respectively headed by Harriman, Interior Secretary Julius Krug, and CEA chairman Edwin Nourse, to study the Marshall Plan's impact on economic aid, U.S. resources, and products and prices. Truman did not formally endorse the Marshall Plan until June 26, just as preliminary negotiations were beginning in London.[36]

The president did not want Russia included. His Truman Doctrine speech in March had set out his anticommunist position, and in May he told news analysts that the Soviets never kept their agreements and now would get only "one language" from him. Then on June 22 the Soviets, who had likened the Marshall Plan to purchasing Europe wholesale instead of nation by nation under the Truman Doctrine, surprised the president and others by accepting an Anglo-French offer to join the negotiations in Paris. But, Truman said, the Soviet-American divide remained as deep as any that had ever existed between nations, even if the Russian response was a "ray of light."[37]

But it quickly dimmed. To begin, even the British found in preliminary talks with Clayton that the U.S. emphasis on balanced budgets, stabilized and convertible—at fixed rates—currencies, and guarantees for American commerce in areas where ERP countries would use dollars for purchases resembled the terms imposed on former enemies such as Italy. Further, Bevin complained that U.S. insistence on a Continental rather than national approach to aid relegated Britain to "just another European country." This approach would appeal even less to the Russians, who had suffered the most wartime destruction. Moreover, the British noted, Clayton's refusal to include the Russians in the short-term food-fuel-fibers program meant that they "would not play" in the Marshall Plan; nor would the Russians meet ERP's standard of World Bank membership since this required revealing gold holdings and other vital economic statistics.[38]

Initial Soviet reaction to the prospective Marshall Plan was extremely suspicious but not without interest in participation and willingness to have Eastern European states take part. Still, the ambiguity of Marshall's speech made it difficult to know whether the U.S. was tendering a serious invitation or proposing to foster Anglo-French collaboration as a prelude to forging a Western European bloc directed at Moscow, as Ambassador Novikov initially wrote from Washington. So too did Molotov, who read and underlined passages in Marshall's speech, believe that the aid offer derived largely from U.S. concern about the impact of Europe's economic decline and that the warning that nations should not seek to profit from Europe's economic difficulties was aimed at Russia. But just as U.S. officials believed that they could not exclude Russia from the initial invitation, the Soviets could not refuse to participate, especially given Eastern Europe's desire for aid, lest they be held responsible for Europe's new division.[39]

Molotov also commissioned a study from the prominent Soviet economist, Evgenii Varga, who said that the Marshall Plan was intended to forestall an economic crisis in the U.S. by extending credits to foreign nations even if they could not repay them. He said that the U.S. was insisting on an all-European aid plan for several reasons, including to put forward a demand to unify Germany economically, to establish a united front in dealing with the Soviet Union, and to try to remove the "iron curtain." But he did not reject participation. He thought that the Russians might bargain hard to gain the credits that the U.S. had to extend in order to sustain its foreign trade.[40]

Even before reading the report the Soviet leaders decided to go to Paris. Apparently they believed it would be best to focus on Marshall's call for Europe to take the initiative and to try to shape the terms to Russia's advantage, perhaps even securing—Molotov briefly hoped—Lend-Lease-style aid. The foreign minister wrote the instructions, presumably approved by Stalin, that said they were to insist on a nation-by-nation program. There was to be no infringement of national sovereignty, no traditional use of Eastern Europe as a raw materials supplier for Western Europe, and no use of Germany's resources until its reparations payments were settled and the Russians given access to Ruhr industry. Molotov also instructed the Eastern European nations to plan to participate and to make their claims just as other European nations had.[41]

The Soviets acted largely as expected in talks with the British and French in Paris starting on June 27. Still, Molotov's large delegation and initial mild speech suggested that the Russians did not wish to provide reason for the British and French to break with them. But the foreign minister's opening gambit that the Russians should ask the U.S. to state what "exact sum" it would advance and whether Congress would appropriate the funds drew Bevin's rejoinder that in a democracy the executive branch did not speak for the legislature, nor did debtors fix terms for creditors. First, Bevin instructed, they had to formulate a European recovery program.[42]

Molotov then argued that inquiry into European nations' resources violated their sovereignty. He contended that Germany could not be included in ERP until the CFM settled that nation's future, especially reparations payments and level of industry. Most important, he insisted that each ERP nation should assess its needs, with the total for Europe conveyed to the U.S. Bevin and Bidault retorted, however, that the Soviet position did not meet Marshall's requirement that every European nation's resources had to be available to benefit the Continent as a whole and that Germany, especially its coal, was vital for Europe. (The French, in fact, were soon ready to raise Germany's industrial level and to devote it to European recovery, not reparations.) Finally, they insisted that to ask the U.S. to fund Europe's requests without a common plan was to ask for a "blank check."[43]

Bevin held that the Soviets meant only to "sabotage" ERP. He expected, "even wished for," the talks to fail. Bidault was of like view. He thought Molotov was delaying only because Russia's "hungry satellites are smacking their lips" at the prospect of American aid. Then on June 30 Soviet intelligence provided Molotov with a summary—which was accurate—reporting that the prior secret Anglo-American talks in London had envisioned the Marshall Plan as reconstruction of Western Europe and western Germany, with no current production reparations for Russia. The foreign minister suspended talks for two days. Bidault then made a final effort at a compromise on July 2, which included use of German resources and European economic coordination, with the U.S. providing "a supplement." But this was intended mainly to placate French Communists and public opinion. The talks ended the next day. Molotov informed Stalin that no "joint decision on the substance of the issue in question" was possible and then warned Bevin and Bidault that a Continental program meant big-power (U.S.) domination of Europe, which would divide the Continent into two camps. Bidault countered that the Soviets were dividing Europe. The next day the British and French invited all European nations to Paris on July 12 to discuss reconstruction.[44]

U.S. officials, as a British diplomat in Washington reported, expressed widespread relief at Soviet rejection of Marshall Plan talks. Truman publicly derided the "folly of nationalism," and he and Marshall applauded the Anglo-French decisions. They also ruled out use of ECE because of Russian membership.[45]

Meanwhile, uncertainty reigned in Moscow. On July 5 and July 6 the Soviets informed the Eastern European states that it would be best if they attended the Paris conference to uphold the Soviet view of nation-by-nation reconstruction. In fact, Molotov went so far as to inform Marshal Tito, who had rejected the Anglo-French invitation, that Yugoslavia should take part in order to reject the kind of credits the U.S. was offering. Then the Yugoslavs should "rebuff" the U.S. and its Anglo-French "satellites" by quitting the conference and "taking with you as many delegations of other countries as possible."[46]

Within twenty-four hours the Kremlin reversed itself, however, and requested that the Eastern European governments refuse to attend the Paris conference. The reason for this is uncertain, although one scholar has written that it may have marked a return to prewar attitudes of not taking part in European collective initiatives. It is also true that the Marshall Plan would have drawn Eastern Europe's economies into a Western European nexus and made the Soviets feel vulnerable. As Molotov recalled—exaggeratedly—they could not rely on the Czechs and Poles, and "the imperialists were drawing us into their company, but as subordinates. We would have become completely dependent on them without getting anything in return."[47]

Regardless, the Eastern Europeans, including the Yugoslavs and Poles, acceded to Stalin. But Klement Gottwald, the Communist president of Czechoslovakia, said that his government's prior acceptance was too well known to be withdrawn. An angry Stalin demanded a meeting in Moscow, and on July 9

Gottwald and his ministers flew there. Stalin then insisted that the Paris conference was intended to isolate Russia and to make German rehabilitation, especially of the Ruhr, the core of the Western bloc. He said that Czechoslovakia was being used as a "tool" against the Soviet Union, which could not allow that. Nor would he yield to Czech assurances that they would never act against Soviet interests.[48]

Following Gottwald's return to Prague on July 11, the Czech government, after a long meeting, bowed to the inevitable and canceled its acceptance of the Paris invitation. Foreign Minister Masaryk apparently told friends that he had gone to Moscow as the foreign minister of an independent sovereign state, but "I returned as a lackey of the Soviet Government." At the same time, Ambassador Smith reported from Moscow that the Czech reversal under Soviet orders "is nothing less than a declaration of war by the Soviet Union on the immediate issue of control of Europe." There had been a lot of "plain speaking" in the Kremlin, Smith added, and Stalin had never before been so hard on his satellites. But now the "lines are drawn," and U.S. failure to meet the Soviet challenge would have repercussions around the world.[49]

There was a certain logic and inevitability to the American-Soviet divide over the Marshall Plan in July 1947. Neither Truman nor Marshall, nor the State Department—including Kennan and Bohlen—wanted to include the Soviets. As the British were quick to note, the U.S. refused to compromise, put almost exclusive emphasis on "what Russia should give," and left the impression that Soviet participation—whose sole purpose was thought to be "sabotage"—had been discounted from the outset. For Americans, as Lord Inverchapel wrote, "[T]he Communists have so successfully replaced the Nazis" as the threat to world peace that it was best to revive Germany with a modicum of Anglo-American control.[50]

Further, the Truman administration did not believe that the Soviets would permit U.S. oversight of their finances, industrial production, and resources. Nor did it think that Congress would appropriate major foreign aid if it benefited the Soviet Union. As Masaryk exclaimed, "Do you see Truman and Congress forking out billions of dollars to Enemy Number One, communist Russia, from whom we all have to be saved?" Moreover, Russian involvement in ERP might have fatally burdened the task of moving Britain and France to accept a revived and integrated European (and German) economy that would include supranational institutions for economic planning and administration. Thus, as historian Michael Hogan has established, it was not only "containment" but also the strategy of economic integration that militated against Soviet involvement in ERP.[51]

Stalin's action, from his perspective, was virtually foreordained, although far less a declaration of war than a calibrated defensive reaction. Since the war's end, there had been no accord with the U.S. on a loan, credits, or German reparations. His February 1946 speech had pointed to Russian reconstruction through Five-Year Plans that emphasized heavy industry and Russian autonomy rather than consumer goods and world trade, and garnered reparations and resources from former enemy (now "satellite") states. The Soviets had little reason to promote Western European–western German recovery. Nor did they have reason to devote their resources to that end. They knew that they could not compete with U.S. production, or the dollar, anywhere in Europe. They also feared, for security reasons, permitting U.S. oversight of their economy through ERP–World Bank reporting requirements. Thus, as the Russian scholar Mikhail Narinsky has written, Stalin and Molotov viewed the Marshall Plan as designed not only to unify Western Europe but to undermine Soviet influence in Eastern Europe.[52]

Most significant, Stalin determined to end dealing with the Western nations and to tighten his control over Eastern Europe. During the summer the Soviets pressed their "Molotov Plan," bilateral trade treaties with Eastern European nations designed to preclude their commerce with the West and to keep them within Russia's political orbit. They also rigged the elections in August in Hungary to assure a Communist plurality. In mid-September Andrei Vishinsky, Soviet delegate to the UN, denounced the Marshall Plan as a "variant" of the Truman Doctrine intended to forge an anti-Russian bloc.[53]

Then from September 22 to September 27 representatives from the Soviet Union, Eastern Europe (except Albania), France, and Italy met in Szlarska Poreba in Poland to form the Communist Information Bureau (or Cominform, successor to the defunct Communist International) to "coordinate" foreign policy. At the initial session, Politburo spokesman Andrei Zhdanov delivered his report "On the International Situation," which in some respects echoed the Truman Doctrine. He proclaimed—in a passage approved by Stalin and inserted at the last moment—that the world was now divided into "two camps," with Russia leading the democracies and the U.S. heading the "antidemocratic camp" committed to global imperialism. The Marshall Plan, he said, was an important part of the U.S. strategy to forge a Western European alliance that would serve as a "jumping-off place for attacking the Soviet Union."[54]

Although Zhdanov also stated that both socialism and capitalism would continue to exist for a long time and that Soviet and capitalist-nation cooperation was possible under conditions of reciprocity and adherence to agreements, this prospective spheres-of-influence approach was effectively ended. Henceforth, he would insist, Communist parties should no longer cooperate with bourgeois parties or, as in the past, join an anti-Fascist coalition. Instead, the

Soviet Union and its allies had to take resolute and unilateral action to oppose the Marshall Plan and other American, or Western, imperialist policies. In effect, as historians have noted, the Marshall Plan served to precipitate Stalin's instituting a major change in grand strategy. The Soviets were abandoning the concepts of separate national roads to socialism and pluralistic governments in Eastern Europe or France and Italy. The Eastern European states were now expected to subordinate themselves in foreign and domestic policies to the Soviet Union, and the Communist Parties in France and Italy were to take every action they could to disrupt or to destroy the incipient Marshall Plan or other collaborative arrangements between or among capitalist states. Confrontation in a bipolar world was the order of the day.[55]

III

The Truman administration did not doubt that Soviet-American rivalry was global. Kennan's soon-classic anonymous article, "The Sources of Soviet Conduct," had already appeared in *Foreign Affairs* in July. "Mr. X" (whose identity was quickly revealed) emphasized the ideological and psychological bases of the Soviet Union's policy and insisted that its ambitions were unbounded and that there was almost no chance of settling conflicts through negotiations. He likened Soviet political action to a fluid stream that filled every available basin of world power and stated that U.S. policy toward Russia had to be long-term "containment," or the "adroit and vigilant application of counter-force" at constantly shifting geographical and political points. Although neither Truman nor Marshall saw the article in advance—Kennan later said that "certainly I don't think [Truman] grasped my position"—it was quickly perceived to be Truman administration doctrine, with an emphasis on military, rather than political or ERP-style, containment. Later Kennan said that he regretted that his "ambiguous" reference to counterforce was interpreted as military force and that he had failed to say that he did not intend that the U.S. should undertake containment everywhere in the world.[56]

Syndicated columnist Walter Lippmann soon wrote a dozen articles—republished in fall 1947 as *The Cold War: A Study in U.S. Foreign Policy*—that criticized Kennan's essay for emphasizing ideology over concerns about defense and the balance of power in Soviet foreign policy. Lippmann was also critical of Kennan for proposing a military response to the Soviets instead of mutual withdrawal of forces. He took Kennan to task for encouraging the U.S. to undertake containment on a global scale instead of distinguishing areas of vital interest from peripheral ones.[57]

Despite the Lippmann critique, the die was cast. As Under Secretary Lovett told a high-level State–War Department meeting that included Chief of Staff General Eisenhower on August 30, "[T]he world is definitely split in two." He said that the three western zones of Germany should be regarded not as part of Germany but of Western Europe and treated as part of the Marshall Plan program for that region. At the same time, the group also approved State Department counselor Bohlen's memorandum positing that since the war's end, "two worlds instead of one" had developed and that the "free" and Soviet worlds were headed toward a "showdown crisis" with little chance of resolving it short of hostilities. Thus the U.S. had to consolidate the free world "politically, economically, financially, and . . . militarily."[58]

To this end, the president on July 11 had already approved a new directive, JCS 1779 (replacing the stringent JCS 1067 of May 1945), for U.S. governance of Germany. JCS 1779 reaffirmed the first-charge principle, General Clay's halt of reparations exchanges, and called for Germany to be self-sustaining and economically integrated into Europe. Truman and his Cabinet decided no longer to brook Anglo-French resistance to increasing German food rations and production. They pressed Britain to raise Germany's industrial level in Bizonia to that of 1936 (rather than 1932), including an increase in annual steel production from 7.5 million to 10.7 million tons.[59]

French protests delayed announcement of this accord. But in mid-August Harriman told Truman, who clearly agreed, that if Germany was to be reintegrated and used as a "bulwark" against Communist advance westward and as a "base" for penetrating democratic ideas into Eastern Europe, it was necessary to halt denazification (to put Germany's "best brains" back to work), decartelization, reparations removals, and French obstruction in the guise of military fears. The time had come to step up German production, reform the currency, and establish a federal German government.[60]

Tough U.S. negotiating led to Anglo-French accord on Germany's new industrial level, which could be the basis for its ERP contribution. The British also gave up plans to nationalize coal (Secretary of War Patterson said it was "high time" U.S. management took over Ruhr coal production—even if Russia charged imperialism) and accepted U.S. predominance in Bizonia. In return, the U.S. assumed most of Britain's occupation costs and "assured" the French that Germany's recovery would not get first priority and that France's interest in controlling Ruhr production would be addressed later.[61]

Meanwhile, the sixteen-nation Conference on European Economic Cooperation (CEEC) that began in Paris on July 12 showed little interest in U.S. ideas about integration, austerity budgets, fixed exchange rates, and tariff reductions. The British resisted transnational coordination to protect their industry, labor, and Commonwealth trade. The French, wedded to reindustrialization under the Monnet Plan, pressed for having international control (no longer ownership) of the Ruhr industry and building their own industry instead of restarting Germany's. The French backed a customs union but knew that Britain was opposed. By mid-August, Lovett complained, the CEEC had produced only "sixteen shopping lists."[62]

U.S. officials also bridled at Britain's announcement in late August that it could no longer exchange dollars for pounds, which augured reducing imports and averting multilateral trade agreements. Harriman proposed to "deal roughly" with the British and to resist their moving further Left. Treasury Secretary Snyder said that Britain's problem was not modernization but lack of incentives, except "dog races, soccer matches and horse racing." Likewise, Truman complained that British problems in Palestine and the Ruhr made them "our problem children," whose decision "to go bankrupt" would end U.S. prosperity, after which "Uncle Joe Stalin can have his way." The president also dreaded calling Congress into special session to seek European aid, especially with CEEC estimates running at $29 billion.[63]

CEEC talks were moved along in late August by the tripartite agreement on Germany's industrial level and by the U.S. permitting CEEC countries—including Bizonia—to set separate national production priorities that would be correlated to "concrete proposals" for area-wide recovery. It was also agreed to focus on "bottlenecks" in coal, grain, and basic industries, and to take steps toward multilateral trade. Britain and France, however, still insisted on excluding Bizonia. Marshall reluctantly acceded to this after Kennan advised that Europe's leaders were politically weak, with their nations divided by "Herculean differences" over Germany and fearful of Soviet pressure. This led to a provisional CEEC Report of September 22 that saluted American "self-help" and mutual aid and stated Europe's economic problems and plans to meet them. The report also summarized each CEEC nation's economic program and agreed to an international review agency that had no power. German recovery was deemed essential but subject to its neighbors' security.[64]

The president was now prepared to invest heavily to gain interim aid as prelude to a long-term program. His administration would use well-run public-political information programs, which were abetted by strong anticommunist, anti-Soviet appeals. As British officials promptly noted, the Americans would stress the "Russian menace" to rally those who did not see the constructive basis for aid and expected ERP nations to stand "shoulder to shoulder" with them to resist "Soviet expansionism." The charges would gain credibility from Cominform activities and then major Communist-led industrial and transport strikes and antigovernment protests in November in France and Italy.[65]

Meanwhile, at a Cabinet Room reception on September 29 Truman, closely following his briefing papers, told congressional leaders that without $600 million in interim aid Europe would go Communist and that it was a "question of how long we could stand up in such a serious situation." The next day he asked the appropriate House-Senate committees to consider European aid. The president and the State Department also encouraged congressmen, with more than 200 responding, to visit Europe. There Bevin warned that without aid perhaps Britain, and surely France, would succumb to Communism—the "only alternative"—and that Soviet policy was a blend of Marxism and imperialism bent on global "ideological conquest." In Paris, Bidault saw a world struggle between "Communism and anti-Communism."[66]

By mid-October White House aides had delineated "The President's Program": multiyear, multi-billion-dollar aid; a halt to European (British) nationalization; and a powerful agency responsible to the president and Congress to handle all of Europe's purchases in the U.S. to avert the bidding that would spur inflation. Truman told the National Conference of Editorial Writers that $16–$22 billion in aid was less than one-third of the $55 billion he had cut from the annual budget when war ended in August 1945. He insisted that the world faced a contest between the Bill of Rights and the Soviet system that made the individual "the slave of the state." If Europeans appeared not to be doing enough, Truman said, that was due to losing the "cream of the crop" of two generations in two wars. But he would do what was "right" and "necessary." Finally on October 23 Truman called that dreaded special session of Congress, to begin on November 17. "Republicats" and some Democrats were trying to "put me in a hole," he wrote, but it was more important "to save the world from totalitarianism than to be president another four years."[67]

By mid-fall the three committees that Truman had established in June under Harriman, Krug, and Nourse reported on European aid, American resources, and the economy. They minimized the cost and inflationary impact of aid and stressed that European recovery and U.S. prosperity were intertwined. Additionally, the recently formed Committee for Marshall Plan Aid to Europe, honorifically headed by former secretary of war Henry Stimson and spearheaded by Acheson and business leaders, waged a nationwide public information campaign, lobbied Congress, and readied committee testimony.[68]

The Soviets could only encourage French and Italian opposition, although Molotov did take occasion on November 6, the thirtieth anniversary of the Bolshevik Revolution, to deliver a fiery speech. He traced the course of Communism in Russia from the consolidation of revolution to its current expanding base in the Soviet Union. He declared it was now time for "all anti-imperialist and democratic" forces to effect the inevitable fall of capitalism, and he warned the "expansionist circles" in the U.S. that had put their faith in the secret of the atomic bomb that "this secret has long ceased to be a secret." The statement had little to do with atomic development, however. Rather it was a part of a "war of nerves" to promote Cominform objectives and opposition to the Marshall Plan, while also disabusing the U.S. of the idea that its atomic monopoly would provide political advantage.[69]

U.S. officials were unmoved by Molotov's statement. In fact, Truman and his aides grew more confident about the U.S. position. Marshall had Kennan prepare a world summary, which the secretary read to Truman and his Cabinet on November 7, stating that the Soviets neither expected nor wanted war and that the "communist menace" in Europe had been halted, due partly to American aid. But to sustain this program, western Germany had to be "kept free of communistic control" and integrated into Western Europe, which meant "making the best of a divided Germany." Further, the Russians' response would be to "clamp down completely" on Czechoslovakia to strengthen the Soviet position in Eastern Europe. But this was "purely a defensive move," and ultimately Russian rule there would "crumble." After the meeting, the president asked Mashall for a full copy of the report.[70]

The next week Marshall told the Cabinet that his foreign-aid testimony to Congress had gone well, except for being drawn down "side streets" on aid for China. Truman's request to Congress on November 17 for $597 million in interim aid was blunt: the future of Europe's "free nations" and U.S. prosperity hung in the balance. Vandenberg wrote that he was "overwhelmed" by the administration's "magnificent" documentation of its case, and not more than twelve senators would vote against the bill, which sailed through Congress by December 15. The aid was trimmed, however, to $540 million, including $18 million for China.[71]

Meanwhile, Marshall prepared for another CFM meeting in late November in London. Before departing, he said that he expected only Soviet "ruses" to get the U.S. out of western Germany in order to open it to "communist penetration" as part of the Soviet plan to dominate the European landmass. Accordingly, U.S. planning for the conference was premised on averting proposals for German economic unity (especially Russian involvement in the Ruhr), for paying current production reparations, or for withdrawing troops. The goal was to find reason to break up the meeting, perhaps over political rights, and then to move forward with integrating western Germany into the Marshall Plan and forming a provisional German government. The British were in accord, and the French were now convinced that they had to go along with their allies in order to influence German policy.[72]

After the CFM meeting opened on November 25, Molotov predictably assailed the Western powers for failing to reform or demilitarize Germany, for not meeting Russian reparations payments, and for plotting to divide Germany. He then pressed in more moderate fashion creation of central agencies, payment of reparations, and formation of a directly elected central government, which would take part in writing a peace treaty. Marshall was unmoved. He held that it was useless to form a government to administer a nation already divided by divergent occupation policies. Thus he reverted to the U.S. demands for a federal regime based on the Länder, with Germany being allowed to join the Marshall Plan but not paying current production reparations. After days of debate, Molotov proffered a compromise on economic unity: to raise Germany's level of industry, limit capital plant removals, and stretch current production reparations payments over twenty years, with zonal barriers coming down after the agreement was in effect.[73]

But as Ambassador Smith (who attended the conference at Marshall's behest) wrote to Eisenhower on December 10, "[T]he difficulty under which we labor is that in spite of our avowed position, we really do not want nor intend to accept German unification in any terms that the Russians might agree to, even though they seemed to meet most of our requirements. . . . However, this puts us in a somewhat difficult position, and it will require careful maneuvering to avoid the appearance of inconsistency if not hypocrisy." In short, the issue for the Americans was more than just their belief that Moscow would not agree to commit German resources to the Marshall Plan. In fact, the Americans preferred to divide Germany and to transform the three western zones into a strong anticommunist redoubt rather than try to negotiate a unified nation that might run the risk of Soviet or Communist influence in western Germany.[74]

Consequently, even after Molotov acceded to the U.S. principle of making the cost of Allied imports into Germany a first charge against export revenue and to making external occupation costs a German governmental debt, Marshall raised the stakes by insisting that shipment of current production reparations be ended as of January 1948. Still, the Americans worried that the Soviets would press an agreement that would look good publicly but frustrate U.S. designs for German and European reconstruction. Molotov bitterly rejected the U.S. position, however, and accused the Allies of bad faith. Marshall rejoined that the foreign minister's behavior reflected on the dignity of the Soviet government. The Americans and British quickly pressed adjournment on December 15, with no date set to reconvene. As Marshall said, "[T]he Russians had at last run against a solid front." The Western powers were now also free to advance their plans to integrate western Germany into the Marshall Plan and to form a western German government. The Rubicon had been crossed.[75]

Upon return to the U.S., Marshall told Truman and the Cabinet on December 19 that Molotov's speeches had been "filled with lies," but now General

Clay was proceeding with currency reform and economic merger in western Germany. Then in a national broadcast the secretary declared that the prospects for German unity were nil and "we must do the best we can where our influence can be felt."[76]

That same day, December 19, Truman requested $6.8 billion in ERP aid for the fifteen months beginning April 1948, and $17 billion during 1948–1952. He minimized the relative cost: 5 percent of the previous war effort and 3 percent of national income for four years. He stressed need for increased trade and stockpiling of resources and assured that the new Economic Cooperation Administration (ECA) would control the use of aid. But the bottom line was the right of European states to live in peace and prosperity, without fear of "totalitarian aggression."[77]

The president reiterated his call for ERP both in his January 12, 1948, annual budget message and at a press conference on January 29. ERP was only 18 percent of the total federal outlay of $37.7 billion, he said, and far less compared to wartime expenditures or current national income. Failure to act meant the advance of totalitarianism and increased defense spending. Further, to commit for only one year was to throw money down a "rat hole": it had to be "all or nothing," although he did not want to be quoted. At the same time, the British remarked, the administration also intended to "thump the Russian drum" because that would permit Congress to see ERP as "containing Russia."[78]

Passage of ERP was virtually assured, although Republican leadership and conservative Democrats would exact compromise on money and structure. Few disputed Marshall's testimony that America's security and way of life depended on revitalizing Europe, although a few critics on the Right such as Senator Robert Taft saw ERP as a "European T.V.A." On the Left, Henry Wallace insisted that the "Martial Plan" would divide Europe and proposed instead a UN reconstruction fund. Meanwhile, Vandenberg, chairman of the Senate Foreign Relations Committee and a strong ERP proponent, persuaded the Truman administration to stop talk of $17 billion in aid and to agree to change its request for $6.8 billion for fifteen months to a comparable $5.3 billion for the first year. The senator would also persuade Truman that ECA could not be located in the State Department but had to be an independent agency with a Cabinet-status administrator appointed by the president with Congress' approval. (Later Vandenberg tactfully told Truman that Congress would not confirm his first choice for the position, Acheson, or Clayton, and then engineered appointment of a Michigan constituent, Paul Hoffman, head of Studebaker Corporation.) The Senate Foreign Relations Committee approved ERP in mid-February, and the Senate, against the backdrop of a crisis over Czechoslovakia, voted the first year's aid by 69–17 on March 13.[79]

The ERP vote gained dramatic, but not determinative, impetus from the crisis in Czechoslovakia in February 1948 and from presidential Cold War politics. The Czechs were led by President Eduard Benes, symbol of prewar democracy and head of the National Socialist Party, and Prime Minister Gottwald, whose Communist Party had won the largest share (38 percent) of the vote in the free elections of 1946. The Czechs followed a postwar policy of nonalignment, in keeping with their 1943 treaty with the Soviet Union. U.S. officials disliked Czech neutrality and economic nationalization policies, and that the coalition government included Communists. After Czech delegates clashed with then Secretary of State Byrnes at a peace conference meeting in August 1946, the U.S. suspended loan negotiations, and Ambassador Laurence A. Steinhardt in Prague continued to insist that denying economic aid would weaken the Communists. The Russians forced the Czechs to decline ERP talks in July 1947, signed a trade treaty with Prague in December, and then shipped part of an agreed 600,000 tons of badly needed wheat. Western-oriented Czechs remained dismayed at the economic hard line of the U.S. toward their country.[80]

Tragedy engulfed Czechoslovakia in early 1948. Fearful that his party would suffer losses in the elections scheduled for May, Vaclav Nosek, the Communist minister of interior (who controlled the powerful State Security Guard), began to purge non-Communists from critical government posts and then ignored a Cabinet order to halt on February 13. Six days later Soviet Deputy Foreign Minister Valerian Zorin arrived in Prague, although he brought the Communists no more than sympathetic support. The next day, February 20, twelve (of twenty-six) non-Communist Cabinet ministers submitted their resignations, believing that Benes had agreed not to accept them but instead would reorganize the Cabinet or advance the elections. The Czech president hesitated, however, leading to five days of national protests, in which the Communists literally outmuscled their opponents. Then Benes, in poor health (he would resign in June, and die in September) and uncertain of the army's loyalty in case of civil war, capitulated to Gottwald's demand for a Communist-controlled government.[81]

Two weeks later, on March 10, the Western-oriented Masaryk was found dead on the street below his foreign ministry apartment. Gottwald's government alleged that the foreign minister had committed suicide, although many believed—rightly so—that the Communists had murdered him. Meanwhile, Stalin added to European tension in late February by insisting that Finland negotiate a defensive pact with the Soviet Union.[82]

At the same time, it must be noted, U.S. officials were meeting with their British, French, and Western European counterparts in London from February 23 to March 6, when they announced initial accord on a federal form of government for western Germany, an international Ruhr authority, and western German integration into the Marshall Plan. Meanwhile, in Berlin Clay continued to dodge agreement with the Russians on four-power currency reform. Then on March 17 Britain, France, Belgium, the Netherlands, and Luxembourg announced signature of the Brussels Treaty, or Western Union—spearheaded by Bevin—a fifty-year mutual-defense pact that also committed these nations to coordinate their financial and economic policies with the Marshall Plan.[83]

The increasing polarization of Europe and U.S. coolness toward the Prague government help to explain why Truman and his aides were not shocked by the Czech tragedy and did not think it meant war. Kennan, of course, had warned during the past November that ERP would probably cause the Russians "to clamp down completely" on the Czechs, and Truman had taken a copy of this report for himself. Now Marshall said that a Communist seizure of power in Czechoslovakia would only "crystallize" their postwar pattern of following the Soviet lead in foreign affairs, and reports from Prague, including from Steinhardt, indicated that the Russians had not concentrated troops on the Czech border or taken direct action through Zorin or otherwise. On March 10 the CIA concluded that neither Czech nor Finnish events signified change in Soviet tactics or policy and that the "psychological reaction to the Communist coup in Prague appears to have been out of all proportion to its actual significance." Or as Bevin wrote, "[T]here is nothing we can do" about Czechoslovakia, except be strong so that no one ever thinks of dealing with the Soviets. And remember never to let Communists into a government "in the vain hope that they will play according to the Westminster rules."[84]

Thus Truman's initial public responses to the Czech coup were restrained. He joined Anglo-French condemnation of a one-party dictatorship in Czechoslovakia but denied prospect of a Western military alliance even though formal talks were under way. He lamented that Czechoslovakia and Finland were "down the drain" and said that he lacked "facts" to comment on Masaryk's death.[85]

Nonetheless, the demise of Czech democracy "crystallized" the darkest views of the Soviet Union, inflamed public-political rhetoric, and galvanized ERP support. This was so despite lack of overt Soviet action and the fact that the Czech Communists did most of the "dirty work" in destroying Czech democracy. Truman, Steinhardt, and many others believed that Stalin and the Czech Communists had conspired to precipitate the 1948 crisis and executed their "putsch" exactly as Hitler and the Czech Nazis had done a decade earlier. From the American viewpoint, France, Italy, and Austria were the next targets of "fifth column aggression supported by external force, on the Czech model."[86]

Indeed, on March 3 Truman raged privately that "we are faced with exactly the same situation with which Britain and France were faced in 1938–9 with Hitler. A totalitarian state is no different whether you call it Nazi, Fascist, Communist or Franco Spain." He reiterated his constant refrain that he had gone to Potsdam with the "kindliest feelings" toward the Russians but that they had "cured" him by breaking every agreement since then. Still, he hoped matters would end peacefully, but he had "a decision" to make and would not shy from it.[87]

Similarly, Churchill told the Bevin government that if the West did not resist the Russians firmly in the next weeks there would be a "gradual slipping into war" as in the 1930s. From Berlin, General Clay informed Ambassador Lewis Douglas in London that "for the first time he really thought that the Russians wanted war soon." But British officials saw no evidence of Soviet war readiness, although Bevin told his Cabinet on March 3 that the Russians sought to dominate Eurasia and then "the whole World Island."[88]

Two days later Clay, known to say that he did not expect war with Russia for at least ten years, reiterated by cable to General Stephen I. Chamberlin, head of intelligence for the Army General Staff, that he had detected a subtle change in Soviet behavior that now led him to feel that war with the Soviets might come with "dramatic suddenness." Clay really sought to buttress the military's effort to get more money from Congress, including for UMT. But his cable, coming when forebodings were running high, ignited a "war scare" among Washington officials that critically shaped how Truman made his case for ERP to Congress and the nation.[89]

Truman was scheduled to address a St. Patrick's Day rally on March 17 in New York. By March 5 White House aide Elsey was adamant that "the president *must*" make a strong speech, a "dramatic declaration" that would raise his prestige as well as that of the U.S., and that he was best when "mad" rather than merely for "good things." Elsey proposed talking about Russian-American relations, including a "roll call" of nations that the Soviets had "swallowed," and urging support for ERP and military aid for Europe. He also proposed criticizing Wallace (now a declared Progressive Party presidential candidate) for calling for a Truman-Stalin summit.[90]

Clifford, who was both White House counsel and campaign strategist, agreed. Having concluded months earlier that Truman's election in 1948 depended greatly on pursuing a tough line toward the Russians and gaining public support through a "sense of crisis" (but not war), Clifford wanted a "peroration" that emphasized "free men and women" confronting the Soviet threat to "their liberty and to their God." Marshall dissented, however. He told Truman and the Cabinet on March 5 that Vandenberg had ERP "well in hand" in the Senate and that the Europeans had agreed to western German participation in ERP and were progressing on German political-economic structure. The secretary recognized problems—Czechoslovakia, Finland, and Italy—but concluded that just because the world was a "keg of dynamite—HST shouldn't start it."[91]

Truman was uncertain. He wanted ERP and expansion of military manpower and spending. Thus he noted on Marshall's report, "Shall we state the case to Congress—name names and call the turn. Will Russia move first? Who pulls the trigger? . . . Then where do we go?" But after Masaryk's death the president left a Cabinet meeting on March 12 ready to "take the bull by the horns and reemphasize his leadership," despite Marshall's caveats about arousing public passion and belief that the U.S. should not take a position it would have to reverse—"that would be tragic." On March 15 Clifford and Elsey persuaded Truman to give a hard-line speech for ERP in New York, but Marshall insisted that Congress was a more appropriate forum. He promptly drafted a temperate address. Truman agreed with his aides that "it stank."[92]

The president had made his "decision": to warn the country lest it be "sunk" as in 1941, he told his staff. Further, he wrote Eleanor Roosevelt on March 16 that he and FDR had done all they could from Yalta to Potsdam to please the Russians—but they only treated U.S. officials in Eastern Europe like "stableboys" and established totalitarian governments there. "Russia has not kept the faith with us," he said, and now he would put "the facts" to Congress and the people.[93]

The president addressed a joint session of Congress shortly after noon on March 17, the day Britain and its allies signed the Brussels Treaty. For the first time, Truman publicly blamed the Soviet Union for causing the Cold War. Current world problems were not the natural aftermath of world war, he said, but the fault of "one nation" that used its veto to obstruct the UN and sought to destroy democracy and independence in Central and Eastern Europe—the death of Czech democracy shocked civilization—and dominate the Continent. He praised the Europeans for the Brussels Treaty and for promoting economic collaboration and urged Congress to pass ERP, enact UMT, and temporarily restore the draft.[94]

Truman reiterated his speech, with more of Clifford's language, later that night in New York. He called for ERP, UMT, and the draft and added a "roll call" of Soviet-dominated nations from the Baltic to the Balkans. He turned up his presidential political rhetoric by insisting that he did not want the support of "Henry Wallace and his Communists," reading him out of the Democratic Party, as Truman noted. He concluded that the issue that confronted the world was "tyranny versus freedom," and warned that Communism sought to deny man's "right to govern himself" as well as the "very existence of God." Thus

Americans had to be prepared to "take risks" to secure peace. Canadian prime minister Mackenzie King recorded that this was a "day that had its place in history," signifying that differences with the Soviets would no longer be settled by conciliation but "by force" if the Russians did not back down.[95]

The House Foreign Affairs Committee promptly voted $5.3 billion in European aid, and as public support grew, Republican (and anticommunist) leaders pushed through the full House a $6.2 billion omnibus aid bill on March 30 that included an additional $570 million for China and $275 million for Greece and Turkey. At their reconciliation conference, Senate leaders gave way to the House's omnibus aid approach, and on April 3 Truman signed the new Foreign Assistance Act. Late in June both the Senate and House appropriations committees would vote an actual $6 billion in aid; including $4 billion for ERP, $1.3 billion for occupied areas (mainly Germany), $225 million for Greece and Turkey, $400 million for China, and $106 million for international aid organizations. Overall, during 1948–1952 Congress would expend about $13 billion in Marshall Plan aid.[96]

IV

In April 1948 Truman told a conference of business-magazine editors that "ERP is the greatest step we have taken lately in the interests of peace" and that if it succeeded, "we will raise the Iron Curtain by peaceable means." ERP augured a European "economic union—customs union," the president said, which meant that "there will be nothing for the Iron Curtain to do but go up" because the people behind it could not get along without Western commerce. Seen from a half-century's perspective, it is tempting to conclude that Truman was more right about ERP than his critics then or later and that one might draw an historical line from creation of ERP in 1947–1948 through formation of the European Coal and Steel Community (ECSC) in 1951, the European Economic Community (EEC) in 1957, and the start of the integrated European Community in 1992. Meanwhile, the tumultuous years 1989–1991 brought the collapse of Communist regimes in Eastern Europe, the destruction of the Berlin Wall and Germany's unification, and finally, the demise of the Soviet Union in 1991. Thus the Iron Curtain was raised.[97]

The road of history is more tortuous than direct, however, and the many East-West conflicts and crises of the past five decades suggest that the ties between events of 1947–1948 and 1992 are tenuous. In fact, ERP may have deepened the East-West divide and not effected Western economic or political integration in the way, or with the speed, that Marshall Planners intended or envisioned in 1947.

ERP did not cause the iron curtain to rise, at least not in the near future, so much as it spurred Moscow to "clamp down" politically in Czechoslovakia and then throughout Eastern Europe. The Soviets also established in January 1949 their rival to ERP, the Council for Mutual Economic Assistance, or Comecon. Comecon proved to be little more than a "symbolic facade" during the Stalin era, during which time it actually extracted about $14 billion in deliveries from Eastern Europe, a sum equal to about what the U.S. expended in Europe. Further, by 1952 the Soviets, through bilateral trade treaties, forced Eastern Europe to carry on 80 percent of its trade with them, a pattern that the Truman administration caused to be heightened by sharply curtailing U.S. loans to, or trade with, the Eastern bloc. Meanwhile Western Europe maintained its Eastern bloc trade at about 50 percent of its 1938 level.[98]

More important, the already scant prospect for German unification virtually vanished because ERP rested on western German reconstruction and contributions while denying the Soviets access to Ruhr industry and the reparations they regarded as their due. As Stalin said in early 1948 to Yugoslav emissary Milovan Djilas, "The West will make Western Germany their own, and we shall turn Eastern Germany into our own state." In effect, the U.S. policy makers perceived German reconstruction as the indispensable means to European recovery and security and were ready to take this decision knowing that it meant Germany and Europe would be increasingly divided into hostile economic and political—and soon military—camps. To some extent the Truman administration's decision to "divide" Germany was less a clear policy choice than a reflection of the reality that the U.S. and the Soviet Union had created during three years of bitter wrangling over Germany. By August 1947 Lovett had expressed the consensus that "the world is definitely split in two." But it is equally true that Truman agreed with Harriman's more pointed assessment that western Germany had to be reconstructed in order to contain the Soviets and to "penetrate" the Eastern bloc.[99]

Truman had more than Cold War reason to be happy about ERP. To begin, in 1948 he was a "lame duck" president, subject to sharp criticism on domestic (especially civil rights and labor) and foreign policy issues from Southern conservatives and Northern liberals in his own party as well as from Republicans, who controlled Congress, assailed foreign aid and taxes, and looked confidently to gaining the White House in November. Thus Truman had to expend his limited political capital shrewdly. He had to muster public-political support for ERP by making excellent use of nonpartisan figures, such as Marshall, the Marshall Plan committee members, and "bipartisan" leaders such as Vandenberg. This is not to say that a modified ERP would not have passed in 1948 or soon thereafter; nor to ignore that Truman's St. Patrick Day anticommunist rhetoric, and tendency "to beat the Russian drum," was excessive. Still, judged in terms of presidential power and legislation, Truman and his White House aides effectively gave maximum public credit to his Olympian-like secretary of state and the vain Vandenberg and mobilized public opinion to effect timely passage of ERP.[100]

ERP accomplishments were significant, although far from what Marshall Planners envisioned. By 1952, Europe's GNP had increased from $120 billion to $159 billion, with industry 35 percent above its 1938 level (ERP's target was 30 percent) and agriculture 11 percent higher than in 1938 (ERP's target was 15 percent). U.S. dollars alone did not gain this result, of course; Europeans provided 80 to 90 percent of the domestic capital formation, as well as the political leadership and skilled and productive workforce, for this initial reconstruction. But debate over whether America's contribution of 10 to 20 percent of reindustrializing capital actually fueled Europe's recovery or only lubricated the engine is less important than that the U.S. demonstrated the vitally necessary commitment to inspire European confidence and to permit the industrial "take off"—or sustain the resurgence already underway—especially given the bitter winter of 1946–1947 and governmental financial-political constraints. In effect, the infusion of U.S. dollars permitted European governments not to have to raise funds to purchase necessary imports by depressing wages or engaging in austerity measures that would have angered their workforces and been politically costly.[101]

The U.S. also profited from ERP because the $13 billion in foreign aid that ECA dispensed to European governments could be spent only on American industrial-agricultural products, thereby invigorating U.S. exports. As ECA deputy administrator (later administrator) William C. Foster wrote in 1949, since U.S. suppliers were the only competitors for ECA funds, "the dollars always come home." Further, European importers, the real purchasers of the goods, paid their governments for them in their national currency, which "counterpart" funds the governments could then spend only on ECA-approved projects. Thus the U.S. sought to influence European national policy—government investment, social spending, and debt reduction—although major influence was limited mainly to weaker states such as Greece and Turkey. Finally, ECA also took 5 percent of the counterpart funds for administration and purchase of strategic materials.[102]

Most significant, ERP provided the framework for the U.S. to co-opt France to accede to German reconstruction, although only after the Americans agreed in the spring of 1948 to keep their troops in Europe, i.e., to occupy Germany, and to create an International Authority to supervise—but not to own, as the French had wanted—Ruhr industry and production. Thus the initial steps were taken toward later Franco-German cooperation, such as the ECSC in 1951. In addition, France's "museum" economy began to modernize, with relative prosperity returned by 1954. Meanwhile the revitalized German "colossus" would both be constrained within a European framework and serve to contain the Soviet Union.[103]

Americans and Europeans, of course, often differed sharply about ERP's purposes. In January 1948, for example, Bevin told his Cabinet that Europe had to collaborate to resist Soviet "penetration" of its affairs. At the same time, however, he also sought a British Commonwealth–Western European Union bloc—or "middle kingdom," to use Michael Hogan's term—that by its "population and productive capacity, could stand on an equality with the western hemisphere and Soviet *blocs*." Thus the British wished to partake of European integration but preserve their world-power status, lead an independent (albeit U.S.-supported) bloc that balanced between the American and Soviet superpowers, and maintain their special relationship with Commonwealth–sterling-area countries and commitment to a socialized domestic economy. Clearly this formidable diplomatic agenda set the British apart, as an Exchequer official wrote, from "the Americans, [who] want an integrated Europe looking like the United States of America—'God's' own country."[104]

Consequently, U.S. and British officials repeatedly clashed about European economic organization. The Americans emphasized free-market forces and supranational economic regulation or integration, and the British insisted on national economic controls and conventional intergovernmental economic cooperation. In 1950 the Americans pressed formation of the European Payments Union (EPU), which was intended to liberalize trade through currency convertibility and reduction of trade barriers and to permit debtor nations to offset trade deficits with any single nation by using their surplus (or EPU drawing rights) with any other European nation. The British agreed to join EPU and to permit limited transferability of sterling. But they also secured a special $150 million guarantee to cover need for gold or dollar payments to the EPU and right to preserve bilateral trade accords. The British drew back from further European integration, which remained largely unfilled except for ECSC, and they did not join the EEC, or Common Market, at its inception in 1957.[105]

Finally, it is clear that the Marshall Plan began to end in November 1950 when the People's Republic of China entered the Korean War. In fact, as early as spring 1949 the Truman administration had started, through military assistance programs, to put European rearmament on a par with economic recovery. After the Korean War widened, most ECA funds were targeted to rearmament. Thus in 1951, three-fourths of the Truman administration's omnibus $8.5 billion foreign-aid package was devoted to military assistance, with ECA subordinated to a State-Treasury-Defense Department International Security Affairs Committee focused on military purposes. Moreover, as European rearmament outran recovery, the result was inflation, and an increasing "dollar gap" and drain on currency reserves. Meanwhile, higher U.S. taxes, shortage of raw materials, and an astronomical leap in military spending from $17 billion in Fiscal Year (FY) 1950 to $53 billion in FY 1951, caused ECA and economic aid to give way entirely in October 1951 to the new Mutual Security Administration, which put near exclusive emphasis on foreign military aid.[106]

Despite the shortfalls, the Marshall Plan proved to be perhaps the most enduring and inspiring foreign policy initiative of the Truman administration. ERP proved highly successful considered solely as a program to help restore European production, revive trade, and limit inflation. At the same time, ERP established a framework to effect Franco-German accord, to foster western German political-economic revival and the security of its neighbors, and to lay the foundation for a half century of Western European political and economic stability and growth. Truman had reason to reflect that "history" would record the Marshall Plan as one of America's greatest contributions to world peace. But in 1948 he still had to confront the dangerous consequences of the division of Germany and of Europe that the ERP had helped to catalyze, and also seek "reelection" as president.[107]

Cat on a Sloping Tin Roof

The Berlin Blockade, 1948–1949

Truman intended to run for president in 1948 despite his complaints about the office's administrative burdens and the abuse he had to take, he said, from "liars and demagogues." He knew that liberal and conservative Democrats sought to find another standard-bearer, notably General Eisenhower or Supreme Court Justice William Douglas. Meanwhile, former secretary of commerce Wallace would organize a new Progressive Party. Truman, however, did not intend to step aside for anyone. In late 1947 he allowed Secretary of the Army Kenneth Royall to sound Eisenhower about the nomination, but that may have been a ploy to gauge Ike's "Potomac fever," the presidential ambition Truman ascribed to many government officials. By this time he enjoyed presidential power and believed, as Defense Secretary Forrestal noted, that it was his duty to nation and party to run, and to effect his "peace program." Truman said he was not a "quitter."[1]

No one knew that better than Clifford, the shrewd White House aide. In November 1947 he had sent to the president his later-famous memorandum "The Politics of 1948." Clifford's analysis anticipated both Henry Wallace as a third-party candidate and the Republicans' choice of New York's moderate governor, Thomas E. Dewey. Clifford's election strategy stressed domestic politics, but also strong presidential foreign policy leadership. He saw "political advantage" to be gained from the "battle with the Kremlin" because the public would unite behind the president as matters moved toward "imminent war." Still, Clifford counseled making policy based on "intrinsic merit," and Truman, despite his charge that Wallace had gone "over to the enemy," was unlikely to promote a foreign crisis for political gain.[2]

Nonetheless, conflict neared in 1948 when the Soviets sought to thwart the American-British-French decision to form a West German state by halting the Allies' access by land to West Berlin. This crisis proved to be a "great divide" over German and European alignment and relations with the Soviet Union. Truman also had to confront the old problem of civilian control of the military and the new, but equally vexing, issue of control of nuclear weapons.[3]

In certain respects, the Berlin blockade proved to be a crisis made-to-order for Truman. He gained high marks at home and abroad for pursuing moderation—neither diplomatic retreat nor military confrontation—in the face of great adversity. He also asserted presidential responsibility for nuclear weapons and generally kept politics out of policy making. But the president did not appear to see or acknowledge the connection between the U.S.-led decision to bring a reconstructed West Germany into a western political, economic, and military condominium and Stalin's decision to impose the Berlin blockade. Truman's quick accord with General Clay's view that "if we move out of Berlin we have lost everything we are fighting for" exaggerated the purpose of Stalin's move as well as the political (and legal) correctness of U.S. policy. It also foreclosed last slim prospects for compromise over Germany and Europe and reinforced the tendency to magnify all conflict and to envision Stalin as Hitler bent on unbounded aggression.[4]

I

The Truman administration had reason to anticipate conflict in 1948 over Germany, and specifically Berlin. ERP success was predicated on increased Anglo-American, and French, cooperation in a reconstructed West Germany, with the Soviets excluded. After bitter adjournment of the CFM meeting in December 1947 signified the virtual end of four-power negotiations on Germany, Secretary Marshall and Foreign Minister Bevin reached accord on need to form a bizonal government—although it was not to be called that, nor created in "unseemly haste"—with the French to weigh melding their occupation zone into "Trizonia." The diplomats agreed as well to revise Germany's level of industry upward and increase its foreign trade (both of which would curtail Russian reparations) and, most crucial, to reform its inflated currency. Clay would make a last effort at currency reform with the Russians, who he thought would go along, although he was prepared to act alone and soon had the new money in hand. Marshall, of course, exulted that the Soviets had "at last run against a solid front."[5]

The new Anglo-American policy meant that there would be two Germanies. U.S. officials expected to pay a price for this. Clay anticipated Soviet "minor annoyances" in Berlin, but he reassured everyone that he had adequate resources to "hold out" for some time. He said he would not ask his government what to do if things became "too tough" until that occurred. But Admiral Roscoe Hillenkoetter, director of the CIG in Washington, informed Truman in late December 1947 that the likely Russian response to unifying western Germany would be "obstructionism" intended to "force the U.S. and other western powers to withdraw from Berlin." The Army General Staff said that the Soviets could do this easily by military action or "administrative difficulties" because Allied access to the city—situated 110 miles inside the Soviet occupation zone—was limited to one highway (from Helmstedt to Berlin), two railroads, and one air corridor. Surprisingly, neither Royall nor Forrestal thought that the army's "information" study required action.[6]

In early 1948, Clay and his British counterpart in Berlin, General Sir Brian Robertson, swiftly reorganized Bizonia's political and economic structures to resemble a formal government. This action triggered Soviet countermeasures in eastern Germany and drew protests from the French, who secured British support for a meeting with the U.S. in London in late February to discuss plans for western Germany. Meanwhile, officials in Washington weighed halting the already-reduced shipment of Russian reparations (largely dismantled German industry), which would increase tension. Significantly, Truman, Marshall, and Clay, as well as Bevin, favored complying with the Potsdam (and subsequent) agreements for both uncompensated reparations deliveries and those exchanged for Soviet-sector goods. They agreed that this would not retard ERP and would gain needed foodstuffs. Bevin was especially concerned that a reparations halt would "exacerbate" conditions in Berlin. But members of Truman's Cabinet, notably Commerce Secretary Harriman, as well as congressional leaders such as Senator Vandenberg, sought to stop deliveries. In mid-February, Truman agreed to continue capital equipment deliveries and to seek Anglo-French accord to end uncompensated deliveries.[7]

Then came the initial conference in London, starting on February 23, of the Western powers to deal with western Germany, notwithstanding Russian protest that their exclusion violated the Potsdam accords. Following two weeks of hard bargaining, the Allies announced their so-called London Program for western Germany on March 6. They agreed in principle to establish a federal form of government, international control of Ruhr production (to assuage the French but also preclude their efforts at annexation), and a military security board to monitor German demilitarization, and agreed to bring western Germany into ERP. In return for French accord, Ambassador Lewis Douglas assured Paris that U.S. troops would remain in Germany "for a long time—until the threat from the east has disappeared." This meant France's protection from both a revived Germany and the Soviet Union. Truman's March 17 speeches to Congress and in New York City confirmed need for U.S. support for European defense.[8]

Still, Bevin would not accede to the U.S. desire to cut off Russian reparations. There was no legitimate basis to end shipment of the relatively small amounts of dismantled machinery legitimately due, and the action would be too provocative, especially regarding Berlin. But over the next months the U.S., urged on by Marshall, Harriman, and Clay, determined to conciliate the western Germans and facilitate their nascent state's cooperation with ERP by sharply cutting back denazification and virtually abandoning decartelization programs. This swept away the last safeguards imposed on Germany by the Yalta and Potsdam agreements.[9]

Despite Marshall's claim that the London Program was only an "interim solution" that did not preclude future four-power agreement on Germany, that prospect was dead. As Ambassador Lord Inverchapel said, the Americans believed that the "division of Germany and absorption of the two parts into rival Eastern and Western spheres is preferable to the creation of a no-man's land on the border of an expanding Soviet hegemony." This outlook was similar, of course, to Stalin's comment—more a statement of fact than immediate desire—to Yugoslavian and Bulgarian Communists in February 1948 that "the West will make Western Germany their own, and we shall turn Eastern Germany into our own state."[10]

East-West tension was further heightened at this time by the Communist coup in Czechoslovakia, and Soviet approaches to Finland for a defense pact and to Norway for a nonalignment accord. Clay sent his "war scare" telegram on March 5, and another the next day to the War Department urging that the U.S. should think of security against Russia first and "against a revived Germany later." Truman then delivered his rousing speeches on March 17 to Congress and to the Sons of St. Patrick in New York in which he blamed the Soviet Union for the Cold War and called for ERP funds, UMT, selective service, and support for the Brussels Treaty. Forrestal said that it was "inconceivable" that the "gang" running Russia would start a war, but he added that the same could have been said in 1939 about Hitler. Soon Anglo-American military planners talked secretly (with the Russians apprised of matters through their spies at the British Embassy) at the Pentagon about a North Atlantic area defense pact. Then on March 30 the NSC proposed a "world-wide counter-offensive" to thwart Russia. NSC 7, a report on "The Position of the United States with Respect to Soviet-directed World Communism," was the first Truman administration document to refer to the "cold war." It recommended maintaining overwhelming atomic weapons superiority, providing machinery to bolster the

Brussels Treaty, or Western Union, building an arms industry, and committing the U.S. to military action if the Soviets attacked the Western Union or other "non-communist" nations.[11]

Meanwhile, in response to the Allied announcement in late January of the forthcoming London Conference, the Russians began to halt American and British trains en route to Berlin. The Soviets allegedly acted to check passenger identity, although this breached prior (1945) oral military accords and past practices. In turn, Clay put armed guards on the trains to bar entry, and the Soviets reverted occasionally to delaying train movements. At the same time, currency reform talks grew testy. Clay proposed quadripartite currency reform, with one printing site in Berlin. He refused all concessions to the Russians, including a second printing site in their zone in Leipzig, or formation of a central financial agency or central bank prior to issuing the new notes. Clay soon said further talks would be superfluous. This led Marshal Vassily Sokolovsky, the Soviet military governor, to deride the U.S. "ultimatum proposal" and insist that the A.C.C. "condemn" U.S. unilateral plans to begin western zonal reform. He noted that the "new printed money is already in Clay's pocket."[12]

Shortly, on March 9, Stalin summoned Sokolovsky and his political adviser, Vladimir Semenow, to the Kremlin to discuss measures to restrict movement of transport and commerce from the western zones of Germany to western Berlin in order to thwart pending formation of a West German government. As Andrei Smirnov, head of the European Department in the Foreign Ministry advised Stalin and Molotov, the Western powers were creating a West German state that they intended to include in a political-military bloc "directed against the Soviet Union and the new democracies." Thus it was necessary to take action, such as calling for a CFM meeting to settle the German question on the basis of the Yalta-Potsdam accords. Failing that, it would be necessary to close off completely the Soviet occupation zone and organize frontier defenses—all of which implied denying the West access to Berlin. In fact, shortly Stalin agreed with Wilhelm Pieck, the head of the SED in East Germany, that prospects for the Communists there would be better if the Americans were forced from Berlin. "Let's make a joint effort," Stalin said, "perhaps we can kick them out."[13]

Despite the rhetoric, the Soviet leader's primary goal was to prevent formation of a powerful West German state integrated into a hostile Western bloc. Any threat to kick the Western powers out of Berlin was intended first as a negotiating tactic to forestall establishment of West Germany. Failing that, Stalin's fallback strategy was to make the U.S. and its allies pay a price for their action by driving them from West Berlin, which would then be incorporated into the Soviet zone. Consequently, in March the Russians acceded to immedi-

ate printing of the new occupation currency while quadripartite work continued on a central financial agency. But the Americans sought reasons to end
the talks. As Frank Wisner, assistant secretary for occupied areas, said on
March 10, they feared that the Soviets would use an agreement to "frustrate"
western Germany's recovery. He proposed to tell Clay that U.S. policy "is no
longer to reach quadripartite agreement on currency and financial reform in
Germany," which would only interfere with economic administration of the
western zones, and that Clay should seek to break off talks within sixty days.
Under Secretary Lovett at once approved this policy change, and the army informed Clay, who readily concurred.[14]

Shortly, Admiral Hillenkoetter again warned Truman of strong Russian reaction to the London Program for Germany. Then after Clay denied Sokolovsky's request for details on March 20, the Soviet military governor declared the
program illegal, and summarily adjourned the A.C.C. Diplomatic adviser Murphy cabled that now the Russians would try to force the Western powers from
Berlin by impeding their "slender communications lines." He warned that withdrawal would cause "severe psychological repercussions" in all of Europe.[15]

The Soviets promptly announced that starting April 1 they would board
Berlin-bound trains to inspect passengers, identify baggage, and issue freight
permits. An enraged Clay replied that his train commanders, as previously,
would supply only passenger lists and freight manifests, and Americans would
identify passengers and vehicles on the Helmstedt-to-Berlin highway. He proposed to the new chief of staff of the army, General Omar Bradley, to increase
the train guard and their weaponry and to shoot—if necessary—to keep Russians off the trains. Clay said that the British agreed, and he and Murphy argued
for a "strong stand" before Berlin life became impossible. Retreat meant disaster in Europe. The Russians did not intend war, the general said, but better to
find out now than later. Further, "there is no middle ground which is not appeasement."[16]

Washington officials were less certain, and more determined not to escalate
the conflict. Truman declined either to appeal to Stalin to avert an incendi-
ary incident or to summon congressional leaders. Bradley, having consulted
widely, instructed Clay not to increase guns or guards—nor to shoot unless
fired upon. The next day the Russians halted three U.S. trains in their zone, letting one proceed after its commander allowed Russian inspectors on board. The
other two train commanders refused Russian entry—but did not try to fight
forward—and soon had to back out of the Soviet zone. Clay, again enraged,
canceled all military trains. But he countered the Soviet "mini-blockade" on
April 2 with a "mini-airlift" from Wiesbaden to supply the 20,000 U.S. forces
in Berlin. He insisted that he could do this "indefinitely."[17]

Clay proposed to push an armed truck convoy through the Soviet highway checkpoint. But Bradley and the British military demurred, if only because the Soviets could halt the convoy by collapsing bridges or by using tanks and cannon. Bradley also said that the Truman administration doubted public willingness to go to war to remain in Berlin. On April 10 he asked Clay whether it might not be best to consider under what conditions the U.S. might withdraw from Berlin to avoid loss of prestige by being forced out. The military governor insisted the U.S. should not move unless driven out. "Why are we in Europe?" he asked, and was persistent that if the U.S. retreated from Berlin, western Germany would be next. "If we mean to hold the continent against communism, we must not budge," Clay said. He added that Russian fear of alienating two million German inhabitants precluded a full Berlin blockade.[18]

In fact, air and ground traffic to Berlin proceeded normally. One Soviet fighter plane did buzz a British transport approaching Gatow airport on April 5, causing both planes to crash and killing all on board. The British commander, General Brian Robertson, ordered fighter escorts for his transports, as did Clay. But after Sokolovsky apologized and pledged no air harassment—the April crash was the only one of its kind over the next year—the escorts were ended and the Soviets quit inspecting trains. Thus, despite confident reports of the Soviet military administration in Berlin that the Western powers were on the defensive and that Clay's effort to build an "air bridge had failed," Stalin evidently did not want to risk war. By mid-April the first Berlin crisis was over.[19]

Meanwhile, the Truman administration, having recently halted sale of strategic materials to the Soviet Union and its Eastern European allies, ordered Clay to cut back strategic reparations for the Soviet bloc. Marshall also proposed an Anglo-American joint note to the Soviets implying use of force— without stating at what juncture or how—to maintain their Berlin position. But Bevin, who publicly affirmed British rights in Berlin, regarded a prior commitment to force as too provocative—"an ultimatum"—especially given Soviet military preponderance there.[20]

Still, on a broader front the NSC proposed a presidential proclamation of U.S. military collaboration with the Western Union, and the British paved the way. Senator Vandenberg acceded to the idea, but concerned that "a Democratic president get all the kudos in an election year," insisted on a Senate resolution. He and Lovett crafted the document, and Senate Resolution 239 was adopted on June 11 by a vote of 64–4. The Vandenberg resolution signified U.S. intent to buttress the Western Union against the Soviets, although this commitment was hedged with language about need to comply with constitutional processes and the UN Charter, and need for collective agreements to be based on self-help and mutual aid.[21]

The Truman administration also appeared to gain politically in Europe. The French committed to Trizonia on April 16. Then in Italy, where for months the State Department and CIA engaged in extensive covert activities—including secret political contributions, arms shipments, pledges of ERP aid, and return of Trieste—to assist Prime Minister Alcide de Gasperi's conservative government, de Gasperi's Christian Democrats defeated the Italian Communists decisively in the April 18 elections. This marked the "turn of the tide in Western Europe," Ambassador Smith cabled from Moscow, while the Allies resumed talks in London to reconstruct western Germany.[22]

Confident State Department officials now weighed having Ambassador Smith signal the Soviets of America's peaceful intent but determination to preserve its position in Europe, including in Berlin. As Lovett instructed Smith, the Russians should not be misguided either by occasional references to "preventive war" against them, or by presidential campaign talk by Wallace that Truman should "sit down with Stalin and make a world agreement." The U.S. sought neither an agreement nor negotiations but only to stipulate the "U.S. position."[23]

Truman approved this narrow *demarche* on April 23. At the same time he told a group of business editors that he had gone to Potsdam in 1945 with the "friendliest feelings" for the war-weary Russians, but he had lost patience because Stalin had broken every agreement within three months. The Russian view was "oriental," or "eastern-minded," he said; "force counts for everything" with them while Eastern European Communists "murdered" their opponents. Thus Stalin's recent "peace claims" were worthless because "all the time he is cutting my throat on the agreements made." Hence the message that Smith conveyed on the president's behalf to Foreign Minister Molotov on May 4 merely disclaimed any U.S. aggressive intentions toward the Soviet Union, while indicating that its policies, especially in Eastern Europe, alarmed the Western nations. But the U.S. would not be deterred from effecting European recovery and collective defense, although the door remained open to compose disagreements.[24]

Molotov's reply on May 10 was "simply our statement in reverse," Smith said. The foreign minister said that Russia's Eastern European alliances were mutual efforts to prevent "repetition" of German aggression. He put the Cold War onus on the U.S. for making ERP and the Western Union hostile to the Soviet Union, establishing military bases on its borders, and halting strategic materials trade. But putting a twist on Smith's words that made it seem the Americans had sought a conference, Molotov said the Soviets still welcomed the U.S. "proposal" to settle differences—and then released notes of their meeting.[25]

This shrewd response raised press speculation, as well as British ire, that the U.S. had proposed bilateral negotiations. Truman and Marshall denied this, but the issue persisted. Wallace publicly proposed a six-point program, comprised largely of arms reduction and increased trade, to initiate American-Soviet talks, and Stalin "accepted" on May 17 on Moscow Radio. Truman fumed to Clifford that he would not deal with Stalin through Wallace, that Russia "never kept any agreement she has made," and "there is nothing to negotiate. What can you do?" On May 20 the president reiterated that the Soviets had broken every agreement made at Yalta and Potsdam. The next day at a key White House meeting, Truman, his Cabinet, and senior diplomats dismissed the Soviet proposals as propaganda.[26]

There matters stood when the London Conference Communiqué of June 7 announced Allied creation of an International Authority to control Ruhr production and distribution, western German economic reorganization (currency reform), ERP participation, and convening of a Constituent Assembly by September 1 to establish a West German constitution and federal government. References to prospective four-power agreement on Germany were meaningless. The Vandenberg resolution came four days later. Truman, campaigning in Oregon on June 11, sought to take the anti-Soviet sting from these measures by casually reiterating his theme that he had gone to Potsdam with "friendliest feelings" toward the Russians and had made "specific" agreements that Stalin—"I like old Joe!"—would have kept but for his being "a prisoner of the Politburo." In a speech the next day at the University of California at Berkeley that White House aides had already modulated, Truman blamed Russia for the Cold War. He exclaimed that "the cleavage that exists is not between the Soviet Union and the United States. It is between the Soviet Union and the rest of the world."[27]

The cleavage fast became a chasm after the centrist government of Premier Robert Schuman and Foreign Minister Georges Bidault got France's National Assembly to ratify the London Program on June 17 by a narrow margin of 297–289. Thus, France committed not just to currency reform in western Germany but formation of a West German government. Clay, along with Robertson and French military governor General Pierre Koenig, promptly notified Sokolovsky on June 18 that the Allies would introduce new currency into western Germany—but not Berlin—on June 20. The Russian commander branded this action illegal, suspended Berlin passenger highway and rail traffic, and closely regulated freight. He then threatened new currency in the Soviet zone in eastern Germany and in all of Berlin, which he said was part of the Soviet zone. Clay disputed this latter point and proposed creating a new four-power currency for Berlin. But Sokolovsky refused. He insisted that Berlin was economically integrated into the Soviet zone and that the Russians would take steps to permit only their currency to circulate in all of Berlin. As everyone recognized, the power to issue currency in an area signified political sovereignty there.[28]

Thus, Clay promptly challenged the Russians on June 23 by announcing new West marks for western Berlin. He did this without consulting Washington and despite French concern that he might precipitate "incalculable consequences." In fact, Clay expected that the Russians would try to "force us from Berlin." But his action—far more political than economic—was intended to underscore Western resolve not only to remain in western Berlin but to administer and govern there separately from, but amid, the Soviet zone. Thus, Clay also readied an armed convoy, with 6,000 troops, to test any Soviet blockade (he reserved decision over action in event of Soviet resistance). In Wiesbaden, General Curtis LeMay, commander of the U.S. Air Force in Europe, prepared for a preemptive strike against Soviet air bases in Germany. Still, Clay did not think that the Russians would go to war, and intelligence reports showed no military preparations. But he thought that they were pressing their limits and, owing more to pride than statecraft, he wanted to call their bluff even though his Berlin staff was divided on this matter. Further, not only the French, but the British military in Berlin and Bevin, were opposed to Clay's action, and the general knew as well that Washington officials would object.[29]

Then on June 24 a Soviet-bloc foreign ministers meeting in Warsaw denounced the London Program for western Germany. They proposed to reopen four-power talks to effect a unified, self-governing Germany, with all occupation troops withdrawn. The Russians—as Clay anticipated—also suspended all highway and rail traffic into western Berlin and curtailed supply of electricity and food from their zone. In turn, the U.S. military governor transformed the already-reduced flow of vital goods and materials from western Germany into an economic counterblockade of eastern Germany. The Berlin blockade had begun.[30]

II

Stalin's primary goal was to call a halt to formation of a powerful West German state allied to the West. He sought to do this by means of the Berlin blockade, which appeared to be the only means at his disposal. This action might open the way to four-power talks over a unified, neutralized, and demilitarized Germany, with the Russians gaining reparations from, if not access to, the Ruhr. If this "All German" strategy failed, then Stalin could pursue his secondary "East German" course, using the blockade to force the Western powers into an embarrassing withdrawal from Berlin and solidifying his control over an East German state that would rival its Western counterpart and extend the Soviet buffer zone.[31]

Regardless of course pursued, Stalin did not intend to push the Berlin blockade to the point of war, especially since the U.S. still held its atomic monopoly and, while the Soviets had a far stronger military balance of power in Berlin, the overall East-West troop alignment in Europe was relatively equal, despite U.S. concern that the Red Army was far stronger. Significantly, while the Soviets shut off ground access between western Germany and western Berlin, they never closed off the air routes or downed a plane, which they could easily have done, and they even cooperated with the Berlin Air Safety Center. Neither did the Soviets try to establish a total blockade to starve out the Berlin occupants, whom they permitted to shop for food and fuel in eastern Berlin and the surrounding countryside. The Russians also turned a blind eye to the varieties of black, gray, and other markets (including mail order) that quickly sprang up and even established Free Shops in East Berlin and Brandenburg that accepted the new West marks from the West Berliners. Further, from June to September 1948 the Soviets permitted hundreds of trucks filled with foodstuffs and bearing Soviet-zone destination papers to unload their goods in western Berlin. In sum, if the Soviets had intended to "win" the Berlin contest, their best opportunity would have been at the outset, when they might have imposed an absolute blockade that would have sharply reduced the time available for the West to organize its airlift—which ultimately supplied only 91 percent of western Berlin's food needs and 78 percent of its coal requirements—and build morale. But Stalin clearly was unwilling to risk war. As the French military command noted on June 24, 1948, the Anglo-American "attitude is based on absolute certainty that the Russians do not want war."[32]

Meanwhile, Truman acted to put his stamp on critical aspects of U.S. policy during the first months of the crisis. Especially during June 26–30 he would make crucial "spot decisions," which he would later claim were not "snap" judgments but derived from being well informed and able to see ahead. Truman would gain credit for his political diplomacy in 1948, although his administration undoubtedly could have done more to prepare for, if not avert, the Berlin crisis. Questions also remain about whether Truman fully grasped the connection between the Western powers' formation of the Brussels Treaty and decision to create a West German government and Stalin's decision to institute the blockade. Further, at the outset of the crisis U.S. policy initiatives came from Clay's military government in Berlin, not from Washington.[33]

The U.S. decision to unify western Germany and to bring it into ERP had effectively ended four-power talks. Now the administration dismissed the June 24 Warsaw proposal to negotiate a unified Germany, free of all foreign troops—this was a new aspect of Soviet policy—as just another ploy to extend Communist control over all of Germany. In addition, U.S. officials brushed off an unofficial Soviet offer, despite Murphy's belief that they wished to bargain, to exchange Berlin territory for Soviet occupation territory in Thuringia and Saxony, thus reverting to the demarcation lines that existed at the end of World War II. But Truman's view, as he had said in May, was that "there is nothing to negotiate. What are you going to do?"[34]

The administration also underestimated the import of Clay's decision to put West marks (or so-called B marks) in western Berlin. The Allies could have managed there even with a Russian-controlled currency. But the Soviets could not have afforded to permit West marks to debase their weaker Soviet marks in eastern Berlin. Hence, when early on June 25 Royall asked Clay to explain his currency policy, the general impatiently said that he had done so in many cables. When next Lovett asked Clay to consider withdrawing his currency, he exclaimed, "[P]lease remember, emphasize—and never stop repeating that currency in Berlin is not the issue—the issue is our position in Europe and plans for western Germany." In sum, Clay inclined to use the currency crisis to combat what he now saw as the larger Soviet agenda to drive the U.S. not just from Berlin but Europe. Thus, when Truman asked for a report on the "currency squabble" on the morning of June 25, Forrestal misled the president by replying that it was not as serious as the press reported.[35]

That same day, Clay again proposed to challenge the Soviet blockade with an armed convoy. He said this would reduce Soviet pressures, despite the convoy's "inherent dangers," because "once committed, we would not withdraw." But Royall said no. So too did the British, for good reason. As Clay later admitted, Soviet forces could have overwhelmed his troops. But he insisted that whereas Washington was "militarily" correct, it was politically wrong because Moscow had been "bluffing." In sum, Clay believed—correctly—that the Soviets never intended to go to war over Berlin, and he sought to capitalize on this.[36]

Clay next turned to his airlift. He was inspired by the British, who had begun to supply their military by air and were weighing civilian aid. Further, Ernst Reuter, leader of the Social Democrats and mayor-elect of Berlin, vowed his followers' resistance to Russian rule. Clay then telephoned LeMay to begin an airlift, although both generals doubted that they had sufficient large transports, or runway capacity at Tempelhof airport, to deliver the 4,500 tons of daily supplies needed for 2.2 million inhabitants in western Berlin. But Under Secretary of the Army General William H. Draper, and his chief planner, General Albert C. Wedemeyer—then on inspection tour in Berlin—thought an airlift feasible, and Clay sought to commit Washington to action. Meanwhile, Murphy would reiterate to the State Department that retreat from Berlin "would be the Munich of 1948" and that the U.S. position in Europe would be "gravely weakened, like a cat on a sloping tin roof."[37]

At the outset, policy initiatives flowed from Berlin to Washington, although Truman and his senior advisers soon took control. Following the June 25 Cabinet discussion of the "currency squabble," the president, Lovett, Forrestal, and Royall quickly agreed that Clay should not comment about "war over Berlin" (especially over currency). They also agreed that sanctions, such as closing the Panama or Suez Canals, would be ineffective and that a protest note would prompt only a "typewriter war." Confusion still remained, however, despite months of research, about whether the U.S. had ever gotten written assurances of ground access to Berlin. Truman had requested this in June 1945, when he proposed to withdraw Anglo-American forces from their advanced positions in Thuringia in exchange for the opening of Berlin to the Allies. But Stalin agreed to the exchange without referring to ground access. Shortly Clay got only an oral agreement from the Russian commander, Marshal Georgi Zhukov. The issue remained static for three years, until June 25, 1948, when Truman and his advisers concluded that "determined steps be taken by the U.S. to stay in Berlin."[38]

The next day the president ordered every available airplane to support Clay's airlift, although Truman had not scrutinized his limited information. Still, the decision did not challenge the blockade so much as circumvent it, with margin left to maneuver. On June 27 senior U.S. officials weighed Allied options: (a) to withdraw in concert from Berlin after Germany's Constituent Assembly met in September; (b) to retain their positions "by all means possible," including armed convoy; or (c) to maintain an "unprovocative but firm stand" and defer a decision. Truman would have to decide, but Marshall made clear that "zero hour" for supplies was still several weeks away and that the U.S. would maintain its "unprovocative but firm stand."[39]

Truman appeared to fix future policy promptly. Meeting with senior aides on June 28 to decide, as Lovett said, whether to remain in Berlin, the president interrupted to say that point would not be discussed. "We were going to stay period," he said. When Royall, always cautious about military realities, suggested that this might require fighting one's way into Berlin, or withdrawing later in greater humiliation, Truman backtracked: they would "deal with the situation as it developed," and "not make a black and white decision now." But he insisted that "we were in Berlin by terms of an agreement and that the Russians had no right to get us out by either direct or indirect pressure." The officials agreed that Clay should seek a currency compromise. At the same time Truman, acting on a suggestion from Bevin, approved sending two squadrons of B-29s to both Great Britain and to Germany, although Marshall's and Bevin's concern not to provoke the Russians delayed dispatch for three weeks. Further, although B-29s were known to be capable of carrying atomic bombs, none of these planes were modified for that purpose.[40]

Truman's "stay period" decision has been labeled impulsive, stemming from his need to show leadership. Clearly he intended to remain in Berlin—short of war. His insistence that the U.S. was there by terms of agreement was technically incorrect but revealing of his outlook. Ground access had never been guaranteed in writing, but the U.S. now argued that it derived from a victorious power's right of occupation or from three years of past practices—the Soviet blockade offended Truman's sense of "contract," of having given one's word. It also seemed to "prove" his frequent charge that Stalin had broken every agreement made since Yalta. At the same time, Truman was not inclined to assess how the Soviets might have viewed the U.S. decision to rehabilitate western Germany as a threat to their security, which led them to react with the Berlin blockade. In that sense, the U.S. did not confront an act of aggression that resembled Hitler's tactics, as Truman said, so much as Stalin's effort either to get the U.S. to call a halt to the formation of a West German government or to make the Americans pay a price for their action by forcing them from Berlin.[41]

Truman felt impelled to preserve the U.S. position in Berlin. He did not consult White House staff nor seek the national limelight. He left it to Marshall to inform diplomats and the public that "We stay in Berlin" and that the U.S. would supply the city by airlift and increase its air strength in Europe while seeking a diplomatic solution.[42]

The president also determined to preserve his control of the atomic bomb, which the 1946 Atomic Energy Act vested in his office. At a full meeting of the Atomic Energy Commission at the Pentagon on June 30, Royall, Forrestal, and Vannevar Bush (who had headed the Office of Scientific Development and Research and advised Truman about the atomic bomb) posited that they did not want to "box in" the president. But the military had to take control of the bomb in order to organize for its use, i.e., determine when and on which targets. David Lilienthal, chairman of the AEC, strongly opposed transferring this power from the president, and the meeting adjourned without consensus. Lilienthal then called Clifford, who put the matter to Truman, who replied that "as long as I am in the White House I will be opposed to taking atomic weapons away from the hands they are now in, and they will only be delivered to the military by particular order of the president issued at a time when they are needed." The issue of atomic control may not have been formally resolved, but it was settled in Truman's mind.[43]

Berlin diplomacy, meanwhile, proved unavailing. On July 3 Sokolovsky said that the Berlin restrictions would remain in effect until the Western powers gave up their plans for West Germany, which Clay took as the first direct Soviet admission of the purposes of the blockade. Three days later the Western powers protested that the blockade violated agreements on four-power admin-istration of Germany, and said that they would not be forced to abandon their rights. The Soviets refused to lift the blockade unless the U.S. and its allies agreed to discuss the London Program for Germany. Marshall refused and re-asserted the U.S. legal litany of rights to occupy Berlin. Molotov replied on July 14 that the U.S. had vitiated its rights by violating the Potsdam accords on A.C.C. rule, reparations, and currency but that the Soviets would open negoti-ations if this included the issue of four-power control of Germany. The U.S. re-jected this as an effort to raise anew the issue of German unity.[44]

Truman held the Russian reply to be "total rejection of everything we had asked for." He briefly despaired, despite having just gained the Democratic presidential nomination that night. Still, the Southern Democrats had bolted the party over civil rights, and many liberals—who would have preferred Jus-tice Douglas—were not happy with Truman or his vice presidential selection, the cautious Senator Alben Barkley of Kentucky. Truman also had to battle to contain military spending. Having seen supplemental appropriations escalate his FY 1949 military budget from $10 billion to $13.5 billion, the president sought to cap FY 1950 military spending at $15 billion, despite Forrestal's in-ability to restrain his service chiefs, whose estimates for global action ran to $23 billion. Finally, Truman curtly told Forrestal in mid-July that it was his "re-sponsibility" to meet the budget target. Meanwhile, the British pressed for the B-29s, and Clay urged an armed convoy to challenge the Soviets.[45]

Truman acted deliberately. Having agreed to dispatch B-29s, he now ap-proved the NSC's formal recommendation on July 15 to send them to Great Britain and Germany. Sixty planes were quickly airborne, with thirty more to follow in August. Not only did the planes lack atomic capacity, however, but neither atomic bombs nor bomb assembly teams were ever sent abroad. More-over, the Russians almost surely knew this, as well as that the U.S.'s atomic bomb stockpile was fewer than fifty. Further, many senior officials, including Marshall, doubted the efficacy of atomic warfare against the Russians. Forre-stal, for example, was scornful of newspaper stories about planes taking off from Maine and flying over the Kremlin, whereupon "Stalin would roll over and quit." In sum, the B-29s were sent more to bolster the U.S. public and the British—keep them from "appeasement"—than to threaten the Soviets, whose behavior did not change, although the U.S. planes may have been an additional deterrent to the Soviets' seriously escalating the crisis by challenging U.S. planes in Berlin's air corridors.[46]

Truman was determined to avert atomic war. On July 15 he acceded to For-restal's wish to discuss physical control of atomic policy but insisted that he would keep any decision to use the bomb in his hands. The president said that he did not intend "to have some dashing lieutenant colonel decide when would be the proper time to drop one." He next met with Forrestal, the AEC, and a large National Military Establishment contingent on July 21. When an NME official opened with a lengthy typed statement, Truman reached for the document and curtly said, "I can read." He cut short Secretary of the Air Force Stuart Symington's claim that the military needed advance control of the bombs—because they might not work—by asking whether they had ever failed to detonate. Lilienthal gave strong support by insisting that the law and past practice provided for civilian control of the bomb and that the president could transfer control whenever he deemed it necessary. Further, Truman implored that the bomb was so "terribly destructive" beyond anything that they had ever seen and that it was used to "wipe out women and children and unarmed people." It was "not a military weapon," he said, and it had to be treated differently from other weapons. And when Royall questioned spending so much money on atomic weapons if they were not to be used, the president said he would study the military's papers but that he had to weigh the bomb's impact on international relations—and this was "no time to be juggling an atom bomb around." Two days later Truman told Forrestal that he would keep control of the bomb and then declared publicly that "every aspect of the atomic energy program required civilian control." This may have enhanced Truman's image with the electorate; creditably, his decision derived from conviction, not politics.[47]

Similarly, Truman held that the U.S. had to remain in Berlin or fail in Europe, as Marshall said on July 19. Both men believed, however, that the blockade resulted from U.S. success in Europe, especially ERP, and from "Russian desperation," reflected in the recent Communist defeat in Finland's elections and in Soviet need in late June to expel Yugoslavia from the Cominform because of its independent ways. U.S. officials took these reversals to mean that Stalin would shy from military action. Further, when Forrestal warned of Russia's military manpower edge, Marshall noted that the U.S. was "much better off" than it was in 1940. Truman concluded that the U.S. would remain in Berlin until all diplomatic means had been exhausted in an effort to avert war. He reiterated this at a second meeting with senior diplomats and advisers.[48]

Finally, summing up his feelings at the day's end, Truman wrote that "I'd made the decision ten days ago *to stay in Berlin*. Jim [Forrestal] always wants to hedge. He's constantly sending me alibi memos which I return with direction and the facts. We'll stay in Berlin—come what may." No matter what caveats others offered, he intended only to "reiterate my 'Stay in Berlin' decision. I don't pass the buck, nor do I alibi out of any decision I make." Later that day he told Forrestal that U.S. policy would "remain fixed . . . until all diplomatic means had been exhausted." In sum, "Stay in Berlin" meant short of war.[49]

Truman now summoned Clay to Washington to resolve the armed convoy issue. The general seemed more convinced than ever that Stalin posed an even greater military threat than had Hitler and that the U.S. had to face down Soviet aggression or there would no next time. Upon arrival on July 21, Clay said that a convoy's prospects had been better in June but that it could still succeed, and that "twenty good divisions" could hold the Russians at the Rhine. But the U.S. could barely muster three, and Marshall and the JCS firmly opposed a ground war. So too did John Foster Dulles, foreign policy spokesman for Republican presidential nominee Thomas Dewey, whom the State Department's "Berlin Group" had just briefed.[50]

Clay spoke mildly when he reported on July 22 to the NSC and senior diplomatic-military officials. He was adamant not to abandon Berlin, and Truman, who was presiding, agreed with him that "if we move out of Berlin we have lost everything we are fighting for." The general also said, however, that use of an armed convoy "might lead to war," and this should not be done "until all other ways have been tried and failed" and the British and French were agreed upon that point. Moreover, Murphy, who was an ardent convoy exponent, declined the "fair chance" he was given to speak to the issue.

Thus Clay emphasized not confrontation but the airlift's success: fifty-two C-54s and eighty C-47s were flying 250 round-trips daily and bringing almost two-thirds of the necessary 4,500 tons of daily supplies. He was optimistic about the longer term. He wanted to have another seventy-five C-54s and to build a second airport. The NSC approved both requests. Further, Clay pointed out that by blaming the blockade on "technical difficulties," the Russians had left "a way out" through a concession. This led Lovett to conclude that although the U.S. had to avoid being "kicked out" of Berlin, it had to be "equally resolute" about a peaceful settlement.[51]

The president had taken this position consistently. He had also became the "ultimate decision-maker" who made the initial "strategic decision" to "Stay in Berlin," and then made or shaped subsequent decisions bearing on "war or peace." As Truman wrote to his sister shortly after the NSC meeting, his greatest fear was that he would win the election and then "have a Russian war on my hands. Two wars are enough for anybody, and I've had two."[52]

III

Truman felt bolstered by White House reports that the public and press overwhelmingly opposed the U.S. being "coerced" from Berlin, although they also favored negotiations, as did the British and Western Union nations. In late July, the State Department dispatched Charles Bohlen, its counselor and head of its

"Berlin Group," to Europe to coordinate Allied diplomacy. Meanwhile, Marshall told Ambassador Smith in Moscow to sound the Soviets who, he reported on July 31, seemed bent on settling. The ambassador and his Anglo-French counterparts met with Stalin on August 2. The Soviet leader told them that he did not intend the blockade to oust the Allies from Berlin but to show how "embarrassed" he was by formation of the West German government. He insisted, however, that because the Allies had created a separate state with its capital at Frankfurt, they had lost their juridical right to be in Berlin, which could not be the capital of all of Germany. He conceded that he could not halt Allied work on a West German state but offered to end the blockade if the Western powers accepted the Soviet mark in Berlin and suspended work on a western German government. Smith balked, and after further negotiations, Stalin suddenly proposed to lift the blockade if the West agreed to use only the Soviet mark in Berlin and simply took note of his "insistent wish" to have the London Program deferred.[53]

Smith, who had taken a hard line toward the Soviets for over two years, reported that Stalin and Molotov, displaying "sweet reasonableness," were anxious to settle. He urged giving some concession on West Germany, such as suspending part of the London Program. But Bohlen, Clay, and others said no. They were convinced that Stalin's real aim was to prevent a West German government and to allow their presence in Berlin only "by sufferance." Marshall then narrowed Smith's negotiating basis by insisting that use of only the Soviet mark in Berlin would require quadripartite control.[54]

Still, by late August Smith neared accord with Molotov and Stalin on a Berlin Communiqué that would have provided for quadripartite control of the Soviet mark in Berlin, removal of the blockade, and then the start of CFM talks on all German issues. But Clay protested its failure to stipulate Allied right to occupy Berlin, and Marshall refused any mention that the CFM might discuss Germany. At the same time, the secretary gave scant consideration to Kennan's PPS proposals, which had been drawn by mid-August, for an all-German settlement that included a single government, quick end to quadripartite machinery, and withdrawal of all occupation forces to Germany's periphery. Kennan hoped this settlement would lead to retrenchment of Soviet power and avert the division of Germany and Europe, given that the "lines of cleavage" had not yet hardened on the Continent. Most important, the Russians were not ready for another war, dissension was rife among their satellites, and anticommunism was running high in Germany. But the Truman administration no longer believed that "German problems" could be resolved except by working with governments that were willing to reach agreement based on "common interest," and fully expected that henceforth the East-West zones of Germany would continue to develop in divergent directions.[55]

Thus the furthest that Marshall would go to reach accord on the Berlin issue was to convey on August 26 four U.S. requirements for any prospective agreement with the Russians. They included "co-equal rights" to be in Berlin; "no abandonment of our position" on West Germany; "unequivocal lifting" of the blockade; and quadripartite control of the Soviet mark in Berlin. Sharp talks in Moscow followed but no communiqué on Berlin; there was only a directive on August 30 that gave the military governors one week to agree to details to effect a four-power Financial Commission to establish control over the Soviet mark and simultaneously to lift the blockade.[56]

Berlin negotiations only frayed nerves. Marshal Sokolovsky evaded Stalin's commitment to a Financial Commission, which Marshall told Truman was of "central importance" and might be the "breaking point" in talks. In Cabinet, Marshall also indicated that the U.S. did not seek a modus vivendi but a determination of whether it was in Berlin by "right" or "sufferance." Meantime, Sokolovsky warned that Soviet planes would clog Berlin's air corridors, and Clay threatened to send U.S. Military Police into the Soviet sector to quell Communist mobs that blocked a City Assembly meeting. By September 6 Lovett, convinced that the Russians sought to dominate Germany, thought that they resisted agreement because the Russians felt they had "lost their shirts" in the Moscow talks. The next day he proposed to ask the Russians bluntly if they intended to honor the Moscow directive; if not, the U.S. would take this "threat to the peace" to the Security Council. The NSC, with Truman presiding, also agreed to warn Russia against clogging Berlin airways and to increase the airlift from 125 to 200 C-54s.[57]

The president said it was "not possible to do business" with the Russians, but he resisted rash action. For example, on September 10 the NSC's report on atomic policy concluded that the military had to plan to use the atomic bomb in case of war, although the president would determine when to use it. Meanwhile, as Lilienthal noted, Forrestal "pushed hard" on the president to "decide that the bomb will be used" and got Marshall to arrange discussion of the issue.[58]

After Forrestal and the military briefed Truman on September 13 on "bases, bombs, Moscow, Leningrad, etc.," he noted that he had "a terrible feeling afterwards that we are very close to war. I hope not," and that "Berlin is a mess." Still, when faced with the question about need to decide in an emergency whether to use the atomic bomb, the president told Forrestal only that he "prayed he would never have to make such a decision, but that if it became necessary, no one need have a misgiving but that he would do so. . . ." Thus, Truman made clear that he would not shy from deciding to use the bomb, but he did not say that he would necessarily use it.[59]

The president's position was far milder than the "unanimous agreement," which Forrestal thought he detected the next night at a meeting with Marshall, Bradley, and numerous major newspaper publishers, that in case of war "the American people would not only have no question as to the propriety of the use of the atomic bomb, but would in fact expect it to be used." Regardless, Forrestal never again asked Truman to assure the bomb's use. Perhaps the secretary thought that war would leave no choice. More likely, he realized that Truman had made clear that he would not act until he had concluded that the moment of decision had arrived.[60]

Nor would Truman give over custody of the bomb. Even when Marshall alluded to that issue again, the president said that he was "most anxious" to defer a decision until after the November election. Forrestal, "still convinced" that the bomb should be in military hands, reserved his right to reopen the issue, but he never did. Probably he realized that Truman had used mention of the election to say politely, given Marshall's presence, that this was no time to let anyone juggle an atom bomb.[61]

Berlin diplomacy remained stalled, however. The start of the Constituent Assembly in Bonn on September 1 to create a West German government diminished Soviet—and American—interest in compromise. The British and French feared rupturing relations, and insisted on a last, but futile, approach to Stalin. Finally, on September 19 Marshall flew to Paris, site of the UN meeting. There Clay reported that he could sustain the Allies in Berlin indefinitely and maintain a reasonable civilian living standard. The British and French agreed to refer the Soviets' "illegal" blockade and "threat to the peace" to the Security Council, which voted the matter to its agenda on October 5.[62]

The Truman administration aimed less at a Security Council settlement than to gain time to strengthen its position in Europe, build a strong West Germany, and avert "appeasement"—or a rash U.S. act in Berlin. In fact, talk about the atomic bomb and preventive war, as well as "taut nerves" in the White House about Truman's election prospects, caused the president to take the suggestion of two new speechwriters that he send his old friend Chief Justice Fred Vinson to "talk peace" with Stalin. Truman prevailed on a reluctant, if flattered, Vinson on October 3. The president then asked Lovett to arrange the Moscow visit and Press Secretary Charles Ross to request radio network time to announce the mission.[63]

Truman informed his White House advisers on October 5. The politically astute Clifford and Elsey objected strongly, but they were in the minority. The president then spoke, belatedly, by teletype to Marshall, whom Lovett had already briefed. The secretary insisted that the proposed mission would undercut his status and diplomacy as well as Anglo-French accord on U.S. policy. The president at once jettisoned his plan, despite urging from some of his aides and his own second thoughts. But when he expressed the latter to Senator Tom Connally, he too opposed the mission. By the time the two men were joined by Senator Vandenberg, a dispirited Truman could suggest only a telephone call to Stalin, an idea readily discarded. Vandenberg suspected that Truman was searching for a campaign "shot-in-the-arm."[64]

Truman was deeply embarrassed when the *Chicago Tribune* broke news of the aborted Vinson mission on October 8. The press challenged the president's competence, excoriated him for playing politics with foreign policy and seeking to appease the Russians, and hinted that Marshall would resign. Publicly, Republican nominee Dewey reaffirmed support for the administration's Berlin policy, but off the record denounced Truman for knowing "considerably less than nothing" about foreign policy. Truman's only defense consisted of his "facts": he had sought peace and the aversion of Soviet "misunderstanding," especially about "atomic problems." He canceled the mission because Marshall had said that it would undercut Allied diplomacy. Marshall denied intent to resign but soon told Truman that for health reasons he would leave by January 1949.[65]

The president was to blame for his public fiasco. He was concerned about Soviet misunderstanding and talk of atomic war, which even the British soon began to mention freely. Truman may also have thought, as others did, that Stalin was a "prisoner of the Politburo" who needed U.S. assurances to settle peacefully. But the president failed to recognize that bilateral diplomacy would undercut Allied unity, and he had sought to boost his campaign, even though his "Stay in Berlin" policy had enhanced his election prospects. Meanwhile, the British and French sought to settle with Russia and feared that the Americans did not.[66]

Regardless, Truman was soon back campaigning. In a speech on October 18 that was originally intended to announce the Vinson mission, he stated that he had hoped to dispel "poisonous" distrust. He aimed at "conciliation"—not "appeasement," nor another "Munich"—he said, and cited the Truman Doctrine, ERP, and forging West Germany as steps toward peace. His later campaign speeches further emphasized European reconstruction and need to contain Communism, and the desire of the Soviets for a Republican victory in order to return the U.S. to "hit-and-run" isolationism and economic downturn. But Truman pledged to "pierce the iron curtain" to bring "truth" to Russia's leaders.[67]

Meanwhile, on October 22 the president approved the NSC's proposal to add sixty-six C-54s to the airlift, despite concern of the JCS about scarce planes and funds. The military leaders also wanted to know whether the U.S. would go to war over a serious Berlin incident, but Truman refused to say. Lovett assured the JCS that the State Department supported their needs. He emphasized that while the U.S. might "not . . . stay in Berlin forever," it would leave only on favorable terms and that "world opinion" protected it from a hostile Russian act. Similarly, Clay, having returned to Washington to allay JCS anxiety, reaffirmed that the airlift was "no longer experimental" and acclaimed its political impact: Germany had become "one of the most anti-communist countries in the world."[68]

Years later the general also extolled Truman for overruling his advisers and privately assuring delivery of the C-54s, but this is exaggeration. To be sure, at "the critical moment" Truman backed a "large and well-supported airlift," and he saw the Berlin crisis as "a political war, not a military one," as Clay said in praise of him. But by late October the president and his chief advisers were already committed to Berlin—but not war over it—and approval of the NSC recommendation was inevitable.[69]

Shortly, Truman also gained his startling come-from-behind presidential victory. He won the popular vote over Dewey by 49.5–44.5 percent and the electoral vote by 303–89. This victory was due chiefly to Truman's relentless campaigning, focus on domestic issues, and strong support from critical New Deal constituencies: labor, agriculture, and crucial minorities in the nation's big cities. The president's handling of the Berlin crisis, despite the Vinson mission gaffe, helped to strengthen his claim to foreign policy leadership. By contrast, one aide to Dewey noted that "the bear got us," meaning that the Republicans lost because they had failed to attack Democratic foreign policy, from Yalta and Potsdam to containment, for being soft on the Russians. That ignores, however, that in 1948 Truman appeared to be doing what the public wanted him to do, namely, sustain a tough policy—short of war—in Berlin and elsewhere. In effect, there would be no more Munichs.[70]

III

In early October the U.S. took the Berlin issue to the Security Council in belief that the Soviets could be isolated there. Three weeks later that body produced a British-crafted resolution demanding the end of the blockade, to be followed by talks on currency reform (use of the Soviet mark in Berlin) and then a CFM meeting to discuss Germany. The Western powers agreed, but predictably the Soviets vetoed the resolution because it made lifting the Berlin blockade a precondition to negotiations. At the same time, the Truman administration again gave short shrift to Kennan's PPS proposal, or "Plan A," to negotiate for a single government for a unified Germany and for withdrawal of foreign troops. In mid-November Truman publicly reaffirmed that there would be no negotiations until the blockade was lifted. Two weeks later the SED established a government for eastern Berlin that claimed to govern the entire city. Meanwhile, Clay pressed western sector elections, over British and French protests. On December 5 nearly 84 percent of the eligible voters turned out despite a Communist boycott. This signified a powerful rejection of the Soviet blockade and German Communism. Berlin was now divided politically and economically.[71]

Soviet and U.S. positions had shifted and hardened over the past six months. As Admiral Hillenkoetter, head of the CIG, correctly told Truman on December 10, the Russians had begun the blockade to win concessions on a German settlement, not to force the Americans from Berlin. But that strategy had failed. Now the Soviets sought their secondary goal of driving the U.S. from the city, which likely would become part of the Soviet sector. But as Lovett told the NSC in mid-December, the airlift, which once had been a "difficult embarrassment," had become a "vital part of our foreign policy" and "the greatest political factor in Europe." Further, "the Berlin situation is war, a showdown," and Americans should no more blink at money or sacrifices now than they had in wartime.[72]

This view precluded compromise. Thus in late December, after a UN committee proposed use of the Soviet mark in Berlin, the Russians accepted, and the British and French proffered amendments. But the Americans balked. They insisted that Berlin was no longer a unified city. Following some diplomatic maneuvering, on January 15 the U.S. formally rejected the UN proposal, declared that the "illegal blockade" had created a divided Berlin, and hinted that soon only the West mark would be used in western Berlin. This repudiated the prior August 30 Moscow directive to establish a four-power currency for Berlin and effectively ended the UN effort to find an acceptable currency agreement for Berlin. Truman later wrote that his administration felt "impelled" to reject the UN proposal, or any four-power accord, because it had concluded that the Russians rarely honored their agreements, and the U.S. did not want to leave the Berliners "at the mercy of the Soviets and their German Communist hirelings."[73]

Truman's hard line paid a quick dividend, especially because the U.S. counterblockade was denying the Soviet zone of Germany vital coal, steel, and machine tools and causing factory closings and severe shortages of consumer goods. Thus on January 30, in reply to queries from Kingsbury Smith, European general manager of International News Service, Stalin proposed to lift the blockade in return for the Allies ending their counterblockade and agreeing to CFM talks on Germany prior to the formation of a West German government. U.S. officials took Stalin's omitting mention of the currency issue—ostensibly the cause of the blockade—as a sign that he wanted to negotiate. Truman at once agreed that Dean Acheson, who had recently succeeded Marshall as secretary of state, should respond. But the president, who had just transferred responsibility for German policy from the military to the State Department, insisted that he would not delay a West German regime. Similarly Acheson, who had moved from proposing Soviet-American atomic sharing in 1945–1946 to promoting the Truman Doctrine in 1947, and was disposed to negotiate only from "situations of strength," held that U.S. interests in Berlin, Germany, and Europe were inextricably intertwined. On February 2 he replied to Stalin only that Allied accord on West Germany did not preclude four-power agreement on all of Germany.[74]

Acheson then had Philip Jessup, deputy chief of the UN mission, secretly approach the Soviet ambassador there, Jacob Malik. By late March they neared accord on holding CFM talks and lifting the blockade-counterblockade, with Jessup insistent that formation of the West German government would continue but would not be completed for some time. The administration kept Jessup's negotiations secret from the military, refused Secretary of the Army Royall's request for an armed convoy to break the blockade, and remained confident of Soviet inaction. On March 20 they finally got Anglo-French accord to declare that the Soviet mark would cease to be legal tender in the western zones of Berlin; the West mark would be the official currency there. The city's division was complete and, Mayor Reuter said, "Berlin belongs to the West."[75]

Shortly, Bevin and Schuman (now foreign minister) went to Washington to formalize the North Atlantic Treaty Organization (NATO) on April 4. This marked the first peacetime alliance for the U.S., although the U.S. limited its commitment to respond to an attack on a member state to acting in accord with constitutional processes and "taking such action as it deems necessary" (instead of Europe's preferred "as may be necessary"). Truman viewed the treaty as "putting the last nail in the coffin of isolationism." The French gained assurance against German or Soviet aggression. The president further assuaged Paris about its Mediterranean concerns by dropping his opposition to including Italy in NATO and by extending NATO's ambit to Algeria.[76]

NATO and ERP spurred France's commitment to Trizonia and to the Washington Agreements of April 8, which included an Occupation Statute for nascent West Germany. The Allies reserved "supreme authority" over critical areas: foreign affairs, trade, the Ruhr, and reparations. But they transformed their military governors into high commissioners and granted West Germany self-government under its Basic Law (constitution) of May 8, with elections scheduled for later in the summer. Meanwhile, the tortuous Jessup-Malik talks continued, with the Soviets trying to forestall formation of a West German government. Truman and Acheson would concede only that this would not occur before or during CFM talks, while Bevin sought "to see Bonn in his pocket" prior to any CFM meeting. The Soviets ultimately gave way on May 5. The four powers announced the end of the blockade-counterblockade as of May 12, with CFM talks on Germany and Berlin to begin on May 23.[77]

The Berlin crisis was over. The U.S. and its allies had won a stunning victory, which also meant there remained only the slimmest prospect to negotiate German unification. During the past months Kennan and his PPS aides had been revising his Plan A for a unified but neutral Germany, with the UN supervising state (Länder) elections prior to the Germans establishing a central government and the U.S. and Soviet Union substantially reducing and withdrawing their troops to "garrison" positions near Germany's borders. The JCS, however, opposed placing U.S. troops in allegedly "indefensible" port cities (they planned, instead, to regroup them east of the Rhine) as long as Russian troops could mass in Eastern Europe. Thus the Defense Department leaked part of Kennan's plan to the *New York Times,* where it appeared on May 12 and drew highly adverse reactions from the British and especially the French, who feared withdrawal of U.S. forces as loss of security against Germany as well as Russia.[78]

For a brief while, Acheson may have been willing to consider German unification. But he allowed Murphy, returned from his post as diplomatic adviser in Berlin, to head an NSC steering committee on German policy. The NSC group rewrote Kennan's Plan A to make a West German government the foundation for any unification, and they eliminated any concessions to the Soviets. Acheson then told the NSC on May 17 that he favored moving ahead with the West German government, and he opposed any merger with East Germany before it was purged of its Red Army and secret-police contingents. He said unity was possible only by "consolidating the Eastern zone into ours." The next day he informed reporters that he intended to go ahead with a West German government "come hell or high water," and on May 19 he told the Senate Foreign Relations Committee that any proposal for Germany would be judged by whether it strengthened Western Europe. Vandenberg asked if this meant that the U.S. intended to offer proposals at the CFM meeting that would bring only a "no" answer from the Soviets and establish a "permanent Cold War." Acheson replied that this was not necessarily the case, but the immediate task was "to see who develops more strength." In sum, from the Truman administration's perspective, better to contest the Soviets over Germany and Europe than to try to negotiate mutual withdrawal and soften the hardening division between East and West.[79]

At the CFM in Paris, the West offered only to have eastern Germany incorporate into West Germany prior to national elections. The Soviets proposed instead to revert to the Potsdam accords, with four-power A.C.C. control of Germany and a Russian stake in the Ruhr. The West rejected this as turning the clock back. Further, in event that Stalin reimposed the blockade, Truman and Acheson inclined to have an armed convoy test Soviet resolve—but not draw Soviet fire! NSC deliberations, however, persuaded the president and secretary merely to continue the airlift and stockpiling. Thus after a month's deliberations, the CFM adjourned on June 20, having reached no agreement over Germany—even about Allied access to Berlin—other than that the blockade was ended.[80]

Truman congratulated Acheson and declared that the U.S. would not jeopardize West Germany's basic freedoms to gain "nominal political unity." West Germans held their first elections in August, and in mid-September Konrad Adenauer, head of the Christian Democrats, became the first chancellor of the new Federal Republic of Germany (FRG). Three weeks later in East Germany, where a People's Congress had previously approved a constitution, the SED proclaimed its governance of the new German Democratic Republic (GDR). Both new governments claimed to speak for all of Germany. The first Berlin crisis had abated, but city and nation—and Europe—were effectively partitioned.[81]

IV

The Berlin blockade proved a major defeat for Stalin and the Russians. Stalin instituted the blockade in an effort to thwart formation of the West German state or, a secondary strategy, to drive the West from Berlin. But he did not anticipate Western resolve, especially that of the U.S., to remain in Berlin, or the success of the airlift and counterblockade. He was not willing to risk war, however, by taking hostile action—such as clogging the air corridors—to break the airlift. He seemed ready to settle by August 1948, when he proposed to end the blockade if the Western powers would agree to use of the Soviet mark in Berlin and then allow the CFM to take up the German issue. U.S. officials were determined to press ahead with their London Program for Germany, however, and in no mood to compromise, even if they did not want war and sometimes worried about the airlift. Finally Stalin's statement in January 1949 opened the way to tortuous negotiations, but these were chiefly concerned with finding a face-saving solution for the Soviets rather than resolving the critical issues, such as currency reform and formation of the West German government, which had led to the Berlin confrontation. Meanwhile, Stalin's actions proved counterproductive: they inspired greater Western unity against the Soviet bloc as well as increased German enmity, especially in the western zones, toward the Soviets and their policies, and Communism.[82]

By contrast, Truman managed to turn the Berlin crisis into a presidential and international success. In retrospect, the crisis seems almost to have been inevitable, given the prior three years of Soviet-American conflict over Germany and then the Truman administration's decision to create a West German state integrated into the Western community. Further, Clay's decision in June 1948 to introduce the West mark into West Berlin raised the issue of sovereignty, as well as financial challenge, at the center of the Soviet Union's occupation zone. At the same time, U.S. military commitment to the recently formed Western Union through nascent (but not so secret) NATO talks and the Vandenberg resolution served to heighten tension.

In fact, as early as December 1947 CIG had warned the president that the Soviets would retaliate over Germany by trying to drive the U.S. and its allies from Berlin. Most officials realized, however, that Russia's real or primary goal was to gain concessions for a German settlement, not to oust the U.S. from Berlin. But U.S. officials had determined to forge a West German state tied politically and economically—and ultimately militarily—to the West, which they viewed as preferable to a unified and neutral Germany. They believed, as Truman said in May 1948, that "there is nothing to negotiate." This outlook, however, also fostered disregard in spring 1948 for Stalin's warnings, such as the mini-blockade, and failure to prepare for a more serious and longer-term Berlin crisis.

Truman left it to Clay to initiate the airlift, while the president rested his case on the narrow legalism that the U.S. was in Berlin by "agreement" (despite belated discovery that no formal accord existed). Most important, the U.S. position—and Truman's exaggerated sense of "contract"—tended to ignore the marked changes that had come about since 1945, the Soviet view of the current German problem, and the intent of the blockade. Similarly, Truman's decision to "stay period"—which was less firm than once believed—lacked real assessment of current conditions or long-term implications. To a great extent, the president's perspective was shaped by a relatively simplistic definition of the situation. Throughout the crisis Truman presumed that U.S. policy was correct and defensive. He saw no connection between the London Program and the Berlin blockade, and he was not amenable to compromise solutions, either on the basis of a four-power currency for Berlin and modification of the London Program or Kennan's more elaborate proposal for East-West disengagement in Germany. In sum, Truman believed that Soviet behavior was wrong and aggressive, and more akin to Hitler's willingness to wage war on sovereign states in 1938 and 1939—as Truman said—rather than an ill-conceived coercive action intended to halt formation of a West German state or solidify the Soviet hold on its sphere of influence.[83]

Truman did manage to make a virtue of some of his predispositions. He demonstrated his determination to sustain the U.S. commitment to Europe and to Allied unity, to avert war, to retain control over the military (especially atomic weapons), and to avoid taking partisan advantage of a foreign policy crisis. He believed that forced U.S. withdrawal from Berlin would seriously undercut its influence in Europe and perhaps ERP, cause Europeans committed to the U.S. to despair, and destroy his presidential standing. He also took great precaution to avert war. As Truman said, the two world wars he had experienced were "enough for anybody."

The president seized upon Clay's airlift to gain time and to circumvent the blockade without shooting. He used his authority to see that Clay got his planes, despite Air Force carping about scarcity or vulnerability elsewhere. By time of the July 22 NSC meeting, Clay had abandoned his provocative quest for an armed convoy and emphasized instead the airlift's growing success and need to exhaust diplomacy.

Similarly, Truman's quick resolve to stay in Berlin was not a "black and white decision"; he would deal with the situation as it developed. With strong support from Marshall, he showed great capacity to withstand the "heat in the kitchen," including that generated by Royall and the army, who sought a more definitive, or traditional, decision either to withdraw or to prepare for battle. The president appeared to firm up the U.S. military position by rapid dispatch of B-29s to Europe. This ambiguous maneuver was intended to signal U.S. seriousness to the Soviets by bringing their cities within range of the bombers, although they were not modified to carry atomic weapons, and the Russians surely knew this. At the same time, however, the planes raised public expectation about U.S. air power—and determination not to be "kicked out" of Berlin—and thereby escalated the Berlin stakes to an exceptionally high level, perhaps more than was justified.[84]

Truman was consistently firm about control of atomic weapons. No matter how often Forrestal, the NME, or key civilian advisers like Harriman argued that the military needed to control the atomic bomb, the president refused to transfer his lawful authority, or prerogative, over this new weapon. As he said on June 30, the military would not get atomic weapons except by "particular order of the president issued at a time when they were needed." He had to weigh both the bomb's horrors and its "impact on international relations," and as Truman told the NSC, this was no time for anyone to juggle an atomic bomb. When military pressure mounted in September, he said that he would not shy from deciding whether to use the bomb, but he did not assure that he would use it.

After the Berlin crisis ended, in July 1949 Truman directed that all military requests concerning atomic weapons be subject to NSC evaluation. As AEC chairman Lilienthal noted, this freed the president from the pressure of JCS-style "no questions asked" requests, which would now be subject to State Department, AEC, and Budget Bureau analysis. Thus Truman set the historic standard for presidential control of atomic weapons, which standard he would have to invoke sooner than he knew during the war in Korea.[85]

Truman did not seek political capital from the crisis. He left major statements to Marshall, provided briefings for Dewey's representatives, and sought bipartisan support. The aborted Vinson mission was naive and smacked of opportunism, and Truman at once gave way to Marshall's protest.

The president's policy paid major political dividends. He was aided significantly by the stunning success of the airlift (as well as the deliberately "incomplete" Soviet blockade), which over 318 days flew more than 200,000 round-trip flights that averaged more than 4,500 tons of daily supplies. U.S. technical prowess enhanced its political prestige, but Truman kept his advisers focused on the policy he sought to pursue, won over the U.S. public, and shored up European resolve and strong anti-Soviet sentiment, especially in western Germany. Moreover, although the Security Council did not condemn Soviet policy, as the U.S. advocated, the Truman administration was still able to demonstrate its peaceful intent and commitment to West Germany and West Berliners.[86]

By January 1949, Stalin was ready for a face-saving solution, and Truman and Acheson responded, albeit deliberately. The administration managed the secret Jessup-Malik talks and kept the British and French in diplomatic tow regarding formation of West Germany. Stalin finally yielded in May to the empty formula that West Germany would not be fully formed before or during the CFM talks in June. Thus U.S. policy appeared so successful in spring 1949 that even Kennan, whose hopes for Soviet-American disengagement in Europe were dashed, was moved to write that Soviet behavior was so "restrained and non-provocative" that it was necessary to ask whether "the fortunes of the cold war have shifted so fundamentally in the past two years that it is now the Russians who are trying to follow, with regard to us, a policy of firmness and patience and unprovocative containment."[87]

Whether that was so remained to be seen. From Truman's perspective, however, his position in Berlin and Europe and his standing as president, which one year earlier might have been likened to that of a "cat on a sloping tin roof," now seemed more secure than ever, although atomic developments in Russia and events in Asia soon would make security seem a chimera.

"To Make the Whole World Safe for Jews"

Truman and Palestine-Israel

Six months after he became president, Truman insisted that Arab-Jewish conflict over Palestine was the issue that most troubled his administration. Zionism, he said in November 1945, "that *is* the sixty-four-dollar question." He predicted that it would remain an electoral issue, and in 1949 he complained that his efforts to gain peace in the Middle East had led to his being "charged with everything from rape to murder."[1]

Palestine policy vexed Truman. The Holocaust that had killed more than six million of Europe's nine million Jews mortified him. He felt obligated, he wrote King Ibn Saud of Saudi Arabia in 1946, to assist the "pitiful remnants" of survivors, even if only to secure haven for 100,000 refugees in Palestine. Similarly, when Senator Walter George of Georgia warned against the use of American dollars or troops in Palestine, Truman rejoined that every congressman should visit Europe's Displaced Persons (DP) camps to see how these people had suffered and that they—like "your ancestors and mine"—depended on the U.S. for help. And when Navy Secretary James Forrestal said that the U.S. could not afford to lose Saudi Arabian oil, Truman snapped that he would not act on the basis of oil but on "what is right."[2]

Truman also criticized Jews who sought to lobby him about the refugee crisis and a homeland in Palestine as "European conspirators." In 1945 he claimed to have told a Jewish group that he could act more boldly only if it would "furnish me with five hundred thousand men to carry on a war with the Arabs," which he opposed. The president bridled at representations from New York, including from Senator Robert Wagner: "I'm not a New Yorker. . . . I am an American," Truman said, and he complained to his Cabinet, "Jesus Christ couldn't please them [the Jews] when he was here on earth, so how could anyone expect that I would have any luck?" He was quick to blame the Jews for thwarting a settlement, said that they behaved badly once they were no longer the "underdog," and in 1949 he berated the new Israeli state's policy toward Arab refugees.[3]

Judgments of Truman's Palestine-Israel policies have ranged as widely as his emotions. Some scholars have denigrated his actions, especially support for a Jewish state, as "squalid" politics that jeopardized American security and ignored Arab claims. Other analysts have contended that any president would have had to respond to Jewish aspirations in the post-Holocaust era and that Truman moved slowly only from supporting a refugee haven to endorsing a Jewish state. Finally, some writers have depicted Truman as hero, citing hyperbole ascribed to Israel's chief rabbi in 1949 that God put Truman in his mother's womb to "bring about Israel's rebirth after two thousand years."[4]

Neither squalid politics nor God's will determined Truman's policies. Initially he resisted involvement in Palestine and said he preferred "to make the whole world safe for Jews," which meant immigration anywhere and no need for a Jewish state. As Palestine conflict escalated, he was persistent that "my soul [sic] interest is to stop the bloodshed." Meanwhile, his diplomatic and military advisers, and Britain and the Arab nations, opposed Jewish refugees—and a state—in Palestine. But the president's action was governed by his sense of moral and political commitment, by advice of shrewd White House advisers, and by the fact that the Jews in Palestine were able to seize the moment. Thus Truman gained a solution where none had seemed possible.[5]

I

In 1915 during World War I, the British promoted an Arab revolt against the Ottoman Empire by promising an independent Arab state. Then in 1917 Foreign Secretary Arthur Balfour declared that Britain favored a "national home" in Palestine for Jewish peoples. At the Paris Peace Conference in 1919, Britain received a mandate, including the Balfour Declaration, over Palestine and its 750,000 Arabs and 65,000 Jews. President Wilson, and then Congress in 1922, endorsed the Balfour Declaration.[6]

British rule in Palestine called for a Jewish Agency to advise on community affairs, and a small Jewish army, the Hagana. Violent Arab protests led Britain in 1922 to split off Transjordan (the area east of the Jordan River under rule of Emir Abdullah Hussein) and to limit Jewish immigration to truncated Palestine to economic absorptive capacity. Few Jews migrated there until Nazi Germany's persecution of European Jewry. By 1939 Jews in Palestine numbered about 500,000, or 30 per cent of the population. Meanwhile, renewed Arab assaults led Britain to send a Royal Commission headed by Lord Robert Peel, which concluded in 1937 that only partition could end the conflict. But the Jews were hesitant, while the Arabs rejected partition and increased their attacks. These were reciprocated by the Hagana and terrorist groups such as the Irgun Zvai Leumi and then the Stern Gang. In May 1939, Prime Minister Neville Chamberlain's government, fearing Arab-German collaboration, issued a White Paper that limited Jewish immigrants to Palestine to 75,000 over five years, curbed land sales, and promised an independent Palestine (Arab state) within a decade.[7]

Winston Churchill attacked Britain's "repudiation" of the Balfour Declaration as "another Munich," but after he became prime minister in 1940, his wartime government sustained the White Paper and forcibly opposed "illegal" Jewish immigration. The Arabs remained neutral, on Britain's side. The Jews, as urged by David Ben-Gurion, head of the Jewish Agency, aided Britain against Germany as if the White Paper did not exist and fought against the White Paper as if there were no war. Meanwhile, in May 1942 at the Biltmore Hotel in New York, the confederation American Zionist Emergency Council (AMZEC) denounced the White Paper and called for a sovereign Jewish commonwealth in all of Palestine. The Biltmore Program, announced just before disclosure of Germany's Final Solution, presaged the intent of the Zionists to forge their own fate.[8]

The Roosevelt administration did little to assist refugees from Nazi persecution and acquiesced in Britain's White Paper. FDR shied from the Biltmore Program, and the State Department, hostile to Zionism and Jewish immigration, was slow to verify the Final Solution. The Roosevelt-Churchill conference at Bermuda in April 1943 proved a "facade for inaction," and in 1944 Roosevelt's aides cited wartime concerns to cause Congress to shelve bipartisan resolutions favoring a Jewish commonwealth in Palestine.[9]

Democratic and Republican Party platforms in 1944 called for unrestricted Jewish immigration to Palestine and a democratic commonwealth there. FDR reaffirmed this pledge, but his aides again got Congress to shelve similar resolutions. In early 1945 State Department officials quoted King Saud as saying that the U.S. and Britain faced a choice between "an Arab land of peace and quiet or a Jewish land drenched in blood." After the Yalta Conference, FDR met with King Saud, who vehemently opposed Jewish immigration, and FDR promised no action hostile to the Arabs.[10]

American Zionists persuaded Roosevelt to reaffirm his support for a Jewish commonwealth, but Arab protests led him to reiterate to King Saud on April 5 his pledge not to take hostile action nor to make a basic decision for Palestine without consulting Arabs and Jews. FDR restated this to other Arab nations on April 12—hours before he died.[11]

Enter Truman, whose early and later writings included "Jew clerk," "Kike town," "smart Hebrew," and "Name's Rosenbloom, but doesn't act it." Truman's close friend and partner in his World War I military canteen and postwar haberdashery was Eddie Jacobson, a Reform Jew from Kansas City. But Jacobson's goals, shared by most American Jews, were secular success and cultural assimilation, not Zionism or a religiously based state.[12]

Truman had decried Chamberlain's White Paper as surrender to the "axis powers," and at Senator Wagner's behest in 1941 he joined the American Palestine Committee to lend moral support to Zionism. He signed its commemoration of the twenty-fifth anniversary of the Balfour Declaration, and at a Holocaust "rescue" rally in Chicago in 1943 proposed to create a "haven" for Jews. This "is not a Jewish problem," he said. "It is an American problem."[13]

Truman also resigned from a group seeking to form a Jewish army because it criticized the Bermuda Conference results, and he cited wartime diplomacy to shy from the bipartisan Senate resolution, sponsored by Wagner and Republican Robert Taft, favoring a Jewish home in Palestine. As vice president, Truman had no voice in FDR's early 1945 diplomacy. But on April 12 he inherited FDR's ambiguous policies, rival Arab and Jewish claims, Britain's contradictory commitments, and great-power rivalries in the Middle East.[14]

II

His first week in the White House, Truman was reminded of FDR's commitment to a Jewish commonwealth by Wagner; Rabbi Stephen Wise of New York, founder of the World Zionist Organization and head of the Zionist Organization of America; and Rabbi Abba Hillel Silver of Cleveland, outspoken Zionist, political ally of Senator Taft, and chair with Wise of AMZEC, which had shaped the Biltmore Program. Meanwhile, State Department officials prodded Truman about FDR's pledges to the Arab world.[15]

Shortly, Truman reaffirmed FDR's promise to consult the Arabs and not to take hostile action. He also hinted that Palestine should be opened to Jewish refugees, especially from DP camps. In late June, Truman approved a commission headed by Earl Harrison, dean of the University of Pennsylvania Law School, to investigate DP camp conditions; while Wagner, along with 54 senators and 250 House members, petitioned him to support a Jewish homeland. At the Potsdam Conference in July, the president asked the British to end their White Paper quota on Jewish immigration.[16]

The new British government of Prime Minister Attlee and Foreign Secretary Bevin sought delay, although their Labor Party had opposed the White Paper and voted for unrestricted Jewish immigration and a sovereign home in Palestine. Upon return from Potsdam to Washington in August 1945, Truman stated that the U.S. sought to "let as many Jews into Palestine as possible." But he recognized need for Anglo-Arab approval for a Jewish state, since "I don't want to send 500,000 American troops to make peace in Palestine." He precluded a Soviet role, while his more cautious secretary of state, Byrnes, told U.S. diplomats in the Middle East to say only that immigration and a Jewish state were being discussed.[17]

In late August, the Harrison Report likened the DP camps and the military's treatment of refugees to Nazi concentration camps and recommended immediate admission of 100,000 Jewish refugees to Palestine. Truman strongly endorsed the refugee proposal, sent the report to Attlee, and reprimanded General Eisenhower, commander of the allied forces in Europe, for the military's poor handling of the DP camps.[18]

The British feared for nation and empire. In autumn 1945 they were the predominant power in the Middle East. They had 200,000 troops in the Canal Zone at their Suez base, a naval presence at Haifa, and air installations at Lydda in Palestine, as well as air bases in Iraq and the Sudan and naval bases in Bahrain and Aden. In Transjordan—which the British administered in association with the Palestine mandate before granting it "independence" in 1946—a British general, John Glubb, commanded the Arab League, then about 8,000 strong. Britain had major oil interests in Iraq, from which oil flowed via pipeline to Haifa, and in Iran, where the Abadan refinery was the world's largest and produced more oil in 1945 than all the Arab states combined.[19]

Most British leaders, including Bevin, presumed that for political, economic, and strategic reasons their nation needed to preserve their long-standing position in the Middle East despite the great costs and problems of doing so. As the foreign secretary would tell the Cabinet in August 1949 after four extremely difficult years, "[I]n peace and war, the Middle East is of cardinal importance to the U.K., second only to the U.K. itself. Strategically, the Middle East is a focal point of communications, a source of oil, a shield to Africa and the Indian Ocean, and an irreplaceable offensive base. Economically it is, owing to oil and cotton, essential to the United Kingdom recovery."[20]

Not surprisingly, in fall 1945 Bevin was loathe to do anything that might offend the Arab world and jeopardize British interests. Thus in response to Truman's support for the Harrison Report, the foreign secretary said that to admit 100,000 Jews to Palestine would incite "grave anti-Semitic policy" in England, cause the Arab world to explode, and rouse dangerous Pan-Islamism. Attlee wrote Truman that to put Jews "at the head of the queue" for immigration would stir violence among other DP camp survivors, violate FDR-Churchill pledges to consult the Arabs on Palestine, and jeopardize Britain in India, where ninety million Muslims "are easily inflamed." The British sought delay, and American aid.[21]

So too did Loy Henderson, director of the State Department's NEA division, seek to alter Truman's course. Henderson regarded Middle East policy as his preserve, was favorably disposed to Arab concerns, indifferent to the plight of Jewish refugees and hostile to Zionism, and was insistent that any U.S. action in behalf of the Jews would move the Arabs toward the Soviets, whom he loathed. For three years he was persistent that Palestine could be neither an Arab nor a Jewish state and that the only solution was British trusteeship, with great-power aid. NEA also insisted that underbuilt Palestine could not accommodate large numbers of Jews and that Truman's "pressure" on Britain violated America's consultative commitment and risked its name worldwide. Further, Henderson circulated a War Department estimate that 400,000 troops would be required to quell an armed Arab uprising and that to deploy U.S. forces would jeopardize demobilization and occupation policies. Meanwhile, Arab nations protested that Jewish immigrants would overrun the Middle East and demanded publication of all FDR–Ibn Saud exchanges. The State Department hesitated and then compromised in mid-October by releasing FDR's April 5 pledge to consult over Palestine.[22]

Truman was lobbied as well by prominent American non-Zionist Jewish groups, who favored Jewish emigration to Palestine but not a Jewish state; by American Zionists, such as Rabbis Wise and Silver, who sought Jewish immigration and a state; and by Chaim Weizmann, head of the World Zionist Organization and president of the Jewish Agency in London, who said that Britain's White Paper violated its mandate terms and League of Nations policy.[23]

Truman deplored "ethnic pressures" on U.S. policy, but he continued to seek admission of Jewish refugees to Palestine. He balked at a "religious" state, however, and feared that a Jewish state would incite "a Third World War." He did not oppose a Zionist state (presumably more secular than "religious") but adamantly opposed sending U.S. troops to Palestine. To gain a political hiatus, Truman acceded in mid-October to Britain's request for an Anglo-American Commission of Enquiry (AAC), and shrewdly shaped its terms of reference. Thus, while Britain proposed to resettle Jewish refugees first in their country of origin (including Germany) and then in nations outside Europe (including Palestine), and to convert its mandate into a trusteeship, Truman insisted that the AAC emphasize Jewish immigration to Palestine and self-governance. He also set an early reporting deadline of April 1946.[24]

At Henderson's request, in early November 1945 Truman met with his

Middle East emissaries. They proposed a more "positive" policy, lest the Arabs turn to Russia, than usual U.S. assurances given to ensure access to Arab oil or calm concerns about "Zionist ambitions." The president promised commercial treaties, technical aid, head-of-state visits for newly independent Lebanon and Syria, and an attempt to avert American-Soviet conflict in the region. But Zionism was "the sixty-four-dollar question," he said. Palestine would remain an American political issue, and a "final solution" might not please everyone.[25]

Truman now said that he still hoped "to get as many Jews as possible into Palestine as quickly as possible," but he balked again at the Taft-Wagner resolution for a Jewish commonwealth because he feared preempting the AAC. He also preferred the more neutral term "Palestine state." But in December Congress passed a revised concurrent resolution favoring Jewish immigration to Palestine and a Jewish national home within a "democratic commonwealth."[26]

Then in late April 1946 came the AAC Report with ten unanimous resolutions. These included promptly admitting 100,000 Jewish refugees to Palestine; to foster a Jewish national home, ending White Paper curbs on immigration and land ownership; transforming a UN trusteeship into a unitary state, "neither Arab nor Jewish"; promoting Arab political-economic development; and disbanding all illegal armies. Truman was elated, especially by the call for 100,000 Jewish immigrants and a Jewish national home, which he believed then—and even in 1948—was the best prospect for a solution. Even Henderson termed the report an excellent compromise, as did Zionist leaders, despite their concern that it did not propose a Jewish state. But Arab opposition, especially to Jewish immigration, was "swift and alarming," U.S. diplomats reported, and NEA said the report jeopardized America's Middle East interests.[27]

Most important, the British refused any Jewish immigration unless the AAC Report was implemented in full. This meant consulting the Arabs, disbanding all illegal armies, and guaranteeing Anglo-American financial and military resources. The British also feared that Palestine talks would disrupt their negotiations with Egypt to preserve a military base there, and promote a Middle East "uproar." Consequently, as Bevin's biographer has concluded, the British balked at the plan that came closer than any other would to offering a Palestine solution that would also have met all of their requirements.[28]

Truman thought the British were stalling. He saw no need to consult further on immigration, now a critical issue because refugees fleeing from Russia and Eastern Europe had raised the number in the DP camps from 50,000 in 1945 to 250,000 at present. The president's views were reinforced by White House aide David Niles, an FDR holdover who handled liaison with minority groups and who was also a strong Zionist; and Major General John Hilldring, assistant secretary for occupied areas, who said the AAC had rejected Britain's prior effort to tie immigration to disbanding armies and Anglo-American resources.[29]

Truman acceded, however, to joint talks in London, led by career diplomat Henry Grady and Labor minister Lord Herbert Morrison, to be followed by Arab-Jewish consultations. The president also formed a State-War-Navy Cabinet Committee to assess the report but instructed Grady that the U.S. would not send troops to Palestine nor act as trustee and that it supported the AAC concept of "No Jewish, no Arab State." Truman did not mention his Cabinet Committee's fuller proposal to explore partition, which offered "the speediest relief from the present impasse." He also sought to start Jewish immigration by offering resettlement costs and other aid, but the British and Arabs refused.[30]

Delay of action on Palestine spurred increased "illegal" Jewish immigration and Irgun and Stern Gang attacks on British officials. The British Cabinet decided on "firm action," and in late June Palestine authorities arrested over 2,000 Jews, including the Jewish Agency leadership and Hagana officials. On July 22 the Irgun blew up the British secretariat and military headquarters at the King David Hotel in Jerusalem, killing ninety-one people. The British made more arrests and deportations and heavily fined the Jewish community. Britain's commander in Palestine, General Michael Baker, declared that this was "punishing the Jews in a way the race dislikes—by striking at their pockets."[31]

British behavior was likened to that of the Nazis and incited bitter complaints to the White House. Truman initially fended off protestors, deplored "terrorism," and sympathized with British need to maintain civic order. At the same time, he implored them to release innocent Jews and to begin to admit Jewish refugees.[32]

The British resisted, asserting that the AAC Report would have a "disastrous impact" on their Middle Eastern interests. They also brushed off Bevin's new conclusion favoring a partition plan that would have tied the proposed Arab province to Transjordan and created a separate Jewish state. Thus the emergent Morrison-Grady Plan of July 24 cast aside the AAC's intended unitary state that would be neither Arab nor Jewish and proposed instead a federal state with autonomous Arab and Jewish provinces, with the latter comprising a tiny fraction of the land and a population only 60 percent Jewish. The British High Commission in Jerusalem would control the central government, including foreign policy, security, and immigration. The only concession to the Jews was admission of 100,000 refugees to their province. Thereafter Britain would restrict immigration to economic absorptive capacity.[33]

Despite the Morrison-Grady Plan's limitations, Truman prepared to approve it because it gained him admission of 100,000 Jewish refugees at only the cost of resettlement. Secretary Byrnes, Under Secretary Acheson, and NEA also pushed the plan. But Jewish leaders and American politicians, including Taft and Wagner, criticized it sharply. The U.S. members of the AAC said that it created an attenuated Jewish ghetto with restrictions that violated League of Nations policy. Then on July 27 James G. MacDonald, an AAC member greatly experienced in refugee work, and New York's senators, Wagner and James Mead, told the president that the Jews would rather lose the 100,000 refugees than accept the plan and that his name would be anathema in history if he supported it. Truman was most defensive: "Well, you can't satisfy these people. . . . The Jews aren't going to write the history of the United States, nor my history." He also denied that Roosevelt had better understood the Balfour Declaration and Jewish feeling: "I am not Roosevelt. I am not from New York. I am from the Middle West." [34]

Three days later, the president devoted his entire Cabinet meeting to Palestine but "got nowhere," he lamented. Acheson, Forrestal, and Byrnes (from the CFM meeting in Paris) pressed the Morrison-Grady Plan. Others resisted, including Treasury Secretary John Snyder and Commerce Secretary Wallace, who said that the Jews expected more than a mere "1500 square miles" and warned that the issue was "political dynamite." Truman agreed but was angry at the Jews: even "Jesus Christ couldn't please them." But when Forrestal broached the issue of oil in Saudi Arabia—where Texaco and Standard Oil of California had established a major consortium, Aramco—the president replied that his only concern was to do "what is right." [35]

Truman believed that the Morrison-Grady Plan was "fair," although he told the British that it needed to gain more political support. He indicated that "our Jewish friends" may have missed their chance to get 100,000 refugees admitted, but his view ignored the Arab League's reiterated "unalterable opposition" to Jewish immigrants or "federal solution or partition" for Palestine. [36]

Thus it fell to White House aide David Niles to warn the Jewish Agency that Truman would "wash his hands" of Palestine unless given a realistic option. This spurred the Jewish Agency's historic decision on August 5 to abandon its Balfour Declaration and Biltmore Program for a homeland or state in all of Palestine, and to propose instead to carve out a small Jewish state that would immediately control its immigration and quickly become sovereign. Acheson, then acting secretary, may have encouraged a representative of the Jewish Agency to think he favored partition of Palestine, but that was not so. Acheson regarded commitment to a Jewish state as contrary to U.S. interests and privately hoped that the Jews would accept a revised Morrison-Grady Plan. Truman and his Cabinet Committee concurred in partition, however, although the president left it to the British, who backed only the Morrison-Grady Plan, to convene an Arab-Jewish conference in London. But the Jews declined to attend unless the issue was partition-statehood, and the few Arab nations that appeared insisted on an Arab state in all of Palestine. "Talks" soon adjourned until December. [37]

Truman despaired that "there's no solution for the Jewish problem," while Zionists urged him to endorse partition of Palestine and a Jewish state. Leading Democrats sought a presidential declaration to avert feared loss of Jewish votes in the November elections, especially in New York State, where Republican governor Dewey was expected to make a pro-Zionist statement to fuel both his current reelection campaign and expected presidential bid in 1948. Truman agreed to make a statement on Yom Kippur eve. The Zionists proposed that he endorse partition, but Acheson and his aides rewrote their proposed text. Truman's statement on October 4 noted his early support for admitting 100,000 Jewish refugees to Palestine, and he now proposed immediate "substantial immigration" and encouraged compromise between the Morrison-Grady Plan for autonomous provinces and the Zionists' call for "a viable Jewish state."[38]

Truman chiefly sought to press Britain to admit Jewish refugees into Palestine and to gain votes for Democrats. His statement, however, was universally interpreted as endorsing a Jewish state, marking a watershed in U.S. support for partition of Palestine. The British and Arabs were furious. So too were militant Zionists, who wanted a Jewish state in all of Palestine. The president stood his ground. "There isn't a reason in the world why One Hundred Thousand Jews couldn't go to Palestine," he wrote Senator George, and then told the British and Arabs that the U.S. had long supported the Balfour Declaration and a Jewish national home, which had no meaning without immigration and settlement on the land.[39]

Still, Truman thought that the situation was "insoluble" and that the Jews "are making it almost impossible to do anything for them." He would act as he saw fit, he wrote, and "let the chips fall where they may," but he would not speak publicly again about Jewish immigration or Palestine. When Bevin visited the White House in December, the president agreed with him that much of the difficulty derived from Britain's having made conflicting pledges to the Arabs and Jews—but "so did we," Truman interjected. Bevin concluded that both sides were "difficult": the Jews wanted their prophets' visions fulfilled, and the Arabs were bent on the status quo. Truman was glad to have the elections over and to leave Palestine policy to others.[40]

III

In January 1947 the British despaired of resolving their Palestine problem; but they managed to start talks with Arabs and Jews in London and also asked the Truman administration for its preferred solution. Acheson said that the most practical choice was partition and second was a compromise between partition and a revised Morrison-Grady Plan that provided Jews with more than just provincial autonomy. Entry of 100,000 immigrants was "essential" for any solution. But Bevin had altered course again, abandoning his recent support for partition. He held that two viable states in Palestine were impossible. The Arabs "implacably" opposed partition, which was enforceable only "at the point of the bayonet," and they could prevent the UN from passing it. The British proposed instead to oversee a unitary state that would have autonomous local governments (cantons), admit 100,000 immigrants over two years, and gain independence in five years. The Arabs, however, rejected Jewish immigration and local self-government. The Jews refused to be denied control over immigration or to be a permanent minority in an Arab state.[41]

The British, overwhelmed by their financial and economic problems and engaged in imperial contraction, suddenly announced in mid-February that they were handing the Palestine issue to the UN with no recommendation. A frustrated Bevin complained that Truman had precluded a solution by injecting the immigration issue in August 1945. U.S. officials fumed at Britain's tossing Palestine to the UN without advice. They worried, Acheson noted, that the Russians would "take the ball" to their advantage and likely veto partition. But Acheson, like Truman, had no answer to "the $64.00 question."[42]

In March, the British imposed martial law to combat Jewish "terrorism" and in April asked the General Assembly to take up Palestine. On May 13 that body established a UN Special Committee on Palestine (UNSCOP), comprising eleven neutral states, none of which was deemed to have vital interests in the Middle East. UNSCOP was instructed to report its recommendations by September 1. Truman was pleased with UNSCOP, but surprised, as were most U.S. and British officials, that the Soviets now took a significant position on Palestine.[43]

The Russians, of course, had a long history of anti-Semitism—including bitter pogroms against the Jews in the 1890s—and anti-Zionism, although from the 1920s through the Second World War the Soviet state was too weak or militarily preoccupied to involve itself in Palestine affairs or challenge British primacy in the Arab world. From summer 1945 to spring 1947 the Soviets took no official stance on Palestine, although they did abet Eastern European immigration to Western Europe. But this probably had more to do with politics in the former region and stirring trouble in the DP camps in the latter area than providing potential supporters for the Jewish community in Palestine. Undoubtedly the Soviets were also unhappy that they had been excluded from the AAC negotiations in 1946.[44]

With the Palestine issue now before the UN, however, Deputy Foreign Minister Andrei Gromyko put Moscow's views before the General Assembly on May 14, 1947. He blamed poor British administration for provoking Arab-

Jewish conflict, referenced the Holocaust horrors and the historical roots of both Arabs and Jews in Palestine, and expressed Soviet preference for a binational or federal state. But should that prove unworkable—as it had—Gromyko offered cautious support for partition, a position the Jewish Agency applauded and the Arabs demeaned.[45]

Gromyko's speech marked a milestone on the road to partition, although reason for this Russian action remains uncertain. The Soviets might have been trying to help dislodge Britain from the Middle East, but that does not explain why they took a position bound to draw Arab ire. Perhaps the Russians, having suffered setbacks along the Northern Tier of the Middle East—Iran, Greece, and Turkey—were using the occasion of Palestine now becoming an international issue before the UN to assert their great-power status to take part in decision making. How much influence they expected to have remains questionable, however. The British still had a grip on Arab favor, Marxism and Islamism did not mix well, and the Jewish community in Palestine, while progressive, was not fully socialist nor of Marxist design. Nor was the Zionist movement especially sympathetic to Communism—indeed, it had far more ties to the American Jewish community. Still, the Russians stated their cautious position and waited on events.[46]

Meanwhile, Truman hoped in vain that UNSCOP could work free of politics. In June, Henderson proposed an eight-year UN trusteeship for Palestine, with a maximum of 12,500 Jewish refugees annually, and then a sovereign state that would be neither Arab nor Jewish but inevitably Arab-controlled. Arab states boycotted UNSCOP, however, and the Jews fostered immigration and battled the British. In July, the British seized the ferry *Exodus 1947* off the Palestine coast and sought to return its 4,500 refugee passengers to France. When nearly all the refugees refused to disembark there, the British decided to intern them in occupied Germany, again spurring charges of "Nazi" behavior. The Irgun, meanwhile, executed two British sergeants, inciting British reprisals and anti-Semitic riots in England.[47]

Truman deplored these events, even complaining that the Jews were behaving "like all underdogs": once on top they were as "cruel and intolerant" as people were to them when they were underneath. Under Secretary Lovett worried that the Palestine conflict was uniting "Moslem Nations, and black and yellow races," and giving "Asiatic countries" the balance of power in the UN. Meanwhile, Henderson secured for himself and George Wadsworth, a like-minded recent ambassador to Iraq, appointment as advisers to the UN delegation. In turn, White House aide Niles got Truman to appoint as his UN liaison General John Hilldring, the departing assistant secretary for occupied territories, who had won credibility with Jewish leaders for his efforts to improve DP camps in Europe. Truman also appointed Eleanor Roosevelt to the delegation. She was neither a Zionist nor proponent of partition but known for her strong support of the UN.[48]

UNSCOP unanimously recommended on August 31 that Britain end its Palestine mandate quickly. The committee's majority (eight nations) report recommended partition into Arab and Jewish states that would gain independence in two years—but effect economic union—with UN administration of an internationalized Jerusalem. A minority (three nations) report proposed a federal state that would become independent in three years. The Jewish Agency strongly supported partition. The Arab Higher Committee denounced both partition and a federal state. An angry Bevin opposed partition, and on September 26 Britain declared that it would soon end its Palestine mandate and withdraw its forces.[49]

Secretary Marshall was not well informed about the Middle East and resistant to partition and a Jewish state. He conceded "surprise" at the quality of UNSCOP's report but feared that partition would prompt "violent Arab reaction," lead to Arab-Soviet alignment, and require U.S. troops in Palestine. Marshall and Lovett proposed to call for further UN study, while Henderson assailed the majority report as "sophistry." Warren Austin, ambassador to the UN, agreed with Marshall that a small Jewish state in Palestine would have "to defend itself with bayonets forever, until extinguished in blood." Eleanor Roosevelt dissented. She doubted Russian opposition to partition and prospects for an Arab-Soviet alliance. She saw the central issue as support for the UN position. General Hilldring urged backing, and amending, UNSCOP's partition plan.[50]

Marshall equivocated. He told the General Assembly on September 17 that the U.S. would give "great weight" to UNSCOP's unanimous resolution to end Britain's mandate and its majority plan for partition. Henderson argued anew for his trusteeship plan. He insisted that "nearly every" diplomatic official and the "overwhelming majority" of non-Jewish Americans who knew the Middle East opposed partition, which would make the U.S. the "foremost" Arab enemy. He also warned that to recognize the principle of a "theocratic racist state" would further divide Jews from Gentiles.[51]

Marshall believed it expedient, however, to take the majority report as a "working basis" to support the UN. On September 24 he decided that the U.S. should support partition in principle, offer territorial amendments to favor the Arabs, and not propose an alternative plan until certain that UNSCOP's majority report could not get the necessary two-thirds majority to pass. Thus the secretary delayed any statement for three weeks.[52]

Meanwhile, Truman's White House aides, Clifford and Niles, questioned

Henderson about his trusteeship plan. Henderson later claimed that they had sought to "humiliate" him but that he resisted until the president said, "Oh, hell, I'm leaving." The NEA chief took this to mean that Truman was not ready to go "all out" for a Jewish state but hoped, in vain, to have the State Department say that partition served American interests.[53]

Henderson exaggerated the inquisitorial nature of his interview and misread Truman, who favored UNSCOP's partition plan but feared stirring public debate with a statement. Truman also said nothing at the first meeting of the newly established NSC on September 26 when Admiral Roscoe Hillenkoetter, now head of the recently formed CIA, presented his agency's "thumbnail" world review alleging that Zionist leaders were exploiting world sympathy to gain a Jewish state despite prospect of an Arab "Holy War" against the West and Soviet control of Arab oil.[54]

Now Forrestal, who believed that oil was the critical element in U.S. plans for war and peace and that Saudi Arabia was one of "the three great puddles [of oil] left," asked at a Cabinet lunch on September 29 whether it might be possible to "lift the Palestine-Jewish question out of politics." For the defense secretary, who was given like many State Department officials to genteel anti-Semitism and firm anti-Zionism, this meant averting partition. Truman was skeptical but thought it might be worth the effort. He was equally cautious when New York's Democratic Party leaders asked him to endorse partition. Similarly, when his longtime friend Eddie Jacobson urged him to speak out on partition so that the "helpless people" in Europe's "Hell holes" might emigrate to Palestine, the president said that the matter was better left to diplomacy. He did approve a statement for Ambassador Herschel Johnson, temporary head of the UN delegation, to make on October 11 declaring U.S. support for partition. But Truman stipulated that the U.S. would not assume Britain's mandate and would contribute only a proportional share to Palestine peacekeeping costs under UN auspices.[55]

Two days later, on October 13, Semen Tsarapkin, the Russian delegate to the UN Ad Hoc Committee on Palestine, stunned U.S. and other officials by announcing Moscow's endorsement of partition, to wit, UNSCOP's majority report. Noting the failure of "Western Europe" to protect the Jews from Hitler and—once again—scoring alleged British misrule in Palestine, Tsarapkin proclaimed that the issue was self-determination, the right of Arabs and Jews to live in Palestine. But given that their conflict had gone beyond conciliation, the only solution was two separate states, with hope that economic union would draw them together.[56]

Once again the Americans were "mystified"—as Lovett said—by Soviet action, while the Jewish community was elated. From Moscow Ambassador

Smith could reason only that the Russians had determined that they could make no inroads in the Middle East in the face of U.S. action in Iran, Greece, Turkey, and the "feudal, anti-Communist ruling class" in Arab states. Hence the Soviets now saw the Jews as "the only immediately useful tool to 'soften up' the area for eventual Communist cultivation," while the British would be driven from the area and Arab-Jewish conflict would permit "covert Soviet aid and incitement."[57]

Meanwhile, the British were angered and argued that the UN could not vote partition without stating who would implement it, but they intended to withdraw by August 1948. The Arabs raised the specter of Middle East carnage and "a third world war"—and hinted at a federal state with autonomous provinces akin to the proposal in the rejected Grady-Morrison Plan. State Department officials, spurred by Henderson, pursued two diplomatic tracks. First, they proposed to revise UNSCOP's plan to include in the new Arab state the largely Arab-populated coastal town of Jaffa and the Negev, a strategically valuable "land-bridge" between Arab states but also an access route for a prospective Jewish state to the Gulf of Aqaba and the Red Sea. Further, Henderson got Marshall to approve an arms embargo on Palestine and bordering states in event of post-partition conflict. This would deny American guns to all sides but advantage the better-equipped Arab states. Second, Henderson and others concluded that the continued U.S. nominal support only for partition would cause it to fail, opening the way for a trusteeship.[58]

The president tried to remain aloof, although Jacobson, frequently lobbying Niles at the White House, noted in mid-October that "Truman fighting entire Cabinet and State Department to put partition over." But Truman also wrote to one senator that he had "struck a match" to 35,000 pieces of Jewish mail and "propaganda" for partition, and in November he complained to another senator that the Jews had "knocked out" the Grady-Morrison Plan and now sought partition, which was practical but unlikely to be voted, while the Arabs seemed to favor a federal solution, which they had rejected in 1946. The Palestine problem appeared "insoluble." But when King Saud wrote Truman in late October that U.S. support for partition meant a "death blow" to its Middle East interests and that the Arabs would destroy any Jewish state, the president asserted U.S. intent to support the UN's "majority views."[59]

Meanwhile, the UN Ad Hoc Committee on Palestine divided into Subcommittee One, led by the U.S. and the Soviet Union, to weigh UNSCOP's majority report on partition, while a second subcommittee fruitlessly assessed UNSCOP's minority report on a binational state, which neither Arabs nor Jews would consider by this time. At White House instruction, U.S. officials on Subcommittee One now urged partition to be effected by July 1, 1948, under British administration. The Soviets proposed that the Security Council—which would allow them a role—implement partition. Curiously, despite the U.S. emphasis on British experience in Palestine, the Attlee-Bevin government concluded that it was "surely playing the Russian game to try to embroil our troops" to enforce a settlement, and they rejected the role. By contrast, the Russians were so determined not to jeopardize a chance for partition that they quickly compromised with the U.S on November 10, agreeing that the British mandate should last until May 1, 1948, after which a UN commission comprising a handful of small states would shepherd the new Arab and Jewish states to independence by July.[60]

Meanwhile, Zionists learned that the State Department sought to have UNSCOP's majority report amended to put the Negev in an Arab state, and they arranged through Niles to have Truman quietly receive Chaim Weizmann on November 19. Weizmann was an eminent chemist as well as longtime president of the World Zionists and the Jewish Agency. He brought maps and agricultural expertise to the White House and apparently persuaded the president of the Negev's strategic value to a Jewish state and of its irrigation prospects. Truman then telephoned Hilldring, who told him of the State Department's proposal. The president replied that the delegation should support UNSCOP's decision to include the Negev in a Jewish state. Hilldring informed the State Department, and Lovett called the White House. Truman said that he had not intended to countermand the State Department but saw no point in having the U.S. stand in a "useless minority." Lovett acceded.[61]

Truman may have secured the Zionists a potential map victory, but the State Department's effort to defeat partition seemed on the verge of success. As the General Assembly neared the critical vote on Subcommittee One's proposal for partition, on November 24 Lovett went to the White House. There he read to the president a personal message to Henderson from a former prime minister of Iraq warning that partition would incur "long-term Arab hostility" toward the U.S. and require American—and worse, Soviet—troops in the Middle East. Lovett also reported that "*Jewish* agencies" were employing "threats" and "bribes" to gain partition votes. He then got Truman to instruct the U.S. delegation not to use improper pressure to gain votes for partition. The next day the General Assembly's Ad Hoc Committee on Palestine voted 25–13 in favor of partition, with 17 abstentions. But this was one vote shy of the two-thirds margin needed to pass at the impending plenary session. Then on November 26 Gromyko reiterated to the General Assembly the Soviet Union's reasons for favoring partition—the only practical solution to Arab-Jewish conflict, he said—and the Zionists managed to get the final vote briefly delayed.[62]

Intense lobbying followed. The Arabs promoted a federal state. An angry

Bevin insisted to Marshall that Britain would not take part in implementing partition nor would he forgive the Jews their "execution of two British sergeants." He also charged that their Balkan émigrés were "indoctrinated Communists." Forrestal showed Senator Howard McGrath, who chaired the Democratic National Committee, the CIA report predicting Arab threats to U.S. security if partition were voted.[63]

Truman looked the other way, however, as his White House aides assisted Zionist efforts. Niles enlisted Bernard Baruch to warn France that it might lose economic aid, and former secretary of state Edward R. Stettinius and Harvey Firestone, head of the Firestone Company, to warn Liberia, dependent on rubber exports, that Firestone would halt expansion there unless Liberia voted for partition. Clifford, along with ten senators and two Supreme Court justices, prevailed on the Philippine government. Overall, White House and Zionist lobbying moved seven of the seventeen nations that had previously abstained to favor partition, while only Greece switched from abstaining to opposing partition. When the General Assembly reconvened on November 28, the Arab delegations sought delay by proposing to consider a federal state in Palestine, but this was rebuffed on grounds that it was merely a resurrection of UNSCOP's minority plan. Next day, at the urging of the U.S. and Soviet delegates, the General Assembly voted 33–13, with 10 abstentions—including Britain—to partition Palestine.[64]

"Mission accomplished," Jacobson noted, but this was premature. Diplomats reported Arab nations' intent to war against partition, and the State Department began to argue partition could not be implemented. Meanwhile, Truman allegedly told Jacobson the "full story" of how "he and he alone was responsible for swinging" the critical partition votes. But the president warned that "pressure groups" would destroy the UN and that the Jews had to show "restraint and tolerance."[65]

IV

The UN partition vote was a recommendation that presumed no need for enforcement machinery. Immediate Arab violence in Palestine, however, created a state of "terror." Arab nations also pledged to take up arms after the departure of the British, who announced on December 11 that their civil administration would end on May 15, 1948, with full withdrawal to be completed by August. The Jewish Communists responded with a policy of "aggressive defense," and David Ben-Gurion soon cabled the Hadassah medical organization in New York that "we are facing war real war." Hostilities soon became nationwide, and in January 1948 the so-called Arab Liberation Army entered Palestine.

Meanwhile, senior U.S. officials who had opposed partition now moved to abort the Truman administration's commitment to that UN program.[66]

Forrestal now took his campaign to remove Palestine from political debate to Governor Dewey, who was evasive. The defense secretary also told Truman in early January 1948 that his service chiefs believed that any future "sustained action" against the Soviet Union depended on control of the Mediterranean. Two weeks later Forrestal testified to a House Armed Services subcommittee that "oil is the lifeblood of a modern war machine" and agreed unequivocally with the statement of Republican congressman Dewey Short of Missouri that partition would anger 350 million Arabs and cause the oil pipelines to be cut. This even though King Ibn Saud had already told the U.S. ambassador in Jidda, J. Reyes Childs, that despite strong Arab opposition to partition, his nation had no intention of acting against its interests by ending oil sales or Aramco concessions. In fact, his government most wanted U.S. military supplies, which Ambassador Childs said would be greatly helpful in gaining extension beyond 1949 of U.S. control of the air base at Dhahran.[67]

In mid-January Kennan sent Marshall a PPS report, prepared in "close collaboration" with Henderson, taking a position similar to that of Forrestal that partition threatened U.S. oil supplies and air bases and that efforts to impose it would meet Arab resistance and bring the Soviets into the region. The PPS recommended seeking a trusteeship. Ambassador Wadsworth pressed similar views on Truman on February 4, and proposed to assure Arab leaders that the U.S. would not try to enforce partition by itself or "disguised" under the UN banner.[68]

The next week Dean Rusk, head of the State Department's UN division, proposed a "New Look" at Palestine. He contended that the UN Charter prohibited use of force to compel a political settlement within a state, and to do this would lose Arab oil and friendship to the Soviets. Rusk, and the PPS again, proposed a UN trusteeship. Marshall told the NSC on February 12 that he was undecided. Forrestal said that to implement partition would require "partial mobilization" and Selective Service. The NSC soon concluded that the U.S. should support only peaceful partition, and its military members urged trusteeship at once. UNSCOP's first special report on February 17 chiefly blamed Arab violence for preventing partition and implored the Security Council not to permit force to thwart UN policy. But at a White House briefing the next day on military preparedness, General Alfred Gruenther of the JCS declared that Palestine intervention would require 80,000–160,000 troops and "partial mobilization," and Forrestal again urged seeking Republican support to preclude military action. The next week Kennan and the PPS told Marshall and Lovett that U.S. security required helping the British to sustain their Middle East strategic position and bases, which would be at U.S. disposal in wartime. This demanded a "fairly radical" reversal of current policy in the Middle East to avert offending the Arab world.[69]

The president remained cautiously committed to partition and angry at both "British bullheadedness" and the "fanaticism of our New York Jews" for allegedly having thwarted the Grady-Morrison Plan in 1946. He told Ambassador Wadsworth that he would not send arms or troops to enforce partition, but he refused "categoric promises" as long as Arab states would not pledge to keep their armies out of Palestine. Truman also refused Jacobson's pleas, intermingled among charges of State Department efforts at "sabotaging" partition, to reaffirm partition or to meet with Weizmann.[70]

The president was equally cool to Forrestal's proposed "nonpolitical" Palestine policy. But the White House was concerned about a congressional by-election on February 17 in a heavily Jewish district in the Bronx, where criticism of Truman's cautious partition policy helped an American Labor Party candidate upset the Democratic candidate. But when Marshall told Truman, about to depart on a Caribbean vacation, that State Department policy was still not fixed, the president advised him to choose the "right one," regardless of politics.[71]

Spurred by Rusk and Henderson's NEA, the State Department cabled Truman on February 21 to approve a speech for Austin proposing Security Council review of the Palestine imbroglio. The key passage, of doubtful legal logic, asserted that the UN Charter authorized use of force to maintain peace against aggression but not to enforce UN recommendations, i.e., partition. The department also asked approval of text, which Austin would hold for a later address, stating that if the Security Council review found that partition required use of force, the U.S. would call for a new trusteeship. The department sought to halt partition—and a Jewish state. As Kennan's PPS concluded on February 24, U.S. failure to reverse its Palestine policy might cause it to become—along with the Soviet Union—military protector of the "Jewish population" against Arab hostility.[72]

Truman did not grasp State Department intent to scuttle partition. He approved Austin's speech but ordered that there be no "recession" from partition. Marshall said that this was not recession, unless one mistakenly believed that the UN could enforce its recommendations. On February 24 Austin called for Security Council review of the Palestine situation. This was agreed on March 5, and three days later Marshall, with Lovett present, got Truman to approve text for Austin to propose a UN trusteeship if the Security Council concluded that it could not gain peaceful partition before Britain's mandate ended on May 15.[73]

Zionists were enraged, but Truman was "very bitter" at them and again refused Jacobson's entreaties for Weizmann. The president blamed his "headache" on "difficult" Arabs, and Jews who sought a U.S. "big stick" policy. Palestine was not solvable, he wrote, but he hoped to gain the UN resolution. And when Senator Francis Myers of Pennsylvania complained that Austin's "weasel worded" and "legalistic" speech obscured America's position, Truman said he was not "ducking" an issue.[74]

Clifford then produced memoranda in early March deploring Austin's "sophistries" that emphasized what could not be done to effect UN policy. Clifford turned on their head State Department arguments that partition threatened U.S. security. Rather, appeasing Arab "aggressors" would deal a "body blow" to the UN, the best agency to consolidate the world's "anti-Soviet forces." Further, a Jewish state would be oriented toward the U.S., not Russia—wealthy Arab rulers knew it would be political suicide to introduce Communist agents into their countries—and the U.S. was the only customer for the Arabs' oil. But to allow an Arab-Jewish war would invite Soviet entry into the Arabian Peninsula as peacekeepers. Truman replied only that partition was "unworkable" without economic union.[75]

Now Jacobson appeared at the White House on March 12 still seeking an audience for Weizmann. Appointments Secretary Matthew Connelly warned him not to mention Palestine to the president, but Jacobson did—and drew angry retorts about Jewish pressures. Later he recalled that at that time Truman seemed as "close to being an anti-Semite" as anyone could. But Jacobson assuaged his old friend by saying that he could withstand public criticism as well as his hero, Andrew Jackson. The president then agreed that after he gave his St. Patrick's Day speech in New York, in which he would blame the Soviets for the Cold War, he would see Weizmann.[76]

Truman received Weizmann on March 18. No official record was kept, although Weizmann recollected that the president committed to "press forward with partition." Truman recalled only that he wanted "justice done without bloodshed" and that Weizmann had fully understood his policy.[77]

Marshall, meanwhile, reiterated to his UN delegation that Truman had approved their tactics, and he told Austin to propose trusteeship as soon as he knew that partition could not be gained peacefully. The Security Council commission soon indicated this. The next day, March 19, Austin, without notifying the White House, proposed suspension of Security Council partition efforts and a General Assembly special session to establish a temporary trusteeship.[78]

The political backlash at this reversal of course was immediate. Truman despaired to be perceived as "a liar and a double crosser," and an aide noted that he was "shocked" and "depressed" at Zionist charges of "betrayal" and capitulation to Arab terror. He also worried that Weizmann would consider him a "shitass." The president sent former speechwriter Samuel Rosenman to reassure the Zionist leader that Truman still backed partition, and he had Marshall state on March 20 that trusteeship was to be "temporary," until a peaceful solution was possible. He also asked Clifford to discover who had created this political mess. The president, naively, refused to believe that Marshall and Lovett knew of Austin's speech but was convinced that "there are people on the 3rd and 4th levels of the State Dept. who have always wanted to cut my throat. They've succeeded in doing it." Someday, he said, he would "clean out" these "striped pants conspirators."[79]

Truman had largely embarrassed himself. He had approved Austin's trusteeship speech on February 21 and March 8. Perhaps some confusion derived from his having indicated that Austin should not act until the Security Council voted not to implement partition by force, whereas Marshall had told Austin to act when he was certain of the UN decision. The difference was timing, but the result would have been the same. This Truman admitted when he told Marshall that his distress was due chiefly to State Department failure to give him the exact time of Austin's speech so that he might have avoided the "political blast" from the press. His primary policy concern was to avert civil or international war and the dispatch of troops to Palestine, whether to restore international peace or to enforce partition. Truman quickly latched on to the idea that a "temporary" trusteeship was not "recession" from partition but a respite to develop a long-term peaceful solution. Marshall feared that UN peacekeeping would lead to enforcing partition and allow the Soviets into the area.[80]

Truman also misjudged State Department officials. They did not seek to cut his throat but that of partition, which they always opposed. Their legalistic trusteeship proposal intended "recession." They had no new, mutually acceptable, peaceful alternative to partition, yet their insistence that the UN could not enforce it gave incentive to the Arabs to wage war to negate UN policy. Department officials also pressed an arms embargo that favored Arabs over Jews.[81]

Truman sought to clarify Palestine policy at a White House–State Department conference on March 24. He indicated he would declare trusteeship to be temporary policy, and he now brushed aside Henderson's claims that partition threatened U.S. interests. White House aides also proposed to lift the arms embargo, but the State Department won a delay to seek a truce. Truman then asked Clifford to draft a statement. On March 25, the president told an overflow news conference that trusteeship was not a substitute for partition but a temporary measure to maintain order—stop the "killing"—after Britain departed on May 15. He urged a truce, which combined with trusteeship might gain a peaceful solution. Only when a reporter pressed him did Truman state that he still favored partition.[82]

Austin soon proposed truce and trusteeship terms but drew no favorable response. Enforcement costs were no less than under partition, although Truman said that he would have the U.S. help implement trusteeship—with Britain and France—to the limit of its ability. Then on April 4 Rusk told the JCS that if the U.S. "did nothing, it was likely the Russians could, and would take definite steps toward gaining control in Palestine through the infiltration of specially trained immigrants." Moreover, U.S. intercession would be strategically advantageous and "give us the opportunity to build bomber fields in the Middle East." The JCS responded that intervention would require a minimum of 104,000 troops, with the U.S. providing about 47,000 of them. But this would require partial mobilization and increased appropriations and overextend U.S. forces. When later, Australia's foreign minister, Herbert V. Evatt, said that the Soviets would also have to be asked to take part, the president said this was "preposterous."[83]

Meanwhile, in April the Jews took their first military offensive to gain control of the territory that the UN had demarcated as their state, and they refused a truce so long as Arab nation troops remained in Palestine. The Arabs remained opposed to Jewish immigration and to Jews sharing in determination of a new Palestine government. The British took the U.S. trusteeship proposal as a ploy for partition and concluded that the only solution was a bloodletting.[84]

Politics and war continued in April. Truman apparently reaffirmed to Weizmann, through Jacobson, his lack of knowledge of State Department intent and his plan to recognize a Jewish state if the UN sustained partition. He also intended to transfer oversight of Palestine policy from Henderson to General Hilldring, recently appointed at the behest of White House aides as Marshall's special assistant. But this gambit failed when Marshall would not accept Hilldring who, like Truman, venerated the secretary and resigned rather than challenge him.[85]

State Department officials still sought a truce to undercut partition. Rusk emphasized to Truman in late April that Jewish leadership was divided over a truce and might reject one, whereas the Arabs were amenable. A somewhat gullible president replied that if that were the case, the Jews "need not expect anything else from us" and, so Rusk reported, told him to "go and get a truce."[86]

A few days later Truman, who wrote Jacobson that his "soul [sic] interest" was to prevent bloodshed, approved Rusk's proposal for Arab-Jewish talks abetted by a ten-day cease-fire and extension of Britain's mandate. The president offered his plane to fly UN mediators to Jerusalem. The Jewish Agency, however, opposed extending Britain's mandate and noted that Arab Higher

Committee officials were not in Palestine. Rusk complained that the Jews intended to form a state. Their military action would make them "actual aggressors," he said, but they would "come running" for UN protection if Arab armies responded. Marshall warned Jewish officials that they were taking a "grave risk" by basing their strategy on "temporary military success" and that they should not look to the U.S. if the Arabs invaded. He also got Truman to approve a statement reaffirming a truce and proposing a UN commissioner, or mediator, for Arab-Jewish talks.[87]

State Department views ran counter to reality in early May. Truce prospects were nil, as Harold Beeley, Britain's chief Foreign Office adviser on Palestine, told Henderson. The Jews opposed trusteeship unless it presaged a state, Beeley said, and the new Jewish state would be able to defeat invading Arabs. Austin reported Arab officials were skeptical about a truce and would "not ever accept a Jewish state." Finally, the State Department's UN adviser reported that everyone had abandoned trusteeship and that only partition would work because *"it would face up to the inescapable fact that a Zionist state already is in being in Palestine."*[88]

Reality was controlling. As Clifford noted on May 4, a Jewish state was "inevitable" as was U.S. recognition, which was consistent with American policy and better done before the Soviets acted. Similarly, Dean Alfange, chairman of the American Christian Palestine Committee of New York, advised that the Jews had shown that they could "implement partition single handed," and the president should recognize the new Jewish state when it came about on May 15. This would strengthen Truman's electoral prospects, UN authority, and the Jewish state's right to self-defense. Clifford, assisted by his own White House adviser, Max Lowenthal, argued likewise to Truman on May 9. So did Eleanor Roosevelt, advising that if the U.S. intended to recognize the Jewish state, it should not "lag behind Russia." And, she added, "I personally believe in the Jewish State."[89]

The president summoned White House and State Department officials on May 12 to settle Palestine policy. Clifford recalled that Truman told him to prepare his recognition case as if he were before the Supreme Court, but this seems exaggerated given Truman's own uncertainty and his penchant to support Marshall. Regardless, Lovett began by assailing Jewish resistance to a truce and looking to make a "behind the barn" partition deal with King Abdullah of Transjordan. Marshall recounted his military warnings to the Jews, and Lovett then asked Truman to approve Marshall's proposal for a truce, a Palestine mediator, and an end to partition efforts.

Clifford argued that there would be no truce. The president should recognize the Jewish state immediately after May 15—before the Soviets acted—and he should state his intention at once and urge UN members to follow suit.

Lovett denounced "premature recognition" as a ploy for votes and as "buying a pig in a poke" because intelligence reports indicated that the Soviets were sending "Jews and Communist agents" from Eastern Europe to Palestine. Marshall challenged Clifford's presence at a foreign policy meeting, eschewed the plan for recognition as domestic politics, and "bluntly" threatened, if he voted in November, to vote against Truman. The president halted the meeting and approved Marshall's tripartite proposal, which was put to the General Assembly the next day.[90]

Clifford bitterly recalled Marshall's "righteous God-damned Baptist tone," although not Lovett's contemptible "pig in a poke" attitude. Truman was noncommittal about recognizing the forthcoming state of Israel at his May 13 news conference and in his reply to Weizmann's renewed appeal. But recognition was not a foregone conclusion. Clifford told Lovett that their White House meeting had decided only against acting before the new Jewish state sought recognition. Now the issue was how to respond to that state's request. Lovett said this was being weighed.[91]

The next morning Clifford pressed recognition on Lovett, insisting that it had to be done quickly if the president were to benefit. Clifford, however, did not tell Lovett, who agreed to a luncheon discussion, that he had already asked Eliahu Epstein, the Jewish Agency representative in Washington, to send a recognition request (already drafted by Democratic-Zionist lawyers) to Truman and to the State Department. Epstein, acting on his own authority, had the emerging state of Israel's request for recognition, within its UN-proposed 1947 borders, at the White House by noontime on May 14.[92]

Meanwhile, at their luncheon that day, Clifford urged recognition on Lovett in lawyerly fashion. With the British mandate ending at 6:00 P.M., he said, there would be no government in Palestine, and "title would be lying about for anybody to seize." Lovett conceded there was no legal bar to recognition but opposed "indecent haste" given likely Arab reaction. Clifford thought delay pointless, saying that the recognition request was en route and that Truman would act. Whether Lovett was then moved to prevail upon Marshall—as Clifford recalled—to notify Truman that he would not oppose recognition is moot. But shortly before 6:00 P.M. Clifford informed the State Department that Truman was about to act. Lovett again sought delay, until the UN voted on Marshall's truce proposal that night, but Clifford refused. Shortly, Rusk telephoned news of Truman's impending recognition to Austin, who left the UN without a word to anyone, allegedly to underscore that recognition was a White House decision. Then at 6:11 P.M. Truman's press secretary, Charles Ross, read a brief statement to reporters announcing de facto recognition of Israel's provisional government, which had proclaimed its existence eleven minutes earlier.[93]

Truman's decision went by ticker tape to the UN, where Philip Jessup, ranking U.S. delegate, informed the startled assemblage, with many delegations angrily expressing lack of confidence in U.S. diplomacy. Nonetheless, Rusk's hasty flight from Washington to New York, allegedly to avert resignation of America's UN delegation, proved unnecessary. Tempers quickly cooled, and the UN shortly voted Marshall's resolution to establish a UN mediator to seek a Palestine truce and to halt work on partition.[94]

Truman's decision to recognize Israel de facto—the Soviets granted de jure recognition the next day, May 15—remains hotly debated. Even Eleanor Roosevelt complained that the abrupt recognition caused "complete consternation" at the UN and greatly embarrassed American delegates, although both Truman and Marshall were not fully apprised of the current status of UN diplomacy. Surely Truman hoped to strengthen his presidential prospects by pleasing Jewish voters. But it is also true that leading Republicans, including Dewey, Taft, and Vandenberg, and a large majority of Congress and governors, favored recognition. Finally, White House staff played exceptional roles as policy advocates and provided Jacobson and Weizmann with access to the president.[95]

Truman's Palestine policy derived from political realities, not campaign concerns. He respected the Balfour Declaration and Jewish desire for a homeland, had great compassion for the "pitiful remnants" of Holocaust survivors, and sought haven in Palestine for 100,000 refugees if only to mitigate frightful DP camp conditions in 1945–1946. But he also bridled at Jewish lobbying, respected Arab nationalism, and sought to avert military conflict in Palestine. His chief interest was to stop the bloodshed. His preferred solution was either the 1946 Anglo-American plan for an autonomous state neither Arab nor Jewish or the successor Morrison-Grady Plan for a federal state with autonomous Arab and Jewish provinces and British oversight of foreign policy and security. But the British scuttled the former plan, the Jews resisted the latter plan, and the Arabs fought against both proposals as well as Jewish immigration, land ownership, and autonomy in Palestine. In 1947 the British handed the Palestine problem to the UN, which voted for partition by more than a two-thirds majority that included the U.S., the Soviet Union, and France. Truman supported both partition and UN authority.

By contrast, State Department officials long disregarded commitment to a Jewish homeland in Palestine, were coldly indifferent to Holocaust victims, antipathetic to Zionism and a Jewish state, and easily given to disparaging Jewish people or intentions. However, they spoke glowingly of Arab nationalism and made as touchstones of their foreign policy the U.S. need to gain Arab oil and to minimize Soviet influence, despite the fact that the Soviets supported partition. Spurred by Henderson, State Department officials challenged all of Truman's policies from the outset—whether immigration or the Anglo-American plan—and bitterly fought partition. They sought to negate the UN decision by seizing on the dubious doctrine that the UN had no authority to enforce partition, thereby giving Arab violence a veto over UN policy. Further, even if they did not intend to deceive Truman with their March 1948 trusteeship proposal, it contravened his order against "recession" from partition.

Similarly, Marshall's tripartite proposal to halt partition, appoint a UN mediator, and gain a truce was also intended to preclude partition, although neither he nor his aides had an alternative solution acceptable to both Arabs and Jews. In fact, by spring 1948 even the British, who were hostile to partition, recognized that only an Arab-Jewish bloodletting could resolve matters. Only the State Department seemed not to have recognized that the Jewish community in Palestine had already implemented partition and would defend its new state against attack by Arab nations.[96]

From the White House perspective, to delay de facto recognition was to deny reality, diminish UN authority, offend a vital domestic political constituency, and permit the Soviets to seize moral and political advantage, which Truman told Eleanor Roosevelt he would not allow. In this latter regard, State Department policy was now hoist by its own Cold War petard of anti-Soviet politics.[97]

Shortly afterwards Lovett complained that Truman's political advisers, having failed to make him the "father" of the new Jewish state on May 12, made him its "midwife" on May 14. Years later Clifford proudly agreed that thanks to Truman's decision the U.S. "*was* 'midwife'" to Israel. Clifford might also have said that the only policy that would have satisfied the State Department was one that did not conceive a Jewish state.[98]

V

Truman's problems heightened after May 15 as five Arab states attacked Israel, which asked the U.S. for de jure recognition, a loan, and lift of the arms embargo. The State Department and Great Britain opposed assisting the beleaguered Jewish state and sought to have its borders sharply redrawn despite the UN partition vote of 1947 that had defined them. Truman sought a principled position, but once again, his inability to grasp the nuances of diplomacy caused him great difficulty.[99]

State Department officials insisted that de jure recognition await Israel's holding elections, although Lovett conceded that no such criterion underlay U.S. recognition policy. But officials aimed to leverage Israel, with Henderson proposing on his own on May 27 that Israel might speed legal recognition by accepting "frontier adjustments." The Israelis refused, however, and fourteen nations soon granted legal recognition. After the presidential campaign began in September, Clifford urged Truman to act. But the president, who in late May had pointedly invited Weizmann to the White House before he departed the U.S. to assume Israel's presidency, had also promised to clear such action with Marshall, who sought to delay legal recognition.[100]

Truman did not consult Marshall upon naming AAC member James G. MacDonald as special representative to Israel. The president also ordered that Henderson, whose arrogant behavior bordered on insubordination as well as anti-Semitism, be removed from his NEA post and sent far abroad as ambassador to India. Truman also gave personal assurance, through Jacobson, that Israel's UN-designated borders "would stick." Moreover, both the Democratic and Republican campaign platforms pledged legal recognition and economic aid and affirmed Israel's borders, with the Democrats stipulating that any border change required Israel's consent.[101]

The president, meanwhile, reluctantly acceded to State Department opposition to a loan to Israel or to lifting the arms embargo, on grounds that the Arabs would view these as a declaration of war, despite the flow of British supplies to the Arabs. Nonetheless, Jewish forces ably defended their state against invading Arab armies until the UN gained a cease-fire on June 11, but the Arabs were in control of the Negev. The UN-appointed mediator, Count Folke Bernadotte of Sweden, then proposed Israel-Transjordan union, with Israel ceding the Negev and Jerusalem (which the UN partition plan had proposed to internationalize) for the western Galilee. Bernadotte's plan marked regression from partition toward the AAC's 1946 proposal of a binational state, however, and met rejection. The Jews would not give up their own state, nor the Negev. Palestinian leaders and Arab nations refused the plan as dividing Palestine between the Jews and Abdullah of Transjordan, with the latter gaining possession of four-fifths of the area of Palestine over which Britain had held a mandate. And even the British, intent on preserving control in the Negev to protect the Suez region, realized the plan was unworkable. Thus, fighting resumed on July 9. Reinforced Jewish troops soon won critical victories and territory in the Galilee, along the Jerusalem–Tel Aviv route, and in the Negev. On July 18 the UN imposed a second cease-fire.[102]

Bernadotte now sought to develop another plan under the aegis of Marshall and Bevin. Meanwhile, Marshall persuaded Truman in late August that Israel's borders had to be redrawn to make it more "homogenous" than under the UN partition plan. The secretary warned that renewed Israeli attacks on Transjordan might bring British intervention, widening the conflict, to Soviet delight. Marshall also assailed Israel's "aggressive tendencies" and "callous mistreatment" of Arab refugees. On September 1 Truman approved his secretary's *de-*

marche, without grasping that a more "homogenous" Israel meant sharp retreat from its UN-voted boundaries, to which Truman, as well as the Democrats and Republicans, were committed.[103]

American and British diplomats shaped Bernadotte's second plan, which again called for Israel to cede the Negev for the western Galilee but reverted to the original UN plan to internationalize Jerusalem. Stern Gang terrorists assassinated Bernadotte on September 16, but his plan was soon released, and at the UN meeting in Paris on September 21, Marshall and Bevin urged acceptance "in its entirety." The Israelis resisted being reduced to a "miniature state," however, while the Arabs opposed any Jewish state, and American Jewish spokespeople criticized the Truman administration for reneging on its commitment to Israel's borders.[104]

Truman was campaigning in the West and did not react to the political storm until September 28, when Jacobson, at Weizmann's behest, joined the president's campaign train in Oklahoma. Jacobson and the White House staff (including Clifford) on board charged that the State Department had undercut the president just as it had in March with its trusteeship proposal. They warned Truman that he would be criticized for breaking his word and lose crucial votes. The president said he "would not budge" from his commitment to Israel's borders despite Marshall, nor endorse the Bernadotte Plan. But the next day, when Clifford telephoned Lovett that Truman intended to reiterate to Marshall his commitment to Israel's borders, the under secretary sharply rejoined that on September 1 the president had approved Marshall's undertaking and had not replied to recent State Department notice of Marshall's intent to endorse the Bernadotte Plan. Shortly, Clifford got Lovett to agree that Truman would declare that the Bernadotte Plan was only a basis for peace efforts, but then the White House counsel dropped the matter.[105]

Marshall sought unsuccessfully to gain Arab-Israeli accord to the Bernadotte Plan without modification. Truman averted comment despite sharp Jewish criticism of his administration and rifts in the U.S. delegation over Marshall's rigidity. On October 17 Truman proposed that Marshall delay further UN debate until the presidential campaign ended. When Lovett demurred, the president made clear his belief that the U.S. delegation had unnecessarily taken the lead at the UN. Later that night Clifford delivered Truman's "request" that the delegation not speak or act without presidential approval. Marshall proposed to comply by stating that the UN had to defer talks to avoid "partisan" pressure during America's elections, but the president rejected this transparent maneuver.[106]

Truman might have said no more on the issue but on October 22 Dewey, his opponent for the presidency, reiterated in a public letter to Dean Alfange that there was Republican support for full recognition of Israel with its UN-sanctioned boundaries. To be sure, Clifford saw Dewey's "error" as Truman's opportunity. But even Lovett recognized that the president had to respond aggressively to this attack on his integrity on the eve of his campaign in Chicago and New York. On October 24 Truman reaffirmed diplomatic-economic support for Israel, proposed to revise the arms embargo, and cited the Bernadotte Plan as only a "basis for negotiation." Four days later at Madison Square Garden, he roundly declared that Israel "must be large enough, free enough and strong enough to make its people self-supporting and secure." [107]

The president had yet again to clarify his position. Recent Israeli advances in the Negev undercut both the Bernadotte Plan, which rested on the lines of force of October 15, and the Marshall-Bevin intent to force Israel to cede the Negev to Transjordan. Marshall now backed a proposed British resolution implying sanctions against Israel if it did not withdraw to its pre–October 15 positions. This aroused strong Democratic protest and caused Truman, once again, to request that Marshall not act without his approval. A perturbed secretary responded that he wished to know to what the president was referring (Britain's revised resolution omitted sanctions) and occasioned Lovett's oft-cited reply that normal diplomatic procedure would resume after the "silly season" ended on November 2. Lovett ignored, however, the extent to which diplomatic inconsistency derived less from campaign politics than repeated State Department efforts to change established policies to which the president, and both political parties, were committed.[108]

Policy discord continued despite Truman's stunning election victory and passage on November 4 of a Security Council resolution calling for Arab-Israeli negotiations but threatening sanctions if Israel did not withdraw from its advanced positions in the Negev. Truman was partly at fault for advocating territorial compromise with no strong commitment to effect this, but Britain and the State Department were chiefly to blame for pressing Israel to cede the Negev even when this defied political-military reality.[109]

Israel had won its war of independence by November and was capable of driving Arab forces from all of Palestine, as U.S. military observers reported. Moreover, as Weizmann contended to Truman, Britain sought to detach the Negev to destroy the UN partition vote, but the Israelis would not depart the area—which they deemed vital to their security and economics—unless "bodily removed." Similarly, Truman's special representative to Israel, MacDonald, confirmed that it was militarily and politically unrealistic for the Israelis to hand over the Negev, and he warned against supporting "Bevin's intransigency." [110]

The president sought policy accord at a November 6 meeting with Lovett and Lewis Douglas, ambassador to Great Britain, who pressed transfer of the Negev to Transjordan as a strategic benefit to the U.S. as well as Britain. Truman reasserted his commitment to Israel's UN-defined borders and no change without Israel's consent. Nonetheless, Lovett emphasized to Marshall—and Truman approved the cable—that the president would not oppose Israel's exchanging the Negev for the western Galilee, now Israeli-occupied territory beyond their original UN borders, and the right to retain Jaffa, as the UN plan had provided. Lovett noted that recent military events made this modified Bernadotte Plan more a practical than an equitable solution.[111]

Marshall pressed Israel's cession of the Negev, hinting at withholding de jure recognition and a loan and warning, "Don't overplay your hand." But the Israelis refused. They rejected the Bernadotte Plan outright and claimed the entire Galilee as well as "modern Jewish Jerusalem." On November 16 a Security Council resolution called for armistice talks, with minimal reference to sanctions if Israel did not pull back its forces. The British were enraged that they might not gain the Bernadotte Plan, while Truman ruled sanctions "out of [the] question."[112]

The U.S. shortly backed Britain's proposal for a Palestine Conciliation Commission (the British feared that Israel would predominate in direct talks with the Arabs), while Israel began a military pullback in the Negev. Lovett thought the time "propitious" for a settlement, provided that the British did not rigidly cling to the Bernadotte Plan or encourage the Arabs to "wishful thinking" about their military prospects. The British wanted the Bernadotte Plan and no negotiations, he said; the Jews wanted negotiations and no Bernadotte Plan.[113]

Truman remained reticent, save to reaffirm to Weizmann his commitment to Israel's UN-defined borders and his hope to foster Israeli–Middle East economic development. No one could foster Arab negotiations with Israel, however, despite even Lovett's mid-December advice to the Egyptians to recognize the "realities" of Israel's existence and military strength and to realize that time to negotiate was "running quite short." Indeed, Israeli forces had trapped Egypt's expeditionary army in the northern Negev at al-Faluja, and seeing no diplomatic prospects and facing military-economic strain, they decided to attack to preclude Egyptian retreat southward. But first, on December 22, they launched diversionary bombing attacks on Egypt's coastal air bases and six days later entered Gaza.[114]

U.S. officials prepared to protest Israel's action and to advise Egypt to negotiate but drew back. The British, however, threatened to retaliate under their 1936 defense treaty with Egypt and to reinforce Transjordan. They also insisted to Truman that wider war endangered Anglo-American strategic interests in the Middle East. The president, who usually discounted British bluster, sent a severe warning to Israel (Prime Minister Ben-Gurion said that Bevin could have written it) to withdraw from Gaza and not to threaten Transjordan—or he would reconsider in full U.S. relations with Israel.[115]

Ben-Gurion and Weizmann, who argued that Israel's war was entirely defensive, immediately assured Truman that the Egyptian incursion was only "hot pursuit" and that the forces had already been ordered withdrawn, but not before Israeli planes shot down five British Spitfires—four over Egypt—on "reconnaissance" on January 7, 1949. The British inclined to military alert in the Middle East. But Egypt's agreement that same day to a cease-fire and armistice talks, and sharp criticism in London of British policy, ended the crisis.[116]

The president now gave short shrift to Bevin's explications, made through Ambassador Oliver Franks, of Britain's strategic need to control the Negev and its lack of confidence in Israel. First Lovett, reflecting the State Department's transformed view, rejoined that strategic security lay in encouraging Israel to a "westward outlook," not in confining it to a "straitjacket" surrounded by "weak Arab enemies" dependent on Britain. Truman was even more blunt: he told Franks that he did not comprehend British anxieties and that the Negev was not worth differing over, nor was it divisible. Privately, Truman said there was "nothing" behind Britain's position "but the bull in the China shop—Bevin."[117]

Soon the Export-Import Bank confirmed Truman's pledge of economic support with a $100 million credit to Israel for agriculture and public works. The president rejected any "deal" with Bevin—that "s.o.b."—who proposed to recognize Israel de facto in exchange for the U.S. recognizing Transjordan and issuing an Anglo-American statement of common policy in the Middle East. Truman did approve a joint statement on seeking Middle East peace and security but canceled it when Bevin set January 26 for recognizing Israel and then briefly delayed.[118]

Meanwhile, following Israel's war-delayed elections on January 25, the president and his new secretary of state, Dean Acheson, moved swiftly to recognize Israel de jure (and Transjordan, as Truman had agreed in August). Truman asked only for enough notice to assure that a "close friend from Kansas City" could be present at the signing, which occurred on January 31. The president then gave his pen to Jacobson, who soon wrote that Truman had "kept his word."[119]

The president had done so. He had refused to renege on the UN partition plan not only to sustain his commitment to a Jewish state but to uphold UN authority. Truman also fulfilled his pledge that Israel's UN-defined borders not be changed without its consent, and he extended economic assistance and de jure recognition, despite delays mainly intended to appease the State Department. In May 1949 he firmly backed Israel's entry into the UN. Finally, it must be noted that Truman hardly played politics with the "Jewish vote" during his presidential campaign. In fact, he would not even have reiterated his commitment to Israel's borders in late October 1948 if Dewey had not attacked the asset the president most cherished: his word.[120]

By contrast, Marshall and his State Department gave only equivocal—at best—support to the UN partition decision and were not straightforward with the president. Their trusteeship proposal of March 1948 sought prolonged delay, really recision, of partition. They also sought to disadvantage the new Jewish state and exact concessions, despite claims to the contrary, by sustaining their arms embargo and withholding de jure recognition and a loan. By contrast, they made no comparable efforts to urge Palestinian Arabs and Arab nations to come to terms with the "realities" of Israel's existence. Thus Marshall, who proved to be militarily as well as politically uninformed in late 1948, appeared to be wedded to "Bevin's intransigency." It was not until Israel won its war of independence that State Department officials such as Lovett would halt their totally unfounded claims that a Jewish state would be inclined toward Soviet or Communist leadership and threaten U.S. national interests, and instead would begin to talk about encouraging Israel to look westward. As John Foster Dulles, then Dewey's foreign policy adviser, wrote at the time, the "lessons" of 1948 demonstrated the division and weakness of Arab states, the fallibility of British judgment, and U.S. need to assume leadership in the Middle East.[121]

Truman, meanwhile, sought to hold Israel to diplomatic account to fulfill its agreements. When armistice negotiations with Egypt foundered over Israel's retaining defensive forces in the Negev near Egypt's border, the president expressed "grave concern" to the Israelis that they not miss the "psychological moment" for accord, which would be key to agreements with the other Arab states. Israel soon signed the armistice with Egypt on February 24, 1949, and armistices with Lebanon, Transjordan, and Syria came during March–July.[122]

Truman also expressed great concern about the postwar territorial division. Israel retained the western Galilee, West Jerusalem and territory running to the coast and south of Jaffa, and a small area in the southern Negev. Transjordan (which became Jordan) annexed East Jerusalem and the West Bank of the Jordan River, most of the territory that would have composed the Arab state envisaged under the UN partition plan. Egypt retained Gaza. Thus Truman could not uphold his position that Israel should not expand its UN borders except through a negotiated exchange. Nor was he able, despite repeated efforts, to gain agreement on internationalizing Jerusalem rather than have it remain divided.[123]

Finally, Truman was deeply distressed at the plight of Arab refugees. He continually urged Israel to permit the return of a sizeable number of some 700,000 Arabs, about half of whom had left by choice or at the urging of Arab leaders during the spring of 1948, when war against the incipient Israeli state was the order of the day. The remaining Arabs then fled, or were driven out, as the Israelis won battles and territory in the latter half of 1948. Thereafter, not even Truman's repeated, personal appeals to Weizmann and offers of financial aid could sway Israel from its contention, formulated into policy in June 1948, that return of the Arabs would pose an unacceptable national security threat. The solution, Israel persisted, was not repatriation but resettlement elsewhere in the Arab world.[124]

Finally, it must be noted that although Israel gained entrance into the community of nations in 1948–1949, no Arab state would recognize Israel or negotiate a peace treaty. Thus, while Truman took pride in having played a vital role in bringing about creation of Israel, he remained unhappy about the disputed postwar territorial division, the plight of Arab refugees, and Arab refusal to negotiate with, or recognize, Israel. Resolution of these issues proved to be beyond his control and awaited three more wars and a half century of tortuous diplomacy and progress toward peace in the Middle East.

"Sand in a Rat Hole"

Double Policy in China

President Truman, like most Americans, knew little about China but admired his nation's missionary and educational work there. He deplored Japan's attacks on China in the 1930s, stated in 1944 that the United States should help China throw off foreign imperialism, and said in 1946 that America's future trade lay in the Pacific.[1]

Truman agreed with the State Department's view in April 1945 that the immediate need to defeat Japan and to gain long-term security required promoting representative government in China and reconciling president Jiang Jieshi's (Chiang Kai-shek) Guomindang (Kuomintang, GMD) government and Mao Zedong's (Mao Tse-tung) Chinese Communist Party (CCP). The Americans supported Jiang's regime but alleged to favor no political faction and sought flexibility if the GMD were to disintegrate. They hoped to moderate British and Soviet claims on Hong Kong and Manchuria, respectively, promote a balanced Chinese economy, and create a Chinese military to maintain postwar security, which required that Jiang's regime gain public support and end the threat of civil war.[2]

Truman soon regarded Jiang's regime as the world's "rottenest," comprising "grafters and crooks," and he likened giving aid to China to "pouring sand in a rat hole." He also deplored China's "so-called Commies," or "bandits," implied that they had "helped the Japs" in wartime, and was persistent that Communism was incompatible with Chinese society. He insisted in 1945 that the U.S. had to take a strong stand in China or else Russia would dominate Asia, and he could not perceive China's civil war apart from American-Soviet conflict. His administration's efforts to mediate GMD-CCP conflict were one-sided, but he brushed off critics of this flawed policy as being more loyal to the Soviet government than to their own.[3]

Truman resisted direct military intervention in China. But after the Communists took power in 1949, he refused to open communication with the incipient People's Republic of China (PRC). His administration challenged the PRC's legitimacy to govern, rejected its claim to Taiwan (Formosa), and permitted Jiang's legions to sustain an American-armed rival regime there and wage aerial and naval warfare against China's new government. Thus, one must conclude that despite the president's stoic recognition that he had "bet on a bad horse" and his desire to minimize the "loss" of China—and notwithstanding recent archival revelations that show greater communication and ideological affinity between Mao and Stalin than previously known—the Truman administration bears responsibility for creating a framework for long-term counter-revolutionary policy toward the PRC well before Sino-American hostilities in Korea precipitated a generation of bitter conflict.[4]

I

The Truman administration inherited a long-standing China problem. Following the revolution of 1911 that ousted the Manchu dynasty, Sun Yat Sen (Sun Zhongshan), spokesman for social democracy in China, was unable to secure control over the new Republic of China. A series of Western-recognized governments continued to rule from Beijing (Peking), while in 1917 Sun established his GMD regime in Guangzhou (Canton). Then in 1924, despite his dislike for Communism and belief that it was inapplicable to China, Sun turned to Moscow and its Comintern agents to restructure his GMD along CCP lines and organize his armies to permit him to gain equality with the central government. Sun died in early 1925, however, and was succeeded by Jiang, whose Northern Expedition finally occupied Beijing in 1928, although his Nationalist Government remained in the more politically hospitable Nanjing (Nanking). Meanwhile, in 1927 Jiang initiated a decade-long military campaign against his current CCP allies, who ultimately took refuge in the northwest province of Yan'an (Yenan) after a devastating six-thousand-mile Long March during 1934–1935.[5]

Unfortunately, not long after gaining power, the GMD became increasingly tied to its military and wealthy business and landowning constituents and failed to develop governmental administration capable of implementing its programs. Tax and land reform laws went unenforced, and the government came to depend on the army to sustain it in power. At the same time, provincial governors, or "warlords," and local elites ruled most of China and forced the vast peasant population to bear the brunt of onerous taxes and conscription, which further eroded the peasantry's support for the GMD.[6]

By the early 1930s U.S. officials in China, such as military attaché Colonel Joseph "Vinegar Joe" Stilwell, reported that Jiang was a dictator whose government neither ruled effectively nor resisted aggression—Japan had attacked Manchuria in 1931 and annexed it the next year—and deployed its best troops to contain the CCP in Yan'an. Finally in 1936 Jiang was forced to form a National Unity government, but Japan's undeclared war that began the following July quickly overran China's major cities and drove the GMD into fortress-like retreat in Chongqing (Chunking) in southwestern China, where it remained until autumn 1945.[7]

President Roosevelt saw China as the victim of "money changers," but he thought it would take years and "several revolutions" to solve its problems. His vague proposal to quarantine the Japanese aggressor in 1937 gained little support, and the relative few supplies his administration provided the GMD were used to protect itself against insurrection.[8]

Japan's attack on Pearl Harbor in December 1941 turned Jiang and his government into symbols of resistance to aggression. Money and supplies flowed freely, and in 1942 Roosevelt sent Stilwell, now a general, back to Chongqing to command the China-Burma-India theater and to serve as Jiang's chief of staff. FDR soon touted China as one of the Four Policemen of the postwar world and said it would line up "on our side" against any adversary in Asia. At Cairo in November 1943 he, Churchill, and Jiang declared that China would regain Manchuria, Taiwan, and the Pescadores from Japan. Then at Teheran FDR got Stalin to endorse the Cairo Declaration, approve China's senior status in a postwar United Nations organization, and confirm Soviet entry into the Pacific war in return for territorial concessions in Manchuria.[9]

Meantime, Jiang largely resisted Stilwell's entreaties to fight aggressively against the Japanese, while U.S. diplomats in the field reported to Washington about the CCP's efficient administration of its area and successful military tactics. This moved FDR to send Vice President Wallace to China in June 1944 to urge Jiang to seek political accord with the CCP. Shortly, Roosevelt also sent the first official U.S. observers, or "Dixie Mission," to Yan'an, from where diplomat John Stewart Service initially reported in July that "we have come into a different country and are meeting a different people." Mao and the Communists stressed three points: (1) their independence from Moscow; (2) their need and desire to collaborate with the U.S. against Japan and in the postwar era ("[W]e cannot risk crossing you—cannot risk conflict with you," Mao said); and (3) their requirement that Jiang broaden his government to include all important parties.[10]

To what extent did Mao speak sincerely in 1944? This is an important determination, especially because he expressed similar views to U.S. officials in later years. Two decades ago historian Michael Schaller judged that whereas

Mao may have deliberately exaggerated the long-term compatibility of Communist and American goals, there is little reason to doubt he meant what he said in 1944. The CCP was in the midst of a struggle for survival against both the Japanese and the GMD, and the U.S. had by far more political, financial, and military support to offer than any other nation, as well as the ability to influence Jiang's behavior, if anyone could do so. Further, the CCP, whose foreign policy was still in the formative stage, had little reason to want to depend solely on the Soviets, who could offer little material support and had a long history of imperial ambition and conflict with China from Central Asia to Manchuria.[11]

Recent writings and newly available Russian and Chinese archival materials sustain this judgment. Mao—who was present at the formation of the CCP in 1921, and by 1944 had become the predominant party leader and policy maker—was a devout Communist and adherent of Marxist-Leninist principles. But he was driven equally if not more so by powerful anti-imperial and nationalist convictions, was highly flexible or pragmatic in thought and action, and was given—he said—to "seeking the truth from the facts." As historian Michael Hunt has stated, Mao was a Chinese populist and patriot who was determined to throw off foreign domination and imperial control in China and to restore the Middle Kingdom to its rightful status in Asia—and in the world. From the 1920s to 1940s he would pursue pragmatic domestic and foreign alliances to achieve his goals, and he remained open to American—or other—assistance consistent with his principles.[12]

During 1919–1921 Mao organized workers and peasants in his native province of Hunan and espoused the anti-imperial sentiments of China's May 4 Movement. He looked to post-1917 Russia as a model and source of support for China as part of the community of oppressed nations. During the mid-1920s, an era marked by intense antiforeign sentiment in China, he cooperated fully with the GMD during its period of unity with the CCP. After Jiang's assault on the CCP in 1927, Mao regarded the GMD as national betrayers and running dogs of the capitalists. From then on he tended to focus on need to organize China's peasantry (contra the Marxist emphasis on industrial working class) and to build powerful base areas that would provide security for the CCP and its People's Liberation Army (PLA) and allow expanding outreach to the population. Mao joined the Long March to Yan'an in 1934 and throughout the decade condemned both Japan for its aggression and the imperial powers for failing to provide China with meaningful support. He backed the Soviet Union's Popular Front concept and in 1937 came around to the National Unity program with Jiang's Nationalist government, although he insisted on retention of the base areas to protect the CCP from "extermination" by the GMD.[13]

Mao justified the Nazi-Soviet Pact of 1939 and Soviet neutrality treaty with

Japan in April 1941 as a consequence of Western appeasement. But while he accepted the very limited financial and economic support that Moscow could offer, he deflected requests from Stalin—who feared an assault from Japan despite the neutrality pact—to undertake major military engagements against Japanese forces. Mao marked the dissolution of the Comintern in 1943 as the end of an era. He and the CCP had to focus on their nation and their revolution, not on developments in the Soviet Union or bordering states.[14]

In this context, the CCP's Central Committee instruction to its comrades in the wake of the Dixie Mission visit in August 1944 is revealing as the CCP's— or Mao's—first comprehensive statement both on foreign policy and on relations with the U.S. In sum, Mao said that the Dixie Mission reflected Allied interest in the new China and in the success of the international united front that had provided for the CCP's development and would allow for "the final victory of the Chinese revolution." Hence, while the GMD remained China's official government, and the CCP could pursue only a semi-independent foreign policy, it was necessary to shed China's traditional xenophobia, cooperate militarily with U.S. officials in hopes of gaining later political and economic cooperation, and try to influence American progressive and middle-of-the-road forces—and even anticommunist diehards. CCP officials should respond to, and make requests for, assistance in a forthright manner, remain "very flexible," and keep their options open. Evidently Mao was forthright with the Dixie Mission in 1944 when he proposed wartime and postwar collaboration with the U.S. and insisted that the GMD had to broaden its government. His outlook also reflected CCP confidence about the future. The misjudgment that occurred at the time was Mao's overestimation of Roosevelt's willingness to deal with the CCP independently or in a contest for power with the GMD.[15]

Nonetheless, Jiang's refusal to respond to a Japanese offensive in southeastern China and to make Stilwell commander of the GMD armies led FDR to send a personal envoy, Major General Patrick Hurley, to Chongqing in September 1944. Formerly secretary of war under President Herbert Hoover, Hurley was vain and arrogant and knew nothing about China except that he wished to be ambassador there. Upon arrival, he denounced British imperialism and Soviet Communism and then connived with Jiang against Stilwell. Early the next month Jiang finally refused Stilwell's appointment and demanded his recall, and Roosevelt deferred to the GMD leader as a head of state. FDR then named as Stilwell's successor General Albert C. Wedemeyer, a firm anticommunist who would defer to Jiang, and appointed Hurley as ambassador to succeed the retiring Clarence Gauss.[16]

At the same time, FDR also wrote off prospects for landing U.S. troops in China to combat the Japanese during the final stages of the war. This would have to be left to the Soviets, he told Stimson, who was of the view that "if we can't get rid of Chiang Kai-shek, we can't get in touch with the only live body of military men there is in China at present, namely the Communists." Still, FDR naively clung to Hurley's view that exclusive aid to Jiang and the GMD could induce them to political reform and collaboration with the CCP.[17]

Thus, Hurley went to Yan'an in early November to negotiate with Mao a proposal—which Hurley had written—to create a coalition government, single army, bill of rights, and GMD-CCP equal access to U.S. military aid. It is uncertain whether Hurley thought this proposal would ultimately be acceptable to the GMD or was merely a ploy to induce the CCP into negotiations. Regardless, Mao literally signed off on the agreement and sent CCP vice chairman and chief negotiator, Zhou Enlai (Chou En-lai) to Chongqing, where Jiang counterproposed that the CCP have only a nominal governmental role and that it disband its armies. Mao angrily rejected this and hinted at releasing copies of the agreement he and Hurley had signed. Enraged, but trapped by his own maneuver, Hurley now allied more closely with Jiang and began to purge the embassy of officials who criticized the GMD or sought to deal with the CCP. At the year's end, Roosevelt could only concur with a lengthy White House report warning that Jiang had brought China near collapse.[18]

Hurley's betrayal outraged Mao and CCP officials, although they continued to court U.S. mediation. Mao and Zhou told a negotiating aide in Chongqing that "we have no intention of splitting with the United States" and would respect Hurley's wish not to publicize their agreement. The CCP, however, would not accede to token representation in a government and hoped that "our American friends" would not compel a change, although all other issues "are negotiable." In fact, on January 9, 1945, Mao and Zhou gave a message to the Dixie Mission, to be forwarded to Washington, proposing to travel there if Roosevelt would receive them as members of a "primary Chinese party." Unfortunately, Hurley discovered the message, viewed it as a CCP effort to circumvent him, and advised FDR against agreeing to the trip.[19]

The president made no reply to the CCP. Instead he sought to resolve his China problem in early February at Yalta. There he convinced Stalin, already committed at Teheran to entering the war against Japan, to join the battle within ninety days of victory in Europe and to continue to recognize only Jiang's regime, a sharp blow to the CCP. In return, Roosevelt agreed that the status quo in the People's Republic in Outer Mongolia would be preserved; and that Russia would acquire the Kurile Islands, recover southern Sakhalin from Japan, and regain former tsarist-era concessions in Manchuria, i.e., lease of Lushun (Port Arthur) as a naval base, internationalization of the port of Dalian (Dairen) and Sino-Soviet operation of the South Manchurian and Chinese Eastern Railroads. FDR also committed to getting Jiang to concur with a Sino-Soviet treaty that would safeguard Russia's "preeminent interests" in Manchuria but recognize China's sovereignty there. Stalin pledged to sign a Friendship Treaty with China.[20]

Roosevelt negotiated the Yalta accords without Jiang's participation—although the latter knew the outlines in advance—not because FDR held the Chinese in contempt, as historian Warren Cohen has said, but because he knew a weak regime when he saw one. The concessions were small price to pay to gain Soviet military collaboration—which the JCS strongly wanted—to minimize U.S. casualties in subduing Japan, to preserve Soviet-American Far Eastern accord, and to keep Stalin and the CCP at arm's length.[21]

For Stalin, who viewed Mao and the CCP as "margarine" Communists and who was angry at their failure to fight Japan aggressively in the year after the German attack on Russia in 1941, the Yalta agreement also served several purposes. The Soviets regained important imperial concessions in Manchuria and created a buffer zone against a potentially hostile U.S. presence there and in North China. The Soviets also gained a continued supply of U.S. military aid and a victor's role in setting terms for Japan's surrender and occupation—all the while preserving a policy of great-power detente.[22]

Meanwhile, civil war erupted between the U.S. foreign service officers in Chongqing and Hurley. On February 28 the former collectively cabled the State Department that the ambassador's one-sided support of the GMD was discredited in China except among Jiang's clique. The only way to avert civil war, they said, was to show willingness to cooperate with the CCP to defeat Japan and force Jiang to share power. Otherwise the CCP would have to look to Moscow. Shortly thereafter, Hurley, having returned to Washington and been apprised of the cable, widely denigrated the CCP and assailed the foreign service officers (soon transferred) as disloyal to him and to the U.S. Then on April 2 he declared that U.S. policy supported only the GMD, implying CCP bad faith in rejecting Jiang's coalition terms. Meanwhile on March 10, Roosevelt belatedly and obliquely replied to Mao's January proposal to visit the U.S with an expression of hope for GMD-CCP accord. FDR said nothing about Hurley's comments and policy nor about Yalta's secret Far East accords. When Roosevelt died on April 12, these problems were bequeathed to President Truman.[23]

II

In spring 1945 the prospect of Russian entry into the Pacific war heightened U.S. concern about Moscow's ambitions in China. Hurley, however, returning to Chongqing via Moscow, reported that Stalin regarded Mao and the CCP as reformers rather than as Communists, supported the U.S. goal of a united, democratic government in China, and was chiefly concerned with having the U.S. hold to the concessions granted to Russia at Yalta. Hurley gave his pledge on this and continued to berate foreign service officers in China who were critical of the GMD.[24]

Nonetheless, Kennan, who was then the chargé in the embassy in Moscow, warned that Stalin intended to restore every tsarist concession in China and dominate every bordering province. Ambassador Harriman said that Stalin sought puppet governments in Manchuria and North China and told Navy Secretary Forrestal, who agreed, that U.S. aid to the CCP meant that ultimately several hundred million people would "march when the Kremlin ordered."[25]

Truman initially inclined to follow Roosevelt's China policy. In May he reassured Foreign Minister Song Ziwen (T. V. Soong) of support for the Cairo Declaration and continued aid but dismissed a proposed Pacific security pact as "power politics." Similarly, Stimson said that concern about Russian entry into the war underscored need for GMD-CCP accord to preclude Soviet machinations and that no action short of war could deny Russia its Yalta concessions.[26]

Truman was delighted at Harry Hopkins' report from Moscow in late May that Stalin accepted the GMD as China's government and as sovereign in Manchuria and sought only to negotiate GMD acceptance of his Yalta concessions before the Soviets entered the war. The president soon apprised Jiang of Yalta's terms, reiterated Soviet-American commitment to GMD rule, and rebuffed GMD efforts to reinterpret Yalta or to have the U.S. become party to a Sino-Soviet treaty.[27]

Sino-Soviet negotiations in June increased American worry about Russian economic control in Manchuria and intent to extend its military zone from Lushun to Dalian. For the first time Secretary of State Byrnes asserted the claim of the U.S., as party to Yalta, to be consulted about a Sino-Soviet treaty. Still, at the Potsdam Conference on July 17 Stalin complained to Truman that the Chinese sought to negate Russia's preeminent interests in Manchuria by refusing to have a Russian director of railroads and Russian majority on the governing board. But after Stalin added that his proposal would not prejudice U.S. interests and that Dalian would remain a free port, Truman claimed to have "clinched the Open Door" in Manchuria. Further, the nearly complete Sino-Soviet treaty was in "better form" than expected, he wrote, thus assuring Soviet entry into the war and saving of many American lives.[28]

The successful atomic tests in New Mexico, however, led Byrnes to believe that he could "out maneuver" Stalin in China by having the GMD stand firm in negotiations so that American use of the atomic bomb would cause Japan to surrender before the Russians entered the war—or Manchuria. "And this will save China" from Stalin, Byrnes said.[29]

Truman, too, thought that use of the atomic bomb would cause Japan to "fold up" before Russia entered the war. But after Chief of Staff General Marshall told him on July 23 that even if the U.S. dictated surrender terms to Japan, nothing could prevent the Soviets from plundering Manchuria, the president advised the Chinese to "carry out" the Yalta concessions but to give no more. He then rushed the Potsdam Declaration to Jiang (but not to Stalin) for his signature, and on August 5 he instructed Harriman to tell Stalin that China had fulfilled Yalta, that Dalian could not be in the Soviet's military zone, and that he wanted a signed protocol reaffirming the Open Door in Manchuria. Truman also acceded to Jiang's request not to assign military commanders to China who were hostile to the GMD or to whom Jiang objected.[30]

The Hiroshima bombing spurred Soviet entry into the war on August 8, one week earlier than Stalin had promised at Potsdam and without the requisite Sino-Soviet treaty. The Soviet leader assured Harriman that he would give Truman his Open Door pledge but insisted that Chinese incompetence required Soviet military control of Dalian. At the same time, Harriman's warning that Stalin's interest in Japanese "war trophies" augured industrial domination of Manchuria provided more incentive to Truman and his advisers to modify unconditional surrender to induce Japan's quick submission—on August 14—in order to contain Russia's advance into Manchuria and claim to an occupation zone in Japan.[31]

Truman's General Order #1 in mid-August directed the Japanese to surrender to the Soviet commander in Manchuria but to Jiang throughout the rest of China, including on Taiwan and in northern Indo-China. Still, General Chu Teh, the CCP military commander, proclaimed his troops' right to occupy the areas that they had liberated. Meanwhile, Stalin hastily concluded negotiations with China. He abandoned military control of Dalian and agreed to have a Chinese chairman of the railway board, to remove his forces from Manchuria within three months, and to support Jiang's government only. Stalin also signed a Treaty of Friendship and Alliance with China on August 14 but said that Truman would have to take his word—no written protocol—on the Open Door in Manchuria.[32]

The Truman administration sought to bolster Jiang's administration, which had made no constructive use of its time in Chongqing to reform itself or plan for the future. It emerged from the war weaker than ever. Its continued corruption and oppressive system of taxation and conscription further alienated the peasant population, while government officials assigned to take control of Japanese administrative and political units and properties in the big cities readily worked with wartime collaborators, enriched themselves, and treated with disdain the population that had stayed put rather than retreat inland during the war.[33]

Meanwhile, the GMD army was in an advanced state of disintegration. It lacked the political-military leadership to take control of the weapons and positions of the two million Japanese forces and one million puppet troops in China, while the CCP army, far smaller than that of the GMD and heavily outgunned, was entrenched in northern and central China. In early August General Wedemeyer, Stilwell's successor, got War Department approval to transport GMD forces to key cities and ports in northern China and Manchuria despite— or perhaps because of—strong CCP presence there. The JCS approved this expanded role on August 10 but cautioned Wedemeyer that the U.S. did not intend to involve its ground forces in a campaign anywhere in China or support the GMD in a "fratricidal war." Wedemeyer promptly ordered his forces to withdraw from any GMD-CCP clashes but cautioned his superiors about the contradictory nature of the U.S. role in China. Literal adherence to averting involvement in a "fratricidal war" would mean withdrawing Jiang's support, he warned, and would jeopardize U.S. political and economic objectives in China. But to assure that the Japanese surrendered only to the GMD might require direct assistance in subduing Communist armed forces.[34]

Truman approved Wedemeyer's operations, which in five months led to transport of 500,000 GMD troops northward and use of nearly 60,000 U.S. Marines to occupy the Beijing-Tianjin (Peking-Tienstin) area. Further, Jiang asked Truman to fulfill FDR's vague, wartime promise at Cairo to equip one hundred Chinese divisions, which Hopkins confirmed were intended "to fight the Japs" and to preserve Jiang's regime. Truman agreed to finish equipping thirty-nine divisions but insisted that they be used only for internal security. Nearly $1 billion in military aid flowed rapidly to the GMD under guise of support for reoccupying Japanese-held territory or by sale of underpriced military surplus.[35]

Still, the specter of civil war loomed. Edwin Locke, the president's representative for wartime production in China and shortly named GMD economic adviser, wrote Truman in August that civil war would be an economic calamity, cause Stalin to rethink his pledge to deal only with the GMD, and severely damage American-Soviet Far Eastern accord. Further, the CCP would win the war because it had great popular support and a superb fighting record, whereas the GMD had neither. Locke urged a concerted great-power effort—or a presidential envoy—to forge a GMD-CCP political compromise.[36]

Hurley agreed but also believed that U.S. support for Jiang combined with Stalin's recognition would inspire GMD reform and compel CCP political concessions. In August the ambassador persuaded Jiang to invite Mao to Chong-qing for talks. The GMD leader would have preferred to attack the CCP, but for the time being he sought to use growing U.S.-Soviet rivalry in China as a means to gain U.S. military aid, transport, and assistance to take over in Manchuria and North China, and to leverage the CCP—unable to count on Soviet aid—into submission through negotiations.[37]

Mao realized this, and initially balked at the talks. Unquestionably the CCP had become increasingly disillusioned with U.S. policy since Hurley's repudi-ation of the Five Point Agreement in 1944. A month before FDR's death the CCP Central Committee concluded that U.S. support for Jiang prolonged his regime and dictatorship and was a bar to successful negotiations. Then in June 1945 the same body concluded that Jiang was preparing for civil war but could not act until Japan was defeated, while the U.S. policy "is to support Jiang, re-sist Japan, and oppose the Communists." The unexpected sudden end of the war against Japan eliminated any U.S. need for CCP forces to contest the Jap-anese. But the Sino-Soviet Pact of August 14—the same day of Jiang's call for talks—was a "dual disaster" for the CCP, as historian Odd Arne Westad has written, because it brought word from Moscow that the Soviets would not support civil war and by terms of their treaty with the GMD they would turn over to them the areas of North China and Manchuria then under Red Army control. Stalin's accord with the GMD showed that he cared far more about So-viet concessions in Manchuria than about revolution in China or its "margar-ine" Communists.[38]

Thus in late August Mao reluctantly decided to go to Chongqing, stating upon arrival that "I have come . . . on the suggestion of the Soviet Union." At the same time, he told his CCP colleagues that he would not accept Jiang's terms "under duress" and that he remained confident that CCP steadfastness, GMD incapacity, and great-power desire for peace could lead to successful ne-gotiations. In short, as Zhou now said, the CCP needed to gain popular support and compel Jiang to compromise, and this required "one part talking and one part fighting."[39]

In Chongqing Mao and Zhou reached loose accord with the GMD to reor-ganize the PLA and to create a representative Political Consultative Conference (PCC) to consider a new constitution and postwar reconstruction. But as Mao departed for Yan'an on October 10, the basic question of political control in the northern provinces that the PLA had liberated was unresolved. Meantime, U.S. Marines moved GMD troops into North China and occupied Beijing and Tian-jin, and there were numerous incidents with the PLA, which harassed transport of GMD troops. The CCP also moved 130,000 forces into Manchuria, while the Soviets refused U.S.-GMD landings in Dalian, an area of Russian special interest—and the CCP blocked landings in Shandong (Shantung) province, which they regarded as a vital link to Northeast China. In November both the GMD and the CCP asked the Soviets to delay their withdrawal from Manchuria. The GMD feared that the CCP would occupy the Soviet-vacated areas, while the CCP now sought Soviet help in occupying key ports in the northeast, building a clandestine munitions complex, and recruiting troops.[40]

U.S. military officials thought that the strength of the PLA was overrated and that Jiang's forces were improving, although the long-term political outlook was uncertain. Nonetheless, in mid-October Wedemeyer, who had returned to Washington for a short stay, told JCS planners that Jiang had sufficient power to cope with the CCP and that there was no need to fear them unless the Russians stepped up their aid, which amounted to very little.[41]

Truman knew that U.S. action was one-sided, but he now told Wedemeyer and Hurley that "my policy is to support Chiang K.C." This led the general to write Admiral Leahy that the president had informed him that U.S. policy would continue to include "full support" for Jiang and the GMD and that "a stiffening policy with regard to the Russians will be undertaken in the Far East." Indeed, the president now began to draft a public statement, relying on War Department information, in which he would state that the GMD had fought "side by side" with the U.S. in the war but that the "so-called Commies not only did not help us but on occasion helped the Japs." He would also doggedly insist that "we are not mixing in China's internal affairs." Disagreement among White House aides, however, about Truman's facts—especially regarding the CCP—caused him to drop the statement.[42]

Still, the president delighted to have Byrnes recall Stalin's terming the CCP "fascists," and did not reply when the secretary proposed mutual Soviet-American troop withdrawal to avert a clash. Moreover, when in mid-November a congressman questioned U.S. action in China, Truman denied American involvement in the civil war but said that the U.S. could not "walk out" of China and leave behind a million armed Japanese. Then he agreed to train 2,300 GMD Air Force pilots in the U.S.[43]

By early November Jiang was pressing Wedemeyer to provide additional air and naval transport to move GMD troops into Manchuria. The general informed Washington that his mission to redeploy GMD troops to disarm and repatriate the Japanese was completed and that he had no authority to transport these forces, which would undoubtedly be used to fight the PLA. Further, the GMD was completely unprepared to occupy Manchuria against CCP opposition, and inept and corrupt GMD administration in North China was turning the populace toward Communists, whom the Soviets were helping to control key areas there and in Manchuria.[44]

Byrnes inclined toward Wedemeyer's view not to provide Jiang with more aid. But War Department officials disagreed, despite their "grave doubts" about Jiang's ability to administer Manchuria, especially if the Soviets aided the CCP. Then we are "in a real mess," Assistant Secretary John J. McCloy said. Thus, the JCS delayed a decision.[45]

One week later on November 14, the GMD attack on the CCP in Shanhai-kuan near the Manchurian border began the battle for that crucial province and gave new urgency to the prospect of GMD-CCP civil war. At the same time, the Soviet officials ordered the PLA to evacuate large cities in North China and purged Communists from urban leadership positions, while Stalin invited GMD representatives to Moscow for economic talks. In sum, Stalin sought to appease Jiang and sustain Yalta-style detente to secure Soviet interests in Manchuria and avert conflict with the U.S. But this also highlighted the contradictory U.S. policy of claiming not to intervene in China's affairs while abetting the GMD assault on the CCP. Thus on November 20, Byrnes questioned the continued presence and purpose of U.S. Marines in China. But Forrestal held that the U.S. was on safe ground so long as it continued to say it was only helping to complete Japan's defeat. Patterson saw "no peril" in increasing aid to Jiang; the 60,000 U.S. Marines, he said, "could walk from one end of China to the other without serious hindrance."[46]

Once again, however, Wedemeyer cabled his deep concerns. Jiang could not unify and democratize all of China, he said, because of lack of organization and inept and corrupt officials. Better he should seek to stabilize South China and, over time, North China, while putting off efforts to regain Manchuria, which could not be done without Soviet and CCP accord. The general also proposed to be relieved as chief of staff to Jiang and to have all U.S. forces in China withdrawn. Shortly he reiterated to Chief of Staff General Eisenhower that the U.S. had to decide whether it was going to follow its stated policy of avoiding involvement in China's "fratricidal warfare," or reverse course and ignore public opinion and the principle of self-determination by providing sufficient air, naval, and ground forces to unify China and Manchuria under Jiang. Or perhaps the U.S. would seek a UN trusteeship over Manchuria to repatriate the Japanese and then withdraw all UN forces and let the Chinese have it out over who governs Manchuria.[47]

Despite the warnings, on November 26 Forrestal and Patterson concluded that from a military viewpoint, GMD control of a unified China best served U.S. interests. They proposed continuing aid and giving more "realistic" directives to military commanders. They claimed to shy from a political view but cautioned that to discontinue GMD aid might appear to be deserting an ally, diminish China's stature, and cause it to break apart. Worse, this would allow

Russia to dominate Manchuria and perhaps North China and thereby achieve Japan's former goals.[48]

Truman felt caught in the middle but unable to "pull out" of China because the GMD would collapse. So too did Forrestal insist on November 27 that the U.S. could not "yank the Marines out of Northern China now," while Patterson questioned Wedemeyer's assessment that the U.S. was involving itself in China's civil war. Byrnes, too, was frustrated, but he told his navy and war counterparts that given the Sino-Soviet treaty and Stalin's pledge to back the GMD, perhaps the U.S. should seek Soviet support to impose a GMD-CCP compromise, telling Jiang to cooperate or lose U.S support. In fact, the State Department was readying such a plan for Hurley, returned to the U.S. again, to take to China, perhaps via Moscow.[49]

That same morning Hurley, who likely feared blame for a failed policy, suddenly resigned, with a demagogic blast that foreign service officers had sided with the CCP and curried favor with British imperialism. "See what a son-of-a-bitch did to me," Truman declared to his Cabinet. He then decried alleged British and Soviet desire to divide China and insisted that unless the U.S. took a strong stand there, the Soviets would replace Japan as the major power in the Far East.[50]

Truman then leapt at a suggestion by Secretary of Agriculture Clinton Anderson to "steal thunder away" from Hurley's resignation by appointing General Marshall, just retired as chief of staff, as the president's special representative to China. Truman so revered Marshall, and was so perplexed about China, that he was prepared to let him write his own directive and vest him with virtual plenary negotiating power. The administration agreed that it was imperative to create a coalition government, ending GMD one-party rule, and a single national army. It was hoped that this would unify China and forestall predicted Soviet advances in Manchuria and North China. Byrnes and the State Department wished to make a truce and an accord on a national political convention preconditions to continue moving Jiang's troops northward; in contrast, Marshall and the War Department wished to give first priority to transporting GMD troops to prevent either the Soviets or CCP from delaying political agreement in order to consolidate their positions in Manchuria.[51]

Byrnes was persistent, however, that the U.S. should withhold transportation and aid from Jiang and deal directly with the CCP over Japanese repatriation if the GMD remained politically intransigent despite CCP compromises. But at a critical meeting on December 11, in which Truman's presence weighed decisively in Marshall's favor, Marshall insisted to Byrnes that a divided China meant Soviet gains in Manchuria and "loss of the major purpose of our war in the Pacific." The general thereby got Byrnes to concede that even if the GMD remained intractable, the U.S. would "swallow its pride and much of its policy" and continue to speed GMD forces northward, although Marshall would keep this intention secret at the outset. On December 14 Truman gave his special envoy a secret, oral agreement, omitted from his China directive, that the U.S. would continue aid to Jiang even if he refused political compromise. Thus, Marshall departed for China with many negotiating carrots, including plans for a military advisory group (MAG) and economic aid to induce Jiang's cooperation. But the envoy brought no comparable diplomatic stick to compel concessions from Jiang, who would exploit this fatal flaw in Marshall's—and Truman's—near impossible mission in China.[52]

III

Truman's declaration on December 15 that China needed to establish a unified government—an oblique admission that the GMD's "one party government" had to end—without foreign intervention was meant to affirm the right of the U.S. to intervene while allaying public concern about doing so. But the presence of U.S. forces in northern China soon drew fire from Stalin and Molotov at the CFM meeting that Byrnes had arranged in Moscow. In response to repeated Soviet inquiries, Byrnes persisted in affirming that U.S. troops in China were there to disarm the Japanese. Stalin said this was also true for his forces in Manchuria, but they did not seem to require so much time to accomplish the task. Molotov pressed more tartly for agreement on mutual troop withdrawal by January 1946, but Byrnes refused to set a deadline. Stalin soon took the edge off both the debate and U.S.-Soviet relations over China by telling the secretary that the Soviets did not object to U.S. troops in China but would merely "like to be told about it." The Soviet leader also acknowledged that Marshall—"one of the few military men who was both a soldier and a statesman"—was the one person who might force a GMD-CCP compromise. Ultimately, on December 28 in their Moscow Conference Communiqué—which would prove helpful to Marshall's early success—the Americans and Russians reaffirmed their commitment to prompt troop removal and a unified but GMD-led Chinese government.[53]

Truman, of course, was displeased with Byrnes' results at the Moscow Conference, and he would confront him about this in early January 1946. Although most of the president's criticisms had to do with Soviet "outrages" in Eastern Europe, Iran, and Turkey, he did say that where once he had wanted the Soviets to intervene in the war against Japan, they "have been a headache to us ever since." He now thought that the U.S. should rehabilitate China under a strong government—presumably without Communists, despite Marshall's avowed purpose—do the same for Korea, and maintain "complete control of Japan and the Pacific."[54]

Marshall, meanwhile, had arrived in China on December 21. Both the GMD and CCP appeared to welcome him. Jiang thought Marshall's appointment meant greater U.S. political and military involvement, especially after learning of JCS plans for a permanent MAG. The GMD's only concern was whether the U.S. would try to halt their attacks on the CCP. Marshall then sought to assuage Jiang by likening Soviet industrial removals from Manchuria to their behavior in Germany, while warning that U.S. aid depended on public perception that both the GMD and CCP sought compromise.[55]

The CCP welcomed the Marshall mission—coming in the wake of the reviled Hurley's resignation—as portending a change in U.S. policy. They took Truman's December 15 statement to mean that U.S. forces would not involve themselves in China's affairs as the British had in Greece, although Mao remained fearful of such intervention until 1950. Meanwhile, the CCP determined to assume a defensive military posture and to take the political initiative for peace by sending Zhou back to Chongqing to negotiate. Marshall also worked to gain CCP confidence, although he insisted that there could not be two separate armies. He refrained from "cracking the whip," he told Truman, but soon got Mao and Zhou to concede continued free movement of GMD troops into northeastern China, which was a great inducement for Jiang to accept a cease-fire on January 10, 1946. Soon after, the PCC that had been established in the fall endorsed a program for constitutional government and social justice. Then on January 31 it resolved to broaden the national government, with GMD membership limited to 50 percent of a national State Council that would convene a newly elected National Assembly in May to draft a constitution.[56]

CCP leaders took this as a "great victory for China's democratic revolution." Their Central Committee promptly informed all regional bureaus on February 1 that the CCP would be joining the government, that there would be a representative congress and responsible cabinet, and civilian control of the military. In turn, the CCP would give up command of the PLA, which would be integrated into a national army. The Communists still feared that Jiang might attack them, and this required "high vigilance." But most important, the Chinese revolution had changed from "military to nonmilitary mass work" and to parliamentary struggle to resolve domestic problems. The CCP was so pleased with the PCC results that they heaped lavish praise on Marshall, the U.S. government, and American-Soviet influence through the Moscow CFM. And once again the CCP hinted at Mao's interest in a trip to the U.S., but Marshall, and Truman, ignored this overture.[57]

In late February Marshall got GMD-CCP agreement to a U.S. plan for demobilization, reorganization, and integration of their armies, with the CCP to evacuate its units from South China and accept a 1 : 5 ratio in a new, nonpolitical national army. Marshall urged Truman to prepare for withdrawal of U.S. forces—despite Russian presence—and then traveled across China. He met with Mao in early March, and the CCP leader pledged to uphold recent agreements despite GMD attacks in Manchuria. Marshall said that CCP special claims in Manchuria had hindered peace talks and that U.S. aid to China—in which the CCP would share—depended on a unified nation. Mao pledged to go anywhere that Jiang proposed for talks, and Marshall told Truman that China was on the brink of unprecedented progress. The president's envoy then departed for Washington in mid-March for six weeks to seek government aid for China. An ebullient Truman said that with more Marshalls, the U.S. could overcome world crises "every hour on the hour." [58]

Marshall's finest hour had passed. The CCP, in reliance on great-power influence and Marshall's mediation, had conceded "first place" to the GMD in a political coalition and shifted the struggle from military to parliamentary means. Marshall banked on GMD reform, and third forces, such as the small, middle-class Democratic League, to hold the balance between the GMD and CCP. But Jiang opposed the PCC accords, especially prospect of a National Assembly with broad powers, and he thought Marshall's pressure for a comprehensive agreement meant that he did not understand China or was influenced by foreign service officers who did not like the GMD. Thus, Jiang seized on the growing U.S.-Soviet Cold War—from conflict over Iran to Churchill's March 5 "iron curtain" speech—and Marshall's long absence from China to vitiate recent accords. Jiang pressed Soviet withdrawal from Manchuria, while his troops attacked PLA positions there and denied access to U.S.-led truce inspection teams. The GMD also negated accord on the PCC resolutions by insisting that its own Central Executive Committee had to approve all National Assembly members. This led to GMD-CCP impasse and delayed that body's meeting. [59]

Jiang disdained negotiating with the CCP even after the Soviets announced in late March withdrawal of their troops from Manchuria within a month. The Americans permitted two extra GMD divisions into the province, and the GMD launched its first major offensive, to forestall PLA occupation of Changchun, a key railway city, and Harbin. By the time Marshall returned to China on April 22, civil war was under way. The Red Army remained aloof and permitted GMD forces to occupy the areas it vacated. Marshall sought a cease-fire but soon told Truman that he blamed GMD stupidity, or Jiang, for failure to achieve one. The general saw no option but to continue supplying them. [60]

As GMD troops moved on Changchun—despite Marshall's effort to neutralize the city—and north toward Harbin in late May, Marshall offered his own plane to Jiang so he could fly to Manchuria to bring his generals under control. But Jiang landed in Shenyang (Mukden) just as GMD troops took Changchun, making the U.S. appear party to the GMD coup. Jiang demanded that the CCP cede Manchuria and that the Americans take final responsibility for ceasefire decisions. Marshall radioed that this virtually destroyed his ability to mediate and—getting no reply—compromised his integrity. Still, Jiang did not return to Nanjing (now the GMD capital) until June 3, when Zhou bitterly charged to Marshall that GMD generals "had the bit in their teeth and the United States was following a double policy."[61]

U.S. failure to restrain Jiang proved costly. At first the CCP viewed his attacks as tactics to gain negotiating leverage, but they soon realized he was bent on civil war. The PLA struck back, retaking Changchun on April 18 (the GMD regained it in mid-May), and Harbin on April 28. Politically the CCP still wished to avoid "deadlock" with the U.S. and to retain "friendly" relations with Marshall, but they believed that direct U.S. aid to the GMD transformed Marshall's mediation into "resultless lip service." Thus the Central Committee concluded in June that presently there was "no hope for peace" and little to do but maintain proper relations with the U.S. while preparing for the inevitable GMD attack.[62]

Marshall knew that Zhou and his colleagues were right. Even the British now said that it was unrealistic to try to mediate with and give aid to the GMD at the same time. Still, Marshall clutched at straws. He got a brief cease-fire in June but admitted to Truman that negotiations were at an impasse and that GMD leaders talked openly of crushing the CCP, auguring protracted conflict and Soviet intervention. Marshall warned Jiang's chief military representative that the U.S. would withdraw its marines, Seventh Fleet, and military aid, and told Jiang that he was pursuing a dictatorial, military policy comparable to that which had led to Japan's destruction. The GMD was unmoved.[63]

In early July Marshall weighed U.S. withdrawal, or serious policy reevaluation, if civil war intensified. But the State Department and military officials, including General MacArthur in Japan, worried about Soviet advances and were persistent that bad as Jiang and his legions were, they were "on our side." Still, Marshall, who had just agreed to succeed Byrnes as secretary of state, might have used his great influence with Truman, who viewed the China scene as "very, very bad," to promote withdrawal or aid cutoff at this critical juncture. Instead, he sought an ambassador to China to help mediate. He inclined to General Wedemeyer but concluded that he was too closely identified with the GMD. Hence, Marshall chose Dr. John Leighton Stuart, a seventy-year-old

China-born missionary and longtime president of Yenching University. Stuart deplored GMD repression but respected Jiang and thought he was the best hope to save China from Communism and Soviet influence.[64]

While Stuart sought to reorganize the GMD regime, Truman warned Jiang on August 10, in the wake of assassination of Democratic League officials and GMD bombing of Yan'an, that allowing "militarists" and "reactionaries" to use force to solve social problems would cause him to "redefine" policy for a U.S. public increasingly reluctant to aid China. Jiang in turn blamed China's problems on the Communists who, he said, sought to impose totalitarianism just as they did in Eastern Europe. The Truman administration backed off. It embargoed sale of small arms to the GMD in August, but then sold it $900 million in military surplus for $175 million.[65]

Marshall soon told Truman that Jiang was "more implacable" than ever and insisted that the CCP rapidly evacuate areas in their control and name in advance their delegates to a National Assembly that the GMD had called—and would control—for November. Meanwhile, in talks with Marshall and Stuart from August to October, the CCP was persistent that the U.S. could not both mediate and aid the GMD, and contended that a cease-fire had to precede negotiations. Marshall and Stuart were "stymied," yet believed that they might "pull the chestnuts out of the crossfire." Truman echoed this vain belief but did nothing to implement it.[66]

Once again Marshall threatened to request his recall if the GMD did not halt their drive on Kalgan, a CCP stronghold and key railway city in North China that Jiang had pledged not to attack. The GMD leader was unmoved. He granted a brief cease-fire, but his forces took Kalgan on October 10. The GMD also called for the National Assembly to convene on November 15, despite a boycott by all other political parties. Meanwhile, Marshall arranged a surprise meeting with Zhou in Shanghai, but the CCP negotiator said that without a return to the conditions of January 1946 in China proper, and June 1946 in Manchuria, negotiations were over.[67]

Marshall told Truman on November 16 that his mission was effectively ended. The president merely reassured that "the Chinese" were to blame for rejecting his wise counsel. Marshall knew that the GMD military, which consumed 80–90 percent of the budget, had blown up negotiations. He warned Jiang that the CCP was too large politically and militarily not to be included in the government, but the GMD leader was more determined than ever to "destroy" the CCP forces. Marshall said this course would bring economic collapse. But he said nothing of the most pressing issue: growing public disapproval of GMD misrule.[68]

Truman allowed Marshall to choose his departure date. The president issued a vacuous China policy statement on December 18 that reiterated the U.S. effort to help China unify itself and gratuitously blamed the CCP for ending negotiations. This drew only bitter CCP riposte for U.S. military support of the GMD. Marshall told Jiang on January 6, 1947, that he was departing for consultations. Jiang warned that although he had accepted Yalta, the Chinese people did not, and that he would never agree to great-power intervention, or trusteeship, in China.[69]

Marshall said little, but his statement upon departing China the next day blamed chiefly GMD "reactionaries" for pursuing a policy of force that destroyed negotiations. He assailed the CCP for "vicious" propaganda and military attacks on Americans and for—technically—ending talks by calling for a return to January 1946 conditions. But he was politically correct to state that the CCP had not appeared irreconcilable in February 1946; nor had it, in fact, in the spring and early summer. Mao had accepted political-military compromise and was ready to seek ultimate victory through parliamentary struggle. But the GMD had opted for military conquest. Still, Marshall, like Truman, naively thought that his "frank statement" would destroy the power of GMD "reactionaries" and give liberals control of the party, weaken the CCP, and cause Americans who doubted Truman's policy to understand that it was not prolonging China's civil war. Meanwhile, CCP officials were deeply embittered by Marshall's failed mediation mission. By January 1947 they looked on any U.S. effort to restart negotiations as a "plot" to strengthen Jiang's military position and to "cheat the people."[70]

IV

Truman was uncertain as ever about policy as U.S. Marines began to withdraw from northern China in early 1947. He told one friend that nothing could be done to prevent Russian domination of Manchuria, then told a proponent of complete disengagement that the U.S. could not go off "half cocked." He then asked Secretary Marshall if it was time to supply ammunition to the GMD. But on March 7, amid Cabinet discussion of aid to Greece and Turkey, he rejected aid to China: "Chiang Kai-shek will not fight it out. Communists will fight it out—they are fanatical. It would be pouring sand in a rat hole. . . ."[71]

Marshall was equally conflicted. His State Department advisers opposed military aid to the GMD and said that economic aid had to await political reform. They proposed only to maintain the modest MAG and transfer some merchant ships. But Patterson and Forrestal raised the specter of Soviet expansion, opposed dealing with the CCP, and pushed for unconditional economic aid and weighing of large-scale military aid.[72]

Marshall still held that the only solution was to "oust the reactionary clique" in the government and install "liberals" from both the GMD and CCP. Ambassador Stuart reinforced this view with reports in spring 1947 of ceaseless GMD political misrule, including on Taiwan. Only "bayonets" sustained the government, whose forces were overextended across North China and Manchuria. But in May Marshall backed off, lifting the 1946 arms embargo. He also agreed to the complete equipping of eight and one-third Air Groups, transfer of naval ships, and "abandonment" of departing marines' arms and ammunition to GMD troops.[73]

The JCS weighed in on June 9 with their long-range study, insisting that to withdraw from China meant Soviet domination there and their ultimate hegemony over Asia. They proposed to offset this with carefully planned, well-supervised military aid for the GMD. But the State Department said that this would mean direct U.S. intervention in China's civil war and Soviet intervention in behalf of the CCP.[74]

Marshall told Truman that the JCS program was "unrealistic." The secretary got his approval instead to send General Wedemeyer on a "fact finding" mission to China during July 22–August 24, with the GMD to be told that economic aid hinged on its reform and U.S. supervision. But when a member of Wedemeyer's mission asked at a predeparture briefing whether GMD's need to broaden its government meant including the CCP, he was told "categorically that Communists would not be included." This marked a major, if unnoted, change in U.S. policy, which had begun with the efforts of FDR and Hurley in late 1944 to seek a coalition government and continued through the Marshall mission in 1946.[75]

The GMD saw Wedemeyer's mission as a "panacea," but his reports catalogued their corruption and ineptitude, including on Taiwan. He candidly told Jiang and his senior government officials that there was need for drastic reforms and that military force alone could not defeat the CCP. Jiang's regime's only reaction was to take offense. Meanwhile, Marshall forwarded Wedemeyer's "clear picture" of matters to Truman and key officials. Wedemeyer's "Report to President Truman" of September 19 critiqued Jiang's administration but insisted that a Communist China, tied to the Soviets, threatened America's freedom and strategic interests. He recommended extensive economic-military aid and advisers and suggested that China invite a UN trusteeship for Manchuria.[76]

Truman responded favorably, but without commitment. Marshall drew back. He wanted Wedemeyer to omit the trusteeship proposal pending study, but the general refused unless the secretary stipulated that Wedemeyer had requested this. Consequently, the Truman administration suppressed the Wedemeyer Report. Why it did so remains a puzzle. Truman later told his counsel,

Clifford, that to have published reports on the GMD "would have pulled the rug out from under them" (Clifford replied that the GMD had "pulled it out from under themselves"). Marshall and the State Department apparently worried that the trusteeship proposal might have required Soviet participation or inspired the Communists in Greece—where the U.S. had intervened unilaterally—to call for UN intercession. But trusteeship was a dead letter. Wedemeyer admitted that he had not discussed it with Jiang, who ignored his hints and had already told Marshall that he would never agree to it. Nor would the CCP, whose recent Sixth Offensive in North China and Manchuria had GMD forces bewildered.[77]

Most likely, Truman and Marshall feared that Wedemeyer's call for extensive aid would have roused a powerful chorus from a growing China bloc that now included House members Walter Judd (MN), Charles Halleck (IN), and Joseph Martin (MA) and Senators Robert Taft (OH), Owen Brewster (ME), Styles Bridges (NH), William Jenner (IN), and Kenneth Wherry (NE). The Truman administration, convinced that it had to act, but determined not to be overwhelmed, thus decided to seek $570 million in economic aid as part of its omnibus foreign aid program to be administered by the ECA. Truman sent a special message on aid to China to Congress on February 16, 1948, while Marshall bluntly told congressional committees about GMD "corruption, inefficiency, and impotence" and said that even a complete takeover of China's government and open-ended commitments of people and resources—all at the expense of America's first priority, Europe—had little chance of success.[78]

Marshall forbade General David Barr, head of the MAG, from assuming strategic or operations responsibility for GMD forces. The secretary also publicly denied that "broadening" the government had meant taking in the CCP. The next day, March 11, Truman said that it had never been the policy of the U.S. government or the Marshall mission to propose taking Communists into the government, a clear denial of past policy. On April 2 Congress voted the China Aid Act, $338 million in economic aid, plus $125 million in military aid to be given at the president's discretion without U.S. supervision—in marked contrast to strict-control policy in Greece. Marshall told Truman that this was "the best plan" to extend aid without further U.S. commitment. The secretary said that he was determined to resist "getting sucked in" and was convinced that the GMD sought an American-Soviet war to drag them out of their difficulties. Meanwhile, the GMD-dominated National Assembly named Jiang as president, with dictatorial power to suppress rebellion.[79]

Nonetheless, by August the CCP neared victory in Manchuria and North China. Stuart now wondered whether the U.S. should abandon the GMD for regional governments or provide military aid to "crush" the CCP. The JCS inclined to military action, but Marshall demurred. He insisted firmly that the U.S. would never again mediate in China or propose coalition government, which—he said amid the pressure of the Berlin blockade—had led only to Communist "engulfment" in Eastern Europe. But the U.S. would do nothing that might encourage the GMD to expect "unlimited aid" or that could be said to prolong the civil war. The State Department's PPS proposed to leave China to its own destiny—"which lies essentially with the Chinese—not with foreigners." The GMD would disappear but a nonmodernized, Communist China posed no security threat, and Soviet ability to use China for its own purposes was "severely qualified." The battle for China's mind would be political and economic, and if the CCP came to power, the U.S. should decide then whether to recognize the new regime.[80]

Truman informed the GMD in late September that he was providing all possible military aid. He averted presidential campaign statements, while Republican presidential candidate Dewey spoke only briefly about additional aid to China or the Russian danger in Asia. Jiang sought to help defeat Truman—and Marshall—with a late October interview in the New York *Herald Tribune* urging more aid and comparing Western failure to halt Japan in Manchuria in 1931 to alleged current failure to resist the CCP and the Soviets. Meanwhile, 400,000 GMD troops, and vast stores of U.S. military equipment, fell to the CCP in Manchuria.[81]

Safely elected, Truman and Marshall decided that despite the GMD's being irreversibly "on its way out" and State Department advice that the U.S. public should now be told the reasons, they would say nothing publicly in order to avoid charges of delivering the "knock out blow." They reluctantly admitted Madame Jiang to the U.S. to deliver final, but vain, pleas for aid as well as to reiterate Jiang's threat that he would look to the Soviets if he did not get U.S. aid. Truman dismissed this threat as coming from "grafters and crooks."[82]

In January 1949 Acheson succeeded the ailing Marshall as secretary of state. Son of an Episcopal bishop and educated at Yale and Harvard Law School, Acheson was an urbane lawyer and diplomat with a Europe-first policy and Western cultural emphasis. He had evolved from a proponent of cooperation with the Soviets to a Truman Doctrine hard-liner, although he professed the need to accept coexistence on a single planet. Acheson shared Truman's and Marshall's disdain for Jiang's regime, but his reserve toward Asians and dislike of revolution inhibited his ability to pursue a new relationship with the CCP. Acheson also got along extremely well with Truman despite their highly dissimilar backgrounds and bearing. The president admired Acheson's loyalty and brilliant manner, and the secretary, taking note of Byrnes' difficulty, took care to gain Truman's prior assent to every undertaking, even if this meant acting like a shrewd lawyer who respected his client's high position but also knew how to present policy options to him that would lead to choices the attorney, or secretary, preferred.[83]

Truman opposed dealing with the CCP. During debate in January 1949 between officials who wished to cut off ECA supplies and foodstuffs to CCP-controlled areas, and ECA administrators who sought to keep a door open to the Chinese people if the CCP would agree to protect ECA operatives, the president insisted at a Cabinet meeting that "we can't be in a position of making a deal with a communist regime." ECA aid ended shortly thereafter.[84]

Truman and the NSC also wished to embargo the China Aid Act's remaining $60 million in military supplies, which officials said the GMD would quickly lose to the CCP. At a White House meeting on February 5 with congressional leaders, however, Senator Vandenberg warned that with the GMD near collapse—Jiang had recently resigned his presidency to General Li Tsungjen—and desperately seeking a settlement, the U.S. could not bear the onus of sealing China's doom to Communism. The president backed off the embargo but ordered informal shipping delays. He and Acheson also resisted a congressional call for a fact-finding mission—the facts were too well known, Truman said—and opposed the bid of Senator Pat McCarran (NV) for an additional $1.5 billion in aid to China. But with the China Aid Act expiring in April, the administration agreed to legislation extending use of unexpended funds to February 1950. When Ambassador Wellington Koo sought a loan to pay GMD troops in June 1949, however, Truman curtly said that he was from Missouri and that the GMD had to prove itself in deeds, not words.[85]

Meanwhile, Mao and CCP officials, confident of final victory, held three major meetings during November 1948–March 1949 to plan their nation's future course. They aimed to carry through their revolution, which meant destroying China's old political structure and building a "New People's Democratic Dictatorship." They also saw need to eliminate dependency on Western imperial nations by increasing trade with the Soviet Union and its bloc. But they intended to sustain the national bourgeoisie for a decade or more to facilitate vital economic reconstruction, which implied prospect of trade with the U.S. and its allies. As Mao said in March 1949, they would trade first with the Soviet bloc but "at the same time we will also trade with capitalist countries."[86]

In terms of foreign policy—now come to the fore of CCP thinking—Mao and his comrades recognized both the confrontation between the U.S. and the Soviet Union and prospects for their collaboration—such as at Yalta—at the expense of weaker states. Mao also believed that the main conflict in the postwar world was not between the two superpowers but between the U.S. and the nations of the "intermediate zone"—in Africa, Asia, and Europe—who were

seeking to throw off imperial controls and forge new, presumably revolutionary, societies. Further, Chinese ethnocentrism and universalism, belief in the
superiority of the Middle Kingdom, led Mao and his colleagues to view their
revolution as in the vanguard of national liberation movements around the
globe and responsible for transforming the U.S.-dominated world order. Thus,
as scholars of modern China have noted, in 1948–1949 the basic principles of
Chinese foreign policy comprised (according to Zhou) intent to "cook their
food in a new way," i.e., put an end to old diplomatic relations; to "clean the
house first before inviting guests," i.e., restructure Chinese society; and to "lean
to one side," i.e., align more closely with the Soviet Union.[87]

This did not mean, however, that a CCP-governed China would seek
conflict with the U.S. In fact, from late 1948 to early 1950 Mao strongly feared
that the U.S. would try to overturn the "New China"—as the CCP referred to
their society—either by direct military intervention, by assisting the GMD, or
by sabotaging its revolution. This view derived in good part from the long history of U.S. opposition to revolutionary movements in China: from the Taiping
rebellion in the 1850s, through the Boxer Rebellion in the 1890s, to the Chinese revolution of 1911 and the nationalist and Communist ferment from the
1920s to 1940s. Nonetheless, the CCP remained cognizant of U.S. economic
and military power, and there still remained the prospect for diplomatic relations—which even Stalin urged on Mao in the spring of 1949—as well as economic cooperation between China's bourgeoisie and the capitalists of the U.S.
and other nations. But nations that sought to deal with the New China, the CCP
determined in early 1949, would have to respect its revolution, negotiate on
the basis of full equality—which meant abrogating the unequal treaties—and
sever all ties with the GMD.[88]

Meanwhile, Mao sought to strengthen his position by aligning more closely
with Stalin, whose expectations of, and assistance to, the CCP were notably
low. For nearly a year the Soviet leader had brushed off Mao's repeated requests
for a meeting in Moscow to gain "advice." But finally in early 1949 Stalin
proposed to send to China a Politburo official, Anastas Mikoyan, who was instructed to listen rather than talk. During secret meetings at CCP headquarters
in Xibaipo in Hubei province during January 30–February 8, Mao and Zhou
said that they were true Marxist-Leninists, not Titoists; that they needed Soviet
reconstruction aid; and that CCP forces had to cross the Yangzi (Yangtze) River
in southern China in order to consolidate their revolution. Mikoyan—presumably speaking for Stalin—made no commitment to aid and advised against
crossing the Yangzi, which would avert confrontation with the U.S., especially
in coastal cities. Instead, he proposed that China might be divided north-south
along ancient (A.D. 420–581) dynastic lines.[89]

Stalin also cabled Mao during January that the GMD had approached him about mediating the civil war. The CCP leader immediately rejected the offer, but shortly acceded after Stalin advised that an outright refusal was tantamount to putting "your trump card on the table" and handing the peace banner to the GMD—and perhaps inviting U.S. intervention. The two leaders then agreed upon a reply to the GMD that included preconditions to negotiations that they knew would be unacceptable, such as exclusion from participation in talks of "war criminals" and nations that had opposed the CCP, namely, the U.S. In short, while some historians perceived the Stalin-Mao relationship as growing closer at this time, it would seem that as late as the winter of 1949—with the CCP upon the verge of complete military victory—the Soviet leader still had little more to offer than conservative advice designed to avert any CCP-U.S. conflict that might compel Moscow to lean decisively to one side, and perhaps jeopardize its railway and port concessions in Manchuria.[90]

Regardless, Stalin's advice did not slow the CCP advance. In early February the GMD fled Nanjing for Guangzhou. Notably, the only ambassador to accompany the Nationalist government was Soviet envoy Nikolai Roshchin, who for the past two years had been trying, without success, to press the GMD to agree to a mediated settlement of the civil war. Then in late April CCP forces crossed the Yangzi and occupied Nanjing, with the Communists now calling for diplomatic and trade relations with all nations. Mao, who had knowledge of private contacts in late March between Ambassador Stuart and Chen Mingshu, a pro-Communist official of another party, evidently believed that the U.S. might take such an initiative. Thus, the CCP leader said he was willing to consider the issue, provided the U.S. ended relations with the GMD, and he instructed military officials in Nanjing to "pay attention to this matter."[91]

Relations with the CCP were not wholly improbable for the U.S., as many American diplomats, businesspeople, and missionaries in China urged maintaining a foothold there. In March Truman said he wished to maintain a "flexible" position, and Acheson, who held that a nonmodernized, Communist China was not a security threat, proposed to wait for the "dust to settle." In May he urged Western nations to adopt a "common front" and to avoid "hasty recognition." But he proposed to apply only traditional criteria for establishing relations: de facto control of the nation, fulfillment of international obligations, and general public acquiescence. Moreover, he did not think withholding recognition should be used as a weapon.[92]

Further, in early February Truman had signed off on NSC 34/1, which urged use of political-economic means to prevent China from becoming an adjunct of Soviet power. Then in early March he approved an Acheson-sponsored policy paper, NSC 34/2, which recognized that the CCP had gained "preponderant power" and would soon control all or most of the nation, with GMD at best remaining a local regime in South China or on Taiwan and claiming international recognition based on "insubstantial legalisms." At the same time, however, the national security managers displayed their cultural arrogance by contending that the CCP leaders had just emerged from "caves to chancelleries," had yet to prove they could deal with urban and national problems, and needed to stop using "vestiges" of American "interventionism" to rationalize Sino-Soviet ties. In fact, if the CCP did not become an independent government, the Truman administration would foster a "new revolution" that might inevitably come to a "test of arms" with the Chinese Communists.[93]

Still, on March 10 Stuart proposed to talk with the CCP. He proposed to try to dissuade the CCP of its misapprehensions about U.S. intentions and to state that if the CCP sought to impose despotism, the U.S. would support an "organized opposition." Acheson approved the meeting in April and warned against threats. But before Stuart acted, Consul General O. Edmund Clubb in Beijing reported on June 1 that Foreign Minister Zhou—using as an intermediary Michael Keon, an Australian journalist who worked for United Press— had sent a message for highest authorities describing a divide between CCP "radicals," who favored aligning with the Soviets, and Zhou-led "liberals," who sought U.S. aid. Clubb, who hoped to promote Tito-like independence from the Soviets, urged a cautious reply. So did Stuart, who wanted to find a CCP intermediary and seize the initiative. Acheson authorized a "plain paper" response: no signature or indication of source. But on June 16 Truman imposed his strict standard "not to indicate any softening toward the communists," who broke contact when Clubb sought more direct contact with Zhou the next week.[94]

Meantime, Stuart used his personal secretary, Philip Fugh, to arrange talks with Huang Hua, a Yenching University classmate of Fugh's and ally of Zhou, who had recently appointed Huang to head the CCP's Aliens Affairs Office in Nanjing, probably with a view to making contact with the ambassador. Mao personally approved the talks in order "to detect the intentions of the U.S. government." He told his envoy to "listen more and talk less," to be serious and cordial, and not to reject the idea of revising China's commercial treaty. Most likely Mao also wished to know U.S. intentions as CCP forces approached Shanghai, China's largest port and East Asia's commercial center. The CCP leader was firm that the "key" to relations was for the U.S. to cut all ties to the GMD and "never interfere with China's internal affairs."[95]

The Stuart-Huang talks produced only statements of principle. The ambassador assured that the U.S. would not intervene militarily in China and expressed doubt that a diplomatic mission would follow the GMD if it went to Taiwan. Otherwise, Stuart insisted that the U.S. had to remain "passive" toward the CCP until it showed that it represented the Chinese people and would abide by international norms. Huang was emphatic about China's right to make its own international decisions and about having the U.S. "discard" the GMD and deal with the CCP on a basis of equality. At the same time, on June 28 he used talk about Stuart's habit of attending Yenching University graduations to say that Mao and Zhou would welcome him to Beijing if he went there now. Stuart took this as a "veiled invitation" to talk directly with the CCP leaders.[96]

The ambassador informed Washington that he saw a unique, and possibly last, chance to explain changing U.S. foreign policy, despite any gain in prestige the CCP might derive from a meeting. Consul General John M. Cabot in Shanghai said America's allies there would welcome Stuart's trip "with open arms" as a means to put the West's viewpoint before "top Communist leaders." So too did State Department officials view the prospective trip as "extremely significant," even if it only provided the occasion for Stuart to demand CCP release of Consul General Angus Ward, under house arrest with his staff in Shenyang since November 1948 for failing to hand over his radio transmitter— which the CCP feared was used to pass information about their troop movements—and now charged with electronic spying.[97]

But Truman quashed Stuart's initiative. The president instructed him on July 1 that "under no circumstance" was he to go to Beijing. As a White House aide noted, Truman was on record as having said that the Communists would not be recognized and "they would not be."[98]

Historians have debated whether Truman's decision may have marked a historic "lost chance" to begin rapprochement with the CCP. The answer is complex. In fact, the best lost chance was Marshall's mission in 1946, when the U.S. might have leveraged the GMD into a coalition government with the CCP and left the two sides to engage in long-term political warfare. By 1949 CCP distrust of the U.S. was extremely great, especially because of its military aid to the GMD. Moreover, no one has been able to find documents to substantiate the Zhou-Keon *demarche,* while it is clear that the CCP were in no hurry to seek recognition from the U.S. unless it cut all ties to the GMD, ended the unequal treaties, and dealt with New China on a basis of equality. Nonetheless, as China scholar Thomas J. Christensen has concluded, in the spring of 1949 Mao was actively considering establishment of relations with the U.S. and was well apprised of the approaches to Stuart, and the CCP would ultimately request Western power recognition. What Mao would not do, however, was revise the goals of his revolution.[99]

By mid-May, in fact, Mao had already decided to send CCP vice chairman, Liu Shaoqi—known to be pro-Soviet—to Moscow to seek aid. And on June 30, two days before Liu's departure, Mao delivered his speech "On the

Principles of Democratic Dictatorship." The Communist leader stated that there was no third road, that China "must lean either to the side of imperialism or to the side of socialism," and that the U.S. and imperialism were dangerous, whereas China and Russia were bound by revolutionary experience and ideology.[100]

It is also true that Stuart's proposed journey may have undercut the "common front" and would have drawn sharp criticism from the China bloc just when the North Atlantic Treaty was before the Senate. Nonetheless, Mao's terms for relations—recognizing PRC sovereignty and cutting GMD ties—were not difficult to meet, and the Truman administration could have weathered public criticism in mid-1949 without losing the NATO treaty or its allies who, Consul General Cabot had reported, welcomed an American approach to the CCP. Further, Truman's veto of Stuart's invitation to Beijing came before word of Mao's speech. In fact, the party leader had a Chinese emissary inform Stuart that it was aimed at CCP faithful—and Stalin—and did not preclude dealing with the U.S., whose power the CCP respected but sought to assure would no longer bolster the GMD. Nor did Mao's words negate his concern that from Yalta onward Stalin had dealt readily with the GMD, sought to secure imperial concessions in Manchuria (which his soldiers had stripped of industrial machinery), backed Mongolian independence, and seemed too ready—as the Mikoyan mission showed—to mediate a GMD-CCP accord to divide China.[101]

Most important, in July 1949 Truman opposed a modus vivendi with the CCP. He not only blocked Stuart's trip to Beijing but at the same time told him to visit the GMD at their new headquarters in Guangzhou before returning to the U.S., which order the ambassador persuaded the president to rescind. Truman and his senior officials seemed unable to conceive how their behavior worsened relations. Rather than deal with the reality of the CCP victory and the roots of its revolution, they threatened to carry out reprisals and to foster "organized opposition" if the Communists—who were also Chinese who recalled their Middle Kingdom traditions—did not conform to American, or Western, standards. And U.S. officials were already excessively worried about CCP intent to dominate Asia.[102]

Worse, the Truman administration did nothing to halt the GMD's "indiscriminate bombing," in American-made planes, of Shanghai and other cities, which began in June and intensified over the next year. The president also said he wanted "strict adherence" to his acceptance of the GMD's illegal "blockade" of China's major ports. He repeatedly said he wanted it to succeed, even though it could not alter the war's outcome but did wreak havoc on civilians, harm evacuation of American nationals, and increase CCP leaning toward Moscow. As Cabot complained in July, the U.S. had rejected every opportunity to place

foreign viewpoints and problems before "top Communists," put those who favored relations with the West in an "impossible" situation, and done nothing to
bridge the "psychological gap," or lessen dangerous misunderstanding, between the CCP and the West.[103]

The gap now widened significantly. CCP vice chair Liu reached Moscow
on July 10. He stated that shortly his comrades would establish a new "people's
dictatorship" that would stand with the USSR in international relations. He
sought to gain Soviet recognition and economic aid and to plan a visit for Mao.
Meantime, New China worried about possible Western intervention but was
ready to combat it, and while willing to trade with imperialist nations on equal
footing, it would reject any preconditions for recognition. Stalin congratulated
the CCP on its victory, gave it responsibility for revolutions in the East, and offered Soviet air protection against GMD bomb attacks on Shanghai. The Soviets also said they would open the way for CCP forces in Xinjiang province—
long a Soviet sphere—in northwestern China and provide a $300 million loan
and technical assistance. Thus the basis was established for CCP-USSR relations and a journey to Moscow for Mao.[104]

Shortly, State Department publication on August 5, 1949, of *United States
Relations with China, with Special Reference to the Period 1944–1949* gave a
bitter public face to U.S.-CCP relations and exemplified counterproductive
U.S. policy. Truman and Acheson had intended this *China White Paper,* comprising 1,054 pages of narrative and documents, to demonstrate to the American public and Congress that the U.S. had given all possible aid to its GMD ally
and thus could not be blamed for its final defeat. The president had even backed
Acheson's decision to include the Wedemeyer Report despite JCS concerns
about its sensitive references to China's strategic value for the U.S. in a conflict
with the Soviet Union. Acheson's letter of transmittal with the White Paper
blamed the GMD for losing the war: Jiang had rebuffed good advice, his government had lost popular support, and the army had lost its will to fight. Nothing could have changed the war's outcome except massive U.S. intervention
and complete command of China's forces, which the Chinese would have resented and the American public would have condemned.

But having made his case for administration policy, Acheson assailed the
CCP for allegedly having forsworn their Chinese heritage and chosen subservience to the Soviets, who masked foreign domination behind the facade of
nationalism. The U.S. thus encouraged the Chinese people to reassert their
"democratic individualism" and to throw off the "foreign yoke" of Russian imperialism, but the U.S. would resist CCP support of Soviet aggression in South
Asia. The next week Truman, asked about recognizing CCP-held areas of
China, said that U.S. policy was the same as always: "[W]e have never been favorable to the Communists."[105]

The *China White Paper* was the administration's most militant anti-CCP statement—a "diatribe"—to date. It was also consistent both with NSC interest in promoting a new revolution in China and some recent stunning State Department proposals to bomb China's coastal cities to show that the U.S. was not a "paper tiger." Mao, of course, was incensed at the White Paper and U.S. policy, and during August–September he published five articles—under a pseudonym—excoriating American aggression against China. He also prepared to lean more closely toward the Soviet Union.[106]

Like it or not, U.S. officials now had to weigh dealing with an emergent CCP government. In February Acheson had presided over drafting of NSC 41, which saw little chance to change this outcome but proposed to use trade controls to leverage the CCP away from the Soviet Union and toward the U.S. In May the secretary said he would apply only traditional criteria to recognition, although he urged a common front and slow movement. There followed the aborted Stuart mission and the China White Paper. Then in mid-September Acheson met with Bevin, who said the British were in no hurry to recognize the CCP, but they wished to protect their large commercial interests and Hong Kong, and perhaps weaken "Russia's grip." Acheson balked at recognition and questioned whether the CCP controlled China. But he said that he inclined to "play for a split between China and the USSR" and admitted that recognition was not much of a "strong card" for negotiations, although he worried about discouraging allies in Southeast Asia.[107]

Ten days later Truman's terse announcement that the U.S. had evidence of a recent atomic explosion in the USSR signified the end of America's atomic monopoly. Then on October 1 Mao proclaimed the People's Republic of China, and Foreign Minister Zhou notified foreign powers of their need to establish normal diplomatic relations. The State Department immediately declined on grounds that the CCP had not promised to recognize international obligations. During October 6–8, however, a State Department–sponsored conference, comprising twenty-five prominent individuals from academic, business, and public-service sectors concluded almost unanimously that the U.S. should recognize the PRC and that this was the only way to normalize relations over time. Similar views came from Ambassador Alan Kirk in Moscow and Consul General Clubb in Beijing. But Acheson resisted recognition, announced the closing of several consulates, and in testimony on October 12 before the Senate Foreign Relations Committee, branded the PRC "a tool of Russian Imperialism." The next day Truman told the visiting prime minister Jawaharlal Nehru—who said that India's proximity to the PRC impelled recognition, but that Chinese nationalism would abate subservience to Moscow—that he wanted non-Communist states to act in concert.[108]

Then on October 24 the CCP—perhaps to demonstrate the PRC's sovereign authority—arrested Consul General Ward in Shenyang for allegedly having assaulted a recently dismissed Chinese employee during a dispute over back wages. During the next six weeks Ward and four colleagues were jailed, beaten, tried without any defense rights, and convicted, with the sentences commuted to deportation in early December. The proceedings enraged Truman, and on November 14 he asked the State Department to weigh a blockade on coal shipments on the China coast—he thought this might also deter British recognition—and said that he was prepared to have the navy sink ships.[109]

Three days later Acheson, returned from a CFM meeting in Paris, rushed with his Far East consultants to the White House, where he said that the U.S. could try either to overthrow the PRC regime or to detach it from subservience to Moscow and encourage "vigorous influences which might modify it." The consultants unanimously endorsed the latter course. Truman concurred, saying that he had gained "new insight" and a "new way" of thinking about Communist success in China. The next day the JCS said that a blockade would be tantamount to an act of war, which might prompt Soviet intervention but not gain release of Ward, who was soon deported.[110]

While U.S.-CCP tension was increasing, the Truman administration, following the advice of Acheson's consultants, was seeking to disengage from the GMD. First, it persuaded Congress, which voted $75 million in aid to the GMD in early October, to allow use of the funds in the "general area of China," while the JCS balked at a military advisory role there. Acheson then dropped plans in the making intended to deny the PRC's expected taking of Taiwan (Kennan had even proposed a military coup to install a regime to replace the GMD) and refused to spend China-area funds there. Similarly, the JCS, although they attributed great strategic value to Taiwan, said that it should not be defended militarily. Further, when Louis A. Johnson, who had replaced Forrestal as secretary of defense in March and who had close ties to GMD officials, now rekindled JCS interest in Taiwan, Acheson argued in late December that the political loss from supporting the GMD outweighed strategic gain. Better that the U.S. should chiefly provide political-economic aid to Asian nationalist movements, he said. The next day the president approved NSC 48/2, a policy paper for Asia that promoted aid to non-Communist states to resist Communism but stipulated that if the PRC took Taiwan, where Jiang had moved and taken control of his government, the U.S. should strengthen its Japan-Okinawa-Philippine defenses.[111]

The president then declared at his press conference on January 5, 1950, that the great powers had agreed at their Cairo and Potsdam Conferences that Taiwan belonged to China, and the U.S. would not intervene there. But prodded by JCS chairman General Omar Bradley, Truman added to his statement that the

U.S. would not seek military bases on Taiwan the qualifying phrase "at this time." Acheson promptly told reporters that this did not alter policy—but then added his qualifying phrase that the U.S. had to be free to act in event of an attack on its forces in the Far East. Still, the secretary told two leading China bloc critics, Senators William Knowland (CA) and Alexander Smith (NJ), that "sheer realities" had to govern policy, that the JCS did not view Taiwan as "vital" to security, and that to risk war to hold the island would fly in the face of America's "preaching of self-determination" in Asia.[112]

Disengagement from the GMD, however, did not constitute engaging with the CCP. Acheson, now citing the Ward case as reason to maintain America's "firm attitude" toward the Communists, refused to consider recognition for the PRC, although by mid-January 1950 twenty-five nations—including Britain, India, Pakistan, and the Soviet bloc—had established formal relations. The U.S. also opposed PRC entry into the UN, prompting the Soviet Union to protest by walking out of the Security Council. Acheson's address at the National Press Club on January 12 shrewdly stated that the driving force in Asia was nationalism, inspired by "revulsion" against centuries of poverty and foreign domination. The GMD had lost the war by failing to meet the Chinese people's basic needs, he insisted. And intervention in Taiwan, which the secretary omitted from America's defense perimeter—and which he said ran from the Aleutians through Japan, the Ryukyus, and the Philippines—would deflect righteous Chinese anger away from the imperial Soviets and toward the U.S. But despite Acheson's providing reason to disengage from the GMD, his White Paper–like insistence that the CCP had merely ridden nationalism to power further dimmed prospects for relations. Similarly, his statement that the U.S. was now assuming Japan's military defense signaled a long-term military presence there that the PRC could view as a security threat, and his contention that an attack on U.S. forces in the Far East might compel it to take Taiwan clearly implied limits on PRC sovereignty.[113]

American animus toward the PRC increased following its January 6 requisition of the military barracks in Beijing of foreign nations—but not of Britain, which had just recognized the PRC—that had built them under a protocol signed after they had crushed the Boxer Rebellion in 1901. From the PRC perspective, the current U.S. legal basis rested on its 1943 "unequal" treaty with the GMD, and the Communists were now determined to put an end to such imperialist-imposed terms. Truman and Acheson asserted U.S. treaty rights, however, and insisted that the barracks had long ago become the American Consulate. They offered instead to exchange a property off consular grounds but threatened to withdraw from China if the PRC persisted.[114]

The PRC rebuffed Acheson's dispatch on January 14, however, and the State

Department ordered U.S. withdrawal—completed in April—from China. Clubb thought that the PRC had overreached in trying to prod U.S. recognition and approval of PRC entry into the UN. But Mao took the U.S withdrawal as "extremely favorable to us" and a sign that imperialist nations would not be able to influence the will of the Chinese people. Regardless, Truman's and Acheson's ultimatum to the PRC was disproportionate to the issue, and they now shelved all thought of recognition. Events soon precluded any future initiative.[115]

PRC and Soviet recognition of Ho Chi Minh's Democratic Republic of Vietnam in late January led the administration to denounce this action and to recognize the French-sponsored regime of Bao Dai in the Republic of Vietnam. The Americans also planned French military aid, which Truman approved in May, to counter possible PRC incursions across the Republic of Vietnam's southern border, but the attacks never occurred. Meanwhile, the administration, stung by House rejection—led in part by the China bloc—of its military aid bill for South Korea, rescued the legislation in early February by again extending to June the expiring China Aid Act, with its unexpended $50 million that now went to the GMD.[116]

Then on February 9, amid loyalty-security hearings, the conviction of Alger Hiss for perjury, and British arrest of atomic physicist Klaus Fuchs for spying for the Soviets, Senator Joseph R. McCarthy (WI) alleged that 205 State Department employees—known to Acheson—were Communists. McCarthy's wild charges, and biting attacks on Acheson as an ersatz British diplomat, spurred a Foreign Relations subcommittee investigation during March–June that led to allegations that China hands (such as diplomat John Stewart Service) and State Department consultant scholars (such as Philip Jessup, Columbia University international law professor, and Owen Lattimore, Johns Hopkins University political scientist) had subverted Far East policy to advance Communism in China. False and perverse as these charges were—and despite Truman's public jibe that McCarthy was the Kremlin's "greatest asset"—policy toward the PRC was further rigidified.[117]

Meanwhile, in November 1949, after eighteen months of approaches, Mao finally got Stalin to invite him to Moscow. The PRC leader departed Beijing on December 6 and was greeted upon arrival ten days later with Soviet accolades and a banquet. But when Mao said that he had long been suppressed in the Communist Party and had nowhere to complain, Stalin retorted that "now you are a winner, and a winner should not be criticized," especially since the Chinese revolution had changed "the whole balance of the world." Still, Stalin only made cautious inquiries about Mao's purposes, who answered evasively that he wanted to achieve something "that not only looks good but tastes delicious."

Shortly, however, Mao apparently indicated need to revise the Sino-Soviet treaty of 1945, but Stalin said this rested on the Yalta accords and that "a change of even one point" might give the U.S. and Britain reason to question all the Yalta terms.[118]

Mao's goal was to gain a formal alliance and Soviet military-economic assistance. But before starting negotiations he sought to be certain that Stalin would treat him, his revolution, and his Middle Kingdom as equals. Thus it took two weeks of Soviet probing before Mao made his purposes clear on January 2, 1950, whereupon Stalin dispatched Molotov and Mikoyan to see him. The Russians quickly agreed with Mao that a treaty was better than a joint communiqué or open statement, and Mao then sent for his chief negotiator, Zhou, whom he told to take his time and travel by train, lest anyone think the Chinese were overly anxious.[119]

Zhou arrived on January 20 and negotiations lasted until February 14. The resultant Sino-Soviet Treaty of Friendship, Alliance, and Mutual Assistance was directed against the revival of Japan's imperialism or aggression and any state—the U.S.—that collaborated with Tokyo. Further, the Chinese got the initially hesitant Russians to agree explicitly that if either China or Russia were attacked by Japan or an allied state, the other would render "military and other assistance by all means at its disposal." At the same time the treaty emphasized Sino-Soviet consultations only on matters of common—rather than international—interest, allowing the Chinese to avert being drawn into faraway conflicts of concern only to the Soviets.[120]

The Chinese also virtually negated Yalta's Far Eastern accords, which they deplored, by getting the Russians to agree to hand over full control of the Manchurian railways and evacuate their troops from Lushun no later than the end of 1952. The PRC would also take control of Dalian, with use of its commercial harbor to be considered after a peace treaty was signed with Japan. A second agreement confirmed the Soviet pledge to Liu in July to provide the Chinese with a $300 million credit, payable over five years at 1 percent interest through deliveries of raw materials, tea, gold, and U.S. dollars. A third, and secret, Additional Agreement provided for Russia to be the only foreign power allowed to undertake financial-economic activities in Manchuria and Xinjiang. While still in Moscow, Mao also ordered over 1,200 planes—including bombers and fighters—and the Soviets began to dispatch a mixed air-defense division to protect China's coastal cities from GMD attacks.[121]

The Sino-Soviet agreements, negotiated from different security and strategic interests, reflected concessions and gains on both sides. By recognizing the success of Mao's revolution, Stalin was able to align China on his side and blunt U.S. predominance in Japan, which was a threat to Soviet security. The cost was direct military commitment to the PRC and divestment of the Yalta concessions, while preserving economic advantage in Manchuria.[122]

The Chinese were bigger winners, despite Russia's providing only minimal economic aid and retaining Manchurian privileges. Most important, China could state that it was no longer isolated, had gained protection against U.S. aggression and that of its allies, and had removed foreigners from its borders. The agreement had allied not only China and Russia but 800 million people from Berlin to Shanghai. Thus Mao and Zhou could claim that they had struck a far better bargain with Stalin than Jiang had in 1945 and drawn a treaty that would compel all nations to recognize the PRC and abrogate the unequal treaties.[123]

PRC adherence to a treaty with the USSR derived largely from its inevitable effort to gain international recognition and security from a perceived U.S. threat. Acheson and other U.S. officials realized that the Chinese had been far less submissive than Stalin expected and that most likely he had retreated on his demands, even if he probably gained some secret concessions. Rather than try to exploit Sino-Soviet differences, however, Acheson—with Truman's advance blessing—launched an all-out attack on PRC leadership. Speaking in San Francisco on March 15, he scorned Stalin's tiny credit and charged the PRC leaders with having sold China's sovereignty and making their nation a "dependency" within the Soviet political-economic orbit.[124]

Ironically, the U.S. now appeared to be in Taiwan's orbit. Truman and Acheson had not only bowed to political pressure to extend aid to China, but the GMD regime unabashedly used U.S.-marked planes to continue indiscriminate bombing of China's cities, such as Shanghai. As Philip Sprouse, head of the Office of China Affairs, complained bitterly on February 16, the bombings were causing the U.S. to be "arraigned before the bar of opinion in China," and the benefits of Truman's January 5 statement on Taiwan had been dissipated. It was "incredible," Sprouse said, that the U.S., rather than halt military aid to this dependent regime, allowed the GMD to "call the turn" on vital interests. Acheson instructed the State Department to be sure that it was "thinking" about halting aid to Taiwan. But he admitted then, and shortly told the British, that the GMD had already told the administration to "go to hell" with its bombing protests.[125]

Neither Truman nor Acheson could conceive of a way out of their China conundrum. They refused to consider recognition, although in late March Acheson directed Clubb to seek talks with Mao or Zhou. But Clubb only got to meet with an Aliens Affairs Office official, who said that the PRC leaders were too busy and that it was "ridiculous" to think of improving relations without recognition. When the PRC also declined interest in a U.S. famine relief program, Truman denounced China's "new taskmasters" as "heartlessly indifferent" to their people.[126]

Conceivably Truman and Acheson believed that the PRC would resolve America's Taiwan problem for them by reclaiming the island militarily. Truman had thought the PRC capable of doing this since autumn 1949, and PRC campaigns in April–May 1950 took Hainan Island and the Chusan Islands. The CIA and many officials now saw the PRC's taking of Taiwan as imminent, although the Communists' small, antiquated navy probably was not up to a major amphibious campaign against this well-fortified island. Moreover, the Americans now undertook to deny Taiwan to the PRC, as Acheson promoted an overall U.S. military buildup that would allow the JCS to commit fully to Taiwan. At the same time, abundant military and increased nonmilitary aid (the latter freeing funds for weapons) flowed to the GMD.[127]

Further, Dean Rusk, the conservative head of the Far Eastern Affairs Office who had been asked by Acheson to take the job to show toughness to the McCarthyite "primitives," sought to "draw the line" in Asia at Taiwan. On May 30 Rusk elaborated a scheme to have the U.S. use its navy and ground forces to "neutralize" Taiwan, sponsor a political coup to replace Jiang (who had reclaimed his presidency on March 1) with former president Sun Li-jen, and seek a UN trusteeship. This increased chances of "early war" with the PRC and Russia, Rusk said, but he favored the risk to sustain a free world.[128]

Truman and Acheson discussed the proposal on May 31, and the president agreed to weigh it. Meanwhile, he had dispatched his own emissary to Taiwan, Karl W. V. Nix, an Ohio businessman whose father Truman knew. Nix reported on June 16 that Jiang was prepared to do anything, even resign, to secure U.S. aid, while Sun pleaded for immediate U.S. action to reverse a desperate situation.[129]

There matters stood when war in Korea began on June 24. The next day Truman met his senior officials at Blair House to weigh their course. He immediately approved Acheson's idea to have the Seventh Fleet sail toward the Taiwan Strait and to seek a UN solution of the Taiwan issue. On June 26 the president and his advisers decided to preclude any possible PRC invasion of Taiwan and to halt Jiang's provocative attacks on the mainland. Truman also proposed to send General MacArthur to replace Jiang, but after Acheson warned that an angry Generalissimo might "throw the ball game," the president left this to "the next step." Truman then announced on June 27 that he was ordering the Seventh Fleet into the Taiwan Strait to prevent any attack on Taiwan and calling on the Taiwanese government to halt mainland attacks. Taiwan's final status, he said, would have to await restoration of Pacific security, a peace treaty with Japan, or UN settlement.[130]

Mao denounced U.S. action as aggression against China, violative both of international agreements and Truman's pledge not to intervene in China's internal affairs, and an act of war that required "full preparations" to thwart

American imperialism. The line between the U.S. and the PRC had been drawn in the Taiwan Strait. The psychological gap had widened into a chasm, and far greater danger lurked than Truman or Acheson imagined.[131]

VI

Truman inherited a vague, difficult China policy in 1945. Amid global war his predecessor had sought to prop up a weak and unwilling ally and avert civil war by spurring a GMD-CCP coalition government. At Yalta FDR had also sought to negotiate the limits of Soviet influence in China. At the war's end, Truman sought to steer the U.S. clear of China's fratricidal conflict and to hold the Soviets to the letter, or less, of Yalta's concessions. But he continued to "support Chiang K.C." by moving GMD armies northward and providing economic subsidies, and he denied that this meant leaning to the side of the GMD against the CCP. In December 1945 he gave Marshall carte blanche to mediate a settlement but subscribed to the secret, perhaps fatal, condition that even if Jiang remained intransigent, the U.S. would continue to aid him. Ironically, Marshall won more respect, and concessions, from the CCP than from the GMD. In early 1946 he appeared near success when he obtained agreement on a broadened government and integrated armies, with the CCP conceding "first place" to the GMD by a wide margin.

But emerging American-Soviet Cold War conflict and Jiang's military offensive against the CCP in spring 1946 brought renewed civil war to China. The GMD ignored Marshall's threats of U.S. withdrawal from China if they did not end their dictatorial policy and accede to a coalition government, and the president and his emissary lacked the resolve to curb Jiang. This cost them their best, and perhaps last, chance to gain accord in China. The CCP concluded that the U.S. was following a double policy by claiming to be mediating while actually aiding the GMD to wage war. Marshall naively believed that his January 1947 bitter farewell statement, aimed chiefly at the GMD, would rouse liberal Chinese to oust their "reactionary" leaders.

Dispatch of Wedemeyer to China in July 1947, with a coalition government ruled out, documented what Truman and Marshall knew about GMD incapacity and corruption but feared to make public. The president and secretary regarded Wedemeyer's proposals for a Manchurian trusteeship and vast U.S.-supervised aid for the GMD to be unworkable. Hence they suppressed his report, leading to charges of cover-up, but sought to show their support for the GMD by showering it with China Act aid and by denying that they had ever sought to include the CCP in China's government.

In fact, from the start Truman and his chief aides viewed the CCP as agents of Soviet power, not as Chinese and Marxists bent on pursuing their own political and national interests that historically were often at odds with Russian/ Soviet interests. The administration ignored that Stalin had not supported CCP revolution in 1945 and preferred to deal with Jiang to protect Soviet imperial concessions in Manchuria. Further, Stalin did not supply large stores of captured Japanese weapons to the CCP until the fall of 1947, or provide Soviet aid until a year later. And as late as winter/spring 1949 he maintained interest in a GMD-CCP settlement.

By then the CCP was on the verge of power. But Truman's insistence that "we can't be in a position of making a deal with a communist regime" defined his attitude toward the CCP, especially regarding recognition. His order on July 1, 1949, that Stuart was not to go to Beijing under any circumstance to talk with Mao and Zhou precluded even de facto dealing with the leaders of the incipient PRC. Truman did this despite the urgings of American diplomats, businesspeople, and missionaries—and other national leaders—to keep the door to China open and the fact that in mid-1949 his administration had the political standing to counter China bloc criticism. To be sure, the indignities the CCP heaped on foreign diplomats, notably Consul General Ward—although his Shenyang office was used for dubious electronic surveillance—lacked civility and raised tempers, especially Truman's. But CCP bad behavior did not justify a blockade or sinking ships, which were Truman's visceral responses before Acheson and realities pulled him up short. Nor did PRC requisition of foreign "military barracks"—an assertion of PRC sovereignty—justify complete withdrawal from China.

The president's, and Acheson's, animus toward the Communists more than CCP behavior or domestic political criticism stymied administration efforts to deal with China's new realities. Truman thought that the Chinese "would never be Communist," and from the White Paper of August 1949 onward he and Acheson were persistent that the CCP had usurped the forces of nationalism to gain power and imposed the "yoke" of Soviet imperialism on the Chinese people, whom the Americans urged to rise up against their new leaders and forge a new revolution.

Truman and Acheson made scant effort to "play for a split" between Mao and Stalin, to encourage the so-called Tito option in 1949–1950. The president never intended to recognize the PRC, and it is doubtful his secretary would have pushed this even after the dust had settled. They were presumptuous to think that they could denigrate "hasty recognition" and take their own time without political consequence. Moreover, by Acheson's traditional recognition criteria, the CCP in 1950 had as much claim to administrative control and public acquiescence in China as the GMD ever did. Nor could the administration escape the consequence of allowing the GMD to engage in an illegal blockade and indiscriminate bombing that could not have been sustained without U.S. material support and political acquiescence. Further, by increasing aid to the GMD and Taiwan defense in spring 1950, the Truman administration affirmed its pursuit of what the CCP called a "two-handed policy": alleging disengagement but intervening in China's affairs. Or as the Americans said, pursuing a "two China" policy, despite private desire to be rid of Jiang.[132]

The Truman administration denied the PRC's presumptive claim to rule Taiwan, negating the Cairo and Potsdam agreements, and further involved the U.S. in China's civil war. This challenged PRC sovereignty and precluded normal relations with the "so-called Communist Chinese Government," which Truman alleged was "nothing but a tool of Moscow." Thus by the time the president ordered the Seventh Fleet into the Taiwan Strait, he had already fixed the matrix for long-term, counterrevolutionary policy toward the PRC, which direct Sino-American conflict in Korea soon catalyzed into a generation of bilateral hostility and Asian wars.[133]

Turning Point

Containment Comes to Korea

President Truman's Cold War diplomacy in the Far East in 1950 soon escalated into unexpected major war. On Saturday evening June 24, word came to the State Department from John Muccio, Ambassador to the Republic of Korea (ROK), that forces from the Democratic People's Republic of Korea (DPRK) had moved south across the 38th parallel, the dividing line between these two states, and staged amphibious landings on South Korea's east coast. Muccio said that the attacks appeared to be an "all out offensive." [1]

Later that night Acheson telephoned Truman, on vacation in Independence, to gain his approval to send a resolution to the UN Security Council calling upon North Korea to withdraw its forces above the 38th parallel. Acheson saw no need for Truman to return to Washington. But news the next morning that North Korean tanks were heading toward Seoul spurred a midday call to the president, who hastily gathered his entourage to fly to Washington. Truman arrived in time to hold an evening conference with his senior civilian and military advisers at Blair House, across from the White House, where they agreed upon "drawing the line" in Korea. The Security Council, meanwhile, voted 9–0 for North Korea to withdraw from South Korea, with Yugoslavia abstaining and the Soviet Union unable to cast its veto because it was boycotting that body, ostensibly to protest its refusal to seat the PRC in place of the GMD. [2]

Rapid U.S. intervention in Korea through the UN and near immediate use of American air and naval forces, and then ground troops, to forestall North Korea's conquest of South Korea was logical on two grounds. First, the U.S. had played a major role in creating the ROK and securing UN recognition for it. Second, the Truman administration was already under fire for having "lost"

China—and presumably Taiwan—and feared that another loss would permit critics of its Asia policy to retaliate by blocking European aid and projected increases in military spending.[3]

Significantly, however, Truman had long subscribed to the overblown conclusion that Korea was a crucial "ideological battleground" of Asia, and backed major economic-military assistance for Korea in 1947 and 1949–1950, despite the consensus that Korea lay outside the U.S. defense perimeter. Further, Truman attributed the start of hostilities in 1950 solely to Soviet-inspired, unprovoked aggression, not to long-standing virtual civil war between two rival Korean regimes. The president quickly analogized North Korea's attack to German and Japanese aggression in the 1930s, and the U.S. response to containment in Greece in 1947. He was persistent that if the Soviets were not halted in Korea, they would "swallow up" Asia and bring collapse upon the Near East and Europe. He also displayed no inclination to seek congressional sanction for his decision to wage war.[4]

Truman's rapid deployment of the Seventh Fleet into the Taiwan Strait augured continued U.S. involvement in China's civil war, and his appointment of General Douglas MacArthur as commander of UN forces in Korea opened his administration to military and political problems abroad and at home. Further, Truman's speeches on July 19 escalated a "police action" against a "bunch of bandits"—or "pagan wolves"—into a struggle for world peace, and he now endorsed a transforming, long-term military buildup. In sum, although events may have moved faster than Truman anticipated in 1950 and compelled certain action, his forceful direction of U.S. foreign policy and military undertakings set the nation on an aggressive course that brought long-term and profound consequences.[5]

I

Korea was a unitary and independent monarchy that had long governed itself largely by Confucian doctrine; paid tribute to the Middle Kingdom of China; and was subject in the late nineteenth century to fierce imperial rivalry between China, Russia, and Japan. After waging war against China and Russia, the Japanese annexed Korea in 1910, and for the next thirty-five years Japan imposed modernization, political repression, and economic-cultural exploitation. Korea emerged from the Second World War with its prospective leadership ideologically splintered and divided among competing groups in exile in the United States; in Chongqing, with the GMD; in Yan'an, with the CCP; in Manchuria; and in Russian Siberia. Virtually all Koreans loathed the Japanese and their Korean collaborators.[6]

The U.S. played only a small role in the international rivalry over Korea until the conferences at Cairo-Teheran in 1943, when President Roosevelt proposed long-term, multilateral trusteeship for Korea, with independence to come "at the proper moment," which the British amended to a vaguer independence "in due course." FDR's trusteeship—his form of containment—presumed Big Four cooperation and aimed ultimately at independence for Korea, which shares a long border with Manchuria and a shorter one—approaching Vladivostok—with the Soviet Maritime Province, and bounds the Yellow Sea, gateway to the concessions the Soviets would seek at Lushun and Dalian. Thus, as a result of Korea's strategic location, it was long perceived both as a dagger pointed at Japan and a pathway for Japan's advances against China and Russia.[7]

At Yalta, Stalin, after confirming that FDR did not intend to station U.S. troops in Korea, quickly acceded to the president's trusteeship concept, although the Soviet leader preferred a shorter rather than longer period. He did not, however, inject Korea into terms for entering the Pacific war. He seemed ready to pursue Russia's pre-1905 strategy of maintaining a balance of power in Korea in order to preclude one nation from dominating there. The Soviet leader reiterated his position in May 1945 to President Truman's emissary, Harry Hopkins, and while negotiating his Manchurian concessions with the Chinese in July. But the Russians, calling Korea an unusual case, also sought a detailed Big Four agreement, including that there be no foreign troops or bases there. Thus, at the outset of the Potsdam Conference a concerned Secretary of War Stimson urged Truman to press trusteeship terms on Stalin to prevent him from using Russian-trained Korean troops to impose a regime on Korea. "This is the Polish question transplanted to the Far East," Stimson warned.[8]

The president did not act, perhaps because he hoped that swift atomic end to the Pacific war would keep the Soviets out of Korea. They raised the issue of Korea on July 22 during a Big Three discussion of trusteeships, but Prime Minister Churchill, testy about Britain's imperial holdings, brushed off the matter. But after the Russian military inquired about coordinating an American-Soviet attack on Korean shores, Chief of Staff General Marshall said that Japanese suicide attacks posed too great a danger to U.S. shipping and that assault ships were unavailable for U.S. landings in Korea. The Soviets were left to liberate Korea militarily.[9]

Atomic bombing of Hiroshima and Nagasaki and Russian entry into the war in early August prompted Edwin Pauley, Truman's friend and reparations negotiator, to urge him to have U.S. forces occupy as much of the industrial areas of Korea and Manchuria as possible. Ambassador Harriman proposed to rush troops to do much the same without regard for Soviet zones of military operation. Secretary of State Byrnes also wanted U.S. troops moved as far north as possible in Korea, and Truman wanted to secure at least one port on the peninsula.[10]

On August 10–11 the State-War-Navy Coordinating Committee (SWNCC), urged on by War Department officials, including Colonel Dean Rusk, recommended the 38th parallel as the demarcation line between the U.S. and Soviet occupation zones in Korea, although this was much farther north than American troops—600 miles away on Okinawa—could have reached if the Russians had contested the terrain. Moreover, the 38th parallel had no political significance and made no economic sense given the industrial-hydroelectric production in the north and agricultural dominance in the south. But the proposed U.S. zone included the Korean capital, Seoul; two-thirds of Korea's 30 million people; and the ports of Inchon and Pusan.[11]

Stalin readily agreed to the proposal and ordered Russian troops to halt their swift advance in Korea at the 38th parallel even before U.S. forces reached Korea on September 8. Japan's rapid collapse had left little time to plan for Korea, and he may have assumed that Russian control in the north assured strategic security and access to Korean industry and hydroelectricity. He may also have sought to show restraint to gain a reciprocal zone in Japan. Still, Stalin had agreed to trusteeship for Korea and evidently sought a balance of competing great-power interests there, not a Polish-style satellite. In fact, the major new factor in Korea in 1945 was the American presence.[12]

The Soviets and Americans behaved badly in Korea. Soviet troops, as usual living off the land and the people, caused a steady flow of refugees across the 38th parallel, while many Koreans whom the Japanese had forced to labor in Manchuria and northern Korea also headed to their former homes in the south. At the same time, Russian military officials curtailed interzonal economic exchange and refused to negotiate with their U.S. counterparts, citing lack of formal agreement on Korea. The Soviets, however, quickly replaced Japanese officials and collaborators with Koreans—including non-Communist, moderate nationalists as well as exiles from Siberia—promoted formation of a Five Province Administration Bureau, and allowed "peoples committees" to promote radical political-economic reform.[13]

The Soviets accepted the Korean Communist Party (KCP), headquartered in the south, but did not promote its activities there. But in September they did arrange for the return to Korea of Kim Il Sung. He was a thirty-three-year-old self-taught Communist and nationalist who was born in Pyongyang but raised largely in Manchuria, where he had waged guerilla warfare against the Japanese in the 1930s. Forced to flee in 1941 to Khabarovsk in the Soviet Maritime Province, he spent the war there as an officer in a multinational military unit. With backing from Soviet military authorities, Kim soon headed the North Korean Communist Party (NKCP). He had one chief rival for power, Cho Man-sik, who was a political nationalist, Christian educator, and leader of the northern branch of the recently created national Committee for the Preparation of Korean Independence (CPKI). This body promoted sweeping reform and a national coalition to head a new Korean People's Republic (KPR).[14]

U.S. policy for Korea was unformed. Truman averted post-Potsdam queries about negotiations with Russians or Koreans, saying only that Korea would become a free country, while the Koreans took the promise of independence "in due course" to mean independence now. U.S. occupation policy, however, resembled that for an enemy nation rather than a liberated one. General John Hodge, head of the American Military Government (AMG), was a hard-nosed, conservative, rural Midwesterner—much like Truman—who had led his troops in bloody Pacific battles. He sometimes spoke disdainfully of Koreans and knew nothing of their passion for national liberation, self-rule, and social change, which he attributed to Communist instigators. Little good advice came from Washington or advisers in Seoul.[15]

Hodge initially retained Japanese administrators, evoking bitter Korean protests and prompting the White House to announce that the practice would soon end. Still, Hodge refused to deal with the aspiring KPR and its proposal for a coalition government, thereby undermining the one political group that might have bridged the sharp Left-Right political cleavage. Instead, Hodge established a repressive Japanese-style bureaucracy, collaborated with the most conservative Koreans, including the newly formed Korean Democratic Party (KDP), and urged return of two rightist leaders, Syngman Rhee and Kim Ku.[16]

Rhee was descended from Korea's royal family, but of modest means. He had earned a doctorate in international law at Princeton University in 1910, was a follower of Woodrow Wilson, and spent most of the next thirty-five years as head of the Korean Commission to the United States campaigning for Korean independence. Ku headed the long-established but narrowly based Korean Provisional Government (KPG) and had spent the war in exile under GMD auspices. Both Rhee and Ku were intense nationalists and virulently anticommunist. Rhee, now seventy years old, looked back to a patriarchal, tightly ordered society, while Ku identified with Korea's wealthiest classes. Rhee returned to Korea in October 1945 and, with Hodge at his side, publicly denounced Soviet rule in North Korea and then got Hodge to expedite Ku's return.[17]

U.S. policy toward Korea moved on two tracks. Hodge tended to create a separate South Korean regime, with Rhee and Ku as bulwarks against Communism, while Secretary Byrnes sought a multilateral trusteeship. The Russians inclined to an independent Korea, provided that it had a neutral, or "friendly," regime, and during fall 1945 avoided conflict with U.S. officials. At the Moscow CFM meeting in December Byrnes pushed a five-year trusteeship, and the Soviets proposed a Joint Commission to consult with "democratic" representatives from all of Korea to form a national provisional government that would then effect a Big Four trusteeship. The Russian proposal, adopted for the most part, gave primacy to creating a provisional government over a trusteeship. But accord on trusteeship, along with agreement on U.S. control in Japan and a unique mediating role in China in exchange for Soviet predominance in Eastern Europe, represented Yalta-style compromise.[18]

The Koreans, however, detested trusteeship. Ku, looking to seize power in the south, promoted strikes against trusteeship and then an attempt to take over the government. Hodge forced him to halt and publicly blamed the Russians for trusteeship, which the general opposed. Hodge also got the KDP and Rhee, who had kept public silence, to form a so-called Representative Democratic Council (RDC) to speak for South Koreans to the AMG and the proposed Joint Commission, and to brand trusteeship a Soviet ploy. The Soviets instructed left-wing groups to support trusteeship, which they could do in the north at minimal cost but which in the south brought political disfavor to the KCP under the leadership of Pak Hon-yong. When Stalin complained that the U.S. was reneging on the Moscow accords, Ambassador Harriman—who really doubted Russian sincerity about the Moscow agreement—reminded Hodge that trusteeship was "Roosevelt's baby" and still official policy.[19]

Truman, of course, wrote off the Moscow accords in early 1946 as "appeasement." He told Byrnes that he was tired of "babying" the Soviets and was of a mind to impose strong central governments in China and Korea. Then after reviewing cables in late February from Hodge reviling the Soviets for imposing Communists and a "blackout" on North Korea and aiming to do the same in the south, the president told his White House staff that "we are going to war with Russia" and that Korea would be one of two fronts.[20]

Neither war nor successful negotiations followed. U.S. policy makers proposed to promote political-economic reform in Korea and to fulfill the Moscow accords. But preliminary American-Soviet military talks to arrange exchange of northern coal and electricity for southern foodstuffs failed largely because the "free market" system in the south and rice exports to Japan left no "surplus" for exchange. On March 20 the Joint Commission opened talks to discuss which Koreans would be consulted about a provisional government and trusteeship. The Soviets insisted on consulting only "democratic" Koreans who supported trusteeship, thus excluding the rightist, antitrusteeship RDC leadership in the south, including Rhee and Ku. The Americans said that this denied free speech, and negotiations deadlocked. The Russian political litmus test derived partly from belief that the U.S. had reneged on the Moscow accords by sponsoring the RDC but also served to rationalize exclusive Soviet control in their zone. The Joint Commission adjourned on May 16 sine die.[21]

Korea's politics were polarized. Kim Il Sung now headed the Communist Party and the new North Korean Interim People's Republic Committee (NKIPC), which he used—along with the backing of the Russian occupiers—to effect social revolution, create a quasi-government, and consolidate his power. His rival, Cho Man-sik, was marginalized for not supporting trusteeship. In the south, Rhee maximized his support through his National Society for the Rapid Realization of Korean Independence (NSRRKI), and touted a separate southern government, with rival Kim Ku deflated because of his aborted coup. Hodge pressed Rhee to moderate his rhetoric about a separate regime and cracked down on Communists and leftists, whom he blamed for Korea's unrest.[22]

U.S. officials slightly regretted the Joint Commission's failure but now sought a separate southern government. They cited policy in western Germany as their model. Notably, Truman's reparations negotiator, Edwin Pauley, on special assignment in the Far East in June, wrote the president that Korea was the "ideological battleground on which our entire success in Asia may depend." He proposed to blame the Russians for blocking Korean unity and to provide assistance, including Japanese industrial equipment, to reconstruct South Korea's economy.[23]

Truman pointedly replied in July that Korea was an ideological battleground and that revised occupation policy would include Pauley's recommendations. The president added that the U.S. would sponsor elections in the south for a legislative assembly, not a separate government, although the former would become that. The Truman-Pauley correspondence, circulated among the secretaries of state, war, and navy, reflected the administration's emergent new policy, which set South Korean elections for mid-October 1946.[24]

Whatever faint hope remained to negotiate a unified Korea disappeared in September after economic conditions in the south led to bitter peasant-worker strikes, which the AMG and brutal Korean police crushed. Against this violent backdrop, Rhee and his extremely conservative supporters won thirty-eight of the forty-five legislative seats in mid-October. In the areas where there had been fraud, Hodge held new elections. But the results were the same, and he appointed forty-five additional, more moderate legislators. Still, Rhee was politically entrenched and unabashedly traveled to the U.S. and to the UN to demand Korean independence and U.S. military withdrawal.[25]

War Department officials, facing budget cuts in early 1947, were intent to withdraw from Korea the 45,000 U.S. troops there, which they held would not impair the Far Eastern Military Command. But the State Department, especially Under Secretary Acheson, viewed Korea's economy as vital to Japan, and in late February an interdepartmental committee held that withdrawal meant "complete political defeat" by the Russians in the one area in the world where "we stand face to face alone." The committee endorsed Acheson's proposed three-year, $600 million aid program, including $250 million in FY 1948.[26]

This immense sum rivaled Truman's dramatic call to Congress on March 12 for $400 million to contain Communism in Greece and Turkey. The next day Rhee congratulated Truman for his historic anticommunist doctrine and proposed that he grant Korea independence and end efforts at a coalition regime. Rhee also drew the analogy that Truman would adopt three years later: "Korea is located in a strategic area similar to that of Greece." The president did not reply to Rhee, but Acheson told the Senate Foreign Relations Committee that the U.S. could be effective in Korea, where "the line has been clearly drawn between the Russians and ourselves."[27]

Truman shied from asking Congress for extensive Korean aid in 1947, but Acheson got the War Department to acquiesce in a reduced three-year program of $540 million, with $215 million for FY 1948. He approved an interdepartmental report positing that there could be no gaps "in our firmness in containing the U.S.S.R.," and that "a firm 'holding of the line' in Korea" would strengthen U.S. positions elsewhere. Still, Secretary of War Patterson was persistent that the U.S. should "get out of Korea at an early date," and Marshall proposed to reconvene the Joint Commission.[28]

Congress balked at Korean aid in 1947, and after Acheson left the State Department in June, the bill was withdrawn. The Joint Commission met during May–August but deadlocked again over Soviet insistence on consulting only "democratic" Koreans who favored trusteeship. The U.S. made a final proposal in August to create separate north-south legislatures that would choose their own representatives—based on population—to form a national legislature to negotiate Korea's independence with the Big Four. But the Soviets held that north-south legislatures perpetuated zonal divisions and that proportional representation favored the far more populous south, where—General Wedemeyer reported—Rhee and his allies impeded any accord.[29]

By September 1947 U.S. officials determined to "liquidate or reduce" their commitment of troops and money to Korea. The Defense Department and JCS stipulated that Korea was of "little strategic interest," and Kennan and the PPS concluded that "[we] should cut our losses and get out of there as gracefully but promptly as possible." Still, numerous officials argued that Korea had become "a symbol to the watching world of East-West" and that the U.S. had to stay for prestige reasons and to deny the Soviets military bases. Finally, Marshall chaired a senior staff meeting that concluded that the U.S. could not "'scuttle' and run" and would explore a Soviet overture for mutual troop withdrawal. But the Americans' chief goal was to take their proposal for separate legislatures and a national government to the UN.[30]

U.S. officials went to the General Assembly, where they predominated and were free from Soviet veto. On November 14 that body passed the U.S.-sponsored resolution to create a UN Temporary Commission on Korea (UNTCOK) to supervise zonal elections by March 31, 1948, and to advise on formation of a national government, with American and Soviet forces withdrawn within ninety days. But the Soviets denied UNTCOK access to North Korea, while Rhee—and even Hodge—sought to use UNTCOK to promote a Rhee-ruled, southern government. When UNTCOK members (Canada, Australia, and India) questioned their mandate to hold elections in South Korea only, the Truman administration said UNTCOK could not "bow the knee" to the Russians, and in February 1948 got the General Assembly sanction for south Korean elections, which Hodge set for May 10.[31]

Creation of a southern government provided means to contain Communism and to withdraw from Korea. This seemed highly desirable given repeated South Korean provocations of North Korea at the 38th parallel and Rhee's campaign charges that Hodge was not supporting a unified, independent Korea. In March, Marshall approved military withdrawal but asked the army to keep a flexible schedule. Shortly the NSC asserted that efforts to stabilize the south were intended to facilitate *"liquidation of the U.S. commitment of men and money in Korea with the minimum of bad effects"* and that the U.S. was to avoid involvement in Korea in order not to have to regard action there by any faction or other power as "a casus belli." On April 8 Truman approved NSC 8, which stated this Korea doctrine.[32]

Rhee and his supporters predominated in raucous elections in May, and he soon became president of the ROK. Hodge, bitter about Rhee, and the AMG departed Korea. Marshall named career diplomat John Muccio ambassador to Seoul, had General MacArthur attend Rhee's inauguration in August, and got the UN to recognize the ROK in December. Truman quickly granted de jure recognition on January 1, 1949. Meanwhile, in September 1948 North Korea formally became a Democratic People's Republic (DPRK), with Kim Il Sung as premier and predominant political authority. His foreign minister was Pak Hon-yong, who had headed the Communists in the south but who fled north in 1948. The Soviets recognized the DPRK in October and soon withdrew their forces that December. But 30,000 Korean veterans from China replaced them, and the new Korean People's Army got heavy weaponry, including airplanes, from the departing Russians. Both the DPRK and the ROK claimed to represent all of Korea. The UN admitted neither state and formed a permanent UNTCOK to seek Korean unity.[33]

The U.S. barely managed its client state. Rhee's repressive rule spurred rebellion, which his police quelled brutally, and soon put about one-quarter of South Korea under martial law. Rhee depended on U.S. support to sustain himself, yet declared that "Koreans must fight Russians" and that North Korea must surrender or have South Korea liberate it from Soviet aggression. U.S. officials worried about Rhee's mental stability and feared that he was opening South Korea to civil war or North Korean conquest. Truman directed economic aid to continue through the ECA, however, although in autumn 1948 Under Secretary of State Lovett held the ECA's proposed three-year $410 million program to be "too rich for my blood." The administration opted for more modest annual aid, and the army planned a December withdrawal, to match that of the Soviets. But Lovett got a six-month delay.[34]

In 1949 Rhee demanded that the U.S. triple the size of his army to 150,000 men. He proposed to invade North Korea, called for a U.S. security treaty and a Pacific-style NATO, and demanded to know whether the U.S. included Korea in its defense perimeter. Ambassador Muccio sought to assuage Rhee and warned him against invading North Korea. Acheson, who had become secretary of state in January 1949, chided Rhee for grave diplomatic breaches.[35]

But the secretary quickly advanced economic aid, and Truman's special message to Congress on June 7 proposed $150 million for FY 1950, part of a three-year $350–$385 million program. The president depicted Korea as a "testing ground" between democracy and Communism, with South Korea's success held to be a "beacon" to North Asians to resist Communism. State Department officials testified to Congress that the "rest of Asia" was watching the Korean aid bill, which House and Senate committees approved in June. But China bloc representatives, embittered in the summer of 1949 at the impending "loss" of China, delayed Congress' vote for six months.[36]

Meanwhile, NSC review of NSC 8 led the JCS to reaffirm that Korea was of little strategic value—MacArthur said it was indefensible—but to agree in late March 1949 to the revised NSC 8/2 conclusion that the U.S. should maintain a well-equipped ROK army of 65,000 troops and provide a military advisory group (KMAG), plus a police force of 35,000 and a small coast guard. This sufficed for internal order and compared reasonably to North Korea's estimated 46,000 troops and 56,000 police and paramilitary forces. The Army Department held that if North Korea attacked South Korea after U.S. troops departed on June 30, the U.S. should seek Security Council sanction and possibly organize broad military collaboration. But the army urged against comparing Greece and Korea: the West had not invested in wartime battles or postwar reconstruction in the latter, and it was not strategically vital. To extend the Truman Doctrine to Korea meant "prodigious effort and vast expenditures" far disproportionate to expected benefits.[37]

Korea lay outside America's Pacific defense perimeter, which MacArthur defined unofficially in 1948 and revealed to a reporter in March 1949. The Pacific had become an "Anglo-Saxon lake," he said. The U.S. line of defense "starts from the Philippines and continues through the Ryukyu Archipelago. . . . Then it heads back through Japan and the Aleutian Island chain to Alaska." State-Defense Department strategy debates soon led in December to NSC 48/1 and NSC 48/2, which called for the U.S. to "contain" and if possible "reduce" Soviet power in Asia and to strengthen defenses in Japan, the Ryukyus, and the Philippines. The NSC recommended continued aid to Korea but left it out of the defense line. This also served to defuse the efforts of Defense Secretary Louis Johnson—who sought to rival Acheson in the Cabinet—to increase aid to the GMD on Taiwan. Truman told Rhee that Korea's best defense was an efficient, compact army.[38]

After Truman's press conference statement in early January 1950 that the U.S. would intercede with respect to the PRC and Taiwan, Acheson gave his National Press Club speech on January 12 on U.S.-Asian relations, in which he blamed the GMD for its failure in China. At the same time he defined the U.S. defense perimeter in the Pacific as running from the Philippines to the Ryukyus to Japan and the Aleutians. In so doing he "omitted" both Korea and Taiwan. But his defense line—which denoted where the U.S. would act alone if attacked anywhere along that line—followed that of MacArthur, the JCS, and NSC 48, and met no public criticism in January 1950. Further, Acheson's statement that people subject to attack elsewhere in the Pacific had to rely on their own defense initially but also had recourse to the world's commitment to the UN Charter, accorded with the military's position. The secretary also balked at saying anything that might spur Rhee, who was still inciting border raids and making claims on the U.S., to undertake provocative action against North Korea.[39]

The next day Acheson told the Senate Foreign Relations Committee that South Korea could handle trouble begun solely by North Korea, and that in event of war the U.S. would act militarily in concert with the UN, although he recognized the prospect of a Soviet veto. When the House unexpectedly defeated the Korean Aid Bill on January 19, the Truman administration cut its first-year request to $120 million and rolled its program into an extension of the China Aid Act, which Truman signed in February. The administration got a second-year $100 million appropriation in June.[40]

Neither aid, nor Muccio's recall in April for White House consultation, halted Rhee's police-state tactics or claims on U.S. defense. Muccio put the best face he could on Rhee's politics and the U.S. commitment to Korea. But in May the Defense Department still held that Korean aid was a political matter because South Korea was of no value to the strategic position of the U.S. in the Far East, and Senator Tom Connally (TX), chairman of the Foreign Relations Committee, said that nothing could prevent the "communists" from overrunning Korea. Rhee denounced the one-foot-in, one-foot-out position of the U.S., but his political standing neared collapse on May 30 when he and his backers suffered sharp defeats in the elections for the National Assembly. Kim Il Sung now proposed to merge the two Korean legislatures and to hold national elections, although this was probably a ploy to undercut Rhee or to cover North Korea's war plans. As far as the CIA could tell on June 19, Kim's regime was firmly entrenched, held military superiority through its heavy weapons, and probably could gain control of South Korea by propaganda and sabotage. The DPRK needed Soviet logistical support for direct attack, but the Russians were unlikely to use their troops—or allow PRC forces—in such an undertaking, preferring instead to subvert the ROK.[41]

II

Truman believed the worst about the Soviets by 1950. This would be evident in his repeated public denunciations of the "new imperialism" and "new tyranny of the Soviet communists" who sought global conquest, albeit at present by subversion rather than military attack. Most important, Truman's views—and decision-making style—were reflected in his order in late January to the State and Defense Departments to reassess U.S. strategic plans in light of Soviet atomic and thermonuclear capabilities and his directive to the AEC to determine the feasibility of a hydrogen bomb.[42]

Unquestionably U.S. detection in early September 1949 of evidence of a Soviet atomic explosion (estimated to have occurred on August 29) spurred heightened debate in Washington about whether the administration had to give greater priority to building a hydrogen—or "Super"—bomb that would be perhaps 1,000 times more powerful than the bombs used against Japan. Scientists had long known of the thermonuclear fusion process that underlay Super, and in 1943 at Los Alamos physicist Edward Teller had proposed to focus on building that weapon. But most scientists thought it necessary first to build a relatively less complex fission, or atomic, bomb. After the war, Secretary Byrnes wanted work to proceed on both atomic weapons and Super, but many of the leading scientists saw no reason to build such an immensely destructive weapon. A secret scientific meeting at Los Alamos in April 1946 showed that a critical design problem remained unresolved, and little progress was made during the next two years.[43]

Moreover, for various reasons the U.S. government did not stress development of Super. Shortly after the war Truman disbanded the Interim Committee and its Scientific Panel, cutting himself off from the best source of advice on nuclear weapons, and as late as fall 1949 he seemed oblivious of work being done at Los Alamos. Most important, for atomic advice he relied on the military, especially General Leslie Groves (former Manhattan Project head) until his retirement in 1948. Thus Truman assumed, as Groves and others did, that the Soviets were at least a decade away from constructing an atomic bomb, despite CIA, AEC, and Pentagon reports that they were likely to have one by mid-1950. When word first came of the Soviet blast in the summer of 1949, Truman was disbelieving and then said that "German scientists in Russia did it." Then after AEC officials verified the atomic detonation, the president insisted that the agency chairman, David Lilienthal, and the detection committee sign a statement that they believed that the Russians had detonated a bomb. Still, the president's statement on September 23 referred only to an atomic explosion.[44]

Finally, the JCS showed little interest in Super during 1945–1949. This derived partly from belief that it was not a military weapon but one of mass destruction and that there were few targets to use it on in Russia. Interservice rivalries also slowed emphasis on nuclear weapons to be delivered by the Air Force. Most important, however, was JCS concern that development of Super would take too many dollars and critical nuclear resources away from increasing their stockpile of atomic bombs, which numbered about 250 in 1949, with each twice as powerful and constructed more efficiently than the 1945 bombs. These new bombs were now viewed as the most vital aspect of the contemplated U.S. air offensive that would serve either to preclude a Soviet attack or retaliate for one.[45]

This was the case despite the fact the JCS' most definitive study, headed by Lieutenant General Hubert R. Harmon, concluded in May 1949 that an atomic attack on the USSR would not cause the Soviets to surrender nor destroy the roots of Communism and might produce "psychological and retaliatory reactions detrimental to the achievement of Allied war objectives." The Harmon Report conclusions disappointed the JCS and Secretary Johnson, who did not inform the president that it had been completed until October. The secretary then managed to suppress the report and, despite several requests from the White House, kept it from Truman, who was never fully exposed to military arguments against an atomic air offensive.[46]

The Soviet atomic bomb, however, forced Washington to confront Super. Lewis Strauss, an investment banker, ally of Teller, and a Truman appointee to the AEC promptly called on his co-commissioners for a "quantum jump" in Super planning. Senator Brian McMahon, chairman of the Joint Committee on Atomic Energy (JCAE), insisted that it would be "fatal" for the U.S. if the Russians developed the bomb first. So too did Air Force Chief of Staff General Hoyt S. Vandenberg tell the JCAE on October 14 that the military believed that Super should be pushed to completion as soon as possible.[47]

Shortly the AEC's General Advisory Committee (GAC), composed of eminent scientists, met in Washington during October 28–30 and unanimously opposed building Super. They cited many technical reasons, including the need for large amounts of tritium (a scarce, radioactive isotope of hydrogen), which they said could be better used to make plutonium for increasingly powerful and mass-produced atomic bombs. But the GAC chair, J. Robert Oppenheimer, and five colleagues based their unconditional opposition to the H-bomb on moral grounds: its vast explosive power and radiation made it a threat to the earth and a "weapon of genocide." Two other GAC members, Nobel physicists Isidor I. Rabi and Enrico Fermi, further denounced Super as "an evil thing," and then proposed that the U.S. state that it would not proceed with the bomb and call upon other nations to pledge that they too would refrain from its development. In effect, Rabi and Fermi proposed a conditional renunciation of Super based on a verifiable ban on thermonuclear testing, which they said was readily detectable at advanced development stages. They also noted that the U.S. had enough atomic bombs to retaliate for production or use of Super. They intended to give Truman a realistic and politically acceptable alternative to building Super.[48]

The AEC soon weighed the GAC reports and opted 3–2 to resist Super. Lilienthal and Commissioners Henry Smyth and Sumner Pike strongly opposed development on technical grounds, lack of military-tactical gain, and likelihood of accelerating the arms race. Commissioners Strauss and Gordon Dean favored Super as possibly providing military and psychological value in deterring an aggressor; they also said they would not resist a secret diplomatic approach to the Russians to try to effect international control. Lilienthal forwarded the AEC and GAC reports to Truman on November 9, and ten days later he designated Lilienthal, Acheson, and Johnson as a special committee ("Z") of the NSC to advise him on the problem.[49]

Meanwhile, on November 21 Senator McMahon sent the president a long and impassioned letter favoring Super and insisting that the Russians were undoubtedly working on it. Two days later General Bradley, chairman of the JCS, said that Soviet possession of Super without U.S. possession was "intolerable" and that U.S. defense planning could not proceed without determining its feasibility. Then on November 25 Strauss wrote Truman that the U.S. had to be as completely armed as any possible enemy and that a Soviet "government of atheists" was unlikely to respond to moral opposition to building Super, which was no more a weapon of mass destruction than the atomic bomb initially appeared to be.[50]

At the same time Acheson talked with many officials, including Lilienthal—his cosponsor of their ill-fated plan for international control of atomic energy in 1946—who firmly opposed building Super for moral and technical reasons. Acheson also spoke with Oppenheimer but claimed to be perplexed by the physicist's desire to try to get the Russians to follow the U.S. example of restraint on Super. "How can you persuade a paranoid adversary to disarm 'by example'?" Acheson asked. Further, domestic politics concerned Acheson. As his science adviser, Gordon Arneson, would recall, the secretary took a contemptuous view of PPS head George Kennan's view that the time might be right to go to the UN to try to get a ban on use of atomic weapons. But so far as Acheson was concerned, even if the U.S. managed to get the Russians to sign a test ban, a congressional buzz saw would defeat the administration and its proposal.[51]

Thus Acheson had little political interest in trying to fight Super. When his Z Committee met for the first time on December 22, he let Lilienthal and Johnson—the latter a no-holds-barred proponent of Super—engage in head-to-head confrontation and then blamed the defense secretary's acerbic nature for the committee's not meeting for another five weeks, until the morning Truman would make his decision. Meanwhile, Acheson sought consensus on a policy of seeking only to establish the feasibility of Super, although he recognized that this would lead to irresistible pressure for development and production.[52]

Lilienthal meantime met privately with Bradley, who held that if America's allies were overrun, all the U.S. had to offer as aid was its atomic stockpile. But he conceded that the bombs were of declining value because both sides would be so badly beaten in an atomic war that it would be of little value to use them. Nonetheless, on January 13, 1950, Bradley signed off as JCS chairman on a memorandum to Johnson urging that the U.S. give top priority to determining Super's feasibility, along with delivery and ordnance issues. Although the JCS said there was no need for a "crash" program, and seemed to defer production, they insisted that the U.S. arsenal had to include a weapon of the greatest capability, namely, "the super bomb." Employing the sports metaphor that "the best defense is a good offense," the JCS insisted that Super would "improve our defense in its broadest sense, as a potential offensive weapon, a possible deterrent to war, a potential retaliatory weapon, as well as a defensive weapon against enemy forces." The JCS also claimed that Super would strengthen U.S. diplomacy, it would be "intolerable" for another nation but not the U.S. to possess Super, and it would shift the psychological balance of power "grossly" in favor of the U.S.—at least until the Russians developed their stockpile. Finally, alluding to the Rabi-Fermi test-ban proposal, the JCS alleged that such a "renunciation" might be construed as unilateral atomic disarmament.[53]

The JCS statement did not deal with Bradley's earlier concern about the utility of atomic or thermonuclear weapons or how they might help effect U.S. limited war aims. Nor did it distinguish defensive from offensive—or first-strike—weapons, resolve concern about the Super's financial and resources impact on other atomic programs, explain what psychological advantage it would provide for the U.S., or reveal why the Rabi-Fermi test ban proposal would be seen as unilateral disarmament. Still, Johnson now had what he wanted, and skirting his Z Committee colleagues, he sent Bradley's memorandum directly to Truman. On January 19 Admiral Sidney Souers, the president's NSC consultant, called Acheson to forewarn that "someone was playing on the unilateral side." But Souers also stated that the president had said that Bradley's memorandum "made a lot of sense and that he was inclined to think that was what we should do." Acheson conceded that Truman should be advised to move forward on feasibility, although it also meant "going quite a long way to committing ourselves to continue down that road." [54]

Truman's mind was made up—in fact, Souers later said, "[I]t had been at the very beginning." But White House officials believed that it was necessary to initiate the discussions among military and scientific advisers in order to show the country that the president made his decisions through an orderly process, not on the basis of "snap judgments." Thus, Z Committee met on the morning of January 31, with Acheson proposing they recommend studying the feasibility of Super, deferring its production pending further study of U.S. foreign policy aims in light of Soviet atomic-thermonuclear prospects, and informing the public about the Super feasibility undertaking. Johnson, however, opposed mention of deferring production, and Acheson and a dispirited Lilienthal gave way, with the latter vainly hoping that perhaps study of U.S. foreign policy aims might take place before any work was done on Super. But Acheson insisted that the pressure for a decision was too great, and "we must protect the president." [55]

Truman then met with his Z Committee, which recommended that the AEC determine the feasibility of Super (but did not warn that this really implied production), that the U.S. assess its foreign policy aims in light of Soviet atomic capabilities and thermonuclear possibilities, and that the president inform the public that the government was going "to continue work"—so that there would not appear to be any new departure—on atomic weapons and Super. The Z Committee also foreclosed the Rabi-Fermi test ban on grounds that the Soviets would never agree to necessary safeguards, although the physicists had said that easy detection of advanced development stages made these unnecessary. [56]

Truman was ready to act, without discussing alternatives. As soon as Lilienthal began to speak against moving forward on Super, the president cut him off and said that there was no alternative to going ahead. The meeting ended after just seven minutes. There was no review of the complex technical, strategic, and political issues that had been the focus of keen debate for the past four months. As Lilienthal wrote immediately after the meeting, his effort at dissent was like saying "'No' to steamroller," and "the Pres. was so clearly set on what he was going to do before we set foot inside the door." Later on Lilienthal would also say that from that day the AEC became "nothing more than a major contractor" for the Defense Department. Meanwhile, on January 31, 1950, the president informed the public that he had directed the AEC to continue its work on all forms of atomic weapons, "including the so-called hydrogen bomb." Four days later Truman told a White House aide that "there actually was no decision to make on the H-Bomb" and that the money had already been allotted to the AEC the previous fall. The U.S. had to make the H-bomb, the president said, even if no one wanted to use it, "if only for bargaining purposes with the Russians." [57]

There was some inevitability to Truman's decision given the politically charged atmosphere in the country owing to the Soviet atomic bomb, the rise of the PRC, and growing congressional and military pressure for action that might reassure an anxious public and seemingly restore U.S. supremacy. Truman was also unlikely to respond to the GAC's moral objections to Super, and he never had put before him for careful consideration the substantive and technical arguments, including the Rabi-Fermi proposal, against proceeding with Super. It is also true, however, that the president was impatient with scientific and intellectual arguments, as well as those who made them, and he inclined to accept JCS views and do what he or others considered to be "realistic." Further, as David Holloway has written, the Russians, who had begun work on their own hydrogen bomb in 1946 without evident soul searching, probably would not have been willing to sign an international accord such as the Rabi-Fermi proposal. [58]

Nonetheless, as Richard Rhodes has said, Truman's belief that he had to start work on Super if only for "bargaining purposes" with the Russians served to inaugurate a dubious presidential tradition of "maintaining and enlarging a threatening nuclear arsenal" that he had no intention of using—except to try to bargain—and that probably served no strategic or tactical purpose. Further, as Rabi later said, Truman did not seem to understand the nuclear weapons problem, and for him to have "alerted the world that we were going to make a hydrogen bomb at a time we didn't even know how to make one was one of the worst things he could have done." [59]

Regardless, just three days after Truman's decision "the roof fell in," as Lilienthal wrote upon hearing that the British had arrested the German-born physicist, Klaus Fuchs, now a naturalized British citizen and head of the Theoretical

Physics Division at their Harwell atomic energy site. Fuchs had come to the U.S. with a British scientific contingent in 1943, worked at Los Alamos in 1944–1946, and attended the secret meeting on Super there in 1946. Now on February 10, 1950, he confessed to spying for the Soviets during and after the war and was soon sentenced to fourteen years in prison under the Official Secrets Act.[60]

Fuchs' arrest inspired immediate claims from Strauss, Johnson, the JCS, and others that the Soviets were ahead on Super, and demands that the U.S. begin an "all-out" development and production program. Fuchs had passed valuable information about plutonium and an implosion-style (Nagasaki) atomic bomb, but the information he had obtained in 1946 on Super would soon be shown to be of no value in building the bomb. Nonetheless, the pressures for Super—the JCS now wanted development even at the expense of atomic bombs—seemed irresistible. Thus on March 9, 1950, Z Committee reconvened (with Dean having replaced Lilienthal as AEC head) and recommended that the president instruct the AEC to continue to make preparations for "quantity production of materials needed for thermonuclear weapons" with no delay between determination of feasibility and possible production. The next day Truman approved the all-out program for Super, with instruction that the decision, unlike that of January 31, be kept secret from the public.[61]

Work on Super moved slowly until a new design was proposed in April 1951, and in May scientists effected a smaller fission-fusion explosion. Truman then gave permission to build a device to test the principle behind the new Super—code-named Mike—in the summer or fall of 1952. Meanwhile, in June Vannevar Bush, who had headed the wartime Office of Scientific Research and Development and now served on—and spoke for—a State Department Panel of Consultants on Disarmament, proposed a delay until 1953. Bush explained the delay as intended to give a new president a chance to try to negotiate agreement for a standstill along the lines of the Rabi-Fermi proposal before the U.S. and the Soviet Union entered into an inevitable cycle of building increasingly fearsome atomic weapons. The science adviser explained that the Russians had not gotten helpful information from Fuchs on Super and still trailed in the race to build that weapon, but that they would gain important information about how the U.S. made its bomb from the fallout of a hydrogen explosion. Further, there was no military rationale for the weapon, and since the start of the Korean War in June 1950, military commanders had stressed need for smaller atomic weapons. Bush also contended that to explode Super as the last act of the Truman administration would send a wrong signal to the world—especially the Russians—whereas postponement had the potential to become a "decisive act of statesmanship."[62]

Truman and Acheson showed interest in the proposal. But strong objections came from the military chieftains, Senator McMahon (who hinted at seeking impeachment), and Teller and his supporters. There was also growing bitterness over the stalemated Korean War, more revelations about Soviet atomic spying, and McCarthyite charges about the administration's failure to confront Communism at home or abroad. Thus the president would go no further than to propose to delay Mike until after the November elections. But protests from officials involved in the countdown at the test site led Truman to give in to the detonation of Mike—ten and a half megatons of explosive—on November 1, 1952, on the Eniwetok atoll in the South Pacific. The U.S. then moved under the Eisenhower administration to test the first "true" hydrogen bomb—fifteen megatons of explosives—in February 1954.[63]

The Soviets meanwhile moved forward with their Super project and own bomb design—effected in 1948—led by physicists Igor Tamm and Andrei Sakharov who, along with others, believed that the U.S. could not be allowed a second monopoly and that it was necessary to restore the balance of power. U.S. test of Mike in 1952 added urgency to the Soviet work on thermonuclear weapons. The Russians tested a single-stage fission weapon that was "boosted" by a thermonuclear reaction on August 20, 1953, and then exploded a "true" Super on November 22, 1955, only twenty months after the U.S. had done so.[64]

Soviet scientists were at once elated by their success, and despaired—like many of their American counterparts—that control of these weapons was not in their hands but those of government officials, who were unlikely to heed their warnings. In fact, shortly after the Soviet test of Super, Igor Kurchatov, who had overseen the Soviet quest for atomic weapons since 1943, exclaimed that the hydrogen bomb "must not ever be allowed to be used," while Sakharov would shortly begin his dissident campaign to halt atmospheric testing. Nonetheless, the U.S.-Soviet race to build intercontinental ballistic missiles capable of carrying atomic and miniaturized thermonuclear weapons to rain mutual destruction upon each other was already under way. That moment for decisive statesmanship, fleeting and politically difficult at best, had passed.[65]

Meanwhile, during the winter of 1950 State and Defense Department officials, led by Paul Nitze, who had replaced Kennan as head of the PPS, readied their analysis of America's global position in light of Soviet atomic-thermonuclear abilities. Nitze was a protégé of Forrestal and admirer of the military, and was convinced that the Soviets meant to defeat the U.S. and were ready to probe "soft spots." NSC 68, "A Report . . . on United States Objectives and Programs for National Security," prepared in great part by Nitze, was sent to Truman on April 7. NSC 68 ranged far beyond its directive and hyperbolically reaffirmed the administration's assumptions that dated from early 1946—

when the president rejected Secretary Byrnes' Moscow accords and Kennan sent his "long telegram"—and that underlay the Truman Doctrine of 1947 and the recent NSC 48 report that extended containment to Asia. But now the emphasis would not be on defending major areas of interest, such as Western Europe, or critical places such as the Turkish Straits, but every area—regardless of size or value—along a defense perimeter that ran around the globe.[66]

NSC 68 posited that the U.S. and the Soviet Union were the world's only two power centers and that the Soviets were animated by "a new fanatic faith, antithetical to our own." The report said that the Soviets sought to solidify their power at home and in their satellites, then to dominate the Eurasian landmass, and ultimately to impose "absolute authority over the rest of the world." Only the U.S. could keep them from their self-appointed goal, but it had to act before the Soviets' further extension of power precluded forming a countervailing coalition. As Robert Lovett, under secretary of state in 1947–1948 and now returned to private life—but a strong NSC 68 supporter—said, "[J]ust because there is not much shooting as yet does not mean that we are in a cold war. It is not a cold war; it is a hot war."[67]

Thus NSC 68 recommended "affirmative" containment, proposing to mobilize the U.S. to develop vast stores of atomic and conventional arms; build major military forces; forge a U.S.-led alliance system; and foster extensive economic-military aid programs, covert operations, and psychological warfare. This preponderance of power would reduce Soviet power on its periphery, promote independent countries in Eastern Europe, revive national aspirations within the Soviet Union, and foster fundamental change in the Soviet system. Nitze did not put a price tag on his programs because he wanted to assess security on its own terms, but NSC 68 envisioned increasing defense spending over five years from Truman's current $14.3 billion to $50 billion, or from 5 percent to 20 percent of GNP.[68]

Critics of NSC 68 said it was too militaristic and overstated Soviet capabilities and intentions. As John Gaddis has written, it established a "negotiating posture that required Soviet capitulation." Defense Secretary Johnson, a fiscally conservative politician-businessman and former American Legion head and assistant secretary of war in the 1930s, initially objected to the rearmament costs. But Nitze garnered support from the diplomatic bureaucracy, the JCS, and Acheson, who later wrote that NSC 68 was intended to "bludgeon the mass mind of 'top government'" so that the president could make a decision and it could be carried out. Acheson also wished to bludgeon Truman to lift his $13.5 billion military spending cap and even engage in deficit spending.[69]

Truman was not ready to be bludgeoned or to decide, although he viewed the world through the same Cold War lens as NSC 68. But the rub, even for a prepared president, was money for the new military mobilization. NSC planners insisted that the funds would come from an expanding economy and increased government revenues. Truman, however, had committed to reduce the defense budget to $13.5 billion for FY 1951 and worried about higher taxes, a diminished Fair Deal, and budget deficits. He ordered that NSC 68 be reviewed and that the report be kept secret, a vain hope as immediate press leaks indicated. Still, during the next months the Budget Bureau criticized NSC calculations, the JCS vacillated, and the president, even while assailing Soviet imperialism and promoting military aid because "the problem of security is world wide," did not seek increased defense spending.[70]

By June 1950 it seemed unlikely that NSC 68 would be decided upon or implemented in the next few years unless—as Acheson would later say with a sense of vindication—the Soviets were "stupid enough" to instigate North Korea's attack on South Korea. The secretary should also have said that NSC 68 shaped the way Truman and his senior officials viewed and responded to this conflict, which soon escalated into a major U.S. war in Asia that became the basis for a vast, long-term military (including Super) buildup.[71]

III

In the early morning of June 25 in Korea, more than 100,000 DPRK troops, armed with Soviet-supplied tanks, heavy artillery, and planes, launched major assaults across the 38th parallel along the Ongjin peninsula northwest of Seoul, to the east at Kaesong and Chunchon, and on South Korea's east coast south of Kangnung. Kaesong fell within hours, and Seoul after three days. Rhee's government and forces retreated south to Taejon.[72]

Truman would never deviate from his June 26 proclamation that the Korean War was the result of North Korea's "unprovoked aggression" and "lawless action," and Acheson never qualified his assertion that "no serious, honest scholar" could ever doubt that Kim's forces attacked without warning, provocation, or justification. President and secretary blamed Stalin for masterminding North Korea's attack, which they saw as a prelude to later assaults in Asia, the Middle East, or Europe, although for diplomacy's sake they initially refrained from public accusation.[73]

The origins of the war were highly complex, however. Both Kim Il Sung and Syngman Rhee had proclaimed their intent to unify Korea—including by military means—under their rule, and their forces had clashed many times at the 38th parallel. Although historian Bruce Cumings has stretched a point by denying legitimacy to the question of who started the Korean War, there is much to be said for his overarching answer that both the U.S. and Soviet Union held sway over Korean regimes and systems that they wished to extend to each other's zones—but could not do so—and that blame for the war must be attributed to "everyone" who took part in the intricate tapestry of events of 1945–1950.[74]

It is now clear, however, that from the time Kim first visited Stalin in March 1949, the North Korean leader pressed for military support to "liberate" South Korea, and he continued to do this until he gained his way. Kim's emphasis on military reunification was not surprising given his soldier's background, the similar view of many postwar Korean revolutionaries, and the fact that Mao was waging war to unify China (although no formal boundary existed between the GMD and CCP). Moreover, Rhee had repeatedly declared his intention to march north and would have done so had the U.S. allowed it. In addition, Kim probably believed the claim of his foreign minister, Pak Hon-yong, who had headed the Communists in the South before fleeing to the North—that an attack against the ROK would cause some 200,000 followers and other guerilla forces to rise up and overthrow Rhee's regime. Finally, Kim's 1949–1950 economic plan was having difficulty, and he probably wanted to bring the wealthier south into a national planning program. In fact, the main purpose of his visit to Moscow in March 1949 was to seek economic help, not to plan a war.[75]

Stalin was of no mind to prompt war in Korea in 1949 or to confront the U.S. When Kim raised the subject with him on March 7, Stalin resisted by citing North Korea's military weakness, the Soviet-American agreement on the 38th parallel, and the prospect of U.S. intervention. And when Kim mentioned ROK assaults on the DPRK, Stalin insisted that "the 38th parallel had to be kept peaceful. It is very important."[76]

Continued North Korean pressure led Stalin to order his embassy in Pyongyang to reappraise the situation. The Soviet chargé, Grigori Tunkin, thought that Kim might win a limited action to seize the Ongjin peninsula and Kaesong, but protracted conflict was inadvisable. He feared that the U.S., because it had failed in China, might now intervene strongly to save South Korea and Rhee. Ambassador Terneti Shtykov was more optimistic. He agreed Kim could not win a full-scale war, but favored limiting action in the Ongjin peninsula and inciting revolution in the south. Better to act now, Shtykov believed, than to allow Rhee to ready his troops for an attack. As for the U.S., the China case and recent troop withdrawals from Korea made intervention unlikely.[77]

Stalin referred the matter to his Politburo, which in September instructed Shtykov to inform Kim that he lacked the requisite military strength for an attack, while limited action might start a war and give the U.S. an excuse to intervene. Thus unification through revolution was the only course. At the same time, Moscow's emphasis on need for greater preparedness led the North Koreans to increase their efforts and to retaliate sharply for an incident near the 38th parallel. But Kremlin leaders reprimanded Shtykov for inciting this action. Then on January 17, 1950, Kim told the ambassador that "I can't sleep at night because I keep thinking of unification," and asked for another meeting with Stalin. The Soviet leader assented and now pledged to help with this "large matter," which required "thorough preparation" and the aversion of "large risk," to wit, U.S. intervention.[78]

Kim and Pak pressed their case in Moscow during March 31–April 25. They insisted that a surprise attack would bring victory in three days, that 200,000 Communists and other guerillas would join the battle, and that the U.S. neither intended nor would have time to intervene. Stalin said that Soviet concerns in the West precluded any aid but that Kim should consult Mao, who best understood "Oriental matters." Still, apparently lacking strong reason to oppose Kim's plan, the Soviet leader said he would put it to the Politburo but also warned that "if you get kicked in the teeth, I shall not lift a finger. You have to ask Mao for all the help." The North Koreans went home, but soon Kim secretly visited Beijing, where he told Mao of his decision to reunify Korea militarily. The PRC leader cabled Stalin for further information on May 14. Stalin replied that due to "the changed international situation" the USSR had consented to Kim's plan, pending Chinese agreement.[79]

Why did Stalin consent, with some reluctance, to the North Korean invasion, and what had changed in the international situation? To be sure, the Soviet atomic bomb increased Stalin's confidence vis-à-vis the U.S. He may well have accepted Kim's view that proper armaments for the DPRK and uprisings in the south would bring quick victory, with the U.S. unwilling or unable to intervene, as indicated not only by the China case and troop withdrawals from South Korea, but Acheson's January 12 National Press Club speech in which he had omitted Korea from America's defense perimeter. Moreover, given that Stalin supported Mao's intent to unify China by taking Taiwan, there seemed little reason to deny Kim a similar option. And a unified Korean satellite would permit the Soviets to strengthen their security in the face of U.S. reconstruction of Japan and current efforts to negotiate a separate peace treaty.[80]

But perhaps more important—ironically—was Stalin's ambivalent view of the CCP triumph in China and the Sino-Soviet treaty. To be sure, Stalin had ceded to Mao the role of presiding over revolution in the East, but that did not eliminate traditional Sino-Soviet rivalry or contention over whether Moscow or Beijing—or Stalin or Mao—spoke for world revolution. Moreover, although the Sino-Soviet treaty of February 1950 bolstered the Soviet Union against third-party attacks, Mao's insistence on eliminating unequal treaties had forced Stalin to yield Soviet postwar gains in Xinjiang and Manchuria, including long-term control over Lushun, Dalian, and the Chinese Eastern Railroad. But now a quick North Korean victory would bring Soviet access to the warm-water ports of Inchon and Pusan and a prospective railroad from Aoji in Korea to Kraskino in the USSR. Further, Soviet control over Korea would delimit PRC influence in Asia and buttress the USSR against Japan and the U.S. And if the U.S. now denied Taiwan to the PRC, or if the U.S. and PRC fought over Taiwan, or in Korea, then the Chinese would be dependent on the Soviets for economic and military aid.

Hence, it seems that Stalin's sponsorship of North Korea's attack in 1950 derived not from a design for global expansion so much as desire to regain the (tsarist) concessions that he had been compelled to retrocede to Mao, to reassert his primacy over the world revolutionary movement, and to strengthen his position in Korea against the U.S. and Japan. And this Stalin proposed to do relatively inexpensively by approving a limited attack in which he promised the North Korean perpetrators—who had their own mind and agenda—nothing more than armaments and military plans. At the same time, he also compelled the Chinese to be complicit in the attack and later to bear the burden for it.[81]

As for the Chinese and North Koreans, there were ideological and political-military links between them, but these did not count for much in early 1950. Korean and Chinese Communists had had close ties since the 1920s, and in the 1930s some Koreans—including Kim, who spoke fluent Chinese—joined the CCP and the Anti-Japanese United Army to wage guerilla war against the invading forces that had suppressed Korea for decades and now were seeking to subjugate China. Approximately 100,000 Korean residents in China joined the PLA to do battle in the northeast. After the war, during 1946–1948, the PLA used North Korea as a base of supply, communications, and refuge in their battle against Jiang and the GMD. Then during 1949–1950 Mao sent more than 50,000 PLA soldiers of Korean nationality back to North Korea.[82]

This was not part of any design for aggression, however. Mao's primary focus in early 1950 was on defeating the GMD on Taiwan (who were assaulting the PRC in U.S.-made planes and ships) and beginning major demobilization of his very large army, reducing military expenses, and starting conversion to a civilian economy. Further, Kim was an intense nationalist who rebelled at Korea's historical deference to the Middle Kingdom of China, and he did not even go to Beijing until Stalin told him he had to gain the support of the PRC for his proposed action.[83]

During Kim's stay in Beijing from May 13 to May 16, he told Mao only that Stalin had approved an attack on South Korea. Kim kept secret all the details about when and how it would occur, and that the Soviet Union was shipping supplies by sea rather than by rail through China in order to keep PRC leaders in the dark. Mao did inquire about possible U.S. intervention. But Kim said this was unlikely or that the war would end first, and the PRC leader apparently assented. Kim also firmly rebuffed Mao's offer to deploy three Chinese armies along the Chinese-Korean borders. In sum, Kim got Mao's cautious blessing for an attack but provided no significant information. In turn, the PRC leader now began to speed preparations to take Taiwan (but had to postpone the operation in mid-June because the buildup took longer than expected) and to effect a successful domestic demobilization-reconversion program. PRC officials were soon taken aback by North Korea's "surprise attack"—as they called it—on June 25, and they remained embittered for years afterwards at Kim's secretiveness and the danger his action brought to China's border. They also did not send any assistance to North Korea until October, when they entered the war.[84]

Stalin, meanwhile, expedited supplies to North Korea and instructed his battle-hardened generals to draft an attack plan. This "all out offensive," as Muccio termed it, was so large and swift that U.S. and UN officials had no reason to believe Kim's later claims that his troops were engaged in a "counterattack." Thus, whatever the long-term causes of Korea's strife, North Korea began this new phase of overt war. And Kim, Stalin, and perhaps Mao as well, all guessed wrong about how Truman would react.[85]

As family and friends noted, Truman was determined to fight even as he prepared to fly from Independence to Washington on June 25. During his cross-country flight, he recalled, he compared "communist" action in Korea to that of fascist leaders in the 1930s and vowed to resist aggression this time. On the way from the Washington airport, Truman said "By God, I'm going to let them have it," which Defense Secretary Johnson strongly supported. But Under Secretary of State James Webb cautioned that the president might first review his senior officials' recommendations. Truman agreed, although the next day—harkening to Rhee's analogy of 1947, if not the JCS warning of 1949—he would tell White House aide Elsey that "Korea is the Greece of the Far East" and that if the U.S. stood idly by, the Communists would take over Iran, or perhaps the whole Middle East. Similarly, on June 27 Truman told a group of congressmen that "if we let Korea down, the Soviets will keep right on going and swallow up one piece of Asia after another," and maybe the Middle East and Europe. If it came to it, he wrote the next day, he would "go all-out to maintain our position."[86]

Intelligence and diplomatic reports unanimously reinforced Truman's view that the Korean conflict was part of Soviet global strategy to test American "resolve" to resist their expansion. As one official said, the Russians saw Asia as their "oyster," to be opened to their domination by destruction of South Korea, and the U.S. had to take more than "half measures" to halt this aggression—

which only MacArthur, initially, doubted was Soviet-led and "all out." So too did British and French officials analogize to the 1930s, likening the attack to Hitler's "plucking the leaves of an artichoke." And shortly when the Norwegian ambassador, Wilhelm Munthe de Morgenstierne, told Acheson that Europe's small nations regarded America's reaction as "a great moment in history," the secretary replied that "it was a turning point in history."[87]

Meanwhile, in the afternoon of June 25 the U.S. sponsored a resolution in the Security Council calling for immediate North Korean withdrawal of its troops above the 38th parallel. Acheson also demanded through diplomatic channels that the Soviets use their "controlling influence" to halt North Korea's attack, although he let the embassy in Moscow soften the words so they did not appear to challenge Moscow directly, but then undercut slim chances for success by publicizing his approach. Regardless, the UN resolution passed 9–0, with Yugoslavia abstaining and the Soviet Union absent because it had been boycotting the Security Council since January, ostensibly to protest that body's failure to seat the PRC in place of the GMD.[88]

Conceivably, Stalin might have ordered his UN delegate, Jacob Malik, to rush back to veto the resolution and succeeding ones. Significantly, however, the Soviet leader ignored Deputy Foreign Minister Andrei Gromyko's and others' advice that he do so, and Malik would not return to the Security Council until it was his turn to chair that body in August. No one is exactly certain why Stalin did not try to thwart the U.S. in the Security Council. Perhaps he thought that North Korea would win swiftly, precluding UN action. He may also have hoped, as some officials suspected at the time, that the U.S. and PRC might come into conflict over Taiwan or in Korea, ending all chances for PRC entry into the UN and leaving Moscow as the spokesman there for world Communism. Moreover, by allowing the U.S. to act under UN auspices, Stalin averted bilateral PRC-U.S. conflict that might have allowed Beijing to invoke the Sino-Soviet treaty and thereby draw the USSR into confrontation with the U.S. In short, if Stalin's initial aim was a quick North Korean victory, a protracted war that produced long-term Sino-American conflict and alienation was also an attractive alternative.[89]

In the meantime, just before Blair House deliberations began on the night of June 25, Webb advised Truman not to move "too fast" and to focus on Acheson's proposals. The president, of course, was most comfortable having his secretary take the lead in policy discussions. He also permitted General Bradley, the JCS chairman, to precede talks by reading to the group a recent MacArthur memorandum urging Taiwan's reinforcement and warning that Communist control of this "unsinkable aircraft carrier" would be a disaster for U.S. strategic interests. But at this critical juncture the president, more than anyone else, put his stamp of firmness on policy making and the decisions that followed.[90]

Acheson opened the conference with four proposals that met no dissent: to have MacArthur send military supplies and a survey team to Korea; to permit U.S. planes to cover evacuation from Seoul and to attack North Korean tanks or planes that interfered; to increase aid to Indochina; and to move the Seventh Fleet in the Philippines toward the Taiwan Strait to preclude a PRC assault on Taiwan, or vice versa. Acheson did not want the U.S. to "tie up" with Jiang and said that Taiwan's future status should be determined by the UN—"or by the Japanese peace treaty," Truman interjected—thus signaling reversion from the long-held Cairo-Potsdam commitments that Taiwan would be returned to China.

Bradley gave quick and strong support to all four proposals. He articulated the consensus that the Russians were not ready for war and that U.S. troops should not be committed to Korea. But the situation there offered as good an occasion as anywhere else for "drawing the line," he said. When Air Force Chief of Staff General Hoyt Vandenberg warned against assuming that the Russians would not fight—and noted the proximity of their air bases, and rights for their jets in Shanghai—Truman asked if the Air Force could knock out Soviet bases in the Far East. Vandenberg replied yes, "if we used A-Bombs."

The president shortly summarized the orders he would issue to effect Acheson's recommendations, with Johnson adding that instructions to MacArthur should not allow him too much authority. Truman also asked for a global review of possible Soviet action and then instructed the Air Force "to prepare plans to wipe out all Soviet air bases in the Far East." He cautioned that this was a request for plans, not action, but it was indicative of his mood. The president stressed that the U.S. was working for the UN and would not act further until it knew whether North Korea would abide by the Security Council resolution calling for its withdrawal from South Korea. Shortly afterwards Truman wrote Acheson that if he had not been able to get a UN special session, "we would have had to go into Korea alone."[91]

Truman remained of tough mind on June 26. He warned North Korea that its lawless action would not be tolerated and told the wavering South Koreans that other nations had defended themselves in more dire straits. Then at his second Blair House meeting, upon hearing that the first Yak fighter had been shot down, he said that he "hope[d] it was not the last," and quickly agreed to lift all restrictions on air and naval action and provide full support for ROK forces. But no action was to be taken north of the 38th parallel, he said, "not yet."

The president next approved moving the Seventh Fleet directly into the Taiwan Strait, said that he wanted to return Taiwan to Japan under MacArthur's command, and then produced the letter he had recently received from Jiang offering to resign if this would clarify Taiwan's governance. For Truman, however, the issue was that this might serve "to get Chinese forces helping us." This led Acheson to warn against further involvement with Jiang or Taiwan's administration. But for the president the idea of using GMD troops, which he had raised before an offer came from Taiwan, would die hard. Meanwhile, he reviewed a proposed resolution to have the UN call for support for the ROK, said that he had done all he could for five years to keep the peace, but now had to act in behalf of the UN, although "I don't want war."[92]

At the White House on June 27, Truman informed congressional leaders of U.S. actions in behalf of the UN in Korea, but on its own in Indochina and the Philippines. Then in a public statement he assailed Communism (at British request the term "centrally-directed communism" was dropped), which he said had moved beyond subversion to "armed invasion," and warned that Communist occupation of Taiwan threatened Pacific security and U.S. forces. That night the Security Council, absent the Soviets, voted 7–1 to pass the U.S.-sponsored resolution urging UN members to assist South Korea to repel North Korea's attack and to secure regional peace and security. There was no mention of the administration's unilateral decision to neutralize the Taiwan Strait. But Mao saw his chance to unify the PRC shattered, and he branded the action as "armed aggression" and tantamount to a declaration of war.[93]

Caution still seemed the order of the day on June 28. Acheson readied a policy statement, in event the Soviets entered Korea, that commitment of U.S. air and naval forces did not imply willingness to fight a wider war and that they were to defend themselves but not aggravate the situation. Truman told the NSC that he did not intend to "back out" of Korea unless military action elsewhere dictated this. But he denied an Air Force request to hit military targets in North Korea and reinforced the order that U.S. forces should not cross the 38th parallel.[94]

The next day the NSC consultants, preparing the Truman-ordered survey, concluded that the Soviets were unlikely to enter the conflict or to spur wider war. The Russians now confirmed this view. In their reply to Acheson's earlier charge to them to restrain North Korea, they stated that they would not intervene in Korea's "internal affairs" and blamed South Korea for the conflict. Uncertainty about the PRC remained, but NSC advisers belligerently held that if PRC troops entered North Korea, the U.S. should bomb them there, and if they entered South Korea—as Kennan said—the U.S. should go north of the 38th parallel and bomb Manchuria. General Richard Lindsay, the JCS representative, seemed mainly concerned not to have ordinary bombing ruin prospects for later use of atomic weapons. But now the JCS sought only to bomb military targets in North Korea.[95]

At his afternoon press conference on June 29, Truman charged that a "bunch of bandits" had attacked South Korea. He readily agreed with a reporter's characterization that the U.S. was engaged in a UN-sanctioned "police action," imagery that fit with his view of the U.S. as a world "sheriff" and his contention that "we are not at war." He refused to comment on use of ground troops or atomic weapons. But at an NSC meeting afterwards, Truman authorized air strikes at military targets in North Korea—MacArthur had begun this on his own—and use of U.S. troops to protect the port of Pusan and air bases in southeast Korea. He wanted the JCS to be "damned careful," however, that their directive, based on Acheson's earlier statement ordering defensive action in event of Russian entry, said nothing that appeared to anticipate war with the Soviets. The goal was to "push the North Koreans behind the line," not to overcommit to actions that might prompt war, or become pretext for PRC intervention, Acheson added. Most important, the JCS directive instructed MacArthur that bombing was to remain well clear of Soviet and Chinese borders.[96]

Despite his caution, Truman inclined again to accept Jiang's recently reported offer of 33,000 GMD troops. But Acheson insisted that having committed a U.S. fleet to protect Taiwan, it would seem incongruous to redeploy the island's likeliest defenders, who also needed to be reequipped. The president was persistent that they take it up with the JCS next day.[97]

Secretary of the Army Frank Pace reinforced Truman's inclination when he telephoned at 4:47 A.M. June 30 to bring word from MacArthur—who had surveyed the Korean front—that disaster loomed unless he immediately deployed a U.S. regimental combat team and readied two divisions in Japan for an early counteroffensive. Truman instantly approved using the combat regiment and, after a 7 A.M. CIA briefing, told Pace and Johnson to weigh giving MacArthur two U.S. divisions and Jiang's two divisions. "What will that do to Mao Tze Tung [*sic*] we don't know," Truman wrote. He did not want an Asian war but suspected, as usual, that the Russians were planning a Black Sea or Persian Gulf attack, and he wanted all the help he could get.[98]

Two hours later Truman informed his senior advisers that he had committed a combat regiment, and he proposed to use GMD troops. Acheson, more candid than earlier, said that this might bring PRC entry into Korea, and perhaps Taiwan. The JCS balked at the quality of Jiang's forces and their need for great logistical-supply support. The president finally backed off. Then with little explanation—and no dissent—he swiftly approved orders to give MacArthur full authority to deploy two U.S. divisions (as part of a larger buildup) and to have the navy blockade North Korea. Shortly Truman told a bipartisan group of fifteen congressional leaders at the White House, and soon thereafter the public, that he had authorized MacArthur to undertake air and naval strikes on North Korea and to use "certain supporting ground units" in the south. The phrasing may not have been intended to deceive, but it obscured the size and scope of the president's commitment of ground forces to front-line conflict in South Korea. As Acheson later wrote, "[W]e were then fully committed to Korea."[99]

Commitment to wage war required congressional authority, as Republican Senator James Kem (MO) said on June 27. In a bitter speech the next day, the leading Republican conservative, Senator Robert Taft, demanded that Acheson resign and that Truman get a congressional resolution approving war, which Taft proposed to sign. Similarly, when congressional leaders met at the White House on June 30, Republican Senator Alexander Smith (NJ) proposed that the president seek a congressional resolution of support, and Republican Senator Kenneth Wherry (NE) twice sharply criticized the commitment of ground forces without Congress' approval. Truman said he would seek Congress' sanction if it proved necessary, but he hoped to suppress the "bandits" in Korea without that. The meeting ended when Dewey Short (MO), ranking Republican on the House Armed Services Committee, interjected thanks in behalf of most of Congress for Truman's leadership.[100]

Truman knew he needed Congress' sanction to commit U.S. forces abroad, but he determined to skirt this. On June 26 he asked Tom Connally, Senate Foreign Relations chairman, about a war declaration. The Texan offered the analogy—appealing to Truman—that police permission was not required to shoot a burglar in one's house and that Congress would tie the president's hands debating any resolution. Hence, he had to act as commander in chief. Truman told Army Secretary Pace that he did not need Congress' approval because "they are all with me," but after the June 30 meeting he asked Acheson to research the issue. The lawyerly secretary provided a list of eighty-seven precedents in which presidents had used troops without Congress' approval. Acheson insisted that Truman had full authority to act as president and commander in chief but proposed that he report his actions to Congress. The secretary also readied a resolution for that body.[101]

At a July 3 meeting, Acheson proposed that Truman give his report to Congress, which should then vote a resolution of support for action taken by the U.S. The secretary said that Truman's action as commander in chief did not require official approval. The president agreed, but Senate Majority Leader Scott Lucas (PA) worried that a full report might appear to be a request for a war declaration. He feared that an irreconcilable minority would prolong debate on any resolution, which Acheson later said would have demoralized U.S. troops. Truman deferred a decision, and a burst of public buying/hoarding made him fear that any message on Korea would spark a call for economic controls. But Acheson persisted about a public report. This led the president to give two addresses two weeks later.[102]

Truman ought to have sought a war declaration or its equivalent. To be sure, a majority in Congress and the public supported his actions during June 26–30. He also took an extremely broad view of his authority as commander in chief and believed, at least initially, that he was engaged in a limited "police action" to defeat "bandits." But neither congressional and public support, nor concern that debate would dishearten troops, obviated need for Congress' authority to deploy forces. Truman might have claimed to have acted in an emergency when he agreed to air and naval action on June 25–26 in South Korea, when he allowed strikes at North Korea on June 29, or when he committed a combat regiment to defend Pusan and air bases on June 30. But when he authorized deployment of two divisions of ground troops—with more in the offing—he knew, or should have known, that he was committing the nation to more than limited police action. Further, Congress was still in session and could have been recalled thereafter. But as White House aide Elsey recalled, Truman was never of a mind to seek a resolution from Congress, and he doubted that Democratic leadership could get one through, despite limited opposition and even Taft's pledge to vote for intervention.[103]

It is also beside the point to say that no resolution would have silenced critics after the Korean conflict turned long, bitter, and inconclusive. In fact, had the president initially sought congressional approval to restore South Korea, this might have given his administration more reason to halt action—or to seek new authorization—before crossing the 38th parallel in October and committing the nation to far wider war than anyone had anticipated in June. But Truman took the easier political course by not seeking congressional sanction. In so doing, he opened the way not only for attacks on "Truman's war" and his presidency, but for his successors to make extravagant claims of presidential power while leading the nation into conflicts that ultimately diminished the stature of the office that Truman revered.[104]

Truman may also have committed himself to greater difficulty than he foresaw in early July 1950 when he formalized the JCS recommendation that MacArthur be named to head the newly established UN Command (UNC). The president did this despite his long-standing dislike of "Mr. Prima Donna, Brass Hat, Five Star MacArthur," who he said was "a supreme egotist who regarded himself as a god," withheld information, and liked to make—rather than carry out—policy. Further, MacArthur was past seventy years old and fully occupied as both head of Japan's occupation and commander of U.S. forces in the Far East. Still, the JCS put forward his name only, and Truman had reason to worry about political repercussions if he passed over the favorite general of the Republican right wing and China bloc. Truman probably also harbored hope that they would sanction his Asian policy if he chose MacArthur.[105]

Thus, as the White House staff readied speeches for the president to deliver to Congress and the nation, they sent advance copies to MacArthur to solicit supportive comments, which arrived with fifteen minutes to spare before Truman's late-night public address on July 19. First, however, the president detailed for Congress his administration's actions during June 25–30, which he said derived from "basic moral principle" and the "lessons from history," namely, that failure to resist aggression in the 1930s spurred only more aggression. He deplored North Korea's "naked, deliberate, unprovoked aggression" and Communist readiness to resort to armed attack. Thus he had to increase military support for the Philippines and Indochina, neutralize Taiwan—without prejudice to a final settlement, he insisted—and strengthen U.S. defense and that of Greece, Turkey, Iran, and NATO. The cost would be $10 billion more in defense expenditures, and—shortly—a request for a $4 billion supplemental military defense appropriation for NATO. He then sketched economic steps to effect increased spending and production of essential materials. This was all the price of providing for the common defense of the free world. And it was a "great state paper," MacArthur had cabled, "the turning point of this era's struggle for civilization."[106]

That night Truman reiterated his message to the nation in more "homely" and briefer form. He denounced North Korea's "raw aggression" and warned that free nations around the world had to stay on guard against such a "sneak attack." He then quoted MacArthur's last-minute report that the battle had been joined in Korea, that the Eighth Army had secured a base in the southeast despite overwhelming odds, and that the enemy's chance to exploit its advantage was gone. The U.S. was committed to remain until the Republic of Korea was restored.[107]

IV

Truman and the U.S. had been joined in battle in Korea long before shooting began in June 1950. Despite earlier FDR-Stalin accord on a trusteeship for Korea, Truman shied from a settlement at Potsdam and the U.S. claimed a favorable occupation zone to the 38th parallel. Stalin acceded either because he had not made his plans or sought a zone in Japan. Truman averted further negotiation, while Hodge fostered reactionary rule in the south and the Soviets fostered Kim Il Sung and Communism in the north. At Moscow in December 1945 Secretary Byrnes got a loose agreement to move toward trusteeship. But the Soviets refused to deal with any Koreans except "democrats" who backed trusteeship, and Hodge undermined trusteeship in the south and supported the authoritarian and virulently anticommunist Rhee.

By June 1946 Truman believed Korea to be an "ideological battleground" that would determine American success in Asia. U.S. officials moved to create a legislative assembly in the south that might become the basis for a separate government, while the JCS did not think Korea worth the cost of its scarce funds and few troops. By the time of the Truman Doctrine and aid to Greece and Turkey, however, the president and Under Secretary Acheson were prepared to commit as much or more money to Korea, where they believed that the line had been clearly drawn between the U.S. and USSR. But Congress balked at the expense, the JCS held Korea to be of "little strategic interest," and in April 1948 Truman approved NSC 8, which stated that it was time to liquidate the U.S. commitment in Korea with minimum bad effects.

The administration made a final effort to negotiate national elections and Korean unity, but the Russians would not put their zone into an electoral contest with the more populous south. The U.S. moved swiftly to get UN sanction to create the ROK under Rhee, while the Soviets supported the DPRK under Kim. Both client states and leaders claimed to represent all of Korea and provoked one another. In 1949 Secretary Acheson proposed increased aid to the ROK, and Truman said that Korea was a "testing ground" between democracy and Communism, despite military persistence that it was far too costly to extend the Truman Doctrine there. Acheson's National Press Club speech in January 1950 expressed the civil-military consensus that South Korea lay outside the U.S. defense perimeter and had to rely on itself and the UN for security. But by spring 1950 the Truman administration had begun to weigh NSC 68, which depicted the Soviet Union as bent on world domination and the U.S. having to build a preponderance of power to deter or resist Soviet-inspired aggression anywhere on the globe.

Stalin provided North Korea with the necessary arms, plans, and advisers, but the attack on South Korea on June 25 was Kim's brainchild and derived from simmering civil war between rival regimes. The Truman administration had good reason to seek a collective response to apparent aggression against a UN-recognized state as well as to avert domestic criticism for another "loss" in Asia. But Truman indicated that he would have gone into Korea alone even if the Security Council had not called for North Korean withdrawal on June 25 and for assistance to the ROK on June 27. Still, the president took the attack as a personal affront and immediately determined to "hit them hard." Moreover, he and his senior officials were unable to conceive of the Korean conflict except as part of a Soviet master plan to test American resolve before committing aggression elsewhere. The president thus drew his analogies to fascist aggression in the 1930s, likened Korea to Greece, and readily applied the doctrines of NSC 68 to "centrally-directed" communism.

The president could argue that he acted as commander in chief in committing air and naval forces in South Korea on June 25–26, striking at military targets in North Korea on June 28, and deploying a combat regiment on June 30. But he also couched his commitment of major ground forces in evasive language and showed no inclination to seek congressional authority to wage war. This denied democratic debate, opened the way to partisan attacks on "Truman's war," and provided bad precedent for future presidents. Moreover, while movement of the Seventh Fleet into the Taiwan Strait on June 26 may have been conceived as a temporary necessity to preclude the further embarrassment of a PRC attack, it also signaled the administration's intent to renege on its pledge to return Taiwan to China and instead to nurture a rival regime on the island. This was a direct challenge to the PRC.

Truman disdained the PRC. He and his senior officials showed little grasp of its legitimate national security concerns and spoke almost cavalierly about bombing the PRC in event it intervened in Korea. Further, naming MacArthur to head a unified military command augured increased difficulty, even allowing for the president's desire to avoid incurring Republican political wrath. In addition to his tendency to disregard orders, MacArthur was an avowed opponent of the PRC and convinced that Taiwan was vital to U.S. defense. His command of forces in Korea was not likely to assure PRC officials that the U.S. did not harbor hostile intentions toward them.

Finally, the rhetoric of Truman's July 19 speeches to Congress and the public essentially escalated a police action against North Korean "bandits" into an issue of U.S. global security and world peace, and foretold major commitment of U.S. resources and GNP to a Cold War buildup at home and abroad. As Acheson mused in July 1950, the issue was no longer just how to restore South Korea but how to guarantee its security after that, and how to keep Taiwan from the PRC. "We have bought ourselves a colt," he said, and neither he nor Truman perceived where it would lead them.[108]

Rollback to Retreat

The Politics of War

During the summer of 1950 President Truman showed no interest in negotiating a Korean settlement until General MacArthur's UN forces had secured a position around Pusan in southeastern Korea or had restored South Korea. Nor would the administration consider broadening negotiations to include the PRC's claim to a UN seat and control of Taiwan. Most important, belief rapidly grew in Washington that the best course would be to march across the 38th parallel to unify Korea. Truman would demonstrate to the Communists that "punishment always followed transgression," and containment would become "rollback" or "liberation."[1]

The president ignored concerns that the PRC and Soviets would view an anticommunist regime in North Korea as a security threat and that the PRC feared U.S. intent to build a rival regime on Taiwan. Truman dismissed PRC warnings of entry into the war as "blackmail," and his hasty trip to meet MacArthur on Wake Island in October was motivated by domestic politics. They focused not on whether the PRC would intervene but on how soon the war would be won. Truman and his advisers paid no heed to PRC vital interests and fear that the U.S. might dominate Asia, where even the British said that America acted like "a law unto itself."[2]

Major PRC attacks in late November 1950 forced rapid U.S./UN retreat. Truman's public comment that use of the atomic bomb was always under consideration was close to the truth and caused British leaders to fly to Washington intent on precluding wider war. The president ostensibly clarified his statement but would give only his "man's word" to consult Prime Minister Attlee before using atomic weapons. And despite Attlee's view that PRC leaders could be both Marxist and nationalist and "not bow to Stalin," Truman was persistent that they were Russian "satellites" who sought to conquer Korea and Southeast Asia.[3]

The president rejected compromise with the PRC in early 1951 to gain a cease-fire and pressed the UN to brand the PRC an "aggressor." He also warned that if driven from Korea, the U.S. would assist GMD action against the PRC and perhaps add a naval blockade and air attacks. But Truman soon recognized the need to end the costly war, while MacArthur sought to "sabotage" cease-fire efforts by demanding that the PRC surrender or face attack. Ultimately the president fired his larger-than-life general in April 1951, but MacArthur's insubordination alone did not cause the crisis. Truman and MacArthur had similar war aims in Korea and similar views of the DPRK and the PRC, and the president and the JCS had long deferred to the general's provocative military tactics. Truman's December 1950 directive to government officials to clear foreign policy statements with the State or Defense Departments was too oblique to contain MacArthur, who would not accept a limited war. But to ensure JCS support while dismissing him, Truman deployed nuclear weapons in the Pacific and gave his new commander there, Lieutenant General Matthew B. Ridgway, qualified authority to strike at the PRC.[4]

Truce talks finally began in July 1951, but the president's personal diplomacy obstructed resolution. In the autumn he refused the standard practice of compulsory exchange of all prisoners of war (POWs) unless the PRC made "some major concession." Then in February 1952 he insisted on voluntary repatriation only, in part to embarrass the PRC politically, and he held to the futile belief that he could either coax agreement or coerce the Communists by saturation bombing.[5]

Meanwhile, beneath the facade of calm crisis management in 1952, Truman fantasized about giving Russia and China ten days to quit Korea or face "all out war" in which he would destroy their major cities from St. Petersburg and Moscow to Vladivostok and from Beijing to Shanghai. "This is the final chance for the Soviet Government to decide whether it desires to survive or not," he fumed. Truman did not intend atomic war, although this was not inconceivable in a heated election year.[6]

Resolution of the Korean War did not come until President Eisenhower's administration settled in July 1953 on terms similar to those that had eluded Truman, including release of nonrepatriated POWs as civilians. But Korean War costs in human life and national treasure were enormous. The U.S. had also set the stage for its long-term commitments to South Korea, Taiwan, and Indochina, while relations with the PRC were embittered for a generation.

I

In July 1950 the Truman administration quickly agreed to MacArthur's requests for eight divisions, nearly all available U.S. ground forces. Shortly, the president's "great state paper" of July 19, requesting $10 billion for defense, augured a long-term military buildup. A week later Truman ordered the NSC to ready a recommendation on NSC 68 by September 1, and he asked Congress for a supplemental $4 billion for NATO allies under the Military Defense Assistance Program (MDAP). Congress appropriated the money on September 22. The next week Truman approved NSC 68, which called for five years of defense spending at $50 billion annually, a level reached when Truman requested an additional $17 billion for defense on December 1. As Acheson testified to Congress, modern weapons eliminated former barriers between the U.S. and predator nations, and America now stood like a person who, "on the death of parent, hears in a new way the roaring of the cataract."[7]

The Korean War provided a catalytic framework for developing a Cold War economy, but it did not preclude seeking a negotiated settlement. North Korea was not interested, however, while its forces moved swiftly southward, destroying nearly half of the ROK army and overwhelming poorly equipped, inexperienced U.S. soldiers. On July 26 MacArthur flew to Korea to order General Walton Walker's troops virtually to "stand or die" along the Pusan perimeter— a line about fifty miles wide and one hundred miles deep—on the southeastern tip of the peninsula. Then infusion of U.S. troops, modern equipment, and increasing air power began to turn the tide of battle. On August 31 Truman wrote that "we have met the challenge of the pagan wolves," although it would take another week of bitter struggle before UN forces dealt the overextended DPRK army its first major defeat and readied their own counteroffensive.[8]

The president kept his diplomatic options open, but he and Acheson strongly opposed British and Indian proposals in July that sought to initiate Korean talks that might gain Russian good offices by weighing a UN seat and control of Taiwan for the PRC. When Bevin said that world opinion stood with the U.S. on Korea but not with regard to the PRC's issues, the president and secretary sharply rejoined that they would not retreat from either Truman's or the UN's June 27 commitment to resist aggression in Korea. Nor would they pay any price for PRC or Soviet help, with the Kremlin unmoved to act so long as the North Koreans were advancing. But the Americans vented excessive ire toward the PRC and alleged that it was spreading aggression across South Asia. They also feared that dealing with the PRC would invite public attack and jeopardize military aid for NATO.[9]

The president sought to stay his course in Korea and avert conflict with the PRC. But he undercut this effort to neutralize the PRC by approving $125 million in military aid and a military mission for Taiwan on July 27, and then by not fully reining in his Far Eastern commander. The administration had resisted MacArthur's proposal to make Taiwan central to the U.S. Pacific defense perimeter and to use GMD forces in Korea, but then agreed that the general— or preferably one of his senior officers—might go to Taiwan to assess its defense. Without a word to Washington, MacArthur went there on July 31 to hail the coordinate political-military interests of the U.S. and Jiang. There were also reports that the general planned to commit three jet fighter squadrons to the island, raising PRC fear that the U.S. intended to strangle the new China.[10]

Truman was furious at MacArthur. He had Defense Secretary Johnson and the JCS inform MacArthur that only the president could order "preventive action" against the PRC and that no U.S. troops or planes were to be committed to Taiwan's defense. Truman also dispatched Averell Harriman, recently recalled as Marshall Plan administrator to be his special assistant, to Tokyo to make clear to MacArthur that whereas the administration might try to employ the UN to establish an independent government on Taiwan, it would not permit Jiang to use the island to relaunch civil war on the mainland. The general accepted the president's position, "but without full conviction," Harriman recounted. MacArthur soon alleged that proponents of "defeatism and appeasement" had misrepresented his Taiwan trip. Still, Truman was highly pleased with Harriman's report and reassured MacArthur that he had always had the president's full confidence.[11]

Further, Truman inclined to support MacArthur in mid-August when U.S. B-29s bombed the North Korean port of Rashin, seventeen miles from the Soviet border and one hundred miles from Vladivostok. State Department officials and the British protested that this action ignored the president's June 29 directive that bombing operations were to stay "well clear" of Soviet and PRC borders and could not halt the flow of oil to DPRK forces from Rashin because oil and other supplies could be shipped instead from Vladivostok. The president seemed to concur in the diplomats' caveats during August 17–18, but at a Cabinet meeting he suddenly told General Bradley that the military was to "go after any target" being used to supply DPRK forces. Thus when the JCS again raised the issue in early September, Acheson cautioned the president with Kennan's argument that the Soviets had "pathological sensitivity" about their borders. But the JCS did not withdraw their target directive until late September, on the eve of the UN advance into North Korea.[12]

Meanwhile, Truman struggled to contain MacArthur over Taiwan. The president's policy of "neutralizing" the island with the Seventh Fleet—while aiding Jiang—had recently come under fire at the UN from the Soviets, who had ended their boycott. The PRC called on the UN to condemn the presence of U.S. "invading forces" on Taiwan. On August 25 Ambassador Warren Austin, speaking for Truman—who shortly reiterated his position in a public letter to Secretary General Trygve Lie—stated that the U.S. did not intend to infringe PRC sovereignty or territory or prejudice Taiwan's future status, but would welcome UN consideration of the issue. That night Acheson received a press release of a speech to be read in MacArthur's behalf at a Veterans of Foreign Wars meeting in Chicago on August 28 declaring Taiwan to be the center of the U.S. defense perimeter, warning that control of the island by a hostile power threatened U.S. security, and hailing Jiang as a vital ally.[13]

Acheson briefed his staff about MacArthur's "insubordination" on August 26 and had Harriman inform Truman. The president then read MacArthur's text to his senior advisers and "decisively repudiated" the general's speech. Secretary Johnson and Army Chief of Staff General Lawton Collins (who had recently been in Tokyo) disclaimed prior knowledge of the address, and Acheson and Harriman said that its release would be a "catastrophe." Truman told Johnson to order MacArthur to withdraw the speech, but shortly Johnson called Acheson to ask whether "we dare" to send a withdrawal order. The defense secretary proposed instead an after-the-fact statement that MacArthur's speech was "one man's opinion." Acheson insisted that the issue was "who is the president of the United States?" White House staff and Harriman demanded that the order be in writing, and preferably from the president. Truman called Johnson to dictate a brief presidential order for MacArthur. Johnson dawdled still, while Acheson and Harriman weighed whether Truman might be asked to reconsider—until the president informed them that he had "dictated what he wanted to go" and that it should. But to soften the blow, Truman added a personal note to MacArthur conveying his UN statement on Taiwan.[14]

MacArthur withdrew his speech, insistent that it was his personal opinion only and was meant to support the president's policy. Truman declared the incident "closed" and added that the Seventh Fleet in the Taiwan Strait was only "flank protection" for UN forces. Later he wrote that he seriously weighed relieving MacArthur of his Korean military command but did not want to hurt him by seeming to demote him. Equally clear, Truman feared to start a domestic political firestorm or to jeopardize a highly risky military invasion just agreed upon.[15]

Thus he drew back, but two weeks later he fired Johnson, who was a hawkish ally of MacArthur concerning Taiwan and an opponent of Acheson. But Acheson had maneuvered deftly during the crisis to underscore the president's authority and to keep MacArthur and Johnson on the political hook. Thus in mid-September, with major Korean action and NATO negotiations under way, Truman turned again to the person he most revered, George Marshall, to head the Defense Department.[16]

II

Since early in the war MacArthur had been urging an amphibious counteroffensive far behind North Korean forces to cut their supply lines and trap them between UN troops in the northwest and around Pusan. In late July he proposed such an invasion at the port of Inchon, 20 miles west of Seoul and 180 miles behind enemy lines. The JCS worried about the exceedingly high, rapidly receding tides that might mire attacking ships in the mud and DPRK defenses on Wolmi-do, the 350-foot-high, heavily fortified island that commanded Inchon harbor. At a meeting in Tokyo on August 23, MacArthur persuaded General Lawton Collins and Chief of Naval Operations Admiral Forrest Sherman that the operation's difficulties ensured surprise and success. The JCS soon approved, then balked in early September, but with Truman's backing finally acceded. On September 15 MacArthur's UN forces—70,000 personnel on 260 ships with heavy air power—launched their attack. They quickly seized Wolmi-do, then took Inchon, and nearby Kimpo Airbase. In late September they recaptured Seoul and reinstalled Syngman Rhee's government. Meanwhile, General Walker's troops broke out of their Pusan beachhead and drove DPRK forces to frantic retreat toward the 38th parallel. The Inchon invasion was a spectacular success, and MacArthur gained near-hero status. The only question remaining was whether to carry the war into North Korea.[17]

The president may have implied the answer in his ambiguous June 26 response at Blair House to his military chieftains' query about whether they could strike north of the 38th parallel: "not yet." Opinion rapidly grew to drive into North Korea, destroy the Communist regime, and unify the nation. On July 1, John Allison, head of the Northeast Asian Affairs office, wrote that permanent peace was impossible so long as that "artificial barrier" remained and that the UN's June 27 resolution calling for restoration of peace and security in the area implied the right to go as far north as the Manchurian border. Dean Rusk, now assistant secretary of state for Far Eastern affairs, agreed.[18]

Similarly, Republican spokesman John Foster Dulles, then employed by the administration to negotiate a peace treaty with Japan, insisted that the U.S. could not allow the aggressor "asylum" in North Korea. MacArthur contended on July 13 to Generals Collins and Vandenberg that North Korean forces had to be destroyed, not just driven from the south. "We win here or we lose everywhere," he said; but "if we win here we improve the chances of win-ning everywhere." Meanwhile, ROK officials, especially Rhee, publicly urged that Truman have the UN march north to "slaughter" the enemy and to unify the nation.[19]

The president ordered the NSC to study the issue. Shortly Kennan and the PPS held that despite public desire for a "final solution" to the Korean problem, action north of the 38th parallel posed far greater risk of conflict with the USSR or PRC, and that the U.S. should limit itself to its UN mandate to repel aggres-sion, force North Korean withdrawal, and leave further decisions to the UN. Nearly every other government quarter disagreed. On July 24 Allison led the State Department argument that the DPRK in Korea had no legal status, that the Soviets' real strategic goal was not Korea but Japan, and that "appease-ment" would gain nothing. He said that the U.S. had to stand up even at risk of global war to what the president had called "raw aggression." Similarly the De-fense Department insisted that the U.S. had to fulfill Korea's aspiration for unity, which would be a step toward "reversing the dangerous strategic trend" of the past year. MacArthur strongly reiterated his view, as expressed earlier to Harriman, that North Korean forces had to be destroyed, that neither the USSR nor PRC would intervene, and that "victory is a strong magnet in the East" and it would shape Asia's political future.[20]

Meanwhile, at the UN on August 17 Ambassador Austin asked rhetorically whether only a part of Korea was to know freedom and emphasized the UN's moral obligation to unify that nation. The next week Navy Secretary Francis Matthews publicly urged that the U.S. become "the first aggressors for peace" and initiate war against North Korea. The PPS now retreated to calling for the U.S. to seek a negotiated settlement before invading the north, while Kennan, departing the State Department, counseled Acheson that it was not necessary to establish an anti-Soviet state in all of Korea. He also cautioned that Mac-Arthur had been given too much latitude regarding policy statements and mil-itary operations and that U.S. involvement with a rival China regime or with the French in Indochina portended disaster.[21]

Finally, there was domestic political pressure to go north, given sharp Re-publican attack, spearheaded by Senator McCarthy, that American boys were dying on the battlefield because the Truman administration had given Russia the "green light" to grab China, Korea, and Taiwan. There was also a growing chorus of moderate opinion, including editorials of major urban newspapers, that return to the status quo was impossible and that at least part of North Ko-rea had to be occupied. Such action would also bolster the Democrats in the November elections.[22]

Truman had likely made up his mind by August 8, when he wrote a friend that they were "over the hump" in Korea and that if the Russians did not inter-vene the situation "ought to be cleared up before many months." NSC officials soon concluded that there was no time for delay given the president's desire for a decision and the military's need for time for a buildup. On August 25 they decided that "roll-back" should be approved, that UN forces should stay "well clear" of Soviet and PRC borders—military operations were to be limited to the "narrow neck" at the 39th parallel—and war with Russia should be avoided. On August 31 Truman publicly disclaimed knowing whether UN troops would enter North Korea, but the next day, in his national address hail-ing the UN for repulsing Communist aggression, he said that Korea had a right to be free, independent, and united.[23]

Officials now produced the first draft of NSC 81, which proposed to gain UN approval for "liberation" of North Korea, with ROK forces to lead the northward march, provided that no Soviet or PRC troops were in the area and chances for success were reasonable. Truman and Acheson soon agreed to the final version of NSC 81/1, which directive allowed MacArthur to advance UN—but not U.S.—forces to PRC (Yalu River) and USSR (Tumen River) borders. The president signed the document on September 11. Four days later MacArthur launched the Inchon invasion, and two weeks later UN forces were at the 38th parallel.[24]

Truman continued to dissemble about intent to cross that line because he did not want U.S.-led action to appear unilateral, and he sought to avert UN de-bate. But by mid-September the U.S. had persuaded the British to sponsor an authorizing resolution, and within two weeks the JCS had readied their military directive for MacArthur's UN troops to cross the 38th parallel to destroy North Korea's forces, provided that neither Soviet nor PRC troops had entered or threatened to do so. MacArthur was constrained not to allow his troops to cross USSR or PRC borders or engage in air or naval action against China or Russia. He was to keep non-Korean troops from their borders "as a matter of policy," and in event of "major" Soviet action in Korea, he was to act defensively and notify Washington. If the PRC entered South Korea (the north was unmen-tioned), action was to continue as long as successful resistance was possible.[25]

Acheson knew the orders were too loosely drawn but told an aide he was unwilling to "take on" the JCS. Truman approved the directive on Septem-ber 27, and the JCS sent it to MacArthur, who wired back that he would split his forces, sending the Eighth Army along the west coast to capture Pyongyang and the X Corps to make amphibious landings on the east coast at Wonsan. The JCS approved, and Marshall added a personal note on September 29 telling MacArthur to "feel unhampered tactically and strategically to proceed north of the 38th parallel." The general, taking license, replied that "all of Korea" was open for military operations until the enemy capitulated. On October 1, at White House instruction, he called on North Korea to surrender.[26]

ROK forces had already begun to cross the parallel. Meanwhile, Britain and seven cosponsors submitted to the General Assembly (where the Soviets had no veto) their U.S.-approved resolution calling on the UN to take all appropriate steps to ensure stability in Korea, hold unifying elections, and then withdraw its troops. The Soviets proposed instead an immediate cease-fire and withdrawal of foreign troops, with elections to follow. India sought to reconcile the two resolutions. But U.S. influence prevailed to defeat the Soviet and Indian measures, and on October 7 the General Assembly passed the British-sponsored resolution. The U.S. First Cavalry Division was already advancing into North Korea.[27]

The president fully supported the U.S.-made decision to cross the 38th parallel to destroy the DPRK regime and to unify the nation. Outraged at North Korea's initial attack, he was determined not only to repulse "raw aggression" but to demonstrate to the Communist aggressors his long-held biblical conviction that "punishment always followed transgression." Acheson told the Cabinet on September 29 that now Korea could be used as "a stage to prove to the world what Western Democracy can do to help the underprivileged countries of the world." The JCS and diplomatic-military bureaucracy, except for Kennan and a few others, saw opportunity to deal a defeat to the Soviets and PRC and transform containment into "roll-back" or "liberation." As historian Melvyn Leffler has said, the "taste of victory," and hubris, impelled Truman and his advisers to seek preponderant American power in Asia.[28]

Power and hubris also caused the Truman administration to disregard PRC concerns about the U.S. advance northward. From the start of the war, U.S. officials worried chiefly about Soviet intervention. They assumed that the PRC was weak, a Soviet vassal, and focused on domestic problems and Taiwan. During July the PRC pursued a quiet "watchful waiting" policy about Korea. But PRC officials also created the Northeastern Border Defense Army (NBDA) and doubled PRC troops in Manchuria to 250,000. MacArthur's July 31 visit to Taiwan and bombings of Rashin in August raised China's fears. Mao told his Politburo that if the "U.S. imperialists" won in Korea, they "may get so dizzy with success that they may threaten us." On August 20, Foreign Minister Zhou stated that the PRC had to worry about the war's outcome in neighboring Korea and demanded a PRC seat on the Security Council when it discussed Korea.[29]

U.S. officials took the PRC military buildup to mean infiltration, not intervention, in Korea. Typically, in his September 1 address Truman denied U.S. hostile intent toward the PRC and said that he hoped the Chinese would not be "misled or forced" into fighting their American "friends." Acheson was more condescending. He stated on national radio on September 10 that the PRC was "intelligent enough" to know better than to take action that might lead to its "dismemberment and destruction." PRC intervention would be "sheer madness."[30]

The Inchon invasion accelerated PRC war preparations. Mao vacillated over aid for North Korea, while U.S. bombing of Manchuria on September 23 heightened PRC anger and led to its charge that this action, combined with U.S. aid to Jiang and intransigence over Taiwan and a PRC seat in the UN, portended an attack on China. Truman and Acheson grudgingly offered compensation for the "accidental" bombing.[31]

Washington now received numerous warnings, especially from India, that the PRC would enter the war if UN forces crossed the 38th parallel. But U.S. officials presumed that the PRC's only chance to intervene successfully was before Inchon. Further, Truman and Acheson were angry with Prime Minister Jawaharlal Nehru for recognizing the PRC and opposing UN action in North Korea, and viewed his ambassador to Beijing, K. M. Panikkar, as a PRC agent. They concluded that China was engaged in a "war of nerves" to keep India from backing the pending UN resolution to enter North Korea.[32]

On September 30 Zhou declared that the PRC would not allow Korea to be "savagely invaded by the imperialists," and early on October 3 he summoned Panikkar to the Foreign Ministry to warn that if U.S. troops entered North Korea, "we cannot sit idly by." Zhou also indicated PRC interest in Nehru's recent proposal to have the UN, with the PRC included, deal with Korean unity but not send forces northward.[33]

Numerous diplomats held Zhou's warnings to signal PRC willingness to risk "World War III." But Acheson curtly denied the PRC's right to take part in the Korean "poker game" unless it put up more than indirect warnings—likely "bluff," he said—and held that it was too late to halt the process. MacArthur dismissed Zhou's warnings as "pure bluff," and Truman later dismissed them as a "bald attempt to blackmail" the UN. The Americans pressed the UN to cross the 38th parallel; MacArthur again called for North Korea's surrender; and the JCS amplified their earlier directive to him, stating that in case of use of PRC forces anywhere (not just in the south) in Korea, he should continue military action as long as chances for success were reasonable. But he was not to strike at China without Washington's approval. On October 10, the PRC Foreign Ministry publicly warned that China could not permit America's "invasion" to threaten its security.[34]

That day Truman announced that he would make a quick trip to meet with MacArthur ("God's right hand man," he wrote privately), to discuss the final phase of the Korean War. In his *Memoirs,* Truman implied that he sought to educate the general, who had not returned to the U.S. in fourteen years, about public opinion. But White House staffers had promoted the trip as good election-year politics, with the president at first resisting this "showmanship." Then on October 8 two U.S. jet fighters overflew the Soviet border and strafed an air base near Vladivostok. Thus, Truman may have decided to meet with MacArthur to signal control of his war making. Still, the president largely undertook a "political junket," as MacArthur said, and without Acheson, Marshall, or the JCS, except for Bradley.[35]

Truman arrived at Wake Island at dawn on October 15. He recalled a cordial greeting from the general—"shirt unbuttoned and wearing a greasy ham and eggs cap that evidently had been in use for twenty years"—but there was no salute. During an hour's private talk, MacArthur assured Truman that the war was won, that the "Chinese commies" would not attack, and that U.S. troops could be sent from Korea to Europe in January 1951. He also apologized for any embarrassment that his withdrawn VFW speech had caused and disavowed political ambition.[36]

MacArthur reiterated for the president's entourage that the war would be over before Christmas and laid out his battle plan. Truman asked what were the chances of PRC or Soviet intervention, and MacArthur replied "very little." They might have intervened decisively at the outset, he said, but no longer. The PRC had no air force, could not move more than 60,000 troops across the Yalu, and if they headed south there would be the "greatest slaughter." The Russians had a good air force but few available troops, and a mixture of Russian planes and PRC troops would not work: "We are the best."

MacArthur called on the president to announce a Truman Doctrine for Asia, and both men derided the French for not fighting hard enough in Indochina. Truman cut off questions about Taiwan: "[T]he General and I are in complete agreement." MacArthur then said that he would put only ROK forces near PRC and Soviet borders—with other troops "pulled back"—and Truman pledged to support Rhee's government: propaganda could "go to hell." The ninety-minute meeting ended. The president then presented MacArthur with a fourth Oak Leaf Cluster, and candied plums for his wife, and hailed the prevailing "complete unanimity of view."[37]

Both men were elated. MacArthur had suavely told Truman what he wanted to hear. There was no new information or issues. The general was likely convinced that he had the full support of Truman, who returned to the U.S. on October 17 and declared that there was no substitute for conversation with the field commander, who had more information at his fingertips than anyone else. He said that their conference underscored the UN's historical action: "united humanity against aggression." Truman praised the Wake Island meeting to

Acheson and others, said he now understood the situation better, and impressed his aides as having a new and favorable view of MacArthur. When a reporter asked about possible differences over Taiwan, Truman—"eyes blazing"—retorted that it was a pity reporters could not understand the ideas of "two intellectually honest men" and that he wished the press were as loyal to the president and his foreign policy as was MacArthur. As for continued U.S. defense of Taiwan until the UN, then weighing the issue, reached a disposition, that "was a river we have not come to."[38]

Nor had Truman considered, as one adviser feared, that PRC leaders might now feel compelled to preemptive action in Korea because the Wake Island meeting, following the UN decision to cross the 38th parallel, signaled a major U.S. move, perhaps an attack on Manchuria. Further, on September 30 desperate DPRK leaders beseeched both Stalin and Mao to intervene directly or to organize volunteer units in China. Stalin did not want to engage the U.S. directly; he appealed instead to Mao to commit five or six divisions of volunteers toward the 38th parallel, and even offered joint control over DPRK and volunteer forces.[39]

According to available Chinese sources, Mao promptly told the Standing Committee of his Politburo that the issue was not "whether but . . . how fast" the PRC should enter the war. Then he immediately cabled Stalin that to forestall an "American rampage" and to preserve a favorable balance in the "entire East," Chinese volunteers would be in Korea within two weeks. Mao requested only weapons and air cover, while Zhou issued his early October warnings of PRC action, which the U.S. disregarded.[40]

Recent Russian archival revelations question the published Chinese version of Mao's October 2 cable or whether it was ever sent. Russian documents indicate instead that Mao—who faced sharp Politburo objections to intervention—cabled Stalin that PRC troops were too few and too poorly armed to fight, and their presence might provoke war with the U.S. as well as compel Russian entry under the Sino-Soviet pact. Thus Stalin, taken aback by Mao's turnabout, pressed his UN resolution for a cease-fire, which the U.S. defeated, and—briefly—began to resign himself to the DPRK's demise. "So what?" he said. "Let the United States of America be our neighbors. They will come here, but we shall not fight them now. We are not ready to fight." But he also increased pressure on Mao, insisting that the U.S. was neither ready nor able to confront the PRC and USSR and that China could now take Taiwan. And if the U.S. did fight, better war be waged now than later, when Japan and South Korea would be rearmed. Further, the USSR would provide air cover for the PRC and honor its Sino-Soviet pact commitments.[41]

Stalin's message bolstered, or goaded, Mao to action. During a series of meetings with his enlarged CCP Central Committee, the Politburo, and senior military officers, resistance to PRC intervention ran high, including from Zhou and Lin Biao, noted commander of the Fourth Army that had fought in Manchuria in the civil war. They and others argued that the PRC needed time for economic-political reconstruction and that the PLA lacked weaponry to match U.S. forces and had no assurance of air cover or logistical support in Korea. Mao drew support from allies he had summoned, such as Peng Dehuai, who had cofounded the PLA with him and commanded its Northwest Military Region— and was the PRC leader's choice to head forces to go to Korea. Peng quickly concluded that no concessions would stop the "tiger," who wanted to "eat human beings." China had to send troops to Korea. Or as Mao said, if the PRC did not do so, "the reactionaries at home and abroad would be swollen with arrogance when enemy troops press to the Yalu border." Thus the time had come for the "Great Movement to Resist America and Assist Korea."[42]

Mao was also confident that prospective Soviet action under its treaty with the PRC would keep the war limited and nonnuclear, that the ROK army was weak, and that the massive PRC army would inflict heavy casualties on the Americans and cause Washington to settle on favorable PRC terms. Thus on October 8—the day after the UN authorized its troops to cross the 38th parallel—Mao ordered the NBDA to become the Chinese People's Volunteers (CPV) and to enter the war. He cabled his decision to an ecstatic Kim and dispatched Zhou and Lin Biao to meet with Stalin October 10–11 at his villa on the Black Sea.[43]

Whether these emissaries sought to bargain with Stalin or derail Mao's plan is uncertain. Zhou opened the talks by stating that the PRC was ill-equipped to fight and subject to reactionary opposition and a U.S. declaration of war. Stalin, who had heard these arguments earlier from Mao and knew of Zhou and Lin's views, rejoined that the Soviet Union was still too weak from the Second World War to fight but that the PRC could take on the U.S., which would get no help from Germany, Japan, or even Britain and would not dare to trigger the Sino-Soviet pact. It was also in China's vital security interest to keep the U.S. from its borders.

Zhou did not flinch, even as Stalin charged that the PRC would bear the onus for the demise of socialism in Korea. But when the Soviet leader proffered the stark option of evacuating the remnants of the DPRK leadership and army to China and the USSR, an apparently shocked Zhou backed down. He inquired about Soviet weapons and air cover. Stalin quickly agreed to these, although he soon made clear that the latter would not be available for a couple of months. Still, he cabled his embassy in Pyongyang to begin to assist Kim to prepare to evacuate. But this proved unnecessary because on October 13 a reassured Mao persuaded his Politburo that confrontation with the U.S. was inevitable, and that it was better to fight before the DPRK retreated to China. That evening he informed Zhou that his decision was "favorable to China, Korea, the East, and the world." Mao spent the next five days developing war plans and issued his final order for the PRC to enter Korea on October 19. That night the first CPV crossed the Yalu, destroyed a ROK battalion six days later, skirmished with UN forces until November 7, and then broke contact, perhaps with slight hope the UN would call off its advance to the Yalu.[44]

Mao's decision for war rested on a powerful confluence of factors. These included a long history of conflict with the U.S., national security and sovereignty concerns, and ideology. PRC leaders had felt betrayed by the U.S. at least since Marshall's failed mission in 1946 and by U.S. support for Jiang's warfare as late as 1950. They viewed the denial of Taiwan as violative of past agreements and their sovereignty and suspected U.S. intent to build a rival government there. The MacArthur-led military advance toward the Yalu, combined with bombings of Manchuria and prospect of an anticommunist regime in all of Korea, posed a major threat to China's national security and the Marxist revolution that Mao and his compatriots sought to bring to their country. Thus Mao concluded that it was necessary to protect, or even advance, revolution at home and abroad and, in so doing, as Shu Guang Zhang has said, transform a danger or crisis into an opportunity.[45]

Despite his own vacillations and strong Politburo and military resistance to war, Mao trumpeted the advantages that his large, morally inspired army would have in fighting an overextended and unmotivated U.S. enemy, minimized the efficacy of atomic weapons, and insisted that the PRC was acting in behalf of revolution—or the exploited people—in the East, perhaps the world. Most likely he would not have taken this audacious step if the U.S. had not crossed the 38th parallel, although the issue may be debated. But prior to October 1950 the CCP leadership had never shown intention to use military force, or to conspire with the Kremlin, to upset the status quo in Asia or drive the U.S. from the area. They concluded, however, that it was better to fight now than to risk having to do so after the "tiger" reached the Yalu.[46]

Meanwhile, MacArthur announced on October 24 his intent to use "any and all ground forces" throughout North Korea. When the JCS queried this violation of his September 27 directive to keep non-Korean forces from Sino-Soviet borders, he said that this had been stated as "policy," not a "final" order. He also cited Marshall's having told him to feel "unhampered" in deploying his forces and claimed that this was fully discussed at Wake Island, although his vague language there probably misled everyone. Still, on October 26 Truman stated that only ROK forces would occupy border areas.[47]

The JCS backed down and the president, apparently uninformed, said nothing. MacArthur advanced his troops, while in the State Department Clubb warned that the PRC was unlikely to commit only a small force to be "bloodied and thrown out" and probably intended a major assault. MacArthur doubted this but confessed uncertainty. He also ordered bombing of every village, city, and factory in the northern part of North Korea, as well as the Korean side of the bridges across the Yalu, action that assured border overflights and bombing of Manchuria. He did not inform Washington, but word came from his air commander, General George Stratemeyer. State and Defense officials doubted the bombing's utility and feared it would anger America's allies and defeat efforts to get a UN resolution urging the PRC to stay out of the war.[48]

On November 6 Acheson called Truman, then in Missouri, to vote the next day. He inclined to allow the bombing but wanted more information. He ordered the mission postponed and no further bombing within five miles of the Yalu. The JCS cabled MacArthur, who fired back that men and materiel were "pouring across all bridges over the Yalu," and that to halt his bombing mission would cause a "calamity." He insisted that the decision be put to the president.[49]

Truman confronted a near *fait accompli* on election eve, with the Democrats' Asian policy—and especially Acheson—under sharp political attack. Predictably he gave the "go-ahead" based on military necessity but had the JCS convey the requirement to remain within UN directives and not to violate PRC territory or airspace. Still, MacArthur was free to advance U.S. troops to the PRC border and to bomb massively there. He then pressed for permission to pursue hostile planes that sought sanctuary in Manchuria. Truman, Acheson, and the JCS inclined to allow limited "hot pursuit." But the president reluctantly said no after soundings at the UN drew strong objections.[50]

Fear of wider war, and a CIA report on November 8 that the PRC had 30,000–40,000 troops in North Korea and could move in another 350,000 within thirty to sixty days, led the JCS to tell MacArthur it might have to reconsider his military directive. This augured slowing or halting his advance and seeking to negotiate with the PRC, perhaps to establish a buffer zone in northern Korea, a British-promoted idea that appealed to Acheson and others. But MacArthur warned against either weakening his UN mission to destroy DPRK forces or postponing his planned attack on November 15. He assured he could prevent the PRC from reinforcing its troops in Korea and analogized the British proposal to appeasement of Hitler at Munich in 1938.[51]

The JCS were uncertain whether the PRC intended only to protect its electric power plants on the Yalu or to drive the UN from Korea. At an NSC meeting on November 9 they outlined three options: (1) withdrawal of UN forces; (2) establishment of defense lines at present positions; and (3) continued advance, with MacArthur's military directive unchanged and the State Department seeking a political settlement. The JCS doubted that MacArthur could halt PRC movement across the Yalu and worried about draining resources from Europe and NATO. The generals favored the third option, as did Acheson, who offered the weak suggestion that MacArthur at least keep his troops from Soviet borders. No one proposed to halt MacArthur, who held that his drive would succeed quickly, although he said that if the PRC entered Korea first, it would be militarily necessary to bomb key points in Manchuria, bringing Soviet entry.[52]

The next week Acheson and Rusk publicly disclaimed U.S. designs on Manchuria or Yalu territory, and on November 16 Truman stated that the U.S. held China's territory inviolate and had "never intended" to carry hostilities to the PRC. But U.S. officials cared less about PRC fears of attack than their allies' fears that American action would prompt PRC intervention. Acheson hoped to preclude this, and calm diplomatic nerves, at a Pentagon meeting on November 21. But he agreed first that MacArthur's directive should not be changed and that the general should be allowed to "probe" PRC intentions. Marshall preferred to gain military success before making proposals, and the JCS thought that if the Chinese entered it would be necessary to "hit them in Manchuria." Thus the conferees proposed only to have MacArthur pull back his forces from the Yalu to defensible high ground *after* they had defeated the enemy. But he balked, insistent that everyone knew the risk of PRC entry from the day U.S. forces were committed to Korea.[53]

Efforts to open cease-fire talks got nowhere. Then MacArthur launched his "home by Christmas" invasion on November 24. Within two days 200,000 CPV and 50,000 North Korean troops counterattacked through the mountain terrain that divided advancing UN forces, driving them into rapid and bitter retreat. "We face an entirely new war," completely beyond the control and strength of this command, MacArthur informed the JCS early on November 28. The last chance to avert disastrous wider war was gone, as Acheson would lament ever after.[54]

III

Truman resisted declaring a national emergency, and his advisers reinforced him at a White House NSC meeting on November 28. Marshall, the JCS, and Acheson proposed to maintain unity with the UN, develop a strong defense line in Korea, and promptly "get out with honor"—handing control to the ROK—in order to build Western European defenses. They resolved not to fall into the "Russian trap" of war with China. This meant they had to "localize" the fighting, and not strike at Manchuria, which would bring greater PRC—and Soviet—intervention. The Korean War was only one part of the worldwide struggle with the Soviet Union.

Truman said the U.S. could "hold the line," and he pledged to "meet the facts and conditions" in Korea. He blamed a press campaign of "vilification and lies" about his Asian policy—and about Acheson—for bringing Democratic defeats in the November elections and being "Russia's best asset" in the expanding war. The president had grave doubts about MacArthur's statements but still respected his abilities and determined that he not "lose face" over his "home by Christmas" campaign. Above all, Truman wanted NSC 68 to be funded, which Bradley later said was the most important decision of that meeting.[55]

The president also called a press conference for November 30 to state that the UN would not quit Korea and to warn the PRC not to serve "Russian colonial policy in Asia." He indignantly denied that MacArthur had exceeded his orders. But after a reporter inquired about whether Truman's stated intent to use "every weapon that we have" included the atomic bomb, he said that "there has always been active consideration of its use." And when asked again whether the bomb's use was under consideration, he said it "always has been," and added that although U.S. action in Korea depended on UN decisions, the field commander always controlled the use of weapons.

White House staff rushed out a clarifying statement that possession of a weapon always implied weighing its use, but the July 1946 Atomic Energy Act specified that only the president could authorize use of nuclear weapons, and he had not done this. Clearly Truman, under stress and often imprecise at press conferences, had been led on by the reporters' questions. He had not remembered the 1946 law or that after the Berlin crisis he had ordered that military requests for atomic weapons go first to the NSC, freeing the president from direct JCS-style pressure.[56]

Nonetheless, Truman's comment about always weighing use of the atomic bomb may have been a veiled threat to the PRC. Use of the bomb against Soviet air bases had been briefly broached at the Blair House Conference on June 26. The president had declined Bradley's request to give MacArthur control of atomic weapons on July 9 but shortly sent nuclear-configured bombers—without atomic cores—to England and then to Guam. The planes returned before PRC forces entered Korea in mid-October. Then on November 4, PPS director Paul Nitze concluded that although tactical use of atomic bombs against CPV troop concentrations in Korea might deter further intervention, there were few targets and the bombs would not be militarily decisive. But they would rouse Asians against the U.S. and might bring Soviet intervention—especially if used strategically against China. Similarly, John Emmerson of the Far Eastern Affairs Office warned that "repetition of Hiroshima and Nagasaki" would bring disastrous consequences and that the bomb should not be used unless it was absolutely necessary, and certain, to produce decisive results that could be gotten no other way.[57]

Another military study in late November proposed use of the atomic bomb to prevent overrunning of U.S. troops. But the JCS opposed any action against the PRC that might prompt Soviet entry because the only recourse would be the bomb, whose effectiveness in the field was unknown, as Marshall told Truman on December 1. JCS planners briefly sanctioned the bomb's use to prevent a disaster during evacuation of UN troops, but this proved unnecessary.[58]

Truman's atomic bomb statement had produced heated foreign reaction. Prime Minister Attlee immediately announced he would fly to Washington. He was intent on precluding wider war and seeking joint control of atomic decisions. The demoralized Truman administration also hoped to limit the war, although at the start of State-Defense meetings of December 1–3, Acheson could suggest only to seek a demarcation line to permit both the U.S. and PRC to leave Korea. General Collins advised that Korea was "not worth a nickel" given Soviet power in Siberia. JCS Chief Bradley warned that to expand the air war to Manchuria might prompt Soviet entry and lead them and the PRC to end their unstated policy of not bombing U.S. air bases in Korea or Japan. Acheson agreed that to strike at the PRC was to invite Soviet entry. He also opposed fighting the "second team" because the "real enemy" was the Soviet Union. Thus, there was strong consensus that Korea was "not decisive" for the U.S. and that it was best to regroup and seek a cease-fire, perhaps being "lucky" enough to regain the 38th parallel.[59]

Truman found the situation *"very bad."* He readily approved JCS instructions on December 1–2 to MacArthur (whom he was bent on extricating from his "serious trouble") to abandon the northeast area above the 39th parallel and to make his primary goal preservation of his troops, establishing beachheads near Korea's "narrow waist" just above the 38th parallel. But MacArthur retorted that this required great reinforcements of U.S. and GMD troops and striking at Manchuria, with the JCS rewriting his "completely outmoded" military directives. He also told *U.S. News & World Report* that Washington's refusal to permit hot pursuit into Manchuria was an unprecedented "enormous handicap" and that refusal to allow him to fly over, and now bomb, Manchuria permitted the PRC to mass its forces undetected and shield their supply lines.[60]

MacArthur's attack on administration policy and promotion of wider war deeply angered Washington officials, who also despaired at the implication that the U.S. was too weak to halt its enemy or to contain its own field commander.

General Ridgway, deputy chief of staff of the army, hinted that MacArthur should be relieved of his command, and Assistant Secretary Rusk suggested sending Collins to command the troops in the field. But the JCS were of no mind to act, and Truman—who later said that he should have fired MacArthur "then and there"—claimed that he did not want the failed offensive to appear to have brought dismissal. The president and his advisers sent Collins to consult MacArthur, and on December 5 Truman issued a directive to all civil-military personnel to gain State or Defense Department clearance for all foreign policy statements. MacArthur was unlikely to respect this routine, oblique order.[61]

Still, administration officials became more resolute about Korea. They analogized the situation to Britain's resistance in 1940 and grew convinced, as Kennan said, that the Soviets would mercilessly exploit their withdrawal, or even efforts at a cease-fire. The Americans also took a hard line during their December 4–8 talks with the British, who they darkly judged desired to seek accord with the PRC and scuttle Asia to preserve their interests in Europe.[62]

The president was most feisty in rebutting Attlee's contention that the PRC leaders could be Marxists and nationalists and "not bow to Stalin," and that PRC claims to a UN seat and control of Taiwan had legitimacy and might provide a basis to settle in Korea. Truman steadfastly held that China's leaders were "complete satellites" of the Soviets, and he refused to discuss political conditions—a PRC seat in the UN or Taiwan's status—to gain a cease-fire. Nor would the U.S. withdraw and leave their Korean allies to be "murdered." If the PRC won in Korea, "then it would be Indochina; then Hong Kong; then Malaya." The president would rather "fight it to a finish," and if the PRC drove the U.S. out, he would have it branded an "aggressor" and perhaps harass it militarily, including with aid from GMD forces. The U.S. did not want war, he said, and he had restrained MacArthur over Manchuria and Vladivostok. But "the only way to meet communism is to eliminate it," he said. The Russians understood only a "mailed fist," and "that is what we are preparing for them." As for the British, Truman concluded privately that they seemed to think that "all should be given up in the Far East to save Europe. I said no!"[63]

The president's advisers, especially Acheson, insisted that the U.S. had to have a "single foreign policy for both sides of the world" and that to adjust to China's "aggression" meant giving in to "aggression everywhere." They refused to widen cease-fire talks to include political issues. Acheson and Bradley now said that it was necessary to "hold the line" over Taiwan, lest the Filipinos and Japanese "run for cover" and the U.S. public conclude that all the gains of the Pacific war had been lost. This militarily vital base could not be left in "enemy hands."[64]

Truman also rejected joint control of the atomic bomb, although he garrulously said that since the U.S. and Britain had always been "partners," he would always consult about the weapon's use. But when Attlee asked him to put this in writing, the president insisted that "if a man's word wasn't any good it wasn't made any better by writing it down"—which entire exchange the Americans insisted be deleted from the record.[65]

The Truman-Attlee Communiqué of December 8 agreed to a UN quest for a cease-fire but rejected linkage to political issues and noted their differing views over a UN seat for the PRC and their desire to settle Taiwan peacefully. Accord on use of the atomic bomb was relegated to pious hope it would never be needed, with the U.S. to keep Britain "informed." The only U.S. concession was to delay seeking to have the UN condemn the PRC and Russians as aggressors and invoke sanctions. But Acheson insisted that it would soon be necessary to "remove the fig leaves" that hid Soviet direction of the war. Attlee consoled himself about the limits of British influence: they were "unequal in power" but "equal in counsel" with the U.S. and had been "lifted out of the European queue." White House aide Elsey groused that the "limies are tough" about Taiwan and on having "Chinks in the UN." As for the bomb: "[W]e've been raped."[66]

At the same time, Collins returned from Japan and Korea to report that UN forces were not in critical condition, that the Eighth Army could dig in south of Seoul and the X Corps on the east coast could be evacuated by sea to Pusan. Moreover, despite Stalin's urging, Mao resisted having the CPV try to drive U.S. forces from Korea. The CPV did not challenge their retreats the next week, although Truman worried that "it looks like World War III is here," and the CIA informed him that the Soviets might be planning a major war. On December 15 Truman declared a national emergency, chiefly for domestic psychological reasons. But this allowed the likes of Senator Taft—who knew that the buildup was largely intended for Europe—to promote a "great debate" over the president's right to send troops abroad without Congress' authority.[67]

Truman's diplomacy remained uncertain. In December the administration pressed for a UN-sponsored cease-fire without political preconditions but with a military inspection commission assured of access to all of Korea. The Chinese rejected this because it ignored political issues (a UN seat and Taiwan). UN officials pressed forward with a cease-fire to be followed by a political conference. The U.S. agreed to preserve UN unity but hoped that the PRC would refuse, which it did on January 13, 1951, two weeks after launching a New Year's offensive across the 38th parallel. The PRC contended that the U.S. would use the cease-fire for "breathing space" and then engage in "endless" political talks. The administration, spurred by House and Senate resolutions branding the PRC an aggressor, got the UN to pass a like measure, with sanctions deferred, on February 1. But this "aggressor" resolution only slowed efforts to settle with the PRC and underlay its long-term alienation from the UN.[68]

Military policy was also unclear. From mid-December the JCS inclined to withdraw from Korea, even after General Ridgway (who took command of ground troops when General Walton Walker died in an accident) rallied UN forces to create a relatively stable position. But MacArthur pressed for major reinforcements, again requesting GMD troops, and on December 24 proposed to respond to PRC- or Soviet-enhanced action by dropping over thirty atomic bombs on "retardation targets," invasion forces, and Manchurian air bases.[69]

Truman did not want to escalate or to withdraw from Korea and "leave our friends there to be murdered." He agreed with Acheson that the U.S. should make the war so costly for the Communists that they would negotiate its end. The JCS rewrote MacArthur's directive on December 29: there would be no additional forces, and "Korea was not the right place to fight a major war." He was to defend successive positions until necessary to undertake "orderly withdrawal." The general fired back his preference to blockade and bomb industrial China and employ GMD forces. He doubted that the Soviets would intervene and argued that the best defense of Europe was in Korea.[70]

The JCS responded on January 9, 1951, that Korean policy was unlikely to be changed and the U.S. would not attack China unless it first struck U.S. forces from outside Korea. MacArthur was to retreat to successive defensive positions until he had to withdraw to Japan. Once again the general appealed over the JCS to the president to ask whether U.S. "political policy" was to maintain military presence there indefinitely, or for a limited time, or to leave promptly. MacArthur insisted that the limitations imposed on his command made its military position untenable, but if political conditions so dictated, the command would hold until its "complete destruction."[71]

Truman and his advisers were astounded at MacArthur's "disloyal" effort either to pass the buck or to widen the war. But at Acheson's prompting, Truman added to the JCS orders a long, conciliatory letter—"not to be taken in any way as a directive"—on the need to limit the Korean War and to build long-term resistance to the "main threat," the Soviet Union.[72]

The JCS also sent Collins and Vandenberg to consult with MacArthur on January 12 bearing a JCS contingency paper with proposals similar to MacArthur's for air and naval action against the PRC. Despite MacArthur's later claims, however, this plan was unlikely to be executed, barring an attack from outside Korea on U.S. troops. Regardless, Collins again reported that conditions were far less critical than MacArthur had said. By March Ridgway had repulsed the PRC's third offensive and gotten UN forces back to the 38th parallel. The JCS withdrew their contingency plan, and the administration looked to settle. Truman refused to say whether the UN would recross the 38th parallel, insistent that this was a "tactical matter" for the field commander. He declined comment on MacArthur's March 7 and March 14 statements—neither one was cleared with the Defense Department—that to halt at the 38th parallel would bring "savage slaughter" of Allied forces.[73]

The administration opened itself again to MacArthur's maneuvers when it informed him on March 20 that it sought to settle and wished to know what had to be done to secure his forces. He responded with a public statement on March 24 that despite the inhibitions imposed on UN forces, they had "brilliantly exploited" enemy weakness, that the PRC was incapable of modern warfare, and that the UN might soon carry the war to China. He invited the PRC's military commander to meet with him in the field to capitulate.[74]

Truman and his advisers were furious at this effort to usurp the president's policy-making authority, which caused him to suspend negotiation efforts. "I'll show that son-of-a-bitch who's boss," Truman raged, and he later said that "my mind was made up" to relieve MacArthur even before there was a "next incident." So too did Deputy Defense Secretary Lovett—and everyone else—think it "perfectly obvious" that anyone other than MacArthur would have been fired at once. But they feared that Truman would appear to be "on the side of sin" if he challenged the popular general's statement. The JCS only forwarded to MacArthur a reminder from the president of his December 1950 directive to gain Defense clearance for public statements, and ordered the general to report any PRC interest in negotiations. MacArthur told an aide to "file this one with the others."[75]

The "next incident" came quickly. In a speech in early February, House minority leader Joseph Martin (MA) had called for use of GMD troops against China and then wrote MacArthur for comment. On April 5 Martin read to Congress MacArthur's deliberately nonconfidential response of March 20 stating that he fully agreed with the idea to use GMD troops, that force had to be met with maximum counterforce, and that to lose Asia was to lose Europe. Further, Martin was right to have said "there is no substitute for victory."[76]

"The situation with regard to the Far Eastern General has become a political one," Truman deduced from news stories on April 5. He concluded that MacArthur had used Martin to shoot "another political bomb." This was "the last straw": "rank insubordination." The president summoned his "Big Four"—Acheson, Marshall, Bradley, and Harriman—to deliberate but noted that "I've come to the conclusion that our Big General in the Far East must be recalled. I didn't express my opinion or make known my decision." Truman later said that the Big Four unanimously favored firing MacArthur. In fact, Acheson first wanted to build a consensus to deflect political attacks, Bradley wanted to consult the JCS, and he and Marshall proposed to consult MacArthur or order him to keep silent. Acheson rejected these options.[77]

Yet that same day Truman approved the JCS request to authorize MacArthur to strike at PRC planes and air bases in Manchuria and Shandong if they attacked U.S. forces from outside Korea. Further, during April 6–9 the president approved the JCS request to transfer nine atomic bombs to the Air Force and Strategic Air Command on Guam and Okinawa despite objections of AEC chairman Gordon Dean and others to putting nuclear weapons within MacArthur's proximity. To assuage concerns, Truman agreed that the NSC would deliberate before these bombs were used and precluded their use in northern Korea, where the terrain made them ineffective. And Bradley withheld from MacArthur both Truman's contingent approval to strike at China and order to ship nuclear weapons to the Pacific on April 10. Still, Truman felt the need to run military-political risk to assure JCS support in relieving MacArthur. By law he also had to notify the Congress' JCAE of his action, adding risk of leaks and public pressure to use atomic bombs.[78]

Truman reinforced his resolve to relieve MacArthur by reviewing an aide's notes of President Lincoln's firing in 1862 of his insubordinate general, George McClellan, and by talking to political friends and leaders. Vice President Barkley urged firing, while Chief Justice Fred Vinson, House Speaker Sam Rayburn, and Senate and House majority leaders Ernest McFarland and John McCormack inclined to caution. By April 9 the JCS joined the Big Four in agreeing to dismiss MacArthur for insubordination, narrowly defined as being out of sympathy with administration policy and violating the president's December 1950 directive to gain clearance for public statements. Only then did Truman reveal his decision and instruct that MacArthur be removed from all of his commands, to be replaced by Ridgway. Army Secretary Frank Pace, then in Korea, was to go to Japan to convey this personally to MacArthur.[79]

Truman told his White House staff early on April 10. He called MacArthur "a worse double crosser than McClellan" but would say nothing publicly until Pace informed him in Tokyo. Then a Pacific communications foul-up and an evening press inquiry to the White House led to fear that MacArthur might learn of the impending action and resign first to embarrass the administration. This led to a hasty White House news conference and release at 1:00 A.M. on April 11 of Truman's order dismissing MacArthur for not giving "wholehearted support" to administration policy and breeching his constitutional duty to be governed by higher civilian authority policies and directives.[80]

Publicly Truman sought to explain the dismissal not as a constitutional is-

sue but as a result of the general's disagreement with the administration's lim-
ited-war policy. Truman defined this as U.S. resistance to a Soviet-led effort to
conquer Korea as part of its "monstrous" global conspiracy but avoidance of
war with China. Truman also made clear that the people who had said that the
PRC would not fight in Korea would not now persuade him that the Soviets
would not intervene if the U.S. attacked China.[81]

MacArthur's firing produced the "explosion" Truman expected. Senator
McCarthy said that the "son-of-a-bitch [Truman] should be impeached," and
Senators William Jenner (IN) and Richard Nixon (CA) charged that the firing
was directed by, or benefited, the Soviets and their allies. Hearst, McCormick,
and Scripps-Howard newspapers were highly critical; some major papers—the
New York Times and *Washington Post*—were supportive. Truman noted the immediate arrival of "telegrams and letters of abuse by the dozens," and the first
week's 13,000 letters ran more than 2 : 1 against him. But by late April the heavy
mail was nearly even, and polls showed public sentiment to be 7 : 3 against war
with China. The decision to explain MacArthur's firing in terms of need to fight
a limited war had succeeded.[82]

Truman believed he could ride out the storm over MacArthur's firing. He
told a White House aide that he could "do nothing else and still be president of
the United States" because the issue was civilian control of the military, although the charge was limited to MacArthur's insubordination. "There can't be
two policy makers at the head of government," Truman wrote in April 1951.
He was sorry to reach "a parting of the ways with the big man in Asia," he told
Eisenhower, but "he asked for it and I had to give it to him." Still the president
insisted that Democratic congressional leaders accede to Joe Martin's unilateral
invitation to MacArthur to address a joint session of Congress, and he ordered
a military honor guard for the general's cross-country travel from San Francisco, with Marshall and JCS greeting him at Washington National Airport.
The president did not greet him at the airport and in his place sent only his military aide, General Harry Vaughan, who was not well respected. White House
staff drafted a gallows-humor welcoming schedule that envisioned MacArthur
wading ashore from a submarine, the burning of the constitution, the lynching
of Acheson, and giving a "21 atomic bomb salute" for the general.[83]

MacArthur's address to a joint session of Congress on April 19 was the-
atrically stunning, and interrupted by applause thirty-four times. In Olympian
style, he insisted that the U.S. could not appease or surrender to Communism
in Asia any more than it could in Europe and that the administration had imposed unacceptable military constraints on his command by denying hot pursuit and use of a blockade and GMD forces against China. (He said nothing of
his proposals to drop atomic bombs on industrial China and to use GMD forces

in Korea.) He alleged that the JCS agreed with his strategy and that war's object was not prolonged indecision but "victory." He said he could not answer his "gallant" soldiers' questions about why advantages had been surrendered to the enemy. Now he was closing fifty-two years of military service, and as the ballad had it, "Old soldiers never die; they just fade away," as would he, "an old soldier who tried to do his duty as God gave him the light to see that duty. Good bye." MacArthur exited to a massive parade and reception by 6,000 Daughters of the American Revolution, and a parade the next day in New York witnessed by 7.5 million people, followed by a national speaking tour.[84]

The president left it to his senior advisers to explicate policy to a joint Senate Foreign Relations and Armed Services Committee hearing on the "Military Situation in the Far East" during May–June. The administration prepared questions for friendly senators to ask to expose the dangers of MacArthur's wider war strategy and his lack of grasp of America's global responsibilities, and leaked a transcript of the Wake Island talks. The general was allowed to testify first and at length. He denied military or political error, blamed faulty intelligence for failure to anticipate PRC intervention, and again assailed the administration for curbing his military tactics. MacArthur also said that knowledge of how the USSR would react to a U.S. attack on the PRC was beyond his purview as a theater commander—which was the administration's point about their need to contain the war. He also denied intent to usurp presidential authority.[85]

Marshall, Bradley, and the JCS countered MacArthur, especially his surmise that the Soviets probably would not give significant aid to a China under attack. But for national security reasons, the administration excised information from the public record that would have undercut MacArthur's position by showing how risky wider war would have been given the great air and submarine power of the Soviets and PRC in northeast Asia and the "shoestring" nature of the U.S. air operation. The JCS also revealed that while the U.S. resisted attacks on PRC or Soviet territory, the latter two had refrained from bombing U.S. air bases and ports in southeastern Korea and Japan. Bradley also stated that the JCS had shelved their contingency plan to attack China, but now Ridgway had qualified authority to use atomic weapons against China in event of a major assault from outside Korea. Most telling was Bradley's comment that the Soviets were the main threat and that to fight China "would involve us in the wrong war, at the wrong place, at the wrong time, and with the wrong enemy."[86]

Acheson concluded the administration's case with a long defense of post-1945 China policy, the main focus of Republican attack after MacArthur's Korean War strategy was undermined. The secretary held that Truman's firing of

MacArthur rested on the president's sole authority to conduct foreign policy and power as commander in chief to issue orders that had to be obeyed. More dubious, if uncontested, was the secretary's contention that the decision to cross the 38th parallel was not intended to effect Korean political unity but necessitated by need to destroy enemy forces, and that PRC entry resulted not from this action but MacArthur's deployment of troops near the Yalu.[87]

The president won the public-opinion battle over his right to relieve MacArthur and to refrain from war against the PRC. The public soon tired of the hearings, and political allies reported that MacArthur on tour was "fading away"—a "drug on the market," Truman noted. In August the senators sent the record of their hearings to the full Senate, but issued no final report. Eight Republicans proffered a de facto minority report conceding presidential authority but deploring the circumstances of MacArthur's firing. In fact, Truman's popularity never recovered from this imbroglio, and administration policy rigidified. Marshall stated that the U.S. would never recognize the PRC or allow it to control Taiwan, and U.S. aid to the GMD would continue. Rusk publicly branded the PRC a Soviet puppet, in his words, a large-scale "Slavic Manchukuo."[88]

IV

Despite the rhetoric, the Truman administration sought to settle the Korean War along the 38th parallel but believed that first it had to halt the Communists' spring offensive lest it be seen as "leading from weakness." After Ridgway's forces battered the CPV, Acheson told the senators holding the MacArthur hearings in early June that the U.S. was amenable to a cease-fire at or near the 38th parallel. The U.S. also used a chance encounter between members of its UN delegation and Ambassador Malik to begin exploratory talks.[89]

Kennan conveyed U.S. interest in a military armistice with no link to political issues with the PRC. Malik expressed Soviet interest in a "peaceful solution" without insisting on withdrawal of foreign troops from Korea. Kennan urged a Washington initiative: the Soviets wished to avert conflict with the U.S. but would soon cause "trouble" if the Korean fighting continued. In fact, the USSR sought to halt the war, or preclude escalation that would bring hostile forces to its borders and increase Western unity. The PRC found the conflict too economically costly and caused too great a dependency on the Soviets, who demanded hard currency for outdated weapons. PRC war aims were limited: restoration of the 38th parallel and political status quo ante, and withdrawal of foreign troops. DPRK and ROK leaders sought to battle to the end.[90]

By late June Truman was persuaded that the "Russians are tired of the Korean affair and want to quit. We'll see." On June 23 Malik announced on a UN-sponsored radio program that the Soviets favored discussion between the belligerents to gain a cease-fire and mutual withdrawal from the 38th parallel. He did not mention foreign troop withdrawal, a PRC seat in the UN, or control of Taiwan. The PRC's *People's Daily* "strongly endorsed" this proposal. Truman announced support of a peaceful resolution if it ended "aggression" in Korea and achieved "security." Acheson told the House Foreign Affairs Committee that the U.S. would settle for Communist withdrawal above the 38th parallel and security for the ROK. The Russians proposed direct UN and Communist military command talks, and Bradley won reluctant JCS support by insisting that U.S. failure to act would undercut UN and public backing.[91]

Truman soon agreed to allow Ridgway to accept a proposal from the Communists to meet at Kaesong, an ancient capital in "no man's land" just south of the 38th parallel, but stipulated that every U.S. decision would be made in Washington. He suspected—wrongly—that the Communists sought a respite only to prepare another offensive. He also shared Defense Department concern that talks might undermine rearmament and publicly persisted in stating that the Soviets sought global conquest.[92]

Talks began on July 10. The U.S. (ostensibly UN Command) negotiators, led by Admiral C. Turner Joy—who disdained bargaining with the "evil" Communists—stipulated that they discuss only cease-fire matters. The Communists, led by North Korean General Nam Il and the "real power," PRC chief of staff General Hsieh Fang, proposed an immediate cease-fire; mutual withdrawal of troops from the 38th parallel and then withdrawal of all foreign troops from Korea; repatriation of all POWs; and then discussion of settlement of the Korean War. U.S. officials, despite Acheson's earlier statements, refused the 38th parallel as a demarcation line and sought a more northern position, and dismissed foreign troop removal as a political issue. They also rejected post-armistice repatriation of all POWs ("all for all"), although this practice was called for by military custom and the Geneva Convention of 1949, which the U.S. had signed (but not yet ratified) and had agreed to abide by in 1950. Sensing that many Communist POWs did not want to be returned, U.S. officials hoped to exact concessions before exchanging some 150,000 Communist POWs for about 16,000 UN POWs.[93]

Acheson applauded Ridgway for meeting the Communists "head on," and on July 19 declared that U.S. troops would remain in Korea to guarantee against "aggression." The JCS proposed that if negotiations ended, UN forces should invade North Korea, bomb along the Yalu, undertake hot pursuit into Manchuria, and blockade China. Finally, after two weeks of posturing, U.S. and Communist negotiators proposed to fix a demarcation line to allow a cease-fire; to establish a body to monitor the cease-fire; and to make arrangements for the POWs.

The U.S. pressed the current battle line—a demarcation line well north of the 38th parallel—as vital to ROK security and just compensation for halting the air war on North Korea. The Communists cited Acheson's earlier statements about the 38th parallel and refused any hint of UN victory. Negotiations broke off in late August, and resumed on October 25 at Panmunjon.[94]

The Communists backed off the 38th parallel as a demarcation line and proposed instead the battle line at the time an armistice was agreed. The U.S. pressed the current—and advantageous—battle line, and the Communists acceded, although debate raged over disputed areas. Ridgway then reverted to the battle line at the armistice so that the UN could continue to fight for territory. But the JCS thought the Communist position reasonable and got Truman to order Ridgway to agree to the current battle line provided all other issues were settled within thirty days. Washington prevailed, and on November 27 the current battle line was agreed to be the demarcation line. This meant a de facto cease-fire because neither side would want to battle for new territory that would have to be returned when an armistice was signed.[95]

Truman was not of conciliatory mind, as the difficult POW issue showed. Acheson believed that the Geneva Convention required all-for-all repatriation, but the JCS inclined to voluntary repatriation to wage "psychological warfare" against the Communists. Ridgway wanted a 1:1 exchange of POWs to prevent the Communists from regaining a large number of their troops, although he was amenable to all for all to ensure early return of all U.S. and ROK troops. But in late October Truman refused all for all. He said that Communist POWs who had cooperated with the U.S. would be "immediately done away with" upon return and that it was unfair to exchange some 150,000 Communist POWs for 16,000 UN POWs. Under Secretary of State James Webb cautioned the president that he might wish to reconsider if the POW issue was the final barrier to an armistice. But Truman doubted this, unless the U.S. got "some major concession" not otherwise obtainable. This view caused one official to note need to "educate the Pres. a little on the POW problem."[96]

Truman was resistant. Even after Ridgway got State and Defense Department concurrence to all for all exchange, the president gave his "strong view" that the U.S. insist "vigorously" on 1:1 exchange, short of breaking negotiations. After this was completed, he said, he might permit repatriation of the remaining Communist POWs on a voluntary basis. But he would make the "final decision."[97]

Truman grew angry at the Communist buildup of ground and air forces—including over 200,000 PRC troops and use of the superlative Russian MIG-15 jet fighter—and their negotiating demands to be able to repair their airfields free from attack and to ban a post-armistice UN troop and equipment buildup. He insisted that the U.S. had "expended lives, tons of bombs, and a large amount of equipment to bring these people to terms." On December 10 he cut short a Key West vacation to address his senior officials in a Cabinet Room meeting. The president said that if the Communists drove the U.S. from the peninsula, "our whole career in Korea would have been wasted," and that at Panmunjon "they have been making the demands and we the concessions." Bradley replied that the Communists had made "very big concessions" by giving up the 38th parallel as a demarcation line and ceding Kaesong and that the U.S. had mutual interest in unchallenged airfield and road repair. Air Force Secretary Thomas Finletter reminded the president that the U.S. had achieved its goals in Korea by repelling aggression and upholding the UN, and it should "not try to rub their [Communist] noses." Truman reluctantly acceded to Bradley's proposal to continue to negotiate and wanted Allied support to warn the PRC that if it violated an armistice, "we will go all out against China."[98]

A Communist proposal to permit UN troop rotation in exchange for repair of airfields—the "key" issue, Admiral Joy vainly believed—raised hopes for an armistice. The thirty-day deadline based on the November battle line was extended to mid-January 1952. Meanwhile, in mid-December Truman and his advisers formalized in NSC 118/2 Bradley's "greater sanction" concept, a proposed warning—never made public—that Soviet or PRC aggression against an armistice would be met by U.S. and Allied military reaction "outside Korea." Or as the British softened the language, the reaction "would not necessarily be limited in geographical scope."[99]

Armistice talks then suffered a major setback in early January 1952 when the U.S. introduced the concept of voluntary repatriation of POWs, an idea gaining favor among politicians and others as means to undermine loyalty of Soviet or satellite-nation troops. The Communists denounced the proposal as "absurd" and vowed to "fight to the end" the U.S. idea to give Chinese POWs the option of returning to Taiwan. Meanwhile, Churchill, having recently returned to office, visited Truman in early January. The prime minister reassured the president that his decision to intervene in Korea had been the "turning point in East-West relationships." But Churchill opposed "all out war" against China, especially use of atomic weapons in Korea or China. Bradley replied that there were no suitable targets, and Acheson admitted that U.S. hope to split the PRC from the Soviets was ended. Still, Truman was persistent that the British did not grasp the U.S. effort to "localize" the Korean War and to meet any prospective PRC attack on Southeast Asia.[100]

Truman wrote bitterly in late January that negotiating with the Communists was akin to dealing with the heads of numbers rackets or dope rings—they had "no honor and no moral code." Drawing on Bradley's "greater sanction," he imagined giving the Soviets and the PRC a ten-day ultimatum to quit the war in Korea or the U.S. would blockade China and destroy every military base in Manchuria. He raged that the Russians had broken every agreement from Teheran to Potsdam, raped "Poland, Rumania, Czeko-Slavakia [sic], Hungary, Estonia, and Latvia, and Lithuania," and turned three million Second World War POWs into "slave labor." But the Soviet leaders could "get the Chinamen out of Korea" and stop supplying the "thugs" attacking the free world. If not, there would be "all out war" and every major city from St. Petersburg to Moscow to Vladivostok and from Mukden to Pekin[g] to Shanghai would be eliminated. "This is the final chance for the Soviet Government to decide whether it desires to survive or not." [101]

Probably Truman did not intend atomic war, although pressure for atomic strikes was ever present and likely to increase in a heated presidential election year. At the same time, the sense of moral and military superiority of the president and his administration narrowed prospects for resolving differences, especially regarding POWs. In February Acheson urged Truman to endorse voluntary repatriation even though the secretary recognized the primacy of the Geneva Convention and admitted that deadlock on the POW question might endanger Allied POWs. But now Acheson, perhaps deferring to his "client," stressed that voluntary repatriation would gain U.S. public and political support and be viewed as consistent with American morality and "psychological warfare" against "Communist tyranny." Lovett, now secretary of defense, was dubious, but unwilling to challenge Acheson, because senior military officials were divided on the issue. Thus Truman approved voluntary repatriation, or opposition to "forcible" repatriation, as U.S. policy. He also stated that officials might seek a compromise but if the choice had to be one of voluntary or forcible repatriation, Truman's mind was long made up. [102]

Deputy Assistant Secretary of State U. Alexis Johnson and Army Vice Chief of Staff General John E. Hull then went to assess POW camps on Koje-do Island off Pusan. Conditions were frightful in the badly overcrowded compounds, overseen by tough ROK and GMD (from Taiwan) guards. Hull and Johnson reported that "mutiny was in the air," but that only about one half, or 11,500 PRC and 5,000 North Korean POWs, would "violently" resist repatriation. Thus the U.S. might skirt forcible repatriation by omitting these objectors from their official POW lists, although Ridgway warned that this violated the Geneva Convention and might cause U.S./UN POWs to be held back. The PRC was also unlikely to allow its soldiers, many of whom had been in the GMD army, to opt to return to Taiwan. [103]

The president concluded at a White House meeting on February 27 that voluntary repatriation was the "final U.S. position." He insisted that the U.S. screen all POWs and remove from its lists those who opposed being repatriated. Remaining POWs would be exchanged on an all-for-all basis for Com-munist-held POWs. Only Chief of Naval Operations (CNO) Admiral William Fechteler warned (as had Ridgway) that this policy might jeopardize return of U.S. POWs, although Acheson, back from a NATO meeting, reported that no U.S. ally opposed this policy. In fact, in Cabinet the British agreed to give it "full support." [104]

Truman deplored harsh Soviet treatment of returned POWs after the Sec-ond World War. But his current decision rested mainly on his sense of moral superiority toward the Communists and their seeming need for forcible repa-triation, and his desire to gain a "psychological" Cold War victory at home and abroad. He and his aides assumed that U.S. power could force the Communists to accept the U.S. position and greatly underestimated the number of POWs who would refuse repatriation. No one had tried to "educate" the president on the POW issue, explaining how he might have gained public support for all-for-all exchange by citing the Geneva Convention, concern for rapid return of American POWs, and need to end the costly Korean conflict.

Meanwhile, the Communists publicly exploited the POW camp problems and mounted a propaganda campaign alleging that the U.S. was waging bacte-riological warfare. The charge originated with PRC field commanders' erro-neous explanation of the outbreak of cholera and plague among their troops but was continued even after Beijing knew the truth. Acheson proposed a Red Cross investigation, which the Communists rejected as biased, but interna-tional criticism of the U.S. continued. On April 1 the U.S. told the Communists that approximately 116,000 POWs could be repatriated to them. The Commu-nists implied that this might suffice for a settlement and that the U.S. omit from its POW lists those reclassified as "civilian internees" or DPRK soldiers of southern origins. But all PRC soldiers had to be returned. [105]

Upon screening, however, the U.S. found only 70,000 Communist POWs willing to return. U.S. officials knew that GMD guards brutally intimidated POWs to refuse repatriation and, by May, rescreening raised willing repatri-ates to about 82,000. Clever list keeping might have raised the number to 100,000, a figure the Communists might have accepted if this included all of the 20,000 PRC POWs. But on April 19 Ridgway, anxious to embarrass the Communists, gave them the 70,000 figure and held to this number for months, while the Communists assailed the U.S. for reneging on its commitment of 116,000 POWs. [106]

The administration sought to avert an impasse, and avoid focus on the POW issue as the bar to an armistice, with a three-point package proposal derived from months of negotiations. On April 28 Ridgway proposed an agreement based on a four-member Neutral Nations Commission (composed of Poland,

Czechoslovakia, Sweden, and Switzerland) to monitor the armistice; unrestricted North Korean airfield repair; and no forcible exchange of POWs. The Communists accepted the trade-off terms—armistice supervision for airfield repair—but demanded return of virtually all their POWs. Neither side would budge on the POW issue, and on May 7 the negotiators declared deadlock.[107]

Truman publicly declared forced repatriation "unthinkable," repugnant to American principles: "We will not buy an armistice by turning over human beings for slaughter or slavery." At West Point on May 18, he reiterated that "we won't buy an armistice by trafficking in human slavery," and privately denounced the negotiations as "propaganda sounding boards for the Commies." He again vented his anger at the Soviets for having murdered over a million German and Polish POWs in the Second World War, having broken every agreement from Teheran to Potsdam, and having "no morals, no honor." And once again he imagined giving the Soviets an atomic ultimatum: "[A]ccept our fair and just proposal or you will be completely destroyed."[108]

Truman was also distraught that on May 7 rioting Communist POWs on Koje-do Island seized the U.S. commander, General Francis Dodd, who had gone into the compound to discuss repatriation. His second in command, General Charles Colson, soon secured Dodd's release by publicly stating that UN forces had killed or wounded some POWs. The Truman administration was embarrassed, and angered by the Communist propaganda that intensified in June after the new U.S. commander, General Haydon Boatner, had to use great force—killing forty-one POWs—to restore order in the POW compounds.[109]

Rhee meanwhile proposed to Truman that he sign a mutual-security treaty with the ROK. Acheson opposed making any response, but Truman, afraid to seem discourteous, opted to convey informal assurances of security. Rhee now declared martial law in Pusan (the temporary capital), began to arrest his political opponents, and brushed off U.S. protests. Then on June 2, sensing that the National Assembly would not reelect him to the presidency, he threatened to dissolve that body if it did not pass a constitutional amendment calling for election of the president by popular vote, which he knew his police could control.[110]

Truman cabled Rhee that these shocking events threatened to make a "mockery" of UN sacrifices in Korea. But the ROK president rejoined that Truman was "ill-informed" and that the U.S. Embassy seemed to be siding with "Communist conspirators." Rhee dropped his threat to dissolve the National Assembly but otherwise continued his "reign of terror," as Acheson termed it, to promote his reelection. U.S. officials feared civil war in South Korea and ordered General Mark Clark (who had replaced Ridgway in May) to prepare to seize the government and put Rhee in custody until martial law was ended and political-civil rights were restored. The military coup never came to pass, however, because Rhee's police and goon squads cowed the National Assembly on

July 3 into passing his constitutional amendment, and the next month he won overwhelming reelection.[111]

The Truman administration, meanwhile, tried to bomb its way to an armistice. On June 19 the president approved a JCS order removing restrictions on bombing North Korean hydroelectric plants on the Yalu River, and on June 23–27 air and naval forces attacked five installations. This caused a two-week blackout in North Korea and curtailed Manchuria's electric supply. But it also produced British protest that the U.S. had broken its pledge to consult before taking drastic action. The U.S. lamely replied that time was too short to consult and that the bombings were on the Korean side of the Yalu.[112]

The U.S. increased military pressure by heavily bombing Pyongyang on July 11, and ten days later Admiral Arthur Radford, commander of the Pacific Fleet, ordered a show of force of one hundred naval jets off the China coast that even Acheson disapproved and Lovett called "sophomoric—just crazy." Still, in mid-July the JCS granted Clark's request for a squadron of F-84 jets with atomic capability. Truman then approved bombing, to be carried out on September 1, of military targets in northeast Korea, a few miles from the Manchurian and Soviet borders. The president maintained during bombing protests that the "free nations" of the world were resisting Soviet aggression and had shown that they would never again walk the "dreary road of appeasement." Nor would the U.S. allow the Communists to force return of their POWs to "slavery and almost certain death."[113]

Behind the bluster, the administration sought to break the deadlock by raising the offer of repatriable POWs from 70,000 to 83,000. The Communists suggested compromise at 100,000–110,000, including all PRC prisoners. There matters stalemated. Truman thought to gain a propaganda victory by supporting a Bradley-JCS idea to invite PRC officials to Koje-do Island to repatriate willing POWs, but General Clark insisted that the PRC would terrorize POWs into returning. Shortly, Acheson weighed an approach to the USSR, but Kennan, now ambassador to Moscow, said that the Soviets would already have acted if they deemed it in their interest.[114]

In August State Department officials continued to weigh having Truman propose an armistice based on the points already agreed, including exchange of 83,000 Communist POWs for 16,000 UN POWs, with post-armistice negotiations to resolve the fate of POWs resisting repatriation. Nitze said that would allow the Communists not to have to agree in advance—as U.S. negotiators had insisted—to nonforcible return of POWs. Then on September 2 President Miguel Aleman of Mexico proposed through the UN an immediate armistice–POW exchange, with nonrepatriates sent to neutral nations as political refugees.[115]

Nitze, Kennan, and other officials wished to move forward, but Clark, the

JCS, and Robert Murphy, now Ridgway's political adviser in Japan, opposed a presidential statement, despite belief that Aleman's idea was a step toward an armistice. But at a Cabinet meeting on September 12, Truman agreed with Lovett's argument that the U.S. should not retreat on issues to get an armistice and that if the U.S. stayed firm, "we can tear them [the Communists] up by air."[116]

Three days later Truman met with the JCS and senior Defense Department officials who, led by Lovett, opposed any proposal. They insisted that the Communists were influenced "solely by force" and would take any offer as a sign of weakness and seek more concessions. Admiral Ruthven Libby, assistant CNO and former armistice negotiator, likened the Communists to "talking animals," incapable of equitable compromise. The president concluded that there was no prospect of an armistice and no alternative to increasing military pressure. The Panmunjon delegation had to present a summary of the U.S. position and then "walk out" of negotiations with no hint of returning unless the Communists made a substantive reply.[117]

Acheson struggled to get around the military's position. He believed that there was only "a one-in-a-thousand" chance that the Communists would permit POWs to be sent to neutral nations. He also suspected that the military opposed an armistice because they feared that they would have to "bring the boys home" while the Communists would reinforce their troops. The next day Lovett stood fast that the U.S. offer only a summary position at Panmunjon and, failing a substantive reply, walk out and also increase military pressure. Acheson agreed to increased pressure but wanted the U.S. to show that it had "exhausted every reasonable effort." Lovett was unmoved, and Acheson concluded that Truman had to choose which position to take.[118]

The president and senior officials held their fateful meeting on September 24. Acheson, sensing resistance all around, sought a self-defeating consensus. He said that State and Defense views did not differ on nonforcible repatriation or need for a summary stance at Panmunjon. But the U.S. had to convince its allies that it had acted rightly. The issue was how to offer terms acceptable to the Communists that would not weaken the U.S. negotiating stance or post-armistice military position. Truman was not encouraging. He would not do "anything in the world to get an armistice" because he feared a repeat of 1945—when Americans "tore up our military machine"—and now he wanted a buildup. Military officials fiercely opposed post-armistice negotiations on nonrepatriable POWs. They wanted increased military pressure and restatement of America's April 28 package proposal.

The president agreed. An armistice would do "no good" unless we "wipe the slate clean." The Communists had to be given "about ten days to accept" the package proposal; otherwise the U.S. had to "be prepared to do the things that seemed necessary." Truman said that he had been "trying to prevent World War III and that he would hate to end his political career by bringing it on, but we cannot give in on principle." The issue was decided. Acheson asked only that Truman not issue an "ultimatum" by stating in advance what action he would take if the Communists refused his proposal. But when Air Force Secretary Pace asked how long after the deadline should increased military pressure begin, the president said "immediately." Shortly he instructed Clark to put the tripartite proposal to the Communists with "utmost firmness": no debate, an October 8 deadline, and maintenance of military pressure.[119]

On September 28 U.S. negotiators proposed a four-power commission of neutral nations to monitor the armistice; unfettered airfield repair; and nonforcible POW repatriation. The Communists responded with a military offensive, and soon rejected the proposal and insisted on repatriation of all of their POWs. The U.S. declared an indefinite recess. Truman administration efforts to negotiate a settlement were ended. In early October the president proclaimed that "we are fighting in Korea so that we won't have to fight in Wichita."[120]

The next week Acheson proposed a UN resolution proclaiming nonforcible repatriation for all POWs, and gained twenty cosponsors among NATO and Commonwealth allies. Indian delegation member V. K. Krishna Menon pressed a deliberately vague resolution to have a four-power Repatriation Commission, following Geneva Convention practices, take responsibility for the POWs, with a fifth nation as "umpire" to help decide disputed cases within ninety days. POWs who still refused repatriation would be turned over to a political conference. Many U.S. allies liked this idea, but Acheson demanded nonforcible repatriation and a time limit for final release, lest the Communists, he said, harangue nonrepatriates into returning. The secretary told Truman that Menon's resolution was akin to "strike settlement lingo," which seems "to give the U.S. the words and the other side the decision." Acheson further reassured the president by deploring U.S. allies for accepting the idea of the Civil War general who said that "if you can't lick 'em, jine 'em," whereas "you are going ahead with General Grant to 'fight it out on this line if it takes all summer.'" Truman instructed the U.S. delegation to stick to nonforcible repatriation.[121]

Acheson also urged the president to gain support from General Eisenhower, now the Republican presidential nominee. During 1952 he had supported U.S. intervention in Korea but accepted his party's platform assailing Democratic foreign policy as "negative, futile and immoral." In the campaign he criticized the Truman administration for having "abandoned" China to the Communists and "written off" much of Asia—although Truman quickly rejoined that Eisenhower was chief of staff in 1947 when the JCS determined to withdraw from Korea. Then on October 24, 1952, Eisenhower pledged that if elected he would "go to Korea." An angry Truman thought that would achieve nothing useful. But after Eisenhower's victory at the polls and a White House transition meeting, the president-elect endorsed Truman's nonforcible repatriation policy. Acheson warned the British that if they supported Menon's resolution there would be "no NATO, no Anglo-American friendship."[122]

But Menon gained more support for his resolution by agreeing that POWs resisting repatriation would be transferred to the UN for their maintenance. The U.S. acquiesced, but the Soviets "set everyone . . . on their ears" by assailing the proposal, perhaps because it implied nonforcible repatriation or because they feared that the PRC, hurting economically, might accept nonforcible repatriation for DPRK—but not PRC—POWs, while U.S. allies would back the resolution as the only alternative to an expanded war. Despite Menon's objections, Acheson pressed UN responsibility for the ultimate "disposition" of unrepatriated POWs, and he also expected to fight the Russians over whether the Geneva Convention meant repatriation "by force." But he felt that he had gotten "most of what we needed."[123]

The UN rejected Soviet efforts to "amend" Menon's resolution to declare an armistice on the basis of points already agreed, and then voted the resolution by 53–5 on December 3. The Americans took this as a victory for nonforcible repatriation, despite deferral of their twenty-one-power resolution, while prospect of a "greater sanction" against the PRC ended. The PRC and DPRK rejected the UN resolution, however. Meanwhile, Eisenhower visited Korea in early December, deliberately meeting only briefly and privately with Rhee and giving Clark no chance to press his plans to attack the PRC. Upon return to the U.S., Eisenhower said little. He met with MacArthur but declined his proposals for "atomic bombing" of China. Truman said MacArthur had no solution except "all-out war in the Far East," and the president now called Eisenhower's recent trip to Korea "demagoguery," intended solely to fulfill a campaign pledge.[124]

The real problem, Lovett said in a Cabinet meeting, was that PRC and DPRK forces were entrenched in the mountains and the PRC had jet bombers that could not be knocked out without bombing above the Yalu—and "if we do that then it might be World War III." Thus Truman could tell a National War College assemblage on December 19 only that U.S. foreign policy had met its "greatest test" by repulsing the Communists' attack on South Korea and that the Communists had rejected a UN-proposed "honorable end" to the war. The president reiterated this in his final State of the Union address on January 7, 1953, and in his Farewell Address on January 15. He analogized Soviet-inspired aggression in Korea in 1950 to German and Japanese aggression in the 1930s and applauded that "where free men had failed the test before, this time we met the test." He also opposed use of an atomic bomb to end the war: "We are not made that way. We are a moral people," and atomic war was "unthinkable." He did not mention military concern about suitable targets or Soviet retaliation.[125]

V

Harry Truman left the White House in January 1953 bitterly frustrated despite his private claim to have "knocked the socks off the Communists in Korea." President Eisenhower had no plan to end the war and would need several months to develop a course of action. His State of the Union declaration on February 2 that the Seventh Fleet in the Taiwan Strait would no longer shield the PRC was bluster. Further, despite his and Secretary of State Dulles' talk at an NSC meeting about need to break down the "false distinction" between atomic and conventional weapons, General Bradley cited Allied opposition and pushed the matter aside. The NSC also refused General Clark's request to bomb Manchurian air bases.[126]

Then Stalin died on March 5. His successor as premier, Georgi Malenkov, initiated a "peace offensive," insistent that U.S.-USSR issues could be settled without war. The Soviets also pressed compromise upon the PRC, which was amenable because it was spending 60 percent of its tax revenue on defense rather than desperately needed modernization. The famine-stricken DPRK was too weak to resist. On March 28 Communist negotiators, taking up a prior suggestion of the Red Cross and Clark, proposed to exchange sick and wounded POWs, and in a cable to the UN Zhou proposed to resume full negotiations. Exchange of sick and wounded, Operation Little Switch, was soon effected, with armistice talks resumed in late April.[127]

Meanwhile, during February–May, NSC and JCS officials worked out six scenarios for increased warfare within Korea and outside of it. Five scenarios included use of atomic weapons and air and naval assaults on the PRC. But every plan had serious drawbacks, including risk of Soviet atomic retaliation and general war. Further, the British began to back off any "greater sanction" against the PRC. Even Dulles saw need for the U.S. to settle the war.[128]

In late April Communist negotiators proposed repatriation of all willing POWs within two months after an armistice was signed; nonrepatriates would be sent to a neutral nation to discuss return with home-state agents; after six months, a post-armistice political conference would determine the fate of remaining nonrepatriates. Clark pressed to know which neutral state would take custody of the POWs, to reduce their stay to two months, and to set a definite date for their final release to an available nation of their choice.[129]

The Communists offered significant concessions on May 7. They dropped the neutral-state idea and proposed that custody screening for repatriation be done by a Neutral Nations Repatriation Commission (NNRC) composed of Sweden, Switzerland, Czechoslovakia, Poland, and India. But a political conference would still make final disposition of remaining nonrepatriates. Clark saw the similarity to the UN-Menon resolution and accepted the NNRC concept but wanted decisions made by unanimous vote (ending undue U.S. worry that India would always side with the two Communist states). He also pressed to reduce the screening period to two months and set a date for final release of nonrepatriates as civilians. But the Communists, opposed to the final release terms, refused agreement.[130]

The U.S. then pursued carrot-and-stick policy, beginning on May 13 with massive bombing of North Korea's irrigation dams to flood spring plantings and disrupt food supplies and rail transport. Eisenhower agreed to increased ROK military aid, including U.S. forces in post-armistice Korea, and Clark updated "Operation Everready," a plan to remove Rhee from power if he acted to thwart an armistice. The JCS, meanwhile, planned to expand the war against China and sought authority over atomic weapons, but Eisenhower held back. Dulles, in India, told Nehru that the U.S. "would probably make a stronger rather than lesser military response," but despite Dulles' later claim, it is doubtful Nehru passed along an atomic warning to the PRC.[131]

On May 25 U.S. officials gave a final offer to the Communists with four concessions: after an armistice, Korean POWs would not be released but given to the NNRC and treated the same as Chinese POWs; NNRC decisions would be by majority vote; the custody period would be ninety days; and a political conference (or the UN, if the Communists preferred) would make final disposition of remaining nonrepatriates within thirty days, after which POWs would be released. The U.S. set a reply time of one week, or negotiations would be ended.[132]

The Communists rejected UN disposition of the POWs, but agreed to study the other terms. The U.S., through Ambassador Charles Bohlen in Moscow, informed Molotov that these proposals went to the "extreme limit of possible concessions." On June 4 the Communists substantially accepted the U.S. terms, including final release of POWs as civilians, which "far exceeds our most optimistic expectation," Dulles wrote Eisenhower. Reference terms for the POW issue were quickly drawn, and by mid-June accord neared on a demarcation line and demilitarized zone.[133]

The U.S., and belatedly Truman, had won on the issue of voluntary, or nonforcible, repatriation of POWs. Why the Communists conceded is uncertain. Clearly, the post-Stalin Soviet regime sought improved relations with the West, confronted increasing political-economic unrest in Eastern Europe—including revolts in East Berlin in June—and had to provide costly aid for the PRC, which was prepared to continue the war but greatly needed to begin its first Five-Year Plan in 1953. Moreover, the PRC had shown the world that it could stand up to the West. Devastated North Korea had to follow its senior allies. As for atomic threats, the U.S. did not make any in spring 1953, nor was the PRC ever intimidated by such threats.[134]

Rhee now sought to "torpedo" an armistice with his planned release of 25,000 Communist POWs on June 18. Eisenhower told the NSC that "we seem to have acquired a new enemy" and briefly weighed saying "goodbye" to Korea. But withdrawal was viewed as too politically embarrassing. Instead, the U.S. rebutted Allied and PRC charges of complicity with Rhee's action and warned him that noncooperation would cause the U.S. to effect a separate armistice. An unrepentant Rhee now demanded that the U.S. sign a security pact prior to an armistice; increase economic and military aid; keep NNRC forces (to guard POWs) out of South Korea; and pledge U.S. military support for an ROK advance northward if the post-armistice political conference did not gain removal of PRC forces from Korea and unify the nation.[135]

Eisenhower again weighed a separate armistice and considered leaving Korea but sent Assistant Secretary Walter S. Robertson to Seoul to negotiate. Robertson saw Rhee as a "fanatic" capable of leading Korea into "national suicide," but the emissary got Washington to assure economic and military aid (for twenty divisions) and encouraged Eisenhower to get Senate leaders to commit on a defense pact. The president made this pledge public on July 6, and on July 10 the ROK leader assured Eisenhower that he would not obstruct—but also not sign—an armistice. The Communists launched an offensive to give the ROK "a bloody nose" and to dispel notions of a northward march, while Eisenhower still worried that Rhee intended to "run out" on his commitment. Hence the president pledged a U.S. military response in "a clear case of aggression" against the ROK and also requested an immediate $200 million aid appropriation.[136]

Finally on July 27, the chief UN (in fact, U.S.) and Communist negotiators signed the armistice, in silence, at Panmunjon, with respective military commanders countersigning at their headquarters. Congress shortly voted $200 million for South Korea, and the sixteen UN nations with troops there released their "greater sanction" statement warning that they would not confine their response to an attack in Korea to the peninsula. In Seoul on August 8, Dulles signed a U.S.-ROK mutual-security pact. Meanwhile, Operation Big Switch saw exchange of about 76,000 Communist POWs (70,000 North Korean and 5,600 Chinese) for 12,700 UN POWs (including 3,600 Americans and 7,500 South Koreans). Some 22,500 Communist nonrepatriates were turned over to the NNRC and ultimately released as civilians. About 350 UN nonrepatriates refused to return home.[137]

Meanwhile, the U.S. used its influence at the UN to limit the post-armistice political conference to the belligerent powers and the Soviet Union, but by excluding India—partly to placate Rhee—the U.S. earned considerable enmity as an ROK "satellite." Regardless, the political conference could not effect a unified Korea, and it adjourned in June 1954, leaving the nation as bitterly divided as it was in 1950, and as it would remain for decades to come.[138]

If U.S. officials had not anticipated North Korea's attack in June 1950, neither had Stalin nor Kim Il Sung anticipated how quickly Truman would decide not only to restore South Korea but to punish Communist transgression by sending MacArthur's forces across the 38th parallel to destroy the DPRK and unify the nation. In the heady rush to expand containment into rollback, however, Truman and his senior advisers ignored advice from Kennan and the PPS that the USSR, and especially the PRC, might perceive establishment of an anti-Communist state on their borders as a security threat. Most significant, the president and his aides did not comprehend how PRC leaders viewed the world, i.e., why they had reason to fear MacArthur's unconstrained northward advance as a harbinger of U.S. intent to build a rival regime on Taiwan—now shielded by the Seventh Fleet—and to coordinate an attack upon China and its revolution.

It is also now known that Mao hesitated to intervene in Korea as late as his October 2 cable to Stalin, while Zhou sought to warn the West that the PRC could not sit by idly. But the president brushed off PRC warnings as "bluff" or "blackmail." He was highly pleased at his Wake Island meeting, where MacArthur told him what he wanted to hear, namely, that the PRC would not intervene—and would be "slaughtered" if it did—and that war would soon be won. MacArthur was now free to continue his provocative march north and bombings along the Yalu. In sum, Truman's political myopia, and that of his advisers, precluded their grasping the PRC leaders' determination to define and to defend their revolution, vital interests, and new role as protector of Asia's oppressed nations.[139]

Major PRC intervention in late November 1950 forced America's bitter retreat and led to Truman's ill-considered comments, and half-veiled threat, that use of the atomic bomb was always under consideration and that control rested with the U.S. theater commander. The White House immediately clarified these statements, while British leaders flew to Washington to preclude wider war. In fact, use of the atomic bomb on Soviet air bases had been raised on June 26, and Truman had sent nuclear-configured bombers to Britain and Guam in July, although these had returned. Discussion continued about nuclear weapons, but their use was resisted because of concern about Soviet retaliation, lack of good targets, and likely objections from American allies and Asians over repeat of Hiroshima and Nagasaki.

Nonetheless, at his December 1950 summit with Attlee, an unhappy president gave only his "man's word" that he would consult before using atomic weapons. He disputed the British view that the PRC leaders could be both Marxists and nationalists and "not bow to Stalin." Truman wrongly insisted that the Chinese were "complete satellites" of Russia bent on conquering Southeast Asia, and the only way to meet Communism was to "eliminate it." That winter he refused negotiations with the PRC prior to a cease-fire and would not consider expanding talks to include recognition of the PRC and control of Taiwan. The U.S. also threatened wider war against China and pressed the UN to brand it an "aggressor" in February 1951, all of which precluded prospect for an early armistice.

Meanwhile, Truman's directives to military officials to clear their statements with the Defense Department, and JCS directives to MacArthur that Korea was not the right place to fight a major war and that he should report any PRC interest in negotiations, were not precise enough to bar the general's undercutting of administration efforts to find a basis for armistice talks. His provocative demand in March 1951 that the PRC military commander surrender to him or face destruction ("sabotage," Truman said) precipitated the crisis that soon led the president to fire his larger-than-life commander. This action took courage, but MacArthur's insubordination alone did not cause the crisis. The president's and MacArthur's views and war aims regarding Korea and the PRC were similar until Washington officials decided in winter 1951 that they had to extricate the U.S. from the costly conflict. But failure to rein in MacArthur earlier—over Taiwan, or on how he sent his troops to the Yalu and bombed there or pressed wider war against the PRC—allowed the general to try to impose his will on U.S./UN policy in spring 1951. Finally, Truman had to fire "the son-of-a-bitch," at great and unrecoverable political cost to his presidency.

Further, to respond to a Communist buildup and to assure JCS support while dismissing MacArthur, Truman transferred atomic weapons to the Air Force in the Pacific and authorized his new theater commander, General Ridgway, to retaliate in event of attacks on U.S. forces from outside Korea. The president also had to inform Congress' JCAE—which included hawkish critics of his Asian policy—of this deployment, while MacArthur electrified the nation with speeches insisting that there was no substitute for victory.

The administration, with Soviet assistance, finally initiated cease-fire talks in June 1951. But it took two years of wrenching diplomacy and bitter fighting to effect a formal armistice in July 1953. The president, who insisted that every decision would be made in Washington, greatly complicated diplomacy in fall 1951 by refusing standard military practice and the Geneva Convention protocol of exchange of all POWs unless the PRC made a major political concession, which it refused. No one seriously attempted to "educate the Pres."—least of all Acheson—who in winter 1952 advised Truman to make nonforcible, or voluntary, repatriation the irreducible U.S. position, despite knowing that this might deadlock negotiations.

Truman's position derived partly from moral concerns and from anger at harsh Soviet treatment of POWs returned to Russia after the Second World War. But the president also sought to wage psychological warfare against the Communists and to gain political victories that he could not win on the battlefield. He mistakenly presumed that he could either coax the Communists to agree to his position by allowing them to repair their airfields, or coerce accord through brutal saturation bombing of their dikes and transportation system. Instead, Truman heightened PRC fears of U.S. hostility and intent to retain POWs to strengthen the GMD on Taiwan, prolonged the war by two years—during which time the U.S. absorbed nearly half of its wartime casualties—and angered NATO allies and Asian nations. The protracted Korean conflict also generated significant domestic political bitterness that contributed significantly to the defeat of the Democrats and repudiation of Truman at the polls in November 1952.[140]

Meanwhile, beneath the facade of calm crisis management, Truman fantasized about giving the USSR and PRC ten days to quit Korea or face "all out war" in which he would destroy their major cities from St. Petersburg to Moscow to Vladivostok, and from Beijing to Shanghai. The Soviets, he said, had to decide whether they wanted their government to survive. Truman, who was not a man of apocalyptic vision and who considered the two world wars he had experienced enough for anyone, did not want atomic war. But by 1952 he was ready to go "all out" against the PRC if it undertook major escalation in Korea, and it is not inconceivable that political and military circumstances in an election year—in which MacArthur sought the Republican nomination—might have driven or tempted a president to an atomic strike.

Regardless, Korean War costs proved staggering. Americans suffered over 35,000 deaths and 100,000 casualties. South Korea's deaths and casualties exceeded 1 million and those of the PRC and North Korea combined were more than 1.5 million, with all of Korea physically devastated. The U.S. expended $70 billion on the war, and Truman, who prided himself on containing military spending, submitted a military budget for FY 1953 of $53 billion, four times that of 1949 and nearly equal to the 20 percent of GNP envisioned in NSC 68.[141]

Further, the Truman administration had set the stage for long-term political-military commitments to South Korea (despite the dictatorial Rhee's outrageous treatment of the U.S. as a "satellite") and to the GMD on Taiwan, and to funding France's widening war in Indochina. The PRC was now bitterly alienated from the U.S. and more closely tied than ever to the USSR, McCarthyism was rampant in America, and the State Department would soon be purged of its experts on Asia, where greater tragedy lay ahead.

Double Containment

America over Europe Divided

The U.S. and the Soviet Union both deemed the fate of postwar Germany crit-ical to their national security. But President Truman and Secretary Acheson saw little to negotiate with the Russians on this crucial matter during 1949–1952. The U.S.-sponsored ERP of 1947 rested on an economically recon-structed West Germany cooperating with Britain and France, and in March 1948 Washington assured the latter that American troops would remain in Ger-many until the threat from the East was gone. The Berlin blockade confirmed Truman's view that it was "not possible to do business" with the Russians.

Prior to the CFM meeting in spring 1949, Acheson insisted that the U.S. in-tended to create a West German government "come hell or high water" and that Germany could be unified only by consolidating the East into the West based on the incipient Bonn constitution. He resisted the idea of U.S.-Soviet troop withdrawal from, and neutralization of, Germany. At the CFM meeting he re-jected Soviet proposals to revert to the Potsdam accords of four-power control because this would have precluded West German–Western European integra-tion. Shortly, Truman declared that the U.S. would not sacrifice West Ger-many's basic freedoms to gain "nominal political unity." Formation in fall 1949 of the Federal Republic of Germany (FRG) and German Democratic Republic (GDR) affirmed division of Germany and of Europe.[1]

When the president asked about "the struggle with the USSR for Ger-many," Acheson replied that the outcome depended on U.S. willingness to bear military and financial burdens, and Anglo-French agreement to relax West Ger-many's Occupation controls. Acheson pressed this on the allies, both to antici-pate West German demands for concessions and to preclude prospect that a unified Germany might revert to its 1920s "Rapallo strategy" of playing Russia against the West. He was also won over by West German Chancellor Konrad Adenauer, who was determined to build a powerful state allied to the West rather than negotiate with East Germany or Russia.[2]

Truman's dictum that the Russians understood only "divisions"—or "force," as he later told the French—reflected administration consensus in 1950. Acheson and the drafters of NSC 68 insisted on need to build "situations of strength" to bargain with the Russians. Adenauer advocated a "policy of strength" as the precondition for talks, and even the more flexible British foreign secretary, Bevin, said that although he would seize any opportunity to end the Cold War, it was "useless to negotiate from weakness."[3]

The Truman administration sought to revitalize West Germany economically even at the price of a divided nation. But military strength—"divisions"— posed a harder issue. In January 1950 Truman had approved developing the hydrogen bomb, and then came NSC 68's call for a vast military buildup. Further, U.S. military planners concluded that defense, rather than liberation, of Europe required placing fighting forces as far east as possible, at the Elbe, not the Rhine. NATO, however, was still only a political statement of defense, and member nations had done little to meet their Medium Term Defense Plan of ninety divisions by 1954. Only the U.S. and West Germany could provide requisite troops. But during Senate hearings on NATO in spring 1949, Acheson, and later Truman, foreswore any plan to send "substantial" U.S. forces to Europe, and they affirmed intent to keep Germany disarmed and demilitarized.[4]

In spring 1950, however, JCS planners insisted that the U.S. had to send more troops to Europe and rearm Germany to defend against the Soviets, who had ground force superiority, the atomic bomb, and support from increased numbers of paramilitary East German police. But Truman feared that German rearmament might lead, as per the interwar era, to creation of a "war machine," and Acheson worried that it would upset European politics.[5]

But start of the Korean War in June 1950, which led Truman to accede to NSC 68, also sped him and Acheson to accept the JCS's "single package" for Europe's defense: a supreme (U.S.) commander for NATO, more U.S. divisions to Europe, and German rearmament. At a CFM meeting in New York in September 1950, Acheson dropped the rearmament "bomb at the Waldorf" on the British and French. The former acceded reluctantly, but the recalcitrant French responded with Prime Minister Rene Pleven's complex plan to create a European Defense Ministry and European Army that would integrate small German troop units. Adenauer agreed to the FRG's limited rearmament as a means to gain its equality of status with its new allies.[6]

The U.S. brokered a compromise to integrate small German regimental combat units (RCUs) into a European Army that would be joined to NATO, now commanded by General Eisenhower. The U.S. thus sought to transform NATO into an alliance that would contain both the Soviet Union and West Germany, but commit the latter's manpower and resources to the West without allowing its own general staff or army. Truman also touched off political debate by claiming authority to send U.S. troops abroad without Congress' approval.[7]

In 1951 Eisenhower urged Europeans to eschew neutralism and to put German divisions under his command. At the same time, two-track allied negotiations proceeded at Bonn, where the U.S. and the FRG sought entry of German divisions into NATO, and at Paris, where the French pressed integration of small German units into a supranational European Army, or later, European Defense Community (EDC). Meantime the FRG pressed the allies to transform their 1949 Occupation Statute into a contractual relationship, while the Russians sought a CFM meeting to discuss Germany's demilitarization-neutralization. The U.S. opted for a contractual agreement with the FRG as the price of German rearmament and Western alignment, but balked at talks with the Russians. As Acheson said, Yalta and Potsdam were "dead."[8]

By summer 1951 U.S. officials concluded that the French-designed EDC offered the fastest route to German rearmament. In July Truman approved NSC 115, which called for integrating small German divisions into an EDC army that would be consigned to NATO's command, and negotiation of contractual agreements that would grant the FRG sovereignty but assure allied rights regarding intervention in the FRG, stationing of troops, Berlin, unification, and lost territories. The allies also created a Temporary Council Committee (TCC) to devise equitable "burden sharing" for NATO-EDC defense plans.[9]

Contractual negotiations moved slowly. The U.S. wanted a German commitment to Western defense to precede a political settlement. The Germans wanted a political accord prior to guaranteeing a defense contribution. So too did rearmament talks drag, despite Truman's insistence that "we must have the Germans" in NATO-EDC. But the French wanted security guarantees in case a rearmed FRG quit EDC, and they also weighed talks with the Soviets to demilitarize and reunify Germany. Finally, at a NATO Council meeting in Lisbon in February 1952 Acheson effected a "grand slam": accord on FRG troop commitments to EDC and financial contribution to Western defense. The French were assuaged by delayed FRG entry into NATO and U.S. assurances that it had an "abiding interest" in EDC's integrity and that U.S. troops would remain in Europe and military aid would flow to Paris.[10]

These developments prompted Stalin's Note of March 1952 proposing a sovereign, united, economically revived, and rearmed—but neutral—Germany. Whether he meant to effect great-power detente over Germany or to throw a "golden apple" of discord—as Acheson said—into the Western camp to derail West German integration and rearmament remains seriously disputed. Regardless, by 1952 Truman, Acheson, and Adenauer had no interest in negotiating the political-economic advantages over Russia they were soon to gain in Germany and Europe. They sought to unify Germany by victory of the West over the East, with the Red Army contained within Russia's borders.[11]

The Americans, however, could not merely say no to Stalin's offer. Instead, they proposed UN-sponsored elections in all of Germany as a basis for negotiations, with a unified Germany able to join any alliance, including EDC. Predictably the Soviets rejected this, and tortuous diplomatic exchanges ensued. Meantime, U.S. officials pressed to conclude Germany's contractual agreements and formation of EDC in late May. The Soviets denounced the Western accords and told GDR officials to begin to seal off East Germany. The Truman administration thus won the "battle of the notes," and bound the FRG and its vast resources to the West. But ultimately French refusal to ratify EDC caused it to fail from the start. Germany and Europe remained more divided than ever along Cold War lines, which Truman blamed on Soviet design.[12]

I

In early 1949 Truman transferred primary responsibility for German policy from the U.S. military to Acheson and the State Department. The president and secretary never wavered about need to integrate western Germany into Western Europe, even if this precluded German unification and withdrawal of Soviet troops from East Germany. When the NATO treaty was signed in Washington in April 1949, Acheson got Bevin and Foreign Minister Robert Schuman of France to agree to modify occupation policy to give the Germans greater control over their government and economy, to conduct allied policy through high commissioners instead of military governors, and to unite France's zone with Bizonia. Bevin hailed this "remarkable" accord on Germany as a high point in Anglo-French relations. Truman said it was the "best thing" his administration had done. The next month, prior to attending a CFM meeting to conclude Berlin blockade talks, Acheson told the Senate Foreign Relations Committee that the incipient Bonn government was the only basis for German unification, which was "not an end in itself." Proposals for East-West unity would be judged on how they strengthened Western Europe.[13]

The CFM made no progress toward German unity, and Acheson was delighted that the Soviets did not propose mutual troop withdrawal. The western Germans soon formed their Federal Republic, and in September the conservative Adenauer became the FRG's first chancellor after his Christian Democratic

Party (CDP) won a narrow victory over Kurt Schumacher's Social Democratic Party (SPD). Adenauer, mayor of Cologne in the 1920s, had been dismissed by the Nazis in 1933 and lived quietly to the war's end. He espoused capitalism, was strongly anticommunist, disdained the Prussian East, and believed that the Soviets would never loosen their grip on East Germany. From 1945 he held that western Germany's only course was to ally with the West to gain unity by Cold War victory over the East. By contrast Schumacher, an ardent nationalist, Marxist, and democrat who spent ten years in a Nazi concentration camp, gave highest priority to German unity and creation of a socialist state in a social-democratic Europe. Meanwhile, in East Germany the Communist-led SED proposed its own constitution in spring 1949, and in October the People's Congress proclaimed the GDR, with Wilhelm Pieck as president and Otto Grotewohl as prime minister. The Soviets replaced their military government with a high commission.[14]

That fall Acheson continued to press the British and French to integrate the FRG into the West. In November the high commissioners, meeting at the luxurious Petersberg Hotel near Bonn, negotiated agreements with Adenauer that provided for FRG membership in the World Bank, IMF, International Ruhr Authority, and the newly created Council of Europe. The allies also agreed to curtail dismantling of oil, rubber, and steel facilities. Meanwhile, Acheson visited the FRG and found great concord with Adenauer's view that the Soviets never negotiated in good faith and would never willingly leave East Germany.[15]

While the Petersberg Agreements were being drawn, the Soviet announcement that Polish-born Russian Marshal Konstantin Rokossovsky had been made Poland's defense minister spurred rumors that the West would rearm the FRG. Bevin and Schuman adamantly opposed this, and Truman and Acheson denied any such plan. But in December Adenauer, interested in negotiating leverage, told a U.S. reporter that the allies' obligation to defend the FRG meant that they should permit it to have its own forces under European command. But the chancellor's idea was sharply criticized in the FRG as likely to revive militarism and harm prospects for German reunification and European reconciliation.[16]

U.S. military officials continued to press German rearmament, despite resistance from Truman and Acheson. JCS chair General Bradley said that Soviet atomic capability precluded Normandy-style landings to liberate Europe, and allied military planners said that NATO's 12 divisions were no match for 175 Soviet divisions (a greatly exaggerated figure, although the Red Army had 25 divisions in East Germany) and increasing, well-equipped GDR police forces. By spring 1950 the JCS insisted that only the FRG's "early rearming" and entry into NATO could provide sufficient combat-ready troops to fight the Soviets deep in German territory. The JCS recommended ending the FRG's economic controls and demilitarization, persuading France that a revitalized Germany was a lesser threat than the Soviet "menace," and creating a federal police force, as Adenauer wanted, that could be the basis of future rearmament. British military officials agreed, but feared French reaction. They promoted an enlarged police force to keep domestic order and defend against East Germany.[17]

Truman worried that a German police force would frighten France and become the basis for a "military machine" that might ally with Russia to "ruin the rest of the world." He strongly supported Acheson's protest to Bevin—who seemed to be fostering Adenauer's police plans—that the British were "seriously misinformed" if they took American accord on a small internal security force to mean that the U.S. could be "brought into line quickly" regarding FRG rearmament.[18]

The president was dead set against the latter. Upon receiving JCS reports in June favoring FRG rearmament and cooperation with Franco's Spain, he labeled both reports "decidedly militaristic" and "wrong as can be." He cautioned Acheson that FRG rearmament would give France a "severe case of jitters" and that he did not want to repeat the post–World War I "mistake" of allowing Germany to train 100,000 officers, ostensibly to preserve order, who became the basis for the "greatest war machine" in Europe's history. Acheson, too, publicly favored German demilitarization, although he misled on June 5 when he stated that demilitarization policy was not being "revalued."[19]

Ironically, the French may have provided impetus for the U.S. to "revalue" its policy. On May 9 Foreign Minister Schuman proposed a striking plan to pool French and German coal and steel production—the "basis of rearmament," Adenauer said—under common market conditions and control by an international high commission. The Schuman Plan was an effort to forge an economic balance of power between France and Germany—by eliminating the supremacy of the latter's industry—and create the basis for political goodwill. This was also France's way of engaging constructively with Germany, which drew plaudits from President Truman and U.S. officials. Ultimately, the Schuman Plan, after considerable debate, would be formalized by treaty in April 1951 as the European Coal and Steel Community, which the U.S. high commissioner to Germany in Bonn, John J. McCloy, said was necessary to present "a united front against the East."[20]

In effect, the Schuman Plan provided reason to view the FRG in a more peaceful light and to hasten its "re-introduction into the community of life," as Acheson defined the U.S. goal. U.S. officials insisted that the French, who wanted to wait upon the success of the Schuman Plan, could now approach

German "problems," such as rearmament, in a way that previously was "impossible." Hence, while neither the U.S. nor the West German government formally favored FRG rearmament in June 1950, the FRG could be more firmly integrated and prepared to take its "normal" place in Europe. Further, France's desire to strengthen NATO led it to propose that each member nation appoint a permanent deputy to its Council to deal with NATO's business. At first Acheson said this gave too much authority to the deputy and to NATO. But to rally America's allies to firmer Cold War posture, he agreed to appoint Charles M. Spofford, a relatively unknown New York lawyer, as permanent deputy to NATO on June 24.[21]

Hours later war came in Korea. Anxiety soon ran high that North Korea's invasion was a harbinger of similar attacks by Soviet satellites. From Bonn, McCloy reported panic among FRG leaders, with GDR propaganda threatening to try them all before people's courts. McCloy, who opposed FRG rearmament and regarded Adenauer as "weak," now proposed to offset "continued bad news from Korea" by allowing Germans to enlist in the U.S. Army and to tell them that if need arose, "we would permit them to fight [collectively] shoulder to shoulder with us." McCloy also said publicly that in event of a Korean-style attack, FRG citizens had to be given the means to defend their own soil.[22]

State Department officials acceded to use of FRG personnel in allied forces but said that rearmament would create "high tension" with the Soviets—and French—and provoke "an armaments race with Germans against Germans." It would be better to wait until U.S. reforms had gained "the right kind of Germany" integrated into a stronger Europe with a European or North Atlantic command more accepting of "balanced" forces. Meanwhile, the JCS, strapped for troops and money by the Korean War, pressed for more U.S. aid to Europe and a greater European contribution to NATO's Medium Term Defense Plan. Truman promptly agreed on July 21 to seek at least $4 billion in European military aid as part of a $10 billion defense supplement and, if need be, to extend ERP beyond 1952. The president told his pessimistic defense secretary, Johnson, that he had been in tougher situations before and was sure Congress would go along.[23]

Truman also asked Acheson on July 25, "[H]ow can German manpower be used without establishing a German Army?" The next week the secretary said that the question was no longer whether but how to rearm Germany without creating its own general staff, army, and Ruhr supply center that would make it the balance of power in Europe—past "mistakes" that the president agreed were not to be repeated. Acheson proposed a European or North Atlantic command and army, with German soldiers who would take orders from NATO, not Bonn.[24]

U.S. officials now urged incorporating Germans into a European Army that would defend against both the Soviets and "further German aggression" and also increase FRG integration and sense of "a real European community." In August Churchill publicly proposed a European Army. Acheson was elated and wished to link the European Army to NATO. But he also insisted that NATO planning was "hopeless" and that the U.S. had to take responsibility for establishing a unified NATO staff—and eventually command—and commit additional U.S. and British troops to Europe. Truman fully assented.[25]

Meanwhile, Adenauer was insisting that Stalin intended to take Germany at least cost, namely, by use of well-armed GDR police. The chancellor openly called for an independent, 150,000-strong German "defense force." Truman replied that German rearmament was "quite impossible" aside from an integrated European force. Acheson agreed.[26]

The JCS, however, held that to create and command an army of different nationalities would be too politically complicated and militarily inefficient and that cautious Europeans would delay rearming Germany. The JCS pressed their indivisible "one package" for Europe: a supreme commander (likely U.S.) for NATO; dispatch of four more divisions from both the U.S. and Britain; and creation of ten to twelve FRG divisions to be placed under NATO command. Acheson opposed immediate German rearmament but thought that after establishment of a NATO unified command, the "inevitable logic of mathematics" would demand inclusion of the FRG. But the Pentagon stood firm, while McCloy—who lobbied Truman—and others argued for immediate German participation.[27]

The president instructed Acheson and Johnson to resolve State-Defense differences. The JCS were persistent that without FRG forces present NATO plans meant "complete disaster" for any U.S. commander and troops in case of Soviet attack. Acheson felt "outflanked" and saw no choice but to accept immediate German rearmament to gain Pentagon support for a unified NATO command. On September 8 he and Johnson jointly recommended to Truman a supreme commander and integrated staff for NATO; dispatch of four to six U.S.—and also British—divisions to Europe; and all troops, including ten to twelve German divisions, to be combined into a European defense force composed of national units and commanders but subject to NATO control. The U.S. would also offer the lure of an integrated production and supply board. After three days of discussion, the president agreed to the "one package," which made a U.S. commander of NATO and U.S. forces contingent on German rearmament. But to avoid appearing to bow to European pressure, on September 9 Truman announced that he would provide "substantial increases" of U.S. forces to Europe, assuming similar allied responses.[28]

Acheson dropped his "bomb at the Waldorf" three days later at a CFM meeting in New York. The secretary viewed recent JCS tactics as "murderous" and knew that failure to give more notice to his British and French counterparts, Bevin and Schuman, made the negotiation a virtual ultimatum. But Acheson would argue that the Europeans stood to gain greatly from America's "absolutely unprecedented" commitment to station its forces abroad in peacetime in an integrated force, and from a U.S. commander of NATO. He boasted that this was part of the "revolution in American foreign policy" that Truman had brought.[29]

On the first day Acheson insisted that defense of Europe far to the east had to include FRG troops integrated into a European force. Bevin resisted German rearmament but wanted military aid and a U.S. commander for NATO. He said that the Germans were likely to refuse to commit their soldiers to an integrated defense force—or drive too hard a bargain. He proposed to create Adenauer's desired federal police and to continue to bring Germany into the "community of nations." Schuman rejected federal police as the basis for an army, which would be "fatal" for any French government to accept—and talked only of a small, state-run police force.[30]

Acheson proposed a state police subject to federalization, and more Indochina aid for France, in exchange for allied agreement in principle to rearm Germany, with implementation delayed. But no inducement, or reminder of Truman's revolutionary foreign policy, could move Schuman. Acheson, angry that U.S. allies "were prepared to accept what we offered" but "not what we asked," declared "impasse" on September 17. He retained slight hope that arrival of the defense ministers, and Truman's firing of Defense Secretary Johnson and replacing him with George Marshall—revered symbol of World War II cooperation—might provide a way out.[31]

Shortly, Acheson told an approving Truman that he had gotten allied accord to end the state of war with Germany, modify its Occupation Statute to grant more sovereignty, create state police subject to federal control, and hold the Soviet Union responsible for any GDR attack on Berlin or West Germany. But not even Marshall's explication to Defense Minister Jules Moch, whose son the Nazis had tortured and executed, and the U.S. offer to make a private deal on FRG rearmament, could move the French to allow FRG forces in NATO. They insisted that French rearmament, and U.S. aid, had to be advanced before the FRG could contribute even resources to NATO, and FRG participation in that body was out.[32]

Truman and Acheson continued to look to more military aid to bring France's accord. They did not anticipate Prime Minister Pleven's complex proposal on October 24 to create all-European political institutions and a Defense Ministry, and then a 100,000-man NATO-commanded European Defense Force (or Community, EDC), comprising mixed contingents, with Germans eventually integrated in small 1,000-man battalions. The Pleven Plan, modeled after the supranational Schuman Plan, was contingent on German ratification of the European Coal and Steel Community and offered delayed, second-class status to the FRG, which would not be a member of the NATO Council or be allowed to have its own army. The French also proposed to agree to a Soviet proposal for four-power talks on Germany. Not surprisingly, Acheson and Marshall found the Pleven Plan "very vague" and designed for "infinite delay." As historians have said, it was intended to rearm Germans but not Germany and to satisfy U.S. desire for German rearmament and French desire to prevent this.[33]

Still, McCloy and others saw virtue in the Pleven Plan's prospect for limited FRG rearmament. This would appease the French and assuage the Russians by forgoing a more aggressive NATO design. Adenauer was won over to limited rearmament, provided German soldiers were not just "cannon fodder," as a means to bargain for German sovereignty. Similarly, Schumacher and SPD opponents went along, although the SPD also branded the CDU as the party of rearmament during the November elections. Further, some CDU officials, and many Germans who said *"ohne mich"*—or "include me out"—continued to oppose rearmament in principle, or as the death knell of reunification.[34]

The Truman administration now opted for the Pleven Plan to gain limited German rearmament and to maintain European unity on the Korean War in the face of PRC intervention and MacArthur's calls for wider war. Late that October the president obtained Eisenhower's private commitment to be his designee as NATO's supreme commander. In December Spofford, the U.S. representative to NATO, gained European agreement, despite JCS objection, to limit FRG rearmament to 6,000-man RCUs, whose total would not exceed 20 percent of EDC forces. The French agreed to FRG units entering EDC before it was fully operational.[35]

Acheson still had to endorse the Pleven Plan in December in order to get the French to ratify the Spofford Compromise. He also proposed to let the Germans "stew for a while" rather than start military negotiations that, he warned, they might use to wrest occupation concessions. Finally, at a NATO Council meeting at midmonth the foreign ministers agreed to an overall integrated defense plan. Truman then formally designated Eisenhower, commander of U.S. forces in Europe, as NATO's supreme commander, and announced that he would send additional U.S. troops to Europe. The NATO ministers also agreed to two-track negotiations on German rearmament. The Allied High Commissioners in Bonn would deal with FRG entry into NATO under the Spofford Compromise, and diplomats in Paris would explore formation of EDC. The U.S. also agreed to French desire to weigh four-power accord on Germany. But Acheson insisted that the Yalta-Potsdam basis for negotiations was "outmoded and dead."[36]

II

The president's announcement that he intended to send troops to Europe spurred "great debate" over his constitutional authority and U.S. policy. In a televised address on December 20, former president Herbert Hoover declared that U.S. policy should focus on hemispheric defense, using air and sea forces to protect the Atlantic and Pacific Oceans and Britain, Japan, the Philippines, and Taiwan. He insisted that to send more troops to the Europeans before they had armed themselves against the "Red tide" would invite "another Korea." Acheson immediately declared that U.S. "withdrawal" to the Western Hemisphere would open Europe to Soviet conquest and that NATO allies now were in accord on integrated defense and German rearmament. The president brushed off Hoover's comments as a return to "isolationism."[37]

Then on January 3, 1951, House Republican Frederic Coudert (NY) offered a resolution requiring the president to obtain Congress' approval to send troops abroad. Five days later Senator Kenneth Wherry (NE) proposed to prohibit dispatch of troops to Europe for NATO purposes before Congress acted. Meanwhile, on January 5, Senator Taft—then the leading contender for the Republican presidential nomination—likened Truman's NATO commitment to his having sent troops to Korea in June without consulting Congress. Taft held the president's pending action to be unconstitutional, and provocative because there was no evidence of Soviet intent to invade Europe. Taft would allow a few divisions for NATO and offered to discuss this with Truman or his designee. Senator Connally, chairman of the Foreign Relations Committee and spokesman for the Democrats, said that he was certain the administration would consult Congress about troop commitments.[38]

Truman was dismissive of restraint on his foreign policy power. On January 4, and again on January 11—after Connally's comment—the president emphasized that as commander in chief he could "send troops anywhere in the world"—to reinforce those in Germany, or to NATO. As for Congress, he added, "I don't ask their permission, I just consult them." He offered to talk about this with any interested senator but ignored Taft's feeler. Perhaps Truman viewed him as a "hopeless" isolationist or did not want to reinforce his presidential candidacy.[39]

Meanwhile, in his State of the Union address on January 8, 1951, the president denounced the new Soviet imperialism as worse than that of the tsars and said that the Soviets' conquest of Western Europe would double and triple their coal and steel production and let them command more troops than the U.S. could ever equal. They could dominate the world by "swallowing up" America's allies, he said. Defense of Europe was defense of the "whole free world." Soon Eisenhower returned to Washington to tell the Cabinet and Congress that the Soviets would not start a war that they knew they could not win, and that 350 million Westerners had no reason to fear "190,000,000 backward Russians," whose only advantage was unity—enforced by bayonet. But if the West armed fifty or sixty divisions, including ten from the U.S., it could "tell Russia to go to hell."[40]

Truman authorized Marshall to testify to Congress in mid-February that the U.S. intended to add only four more divisions to the two already in Germany, bringing U.S. forces in Europe to 180,000. Acheson then emphasized need to build forces to prevent a repeat of Soviet aggression through a satellite as in Korea. The secretary also persisted in the dubious assertion that from the founding of the Republic the courts had always upheld the president's right to send troops abroad. Truman then informally assured congressional leaders that he did not intend to send more than four new divisions—Eisenhower warned him that this was not a "permanent solution"—but that "I'll be damned if I am going to let Congress limit me," or a successor.[41]

Truman also knew that the raging Korean conflict limited the number of divisions he could raise for Europe. His administration did muster the votes to defeat the Wherry resolution, while expediency dictated acceptance on April 5 of a sense-of-the-Senate resolution, for which even Taft and other Republicans could vote, that approved Eisenhower's appointment and assignment of four divisions to his command but required Congress' approval for additional troops. The president was also constrained not to send any troops until the JCS certified that European nations were progressing toward an integrated defense. That same day Truman, starting his five-day countdown to fire MacArthur, hailed the support for NATO but said nothing about Congress' limiting his authority to deploy troops to four divisions. The "great debate" thus ended with bipartisan backing for the administration's NATO-European policy, but the president's authority to dispatch troops "anywhere in the world" remained in dispute.[42]

Meanwhile, the USSR and its Eastern European allies, at a meeting in Prague in late October 1950, had protested FRG rearmament. First they proposed an all-German Constitutional Council (GCC) with equal FRG and GDR representation. Then on November 3 the Soviets requested a CFM meeting to discuss German demilitarization. At the end of the month, GDR Prime Minister Grotewohl wrote Adenauer to advance the idea that a GCC might become the basis for a provisional government of a unified Germany. In mid-December the Soviets reiterated to the British and French that FRG rearmament violated the Anglo-Soviet and Franco-Soviet treaties.[43]

The Soviet initiative, or "peace offensive," coming in the wake of the PRC advance and UN retreat in Korea, may have been intended chiefly to exploit U.S. anxiety and policy rifts with its allies, as well as France's fear of German rearmament. Regardless, Acheson quickly concluded that the Soviet proposals were "unacceptable," intended only to delay FRG rearmament and Western defense. He held that a CFM meeting to discuss Germany was no more likely to succeed than had the fruitless one at the end of the Berlin blockade in May 1949. If the Russians were serious, they had to posit a more complete agenda—an Austrian peace treaty and an end to conflict with the PRC in Korea—to reduce East-West tension.[44]

Adenauer too had little interest in the Soviet proposals, except to press the West to relax occupation controls. The British expressed mild interest in the Soviet proposals, if only to demonstrate for public opinion that they did not fear to negotiate. But they saw only "slight" chance for a successful meeting, and the agenda had to be broader to include discussion on more than German demilitarization. Prime Minister Attlee also believed that the U.S. would view any step that might delay FRG rearmament as a "radical change in policy." He decided not to press Truman during his hastily convened visit to the White House in early December 1950. The president had already agreed to accept the Spofford Compromise and to send Eisenhower and U.S. troops to Europe. "Any sign of drawing back," Attlee said, would be "fatal" to Anglo-American partnership.[45]

The British judged Truman correctly. For example, he received Pleven in late January 1951 to strengthen the premier's standing in French politics and to balance Attlee's visit, despite knowing that the French would propose four-power talks on Germany and insist that Soviet fear of FRG rearmament would dispose them to make concessions. But the president would not bend. He sought to strengthen France's resolve by declaring it to be under America's atomic umbrella and bragged that the U.S. had a "phenomenal" atomic lead over the Russians. He restated his claim that he had the power to send troops to Europe and that the U.S. sought FRG-Western European integration. We "must not agree on a neutralized and demilitarized Germany," Truman said. And in reply to French concern that the West do nothing to preclude talks with Moscow, he stated that "we could not allow the Russians to get us into the position of holding up or delaying our military build-up. The Soviets respect only force and we must go forward to get the force that they will respect."[46]

Shortly, the U.S. averted reply to a Soviet suggestion on February 4 to agree to limit the size of NATO forces even though this proposal implied USSR acceptance of NATO. The administration also gave minimal response to a GDR proposal on March 2 urging a four-power peace treaty to unify, democratize, and demilitarize Germany, and to Soviet entreaties in spring 1951 for a CFM meeting to focus on German demilitarization, withdrawal of foreign troops, and East-West reduction of forces.[47]

Truman and Acheson opposed a demilitarized or neutralized Germany. State Department specialists said that the Soviets would not relinquish control of the GDR, or that they would try to absorb a unified country. Other officials held that German neutralization would discourage French and Western European rearmament. Thus Germany was not a "negotiable item" and "could not be bartered for easing tensions." Further, an Austrian peace treaty and Soviet withdrawal from its Eastern European satellites were "prerequisite" to agreement on Germany. Or as Acheson told the Cabinet on February 9, Soviet armament of its satellites had caused the current tension and "the best point of discussion would be the re-armament of Western Europe."[48]

The U.S. did agree to talks in Paris in spring 1951 to weigh a CFM agenda but insisted on taking up an Austrian peace treaty, propaganda constraints, and arms reduction before dealing with Germany. The Russians sought first to focus on Germany—fulfilling the Potsdam agreements on demilitarization, troop withdrawal, and neutralization—and then reduce international tension. The West rejected this, as well as the Soviets' added insistence on discussing NATO and U.S. military bases in Europe and its proposal for a CFM meeting with no stated agenda.[49]

The U.S. finally proposed its so-called triple play: an offer of three separate agendas, each with some mutually desired items but none that included the NATO/U.S. bases issues. The Americans and British insisted that these were beyond CFM purview and resulted from Soviet-induced tensions. Predictably the Soviets balked, and the West continued to wrangle only until the June 17 elections in France, where the anti-Soviet right wing made major gains, the centrists slipped, and the Communists lost heavily. The West promptly adjourned CFM agenda talks.[50]

Meanwhile, inter-Allied negotiations over FRG rearmament and revision of occupation terms moved slowly. Although Truman and Acheson wanted FRG rearmament to follow from political-economic integration, in December 1950 the NATO Council had committed to rearmament talks at Petersberg and Paris. Eisenhower then spent January 1951 touring NATO capitals to urge greater commitment to defense, implying German rearmament. It was time to let "bygones be bygones," he remarked to FRG officials concerned about lingering World War II animus toward them. Upon return to the U.S. at the end of the month, he told Truman and the Cabinet that he wanted German troops under his command—he had "good reason to know what kind of fighters they made"—with no conditions attached. He said he "did not give a damn" about Franco-German quarrels, which they had to resolve themselves.[51]

The JCS pressed to have the FRG enter NATO with a 500,000-man army composed of full, 15,000-man divisions. The French, however, feared an FRG with its own national army and defense establishment. They pushed their Pleven Plan, which proposed to create a European Defense Ministry and integrated army. German forces would be limited to 100,000 troops, organized in regiments smaller than the Spofford Compromise's 6,000-man RCUs, which would be integrated into large mixed-national divisions constituting the European Army. The Germans would not have a Defense Ministry or general staff, nor be NATO members. The British further slowed prospective German rearmament in February 1951 by insisting on prior allied rearmament, strengthening of forces in Germany, safeguards against a reemergent German threat, and agreement on a fixed level of FRG contribution to Western defense.[52]

During February–June 1951 at Petersberg, the Allied High Commissioners and German officials focused on bringing the FRG and its divisions directly into NATO, while in Paris the French pushed their Pleven Plan to integrate German soldiers into a European Army, or EDC. Acheson and the JCS, however, held EDC to be militarily unrealistic, despite Truman's praise for its model, the recently approved Schuman Plan. On June 6 the Petersberg negotiators, hewing to German plans, proposed to create a German Defense Ministry, Inspectorate General (to command 250,000 German troops), and twelve heavily armed, mobile divisions to be assigned to NATO on equal basis with all other forces.[53]

The Paris talks deadlocked, meanwhile, over the Pleven Plan, whose integrationist plans Acheson and FRG officials took to be a ruse to postpone German rearmament. The French, however, refused to accept the Petersberg plans for German rearmament. Similarly, McCloy and Ambassador David Bruce in Paris resisted formation of a German national army that would enter NATO. They preferred an integrated European Army that would "contain" German rearmament, foster European unity, and ultimately allow withdrawal of U.S. troops from the Continent. McCloy and Bruce won over Eisenhower who, despite his preference to have German divisions in NATO, sympathized with French security concerns and was frustrated by the politics of negotiations. He, too, viewed U.S. withdrawal as inevitable, and by June 1951 concluded that NATO required a "spectacular success" and that European security would not be settled "until there exists a United States of Europe." Most important, he held that allied failure to safeguard Western Europe meant not being able to "get Germany wholeheartedly on our side in the struggle against communism."[54]

McCloy returned to Washington in June to confer with Truman and State and Defense officials about reconciling the Pleven Plan for a European Army with the Petersberg plans for FRG entry into NATO. McCloy insisted that he would warn the French not to interfere with Eisenhower's command of troops or delay German rearmament, but France's security concerns had to be met before it would agree to FRG political-military equality. Similarly, Ambassador Bruce's "long telegram" in early July urged merging of the Paris-Petersberg plans and creating a European Army as the best way to build Western defense, gain a German contribution, and move the FRG toward sovereignty.[55]

Despite his skepticism about the Pleven Plan, Acheson was convinced by July 6 that the French would never agree to FRG rearmament-sovereignty without safeguards and that deadlock raised the "greatest question of German adherence to the West." Hence it was necessary to create a European Army nominally commanded by Eisenhower but assigned to NATO's Central Sector commander, France's General Alphonse Juin. This would also foster accord on European defense institutions and FRG sovereignty. Finally, on July 18, at Mc-Cloy's urging, Eisenhower cabled Marshall that he supported a European Army and securing an FRG contribution to Western defense, and offered to do all he could to break the impasse.[56]

Eisenhower's intercession removed military objection to the Pleven Plan and spurred the Paris negotiators to produce in late July the framework for a supranational EDC with a European Army (now European Defense Force, or EDF). The six member nations—France, the FRG, Italy, Belgium, the Netherlands, and Luxembourg—would have equal status and share common supply systems and armaments programs. The general and his advisers soon worked out organizational details, with EDC subject to Eisenhower's command. Meanwhile, Acheson decided to "go all out" for EDC, as called for on July 30 in NSC 115. Truman approved three days later.[57]

The Truman administration was highly anxious to reach closure on EDC, which would allow the U.S. to rearm and to control the FRG, to contain the Soviets and their satellites, and to predominate in Europe. As the British noted, the Americans favored EDC even more than officials in London had realized. Acheson pushed the British and French to agree to rapid German rearmament—even before EDC institutions were operative—and to restore virtual FRG sovereignty, and eventually to admit the FRG into NATO. The British wished to move more slowly and to preclude FRG control of its own forces. The French wanted EDC institutions up and running before they granted German rearmament or sovereignty, and before France gave up its national army.

The Germans, having reluctantly acceded to the EDC formula, thought that even provisional EDC accord sufficed to permit them to create their own defense institutions and armed forces, which reflected reversion to their Petersberg plans.[58]

Military talks moved slowly, although at U.S. urging the NATO Council in October created a Temporary Council Committee (TCC), headed by "three wise men" (Averell Harriman, then Truman's special assistant; Sir Edmund Plowden, head of the British Economic Planning Board; and Jean Monnet, father of the Schuman Plan), to assess each nation's contribution to NATO's defense and set burden-sharing principles for EDC. By year's end the TCC had estimated equitable national contributions—save that of the FRG—to the common defense.[59]

Similarly, German contractual talks were snarled. Since the war's end the Western allies, by virtue of their conquest, had assumed "supreme authority" over occupied Germany and the right to intervene in an emergency. The Adenauer government now regarded supreme authority as violative of its sovereignty and indicative of distrust of the FRG. But the French would not allow FRG sovereignty until EDC was fully formed and the FRG's Western defense contribution assured. The FRG insisted that contractual sovereignty come first. Negotiations languished in 1951, but by summer U.S. officials saw need to make the Germans "enthusiastic members of our club." Accord on EDC and TCC estimates then spurred allied accord on FRG control over its own foreign and domestic affairs, except where the new agreement stipulated otherwise, thus preserving "supreme authority" by other words. The allies also retained their right to intervene in Germany, with the FRG able to appeal to the NATO Council.[60]

Acheson was adamant that the allies retain all rights held since 1945 pertaining to stationing of their troops, Berlin, unification, and a peace treaty. The Germans were not to be allowed to deal directly with Moscow or its agents on these issues, including "lost territories." Thus, when in September 1951 GDR Prime Minister Grotewohl again called for free elections to establish a German National Assembly—this time without insisting on equal GDR-FRG representation—the U.S. encouraged Adenauer's inclination to derail the initiative by proposing UN-supervised elections, which the GDR was sure to refuse. In October Truman, anticipating Churchill's return to power and likely call for Big Four meetings, said that he was "firmly" against any meeting because it was bound to discuss Germany.[61]

The next month the U.S. and its allies reached an interim "General Agreement" giving the FRG "practical" sovereignty. The allies retained control over matters that required dealing with the Soviets, as well as the right to keep their troops in the FRG for occupation and defense purposes. As Acheson told Truman, "[O]ur security against Germany for the future lies in tieing [*sic*] Germany to the west in every possible way through such institutions as the Schuman Plan, European defense force, and eventually NATO." But now the allies had to agree on the "sovereignty" that the FRG craved, as well as its defense contribution. The latter was vital, since the British and French insisted that they could not pay "one cent" for troop support in Germany, and Truman feared that a $15 billion budget deficit for FY 1953 would undermine all his administration had done in Europe since 1947.[62]

U.S. urgency about a final agreement on Germany and EDC was evident when Prime Minister Churchill visited the White House in January 1952. Churchill offered his usual fulsome praise about Anglo-American intent not to "dominate" the world "but to save it," and lauded Truman's intervention in Korea. Churchill offered to help with EDC but clearly intended to sustain Britain's decision to stay out. He deplored the Pleven Plan's integrationism, which he said did not strengthen armies by binding them together like sticks so much as turn them into a "bucket of wood pulp." Finally, he insisted that the Soviets feared Western friendship more than enmity. Thus, while he wanted the West to strengthen itself to force the Soviets to seek its friendship, his goal was a heads-of-state meeting.[63]

Truman by contrast emphasized need to "build a position of strength so that it would be possible to talk to the Soviets in a language they can understand." This meant "being strong enough to enforce the peace"—and he was adamant that "we must have the Germans." He did not want to meet with the Soviets—except in the unlikely event they would meet in the U.S.—and he was "not willing to give over the whole world to them, not so long as he was president."[64]

Acheson pressed an agreement with the FRG—or "we will lose Germany to the Soviets." He did not think that they would strike at Europe so much as work through their satellites. But he insisted that it was necessary to "create sufficient force to make it too dangerous for the Russians to undertake any action in Europe." There was no alternative to EDC and an FRG defense contribution, or to granting the FRG equality and lifting controls on its industry. The Americans also insisted, over Churchill's protests, that NATO (and EDC) be located in Paris, not London, and that an American, not British, admiral head its Atlantic command.[65]

The Americans were also intent to allay France's fear of being overwhelmed by the Germans in EDC and to meet its demand for an Anglo-American guarantee in case the FRG pulled its forces out of EDC. The French sought to exclude the FRG from NATO and to impose sweeping restrictions on FRG weapons production. Further, French appointment in late January of an ambassador to the coal-rich—but territorially disputed—Saar in an effort to forge economic union threatened future negotiations, with the FRG countering French demands with its own claims to sovereignty and equality.[66]

Truman told Acheson that he wanted accord on Germany and EDC within a month. Then at a foreign ministers meeting—with Adenauer included despite French protest—in London in mid-February, the secretary gained agreement on most issues. The French were persuaded to shelve the Saar matter until conclusion of negotiations on FRG sovereignty and EDC. At the same time, the Germans agreed to self-restraint on atomic, biological, chemical, and heavy land, air, and sea weapons, and to allowance of EDC curbs on weapons production in strategically "forward" areas of Germany. Acheson was persistent that the Truman administration could not ask Congress for further guarantees of French security—in case the FRG quit EDC—but he said that U.S. troop commitment to European defense guaranteed EDC. France backed off its demand for a British guarantee, which would have underscored their not joining EDC. Acheson also linked the FRG to NATO by proposing an EDC Council, including the FRG, to parallel NATO's. The FRG would be allowed to call a joint meeting whenever a question of its participation arose, as NATO nations could do in cases involving their security. The FRG's defense contribution was the only unresolved major issue.[67]

Acheson quickly concluded Western defense agreements at a NATO Council meeting in Lisbon on February 20–26. Having had time to weigh the TCC estimates and the political cost of refusal, Adenauer agreed to a $2.6 billion contribution through EDC in return for reduced occupation charges and commitment of twelve German divisions. The NATO Council extended its collective defense treaty guarantee to EDC, the French acceded to the London security controls on Germany, and the U.S. pledged its abiding interest in the integrity of EDC—and an additional $600 million in aid for France's rearmament and war in Indochina. The U.S. also obtained admission of Greece and Turkey into NATO. An "exultant" Acheson cabled Truman that "we have something pretty close to a grand slam."[68]

From the U.S. viewpoint, the success was real, with EDC and the contractual agreement between the allies and the FRG ready to be concluded. But four days later the French government of Edgar Faure had to resign after asking for a 15 percent tax increase to meet its Lisbon defense pledges, most of the Lisbon agreements soon dissipated, and in March a proposal from Stalin threw into high relief the Western powers' differing views over how to deal with their Soviet—and German—problems.[69]

III

From the fall of 1950 through January 1952 the Truman administration had shown no interest in Soviet overtures to gain accord on an agenda for a CFM meeting to focus on Germany, and similarly had rebuffed—through Adenauer—GDR overtures for all-German elections to a National Assembly that might ultimately lead to unification. Whether Soviet-GDR initiatives were sincere or efforts to capitalize on U.S. difficulties during the Korean War is moot. Regardless, Truman and his aides were bent on linking West Germany to the U.S. and its allies through the Schuman Plan, EDC, and NATO, and granting the FRG increasing sovereignty while retaining critical occupation rights there. Neither Truman nor Acheson was the least interested in German neutralization or demilitarization, and in January 1952 the president had made clear to Churchill that he did not want a Big Four meeting.

Then on March 10, 1952, the Soviet Foreign Ministry delivered a note, surely approved by Stalin, to the American, British, and French Embassies in Moscow calling for the Big Four to prepare a peace treaty with an "all German Government" that would be submitted to all nations that had fought Nazi Germany. Stalin's Note represented the most complete proposal he had ever put forth on Germany: formation of a unified, independent, democratic and neutral state, with all foreign troops withdrawn within a year. Germany's borders would conform to those "agreed" at the Potsdam Conference (including the Oder–western Neisse border with Poland), and all citizens—including former Nazi and military officials, except those convicted of crimes—would have civil and political rights. Germany would not be allowed to join any "coalition or military alliance" directed against nations that had fought Hitler's regime, but it could develop unrestricted world trade; maintain land, sea, and air forces for defense; produce war materials as agreed by treaty; and join the UN.[70]

The precise purpose of Stalin's Note remains in dispute. It might have been a serious proposal to reduce great-power conflict over a divided Germany and two sovereign states, or an initial gambit to test the waters for a settlement. It might also have been a diplomatic tactic to forestall the German contractual agreements, FRG rearmament, and EDC, or a propaganda ploy—aimed largely at the German populace—to undermine the Adenauer government and its increasing alignment with the West. To be sure, Stalin made his proposal only after the West's successful London-Lisbon negotiations, with the German agreements and formation of EDC near conclusion. Thus there is reason to believe he sought to stir fractious political debate among the allies, within the FRG—where many Germans and opponents of Adenauer preferred hope of reunification to rearmament—and within France, where fear of a rearmed Germany always ran high. But from a national security perspective, Stalin also had reason to make a last effort to preclude formation of a sovereign, rearmed, and industrially strong FRG integrated into a U.S.-led alliance system hostile to the Soviet Union.

It is, in fact, the latter concern that provides some basis to think that there was a serious side to Stalin's proposal, i.e., that his new "calculation of forces" led him to conclude that the USSR (and the U.S., if it was to be tempted to negotiate) stood to gain from a unified but neutral and only defensively rearmed Germany. This would permit the Americans and Soviets to disengage in all of Germany and diminish their confrontation over the two German states, each of which was currently being tugged to join a rival and increasingly militarized bloc. From Stalin's perspective there was also danger that ultimately an economically more powerful FRG would exert a strong westward pull on the GDR. The Soviet proposal also reduced the prospect that a fully rearmed FRG might "break out of American bondage," as Stalin said in his early 1952 article, "Economic Problems of Socialism in the U.S.S.R." And while the Soviet leader contended in this case that a rearmed Germany was more likely, as in the 1930s, to fight its capitalist rivals than to fight the USSR, he still had to worry that it might repeat its June 1941 action to seek "lost" territories or renew territorial ambitions in the east. Most important from Moscow's viewpoint, withdrawal of U.S. forces from a neutral Germany would reduce American power on the Continent and lessen any threat to the Soviets. As Deputy Foreign Minister Andrei Gromyko—who presided over formulating the Stalin Note—said, or hoped, the initiative would strengthen both opposition to "remilitarization" of West Germany and proponents of unification, and "unmask" the West's aggressive intentions.[71]

Truman was at Key West trying to shed a bronchial infection when the Stalin Note reached Washington. Acheson immediately assured him that he would keep him apprised of deliberations and clear critical responses to the Soviets. The secretary also said that the Stalin Note "has the usual apparent hooks in it" and was designed to appeal "primarily to the Germans and to impressionable opinion generally," and that since the Lisbon meeting he had "expected such a last ditch effort to prevent German integration." He thought it would be "ill advised" to turn it down "out of hand," but he soon likened the Soviet offer to tossing a "golden apple" of discord over the iron curtain to sow allied conflict. Both Truman and Acheson opposed neutralizing Germany. They had resolved to build allied political-military strength in Europe, with the FRG integrated into this system. The secretary told the president, "[Y]ou are missing no sensational weather here, physical or political."[72]

The British, too, suspected that Soviet purpose was to start protracted talks to delay the German agreements and EDC indefinitely, although Eden recognized that the Stalin Note "in both tone and substance worked considerable advance" upon prior Soviet proposals and perhaps signified that now they were "prepared to pay a bigger price" to prevent FRG integration. But the British opposed dealing with the Stalin Note on its "merits." They proposed—as Adenauer had when the GDR called for an all-German Assembly—to require that the UN specify that firm basis for free elections existed in all of Germany before weighing means to unify the nation.[73]

Adenauer had no interest in neutralization or negotiations with the Soviets or GDR. He wanted to build a strong, Western-oriented FRG that could ultimately negotiate reunification on its own terms with the GDR. He told the Western high commissioners that a four-power conference would only slow FRG integration and EDC, although "a purely negative answer" would have bad psychological effect. He proposed instead to "show up the Russian note" by posing "precise questions" about whether the Soviets would allow a UN Commission to investigate election conditions in the GDR, or whether Germany would be restricted from joining the Schuman Plan or EDC. Further, the Russians had to understand that "no German Government" could accept the Oder–western Neisse boundary with Poland: Germany's eastern borders had not been set at Potsdam. In sum, Adenauer's quick dismissal of the Stalin Note and remark that "it would make no difference whatever" to his government's policy, led his minister for all-German affairs, Jacob Kaiser, to reprove him as "more American than the Americans." But Kaiser was the only minister to oppose the chancellor.[74]

McCloy, too, regarded the Kremlin "propaganda blast" as designed to stir German nationalist sentiment over unification in order to impede rearmament, but he shied from a purely negative reply. He emphasized need for a UN Commission to conduct all-German elections, to insist on Germany's right to join a European defense community, and to avert issues that would permit a "Soviet exercise in sophistry." Similarly, U.S. officials in Moscow insisted that the Soviets meant to delay Western rearmament and FRG integration and would not give up control of the GDR. The French thought that the Soviets sought to preclude FRG integration by offering a unified but neutralized Germany that at least "would not be entirely on side of west in east-west questions." They, too, insisted on UN-supervised national elections and on the new government's being able to set its own policy pending a peace treaty and being free to join a coalition.[75]

Finally, it must be noted that although the Truman administration had recently coaxed Kennan out of his eighteen-month leave of absence from the

State Department to become ambassador to Moscow, with Senate confirmation hearings held during February–March, no one consulted America's most experienced Soviet expert about Stalin's Note. Further, when Kennan called on Truman on April 1, the president said only that he "never believed" that the Soviets wanted another great war but otherwise gave "no instruction of any kind" to his new envoy. The next day Acheson was decidedly reserved in his meeting with Kennan and "said nothing" to give "any clue" about policy.[76]

Kennan, concerned to have no instruction about critical problems "such as Germany"—just when it seemed to him that the Russians showed "some willingness" to start discussions—soon arranged to meet with Acheson and his advisers in mid-April. But the ambassador was disappointed again by Acheson's brief, unresponsive reception. Kennan told the policy makers he was upset at evident U.S. failure either to state frankly why it disliked the Soviet note or to propose American ideas for German unification even while pushing the Bonn agreements. Acheson replied that the U.S. could say nothing to distract from the German agreements and EDC because failure to effect them in the next weeks meant "our whole European policy would suffer a grievous setback." This confirmed for Kennan that "we had no interest in discussing the German problem with the Soviet government in any manner whatsoever."[77]

Truman and Acheson intended to get the allies to give short shrift to the Stalin Note. The secretary initially proposed to say only that the four powers could not impose a peace treaty on Germany, that UN oversight of national elections for a new government was a precondition to treaty talks, and that the Soviets should show good faith by concluding an Austrian treaty. The British and French, however, now wished, if only briefly, to take the Stalin Note more seriously, at least to determine if a new German government would be independent of four-power control. But Acheson was adamant that the West "drive ahead" with finalizing the German agreements and EDC and that their reply should be "as simple as possible," with no questions about a unified Germany or peace treaty terms.[78]

Adenauer, meanwhile, pressed the high commissioners to insist on the FRG's right to join the Schuman Plan or EDC and to reject the Potsdam borders. Then at a meeting in Paris, Eden, Schuman, and Adenauer agreed to insist that UN-supervised national elections be held, that a new government be independent, and that German borders be set at a peace conference. They discounted formation of a German national army as a "step backwards" in European relations, but Germany had to be permitted to join the "defensive European community." Truman approved, and on March 25 the allies delivered identical notes to the Soviets.[79]

The blunt Western reply would not close the matter, to no one's surprise.

Acheson guessed at a Soviet request for a four-power meeting; State Department planners said that the Soviets might even permit UN-supervised elections, albeit illusory "Potemkin village" affairs, to create an "Austrian-type situation." If so, the U.S. should make clear that the "unification game . . . will be played seriously and to a conclusion"—with the Russians likely to back down. In West Germany, meanwhile, proponents of reunification and critics of Adenauer's exclusive Western orientation caused the Bundestag to resolve on April 3 that the FRG should ask the four powers to conduct free elections to create a unifying National Assembly.[80]

The formal allied response seemed to anger Stalin or to confirm his darkest views about Western intentions. Regardless, at a Kremlin meeting on April 7 with his Foreign Ministry heads and the leaders of the GDR and SED, he said it was now clear that the West would not accept any proposal the Soviets made over Germany, or remove their troops. "The Americans need their troops in West Germany to hold Western Europe in their hands," Stalin said, and while they say they wish to defend against Russia their "real goal" is "to control Europe." He expected the U.S. to draw a rearmed FRG into NATO and said that "Adenauer is in the pocket of the Americans." He implored the GDR officials that it was time to "organize your own state" and to regard its demarcation line with the FRG as a "frontier, not as a simple border but a dangerous one" that required increased protection. Whatever remote chance there might have been for fruitful negotiations was virtually dead.[81]

Stalin's pique was partly concealed, however, in the Soviets' reply to the West on April 9. The Russians chided the West for rejecting their draft treaty without proposing another one, and persisted in their demands that a unified Germany conform to the Potsdam borders, remain outside an alliance, and be limited to raising an army for defense only—a condition that would undermine EDC. But for the record, the Russians kept negotiations alive by proposing that the Big Four sponsor all-German elections and begin peace treaty talks. Acheson and the allies, however, saw this as a ploy to delay FRG integration, although the secretary, with Truman's approval, suggested calling the Russian bluff by having the four powers' high commissioners discuss having an "impartial Commission" arrange all-German elections.[82]

Eden inclined to go along but then feared that the Berlin meeting would delay the German agreements and EDC. Adenauer, after weighing the matter for a day and "through half the night," was even more certain that the meeting "would be a mistake" because his Cabinet would not let him sign the agreements until they knew whether the Soviet offer of free elections was sincere. Moreover, his opponents and some government members would insist that negotiations, which the Russians could prolong, be concluded before finalizing the agreements and EDC. Similarly, Mayor Ernst Reuter of Berlin balked at negotiations with the Soviets.[83]

Acheson and Truman thus agreed that the allies should insist that the UN, or an impartial commission, sponsor elections to form an all-German government that would play its "full part" in treaty negotiations, remain independent of the four powers, and be able to join a European defense community. This reply to Moscow on May 13 produced not unexpected, bitter Soviet charges on May 24 that Western emphasis on electoral preconditions was intended to delay peace treaty talks, and that the pending agreements with Adenauer's government revealed Western intent to "legalize the re-establishment of the German army headed by Hitlerite generals" and strengthen the aggressive character of the North Atlantic powers seeking unity with the "German revanchists."[84]

"We have won the battle of the notes," Eden now told Acheson, who found the Soviet reply "feeble." Even Kennan jeered at the "remarkable weakness" and "injured sweet reasonableness" of the Soviet note. Indeed, Russian recriminations revealed that they knew they could not block the impending German agreements and EDC, which signaled near permanent East-West division. If there was any doubt, Stalin, having told GDR leaders on April 7 to organize their own state, now began to seal off the Soviet zone of Germany from the West, likely intending to create a "full-fledged satellite."[85]

The Soviet blast also provided final incentive, if any was needed, for the Western powers and FRG to sign the agreements and EDC treaty then being hammered out in Bonn and Paris, respectively. Negotiations were intense during April–May, with Truman bent on submitting agreements to Congress before it adjourned for the summer and the forthcoming election campaign all but officially ended his presidency. Thus on May 22, two days before officials concluded that they had won the battle of the notes, Acheson flew to Germany to conclude what he considered the most critical undertaking of his term as secretary.[86]

Talks in Bonn were led by McCloy, who would conclude that the final agreements barely resembled the original proposals owing to allied concessions and need to recognize the FRG's demand for "full equality"—and during one mid-May session he exclaimed "this is now the 122nd concession the Allies have made to the Germans." In fact, Adenauer skillfully exploited the tight U.S. deadline and pressure from German nationalists, who quickly branded retention of occupation-style controls as "Versailles" and assailed any obligations that might impede unification. Thus the allies abandoned or scaled back civil service and industrial and banking decartelization-deconcentration reforms, and brokered a compromise between British and French demands for a high FRG contribution to Western defense and German desire to spend more on their own rearmament. This led to a sliding-scale agreement that initially emphasized Anglo-French rearmament ahead of German, but the cost was further concession on decartelization, deconcentration, and lessened reparations.[87]

McCloy did prevent the Germans from last-minute balking at agreed reparations terms for Jewish Holocaust victims, while the allies, despite revocation of the Occupation Statute, retained nearly all of their former powers pertaining to emergency intervention, stationing of forces, Berlin, unification, and a peace treaty. They further assured that in event of unification, the FRG would not transfer its powers to any new government that would not agree to abide by the FRG's international obligations, thus precluding FRG-GDR deal making that might alter Germany's relationship with the West. Acheson gave reciprocal assurance in a side-letter to the FRG that the West would not impair its sovereignty.[88]

The foreign ministers then sought to finalize EDC, when the French again pressed for an Anglo-American security guarantee in event rearmed Germany seceded from the new defense group. The British inclined to assuage the French, but Truman and Acheson knew that their "dying" administration could not get the Senate to ratify such a new commitment. They agreed only to a joint declaration with Britain that they had an "abiding interest" in EDC's integrity and regarded a threat to it as a threat to their security. The French reluctantly acceded, and the German agreements and EDC were signed on May 26–27 in Bonn and Paris, respectively.[89]

Ironically, response to the agreements in the U.S. was more positive than in Germany, where many critics argued that the new ties to the West precluded unification. In France, the Left charged that the agreements fostered anti-Soviet alignment, and the Right—including General de Gaulle—claimed that they ceded too much to the FRG. Still, at least one historian, Thomas Schwartz, has judged that the Bonn accords were the "crowning achievement" of the Truman administration's German policy. The president lauded the accords as enabling the FRG to participate fully in the "family of nations" and providing for Europe's common defense and increased unity. He promptly submitted the agreements and protocol (negotiated earlier at Lisbon) establishing reciprocal NATO-EDC security guarantees for ratification, and on July 2 the Senate complied.[90]

Acheson was "astounded" in early June, however, to learn that the French had gained British assent to respond to the Soviets' May 24 note with a proposal for a four-power meeting to set terms for all-German elections and formation of a government, although peace treaty talks would have to await establishment of a German government. He complained to the British that the Truman administration had premised submitting the German agreements and NATO-EDC protocol to the Senate on not having four-power talks, and that the Russians would expand even the most limited agenda. He wanted no proposal except one that would result "in a clear Soviet refusal of a meeting on reasonable terms." Similarly, Adenauer, who now held that the Bonn agreements made the FRG an equal partner, opposed any meeting with the Russians unless they assured that return to four-power, or Potsdam, controls was a dead letter, and that the FRG was sovereign and had the right to join a Western defense system. He also told Acheson that the Bundestag would not ratify the Bonn agreements while negotiations were under way with the Russians.[91]

Acheson had to find a compromise between his and Adenauer's kindred views that opposed negotiations with the Soviets and those of the French, whose National Assembly would not ratify the accords unless assured that the West had made every good-faith effort to negotiate with Moscow. The secretary thus fostered a "reasonable" proposal intended to draw Russian rejection. At a CFM meeting in London in late June, he gained French accord to propose to negotiate with the Soviets solely on the issue of establishing an impartial commission to assess prospect for free elections in all of Germany. The allies would still insist, however, that the Soviets stipulate that a new German government would be free of four-power control and able to join a European defense system. As Acheson confidently cabled Washington, "whole tenor of note puts onus on Sovs sufficiently to make it unlikely that Sovs will agree to mtg on terms proposed."[92]

After Acheson assured Adenauer that the West would not deal separately over Germany with the Russians, and calmed French concern about FRG influence on Big Four talks, Kennan transmitted the allied note to the Soviets on July 10. As expected, their reply two weeks later assailed the West for signing the separate German agreements and EDC in "flagrant violation" of the Potsdam accords, delaying discussion of German unification and a peace treaty, and inviting the FRG to join the "aggressive" North Atlantic bloc. The Russians again called for a four-power meeting, including FRG and GDR representatives, with a broad agenda: a German peace treaty, formation of a government, and then free elections.[93]

U.S. officials readily concluded that regardless of what the Soviets may have intended with their first note in March, they no longer wanted four-power talks. Their attack on the Bonn agreements and EDC showed that they regarded these as *"faits accomplis."* Now they sought only to foment "political trouble" and offered terms for a meeting that the West had repeatedly rejected. The U.S. replied in late September that "conditions had radically altered since the Potsdam Agreement of 1945," and that the Big Four could not "dictate" a German peace treaty. Talks were not possible until free elections, which seemed to mean one thing in the West and another in the "Soviet vocabulary," were held to elect an all-German government that would negotiate a peace treaty. The Soviets made no further reply. The "battle of the notes" had reached its anticlimactic closure.[94]

IV

Prospect for accord over Germany on the basis of the Soviet proposal of March 1952 was remote, but not solely because Stalin—as Vojtech Mastny has said—sought only to negotiate either a unified, "pro-Soviet though not necessarily communist" Germany or, next best alternative, effect a full-fledged satellite in East Germany. To be sure, Stalin's emphasis on Big Four talks based on the Potsdam framework was better suited to 1945–1948 than the radically altered conditions since then that included formalization of the FRG, NATO, the Schuman Plan, and an impending EDC. Still, even in 1952, Stalin's German policy was not set in concrete. As Henry Kissinger has pointed out, the Soviet leader had not recognized the GDR regime as a completely sovereign state and gave it a status distinct from that of his Eastern European satellites in order to use it as a bargaining chip in negotiations over Germany.[95]

Moreover, Stalin did not fully reject negotiations with the West and order the GDR's "satellization" until early April 1952, following allied rebuff of his note. This is not to say that U.S. acceptance of the Potsdam framework for negotiations would not have risked undermining both the intensely pro-West Adenauer government and ratification of the Bonn agreements and EDC. Further, Congress and the public would have been confused about administration efforts to foster FRG–Western European integration. But these problems might well have been overcome by explication of the benefits to be derived from resolving the problem of a unified Germany and slowing the rush to Cold War political divisions and military alliances.[96]

Truman, however, did not want to negotiate with Stalin, who he insisted broke every accord and respected only "force." Nor did the president seek a neutralized or demilitarized Germany. He was convinced that a rearmed FRG was as critical to NATO-EDC as an economically resuscitated FRG was to Western Europe's recovery. He and his senior aides largely paid lip service to the idea of a unified Germany, unless it came on exclusively U.S. terms. In fact, officials worried that a unified Germany might play East against West and/or dominate its smaller neighbors, and it might also choose a socialist Schumacher/SPD government rather than the conservative and politically reliable

Adenauer/CDU government. Truman was also content to leave German negotiations, as distinct from Korean armistice talks, to Acheson, whose "situations
of strength" strategy rested on a significant FRG contribution to NATO-EDC.[97]

From the outset, Acheson viewed Stalin's Note as an apple of discord intended to upset FRG integration and the "grand slam" that he had gained at Lisbon on Western rearmament. He held that the Potsdam framework was "dead,"
and he would proffer only "reasonable" terms that he knew the Soviets would
bear the onus for rejecting. Hence, he emphasized UN-sponsored all-German
elections as a precondition for peace treaty talks and insisted that the new Germany remain free to join any alliance, i.e., NATO-EDC. This precluded Germany's neutralization-demilitarization and hinted at its enlistment in an anti-
Soviet, NATO-led axis. Stalin was not likely to accept this.

Similarly, Adenauer based his "policy of strength" on aligning the FRG
with the West and unifying Germany on Western terms. He vehemently opposed the Potsdam framework, especially mention of the Oder–western Neisse
boundary with Poland, and he resisted negotiations with the GDR or Soviets,
except to prompt concessions from the West. He thought that Stalin would
never loosen control of the GDR and sought to neutralize Germany only as a
means to dominate the unified state. The British held Stalin's proposal to be
more advanced than previous ones, but they were unwilling to endanger the
German agreements or EDC, or U.S. aid and military commitment to Europe.
The French were too weak to lead and depended on U.S. aid to sustain their
struggle in Indochina.

Thus, while it cannot be said with certainty that U.S. failure to deal more
positively with Stalin's Note was truly a lost opportunity to negotiate German
unification, it is clear that the Truman administration, as Melvyn Leffler has
pointed out, preferred to co-opt and integrate West German economic and military power into an alliance that would prevent the Soviets from threatening
Western Europe. In so doing, however, the U.S. averted exploring an option that
might have left Germany and Europe less divided and less dependent on the
two nuclear superpowers and their impending military alliances. As Kennan
recorded in September 1952 after talking with U.S. officials tied to NATO, they
were basing policy on the German agreements and EDC and refused to con-
template withdrawal of U.S. forces from Germany "at any time within the fore-
seeable future under any conceivable agreement with Russia." This meant
"continuance of the split of Germany and Europe."[98]

The Truman administration, however, could not get the Germans or French
to ratify EDC before leaving office in January 1953, although the FRG complied in March. Nor could the new president, Eisenhower, and Secretary of
State Dulles, move the French. Then Stalin's death on March 5 seemed to lessen

incentive for increased European defense. His successors immediately began to speak about "peaceful coexistence" and hint at greater flexibility over Germany, while Churchill resumed his call for a Big Four meeting. Eisenhower's "Chance for Peace" speech on April 16 deplored the costs of Cold War militarization, but he held to his campaign slogan of "liberation" of peoples in the Soviet orbit and to Truman's policy that elections for a new German government, able to join NATO-EDC, had to precede peace treaty talks. Eisenhower called for a Russian show of good faith by signing an Austrian treaty and helping the U.S. to effect an "honorable armistice" in Korea.[99]

Soviet intervention in the GDR in June with troops and tanks to crush nationwide uprisings against the Communist regime—begun as worker protests in Berlin—further impeded Big Four talks. Eisenhower said that now he would not attend a summit, although in July the U.S. and Britain jointly proposed a foreign ministers' meeting to discuss Germany. But this initiative was to convince the French to ratify EDC by showing that all diplomatic avenues had been explored, and to bolster Adenauer and the CDU in the FRG's September elections. The U.S., meanwhile, orchestrated a psychological propaganda campaign and food relief program to undermine the GDR, while the NSC held that a neutralized Germany with U.S. forces withdrawn was too great an economic and strategic loss. Rather, U.S. policy favored a unified Germany "allied to the free world," which would "represent a major step in rolling back the iron curtain." Ironically, however, the USSR's intervention in the GDR now raised its stake in preserving that regime and strengthened the bargaining power of Walter Ulbricht, the dictatorial general secretary of the SED, who blamed the June riots on U.S. propaganda.[100]

Adenauer's sweeping reelection in September seemed to augur four-power talks that might spur the French to ratify EDC. Dulles also proposed to Eisenhower a "spectacular effort to relax world tensions" based on U.S.-Soviet troop withdrawal from Europe. But Adenauer's victory led to hardened negotiations with France over control of the Saar and talk about creating a German national army as an alternative to EDC. Privately, the chancellor feared that four-power talks might lead to a Soviet-American deal unfavorable to the FRG.[101]

Further, Dulles' troop withdrawal ideas, based on an emerging "New Look" that favored atomic weapons for defense over more costly buildup of conventional forces, aroused European concern that U.S. atomic retaliation against Soviet action would bring massive destruction to the Continent. In late November, Dulles sharply reasserted to Adenauer the U.S. commitment to German integration and EDC but insisted that maintaining Franco-German amity was the basis for continued pouring of U.S. resources into Europe. The secretary urged German concessions on the Saar to spur France to ratify EDC. Adenauer's silent reaction to Dulles' critical points suggested that the message had gotten through, while the Soviets now accepted Western terms for four-power talks on Germany in Berlin. Still, in mid-December Dulles warned NATO allies that failure to implement EDC would prompt an "agonizing reappraisal" of U.S. policy in Europe. But this policy reversal was correctly perceived as "bluff."[102]

The meeting of the Big Four Foreign Ministers in Berlin during January–February 1954 was a standoff. Eden promoted Western plans for free elections in Germany, formation of an all-German government, and peace treaty negotiations with security guarantees, while Dulles was persistent that Germany be allowed to join a "defensive" EDC. The Soviets insisted that Germany could be unified only within the framework of a European security pact that ended NATO-EDC and that "free elections" had to follow Eastern Europe's model, which excluded "fascistic" and "militaristic" groups from parliamentary processes. The Soviet position, which bore no resemblance to the Stalin Note, reflected their preference now for a divided Germany—they gave the GDR sovereignty in March—over a unified nation that might join a Western alliance.[103]

U.S. officials were delighted to be able to argue that there was no alternative to EDC. The British and Germans stepped up their commitments, but the French continued to fear German domination—in or out of EDC—and refused to consider dissolving their national army. Nor would they be moved by increased, or threats of lowered, U.S. aid for Indochina. French defeat in May at Dienbienphu in Vietnam finally led Prime Minister Pierre Mendes-France to propose that his country become a member of EDC if it revised its supranational structure, the British joined, and the French army retained its autonomy. But the U.S. successfully urged the EDC nations to reject this proposal and threatened to rearm Germany without French participation. In August 1954 an angry French National Assembly rejected EDC.[104]

U.S. officials were furious but should not have been surprised. EDC really allowed the U.S. to contain both France and Germany within a supranational alliance structure that would also defend against the Soviet Union, but with France denied the independent policy voice and army that it deemed appropriate. Ironically, French slaying of EDC prompted the British to promote German and Italian membership in the Western European Union (WEU) of 1948. The U.S. recommitted to defend Western Europe, and the FRG renounced manufacture of atomic, chemical, and biological weapons and accepted WEU limits on its troops and manufacture of heavy weapons. The allies also agreed to have the FRG enter NATO, with German forces assigned to NATO's integrated command.

The allies further revised Germany's agreements to enhance its sovereignty and Adenauer's standing, and the FRG renounced use of force to effect territorial changes. The French were too weak to resist this tide, and Russian offers in late 1954–early 1955 to negotiate German unification—and demilitarization—on the basis of the Eden Plan met stiff Anglo-American resistance. On May 8, 1955, exactly one decade after Nazi Germany's unconditional surrender, the FRG regained its sovereignty and entered NATO. The next week the Soviet Union and its seven Eastern European allies signed their Warsaw Treaty Organization. The political, economic, and military division of Germany and Europe, under American and Soviet aegis, was now complete and would persist for the next thirty-five years.[105]

But from Truman's perspective, as he said in December 1952, his administration had done all it could to foster world peace—"never was a greater or more enlightened effort expended for a noble purpose"—and to resist Soviet and Chinese aggression. If the American people remained patient, he persisted, they would realize their goal of a just and lasting peace.[106]

Conclusion

Truman and Another Such Victory

No one leader or nation caused the Cold War. The Second World War generated inevitable Soviet-American conflict as the world's two most powerful nations, with antithetical political-economic systems, confronted each other on two devastated, war-torn continents. The Americans, who emerged from the war with their nation unscathed, their economy burgeoning, and having suffered relatively few war deaths (about 400,000), would seek to fashion a world order friendly to their liberal politics, capitalist economy, and global strategic interests. They would also seek to achieve maximal national security by preventing any nation from severing U.S. ties to its traditional allies and vital areas of trade and resources, and to avoid 1930s-style "appeasement."[1]

So too would the Soviets seek to shape a world order friendly to their Communist regime. They sought to establish maximal national security by restoring their historic 1917 borders, maintaining oversight of the governments and foreign policies of nations along their European borders, and exacting recompense from Germany and its former Axis allies for staggering wartime damages. These included the deaths of more than 20 million Russian soldiers and civilians, and destruction of tens of thousands of cities and towns and the better part of the nation's industrial and agricultural capacity. To be sure, Stalin was a brutal dictator who directed a murderous regime. But there is no evidence that he intended to march his Red Army westward beyond its agreed-upon European occupation zones, and he put Soviet state interests ahead of desire to spread Communist ideology. He was also prepared to deal practically with the U.S., whose military and economic power he respected.[2]

President Truman inherited an expedient wartime alliance that already stood on shaky ground at Yalta in February 1945 and grew more strained over Soviet control in Rumania and Poland, while U.S. surrender talks with German officials at Bern roused Stalin's fears of a separate peace. New to office and wholly inexperienced in foreign affairs, Truman could rightly lament that "they didn't tell me anything about what was going on." Thus, he had to depend on advisers whose views ranged from Harriman's belief that it was time to call a halt to the Russians' "barbarian invasion" of Europe to counsel from Roosevelt's emissaries, Davies and Hopkins, that it was necessary to put Soviet-American differences in perspective in order to try to preserve long-term accord.

To his credit, Truman strove to measure up to the awesome responsibilities of the presidency and to have the U.S. assume global responsibilities that it had never before shouldered. He favored creation of the UN and held that he wanted to "keep all of my engagements with the Russians" because they were "touchy and suspicious of us," although "World Peace" depended on mutual cooperation. He fostered extensive foreign aid and reconstruction and pushed European cooperation and integration. He also sought to retain civilian control over nuclear weapons and to constrain military spending, and—having already witnessed two wars—he strongly wished to avert a third. He would take on a major "police action" to halt aggression and preserve the independence of South Korea—a nation recognized by the UN—and after he recognized his "overreach" in trying to punish North Korea by using military means to unify the peninsula, he sought to return to the status quo ante.[3]

There is merit in the contemporaneous judgment of the liberal head of the AEC, David Lilienthal, in July 1948—when Truman was under fire from conservatives and liberals in his party who sought to deny him the Democratic presidential nomination—that "Truman's *record* is that of a man who, facing problems that would have strained and perhaps even floored Roosevelt at his best, has met these problems head on in almost every case. The way he took on the aggressions of Russia; the courage in calling a special session of an antagonistic Congress controlled by the opposition to put through an extensive program for the restoration of Europe; his civil rights program, upon which he hasn't welched or trimmed—my God! What *do* these people want?" And as for the charge that key foreign policy advisers were ultraconservative, "who put Forrestal, and Harriman and Lovett in public life . . . for the first time but FDR himself?" In Lilienthal's view, it was time for perfectionist liberals and reactionaries to stop hounding Truman, "a real man."[4]

This judgment, which has been amplified in recent years by Truman biographers and triumphalist historians of the Cold War, nonetheless greatly underestimates the extent to which the president, from the Potsdam Conference

through the Korean War, significantly contributed to and exacerbated the growing Cold War and militarization of U.S. foreign policy. Clearly, Truman's insecurity with regard to diplomacy and world politics led him to seek to give the
appearance of acting decisively, and reinforced his penchant to view conflict in
black-and-white terms and to divide nations into free or totalitarian societies.
He shied from weighing the complexities of historic national conflicts and local or regional politics. Instead, he attributed nearly every diplomatic crisis or
civil war—in Germany, Iran, Turkey, Greece, Czechoslovakia, China, and Korea—to Soviet machination and insisted that the Soviets had broken every
agreement and were bent on "world conquest." To determine his response, he
was quick to reach for an analogy, usually the failure of Western powers to resist Germany and Japan in the 1930s, and to conclude that henceforth he would
speak to the Russians in the only language he thought they understood: "divisions." This style of leadership and diplomacy closed off both advocates and
prospects for more patiently negotiated and more nuanced or creative courses
of action.

At the same time, Truman's presumptions about the political-economic-
military-moral superiority of the U.S. led him to believe that he could order the
world on America's terms, and he ascribed only dark motives to nations or
leaders who resisted its will. Monopoly control of the atomic bomb heightened
this sense of righteous power. Thus he set sail for Potsdam in July 1945 determined to advance only American interests and highly disposed to atomic diplomacy. He believed that use of the bombs on Japan would allow the U.S. to "out
maneuver" the Russians in China, i.e., negate their Yalta concessions, and prevent them from getting in on the "kill" of Japan, or its occupation. The bomb,
his ace in the hole, also reinforced Truman's determination to deny the Russians any fixed sum of reparations—despite the Yalta accords and Germany's
capacity to pay—and access to the Ruhr by allowing Byrnes to negotiate to impasse over this issue. The secretary then imposed his zonal reparations ultimatum on the Soviets. This policy served to increase East-West divide and diminished prospects of reunifying Germany.

Truman won his hand at Potsdam. But use of two atomic bombs on Hiroshima and Nagasaki—the second was absolutely not militarily necessary—
showed that for the president, and Byrnes, the prospect of political gain in
Europe and Asia precluded serious thought about not using the bombs. The
Russians may also have been led to conclude that the bombs were directed at
them, or at their ability to achieve their strategic interests, including a "paltry"
$10 billion in German reparations. Regardless, Stalin would not be pressured;
he gave orders to speed development of a Russian atomic bomb, while the Soviets also dug in their heels diplomatically.

In September 1945, Truman backed Byrnes' "bomb in his pocket" diplomacy at the London CFM, which deadlocked over Soviet control in Eastern Europe and U.S. control in Japan. The Russians should be told "to go to hell," the president said. He also sided with "ultranationalist" advisers who opposed international atomic sharing. He believed that the U.S. was the world's atomic "trustee," that its technological-industrial genius assured permanent atomic supremacy, and that other nations would have to catch up on their own. In spring 1946 Truman undermined the Acheson-Lilienthal plan for international control and development of atomic resources by naming Baruch as chief negotiator. His emphasis on close inspections, sanctions, no veto, and indefinite U.S. atomic monopoly underscored Soviet atomic disadvantage and virtually assured their refusal. Neither Truman nor Baruch, nor U.S. military officials, would give up control over their "winning weapon," or take a calculated risk to avert an otherwise inevitable arms race. Sadly, neither they, nor Stalin, saw the bomb as a common danger to the human race.

Meanwhile, Byrnes' diplomacy in Moscow in December 1945 had produced Yalta-style accords on a European peace treaty process, Russian predominance in Bulgaria and Rumania, U.S. primacy in China and Japan, and compromise over Korea. Soviet disputes with Iran and Turkey were set aside. But Truman took this accord to be appeasement, criticized his secretary, and said that the Russians understood only an "iron fist" and that he was tired of "babying" them. Thus Truman's personal Cold War declaration came six weeks before Kennan's "Long Telegram" and Churchill's iron curtain speech.

Strong U.S. protests in 1946 caused the Russians to withdraw both their troops from Iran and their claims to joint defense of the Turkish Straits. Stalin evidently did not seek to annex Azerbaijan or foster a separatist state. Rather, he sought to reassert traditional Russian influence and gain an oil concession to put the USSR on equal footing with the U.S. and Britain. But Truman and Byrnes rejected this. They decided to let the Russians have it "with both barrels" at the UN. The Soviets withdrew from Azerbaijan under cover of an oil agreement that ultimately Teheran never ratified, while the U.S. declared Iran and its oil to be major strategic interests and began to underwrite the shah's government militarily. The president would also reference the Iran case when he confronted problems in Greece.

As for the Soviet note to Turkey in August 1946 calling for revised governance of the Straits, Truman said he was ready to follow his policy of military response "to the end" to determine if Russia intended "world conquest." This despite the fact that the Soviets had begun to withdraw from the Balkans and no one—including the Turks—expected them to launch an attack. U.S. action rested on its plans to integrate Turkey into its strategic planning and to use it as a base of operations against Russia in event of war. Shortly, Truman approved a Mediterranean command that led to the U.S. becoming the dominant naval power in the region by year's end.

Meanwhile, Truman ignored both Wallace's proposals to promote economic ties with Russia and his questions about U.S. global military expansiveness. The president then fired his commerce secretary after he publicly challenged Byrnes' Stuttgart speech in early September 1946 propounding West German reconstruction and continued U.S. military presence there. The firing was reasonable, but Truman contributed to the imbroglio by failure to address the significant issues Wallace had raised, while the president's rage at him as "a real Commy," and at "parlor pinks" as a "sabotage front" for Stalin, was excessive.

At this same time Truman accepted at face value Clifford's "Russian Report" and accompanying "Last Will of Peter the Great." The report was a hasty White House compilation of apocalyptic projections of Soviet aim to conquer the world by military force, which the president's aides put forth in "black and white" terms to appeal to him and to justify a vast military buildup. Similarly, the will was an old forgery purporting to show that Tsar Peter—read Stalin—had designs to conquer Eurasia by subversion and force. Truman continued to cite this document even after he had been informed that it was spurious. Further, as Clifford recalled, it was a short step from the Russian Report to Truman's epochal request in March 1947 for military aid to Greece and Turkey to help "free peoples" fight totalitarianism.

In enunciating his Truman Doctrine, the president vastly overstated the global-ideological aspects of Soviet-American conflict, insisted that the Russians had broken every agreement since Potsdam, and added in fall 1947 that "if Russia gets Greece and Turkey," it would get Italy and France, the iron curtain would extend to western Ireland, and the U.S. would have to "come home and prepare for war." Truman's fears were excessive. Stalin never challenged the Truman Doctrine or Western primacy in Greece, and he told Yugoslavia's leaders in early 1948 to halt their aid because the U.S. would never allow the Greek Communists to win and break Anglo-American control in the Mediterranean. When Marshal Tito balked, Stalin withdrew his advisers from Yugoslavia and expelled it from the Cominform.

Perhaps U.S. officials feared that Britain's retreat from Greece might allow the Soviets to penetrate the Mediterranean, or that if Greek Communists overthrew the reactionary Greek regime they might align Athens with Moscow. Evidence for this remains thin. In fact, EAM had deep roots in Greek society and its triumph did not portend a state that would have marched to Stalin's drumbeat any more than did Tito's or Mao's. Further, the Truman administration's costly—and almost exclusively military—policy never addressed the causes of Greece's civil war. Instead, it helped to sustain in power for three decades repressive regimes that persecuted their opponents and denied them basic rights. Equally important, Truman's rhetorical division of the world into "free" versus "totalitarian" states, as Gaddis once said, created an "ideological straitjacket" for U.S. foreign policy and an unfortunate model for later interventions. This includes Korea—"the Greece of the Far East," as Truman would say—French Indochina, and a host of other nations by other presidents in the decades to come.

The Truman Doctrine led to the Marshall Plan in June 1947, but they were not "two halves of the same walnut," as Truman claimed. State Department officials who drew ERP differentiated it from what they viewed as his doctrine's implications for economic and ultimately military warfare. Initially, the Soviets assailed the Marshall Plan as an effort to purchase Europe wholesale, although there was brief interest in participating if the U.S. offered a generous Lend-Lease style arrangement, a most unlikely event. As the British quickly saw, however, Soviet participation was precluded by U.S.-imposed financial and economic controls and by the integrated, Continental approach to aid rather than nation-by-nation basis that would have benefited war-devastated Russia. In direct talks in Paris, U.S. officials refused concessions, focused on resources to come from Russia and Eastern Europe, and insisted on German contributions to ERP ahead of reparations payments or a peace treaty—and then expressed widespread relief when the Soviets rejected ERP for themselves and Eastern Europe.

The Marshall Plan helped to spur American-European trade and Western European recovery, bring France into camp with Germany and satisfy French economic and security claims, and revive western Germany industrially without unleashing the 1930s-style "German colossus." The Marshall Plan was also intended to contain the Soviets economically, preclude German-Russian bilateral dealings, and provide the U.S. with access to its allies' domestic and colonial resources.

The Marshall Plan's excellent return on investment, however, may have cost far more than the $13 billion expended. As Lovett said in August 1947, "[T]he world is definitely split in two," while Kennan forewarned that for defensive reasons the Soviets would clamp down on Czechoslovakia and Eastern Europe. Indeed, Stalin evidently viewed the Marshall Plan as signaling a U.S. effort to predominate over all of Europe, and the Soviets undertook a comprehensive strategy shift that led to rigging elections in Hungary, Zhdanov's "two camps" approach to world policy, creation of the Cominform, and support for the Communist coup in Czechoslovakia in February 1948. Truman in turn concluded that the Western world confronted the same situation it did a decade earlier with Nazi Germany, and his bristling St. Patrick's Day speeches in March 1948 put sole onus on the Soviet Union for the Cold War. Then Anglo-American talks at the Pentagon would culminate in NATO in April 1949.

Meanwhile, the U.S. decision to make western Germany the cornerstone of ERP virtually precluded negotiations to reunify the country. In fact, when Marshall proposed during a CFM meeting in spring 1947 to offer current production reparations to the Russians to induce agreement to unify Germany, the president sternly refused, despite the secretary's complaint about lack of "elbow room" to negotiate. By the time of the next CFM in late 1947, U.S. officials neither wanted nor intended to accept German unification on any Russian-proposed terms even though they met most U.S. requirements, as Ambassador Smith wrote.

By then the U.S. was on to its London Conference program to create a West German state. As Stalin said in February 1948, "The West will make Western Germany their own, and we shall turn Eastern Germany into our own state." In June the Soviet dictator initiated the Berlin blockade to try to forestall the West's program. But Truman determined to "stay period," convinced that to withdraw from Berlin would seriously undermine U.S. influence in Europe and ERP and destroy his presidential standing. He also determined to avert military confrontation.

But the president saw no connection between the London Program and the blockade. Further, his belief that "there is nothing to negotiate," and his accord with Clay's view that to withdraw from Berlin meant "we have lost everything we are fighting for," exaggerated the intent of Stalin's maneuver and diminished even slim chances for compromise on Germany. This meant refusing to consider a four-power currency for Berlin and modification of the London Program, as well as rejecting Kennan's more complex "Plan A" for a unified, neutralized state with U.S. and Soviet forces withdrawn to its periphery. As Marshall said in August 1948, there would be "no abandonment of our position" on West Germany.

Eventually Truman and the airlift prevailed over Stalin, who gave in to a face-saving CFM in May 1949 that ended the blockade, with nothing else agreed. Truman's new secretary of state, Acheson, now said that the U.S. intended to create a West German government "come hell or high water" and that Germany could be unified only by consolidating the East into the West on the basis of its incipient Bonn Constitution. Similarly, Truman said in June 1949 that he would not sacrifice West Germany's basic freedoms to gain "nominal political unity."

The president also showed no interest when in March 1952 Stalin proposed a Big Four meeting to draft a peace treaty for a united, neutral, defensively rearmed Germany free of foreign troops. Whether Stalin was seeking an all-German settlement to reduce great-power conflict over a divided nation has been debated. His note came only after the U.S. and its allies were near contractual accord on West German sovereignty, and Acheson had just negotiated his "grand slam" providing for German forces to enter a proposed EDC linked to NATO and an FRG financial contribution to Western defense. Acheson held that Stalin had thrown a "golden apple" of discord over the iron curtain to forestall a sovereign, industrially strong, and rearmed West Germany joining a U.S.-led alliance system.

Truman gave full sway to Acheson, who hesitated to reject Stalin's offer out of hand. But he insisted that the Allies "drive ahead" with the German contractual agreements and EDC and, with Adenauer's help, crafted uniform Allied replies with conditions that he knew Stalin would reject. Further, although Truman and Acheson had just coaxed Kennan to become ambassador to Moscow, they never asked his advice nor gave him a policy clue, leading him to lament that "we had no interest in discussing the German problem with the Soviet Government in any manner whatsoever."

Stalin, meanwhile—following initial Western rebuff of his note—told East German leaders in April 1952 that the West would never accept any proposal they made and that they had to organize their own state and protect its border. The U.S. won the "battle of the notes," although exchanges continued. But the Allies concluded the German agreements and EDC in late May, and when the French shortly reverted to proposing a four-power meeting on Germany, Acheson shaped the note to "make it unlikely that Sovs will agree to mtg on terms proposed."

Prospect for accord on Germany based on Stalin's Note was remote, but not just because the Russian ruler aimed to create either a unified pro-Soviet though not necessarily Communist Germany, or a full-fledged East German satellite. Neither Truman nor Acheson had any interest in a unified, neutral, or demilitarized Germany. They now believed that a rearmed FRG was as vital to NATO as West Germany was to ERP. They sought to create situations of strength by integrating West German economic and military power into a Western alliance system. German unity was possible only on the basis of West over East. As Kennan said again in fall 1952, U.S. officials saw no reason to withdraw their forces from Germany under any conceivable agreement with Russia. This meant that the "split of Germany and Europe" would continue, as it did for the next forty years.

II

In Asia as in Europe the Truman administration pursued a policy of containment that became "liberation" or "rollback," with fearful consequences. The president contributed significantly to the tragic conflicts that soon enveloped Asians and Americans through his lack of understanding of Asian politics and nationalism, his sense of superiority toward Asians and tendency to demonize those who did not bend to American will, and his visceral anticommunism.

In spring 1945 Truman was content to continue aid to Jiang's GMD government and urge that it broaden its political base in order to avert civil war with Mao's CCP. Truman also came to see Jiang's government as the world's "rottenest," realized that it "would not fight it out," and likened aid to China to "pouring sand in a rat hole." But at the same time he deplored China's "so-called Commies" and later branded the CCP "a bunch of murderers." Truman's parochial worldview led him to believe that Chinese society would never adapt to Marxism, and he never saw the extent to which Mao and the CCP had come to represent powerful aspirations of the Chinese people, who were bent on throwing off foreign domination and imperial control in China and restoring their nation—the Middle Kingdom—to its rightful status in Asia, if not the world.

Most important, Truman could not perceive China's civil war apart from the American-Soviet Cold War. He was relieved to learn in early 1945 that Stalin accepted GMD sovereignty over China, wanted only his Yalta concessions, and would respect the Open Door policy. But Truman quickly accepted hard-line War Department advice and insisted that the U.S. had to take a strong stand in China, or Russia would dominate Asia. He sought to outmaneuver Stalin and Mao by moving 500,000 GMD troops to occupy North China and providing major military aid, including 60,000 U.S. Marines who occupied Beijing-Tianjin and skirmished with CCP forces. "My policy is to support Chiang K. C.," Truman persisted, and he ignored Byrnes' proposal to seek mutual Soviet-American troop withdrawal.

In December 1945 Truman sent Marshall to mediate in China and seek a coalition regime. But the president agreed to his call for a secret codicil assuring military aid to the GMD even if it remained intransigent, a fatal flaw in the general's near-impossible mission. In early 1946 Marshall did gain accord on a broadened government and integrated armies, with the CCP conceding "first place" to the GMD. But Marshall's inability to constrain Jiang from renewing civil war against the CCP that summer cost the U.S. its last best chance to unify China. The CCP was left to conclude that the U.S. was following a double policy of claiming to be mediating while aiding the GMD war against them. Meanwhile, Truman derided critics of his China policy as people who "are more loyal to the Russian government than they are to their own." And in 1948 he denied that efforts to get Jiang to broaden his government ever meant including Communists, who believed only in a "totalitarian state."

Later on Truman said that common sense had held him from major military intervention, given China's size, Jiang's weakness, and Mao's consolidated strength. True enough; but the president also feared that loss of American lives and money would harm his 1948 election campaign while Jiang, unlike his counterparts in Greece, did not request intervention, which portended U.S. control of his regime's army and finances.

More important, Truman opposed dealing with Communists under any circumstance. In January 1949 he insisted that ECA halt delivery of supplies and foodstuffs to CCP-controlled areas rather than try to keep a door ajar to the Chinese people. Shortly the president signed NSC policy papers that recognized the inevitability of a CCP victory, but U.S. officials arrogantly posited that the Communists had just emerged from "caves to chancelleries" and had yet to prove they could govern effectively. Further, if they did not remain independent of Moscow, the U.S. would foster a "new revolution" that might come to a "test of arms" with the CCP.

Truman's narrow perspective militated against flexibility, and he resisted opening channels of communication with the CCP. In early June 1949, after Acheson agreed to limited contact by Clubb and Stuart with Chinese officials alleged to want to talk with the U.S., the president imposed his strict sanction "not to indicate any softening toward the communists." He then refused to allow Stuart to accept an invitation to go to Beijing for talks and had to be persuaded to retract his order that instead the ambassador visit the GMD at their new Guangzhou headquarters before returning to the U.S. As a White House aide noted, the president would not recognize the Communists.

Whether this marked a historic lost chance to try to begin rapprochement with the CCP in summer 1949 has been long debated. To be sure, Mao was in no hurry to seek U.S. recognition and would have insisted that it cut its ties to the GMD. New evidence suggests, however, that Mao was amenable to dealing with the U.S. provided it recognized CCP sovereignty and did not ask that it give up the goals of its revolution. Undoubtedly Truman would have come under political fire from the China bloc if he did this, but in 1949 his administration was capable of withstanding the attacks, especially since America's NATO allies would have welcomed the U.S. approach to the CCP.

Rather than deal with the impending CCP victory, however, the Truman administration did nothing to halt the GMD's indiscriminate bombings in American-marked planes of Shanghai and other cities, which would continue until mid-1950. The president also repeatedly called for "strict adherence" to his acceptance of the GMD's illegal blockade of China's major ports, although none of this action could alter the outcome of the civil war but could wreak havoc on civilians and harm evacuation of Americans. This policy precluded talks with any Communists and any prospect of lessening dangerous misunderstandings.

Finally, Truman agreed completely with the counterproductive Acheson–State Department White Paper of August 1949. Although this documentary compilation was intended to mollify the China bloc and other lobbyists for Jiang by demonstrating past U.S. support for the GMD, Acheson's letter of transmittal was a "diatribe" that charged the CCP with having foresworn its Chinese heritage, said it had no legitimacy to govern, and urged the Chinese people to throw off their Russian "yoke." This message ignored that there had been centuries of Russia-China conflict, that Stalin had not supported the CCP revolution nor provided significant military aid until 1948, and that he had remained interested in a GMD-CCP settlement as late as spring 1949. The White Paper only incensed Mao, who now prepared to lean more toward Moscow.

Further, despite Acheson's claim in September 1949 that the U.S. intended to "play for a split" between the CCP and the Soviets, the secretary responded to Mao's October proclamation of the PRC and call for relations with all nations by ignoring the traditional criteria for recognition, closing numerous consulates, and branding the PRC a tool of Soviet imperialism. And despite Truman's claim in November 1949—after his meeting with Asian specialists—that he had gained "new insight" and a "new way" of thinking about Communist success, when the PRC asserted its sovereignty by requisitioning foreign military barracks in Beijing in January 1950, the U.S. invoked a protocol drawn a half century earlier when Western powers had crushed the Boxer Rebellion. Then in spring 1950 the U.S. withdrew completely from China.

Meanwhile, Truman heartily approved Acheson's charge that the PRC had sold its sovereignty by signing a defense treaty with the Soviets in February 1950, even though the pact included Soviet return of its Manchurian concessions by 1953 and a small credit for the PRC, and limited the PRC's commitment to aiding the Soviets to matters in which they had common interest. The treaty also allowed Mao to say that he had expelled all foreigners from China and gotten better terms from Stalin than had Jiang in 1945 in fulfilling Yalta. Further, the Truman administration now bowed to Congress' pressure to maintain aid to the Taiwan-based GMD, whose continued bombings of the mainland raised the specter of the U.S. allowing a client state to call the turn on its vital interests and cause it to be vilified by the Chinese people. Acheson also had to admit that the GMD had told the administration to "go to hell" with its bombing protests.

The Truman administration involved itself even more deeply in China's civil war in spring 1950 by allowing the JCS to commit to Taiwan's defense. In addition, State Department officials soon proposed to stage a coup to be rid of Jiang and put the island under UN trusteeship, even at the risk of "early war" with the PRC and Soviet Union. Truman sent a family friend to Taiwan to assess matters, but the start of the Korean War in June 1950 precluded action. However, the president's quick ordering of the Seventh Fleet into the Taiwan Strait led Mao to denounce the maneuver as violative of the Cairo and Potsdam accords and an act of war. Perhaps it was not the latter, but Truman's China policies had already fixed the matrix for long-term, counterrevolutionary policy toward the PRC, whose complex origins and present concerns he never understood. From his parochial perspective, as he said in July 1950, the Chinese Communist government was "nothing but a tool of Moscow just as the North Korean Government is."

Truman made his most fateful decisions during the Korean War, which he attributed solely to Soviet-inspired North Korean unprovoked aggression against South Korea, and not to bitter conflict between two regimes struggling for supremacy. He said that if the U.S. did not aid South Korea, the Soviets would "swallow up" Asia and that would cause "collapse" in the Near East and possibly Europe. Stalin, of course, had supplied advisers, military plans, and equipment for North Korea. He may also have seen—ironically—a North Korean victory as a way to gain access to warm-water ports at Inchon and Pusan as compensation for the concessions he now had to return to the PRC. Stalin might also have sought to strengthen the USSR against the U.S. and Japan. But the invasion was the brainchild of Kim Il Sung, who spent a year persuading Stalin, and then Mao, that victory would come swiftly and without U.S. intercession. Kim also kept Mao in the dark with respect to timing of the attack.

Truman's immediate decision to intervene to preserve South Korea's UN-recognized independence—and to protect his administration from criticism over another loss in Asia—was logical, although it surprised Communist leaders. He determined that this new aggression could not go unchecked. But he and other officials were too quick to analogize North Korea's attack to German and Japanese action in the 1930s and to conclude that it was part of a "centrally-directed" global Communist challenge. It is also true that Truman long believed that Korea was the "ideological battleground" of Asia, approved more military aid for South Korea than for Greece during 1947–1950, and in 1949 signed NSC 48/2, which extended containment to Asia and exaggerated the link between U.S. success in Korea and its global security. Truman's movement of the Seventh Fleet into the Taiwan Strait augured intent to deny Taiwan to the PRC, and he had to be dissuaded from using Jiang's troops in Korea. Further, the president not only opened himself to charges of "Truman's war" but also set a dangerous precedent by not pausing to gain Congress' approval to act in June 1950, especially after he committed two divisions on June 30. As a White House aide said, Truman was not of a mind to ask for Congress' consent.

Even more unfortunately, the president's July 19 speech escalated a U.S./ UN "police action"—against "pagan wolves"—into an issue of U.S. security and world peace. He now called for a major military buildup and soon signed NSC 68, which proposed to spend 20 percent of the GNP on the military and wage global Cold War. The president also quickly acceded in August to hard-line views proposing to send U.S./UN forces—led by a provocative general who regarded Jiang as an ally and the PRC as an enemy—across the 38th parallel to vanquish North Korea and to unify the nation militarily. Thus Truman would demonstrate his biblical conviction that "punishment always followed transgression," while containment would become "liberation" or "rollback." And as Leffler has written, America would establish its preponderant world power.

Truman ignored early warnings that the PRC would view as a threat to its security and its revolution MacArthur's unconstrained northward march and prospect of establishment of an anticommunist regime on its border. He also dismissed PRC worry that the U.S. would build a rival Chinese regime on Taiwan, which MacArthur had already proclaimed vital to America's defense perimeter. Truman further disregarded PRC warnings of entry into the war in early October as "blackmail" and never believed that it would fight—which we now know Mao chose to do only after being goaded by Stalin and overcoming strong opposition to war, including from Zhou and military leaders. The president was also "highly pleased" with his Wake Island talks with MacArthur, which focused not on PRC actions but on how soon the war would be won. Truman's political myopia precluded his grasping PRC determination to define and defend its vital interests and its revolution, and its fear that U.S. conquest of North Korea would allow it to dominate Asia where, even the British complained, the U.S. acted like "a law unto itself."

Major PRC attacks in late November 1950 forced America's bitter retreat. Truman's ill-considered comment, or half-veiled threat, that use of the atomic bomb was always under consideration caused British leaders to fly to Washington intent to preclude wider war. In fact, atomic attack against Russia was first hinted at in June, and Truman had sent nuclear-configured bombers (without atomic cores) to England and Guam in July. The issue of atomic strikes arose again in his Cabinet meeting in early December and several times thereafter. But they were resisted chiefly because they were seen to be ineffective, would alienate NATO allies and Asian nations, and perhaps incur Soviet retaliation. Still, at his summit with Attlee the president would give only his "man's word" that he would consult before using atomic weapons. And despite Attlee's view that PRC leaders could be both Marxist and nationalist and "not bow to Stalin," Truman clung to his view that China's new leaders were "complete satellites" of Russia who sought to conquer Korea and Southeast Asia.

U.S. officials soon sought to halt the costly Korean conflict if only because they did not want to fight the "second team," the PRC, when the "real enemy" was the Soviet Union. But the president stubbornly refused compromise in early 1951: no negotiations with the PRC before a cease-fire; no recognition of the PRC, nor a UN seat; and no halt of U.S. aid to the GMD. Further, if the PRC drove the U.S. from Korea, the U.S. would mobilize the GMD, blockade China, and attack by air. Truman also pressed the UN to brand the PRC an "aggressor" in February 1951, precluding an early settlement.

Truman then faced MacArthur's apparent intent to "sabotage" the administration's cease-fire efforts when the general publicly demanded in late March that the PRC capitulate to him or face destruction. Following release in early April of MacArthur's letter stating that there was "no substitute for victory," Truman bravely fired his larger-than-life field commander. But MacArthur's insubordination was not the sole cause of the crisis. The administration had failed to rein him in for his provocative public comments and battlefield tactics since August 1950, and Truman's December 1950 directive to all military commanders to clear statements with the Defense Department was not pointed enough toward MacArthur. Further, the president's view of the PRC and North Korea, and his early war aims, were similar to MacArthur's. (And MacArthur's proposals to strike at the PRC were not too different from recent JCS ideas.) The basic disagreement between the president and general derived from Truman's political realization that he had to quit the war.

Moreover, to gain JCS support while firing MacArthur and to respond to a PRC buildup, Truman again deployed atomic bombers and nuclear weapons to Guam and approved a directive for retaliation against air attacks from outside Korea. He then sent another nuclear deployment to Asia and gave his new military commander, Ridgway, qualified authority for atomic strikes in event of a major attack from the PRC. MacArthur meantime electrified Congress and the nation with speeches stating that the purpose of war was victory.

Finally, the president's personal diplomacy obstructed armistice talks. In October 1951 he overrode standard military practice and U.S. commitment to the 1949 Geneva Convention provisions, and rejected "all for all" compulsory exchange of POWs unless the PRC made a major concession. Then in February 1952 he insisted on voluntary repatriation only of POWs. He did so partly for moral reasons but equally because he believed that he could gain his way either by promising to permit North Korea to repair its airfields or by brutal conventional bombing. He agreed with Lovett that "we can tear them [the Chinese and Koreans] up by air." But the president's narrow view succeeded only in transforming the POW issue from one that could have been resolved in a few months of hard bargaining to one that produced indefinite stalemate. Thus, fighting would continue until the Eisenhower administration gained a compromise in July 1953 that turned unrepatriated POWs over to a neutral-nations commission.

Meantime, beneath the facade of calm crisis management in 1952, Truman fantasized about giving Russia and China ten days to quit Korea or face "all out war" in which he would destroy all of their major cities and give the Soviet government its final chance to decide whether it wished to survive. Truman may not have intended atomic war, but he had created a dangerous situation, especially for a heated election year.

Korean War costs were staggering in terms of American, Chinese, and Korean lives lost and devastation wreaked on Korea. Meanwhile, U.S. military spending soared to NSC 68's projected 20 percent of GNP. The stage was also set for long-term U.S. political-military commitment to South Korea, to the GMD on Taiwan and the French in Indochina, while U.S.-PRC relations were embittered for a generation to come. Further, the Fair Deal was dead, McCarthyism was rampant, and Truman departed the presidency with extremely low public regard and with the U.S. on Cold War footing at home and abroad for years to come. Still, in his unpublished Farewell Address, Truman claimed that "Russia was at the root" of every problem in Europe and Asia and that his administration had saved countless countries from Soviet invasion and "knocked the socks off the communists" from Greece to Korea.

In conclusion, it seems clear that despite Truman's pride in his knowledge of the past, he lacked insight into the history unfolding around him. He often could not see beyond his immediate decision or visualize alternatives, and he seemed oblivious to the implications of his words or actions. More often than not he narrowed rather than broadened the options that he presented to the American citizenry, the environment of American politics, and the channels through which Cold War politics flowed. Throughout his presidency, Truman remained a parochial nationalist who lacked the leadership to move the U.S. away from conflict and toward detente. Instead, he promoted an ideology and politics of Cold War confrontation that became the modus operandi of successive administrations and the U.S. for the next two generations.

Notes

Journal Abbreviations

AHR: American Historical Review
DH: Diplomatic History
IS: International Security
JAH: Journal of American History
PHR: Pacific Historical Review
PSQ: Political Science Quarterly

Preface

1. Kirk H. Porter and Donald Bruce Johnson (eds.), *National Party Platforms, 1840–1960* (Urbana, 1961), 497; Donald R. McCoy, *The Presidency of Harry S. Truman, 1945–1953* (Lawrence, 1984), 297.

2. Arthur M. Schlesinger, "Our Presidents: A Rating by 75 Historians," *New York Times Magazine,* July 29, 1962, 10–14; Morton Borden, *America's Eleven Greatest Presidents,* 2nd ed. (New York, 1971), v–ix; Merle Miller, *Plain Speaking: An Oral Biography of Harry S. Truman* (New York, 1973), and Robert H. Ferrell, *Harry S. Truman and the Modern American Presidency* (Boston, 1983), 187–192; Roy Jenkins, *Truman* (New York, 1986), 7; David McCullough, *Truman* (New York, 1992), esp. 992 for "His Odyssey"; Melvyn P. Leffler, *A Preponderance of Power: National Security, the Truman Administration, and the Cold War* (Stanford, 1992); Robert H. Ferrell, *Harry S. Truman: A Life* (Columbia, 1994); Alonzo L. Hamby, *Man of the People: A Life of Harry S. Truman* (New York, 1995); an incisive, highly critical exception to this view on foreign affairs is William E. Pemberton, *Harry S. Truman: Fair Dealer and Cold Warrior* (Boston, 1989).

3. Diary entry for July 26, 1945, in Robert H. Ferrell (ed.), *Off the Record: The Private Papers of Harry S. Truman* (New York, 1980), 56–57; John Lewis Gaddis, "The Tragedy of Cold War History," *DH,* 17 (Winter 1993), and idem, *We Now Know: Rethinking Cold War History* (New York, 1997); see also Vojtech Mastny, *The Cold War and Soviet Insecurity: The*

Stalin Years (New York, 1996), and Vladislav Zubok and Constantine Pleshakov, *Inside the Kremlin's Cold War: From Stalin to Khrushchev* (Cambridge, 1996), esp. 9–35.

4. Walter LaFeber, *America, Russia, and the Cold War, 1945–1992*, 7th ed. (New York, 1993), 20–21; for discussion of new sources, see Symposium, "Rethinking the Lost Chance in China," *DH*, 21 (Winter 1997), 71–115, and Symposium, "Soviet Archives: Recent Revelations and Cold War Historiography," *DH*, 21 (Spring 1997), 216–305; Melvyn P. Leffler, "The Cold War: What Do 'We Now Know'?" *AHR*, 104 (Apr. 1999), 501–524; see also idem, "Inside Enemy Archives: The Cold War Reopened," *Foreign Affairs*, 75 (July/Aug. 1995), 120–135.

5. On Stalin's policies, see David Holloway, *Stalin and the Bomb: The Soviet Union and Atomic Energy, 1939–1956* (New Haven, 1994), Carolyn Kennedy-Pipe, *Stalin's Cold War: Soviet Strategies in Europe, 1943–1956* (Manchester, 1995), Norman M. Naimark, *The Russians in Germany: A History of the Soviet Zone of Occupation, 1945–1949* (Cambridge, 1995), and Dmitri Volkogonov, *Stalin: Triumph and Tragedy* (Rocklin, 1996).

6. Michael H. Hunt, *The Genesis of Chinese Communist Foreign Policy* (New York, 1996); see also Odd Arne Westad, *Cold War and Revolution: Soviet-American Rivalry and the Origins of the Chinese Civil War, 1944–1946* (New York, 1993).

7. Sergei Goncharov, John W. Lewis, and Xue Litai, *Uncertain Partners: Stalin, Mao, and the Korean War* (Stanford, 1993).

8. Alexandre Y. Mansourov, "Stalin, Mao, Kim, and China's Decision to Enter the Korean War, September 16–October 15, 1950: New Evidence from the Russian Archives," Cold War International History Project (hereinafter CWIHP), Woodrow Wilson Center, Washington, D.C., *Bulletin: The Cold War in Asia, 6–7* (Winter 1995/1996); see also Chen Jian, *China's Road to the Korean War: The Making of the Sino-American Confrontation* (New York, 1994), Thomas J. Christensen, *Useful Adversaries: Grand Strategy, Domestic Mobilization, and Sino-American Conflict, 1947–1958* (Princeton, 1996), Shu Guang Zhang, *Deterrence and Strategic Culture: Chinese-American Confrontations, 1949–1958* (Ithaca, 1992), and idem, *Mao's Military Romanticism: China and the Korean War, 1950–1953* (Lawrence, 1995).

9. Thomas G. Paterson, "Toughness: Truman's Style of Diplomacy," and "Consent: American Public Opinion, Congress, and the Cold War Mentality," in *On Every Front: The Making and Unmaking of the Cold War*, rev. ed. (New York, 1992), 119–139, 140–163; see also idem, "Harry S. Truman, American Power, and the Soviet Threat," in Thomas G. Paterson, *Meeting the Communist Threat: Truman to Reagan* (New York, 1988), 35–53.

10. James MacGregor Burns, "A Note on the Study of Political Leadership," in *Roosevelt: The Lion and the Fox, 1882–1940* (New York, 1956), 486–487.

Chapter 1. Independence to Washington

1. Harry S. Truman, *Memoirs*, 2 vols. (Garden City, 1955–1956), I: *Year of Decisions*, 120.

2. Three major biographies that provide details of Truman's early life are McCullough, *Truman*, 15–138, Ferrell, *Truman*, 1–90, and Hamby, *Man of the People*, 3–82; still useful, especially for anecdotal material, are Jonathan Daniels, *Man of Independence* (Philadelphia, 1950), Alfred Steinberg, *The Man from Missouri: The Life and Times of Harry S. Truman* (New York, 1962), Harold F. Gosnell, *Truman's Crises: A Political Biography of Harry S. Truman* (Westport, 1980), and Richard Lawrence Miller, *Truman: The Rise to Power* (New York, 1986).

3. Daniels, *Man of Independence*, 59–60; Hamby, *Man of the People*, 18–19, 41–42.

4. Truman, *Year of Decisions*, 113–118; Truman quoted in M. Miller, *Plain Speaking*, 46; Bert Cochran, *Harry Truman and the Crisis Presidency* (New York, 1973), 27–29, and James David Barber, *The Presidential Character: Predicting Presidential Performance in the White House* (Englewood Cliffs, 1972), 250–253; see also Ferrell, *Truman*, 10, 16, and Hamby, *Man of the People*, 14–16.

5. Robert H. Ferrell (ed.), *The Autobiography of Harry S. Truman* (Boulder, 1980), 6, 8, 36.

6. Truman's view of powerful men in entry for June 7, 1945, Eben A. Ayers Diary, Box 25, Eben A. Ayers Papers, Harry S. Truman Library, Independence, Mo.; "fakirs" in diary entry for July 16, 1948, in Ferrell (ed.), *Off the Record*, 144; "professional liberals" quoted in Margaret Truman, *Truman* (New York, 1973), 8; "striped pants boys" in entry for June 7, 1945, Ayers Diary, Box 25, Ayers Papers; "son of a bitch" for de Gaulle in entry for May 4, 1945, Ayers Diary, Box 25, Ayers Papers; for Stalin, in Fletcher Knebel and Charles W. Bailey II, *No High Ground* (New York, 1960), 1–2, and Truman to Acheson, Mar. 15, 1947, Ferrell (ed.), *Off the Record*, 348–349; for Bevin, entry for Jan. 15, 1949, Ayers Diary, Box 26, Ayers Papers; on Truman and Molotov, cf. Truman, *Year of Decisions*, 79–82, and Bohlen Memorandum, Apr. 23, 1945, U.S. Department of State, *Foreign Relations of United States, Diplomatic Papers, 1945*, 9 vols. (Washington, D.C., 1967–1969), V, 256–258 (hereinafter *FR year*, and volume); on Truman and Byrnes, Truman to Byrnes, Jan. 5, 1946, President's Secretary's File (hereinafter PSF), Box 333, Harry S. Truman Papers, Truman Library, and Robert L. Messer, *The End of an Alliance: James F. Byrnes, Roosevelt, Truman, and the Origins of the Cold War* (Chapel Hill, 1980), 157–160.

7. Truman, *Year of Decisions*, 116, and Ferrell (ed.), *Autobiography*, 33; for examples of Truman's moralizing, see Truman Remarks at Caruthersville, Oct. 7, 1945, and Truman News Conference, Apr. 6, 1946, in *Public Papers of the Presidents of the United States: Harry S. Truman*, 8 vols. (Washington, D.C., 1961–1966), I, 378–381, and II, 181 (hereinafter *PPHST*), and M. Truman, *Truman*, 8.

8. Ferrell (ed.), *Autobiography*, 3, 5, and Truman, *Year of Decisions*, 122.

9. Truman, *Year of Decisions*, 119–120, and Truman Memorandum, May 14, 1934, Ferrell (ed.), *Autobiography*, 136–137; see also Ferrell, *Truman*, 20.

10. Truman, *Year of Decisions*, 168, and Ferrell (ed.), *Autobiography*, 30; see also Ernest R. May, *"Lessons" of the Past: Use and Misuse of History in American Foreign Policy* (New York, 1973), 50–51, and Richard E. Neustadt and Ernest R. May, *Thinking in Time: The Use of History for Decision-Makers* (New York, 1986), 134–148.

11. Ferrell (ed.), *Autobiography*, 12, 17; Steinberg, *Man from Missouri*, 29–30; Hamby, *Man of the People*, 18.

12. Ferrell (ed.), *Autobiography*, 17–23, 27; Ferrell, *Truman*, 26–36.

13. Ferrell (ed.), *Autobiography*, 30–36.

14. Ferrell, *Truman and American Presidency*, 15; Truman to Elizabeth ("Bess") Wallace, Dec. 31, 1910, Jan. 10, May 23, and Nov. 28, 1911, and Aug. 18, 1914, in Robert H. Ferrell (ed.), *Dear Bess: The Letters from Harry to Bess Truman, 1910–1959* (New York, 1983), 18–20, 35–36, 61–62, 172; Ferrell (ed.), *Autobiography*, 55, 130.

15. Truman to Bess Wallace, June 22 and Oct. 16, 1911, Sept. 8, 1914, Oct. 28 and Nov. 3, 1917, and Feb. 3, Mar. 10, and Mar. 27, 1918, in Ferrell (ed.), *Dear Bess*, 39, 52–53, 174, 233, 234, 242–243, 248, 253–254; see also Truman to Bess and Margaret Truman, Aug. 9, 1930, and Truman to Bess Truman, July 6, 1938, and July 7, 1941, ibid., 341, 385, 460.

16. M. Truman, *Truman*, 53–55; Ferrell (ed.), *Autobiography*, 127; Hamby, *Man of the People*, 16; Margaret Truman, *Bess W. Truman* (New York, 1986), 17–19.

17. Hamby, *Man of the People*, 134–138; Truman to Bess Wallace, July 12, 1911, Aug. 29, 1916, and May 27, 1917, in Ferrell (ed.), *Dear Bess*, 40, 210–211, 215; Truman, *Year of Decisions*, 126–127, and Ferrell (ed.), *Autobiography*, 36–37.

18. Ferrell (ed.), *Autobiography*, 30, 41, 128; Truman to Bess Truman, July 14, 1917, in Ferrell (ed.), *Dear Bess*, 223–225.

19. Ferrell, *Truman*, 60–61.

20. Steinberg, *Man from Missouri*, 42–45; Truman, *Year of Decisions*, 128–129, and Ferrell (ed.), *Autobiography*, 42–44; Hamby, *Man of the People*, 62–65.

21. Truman to Bess Wallace, Mar. 27, 1918, in Ferrell (ed.), *Dear Bess*, 253–255; Ferrell (ed.), *Autobiography*, 46; Daniels, *Man of Independence*, 95–96.

22. Truman to Bess Wallace, Oct. 30, Nov. 1, and Dec. 14, 1918, and Jan. 21 and Apr. 14, 1919, in Ferrell (ed.), *Dear Bess*, 276, 277, 285–286, 293–294, 297–298; Ferrell (ed.), *Autobiography*, 47–51; Ferrell, *Truman*, 82–84.

23. Daniels, *Man of Independence*, 90; Truman to Bess Truman, Mar. 29, Oct. 11, Oct. 30, Dec. 14, 1918, and Jan. 21, 1918, in Ferrell (ed.), *Dear Bess*, 253–255, 274–275, 275–277, 285–286, 293 ("Miss Liberty" reference in Dec. 14 letter but similar remark in Oct. 11, 1918 letter).

24. Steinberg, *Man from Missouri*, 53–58; Truman, *Year of Decisions*, 133–136; Ferrell, *Truman*, 84–88.

25. Truman, *Year of Decisions*, 137–138; Steinberg, *Man from Missouri*, 63–64; Ferrell, *Truman*, 91–98.

26. M. Truman, *Truman*, 68–69; Daniels, *Man of Independence*, 130–134; Ferrell (ed.), *Autobiography*, 60–61; Ferrell, *Truman*, 99–108.

27. Lyle W. Dorsett, *The Pendergast Machine* (New York, 1968), 71–73; Truman quoted in Ferrell, *Truman*, 109–116.

28. Dorsett, *Pendergast Machine*, 109–110; Truman quoted in John F. Murphy, *The Pinnacle: The Contemporary American Presidency* (Philadelphia, 1974), 39–40.

29. [Truman to Bess Truman, May 7, 1933], quoted in M. Truman, *Truman*, 74–75; this letter is referenced in Ferrell (ed.), *Dear Bess*, 353, but not quoted in full.

30. Ibid.

31. Ferrell, *Truman*, 114–115, 125–128.

32. [Truman Memorandum, May 14, 1934], in William Hillman (ed.), *Mr. President: The First Publication from the Personal Diaries, Private Letters, Papers, and Revealing Interviews of Harry S. Truman, Thirty-second President of the United States* (New York, 1952), 189–190.

33. Daniels, *Man of Independence*, 169–172; Dorsett, *Pendergast Machine*, 112–115.

34. Truman quoted in Steinberg, *Man from Missouri*, 115.

35. Milligan quoted in Daniels, *Man of Independence*, 172.

36. Gene Schmidtlein, "Pursuing the Gleam: Truman's First Senatorial Election," *Whistle Stop* (Harry S. Truman Library Institute Newsletter), 6 (Fall, 1978).

37. Truman, Press Releases, Oct. 11 and Oct. 13, 1934, PSF, Box 239, Truman Papers; Daniels, *Man of Independence*, 175.

38. Truman, *Year of Decisions*, 144; Ferrell, *Truman*, 132; Truman's thirty official appointments with Roosevelt during 1935–1945 are listed in an Office Memorandum, Nov. 4, 1963, Senatorial and Vice Presidential Files (hereinafter SVPF), Box 168, Truman Papers.

39. Steinberg, *Man from Missouri*, 126–128; Ferrell, *Truman*, 132–133.

40. Ferrell (ed.), *Autobiography*, 68, 70; "Yea and Nay Votes of Hon. Harry S. Truman of Missouri in the Senate of the United States," PSF, Box 242, Truman Papers.

41. Daniels, *Man of Independence*, 186–187; Hamby, *Man of the People*, 221–227, 238–239; diary entry for June 12, 1940, *The Secret Diary of Harold L. Ickes*, 3 vols. (New York, 1953–1955), III: *The Lowering Clouds, 1939–1941*, 205–206.

42. Ferrell, *Truman,* 144–147.

43. Ibid., 222; Dorsett, *Pendergast Machine,* 134–137.

44. Hamby, *Man of the People,* 233–236; Ferrell, *Truman,* 148–150; Truman interview with Jonathan Daniels, Aug. 30, 1949, Daniels' research notes, Box 1, Truman Library; see also M. Truman, *Truman,* 117–121.

45. Truman quoted in Steinberg, *Man from Missouri,* 169; Hamby, *Man of the People,* 239–247; James T. Crenshaw, "The 1940 Senatorial Campaign in Missouri," Part II, *Whistle Stop* (Harry S. Truman Library Institute Newsletter), 3 (1980).

46. Howard Davis to Truman, July 16, 1941, PSF, Box 242, Truman Papers; Donald Riddle, *The Truman Committee* (New Brunswick, 1963), 12–20; Ferrell (ed.), *Autobiography,* 75–76; Truman, *Year of Decisions,* 166–168.

47. Robert J. Donovan, *Conflict and Crisis: The Presidency of Harry S. Truman, 1945–1948* (New York, 1977), xiii–xiv; Riddle, *Truman Committee,* passim, esp. 64–67, 122–154.

48. Riddle, *Truman Committee,* 154–165; "Billion-Dollar Watch Dog," *Time Magazine,* 41 (Mar. 8, 1943), 13–15; Stanley High, "Senator Truman Saves a Billion," *The American Mercury,* LVII (Sept. 1943), 356–360, also condensed in *Reader's Digest,* 43 (Sept. 1943), 83–86; Steinberg, *Man from Missouri,* 202–203; see also Ferrell, *Truman,* 157–161, and Hamby, *Man of the People,* 248–254.

49. Truman quoted in M. Truman, *Truman,* 166–168, 184; Ferrell, *Truman,* 168–169.

50. John Morton Blum, *V Was for Victory: Politics and Culture during World War II* (New York, 1976), 279–289; Robert L. Messer, *End of an Alliance,* 12–22; Roosevelt to Byrnes, June 10, 1944, Folder 637, James F. Byrnes Papers, Robert M. Cooper Library, Clemson University, Clemson, S.C.

51. Ferrell, *Truman,* 163–164.

52. Hamby, *Man of the People,* 280–281; Truman, *Year of Decisions,* 191, later claimed that Hannegan showed him a note written by Roosevelt that said, "Bob, it's Truman, FDR," but no such note has ever been found; see also Ferrell (ed.), *Autobiography,* 89 and 135 n. 89; on FDR and Byrnes, Transcript Notes of Roosevelt-Byrnes Telephone Conversation [July 14, 1944], Folder 74, Byrnes Papers; on Wallace letter, John Morton Blum (ed.), *The Price of Vision: The Diary of Henry A. Wallace, 1942–1946* (Boston, 1973), 365–367; FDR had apparently sent Wallace on a trip around the world to Russia and China so that he would be not be in Washington during the critical weeks of political machination prior to the Democratic convention.

53. Ferrell, *Truman,* 167.

54. Ibid., 170–171; see also Ferrell (ed.), *Autobiography,* 90–91, and *Year of Decisions,* 190–191.

55. Truman to Bess Truman, Aug. 18, 1944, in Ferrell (ed.), *Dear Bess,* 509–510; Robert E. Sherwood, *Roosevelt and Hopkins: An Intimate History* (New York, 1948), 881–882.

56. Truman Speech, Feb. 20, 1939, SVPF, Box 1, Truman Papers; Truman "Yea and Nay Votes," SVPF, Box 242, Truman Papers; Truman Speech, Nov. 11, 1937, SVPF, Box 1, Truman Papers.

57. Truman "Yea and Nay Votes," SVPF, Box 242, Truman Papers; Truman Speeches, Apr. 20, 1937, Mar. 7, 1938, and Feb. 20, 1939, SVPF, Box 1, Truman Papers; Ferrell (ed.), *Autobiography,* 74–75, and Ferrell, *Truman,* 153; Wilson D. Miscamble, "The Evolution of an Internationalist: Harry S. Truman and American Foreign Policy," *The Australian Journal of Politics and History,* 23 (Aug. 1977), 273–275, and Truman Speech, Mar. 25, 1939, SVPF, Box 163, Truman Papers.

58. Miscamble, "Evolution of an Internationalist," 270–272; Truman Speeches, Apr. 20. and Nov. 11, 1937, Mar. 7, 1938, and Feb. 20 and Oct. 8, 1939, SVPF, Box 1, Truman Papers; on Moral Rearmament, Truman to Bess Truman, Nov. 11, 1939, in Ferrell (ed.), *Dear Bess,* 428–429, Tom Driberg, *The Mystery of Moral Rearmament: A Study of Frank*

Buchman and His Movement (New York, 1965), 92–93, and Hamby, *Man of the People,* 264–265.

59. Truman Speech, June 30, 1940 (KMOX Radio, St. Louis), *Appendix to the Congressional Record,* vol. 86, Part 16, 4192–4193; diary entry for June 7, 1945, Ferrell (ed.), *Off the Record,* 44–45; Donovan, *Conflict and Crisis,* 293–298.

60. *New York Times,* June 24, 1941; "brave ally" in Richard S. Kirkendall, "Truman and the Cold War," in Gerald G. Steckler and Leo Donald Davis (eds.), *Studies in Mediaevalia and Americana: Essays in Honor of William Lyle Davis, S.J.* (Spokane, 1973), 153–154; see also Daniels, *Man of Independence,* 229.

61. Truman to Bess Truman, Dec. 30, 1941, in Ferrell (ed.), *Dear Bess,* 471; Truman to Myron Taylor, May 19, 1946, Box 1, Myron Taylor Papers, Truman Library; on Russians and agreements, see Truman Note, Mar. 23, 1946, PSF, Box 83, Truman Papers, and Truman to Eleanor Roosevelt, Mar. 16, 1948, in Ferrell (ed.), *Off the Record,* 125–126.

62. Robert A. Divine, *Second Chance: The Triumph of Internationalism in America during World War II* (New York, 1967), 93–98; Hamby, *Man of the People,* 268.

63. Divine, *Triumph of Internationalism,* 146–155; *Congressional Record,* vol. 90, Part 2, 2299–2300.

64. Truman quoted on diplomacy in Hamby, *Man of the People,* 268; liberal despair over FDR's choice of Truman as running mate and duplicity toward Wallace is cited in Gosnell, *Truman's Crises,* 193, and Martin Weill, *A Pretty Good Club: The Founding Fathers of the U.S. Foreign Service* (New York, 1978), 226–227.

65. Truman to Bess Truman, Aug. 18, 1944, in Ferrell (ed.), *Dear Bess,* 508–510; Ferrell, *Truman,* 171–172.

66. *New York Times,* Oct. 11, Oct. 23, Oct. 26, Oct. 28, Oct. 29, Oct. 30, and Nov. 5, 1944; Roosevelt shrewdly asserted that just as a policeman could not summon a town meeting before arresting a housebreaker, an American representative to the U.N. had to be authorized to sanction swift action.

67. Robert A. Divine, *Foreign Policy and U.S. Presidential Elections, 1940–1948* (New York, 1974), 161–164; Truman, *Year of Decisions,* 194.

68. Hamby, *Man of the People,* 289.

69. Steinberg, *Man from Missouri,* 229–230; Truman to Martha Ellen Young and Mary Jane Truman, Apr. 11, 1945, in Ferrell (ed.), *Off the Record,* 13–14; on the Wallace episode, Ferrell, *Truman,* 174–175 (the senators took away the secretary of commerce's authority over massive Reconstruction Finance Corporation funds); on Lend Lease, George C. Herring, Jr., *Aid to Russia, 1941–1946: Strategy, Diplomacy, and the Origins of the Cold War* (New York, 1973), 188–190, and Allen Drury, *A Senate Journal, 1943–1945* (New York, 1963), 409.

70. *New York Times,* Feb. 23, 1945; Truman to Price Wickersham, Mar. 7, 1945, quoted in Kirkendall, "Truman and the Cold War," 164.

71. Stalin to Roosevelt, Mar. 27, 1945, *FR 1945,* I, 165; diary entry for Apr. 2, 1945, in Arthur Vandenberg, Jr. (ed.), *The Private Papers of Senator Vandenberg* (Boston, 1952), 161; Truman to Clem Randau, Apr. 7, 1945, quoted in Kirkendall, "Truman and the Cold War," 164.

72. Bradley F. Smith and Elena Agarossi, *Operation Sunrise: The Secret Surrender* (New York, 1979), 72–124, contend that the U.S. government did not seek to gain a march on the Russians, although Dulles may have had his own agenda.

73. Roosevelt to Churchill, Mar. 11, and Roosevelt to Stalin, Apr. 1, 1945, *FR 1945,* V, 509–510, 194–196; Roosevelt to Stalin, Apr. 4, 1945, *FR 1945,* III, 745–746; Roosevelt to Churchill, Apr. 6 and Apr. 11, 1945, in Warren F. Kimball (ed.), *Churchill and Roosevelt: The Complete Correspondence,* 3 vols. (Princeton, 1984), III: February 1944–April 1945, 617, 630.

74. Truman letter in Steinberg, *Man from Missouri,* 233; Truman, *Year of Decisions,* 6.

75. On Truman and FDR's health, see Ferrell, *Truman,* 175; for accounts of Apr. 12, 1945, see Truman's diary entry for that day, PSF, Box 228, Truman Papers, and Ferrell (ed.), *Off the Record,* 14–16.

76. Truman Press Statement, Apr. 12, 1945, *PPHST,* I, 1; Record [Apr. 12, 1945], in Thomas M. Campbell and George C. Herring (eds.), *The Diaries of Edward R. Stettinius, Jr., 1943–1946* (New York, 1975), 315–316; entry for Apr. 12, 1945, in Vandenberg (ed.), *Vandenberg Papers,* 165; diary entry for Apr. 12, 1945, in Ferrell (ed.), *Off the Record,* 16.

Chapter 2. First Encounters

1. Diary entry for Apr. 12, 1945, David E. Lilienthal, *The Journals of David E. Lilienthal: The TVA Years, 1939–1945,* 6 vols. (New York, 1964–1976), I, 690; Grace Tully, Roosevelt's secretary, quoted in diary entry for May 14, 1945, J. Blum (ed.), *Price of Vision,* 448; diary entry for Apr. 29, 1945, Harold L. Ickes Diaries, Harold L. Ickes Papers, Library of Congress, cited in Donovan, *Conflict and Crisis,* 18.

2. Alben W. Barkley, *That Reminds Me* (Garden City, 1954), 197 (similarly, W. Averell Harriman and Elie Abel, *Special Envoy to Churchill and Stalin, 1941–1946* [New York, 1975], 447–448); diary entries for May 26 and June 4, 1945, Eben A. Ayers Diary, Eben A. Ayers Papers, Box 25, Truman Library; Truman to Eleanor Roosevelt, Sept. 1, 1945, Ferrell (ed.), *Off the Record,* 63.

3. Diary entries for May 14, Sept. 5, Sept. 22, and Oct. 15, 1945, Ferrell (ed.), *Off the Record,* 24, 64, 69, 71–72.

4. William D. Leahy, *I Was There* (New York, 1950), 347–348; diary entry for May 4, 1945, J. Blum (ed.), *Price of Vision,* 440; Ayers Memorandum, Oct. 1951, Historical File, PSF, Box 227, Truman Papers; diary entry for June 29, 1945, Ferrell (ed.), *Off the Record,* 44–45.

5. Truman to Martha Ellen and Mary Jane Truman, May 8, 1945, Truman, *Year of Decisions,* 206, and Truman to Martha Ellen and Mary Jane Truman, Oct. 13, 1945, Ferrell (ed.), *Off the Record,* 69–70; diary entries for Apr. 27 and June 9, 1945, J. Blum (ed.), *Price of Vision,* 437, 459; Truman to "Mamma and Mary Jane," June 13, 1945, Truman, *Year of Decisions,* 293–294.

6. Notes on Truman-Stettinius Meeting, Apr. 21, 1945, Campbell and Herring (eds.), *Stettinius Diaries,* 325, and diary entry for May 25, 1945, Ayers Diary, Box 25, Ayers Papers; diary entry for May 18, 1945, J. Blum (ed.), *Price of Vision,* 452; Morgenthau diary entry for June 1, 1945, quoted in Messer, *End of an Alliance,* 70.

7. Diary entry for Apr. 13, 1945, Ferrell (ed.), *Off the Record,* 16–17; Truman Address to Joint Session of Congress, Apr. 16, 1945, *PPHST,* I, 1–6; Truman, *Year of Decisions,* 326.

8. Messer, *End of an Alliance,* 66, 70; Truman, *Year of Decisions,* 23; diary entry for Apr. 13, 1945, Ferrell (ed.), *Off the Record,* 17; on the Yalta notes, see Byrnes to Truman, Apr. 25, and Leahy to Byrnes, Apr. 28, 1945, Folder 622, Byrnes Papers, and "The Crimean Conference: Minutes of Meetings prepared by James F. Byrnes," Folder 628, Byrnes Papers.

9. Byrnes Speech, Nov. 11, 1939, Folder 6, and Byrnes to Roosevelt, Feb. 17, 1945, Folder 92, Byrnes Papers; Messer, *End of an Alliance,* 32–33, 53–64; Truman on Byrnes in Daniels Research Notes, Aug. 30, 1949, Box 1, Jonathan Daniels Papers, Truman Library, and diary entry for July 7, 1945, Ferrell (ed.), *Off the Record,* 48–49; "Sabotage Press" in diary entries for June 1 and Sept. 1, 1945, ibid., 39–40, 63; "horse thief" in diary entry for Aug. 10, 1945, J. Blum (ed.), *Price of Vision,* 475.

10. Diary entry for May 18, 1945, J. Blum (ed.), *Price of Vision,* 451; diary entry for

June 7, and Truman to Eleanor Roosevelt, May 10, 1945, Ferrell (ed.), *Off the Record*, 44–45, 20–22; Truman to John Garner, PSF, Box 187, Truman Papers.

11. Entry for May 13, 1945, Joseph E. Davies Journal, Box 16, Joseph E. Davies Papers, Manuscript Division, Library of Congress, Washington, D.C., and diary entry for May 18, 1945, J. Blum (ed.), *Price of Vision*, 451; Truman on Stalin in diary entry for Aug. 10, 1945, Ayers Diary, Box 25, Ayers Papers; diary entry for July 17, 1945, Ferrell (ed.), *Off the Record*, 53, Daniels, *Man of Independence*, 278, and Truman to Acheson [unsent], Mar. 15, 1957, Ferrell (ed.), *Off the Record*, 348–349.

12. Notes on Truman-Stettinius Meeting, Apr. 21, 1945, Campbell and Herring (eds.), *Stettinius Diaries*, 324–325, and diary entry for Apr. 27, 1945, J. Blum (ed.), *Price of Vision*, 346; diary entry for May 26, 1945, Ayers Diary, Box 25, Ayers Papers.

13. John Lewis Gaddis, *Russia, the Soviet Union, and the United States: An Interpretive History*, 2nd ed. (New York, 1990), 117–130; Roosevelt to Joseph P. Kennedy, Oct. 30, 1939, in Elliott Roosevelt (ed.), *F.D.R.: His Personal Letters, 1928–1945*, 2 vols. (New York, 1950), I, 379–380, and Roosevelt to William A. White, Dec. 14, 1939, ibid., II, 967–968.

14. Arnold A. Offner, "Uncommon Ground: Anglo-American–Soviet Diplomacy, 1941–1942," in *Soviet Union/Union Sovietique*, 18 (1991), 242–243, 248–249; see also Hugh Phillips, "Mission to America: Maksim M. Litvinov in the United States, 1941–1943," *DH*, 12 (Summer 1988), 266, 268–270; for analysis of the wartime alliance that stresses the need to defeat Hitler, see Robin Edmonds, *The Big Three: Churchill, Roosevelt, and Stalin in Peace and War* (New York, 1991).

15. Churchill quoted in Stephen Merritt Miner, *Between Churchill and Stalin: The Soviet Union, Great Britain and the Origins of the Grand Alliance* (Chapel Hill, 1988), 10, and Churchill, *The Second World War*, III: *The Grand Alliance*, 369–370, 371–373; Churchill to Roosevelt, Mar. 7, 1942, in Kimball (ed.), *Churchill and Roosevelt*, I, 394–395; see also John Charmley, *Churchill's Grand Alliance: The Anglo-American Special Relationship, 1940–1957* (New York, 1995), esp. 48–56, and Warren F. Kimball, *Forged in War: Roosevelt, Churchill, and the Second World War* (New York, 1997), esp. 97–114, 333–334.

16. William Taubman, *Stalin's American Policy: From Entente to Detente to Cold War* (New York, 1982), 18–23, 40; Molotov quoted in Gaddis, *Russia and United States*, 142; on the Second Front, Albert Resis (ed.), *Molotov Remembers: Inside Kremlin Politics: Conversations with Felix Chuev* (Chicago, 1993), 45–46; Stalin quoted in Milovan Djilas, *Conversations with Stalin*, trans. Michael B. Petrovich (New York, 1962), 73, 114; for assessments of Stalin as a realist in foreign policy, see Holloway, *Stalin and the Bomb*, 166–171, and Kennedy-Pipe, *Stalin's Cold War*, 1–7, 9–15, 66–67, 109–110, 192–198; for a view of Stalin's foreign policy as moved by a "revolutionary-imperial paradigm," but constrained by the U.S. and more "defensive, reactive, and prudent" than inspired by a master plan in the postwar era, see Zubok and Pleshakov, *Inside Kremlin's Cold War*, esp. 9–77, 275–282; Mastny, *Cold War and Soviet Insecurity*, concedes that Stalin did not intend to march the Red Army into Western Europe or impose Communist regimes abroad, but contends that he deliberately conjured foreign threats to solidify his domestic control and that ultimately, his insatiable insecurity promoted the Cold War confrontation globally; Gaddis, *We Now Know*, argues that Stalin was heir to the traditions of Ivan the Terrible and Peter the Great as well as of Lenin, killed more people than Hitler did, was unrelentingly expansionistic and ideological, and caused the Cold War.

17. On Stalin and Atlantic Charter, see Anthony Eden, Earl of Avon, *The Memoirs of Anthony Eden, Earl of Avon*, vol. 2, *The Reckoning* (Boston, 1965), 336–337; Stalin quoted in David Dallin, "Stalin and the Prospects for Post-War Germany," in Francesca Gori and Sil-

via Pons (eds.), *The Soviet Union and Europe in the Cold War, 1943–53* (New York, 1996), 187; Eden views in Geoffrey Warner, "From 'Ally' to Enemy: Britain's Relations with the Soviet Union, 1941–1948," in Gori and Pons (eds.), op. cit., 295; on FDR and State Department, Offner, "Uncommon Ground," 247–249.

18. On Stalin and German reparations, Resis (ed.), *Molotov Remembers,* 60, and Naimark, *Russians in Germany,* 10, 141; on "correlation of forces," Resis, op. cit., 51.

19. Vladimir O. Pechatnov, "The Big Three after World War II: New Documents on Soviet Thinking about Post War Relations with the United States and Britain," CWIHP, Working Paper No. 13 (July 1995).

20. On the Katyn massacre, see Adam Ulam, *Stalin: The Man and His Era* (Boston, 1973), 583–584 (the total number of missing Polish officers was at least 15,000), and Richard Overy, *Russia's War: Blood upon the Snow* (New York, 1997), 352–354, which puts the Katyn killings in an even larger context of systematic murder and notes that the Soviet government did not admit its responsibility until the early 1990s; on the Russo-Polish border agreement, see Robert Beitzell, *The Uneasy Alliance: America, Britain, and Russia, 1941–1943* (New York, 1968), 317, 350–351, John Lewis Gaddis, *The United States and the Origins of the Cold War, 1941–1947* (New York, 1972), 144, and Edmonds, *The Big Three,* 381–383, who points out that Stalin's claim to the Curzon Line was strong, although Lwow had a Polish majority.

21. On whether the Russians could have aided the Warsaw uprising, see Gerhard Weinberg, *A World at Arms: A Global History of World War II* (Cambridge, 1994), 709–713, who says yes, and Edmonds, *The Big Three,* 385, who thinks the need for the Red Army halt was legitimate; on the politics of the uprising, see Jan Karski, *The Great Powers and Poland, 1919–1945: From Versailles to Yalta* (Lanham, 1985), 525–531, Krystyna Kersten, *The Establishment of Communist Rule in Poland, 1943–1948* (trans.), John Micgiel and Michael H. Bernhard (Berkeley, 1991), 77–117, and Anna M. Cienciala, "The View from Poland," in Arnold A. Offner and Theodore A. Wilson (eds.), *Victory in Europe 1945: From World War to Cold War* (Lawrence, 2000) 56–60.

22. Karski, *Great Powers and Poland,* 542–564, and Charmley, *Churchill's Grand Alliance,* 109–112.

23. On the Churchill-Stalin agreement in 1944, Albert Resis, "The Churchill-Stalin 'Percentages' Agreement on the Balkans, Moscow, October 1944," *AHR,* 83 (Apr. 1978), 368–387; under terms of their agreement, the British took a 90 percent sphere of influence in Greece, the Soviets got 90 percent in Rumania and 75 percent in Bulgaria, and Hungary and Yugoslavia were split 50–50; ambassador to Moscow Averell Harriman reported on the meetings to Roosevelt, who said he was pleased with the results, in Kimball, *Forged in War,* 290; on Yalta, Diane Shaver Clemens, *Yalta* (New York, 1970), 206–211, and Cienciala, "View from Poland," 61–62; on Molotov on Stalin and the Declaration of Liberated Europe, Resis (ed.), *Molotov Remembers,* 51; on FDR and Admiral William D. Leahy exchange, Leahy, *I Was There,* 315–316.

24. Clemens, *Yalta,* 212–214, and Cienciala, "View from Poland," 61; see also Lynn Ethridge Davis, *The Cold War Begins: Soviet American Conflict over Eastern Europe* (Princeton, 1974), 184–187.

25. Kimball, *Forged in War,* 317–318; *New York Times,* Mar. 2, 1945; on Stalin, Vojtech J. Mastny, *Russia's Road to the Cold War: Diplomacy, Warfare, and the Politics of Communism* (New York, 1979), 255–257.

26. Kimball, *Forged in War,* 320–323; Churchill to Roosevelt, Mar. 8, and Roosevelt to Churchill, Mar. 11, 1945, *FR 1945,* V, 145–150, 157.

27. Roosevelt to Churchill, Mar. 29, 1945, *FR 1945,* V, 189–190; see also Harri-

man, *Special Envoy,* 444; Roosevelt to Stalin, Apr. 1, and Stalin to Roosevelt, Apr. 7, 1945, *FR 1945,* V, 194–196, 201–204; Ciechanowski to Stettinius, Apr. 4, 1945, *FR 1945,* V, 198–201.

28. Roosevelt to Churchill, Apr. 6, 1945, Kimball (ed.), *Churchill and Roosevelt,* III, 617, and Roosevelt to Churchill, Apr. 11, 1945, *FR 1945,* V, 21.

29. Leffler, *Preponderance of Power,* 30–32; Truman to Churchill, Apr. 13, and Truman and Churchill to Stalin, Apr. 16, 1945, *FR 1945,* V, 211–212, 220–221; Truman, *Year of Decisions,* 37–39; on Yalta and Poland, see "Policy Manual for the President," Apr. 16, 1945, PSF, Box 159, Truman Papers, and "Summary of Proceedings and Agreements of the Crimean Conference February 1945," (prepared June 13, 1945, by George Elsey), Folder 623, Byrnes Papers; on Stalin's diplomacy, Harriman, *Special Envoy,* 441–443, entry for Apr. 23, 1945, Davies Journal, Box 16, Davies Papers, and Harriman to Stettinius, Apr. 16, 1945, *FR 1945,* V, 225–226; on Russian concerns about Truman, Mastny, *Russia's Road to the Cold War,* 271.

30. On Harriman, see Daniel Yergin, *Shattered Peace: The Origins of the Cold War and the National Security State* (Boston, 1977), 74–76, and David Mayers, *The Ambassadors and America's Soviet Policy* (New York, 1995), 156–159; "world bully" in Harriman to Hopkins, Sept. 10, 1944, *FR 1944,* IV, 988–990, in which he said that nearly all Russians wanted American friendship and the U.S. needed to strengthen the hand of those around Stalin who were of like mind; see also Harriman to Stettinius, Mar. 26 and Apr. 3, 1945, *FR 1945,* V, 183–184, 196–197; entry for Apr. 20, 1945, Walter Millis (ed.), *The Forrestal Diaries* (New York, 1951), 47.

31. Bohlen Memorandum, Apr. 20, 1945, *FR 1945,* V, 231–234.

32. Truman, *Year of Decisions,* 75; Wilson D. Miscamble, "Anthony Eden and the Truman-Molotov Conversations, April 1945," *DH,* 2 (Spring 1978), 172; Notes of Truman-Stettinius Meeting, Apr. 21, 1945, Campbell and Herring (eds.), *Stettinius Diaries,* 324.

33. Truman Notes for Ayers, May 1951, PSF, Box 229, Truman Papers; diary entry for Apr. 23, 1945, Ayers Diary, Box 25, Ayers Papers; Bohlen Memorandum, Apr. 22, 1945, *FR 1945,* V, 235–237.

34. Minutes of First and Second Meetings regarding the Polish Question, Apr. 22 and Apr. 23, 1945, *FR 1945,* V, 237–255; Anthony Cadogan to Theodosia Cadogan, Apr. 23, 1945, David Dilks (ed.), *The Diaries of Sir Alexander Cadogan, 1938–1945* (New York, 1972), 732.

35. Bohlen Memorandum, Apr. 23, 1945, *FR 1945,* V, 252–255; see also Yergin, *Shattered Peace,* 81.

36. Bohlen Memorandum, Apr. 26, 1945, *FR 1945,* V, 256–258, and Truman, *Year of Decisions,* 79–82; entry for Apr. 23, 1945, Davies Journal, Box 16, Davies Papers; Charles E. Bohlen, who translated for FDR and Truman, says in *Witness to History, 1929–1969* (New York, 1973), 213, that FDR would have said the same thing, only more diplomatically, but does not refer to "carry out your agreements" language; for typical assessments, see Gaddis, *U.S. and Origins of Cold War,* 204–205, and Yergin, *Shattered Peace,* 82–83, but cf. Miscamble, "Truman-Molotov Conversations," 169–170, 180; Harriman, *Special Envoy,* 453–454, reflects that Truman's attack was too vigorous—"a mistake"—but the ambassador said nothing in 1945; Leahy, *I Was There,* 351–352, liked the approach, believing that it might get the Polish government the "appearance of independence."

37. Department of State, Biographical Note on Molotov, Apr. 20, 1945, PSF, Box 187, Truman Papers; for other views on Molotov, see diary entry for Sept. 28, 1945, Walter Brown Diary, Folder 54, Byrnes Papers, William H. Draper Memorandum, July 19, 1948, PSF, Box 157, Truman Papers, and Leahy, *I Was There,* 349; on Stalin, Truman, *Year of Decisions,* 31.

38. Diary entry for Apr. 26, 1945, Harold Smith Diary, Box 1, Harold Smith Papers, Truman Library; Truman to Churchill, Apr. 23, 1945, *FR 1945*, III, 240; Bohlen, *Witness to History*, 213, does not refer to Truman's "carry out your agreements"; on "major milestone," Walter Isaacson and Evan Thomas, *The Wise Men: Six Friends and the World They Made* (New York, 1986), 264, 267; diary entry for Apr. 24, 1945, Vandenberg (ed.), *Vandenberg Papers*, 175–176.

39. Resis (ed.), *Molotov Remembers*, 55; Stalin to Truman, Apr. 24, and Churchill to Truman (and Stalin), Apr. 28 and Apr. 29, 1945, *FR 1945*, V, 263–271.

40. Leffler, *Preponderance of Power*, 32–33; entries for Apr. 30, 1945, Davies Journal and Diary, Box 16, Davies Papers; Davies' book, *Mission to Moscow* (New York, 1941), was published just after the German attack on the Soviet Union; it mainly comprised his dispatches written during Stalin's purges in 1936–1938; the ambassador said there was reason to believe that individuals had plotted against the government, although he deplored the lack of Western legal procedure, including the presumption of innocence and right to cross-examine witnesses; Davies spoke admiringly, however, of the Russian people and said that postwar peace depended on American-Soviet cooperation.

41. Truman, *Year of Decisions*, 10–11; entry for Aug. 6, 1951, Ayers Diary, Box 25, Ayers Papers.

42. Robert A. Divine, *Roosevelt and World War II* (Baltimore, 1969), 58–65; Martin J. Sherwin, *A World Destroyed: Hiroshima and the Origins of the Arms Race*, rev. ed. (New York, 1987), 85–89, 102–103; Holloway, *Stalin and the Bomb*, 96–106; for recent studies of Soviet atomic spying, beginning with that of the refugee German physicist Klaus Fuchs, who came to the U.S. from Britain in 1943, see John Earl Haynes and Harvey Klehr, *Venona: Decoding Soviet Espionage in America* (New Haven, 1999), 304–330, and Allen Weinstein and Alexander Vassiliev, *The Haunted Wood: Soviet Espionage in America—The Stalin Era* (New York, 1999), 185–210.

43. Sherwin, *A World Destroyed*, 90–114, 121–139, and Appendix C, Hyde Park Aide-Mémoire, Sept. 18, 1944, 284.

44. Stimson to Truman, Apr. 24, 1945, PSF, Box 15, Truman Papers; Sherwin, *A World Destroyed*, 162–164, 192, and Appendix I, Stimson: Memo Discussed with President, Apr. 25, 1945, and Appendix J, Groves: Report of Meeting with the President, Apr. 25, 1945, 291–294; Gregg Herken, *The Winning Weapon: The Atomic Bomb and the Cold War, 1945–1950* (New York, 1981), 13–14.

45. Calendar Notes, Apr. 25, and diary entry for Apr. 26, and Transcript Truman-Stettinius Conversation, Apr. 26, 1945, Campbell and Herring (eds.), *Stettinius Diaries*, 336–340; Divine, *Second Chance*, 289–290; on the Ukraine-Byelorussia and Polish issues, Minutes of Eighteenth Meeting of U.S. Delegation, Apr. 27, 1945, *FR 1945*, I, 416–418, and Transcript Truman-Stettinius Conversation, Apr. 27, 1945, Campbell and Herring (eds.), *Stettinius Diaries*, 342–344.

46. Diary entries for Apr. 25 and Apr. 27, 1945, Vandenberg (ed.), *Vandenberg Papers*, 176–177, 180–181; Thomas M. Campbell, *Masquerade Peace: America's UN Policy, 1944–1945* (Tallahassee, 1973), 88–120, 127–129; J. Tillapaugh, "Closed Hemisphere and Open World?: The Disputes over Regional Security at the U.N. Conference, 1945," *DH*, 2 (Winter 1978), 29.

47. Notes on Truman-Stettinius Meeting, Apr. 21, and Transcript of Truman-Stettinius Conversation, Apr. 27, 1945, Campbell and Herring (eds.), *Stettinius Diaries*, 324–325, 342–344; Divine, *Second Chance*, 289–290; Vandenberg to Hatch and Hill, May 1, 1945, Campbell and Herring (eds.), *Stettinius Diaries*, 347; Vandenberg diary entry for Apr. 30, 1945, quoted in David Green, *The Containment of Latin America: A History of the Myths and Realities of the Good Neighbor Policy* (Chicago, 1971), 221; the similar remark that Molo-

tov had solidified "Pan America against Russia" appears in entry for Apr. 30, 1945, Vandenberg (ed.), *Vandenberg Papers,* 182.

48. Minutes of Sixteenth Meeting of U.S. Delegation, Apr. 25, 1945, *FR 1945,* I, 388–402 (esp. 389–390, 397), and Harriman, *Special Envoy,* 455–457.

49. Tillapaugh, "Closed Hemisphere and Open World?" 26–28; Campbell, *Masquerade Peace,* 120–122.

50. Minutes of the Second Four Power Consultative Meeting, May 3, 1945, *FR 1945,* I, 567–568; entry for May 4, 1945, Campbell and Herring (eds.), *Stettinius Diaries,* 348.

51. Entry for May 5, 1945, Vandenberg (ed.), *Vandenberg Papers,* 186–188, and Minutes of Fifth Four Power Consultative Meeting, May 4, Stettinius to Truman, May 6, and Minutes of Five Power Consultative Meeting, May 7, 1945, *FR 1945,* I, 604–606, 610–611, 613–614, 630–631.

52. Vandenberg to Stettinius, May 5, and diary entry for May 7, 1945, Campbell and Herring (eds.), *Stettinius Diaries,* 349–351; Campbell, *Masquerade Peace,* 165–166.

53. Entries for May 8, 1945, Campbell and Herring (eds.), *Stettinius Diaries,* 353, 355–356; Campbell, *Masquerade Peace,* 168–169; Tillapaugh, "Closed Hemisphere and Open World?" 36.

54. Minutes of Thirty-sixth Meeting of U.S. Delegation, May 11, 1945, *FR 1945,* I, 663–673, and Transcript Truman-Stettinius Conversation, May 12, 1945, Campbell and Herring (eds.), *Stettinius Diaries,* 361–362.

55. Minutes of Third Five Power Informal Consultative Meeting, May 12, and Hartley Memoranda, May 12, 1945, *FR 1945,* I, 691–698, 698–706, and Lord Gladwyn, *The Memoirs of Lord Gladwyn* (New York, 1972), 161–162; diary entry for May 12, 1945, Campbell and Herring (eds.), *Stettinius Diaries,* 362–364, and Minutes of Third Five Power Informal Consultative Meeting, May 12, 1945, *FR 1945,* I, 706–707.

56. Minutes of Thirty-ninth Meeting of U.S. Delegation, May 15, 1945, *FR 1945,* I, 719–727; diary entries for May 14 and May 15, and Transcript Truman-Stettinius Conversation, May 15, 1945, Campbell and Herring (eds.), *Stettinius Diaries,* 364–372; *New York Times,* May 16, 1945; Campbell, *Masquerade Peace,* 172–175.

57. Memorandum Grew-Truman Conversation, May 14, 1945, Joseph C. Grew Papers, VII, Houghton Library, Harvard University, cited in Tillapaugh, "Closed Hemisphere and Open World?" 41–42; diary entry for May 23, 1945, Vandenberg (ed.), *Vandenberg Papers,* 197–198.

58. Green, *Containment in Latin America,* 233; entry for May 15, 1945, Campbell and Herring (eds.), *Stettinius Diaries,* 370–371, records Senator Connally's pledge to the Latin Americans that the United States would not allow "*any*" nation" to interfere in Latin America, implying that it would keep out Russia, but also not acknowledging any constraint on the power of the United States.

59. Mastny, *Russia's Road to the Cold War,* 267–268, 270, 273, 282.

60. Memorandum Stettinius-Eden-Molotov Conversation, May 2, 1945, *FR 1945,* V, 272–275, and Summary Truman-Stettinius Conversation, May 2, 1945, Campbell and Herring (eds.), *Stettinius Diaries,* 346; Grew to Kennan, May 3, and Kennan to Grew, May 4, 1945, *FR 1945,* V, 276–278.

61. Truman, *Year of Decisions,* 253–254, and Grew to Truman, May 4 and May 5, 1945, PSF, Box 271 and PSF, Box 272, Truman Papers; Grew Memorandum of May 5 also quoted in Grew to Caffrey, May 7, 1945, *FR 1945,* IV, 448–449.

62. Donovan to Truman, May 5, 1945, Office of Strategic Services Files, Box 15, Truman Papers.

63. Churchill to Truman, Apr. 30, and Truman to Churchill, May 1, 1945, *FR 1945,* IV, 446, 446 n. 76, and Truman, *Year of Decisions,* 216–217; Stephen E. Ambrose, *Eisenhower*

and Berlin, 1945: The Decision to Halt at the Elbe (New York, 1967), 85–86; Hamby, *Man of the People,* 318.

64. Grew Memorandum, May 7, 1945, *FR 1945,* III, 778–779; see also Leahy, *I Was There,* 358–363.

65. Truman to Martha Ellen and Mary Jane Truman, May 8, 1945, Truman, *Year of Decisions,* 206, and Truman Broadcast, May 8, 1945, *PPHST,* I, 48–49; Ayers Memorandum, [?] 1951, PSF, Box 229, Truman Papers: Leahy, *I Was There,* 362–364; Mastny, *Russia's Road to the Cold War,* 276–278; on Russian celebration, and arrest of Germans, entry for May 10, 1945, Harry C. Butcher, *My Three Years with Eisenhower: The Personal Diary of Captain Harry C. Butcher, 1942–1945* (New York, 1946), 836–844, and Stephen E. Ambrose, *Eisenhower: Soldier, General, and President-Elect, 1890–1952* (New York, 1983), 427–428.

66. Churchill to Truman, May 6, and Truman to Churchill, May 9, 1945, *FR 1945: The Conference of Berlin (The Potsdam Conference), 1945,* 2 vols. (Washington, 1960), I, 3–4. Churchill to Truman, May 6, and Truman to Churchill, May 9, 1945, *FR 1945: Potsdam,* I, 3–4.

67. Sherwin, *A World Destroyed,* 187–188; Truman to Eleanor Roosevelt, May 10, 1945, Ferrell (ed.), *Off the Record,* 20–22.

68. Truman to Stalin, May 4, Memorandum Stettinius-Eden-Molotov Conversation, May 4, and Stalin to Truman, May 4 and May 10, 1945, *FR 1945,* V, 281–285, 293; Churchill to Truman, May 11, 1945, *FR Potsdam,* I, 5–6; "U.J." was the Anglo-American way of referring to "Uncle Joe" Stalin.

69. Grew Memorandum for Truman, May 10, 1945, *FR 1945,* V, 1151–1153; Richard S. Dinardo, "Glimpse of an Old World Order?: Reconsidering the Trieste Crisis of 1945," *DH,* 21 (Summer 1997), 266–267.

70. Matthews Memorandum, Apr. 30, and Grew Memoranda, May 10 and May 11, 1945, Truman to Churchill, May 11, and Churchill to Truman, May 12, 1945, *FR 1945,* IV, 1127–1128, 1154–1158; see also Lisle A. Rose, *Dubious Victory: The United States and the End of World War II* (Kent, 1973), 120–124.

71. Churchill to Truman, May 11 (2 cables) and May 12, 1945, *FR 1945: Potsdam,* I, 5–8, 8–9.

72. Herring, *Aid to Russia,* 181–190.

73. Entry for Apr. 26, 1945, Harold Smith Diary, Box 1, Harold Smith Papers, Truman Library; Stettinius to Grew, May 9, 1945, *FR 1945,* V, 998.

74. Transcript Truman-Stettinius Conversation, May 10, 1945, Campbell and Herring (eds.), *Stettinius Diaries,* 358; Grew and Crowley Memorandum for Truman, May 11, and Truman Memorandum for Grew and Crowley, May 11, 1945, *FR 1945,* V, 999–1000; Herring, *Aid to Russia,* 203–205.

75. Truman, *Year of Decisions,* 228, and Daniels, *Man of Independence,* 271; Herring, *Aid to Russia,* 205–206.

76. Ferrell, *Truman,* 201, for "fiasco"; Bohlen Memorandum of Stalin-Hopkins Conversation, May 27, 1945, *FR 1945: Potsdam,* I, 31–52, esp. 32–33, 35.

77. Truman to Emmy Southern, May 13, 1945, Ferrell (ed.), *Off the Record,* 23; entry for May 13, 1945, Davies Journal, Box 16, Davies Papers.

Chapter 3. Preparing for Peacemaking

1. Bohlen, *Witness to History,* 215–216; Harriman, *Special Envoy,* 459; diary entry for May 18, 1945, Ferrell (ed.), *Off the Record,* 30.

2. Diary and journal entries for May 13, 1945, Davies Diary and Journal, Box 16, Davies Papers.

3. J. Blum (ed.), *Price of Vision*, 448; Churchill to Truman, May 13, Truman to Churchill, May 14, and Grew Memorandum, May 15, 1945, *FR 1945: Potsdam*, I, 12–15.

4. Sherwood, *Roosevelt and Hopkins*, 886–887; diary entries for May 18, May 19, and May 22, 1945, Ferrell (ed.), *Off the Record*, 30, 31–32, 35.

5. Diary entry for May 22, 1945, Truman Diary, PSF, Box 333, Truman Papers; see also Hillman (ed.), *Mr. President*, 114–116; Stettinius Calendar Notes, May 23, 1945, Campbell and Herring (eds.), *Stettinius Diaries*, 378; diary entry for May 22, 1945, Ferrell (ed.), *Off the Record*, 35.

6. Truman to Churchill, May 14, *FR 1945*, IV, 1160, and May 16, 1945, PSF, Box 115, Truman Papers (Truman said if allied forces were attacked, they were only to throw the Yugoslavs back to preclude another attack); Truman to Churchill, May 20, 1945, *FR 1945*, IV, 1169–1170; on Eisenhower's plans, drawn at Truman's request, see James F. Schnabel, *The History of the Joint Chiefs of Staff*, I: *The Joint Chiefs of Staff and National Policy, 1945–1947* (Wilmington, 1979), 49–50.

7. Truman to Stalin, May 20, and Stalin to Truman, May 23, 1945, *FR 1945*, IV, 1168–1169, 1172–1173; on Tito speech and Stalin quote, Dinardo, "Glimpse of an Old World Order?" 377–378.

8. Grew to Patterson, May 26, and Patterson to Grew, June 9, 1945, *FR 1945*, IV, 1176–1177, 1182–1183; British Embassy to State Department, May 23, and de Gasperi to Kirk, June 6, 1945, ibid., 1174–1175 and 1179–1180; Mastny, *Russia's Road to the Cold War*, 282; Dinardo, "Glimpse of an Old World Order?" 379–381; see also Schnabel, *History of the JCS*, I, 51–52, which does not mention Stalin's role.

9. Clemens, *Yalta*, 150–158; Grew to Stettinius, May 1, and Caffery to Stettinius (two cables), May 5, 1945, *FR 1945*, IV, 682–683, 685–687; Truman quoted in diary entry for May 4, 1945, Ayers Diary, Box 25, Ayers Papers, and Grew Memorandum of Conversation with Truman, June 5, 1945, Box 7, Grew Papers.

10. Grew Memoranda, May 18, May 19, and May 21, 1945, *FR 1945*, IV, 687–696, 698–699.

11. Diary entry for May 31, 1945, Ayers Diary, Box 25, Ayers Papers; Rose, *Dubious Victory*, 116–118; Grew Memorandum, June 2, 1945, Box 7, Grew Papers.

12. Truman to de Gaulle, June 6, and de Gaulle to Truman, June 8, 1945, *FR 1945*, IV, 734–735, 736–737; Grew Memorandum, June 8, 1945, Box 7, Grew Papers.

13. Hopkins to Truman and Truman to Hopkins, May 28, Hopkins to Truman, May 30, and Stalin to Truman, May 30, 1945, *FR 1945: Potsdam*, I, 86–88; for confirmation that Truman delayed the meeting and let it seem others were responsible, see Elsey Note, June 15, 1945, Box 55, Elsey Papers; on the connection with the atomic bomb, see entry for May 21, 1945, Davies Diary and Journal, May 21, 1945, Box 16, Davies Papers, and Sherwin, *World Destroyed*, 191; Churchill to Truman, June 9 and June 15, and Truman to Churchill, June 11 and June 15, 1945, *FR 1945: Potsdam*, I, 94–95, 98.

14. Bohlen, Memorandum of Hopkins-Stalin Conversation, May 28, 1945, *FR 1945: Potsdam*, I, 41–52; diary entry for May 29, 1945, J. Blum (ed.), *Price of Vision*, 454.

15. Bohlen Memoranda of Hopkins-Stalin Conversations, May 27, May 28, and May 30, 1945, *FR 1945: Potsdam*, I, 24–31, 31–41, 53–57.

16. Truman to Hopkins, June 5, and Bohlen, Memorandum of Hopkins-Stalin Conversation, June 6, 1945, *FR 1945*, V, 326–327, 328–329.

17. Calendar Notes for May 23, 1945, Campbell and Herring (eds.), *Stettinius Diaries*, 377; diary entry for June 2, 1945, Vandenberg (ed.), *Vandenberg Papers*, 201; Grew to Harriman, June 2, 1945, *FR 1945*, I, 1117–1119; journal entry for June 6, 1945, Davies Journal, Box 16, Davies Papers; Memorandum, Hopkins-Stalin Conversation, Sherwood, *Roosevelt*

and Hopkins, 910–912; diary entry for June 7, 1945, Vandenberg (ed.), *Vandenberg Papers,* 207–208.

18. Diary entries for June 7 and June 13, 1945, Ferrell (ed.), *Off the Record,* 44–45, and Truman to Churchill, June 7, 1945, *FR 1945,* V, 331–332; Davies Report, June 12, 1945, *FR 1945: Potsdam,* I, 64–78; Harriman to Truman, June 8, 1945, ibid., 61–62.

19. Diary entry for June 7, 1945, Ferrell (ed.), *Off the Record,* 44–45.

20. Transcript of Truman News Conference, June 13, 1945, *PPHST,* I, 118–127; Durbrow Memorandum, June 13, and Harriman to Stettinius, June 21, 1945, *FR 1945,* V, 338–339, 352–354; Truman to Churchill, July 2 and July 3, 1945, *FR 1945: Potsdam,* I, 733–734.

21. Karski, *Great Powers and Poland,* 622–623; Kersten, *Establishment of Communist Rule in Poland,* 153–160; White House Press Release, July 5, 1945, *FR 1945: Potsdam,* I, 735.

22. Grew Memorandum, June 4, 1945, *FR 1945,* V, 324–325; Harriman to Grew, June 28, and "Suggested . . . Policy regarding Poland," June 29, 1945, *FR 1945: Potsdam,* I, 727–728, 714–716; Truman News Conference, June 13, 1945, *PPHST,* I, 118–127; Kersten, *Establishment of Communist Rule in Poland,* 77–117, argues that Stalin never intended to compromise and that he sought both territory and Communist rule in Poland; Cienciala, "View from Poland," 65–66, emphasizes that U.S. need for Soviet aid in fighting Germany and FDR's desire to bring U.S. troops home quickly after the war led to acceptance of Soviet predominance in Poland.

23. Arnold A. Offner, "Research on German-American Relations: A Critical View," in Frank Trommler and Joseph McVeigh (eds.), *America and the Germans: A 300-Year History,* 2 vols. (Philadelphia, 1985), II, 175–176; Raymond G. O'Connor, *Diplomacy for Victory: FDR and Unconditional Surrender* (New York, 1971), 50–56; Samuel I. Rosenman (comp.), *The Public Papers and Addresses of Franklin D. Roosevelt,* 13 vols. (New York, 1938–1950), XII, 391; John Morton Blum, *From the Morgenthau Diaries: Years of War, 1941–1945* (Boston, 1967), 342, 348–349.

24. Naimark, *Russians in Germany,* 10.

25. Beitzell, *Uneasy Alliance,* 351–353, Kennedy-Pipe, *Stalin's Cold War,* 42–43, and Clemens, *Yalta* 32–33.

26. J. Blum, *Years of War,* 343–374; Gaddis, *U.S. and Origins of Cold War,* 122–125; "planned chaos" in "Directive to SCAEF regarding . . . Germany," Sept. 22, 1944, *FR 1945: Yalta,* 143–154.

27. Kennedy-Pipe, *Stalin's Cold War,* 56, and Clemens, *Yalta,* 140–172, 295–299, 308–309; Clemens, 172, indicates that while the $20 billion figure was not firm, the Russians had reason to believe from talks that the U.S. had committed to $10 billion for them.

28. Stettinius to Roosevelt, Mar. 8, and "Draft Directive . . . for Germany," Mar. 10, Grew Memorandum for Roosevelt, Mar. 23, and Memorandum regarding American Policy for . . . Germany, Mar. 23, 1945, *FR 1945,* III, 433–438, 471–473; J. Blum, *Years of War,* 400–414, 451–457; Frank A. Ninkovich, *Germany and the United States: The Transformation of the German Question since 1945* (Boston, 1988), 21–24.

29. J. Blum, *Years of War,* 460; Jean Edward Smith, *Lucius D. Clay: An American Life* (New York, 1960), 232–235; Douglas quoted in Robert Murphy, *Diplomat among Warriors* (New York, 1964), 251.

30. Grew Memorandum, May 10, 1945, *FR 1945,* III, 508–509; Truman, *Year of Decisions,* 236; J. Blum, *Years of War,* 459.

31. Truman, *Year of Decisions,* 235–236; entry for May 16, 1945, Stimson Diary, Stimson Papers, Sterling Library, Yale University, New Haven, CT.

32. Bruce Kucklick, *American Policy and the Division of Germany: The Clash with Russia over Reparations* (Ithaca, 1972), 126–128; Truman, *Year of Decisions,* 308; J. Blum, *Years of War,* 459; Grew to Stettinius, June 20, 1945, Box 7, Grew Papers.

33. Donovan to Truman, May 5, 1945, Office of Strategic Services Files, Box 15, Truman Papers.

34. J. Blum, *Years of War,* 459; Deborah Welch Larson, *Origins of Containment: A Psychological Explanation* (Princeton, 1985), 191.

35. Henry L. Stimson and McGeorge Bundy, *On Active Service in Peace and War* (New York, 1947), 571–582.

36. Entry for May 16, 1945, Stimson Diary, Stimson Papers, and Stimson and Bundy, *On Active Service,* 582–583; Truman diary entry for May 16, 1945, Ferrell (ed.), *Off the Record,* 25.

37. Elsey Memo [undated], and Grew to Pauley, July 2, 1945, *FR 1945: Potsdam,* I, 453–456, 519–521; Dept. of State, Briefing Book Papers, "Policy toward Germany," June 29, "Germany—Partition," June 29, "The Ruhr," June 27, and "The Rhineland," June 30, 1945, ibid., 435–449, 456–461, 586–589, 591–592.

38. J. Blum, *Years of War,* 461–473.

39. Grew to Winant, June 24, de Gaulle to Truman, June 28, and Churchill to Truman, July 3, 1945, *FR 1945: Potsdam,* I, 612–613, 613 n. 2, 622; see also Melvyn P. Leffler, "The Struggle for Germany and the Origins of the Cold War," German Historical Institute Occasional Paper no. 16 (Washington, 1996), 18–21.

40. Entry for May 8, 1945, Stimson Diary, Stimson Papers; Truman, *Year of Decisions,* 87.

41. Entries for May 10 and May 13, 1945, Stimson Diary, Stimson Papers; Sherwin, *A World Destroyed,* 188–190; Sherwin, op. cit., 37, explains that S-1 was short for a new committee, Section-1, of the Office of Scientific Research and Development (OSRD), created in late 1941 to advise President Roosevelt on policy questions relating to nuclear fission; S-1 Committee members were Stimson, Marshall, Vannevar Bush (head of OSRD), James B. Conant (president of Harvard University and chairman of the National Defense Research Committee); Vice President Wallace was FDR's personal liaison to the committee.

42. Entries for May 14 and May 15, 1945, Stimson Diary, Stimson Papers; see also Leon V. Sigal, *Fighting to a Finish: The Politics of War Termination in the United States and Japan, 1945* (Ithaca, 1988), 110–111.

43. Entry for May 16, 1945, Stimson Diary, Stimson Papers.

44. Diary entry for May 16, 1945, Ferrell (ed.), *Off the Record,* 25; entry for May 21, 1945, Davies Diary, Box 16, Davies Papers; Truman to Bess Truman, July 31, 1945, Ferrell (ed.), *Dear Bess,* 522–523.

45. Stimson to Grew, May 21, 1945, *FR 1945,* VII, 876–878.

46. Entries for May 18–27, May 28, and May 30, 1945, Stimson Diary, Stimson Papers; Leo Szilard, "Reminiscences," in Donald Fleming and Bernard Bailyn (eds.), *The Intellectual Migration: Europe and America, 1930–1960* (Cambridge, 1969), 123–128, 146–148; Sherwin, *A World Destroyed,* 200–202; Szilard was accompanied by Walter Bartky, associate dean of physical sciences at Chicago, and Harold Urey, head of the Manhattan Project's Gaseous Diffusion Laboratory at Columbia University.

47. Grew Memoranda, May 28 and May 29, 1945, *FR 1945,* VI, 545–549; entry for May 29, 1945, Stimson Diary, Stimson Papers; Sigal, *Fighting to a Finish,* 114–115.

48. Entry for May 31, 1945, Stimson Diary, Stimson Papers; Sherwin, *A World Destroyed,* 202–209, Appendix L, "Notes of the Interim Committee Meeting, May 31, 1945," 295–304; Messer, *Byrnes,* 87–88.

49. Gar Alperovitz, *The Decision to Use the Atomic Bomb and the Architecture of an American Myth* (New York, 1995), 170–172, suggests that Marshall's acquiescence in Byrnes' forceful intervention meant that the general and others realized that critical decisions about use of the bomb were being made "elsewhere," i.e., in the White House; more

likely, Byrnes pressed his own view, which coincided with that of Truman and, at this time, Stimson.

50. Entry for June 6, 1945, Stimson Diary, Stimson Papers.

51. Grew Memoranda, June 9 and June 14, and Grew to Hurley, June 18, 1945, *FR 1945,* VII, 896, 901–903, 907.

52. Sherwin, *A World Destroyed,* 210–213; Alperovitz, *Decision to Use the Atomic Bomb,* 187–188.

53. Sherwin, *A World Destroyed,* 214–217.

54. Grew Memorandum, June 15, 1945, Box 7, Grew Papers; Akira Iriye, *Power and Culture: The Japanese-American War, 1941–1945* (Cambridge, 1981), 248–252.

55. Grew Memorandum, June 18, 1945, *FR 1945: Potsdam,* I, 177–178; diary entry for June 17, 1945, Ferrell (ed.), *Off the Record,* 47.

56. Memorandum by secretary of Joint Chiefs of Staff, June 18, 1945, *FR 1945: Potsdam,* I, 903–910 (which makes only brief reference to McCloy's remarks); Forrestal Memorandum, Mar. 13, 1947, PSF, Box 157, Truman Papers (Forrestal recalled McCloy's proposal correctly but mistakenly recalled that he and Stimson were not at this meeting); Sigal, *Fighting to a Finish,* 119–122; on McCloy's role, Isaacson and Thomas, *The Wise Men,* 295–296, and Kai Bird, *The Chairman: John J. McCloy, the Making of the American Establishment* (New York, 1992), 245–247, which adds that Byrnes, who was not invited to the White House meeting, rejected McCloy's proposal without explanation; see also Barton J. Bernstein, "Understanding the Atomic Bomb and the Japanese Surrender: Missed Opportunities, Little-Known Near Disasters, and Modern Memory," *DH,* 19 (Spring 1995), 230–234, and Samuel J. Walker, *Prompt and Utter Destruction: Truman and the Use of the Atomic Bombs against Japan* (Chapel Hill, 1997), 32–42; for full accounting of casualty estimates, see Sherwin, *A World Destroyed,* Appendix U, "War Planners' Casualty Estimates for the Invasion of Japan and Other Options for the Final Pacific Campaign," June 1945, 335–349.

57. Entry for June 19, 1945, Stimson Diary, Stimson Papers.

58. Entries for June 25 and June 26–30, 1945, Stimson Diary, Stimson Papers; Minutes of the Committee of Three Meeting, June 26, 1945, *FR 1945: Potsdam,* I, 887–888; on Bard, Sherwin, *A World Destroyed,* 217, and Appendix O, "Bard Memorandum, June 28, 1945," 307–308.

59. Briefing Book Paper, June 29, and Stimson to Truman, July 2, 1945, *FR 1945: Potsdam,* I, 884, 888–894; entry for July 2, 1945, Stimson Diary, Stimson Papers.

60. Iriye, *Power and Culture,* 253–256; two years later Grew wrote Stimson that he still believed that if surrender could have been achieved "before the entrance of Soviet Russia into the war and the use of the atomic bomb, the world would have been the gainer." He also insisted that Japan's rejection of the Potsdam Declaration on July 28 was "a most unfortunate if not utterly stupid step," too much concerned with diplomatic bargaining; Grew to Stimson, Feb. 12, 1947, Stimson Papers.

61. Entry for July 3, 1945, Stimson Diary, Stimson Papers; Charles L. Mee, Jr., *Meeting at Potsdam* (New York, 1975), 116, 119; Sigal, *Fighting to a Finish,* 130; Minutes of the Combined Policy Committee, July 4, 1945, *FR 1945,* II, 12–13.

62. John Snyder, Sam Rosenman, and George Allen to Truman, July 6, 1945, *FR 1945: Potsdam,* I, 228; Truman to Bess Truman, July 3 and July 6, 1945, Ferrell (ed.), *Dear Bess,* 516–517.

Chapter 4. A Stony Place

1. Truman to Bess Truman, July 16, 1945, Ferrell (ed.), *Dear Bess,* 518, and diary entry for July 16, 1945, Ferrell (ed.), *Off the Record,* 50–53; Truman referred to his "Berlin

White House," but others called it the "Little White House"; on Russian troop behavior, Naimark, *Russians in Germany,* 32–36, 60–140, which deals with the issue of mass rape.

2. Truman to Dean Acheson, Mar. 13, 1957 [unsent], Ferrell (ed.), *Off the Record,* 348–349; diary entries for July 7, July 16, and July 20, 1945, ibid., 48–49, 50–55; Bohlen Notes, July 17, 1945, *FR 1945: Potsdam,* II, 43–47, and diary entry for July 17, 1945, Ferrell (ed.), *Off the Record,* 53, and Truman to Bess Truman, July 25 and July 19, 1945, Ferrell (ed.), *Dear Bess,* 521–522.

3. Diary entries for July 17 and July 18, 1945, Ferrell (ed.), *Off the Record,* 50–54.

4. Entry for July 30, 1945, Stimson Diary, Stimson Papers.

5. Grew, *Turbulent Era,* II, 1425–1426; MacLeish to Byrnes, July 6, Draft Proclamation [July 6], and Minutes of . . . Secretary's Staff Committee, July 7, 1945, *FR 1945: Potsdam,* I, 895–897, 900–901; Grew to Byrnes, July 16, and Grew Memorandum, July 17, 1945, *FR 1945: Potsdam,* II, 1267–1268, and Cordell Hull, *The Memoirs of Cordell Hull,* 2 vols. (New York, 1948), II, 1593–1594.

6. Millis (ed.), *Forrestal Diaries* 74–76; entry for July 16, 1945, Stimson Diary, Stimson Papers.

7. Stimson to Truman, July 16, 1945, *FR 1945: Potsdam,* II, 1322–1323.

8. Entries for July 16 and July 17, 1945, Stimson Diary, Stimson Papers; entry for July 16, 1945, Davies Diary, Box 18, Davies Papers; Grew Memorandum, July 17, 1945, *FR 1945: Potsdam,* II, 1261.

9. Entries for July 15, July 17, and July 18, 1945, Stimson Diary, Stimson Papers; Stimson Memorandum, July 16, and Donald Russell to Byrnes, July 20, 1945, *FR 1945: Potsdam,* II, 1223–1224, 1227–1241.

10. Bohlen Memorandum [Truman-Stalin Meeting, July 17, 1945], Mar. 28, 1960, *FR 1945: Potsdam,* II, 1582–1587.

11. Entry for July 17, 1945, Stimson Diary, Stimson Papers; Truman to Bess Truman, July 18, 1945, Ferrell (ed.), *Dear Bess,* 519; Bernstein, "Understanding the Atomic Bomb," 245–246 says that Truman (and others) thought that the Russian attack and the atomic bomb would cause Japan to cease fighting soon but not immediately, and they were surprised by the surrender on August 15.

12. Entry for July 18, 1945, Stimson Diary, Stimson Papers, and Truman to Bess Truman, July 18, 1945, Ferrell (ed.), *Dear Bess,* 519; Churchill, *The Second World War,* VI: *Triumph and Tragedy,* 640–642; Bohlen Memorandum [Truman-Stalin Meeting, July 18, 1945], Mar. 28, 1960, *FR 1945: Potsdam,* II, 1887–1888, and entry for July 18, 1945, Walter Brown Diary, Byrnes Papers; Holloway, *Stalin and the Bomb,* 126.

13. Entry for July 20, 1945, Brown Diary, Byrnes Papers, and entry for July 28, 1945, Millis (ed.), *Forrestal Diaries,* 78; entries for July 21 and July 22, 1945, Stimson Diary, Stimson Papers.

14. Entry for July 22, Stimson Diary, Stimson Papers; Sherwin, *A World Destroyed,* 229–230.

15. Entry for July 22, 1945, Stimson Diary, Stimson Papers; Harrison to Stimson, July 21, and Stimson to Harrison, July 23, 1945, *FR 1945: Potsdam,* II, 1372–1373; Truman to Bess Truman, July 25, 1945, Ferrell (ed.), *Dear Bess,* 55–56, and entry for July 24, 1945, Stimson Diary, Stimson Papers; Sherwin, *A World Destroyed,* 231.

16. Entries for July 23 and July 24, 1945, Stimson Diary, Stimson Papers; Truman to Jiang Jieshi, July 23, 1945, *FR 1945: Potsdam,* II, 1241.

17. Entry for July 23, 1945, Stimson Diary, Stimson Papers; entry for July 24, 1945, Brown Diary, Byrnes Papers; Harrison to Stimson, July 23, 1945, *FR 1945: Potsdam,* II, 1374.

18. Entry for July 24, 1945, Stimson Diary, Stimson Papers; Potsdam Declaration,

July 26, 1945, *FR 1945: Potsdam,* II, 1474–1476; Truman to Patrick J. Hurley, July 24 and July 25, and Hurley to Byrnes, July 26, 1945, ibid., 1278, 1281, 1282–1283; Jiang asked that he be listed ahead of Churchill and that he be invited to all future conferences on Asia; on July 2, Stimson had recommended asking the Soviet Union to sign if it was already in the war; given the assured Soviet entry, Truman had reason to make the Soviets part of the July 26 threat if he really wished to induce Japan's surrender; see Stimson to Truman, July 2, 1945, ibid., 888–894; on compelling threat, Sigal, *Fighting to a Finish,* 129–130, 139–140.

19. Bohlen, *Witness to History,* 237; entry for July 24, 1945, Walter Brown Diary, Byrnes Papers; see also Truman, *Year of Decisions,* 416, and James F. Byrnes, *Speaking Frankly* (New York, 1947), 263; entry for Aug. 9, 1945, Ayers Diary, Box 25, Ayers Papers, confirms that Truman did not tell Stalin that his new weapon was an atomic bomb.

20. Georgi Zhukov, *The Memoirs of Georgi Zhukov* (New York, 1971), 674–675, Holloway, *Stalin and the Bomb,* 117, and Resis (ed.), *Molotov Remembers,* 56; Truman, *Year of Decisions,* 420–421; see also Knebel and Bailey, *No High Ground,* 124–126.

21. Entries for July 27 and July 28, 1945, Brown Diary, Byrnes Papers, and entry for July 28, 1945, Millis (ed.), *Forrestal Diaries,* 78; on Japanese approach to Russians, Sigal, *Fighting to a Finish,* 145–147, and Foreign Minister Togo to Ambassador Sato, July 28, and Press Conference Statement by Prime Minister Suzuki, July 28, 1945, *FR 1945: Potsdam,* II, 1292–1293; Leahy, *I Was There,* 422; Truman to Stalin, July 31, 1945, *FR 1945: Potsdam,* II, 1333–1334.

22. Sigal, *Fighting to a Finish,* 146–152, 229–230, and Bernstein, "Understanding the Atomic Bomb," 239–241; Translation of Prime Minister Suzuki's Press Conference [July 28, 1945], *FR 1945: Potsdam,* II, 1293.

23. Donovan, *Conflict and Crisis,* 96; *Whistle Stop* (Harry S. Truman Library Institute Newsletter), 7 (Summer 1979).

24. Central Secretariat Memorandum, July 12, 1945, *FR 1945: Potsdam,* I, 500–503.

25. Grew to Pauley, July 2, Briefing Book Paper, June 27, and Joint Strategic Survey Committee Memorandum [June 26], 1945, ibid., 519–521, 586–589, 595–596.

26. Pauley to Maisky, July 13, 1945, ibid., 547–548; [Ben Cohen] Memorandum [July 16, 1945], and Stimson to Truman, July 16, 1945, *FR 1945: Potsdam,* II, 989, 754–757, 990–991; entries for July 16 and July 17, 1945, Brown Diary, Byrnes Papers, and entry for July 16, 1945, Stimson Diary, Stimson Papers.

27. Thomas G. Paterson, *Soviet-American Confrontation: Postwar Reconstruction and the Origins of the Cold War* (Baltimore, 1973), 100–102; C. K. Huston to Walworth Barbour, July 11, 1945, *FR 1945: Potsdam,* I, 831–839; see also Hugh DeSantis, "American Career Diplomats in the Balkans," *PSQ,* 94 (Fall 1979), 480–486.

28. Joint Strategic Survey Committee Memorandum, June 29, 1945, *FR 1945: Potsdam,* I, 755.

29. Naimark, *Russians in Germany,* 10; Gaddis, *We Now Know,* 116–117; Loth, "Stalin's Plans for Postwar Germany," in Gori and Pons (eds.), *Soviet Union and Europe,* 24–26.

30. Entry for July 29, 1945, Millis (ed.), *Forrestal Diaries,* 79; entries for July 16, 19, and 21, 1945, Davies Diary, Box 18, Davies Papers; Truman to Bess Truman, July 31, 1945, Ferrell (ed.), *Dear Bess,* 522–523; diary entry for July 30, 1945, Ferrell (ed.), *Off the Record,* 57–58; Stimson to Truman, July 22, 1945, *FR 1945: Potsdam,* II, 808–809.

31. Entry for July 19, 1945, Stimson Diary, Stimson Papers; entry for July 28, 1945, Millis (ed.), *Forrestal Diaries,* 78, and diary entry for July 30, 1945, Ferrell (ed.), *Off the Record,* 57–58; entries for July 20 and July 24, 1945, Brown Diary, Byrnes Papers.

32. First Plenary Meeting, July 17, 1945, *FR 1945: Potsdam,* II, 52–63.

33. Truman to Martha Ellen Truman, M. Truman, *Truman,* 269; Second and Third Plenary Meetings, July 18 and July 19, 1945, *FR 1945: Potsdam,* II, 88–98, 116–137; on cre-

ation of the Council of Foreign Ministers, see Patricia Dawson Ward, *The Threat of Peace: James F. Byrnes and the Council of Foreign Ministers, 1945–1946* (Kent, 1979), 11–17.

34. Cadogan to Lady Theodosia, July 18, 1945, Dilks (ed.), *Cadogan Diaries,* 765–766; Third Plenary Meeting, July 19, 1945, *FR 1945: Potsdam,* II, 116–137.

35. Fourth Plenary Meeting, July 20, 1945, *FR 1945: Potsdam,* II, 164–182; entry for July 19, 1945, Lord Charles Moran, *Churchill: Taken from the Diaries of Lord Moran* (Boston, 1966), 296.

36. Report by Subcommittee on German Political Questions, July 19, Proposal by U.S. Delegation, July 17, and Meeting of Economic Subcommittee, July 20, 1945, *FR 1945: Potsdam,* II, 784–787, 832–835, 141–142; "Statement of Potsdam Conference," Frederick J. Dobney (ed.), *Selected Papers of Will Clayton* (Baltimore, 1971), 138–139; Resis (ed.), *Molotov Remembers,* 53.

37. Fifth Plenary Meeting, July 21, 1945, *FR 1945: Potsdam,* II, 203–221.

38. Entry for July 23, 1945, Moran, *Diaries,* 298; entry for July 22, 1945, Stimson Diary, Stimson Papers.

39. Entry for July 23, 1945, Stimson Diary, Stimson Papers; entry for July 29, 1945, Davies Diary, Box 18, Davies Papers.

40. Truman Note [1954], PSF, Box 334, Truman Papers; Sixth and Seventh Plenary Meetings, July 22 and July 23, 1945, *FR 1945: Potsdam,* II, 240–268, 290–317.

41. Byrnes-Molotov Meeting, and Sixth Meeting of the Foreign Ministers, July 23, 1945, *FR 1945: Potsdam,* II, 274–275, 276–281; see also Proposal by Soviet Delegation, July 29, 1945, ibid., 913–914.

42. Seventh Plenary Meeting, July 23, 1945, ibid., 290–317.

43. Jonathan Knight, "America's International Guarantees for the Straits: Prelude to the Truman Doctrine," *Middle Eastern Studies,* 13 (May 1977), 243–246; Arthur R. De Luca, "Soviet-American Politics and the Turkish Straits," *PSQ,* 92 (Fall 1977), 503–512.

44. Entry for July 23, 1945, Stimson Diary, Stimson Papers; on Truman's suspicions about Russia and the Straits, see entries for Nov. 19 and Dec. 17, 1945, Ayers Diary, Box 25, Ayers Papers; Seventh and Eighth Plenary Meetings, July 23 and July 24, 1945, *FR 1945: Potsdam,* II, 357–374.

45. Entry for July 23 and July 24, 1945, Moran, *Diary,* 300–306; Ninth Plenary Meeting, July 25, 1945, *FR 1945: Potsdam,* II, 381–391.

46. Truman to Bess Truman, July 25, 1945, Ferrell (ed.), *Dear Bess,* 521.

47. Truman to Bess Truman, July 28, 1945, M. Truman, *Truman,* 278; and diary entry for July 16, 1945, Ferrell (ed.), *Off the Record,* 51–52; Meeting of the Combined Chiefs of Staff with Truman and Churchill, July 24, 1945, *FR 1945: Potsdam,* II, 339–344.

48. Churchill, *The Second World War,* VI: *Triumph and Tragedy,* 631–634, and Leahy, *I Was There,* 409–410; entry for Aug. 2, 1945, Dilks (ed.), *Cadogan Diaries,* 778.

49. Truman to Bess Truman, July 29, 1945, Ferrell (ed.), *Dear Bess,* 522; Byrnes, *Speaking Frankly,* 79; Leahy, *I Was There,* 420–421.

50. Truman to Bess Truman, July 29 and July 31, 1945, Ferrell (ed.), *Dear Bess,* 522–523; entry for July 27, 1945, Brown Notes, Byrnes Papers.

51. Entries for July 28 and July 29, 1945, Davies Diary, Box 18, Davies Papers; see also Carolyn Woods Eisenberg, *Drawing the Line: The American Decision to Divide Germany, 1944–1949* (Cambridge, 1996), 104–105, and Messer, *End of an Alliance,* 107.

52. Ninth Meeting of the Foreign Ministers, July 27, 1945, *FR 1945: Potsdam,* II, 436–443; Eisenberg, *Drawing the Line,* 106.

53. Proposal by Soviet Delegation, July 29, and Truman-Molotov Meeting, July 29, 1945, *FR 1945: Potsdam,* II, 471–476, 913–914.

54. Byrnes-Molotov Meeting, July 30, 1945, ibid., 480–483.

55. Tenth Meeting of the Foreign Ministers, July 30, and Byrnes-Molotov Conversation, July 31, 1945, ibid., 483–497, 510; see also Byrnes, *Speaking Frankly,* 85.

56. Truman to Bess Truman, July 31, 1945, Ferrell (ed.), *Dear Bess,* 522–523.

57. Eleventh Plenary Meeting, July 31, 1945, *FR 1945: Potsdam,* II, 510–540.

58. Kucklick, *American Policy and the Division of Germany,* 161–162; Eisenberg, *Drawing the Line,* 105–113; diary entry for July 30, 1945, Ferrell (ed.), *Off the Record,* 57–58.

59. Marc Trachtenberg, *A Constructed Peace: The Making of the European Settlement, 1945–1963* (Princeton, 1999), 25–29; Trachtenberg also says that this sphere-of-influence idea coincided with Stalin's view that whichever nation occupies a territory imposes its social system on it, Djilas, *Conversations with Stalin,* 114.

60. Trachtenberg's only mention of the atomic bomb is a brief reference in a footnote, *A Constructed Peace,* 28 n. 83; Volkogonov, *Stalin: Triumph and Tragedy,* 500–501.

61. Cadogan to Lady Theodosia, July 31, 1945, Dilks (ed.), *Cadogan Diaries,* 777–778; Twelfth Plenary Meeting, Aug. 1, and Communiqué, Aug. 2, 1945, *FR 1945: Potsdam,* II, 565–585, 1499–1511, and R. Murphy, *Diplomat among Warriors,* 342.

62. Twelfth Plenary Meeting, Aug. 1, 1945, *FR 1945: Potsdam,* II, 566–568.

63. Truman to Martha Ellen and Mary Truman, July 30, 1945; Truman, *Year of Decisions,* 402; Knebel and Bailey, *No High Ground,* 1–2; entry for Aug. 9, 1945, Ayers Diary, Box 25, Ayers Papers, and Research Notes, Aug. 30, 1949, Box 1, Daniels Papers; Stalin on Byrnes in Thirteenth Plenary Meeting, Aug. 1, 1945, *FR 1945: Potsdam,* II, 601, and diary entry for Aug. 10, 1945, J. Blum (ed.), *Price of Vision,* 475.

64. Truman Radio Address, Aug, 9, 1945, *PPHST,* I, 203–214.

65. Entry for Aug. 3, 1945, Brown Diary, Byrnes Papers; Byrnes to Harriman, Aug. 5, 1945, *FR 1945,* VII, 955–956; Truman, *Year of Decisions,* 421–422, Knebel and Bailey, *No High Ground,* 2–3, 228–231; Daniels, *Man of Independence,* 287; Donovan, *Conflict and Crisis,* 96–97; Truman Statement on Use of the A-Bomb, Aug. 6, 1945, *PPHST,* I, 197–200.

66. Truman Radio Report, Aug. 9, 1945, *PPHST,* I, 212; Truman to Samuel McCrea Cavert, Aug. 11, 1945, Official File 92-A, Truman Papers; Truman also replied to a congressman who called for continued atomic bombing that although "Japan is a terribly cruel and uncivilized nation, I can't bring myself to believe that, because they are beasts, we should ourselves act in this manner," Truman to Richard Russell, Aug. 9, 1945, Official File 197, Truman Papers.

67. Entry for Aug. 9, 1945, Ayers Diary, Box 25, Ayers Papers; Harriman to Byrnes, Aug. 8, 1945 (two cables), *FR 1945,* VII, 958–965.

68. Entry for Aug. 9, 1945, Stimson Diary, Stimson Papers; Walker, *Prompt and Utter Destruction,* 186.

69. Robert A. Pape, "Why Japan Surrendered," *IS,* 18 (Fall 1993), 154–201, esp. 156–157, 183–188; Herbert Bix, "Japan's Delayed Surrender: A Reinterpretation," *DH,* 19 (Spring 1995), 217–218; Sigal, *Fighting to a Finish,* 224–226.

70. Sigal, *Fighting to a Finish,* 226–242 (Suzuki quoted on 226); Max Grassli to Byrnes, Aug. 10, 1945, *FR 1945,* VI, 627.

71. Entries for Aug. 10, 1945, Stimson Diary, Stimson Papers, Millis (ed.), *Forrestal Diaries,* 83, and Brown Diary, Byrnes Papers.

72. Diary entries for Aug. 10, 1945, J. Blum (ed.), *Price of Vision,* 473–474, and Millis (ed.), *Forrestal Diaries,* 84; Sigal, *Fighting to a Finish,* 252–255.

73. Harriman, *Special Envoy,* 496–501; Michael Schaller, *The U.S. Crusade in China, 1938–1945* (New York, 1979), 260.

74. Sigal, *Fighting to a Finish,* 256–272; Bix, "Japan's Delayed Surrender," 218–222; Barton J. Bernstein, "The Perils and Politics of Surrender: Ending the War with Japan and

Avoiding the Third Atomic Bomb," *PHR,* 46 (Feb. 1977), 17–22, suggests that the "ambiguous" August 11 proposal inspired Japanese militarists to try to prolong the war.

75. Truman Statement Announcing Japan's Surrender, Aug. 14, 1945, *PPHST,* I, 216–217; General Order No. 1 (prepared Aug. 11, 1945), and Truman to MacArthur, Aug. 14, 1945, *FR 1945,* VI, 635–639, 645–650; on the rejected Japanese terms, Grassli to Byrnes, Aug. 16, MacArthur to Marshall, and Byrnes to Grassli, Aug. 17, 1945, ibid., 668–669, 671–672.

76. Stalin to Truman, Aug. 16, Aug. 18, and Aug. 30, and Truman to Stalin, Aug. 18 and Aug. 27, 1945, Ministry of Foreign Affairs of the U.S.S.R., *Stalin's Correspondence with Roosevelt and Truman* (New York, 1965), 265–269; see also Truman, *Year of Decisions,* 440–443.

77. Truman Radio Address, Sept. 1, 1945, *PPHST,* I, 254–257.

78. Marc S. Gallicchio, *The Cold War Begins in Asia: American East Asian Policy and the Fall of the Japanese Empire* (New York, 1988), 57, 74–76; see also Stanton Memorandum [for Harriman], Apr. 19, and Kennan to Stettinius, Apr. 23, 1945, *FR 1945,* VII, 338–345, and entry for May 14, 1945, Millis (ed.), *Forrestal Diaries,* 57–58.

79. David Robertson, *Sly and Able: A Political Biography of James F. Byrnes* (New York, 1994), 434–435, emphasizes Byrnes' political concerns, but completely underestimates the secretary's diplomatic concerns in Europe as well as in North Asia; on analysis of the number of lives possibly saved, Rufus E. Miles, Jr., "Hiroshima: The Strange Myth of a Half Million Lives Saved," *IS,* 10 (Fall 1985), 121–140, which says that the number of American lives saved was at most 20,000 and likely far fewer; John Roy Skates, *The Invasion of Japan: Alternative to the Bomb* (Columbia, 1994), 244, a close study of military planning, says that the large casualty figures cited by Truman and Stimson were "without basis in contemporary planning"; Truman, *Year of Decisions,* 477, attributes the 500,000 figure to Marshall, but this has never been documented and it is unlikely the chief of staff ever said that; Henry L. Stimson, "The Decision to Use the Atomic Bomb," *Harper's Magazine,* 194 (Feb. 1947), 97–107, says that there could have been 1,000,000 casualties if the war had continued into late 1946 (p. 102), but this article was written at the behest of James B. Conant, a prominent chemist and president of Harvard University who had worked on the bomb project and who wished to prevent future criticism of the use of the bomb; Stimson's article contends that the bomb was the "least abhorrent" way to end the war but does mention his and others' efforts to gain an earlier end by offering to retain the emperor; see also Barton J. Bernstein, "Seizing the Contested Terrain of Early Nuclear History: Stimson, Conant, and Their Allies Explain the Decision to Use the Atomic Bomb," *DH,* 17 (Winter 1993), 35–72, and Walker, *Prompt and Utter Destruction,* 100–102.

80. Bix, "Japan's Delayed Surrender," 223–225, is especially critical of the emperor for being a major war protagonist and refusing to face defeat until the last moment, although Bix also notes (p. 223) that Truman and Byrnes "probably wanted to use the atom bomb rather than diplomatic negotiations"; Sadao Asada, "The Shock of the Atomic Bomb and Japan's Decision to Surrender—A Reconsideration," *PHR,* 67 (1998), 477–512, says that the Japanese leaders failed to translate their clear military defeat into formal political surrender, which the bomb and Soviet entry into the war finally compelled; Skates, *Invasion of Japan,* 257, says use of the bomb against "an already defeated Japan" resulted from the "conflict between America's rigorous insistence on unconditional surrender and the irrational, suicidal, and hopeless nature of Japan's last defenses."

81. Iriye, *Power and Culture,* 263–265; Sigal, *Fighting to a Finish,* 277–281.

82. Alperovitz, *Decision to Use the Atomic Bomb,* esp. 224–291, makes the lengthiest argument that Truman and Byrnes used the atomic bomb to influence the Soviets and to try to control the Asian and European settlement (since atomic power meant ability to control

postwar Germany without Russian forces); Barton J. Bernstein, "Eclipsed by Hiroshima and Nagasaki: Early Thinking about Tactical Nuclear Weapons," *IS*, 65 (Spring 1991), 149–173, esp. 168–170, argues that influencing or intimidating the Russians was only a "bonus" or confirming factor in the bomb's use, and the primary reason was to defeat Japan quickly; Bernstein reiterates the "bonus" argument in "Understanding the Atomic Bomb," 230; Walker, *Prompt and Utter Destruction*, 92–97, agrees that influencing the Soviets was a factor but gives more emphasis to ending the war quickly and also cites justifying Manhattan Project costs, lack of incentives to avert use, and racial-wartime hatreds; he also concedes that it was not absolutely necessary to use the bombs and that they saved, at most, "several thousands" of lives; Bernstein, "Eclipsed by Hiroshima," 164–165, states that Truman's insistence that he would use the bomb only on a military target (diary entry for July 25, 1945, Ferrell [ed.], *Off the Record*, 55–56), was self-delusion, especially since the four listed targets were cities and the fifth target would have been Tokyo, which had already been brutally firebombed in March 1945; see also Walker, *Prompt and Utter Destruction*, 61–62.

Chapter 5. A Personal Declaration of Cold War

1. Truman Press Conference, Oct. 8, 1945, *PPHST*, I, 383; McKellar to Truman, Nov. 6, and Truman to McKellar, Nov. 12, 1945, OF 48, Box 236, Truman Papers; "passionately desirous" of peace in Forrestal to E. Palmer Hoyt, Nov. 1, 1945, cited in Gaddis, *United States and Origins of Cold War*, 269; Calendar Notes, Oct. 22, 1945, Campbell and Herring (eds.), *Stettinius Diaries*, 437.

2. Larson, *Origins of Containment*, 224–226.

3. Entry for July 3, 1945, Brown Diary, Byrnes Papers; entry for Sept. 18, 1945, Harold Smith Diary, Smith Papers, Truman Library; Messer, *End of an Alliance*, 126, questions that Byrnes, prior to departing for the London CFM, actually referred to "little bastards" in the State Department.

4. Sherwin, *A World Destroyed*, 85–86, 284; on secret agreements, see Ronald Campbell to Bevin, Aug. 8, 1945, Nevile Butler Papers, Foreign Office Files Number 800, Piece 534, Public Record Office, London (hereinafter F.O. 800/Piece Number); Attlee to Truman, Aug. 8, *FR 1945*, II, 36–37.

5. Truman to Attlee, Aug. 9, 1945, *FR 1945*, II, 37 n. 1, and Truman Radio Report, Aug. 9, 1945, *PPHST*, I, 212–214; Richard G. Hewlett and Oscar E. Anderson, Jr., *A History of the United States Atomic Energy Commission*, I: *The New World, 1939–1946* (University Park, 1962), 400–401, 406–407, Herken, *Winning Weapon*, 362 n. 31, and McGeorge Bundy, *Danger and Survival: Choices about the Bomb in the First Fifty Years* (New York, 1988), 134–135; Ayers Memorandum [n.d.], PSF, Box 227, Truman Papers; Attlee to Truman, Aug. 17, and Truman to Attlee, Aug. 19, 1945, F.O. 800/535; George Harrison Memorandum, Aug. 18, 1945, Sherwin, *A World Destroyed*, Appendix Q, 314–315.

6. Butler Minute, Nov. 18, and Advisory Committee on Atomic Energy Memorandum, Aug. 18, 1945, F.O. 800/535, and Butler Memorandum, Sept. 12, 1945, F.O. 800/555; entries for Aug. 12–Sept. 3, Sept. 4, and Sept. 5, 1945, Stimson Diary, Stimson Papers.

7. Entries for Sept. 13 and Sept. 17, 1945, Brown Diary, Byrnes Papers; Messer, *End of an Alliance*, 129–130.

8. Stalin quoted in Holloway, *Stalin and the Bomb*, 132; Vladimir O. Pechatnov, "'The Allies Are Pressing on You to Break Your Will . . .': Foreign Policy Correspondence between Stalin and Molotov and Other Politburo Members, September 1945–December 1946," CWIHP, Working Paper No. 26 (Sept. 1999), 2, 24–25.

9. Record of First Meeting of Council of Foreign Ministers (CFM), Sept. 11, Bohlen

Memorandum, Sept. 14, and Seventh Meeting of CFM, Sept. 17, 1945, *FR 1945,* II, 114–123, 163–166, 209–217; Conclusions of a Meeting of the Cabinet, Sept. 11, 1945, Records of the British Cabinet Office, Group 128, Piece 3, Public Record Office, London (hereinafter CAB Group/Piece); entry for Sept. 24, 1945, Brown Diary, Byrnes Papers; Resis (ed.), *Molotov Remembers,* 74, and Fifteenth Meeting of CFM, Sept. 21, 1945, *FR 1945,* II, 297–298.

10. Soviet Delegation Memoranda (4), Sept. 12, Cavendish Cannon Memorandum, Sept. 14, and Bohlen Memorandum, Sept. 16, 1945, *FR 1945,* II, 147–150, 182–185, 194–201; Pechatnov, "Allies Are Pressing on You," 2.

11. Calendar Notes for Sept. 12, 1945, Campbell and Herring (eds.), *Stettinius Diaries,* 418, and entry for Sept. 17, Brown Diary, Byrnes Papers; Bohlen Memorandum, Sept. 20, 1945, *FR 1945,* II, 267–269, and entries for Sept. 20 and Sept. 21, Brown Diary, Byrnes Papers.

12. Entry for Sept. 10, 1946, Davies Diary, Box 22, Davies Papers; Truman to Byrnes [Sept. 22, 1945], PSF, Box 119, Truman Papers.

13. Bohlen Memorandum, Sept. 22, 1945, *FR 1945,* II, 313–315; Truman to Stalin, Sept. 22 (two cables), and Stalin to Truman, Sept. 22 and Sept. 24, 1945, ibid., 328–329, 331–334; Pechatnov, "Allies Are Pressing on You," 5; Bevin quoted in Allan Bullock, *Ernest Bevin: Foreign Secretary, 1945–1951* (New York, 1983), 134.

14. Truman Statement, Sept. 22, Truman Message, Sept. 24, and Truman News Conference, Sept. 26, 1945, *PPHST,* I, 337–341, 342–343, 344–345.

15. Entry for Sept. 26, 1945, Brown Diary, Byrnes Papers, Harriman, *Special Envoy,* 508–509, Memorandum, Stettinius-Byrnes Conversation, Sept. 28, 1945, Campbell and Herring (eds.), *Stettinius Diaries,* 425–427, Twentieth Meeting of CFM, Sept. 25, 1946, *FR 1945,* II, 359, 365–370.

16. Truman to Byrnes [Sept. 25], 1945, PSF, Box 159, Truman Papers; Yergin, *Shattered Peace,* 129–130; Bohlen Memorandum, Sept. 30, 1945, *FR 1945,* II, 487–489.

17. Pechatnov, "Allies Are Pressing on You," 7–8.

18. Truman Press Conference, Oct. 8, 1945, *PPHST,* I, 383–384; Calendar Notes for Oct. 22, 1945, Campbell and Herring (eds.), *Stettinius Diaries,* 437, and diary entry for Oct. 26, 1945, J. Blum (ed.), *Price of Vision,* 501–502; Truman to Bess Truman, Sept. 22, 1945, Ferrell (ed.), *Dear Bess,* 523.

19. Stimson to Truman, and Stimson Memoranda for Truman, Sept. 11, 1945, *FR 1945,* II, 40–44, and entry for Sept. 12, 1945, Stimson Diary, Stimson Papers; diary entry for Sept. 18, 1945, J. Blum (ed.), *Price of Vision,* 481; entry for Sept. 18, 1945, Davies Diary, Box 22, Davies Papers; on "secret ordnance procedures" see Patterson to Truman, Sept. 26, 1945, *FR 1945,* II, 54–55, and on "know-how," see James L. Gormly, "The Washington Declaration and the 'Poor Relations': Anglo-American Atomic Diplomacy, 1945–46," *DH,* 8 (Spring 1984), 130.

20. Dean Acheson, *Present at the Creation: My Years in the State Department* (New York, 1969), 123; see also Herken, *Winning Weapon,* 31, Bundy, *Danger and Survival,* 139, and James Chace, *Acheson: The Secretary of State Who Created the American World* (New York, 1998), 119.

21. Connelly Cabinet Notes, Sept. 21, 1945, Connelly Papers, and Forrestal Memorandum, Sept. 21, 1945, PSF, Box 157, Truman Papers (Millis [ed.], *Forrestal Diaries,* 94–96, gives only excerpts and incorrectly states that "nearly all" accorded with Forrestal; diary entry for Sept. 21, 1945, J. Blum (ed.), *Price of Vision,* 483–485; Wallace to Truman, Sept. 24, ibid., 485–487, Acheson to Truman and Patterson to Truman, Sept. 25, 1945, *FR 1945,* II, 48–50, 54–55, and Abe Fortas to Truman, Sept. 26, 1945, PSF, Box 112, Truman Papers; Anderson to Truman, Sept. 25, Vinson to Truman and McKellar to Truman, Sept. 27, 1945, PSF, Box 112, Truman Papers.

22. Truman to Bess Truman, Sept. 22, 1945, Ferrell (ed.), *Dear Bess,* 523, Herken, *Winning Weapon,* 31–33, and Hewlett and Anderson, *The New World,* 424–426; Attlee to Truman, Sept. 25, 1945, PSF, Box 170, Truman Papers, and Halifax to Bevin and Attlee, Sept. 25, 1945, F.O. 800/535.

23. Truman Special Message, Oct. 3, 1945, *PPHST,* I, 362–366.

24. Truman to Attlee, Oct. 5, 1945, PSF, Box 170, Truman Papers, and entry for Oct. 5, 1945, Smith Diary, Smith Papers.

25. Truman News Conference, Oct. 8, 1945, *PPHST,* I, 383, McKellar to Truman, Oct. 9, 1945, PSF, Box 112, Truman Papers; Truman-Fyke Farmer conversation [Oct. 11, 1945], cited in Herken *Winning Weapon,* 39; Bundy, *Danger and Survival,* 144–145, concedes that Herken's view of Truman as unwilling to share atomic secrets is correct, although he is less critical of Truman.

26. Donovan, *Conflict and Crisis,* 130, and Leffler, *Preponderance of Power,* 95; Minutes of Meeting of Secretaries of State, War, and Navy, Oct. 16 and Oct. 23, 1945, *FR 1945,* II, 59–61, 61–62.

27. Attlee to Truman, Oct. 16, and Truman to Attlee, Oct. 17, 1945, F.O. 800/53; White House Memorandum, Oct. 19, 1945, PSF, Box 172, Truman Papers, cited in Gormly, "Washington Declaration," 130; Truman Address, Oct. 27, 1945, *PPHST,* 431–438.

28. Bundy, *Danger and Survival,* 146–147; Gormly, "Washington Declaration," 132; Byrnes to Truman, Nov. 5, 1945, *FR 1945,* II, 69–73.

29. Bundy, *Danger and Survival,* 147; Holloway, *Stalin and the Bomb,* 157.

30. Hewlett and Anderson, *The New World,* 457–458, 461; Halifax to Sir John Anderson, Sept. 20, 1945, F.O. 800/555; Conclusions of a Meeting of the Cabinet, Confidential Annex, Nov. 8, 1945, CAB 129/5.

31. Bullock, *Bevin,* 286–288; Churchill to Attlee, Sept. 25, 1945, F.O. 800/535; Attlee Cabinet Paper, "International Control of Atomic Energy," Nov. 5, 1945, CAB 129/4.

32. Butler to Campbell, Nov. 15, 1945, F.O. 800/538; Herken, *Winning Weapon,* 63–64, and Gormly, "Washington Declaration," 133–135.

33. Herken, *Winning Weapon,* 64–66; Gormly, "Washington Declaration," 135–136; Truman News Conference, Nov. 15, 1945, *PPHST,* I, 472–475; Vandenberg (ed.), *Vandenberg Papers,* 226–227; Truman-Attlee-King Memorandum, and Groves-Anderson Memorandum, Nov. 16, 1945, *FR 1945,* II, 75–77.

34. Connelly Cabinet Notes, Nov. 16, 1945, Connelly Papers, Truman Library; diary entry for Nov. 16, 1945, J. Blum (ed.), *Price of Vision,* 515–516; Larson, *Origins of Containment,* 234.

35. Leffler, *Preponderance of Power,* 78–79, and idem, "Strategy, Diplomacy, and the Cold War: The United States, Turkey, and NATO, 1945–1954," *JAH,* 71 (Mar. 1985), 808–809; Eduard Mark, "The War Scare of 1946 and Its Consequences," *DH,* 21 (Spring 1997), 388–389.

36. Truman to Byrnes, Oct. 13, 1945, quoted in Larson, *Origins of Containment,* 225; Byrnes to Truman, Oct. 19, and Truman to Byrnes, Oct. 20, 1945, *FR 1945,* VIII, 1255–1256, 1256 n. 69; see also Byrnes to Truman, Sept. 3, 1945, ibid., 1242–1245, and Byrnes to Truman, Oct. 13, 1945, PSF, Box 159, Truman Papers.

37. Wilson to Byrnes, Oct. 27, and Harriman to Byrnes, Oct. 29, 1945, *FR 1945,* VIII, 1262, 1263–1264; Byrnes to Wilson, Oct. 30, and Wilson to Byrnes, Nov. 2 and Nov. 3, 1945, ibid., 1265, 1270–1271, 1271–1272; diary entries for Nov. 19 and Dec. 17, 1945, Ayers Diary, Box 25, Ayers Papers.

38. Yergin, *Shattered Peace,* 180–182, George Lenczowski, *The Middle East in World Affairs,* 4th ed. (Ithaca, 1980), 178–181, and Schnabel, *History of the JCS,* I, 82–84; on U.S. oil interest, see Byrnes to Roosevelt, Oct. 15, 1943, Folder 70, Byrnes Papers.

39. Second Meeting of CFM, Sept. 22, 1945, *FR 1945*, II, 315–316; Yergin, *Shattered Peace*, 182–183; Leffler, *Preponderance of Power*, 79–81; Larson, *Origins of Containment*, 221, 231, 234–236; on Byrnes' view that the Russians were behind the revolts in Iran, diary entry for Nov. 23, 1945, J. Blum (ed.), *Price of Vision*, 519; on Iranian conditions, Murray to Byrnes, Sept. 24 and Sept. 25, 1945, and Kennan to Byrnes, Oct. 1, 1945, *FR 1945*, VIII, 417–419, 424; Murray to Byrnes, Nov. 19, Nov. 20, Nov. 21, and Nov. 25, 1945, ibid., 433, 437–440, 454–455; Byrnes to Harriman, Nov. 23, and Harriman to Byrnes, Nov. 30, 1945, ibid., 448–450, 468–469; on Russian aims in Iran, Natalia I. Yegorova, "The 'Iran Crisis' of 1945–1946: A View from the Russian Archives," CWIHP, Working Paper No. 15 (May 1996), 10–13, and F. Scheid, "Stalin's Reluctant Bid for Iranian Azerbaijan, 1941–1946: A View from the Azerbaijani Archives," Draft Paper for Conference, "Stalin and the Cold War, 1945–1953," Yale University (Sept. 1999), 14–15; Truman comment in entry for Dec. 19, 1945, Davies Journal, Box 22, Davies Papers.

40. Schaller, *Crusade in China*, 264–265, 280–287; "in the middle" in entry for Nov. 19, 1945, Ayers Diary, Box 25, Ayers Papers; diary entry for Nov. 6, 1945, J. Blum (ed.), *Price of Vision*, 506–507, Truman Appointment Sheet Notes, Nov. 15, 1945, PSF, Box 82, Truman Papers, and Truman to Congressman Ellis Patterson, Nov. 16, 1945, OF, Box 62, Truman Papers; Patterson-Forrestal Memorandum, Nov. 26, and Minutes of Meeting of Secretaries of State, War, and Navy, Nov. 26, 1945, *FR 1945*, VII, 670–678, 683–686; for more detailed analysis of Truman's policy, see chap. 12, "Sand in a Rat Hole: Double Policy in China."

41. Patterson-Forrestal Memorandum, Nov. 26, and Minutes of Meeting of Secretaries of State, War, and Navy, Nov. 26, 1945, *FR 1945*, VII, 670–678, 683–686.

42. Schaller, *Crusade in China*, 288–289, Donovan, *Conflict and Crisis*, 149–151.

43. Entry for Nov. 27, 1945, J. Blum (ed.), *Price of Vision*, 519; Marshall Memorandum, Dec. 11, and Truman to Marshall, Dec. 15, 1945, *FR 1945*, VII, 767–769, 770–773.

44. Entries for Sept. 18, 1945, Brown Diary, Stimson Papers; Yergin, *Shattered Peace*, 143–145, and *New York Times*, Nov. 1, 1945.

45. Ward, *Threat of Peace*, 50–51, Harriman, *Special Envoy*, 511–516, and John Balfour (British Embassy in Washington) to Bevin, Feb. 20, 1946, F.O. 800/513.

46. Entry for Thanksgiving Day [Nov. 23,] 1945, Brown Diary, Byrnes Papers, Bullock, *Bevin*, 199–200; and Bevin to Byrnes, Nov. 28, and Bevin to Halifax, Dec. 4 and Dec. 6, 1945, F.O. 800/512; Byrnes Memorandum, Dec. 4, 1945, *FR 1945*, II, 595–596.

47. Harriman to Byrnes, Nov. 27, 1945, *FR 1945*, V, 922–924, and Archibald Clark-Kerr to Bevin, Dec. 3, 1945, *FR 1945*, II, 82–84.

48. Harriman to Molotov, and Molotov to Harriman, Dec. 7, 1945, *FR 1945*, II, 599–600; Memo by Informal Committee, Dec. 10, and Forrestal to Byrnes, Dec. 11, 1945, ibid., 92–97; Butler Memorandum, Dec. 12, 1945, F.O. 800/554.

49. Diary entry for Nov. 28, 1945, J. Blum (ed.), *Price of Vision*, 524; Truman News Conference, Nov. 29, 1945, *PPHST*, I, 513; Byrnes to Winant, Dec. 3, 1945, *FR 1945*, II, 592; Ward, *Threat of Peace*, 57, and Larson, *Origins of Containment*, 235–236, 238; entry for Dec. 8, 1945, Davies Diary, Box 22, Davies Papers; entry for Dec. 12, 1945, Ayers Diary, Box 25, Ayers Papers.

50. Diary entry for Dec. 10, 1945, Vandenberg (ed.), *Vandenberg Papers*, 227–228.

51. Diary entry for Dec. 11, 1945, Vandenberg (ed.), *Vandenberg Papers*, 229; Acheson to Byrnes, Dec. 15, and Byrnes to Acheson, Dec. 17, 1945, *FR 1945*, II, 609–610, 609 n. 81; see also Messer, *End of an Alliance*, 143–144.

52. Truman to Stalin [n.d., but given to Stalin by Byrnes on Dec. 19, 1945], *FR 1945*, II, 687–688; Ethridge to Byrnes, Dec. 8, 1945, *FR 1945*, V, 633–641.

53. Memorandum of Bevin-Byrnes Conversation, Dec. 17, 1945, *FR 1945*, II, 629–632; Bullock, *Bevin*, 200–201; for correspondence about the bases the United States sought, see Halifax to Foreign Office, Nov. 8 and Nov. 10, Bevin to Halifax, Nov. 15 and Nov. 27, and Byrnes to Bevin, Dec. 10, 1945, and Bevin to Halifax, Jan. 11, 1946, F.O. 800/512; record of Stalin-Bevin Conversation, Dec. 24, 1945, *FR 1945* II, 774–776.

54. Memorandum of Stalin-Molotov-Byrnes Conversation, Dec. 19, 1945, *FR 1945*, II, 681–684; Bohlen, *Witness to History*, 248; Minutes of Byrnes-Bevin-Molotov Conversation, Dec. 21, 1945, *FR 1945*, II, 718–719; Acheson to Byrnes, Dec. 20, and Byrnes to Acheson, Dec. 22, 1945, ibid., 707–708, 725.

55. Minutes of Byrnes-Bevin-Molotov Conversation, Dec. 21, 1945, ibid., 717, and Yergin, *Shattered Peace*, 149–150.

56. Minutes of Byrnes-Bevin-Molotov Conversation, Dec. 19, and Memorandum of Stalin-Molotov-Byrnes Conversation, Dec. 23, 1945, *FR 1945*, II, 666–669, 756–758.

57. Byrnes to James B. Conant, Jan. 5, 1946, Folder 626, Byrnes Papers; Record of Byrnes-Bevin Conversation, Dec. 17, Memo by U.S. Delegation, Dec. 18, Fifth Session CFM, Dec. 20, Sixth Session CFM, Dec. 22, 1945, *FR 1945*, II, 632, 663–664, 698, 736–737; Memo of Stalin-Byrnes Conversation, Dec. 23, 1945, and Informal Meeting CFM, Dec. 24, ibid., 756, 762–763; Herken, *Winning Weapon*, 82–84.

58. Bohlen, *Witness to History*, 249; Messer, *End of an Alliance*, 150–151, and Holloway, *Stalin and the Bomb*, 158–159.

59. Memo of Byrnes-Molotov Conversation, Dec. 18, Informal Meeting CFM, Dec. 22, Memorandum Stalin-Byrnes Conversation, Dec. 23, 1945, *FR 1945*, II, 643–645, 727–734, 750–756; Informal Meeting CFM, Dec. 21, and Informal Meeting CFM, Dec. 26, 1945, ibid., 781–795, 801–805; see also Bevin Draft Memo, Dec. 23, 1945, ibid., 758–759, and Ward, *Threat of Peace*, 63–66; on the British having "welcomed" the Balkan accord, see Conclusions of a Cabinet Meeting, Jan. 1, 1946, CAB 128/5.

60. Memoranda of Stalin-Byrnes Conversations, Dec. 19 and Dec. 23, 1945, *FR 1945*, II, 684–687, 750–752; Memorandum by British Delegation, Dec. 24, Byrnes-Molotov Conversation, Dec. 25, Informal Conversation CFM, Dec. 25, Informal Meeting CFM, Dec. 26, and Bevin to Molotov, Dec. 27, 1945, ibid., 771–772, 777–779, 795–797, 805–806, 814–815; Record of Bevin-Stalin Conversation, Dec. 19, 1945, ibid., 688–691; Harriman to Acheson, Dec. 27, 1945, ibid., 815–824.

61. Molotov quoted in Pechatnov, "Allies Are Pressing on You," 14; Acheson on Byrnes, cited in Ward, *Threat of Peace*, 72.

62. Kennan, *Memoirs*, I, 284, 286–288 (for Kennan views on Potsdam agreements, Lend-Lease, economic aid, and atomic exchange, see ibid., 266–269, 296–297); Harriman, *Special Envoy*, 517.

63. Entries for Nov. 28, Dec. 26, and Dec. 28, 1945, Leahy Diary, cited in Yergin, *Shattered Peace*, 155, and Donovan, *Conflict and Crisis*, 159; Larson, *Origins of Containment*, 246; diary entry of Jan. 2, 1946, Vandenberg (ed.), *Vandenberg Papers*, 233–234, Acheson, *Present at the Creation*, 136, and Yergin, *Shattered Peace*, 440 n. 23.

64. Diary entry for Nov. 28, 1945, J. Blum (ed.), *Price of Vision*, 524, and Truman to Bess Truman, Dec. 28, 1945, Ferrell (ed.), *Off the Record*, 75–76; Acheson, *Present at the Creation*, 136, Byrnes to Truman, and Truman to Byrnes, Dec. 29, 1945, PSF, Box 83, Truman Papers.

65. Entry for Dec. 29, 1945, Leahy Diary, cited in Messer, *End of an Alliance*, 157; Daniels Research Notes (Clark Clifford interview, 1949), Box 1, Daniels Papers; Truman's comments in Connelly Cabinet Notes, Dec. 22, 1950, Connelly Papers, and Daniels Research Notes (Truman interview, 1949), Box 1, Daniels Papers; *New York Times*, Dec. 31,

1945, and entry for Jan. 4, 1946, Harold Ickes Diary, cited in Messer, *End of an Alliance,* 262 n. 16.

66. Byrnes to Truman, Jan. 2, 1946, PSF, Box 172, and Truman to Byrnes, Jan. 5, 1946, PSF, Box 333, Truman Papers. Attached to Truman's letter is an undated note saying, "I wrote this memorandum and read it to my Secretary of State. So urgent were its contents I neither had it typed nor mailed it but preferred to read it in order to give emphasis to the points I wanted to make. H.S.T." (Acheson sent Truman the Ethridge Report of Dec. 7, 1945, on Jan. 11, 1946, and suggested it not be made public. [Acheson to Truman, Jan. 11, 1946, PSF, Box 172, Truman Papers.])

67. Truman always claimed to have read the letter to Byrnes in the Oval Office. The president insisted on this to an aide in 1951 (noting that at the end, Byrnes' face was "fiery red"), again when the letter was published by the journalist William Hillman in 1952 in *Mr. President,* and then in Truman's *Memoirs* (ghostwritten by Hillman) in 1955. Byrnes declared in 1952, and ever after, that he never saw or heard of the letter until it appeared in *Mr. President* and that he would have resigned at once had Truman read it to him. Byrnes' view seems nearer the truth. Truman, with his hyperbolic memory, surely exaggerated his verbal dressing-down of Byrnes. But the president, who at first rage might have intended to send the letter (why else sign it?), perhaps used it to inspire or guide himself to make similar points in more moderate tones when he conferred with Byrnes on January 5. See entries for July 26, 1951, and March 17–22, 1952, Ayers Diary, Box 26, Ayers Papers, and Truman, *Year of Decisions,* 551–552; James F. Byrnes, "Byrnes Answers Truman," *Colliers,* Apr. 26, 1952, 15–17, James F. Byrnes, *All in One Lifetime* (New York, 1958), 400–404, and George W. Curry, *James F. Byrnes,* vol. 14 in *The American Secretaries of State and Their Diplomacy* (New York, 1965), 189–190; on Truman-Byrnes relationship, Harriman, *Special Envoy,* 524, and Messer, *End of an Alliance,* 160.

68. Larson, *Origins of Containment,* 226.

69. Connelly Cabinet Notes, Dec. 22, 1950, Connelly Papers, and Pauley to Truman, June 22, *FR 1946,* VIII, 706.

Chapter 6. The Year of Decisions

1. Churchill to Truman, Jan. 19, 1945, quoted in Thomas G. Paterson, *On Every Front: The Making and Unmaking of the Cold War,* rev. ed. (New York, 1992), ix; Truman Radio Report, Jan. 3, and State of the Union/Budget Message, Jan. 21, 1946, *PPHST,* II, 1–8, 36–87; McCoy, *Presidency of Harry S. Truman,* 57–58.

2. Diary entries for Mar. 13 and Mar. 18, 1946, Charles Ross Diary, Box 322, Truman Papers, and entry for Jan. 11, 1946, Millis (ed.), *Forrestal Diaries,* 128–129; Donovan, *Conflict and Crisis,* 180–183, and Hamby, *Man of the People,* 307–308; Ferrell, *Truman,* 221–223, questions Ickes' fairness.

3. *New York Times,* Jan. 9, 1946; Larson, *Origins of Containment,* 251–252.

4. Herken, *Winning Weapon,* 129–131, Messer, *End of an Alliance,* 185–186, and Haynes and Klehr, *Venona,* 168 (the Canadian investigation had been touched off by defection of Igor Gouzenko, a military intelligence code clerk in the Canadian Embassy, in September 1945); Holloway, *Stalin and the Bomb,* 222–223; Marjorie Garber and Rebecca Walkowitz (eds.), *The Rosenberg Case, McCarthyism, and Fifties America* (New York, 1995), 51.

5. *New York Times,* Jan. 23 and Jan. 30, 1946, Kennan to Byrnes, Jan. 27, 1946, *FR 1946,* VI, 683, and Truman News Conference, Jan. 30, 1946, *PPHST,* II, 102–105. See also Athan

Theoharris, "Roosevelt and Truman on Yalta: The Origins of the Cold War," *PSQ,* 87 (June 1972), 239–241, and Messer, *End of an Alliance,* 169–174.

6. Halifax cited in The Earl of Birkenhead, *Halifax: The Life of Lord Halifax* (Boston, 1966), 558; entry for Feb. 28, 1946, Smith Diary, Smith Papers, and entry for Feb. 15, 1946, Ross Diary, President's Personal File (PPF), Box 322, Truman Papers; Truman's mother cited in Yergin, *Shattered Peace,* 163–164, and Messer, *End of an Alliance,* 181–182.

7. Diary entry for Mar. 15, 1946, Beatrice Bishop Berle and Travis Beal Jacobs (eds.), *Navigating the Rapids, 1918–1971: From the Papers of Adolf A. Berle* (New York, 1971), 573; entry for Jan. 24, 1946, Ayers Diary, Box 25, Ayers Papers; entry for Feb. 20, 1946, Leahy Diary, cited in Donovan, *Conflict and Crisis,* 187.

8. Forrestal to Homer Ferguson, May 14, entry for June 30, 1945, and Forrestal to Walter Lippmann, Jan. 7, 1946, Millis (ed.), *Forrestal Diaries,* 57, 72–73, 128; Yergin, *Shattered Peace,* 164–165, and Townsend Hoopes and Douglas Brinkley, *Driven Patriot: The Life and Times of James Forrestal* (New York, 1992), 265–269.

9. Stalin speech in *Vital Speeches of the Day,* 12 (Mar. 1, 1946), 300–304; Holloway, *Stalin and the Bomb,* 150–155; Resis (ed.), *Molotov Remembers,* 8.

10. Yergin, *Shattered Peace,* 166–167, Harriman *Special Envoy,* 546–547, and Larson, *Origins of Containment,* 252–255; H. Freeman Matthews to Acheson and Byrnes, Feb. 11, 1946, cited in Larson, op. cit., 255, and entry for Feb. 17, 1946, Millis (ed.), *Forrestal Diaries,* 134–135; JCS to SWNCC, Feb. 21, and JCS to Byrnes, Mar. 29, 1946, *FR 1946,* I, 1165–1166; see also Schnabel, *History of the JCS,* I, 91–92; even the highly critical Taubman, *Stalin's American Policy,* 133–134, notes "in retrospect" the "innocuous" and "defensive" tone of the speech but suggests that Stalin's three Five-Year Plans coincided with his belief that war would not come for fifteen years, when Germany (and Japan) would be revived.

11. Truman cited in entry for Feb. 9, 1946, Davies Diary, Box 22, Davies Papers, and Larson, *Origins of Containment,* 254; diary entry for Feb. 12, 1946, J. Blum (ed.), *Price of Vision,* 546, and entry for Mar. 25, 1946, Ross Diary, PPF, Box 322, Truman Papers.

12. Herring, *Aid to Russia,* 230–236, and George Herring, "The United States and British Bankruptcy, 1944–1945," *PSQ,* 86 (June 1971), 276–278, and Acheson, *Present at the Creation,* 122; the Lend-Lease law might have been interpreted to allow aid to continue so long as the president deemed it in the national defense; see Paterson, *Soviet-American Confrontation,* 46.

13. Robert M. Hathaway, *Ambiguous Partnership: Britain and America, 1944–1947* (New York, 1981), 186–197; Paterson, *Soviet-American Confrontation,* 147–154.

14. Bullock, *Bevin,* 202–205, Hathaway, *Ambiguous Partnership,* 230–247, and Vandenberg to Dulles, Dec. 19, 1945, Vandenberg (ed.), *Vandenberg Papers,* 230–231.

15. Truman to McKellar, Nov. 12, 1945, OF, Box 326, Truman Papers; Truman Special Message to Congress, Jan. 30, and Truman Statement Mar. 4, 1946, *PPHST,* II, 97–100, 137–138, and Truman to Vinson, June 6, 1946, PSF, Box 132, Truman Papers; Paterson, *Soviet-American Confrontation,* 164–169.

16. Herring, *Aid to Russia,* 144–178, and Offner, "Research on American-German Relations," 175–176.

17. Paterson, *Soviet-American Confrontation,* 46–48, and Export-Import Bank Memorandum, Sept. 21, 1945, and Vinson Memorandum to Truman [undated, but marked "Approved 9/21/45 Harry S. Truman"], *FR 1946,* I, 1405–1408.

18. Gaddis, *United States and Origins of the Cold War,* 259–260, and Paterson, *Soviet-American Confrontation,* 48.

19. Kennan to Byrnes, Sept. 15, 1945, *FR 1945,* V, 881–884, Gaddis, *United States and*

Origins of Cold War, 259–260, and Paterson, *Soviet-American Confrontation,* 48–50; Truman News Conference, Dec. 7, 1945, *PPHST,* I, 528.

20. Harriman, *Special Envoy,* 533–534.

21. Truman News Conference, Feb. 21, 1946, *PPHST,* I, 128; Byrnes to Fedor Orekhov, Feb. 21, 1946, *FR 1946,* VI, 828–829, and Paterson, *Soviet-American Confrontation,* 51–52.

22. Gaddis, *We Now Know,* 193, and Paterson, *Soviet-American Confrontation,* 155; Nikolai Novikov to Byrnes, Mar. 15, 1946, *FR 1946,* VI, 829–830; Wallace to Truman, Mar. 14, Truman to Wallace, Mar. 20, and Wallace to Truman, Mar. 21, 1946, PSF, Box 187, Truman Papers and Truman, *Year of Decisions,* 556; Byrnes to Novikov, Apr. 18, and Luthringer Memorandum for Clayton, May 23, 1946, *FR 1946,* VI, 834–836, 842–843.

23. Byrnes to Novikov, June 13, 1946, *FR 1946,* VI, 844–846; Wallace to Truman, July 23, 1946, Box 18, Clifford Papers, and Elsey Note, July 24, 1946, Box 63, Elsey Papers; Paterson, *Soviet-American Confrontation,* 54.

24. Paterson, *Soviet-American Confrontation,* 55–56.

25. Fraser Harbutt, *The Iron Curtain: Churchill, America, and the Origins of the Cold War* (New York, 1986), 166–167; MacArthur [for Hodge] to Byrnes, Feb. 24, 1946, *FR 1946,* I, 640–642, and entry for Feb. 25, 1946, Ayers Diary, Box 25, Ayers Papers; entries for Feb. 28 and Mar. 10, 1946, Millis (ed.), *Forrestal Diaries,* 141, 143–144, and entry for Feb. 28, 1946, Ayers Diary, Box 25, Ayers Papers; Ambassador Ertegun's ashes were returned on the *Missouri* because no (smaller) cruiser was available; see Bruce Robellet Kuniholm, *The Origins of the Cold War in the Near East: Great Power Conflict and Diplomacy in Iran, Turkey, and Greece* (Princeton, 1980), 335; Churchill to Attlee and Bevin, Mar. 7, 1946, F.O. 800/513, and Leffler, "U.S., Turkey, and NATO," 811.

26. Kennan to Byrnes, Feb. 22, 1946, *FR 1946,* VI, 696–709, and Kennan, *Memoirs,* I, 292–296.

27. On Kennan and his cable, see Kennan, op. cit., Larson, *Origins of Containment,* 255–257, Yergin, *Shattered Peace,* 168–171, Harriman, *Special Envoy,* 548, John Lewis Gaddis, *Strategies of Containment: A Critical Appraisal of Postwar American National Security Policy* (New York, 1982), 19–21, and David Mayers, *George Kennan and the Dilemmas of US Foreign Policy* (New York, 1988), 97–101; Elsey quoted in M. Truman, *Truman,* 309.

28. Mayers, *Kennan,* 100–101.

29. Vandenberg (ed.), *Vandenberg Papers,* 247–251, and Stettinius Calendar Notes, Feb. 28, 1946, cited in Gaddis, *United States and Origins of Cold War,* 306 n. 40.

30. Truman Note, and Overseas Press Club Speech, Feb. 28, 1946, Folder 626, Byrnes Papers; Harbutt, *Iron Curtain,* 172, and Messer, *End of an Alliance,* 192.

31. Donovan, *Conflict and Crisis,* 190; Churchill to Truman, Nov. 8, and Truman to Churchill, Nov. 16, 1945, PSF, Box 115, Truman Papers; Churchill to Bevin, Nov. 13, 1945, F.O. 800/512.

32. Entry for Feb. 10, 1946, Leahy Diary, cited in Harbutt, *Iron Curtain,* 161; entry for Feb. 10, 1946, Halifax Diary, and M. R. Wright to P. J. Dixon, Feb. 16, 1946, cited in Henry B. Ryan, "A New Look at Churchill's 'Iron Curtain' Speech," *The Historical Journal,* 22 (1979), 904.

33. Harbutt, *Iron Curtain,* 162, and entry for Feb. 10, 1946, Leahy Diary, and entry for Feb. 11, 1946, Davies Diary, cited in Larson, *Origins of Containment,* 265; Truman News Conference, Feb. 21, 1946, *PPHST,* II, 130, 133, and Churchill to Attlee, Feb. 21, 1946, F.O. 800/513; Conclusions of a Cabinet Meeting, Mar. 11, 1946, CAB 128/5, and Mason Minute, Mar. 12, 1946, F.O. 371/51624.

34. Byrnes, *All in One Lifetime,* 349; entry for Mar. 7, 1946, Ross Diary, PPF, Box 322, Truman Papers, and Churchill to Attlee, Mar. 7, 1946, F.O. 800/513.

35. *New York Times,* Mar. 6, 1946.

36. Harbutt, *Iron Curtain,* 197–208; Truman News Conference, Mar. 8, 1946, *PPHST,* II, 145–146, 148; diary entry for Mar. 12, 1946, J. Blum (ed.), *Price of Vision,* 558, Truman to Martha Truman, Mar. 11, 1946, cited in M. Truman, *Truman,* 312, and Truman interview, Aug. 30, 1949, Daniels Research Notes, Box 1, Daniels Papers.

37. *New York Times,* Mar. 14, 1946, and Kennan to Byrnes, Mar. 14, 1946, *FR 1946,* VI, 716–717, and Gladwyn, *Memoirs,* 185.

38. Truman News Conference, Mar. 14, 1946, *PPHST,* II, 156, and *New York Times,* Mar. 17, 1946.

39. Larson, *Origins of Containment,* 268–269; entries for Mar. 18, Mar. 19, and Mar. 22, 1946, Ross Diary, PPF, Box 322, Truman to Stalin, Mar. 19, 1946, PSF, Box 188, and Truman Note, Mar. 23, 1946, PSF, Box 83, Truman Papers.

40. Smith to Byrnes, Apr. 5, 1946, *FR 1946,* VI, 132–136, Bohlen, *Witness to History,* 253, and Strobe Talbott (trans.), *Khrushchev Remembers* (London, 1971), 361, 393.

41. Harry S. Truman, *Memoirs,* II: *Years of Trial and Hope* (Garden City, 1956), 94–95, and Yergin, *Shattered Peace,* 179–182; Byrnes to Roosevelt, Oct. 15, 1943, Folder 70, Byrnes Papers, and Stephen L. McFarland, "A Peripheral View of the Origins of the Cold War: The Crises in Iran, 1941–1947," *DH,* 4 (Fall 1970), 333–337; Robertson, *Sly and Able,* 466; see also Kuniholm, *Origins of Cold War in Near East,* 188–208.

42. Scheid, "Stalin's Reluctant Bid for Iranian Azerbaijan," 1–4, 8–10, who points out that Bagirov's goal—not Stalin's—was to unite the Soviet and Iranian provinces of Azerbaijan under Moscow's rule, and Yegorova, "Iran Crisis of 1945–1946," 8–12; Murray to Byrnes, Mar. 23 and Mar. 27, 1946, *FR 1946,* VII, 373–375, and Conclusions of a Cabinet Meeting, Mar. 18, 1946, CAB 128/5.

43. Byrnes, *Speaking Frankly,* 123, and Calendar Notes for Jan. 23, 1946, Campbell and Herring (eds.), *Stettinius Diaries,* 447–448, Hare Memorandum for Stettinius, Jan. 23, and Stettinius to Byrnes, Jan. 30, 1946, *FR 1946,* VII, 307–309, 325–326.

44. Yergin, *Shattered Peace,* 186–187, McFarland, "Peripheral View," 345–347, and Kuniholm, *Origins of Cold War in Near East,* 313–314, 390; Kennan to Byrnes, Mar. 4, 1946, *FR 1946,* VII, 337–339; Yegorova, "Iran Crisis of 1945–1946," 18.

45. Byrnes to Kennan, Feb. 22 and Byrnes to Murray, Mar. 3, 1946, *FR 1946,* VII, 334–336; see also *FR 1946,* VII, 350–354; Kuniholm, *Origins of Cold War in Near East,* 314–315.

46. Rossow to Byrnes, Mar. 5, Byrnes to Kennan, Mar. 5, Rossow to Byrnes, Mar. 6 and Mar. 7, 1946, and Wright Memorandum, Aug. 16, 1965, *FR 1946,* VII, 340–348; see also Kuniholm, *Origins of Cold War in Near East,* 320–321.

47. On Russian troop movements, Yergin, *Shattered Peace,* 189; Truman News Conference, Mar. 8, 1946, *PPHST,* II, 146–147; Harbutt, *Iron Curtain,* 220–221, Harriman, *Special Envoy,* 550, and Truman News Conference, Mar. 14, 1946, *PPHST,* II, 155–156; Kuniholm, *Origins of Cold War in Near East,* 320–324; see also *FR 1946,* VII, 348–349, Mar. 14, ibid., 355–360.

48. Murray to Byrnes, Mar. 24, 1946, *FR 1946,* VII, 377–378; Truman News Conference, Mar. 21, 1946, *PPHST,* 164–165, Byrnes to Bevin, Mar. 21, 1946, *FR 1946,* II, 33, and Stettinius Calendar Notes, Mar. 24, 1946, Campbell and Herring (eds.), *Stettinius Diaries,* 460–461.

49. Harbutt, *Iron Curtain,* 236–237, and Murray to Byrnes, Mar. 23, 1946, 373–375; Yegorova, "The Iran Crisis of 1945–1946," 19; Kennan to Byrnes, Mar. 22, 1946, Box 63, Elsey Papers, and Bevin to Byrnes, Mar. 21, 1946, *FR 1946,* VII, 368–369; Murray to Byrnes, Mar. 25, 1946, *FR 1946,* VII, 379–380; Kuniholm, *Origins of Cold War in Near East,* 328.

50. Harbutt, *Iron Curtain,* 239, 243–245; Byrnes Statement, Mar. 26, and Acheson to Kennan, Mar. 29, 1946, *FR 1946,* VII, 382–383, 393–394.

51. Smith to Byrnes, Apr. 4, 1946, *FR 1946,* VI, 732–736, and Walter Bedell Smith, *My Three Years in Moscow* (Philadelphia, 1950), 50–54; Murray to Byrnes, Apr. 4, 1946, *FR 1946,* VII, 405–407.

52. Smith to Byrnes, Apr. 5, 1946, *FR 1946,* VI, 733–735; *New York Times,* April 7, 1946; Truman Statement to American Society of Newspaper Editors, Apr. 18, 1946, *PPHST,* II, 211–212.

53. Allen to Byrnes, May 25, 1946, *FR 1946,* VII, 484–486, and Editor's Note, ibid., 493; Matthews Memorandum of Bidault-Byrnes Conversation, May 1, 1946, *FR 1946,* II, 204.

54. Truman News Conference, May 9, 1946, *PPHST,* II, 243; Allen to Henderson, June 6 and June 10, 1946, *FR 1946,* VII, 495–496, and McFarland, "Peripheral View," 348–349; Kuniholm, *Origins of Cold War in Near East,* 387–391.

55. Hildring Memorandum to Reid, Sept. 26, 1946, State-War-Navy Coordinating Committee to Hildring, Oct. 12, 1946, *FR 1946,* VII, 515–516, 529–532; Ala to Byrnes, Oct. 15, Office of Near Eastern Affairs Memorandum, Oct. 18, and Allen to Byrnes, Nov. 2, 1946, *FR 1946,* VII, 532–533, 535–536, 544–545; Kuniholm, *Origins of Cold War in Near East,* 392.

56. Allen to Byrnes, Dec. 17, and Byrnes to Allen, Dec. 20, 1945, *FR 1946,* VII, 563–564.

57. Smith to Byrnes, Dec. 27, 1946, *FR 1946,* VII, 566–567; Kuniholm, *Origins of Cold War in Near East,* 393–397; James A. Bill, *The Eagle and the Lion: The Tragedy of American-Iranian Relations* (New Haven, 1988), 37; Paterson, *Soviet-American Confrontation,* 182.

58. Byrnes to Allen, Dec. 10, 1946, *FR 1946,* VII, 563; Forrestal cited in Yergin, *Shattered Peace,* 190; Paterson, *Soviet-American Confrontation,* 182; on Truman and the "ultimatum" issue on April 24, 1952, see Editorial Note, *FR 1946,* VII, 348–349, and Kuniholm, *Origins of Cold War in Near East,* 321–322 n. 45, who confirms that Truman did not send an ultimatum (he might have been referring to Byrnes' notes in March 1946) but says that Truman's "erroneous" recollection indicates the "importance of the crisis in his thinking about how Russia should be treated"; on "Trumanism" in 1952, see Truman Note, May 15, 1952, PSF, Box 333, Truman Papers.

59. Diary entry for Jan. 16, 1946, Lilienthal, *Journals,* II: *Atomic Energy Years,* 10–11; Hewlett and Anderson, *The New World,* 532–533; Holloway, *Stalin and the Bomb,* 161.

60. Herken, *Winning Weapon,* 153–158, Larry G. Gerber, "The Baruch Plan and the Origins of the Cold War," *DH,* 6 (Winter 1982), 71–72; Acheson quoted in Hewlett and Anderson, *The New World,* 548; diary entries for Mar. 9 and Mar. 16, 1946, Lilienthal, *Atomic Energy Years,* 27–30.

61. Bundy, *Danger and Survival,* 159–161; diary entries for Feb. 25 and Mar. 9, 1946, Lilienthal, *Atomic Energy Years,* 23–24, 27–28, and Ross Memorandum [conversation with Acheson], Nov. 2, 1946, *FR 1946,* I, 983–988.

62. Herken, *Winning Weapon,* 130, and *New York Times,* Feb. 17, 1946; Truman Special Message to Congress, Oct. 3, 1945, *PPHST,* I, 362–366, Hewlett and Anderson, *The New World,* 433–438, and Donovan, *Conflict and Crisis,* 133–134.

63. Vandenberg (ed.), *Vandenberg Papers,* 254–261, and Herken, *Winning Weapon,* 133–136.

64. Attlee to Truman, Apr. 16, Byrnes Memorandum, Apr. 18, and Truman to Attlee, Apr. 20, 1946, *FR 1946,* I, 1231–1232, 1232–1233, 1233–1235; Acheson to Truman, May 6, and Counselor Canadian Embassy to Acheson, Apr. 29, and Truman to Attlee, Dec. 28, 1946, ibid., 1244, 1259; Gormly, "The Washington Declaration," *DH* (Spring 1984), 142–143.

65. Truman, *Years of Trial and Hope,* 6–8, 10; Truman Note, Mar. 15, 1946, Ferrell (ed.), *Off the Record,* 87.

66. Acheson, *Present at the Creation,* 154, entries for Mar. 24 and Apr. 20, 1946, Lilienthal, *Atomic Energy Years,* 30–33, 39–40; Baruch to Byrnes, Mar. 13, 1946, *FR 1946,* I, 757–758.

67. Herken, *Winning Weapon,* 158–160 (Baruch-Truman quote on p. 160), Truman, *Years of Trial and Hope,* 8–10, and Truman News Conference, Mar. 28, 1946, *PPHST,* II, 174; Byrnes quoted in diary entry for June 13, 1946, Lilienthal, *Atomic Energy Years,* 59.

68. Baruch Memorandum for Truman, June 6, 1946, *FR 1946,* I, 838–840, and Baruch Memorandum, June 1, 1946, cited in Lloyd C. Gardner, *Architects of Illusions: Men and Ideas in American Foreign Policy, 1941–1949* (Chicago, 1970), 194; "swift and sure punishment" in Byrnes, *Speaking Frankly,* 271; diary entries for May 7, May 17, and May 19, 1946, Lilienthal, *Atomic Energy Years,* 42–43, 49–53; "winning weapons" in *New York Times,* June 15, 1946; see also Gerber, "The Baruch Plan," 70–73; on military view, Leahy to Baruch and Chester Nimitz (CNO) to Baruch, June 11, and Eisenhower to Baruch, June 14, 1946, *FR 1946,* I, 851–856, and Leffler, *Preponderance of Power,* 115–116.

69. Connelly Cabinet Notes, Mar. 22, 1946, Connelly Papers; diary entry for Dec. 29, 1946, Lilienthal, *Atomic Energy Years,* 125.

70. Baruch Memorandum for Truman June 6, and Truman Memorandum for Baruch, June 7, 1946, *FR 1946,* I, 838–840, 846–851; Truman quoted on Stimson in Gardner, *Architects of Illusion,* 195.

71. *New York Times,* June 15, 1946, and Hewlett and Anderson, *The New World,* 576–579.

72. *New York Times,* June 20, 1946, and Holloway, *Stalin and the Bomb,* 162.

73. Hewlett and Anderson, *The New World,* 575–576, Leffler, *Preponderance of Power,* 115–116, and Holloway, *Stalin and the Bomb,* 162–163.

74. Diary entry for June 19, 1946, Vandenberg (ed.), *Vandenberg Papers,* 291; Holloway, *Stalin and the Bomb,* 163, and Herken, *Winning Weapon,* 175–176.

75. Baruch to Truman, July 2, and Truman to Baruch, July 10, 1946, PSF, Box 113, Truman Papers; Herken, *Winning Weapon,* 175.

76. Hewlett and Anderson, *The New World,* 590–591; Notes on Staff Conference of U.S. Delegation to AEC, and Notes on a Conference between Members of U.S. and Canadian Delegations to UNAEC, Aug. 1, 1946, *FR 1946,* I, 869–873.

77. Diary entry for Dec. 14, 1945, J. Blum (ed.), *Price of Vision,* 530, Herken, *Winning Weapon,* 196–197, and David Alan Rosenberg, "American Atomic Strategy and the Hydrogen Bomb Decision," *JAH,* 66 (June 1979), 63–66; Groves Memorandum to Hancock, Aug. 16, Johnson to Byrnes (Gromyko Statement), Aug. 29, and Notes of Meeting of U.S. Delegation to UNAEC, Sept. 10, 1946, *FR 1946,* I, 877–888, 892–893, 906–911.

78. Baruch Memorandum for Truman, Sept. 17, 1946, *FR 1946,* I, 919–929; Wallace to Truman, July 23, 1946, Box 18, Clifford Papers, and Hancock Memorandum, Sept. 19, 1946, *FR 1946,* I, 932–935; *New York Times,* Sept. 21, 1946.

79. Hewlett and Anderson, *The New World,* 606–608; Holloway, *Stalin and the Bomb,* 164–165.

80. Herken, *Winning Weapon,* 189–190; Baruch to Byrnes, Nov. 4, Byrnes to Baruch, Nov. 5, and Acheson to Baruch, Nov. 7, 1946, *FR 1946,* I, 900–992, 995–996, 1000; Ross memorandum [Conversation with Acheson], Nov. 2, and Austin Memorandum, Nov. 26, 1946, ibid., 983–988, 1053–1054; diary entry for Dec. 22, 1946, Lilienthal, *Atomic Energy Years,* 123.

81. Herken, *Winning Weapon,* 191, Hewlett and Anderson, *The New World,* 617–618; in 1947 the Soviets still sought to ban atomic weapons but also proposed an international

commission to inspect atomic facilities engaged in mining materials and producing atomic power, but the facilities would not pass to international control nor would research facilities be inspected; this was too little, too late; see Holloway, *Stalin and the Bomb,* 165.

82. Holloway, *Stalin and the Bomb,* 166–167; Dean Rusk, as told to Richard Rusk, *As I Saw It: Dean Rusk As Told to Richard Rusk* (New York, 1990), 139.

83. Ickes quoted in Gardner, *Architects of Illusion,* 200; Wallace to Truman, July 23, 1946, Box 18, Clifford Papers.

Chapter 7. The Die Is Cast

1. Truman Conference with American Society of Newspaper Editors, Apr. 18, and Truman News Conference, May 9, 1946, *PPHST,* II, 211–212, 243; diary entry for Sept. 18, 1946, J. Blum (ed.), *Price of Vision,* 619, Truman to John Garner, Sept. 21, 1946, PSF, Box 187, Truman Papers, and entry for Sept. 10, 1946, Davies Diary, Box 25, Davies Papers.

2. Smith to Byrnes, Apr. 5, 1946, *FR 1946,* VI, 736, Matthews Memorandum, May 1, 1946, *FR 1946,* II, 204, and Truman cited in McCoy, *Truman Presidency,* 58.

3. Yergin, *Shattered Peace,* 193–200, 219–220.

4. Truman Remarks on Presenting Medal of Honor, Mar. 27, and Truman Address on Army Day, Apr. 6, 1946, *PPHST,* II, 170–171, 185–190.

5. Hoover-Truman Conversation, May 16, 1946, and Department of State, *Union of Soviet Socialist Republics, Policy and Information Statement,* May 15, 1946, cited in McCoy, *Truman Presidency,* 82; diary entry for Sept. 26, 1946, Ferrell (ed.), *Off the Record,* 98–99.

6. Felix Belair *(New York Times),* as recorded in diary entry for June 25, 1946, J. Blum (ed.), *Price of Victory,* 582, Inverchapel to Foreign Office, Aug. 18 and Aug. 26, 1946, F.O. 371/51609 and 371/51610; Truman to "Mamma and Mary," Nov. 11, 1946, cited in M. Truman, *Truman,* 322–323.

7. Dunn to Matthews, Feb. 27, and Dunn to Byrnes, Mar. 13, 1946, *FR 1946,* II, 16–19, 28–29.

8. Eduard Mark, "American Policy toward Eastern Europe," *JAH,* 68 (Sept. 1981), 330, Herbert Feis, *From Trust to Terror: The Onset of the Cold War, 1945–1950* (New York, 1970), 121–122, and Connelly Cabinet Notes, Apr. 19, 1946, Connelly Papers.

9. Diary entries for Apr. 28 and Apr. 30, 1946, Vandenberg (ed.), *Vandenberg Papers,* 266–267, 268–269; Truman used "right attitude" to describe Ambassador Smith's firm view toward Russia, Truman to Wallace, Mar. 20, 1946, PSF, Box 187, Truman Papers.

10. On the CFM meeting, see Ward, *Threat of Peace,* 90–102, Curry, *Byrnes,* 221–222, and Bullock, *Bevin,* 259–264; diary entry for May 6, 1946, Vandenberg (ed.), *Vandenberg Papers,* 276–277; on Byrnes-Molotov exchange, Bohlen Memorandum, Apr. 28, 1946, *FR 1946,* II, 146–147.

11. Pierson Dixon, *Double Diploma: The Life of Sir Pierson Dixon* (London, 1968), 212–213.

12. Diary entry for May 28, 1946, Vandenberg (ed.), *Vandenberg Papers,* 285–286; Curry, *Byrnes,* 222–225, and Bevin to Byrnes, May 29, 1946, *FR 1946,* II, 452–454.

13. On the CFM meeting see Ward, *Threat of Peace,* 103–126, Curry, *Byrnes,* 225–238, and Bullock, *Bevin,* 281–283; diary entry for May 15, 1946, Vandenberg (ed.), *Vandenberg Papers,* 281.

14. Offner, "Research on German-American Relations," in Trommler and McVeigh (eds.), *America and the Germans,* II, 176–177; on "Bolsheviki land-grab," Truman diary entry for July 25, 1945, Ferrell (ed.), *Off the Record,* 55–56.

15. Price to Truman, Nov. 9, Truman to Byrnes, Nov. 21, and Byrnes to Truman [n.d.], 1945, PSF, Box 179, Truman Papers; Patterson to Truman, Nov. 27, 1945, OF 198, Box 687,

Truman Papers; Truman to Secretaries of State, War, and Navy, Nov. 28, 1945, *PPHST,* I, 530–534; *New York Times,* Dec. 7, 1945, and Halifax to Foreign Office, Dec. 9, 1945, F.O. 371/44539.

16. On the Patterson-McCloy-Murphy-Clay reports and disputes with the French, see John Gimbel, "On Implementation of the Potsdam Agreement: An Essay on U.S. Postwar Policy," *PSQ,* 87 (June 1972), 250–253, and John Gimbel, *The American Occupation of Germany: Politics and the Military, 1945–1949* (Stanford, 1968), 56–57; see also Patterson to Truman, June 11, 1946, PSF, Box 179, Truman Papers, and Murphy to Byrnes, Feb. 24, Caffery to Byrnes, Mar. 1, and Murphy to Byrnes, Apr. 4, 1946, *FR 1946,* V, 506–507, 509–511, 536–537; on the steel accord, Byrnes to Clay, Jan. 28, and Clay to Byrnes, Jan. 31, 1946, *FR 1946,* V, 493–494, 494–496; on level of industry, Yergin, *Shattered Peace,* 226, and Conclusions of a Meeting of the Cabinet, Mar. 18, 1946, CAB 128/5.

17. Naimark, *Russians in Germany,* 141–204, 257–258, 317–321, and 351–352; see also Kennedy-Pipe, *Stalin's Cold War,* 93–101, and Zubok and Pleshakov, *Inside Kremlin's Cold War,* 47–52.

18. Eisenberg, *Drawing the Line,* 211–214, and J. Smith, *Clay,* 366–369.

19. Murphy to Byrnes, Mar. 29, and Byrnes to Murphy, Apr. 9, 1946, *FR 1946,* V, 714–715, 717; Naimark, *Russians in Germany,* 329, and Eisenberg, *Drawing the Line,* 215–216.

20. Naimark, *Russians in Germany,* 166–167.

21. Byrnes to Clay, Jan. 28, and Murphy (for Clay) to Byrnes, Jan. 31, 1946, *FR 1946,* II, 494–496; Clay quoted in Eisenberg, *Drawing the Line,* 210; Conclusions of a Meeting of the Cabinet, Mar. 18, 1946, CAB 128/5.

22. Eisenberg, *Drawing the Line,* 212, and J. Smith, *Clay,* 350–354; Gimbel, *American Occupation,* 56–61, and Symington Memorandum (interviews with General Clay, July 25, July 29, and July 30, 1946), PSF, Box 157, Truman Papers.

23. Kennan to Byrnes, Mar. 6, and Smith to Byrnes, Apr. 2, 1946, *FR 1946,* V, 516–520, 535–536.

24. Murphy to H. Freeman Matthews, Apr. 2, 1946, cited in Eisenberg, *Drawing the Line,* 225; see Messer, *Byrnes,* 204–205; Kennan to Offie, May 10, 1946, *FR 1946,* V, 555–556 (H. Carmel Offie worked in Murphy's office in Berlin); Eisenberg, op. cit., 226–228.

25. Ward, *Threat of Peace,* 87; entry for Apr. 19, 1946, Connelly Cabinet Notes, Connelly Papers; Matthews Memorandum, May 1, 1946, *FR 1946,* II, 203–206.

26. Vandenberg Speech, Jan. 10, 1945, Vandenberg (ed.), *Vandenberg Papers,* 132–138; Byrnes, *Speaking Frankly,* 171–174, and Molotov to Byrnes, Apr. 20, 1946, *FR 1946,* II, 83 (there is no record of a Byrnes-Stalin talk on this subject).

27. Bohlen Memorandum, Apr. 28, U.S. Delegation Records, Apr. 29 and May 15, 1946, *FR 1946,* II, 146–147, 165–173, 393–399; text of proposed treaty in ibid., 190–193.

28. Byrnes cited in Yergin, *Shattered Peace,* 226; French and British views in Memorandum of French Delegation at CFM, Apr. 25, and U.S. Delegation Record, May 15, 1946, *FR 1946,* II, 109–112, and Bevin Memorandum, Apr. 15, 1946, and Conclusions of a Cabinet Meeting, Apr. 17 and May 3, 1946, CAB 128/5.

29. Ward, *Threat of Peace,* 91–92, 96–97.

30. Diary entry for Apr. 30, 1946, Vandenberg (ed.), *Vandenberg Papers,* 268–269, and Transcript of Byrnes-Truman Conversation, May 2, 1946, cited in Ward, *Threat of Peace,* 95; Yergin, *Shattered Peace,* 224; U.S. Delegation Record, May 16, 1946, *FR 1946,* II, 433–434; *New York Times,* May 21, 1946.

31. Diary entry for May 28, 1946, Vandenberg (ed.), *Vandenberg Papers,* 285–286; the senator never revealed the name of the diplomat.

32. Ward, *Threat of Peace,* 110–114.

33. U.S. Delegation Record, July 9 and July 10, 1946, *FR 1946,* II, 842–847, 869–873.

34. U.S. Delegation Record, July 9 and July 10, 1946, *FR 1946,* II, 847–850, 869–873;

Byrnes to Truman, July 11, 1946, PSF, Box 179, Truman Papers, cited in Eisenberg, *Drawing the Line*, 238; Byrnes, *All in One Lifetime*, 366.

35. U.S. Delegation Record, July 11, 1946, *FR 1946*, II, 897–898; Byrnes, *Speaking Frankly*, 194.

36. *New York Times*, July 16, 1946; Inverchapel to Foreign Office, July 24 and July 29, 1946, F.O. 371/51607; on the KPD-SPD merger, see for example, Murphy to Byrnes, Mar. 20, and Byrnes to Murphy, Apr. 9, 1946, *FR 1946*, V, 710–712, 717; on reparations, Yergin, *Shattered Peace*, 227–228.

37. Leffler, "Struggle for Germany," 30–32; Conclusions of a Meeting of the Cabinet, July 25, 1946, CAB 128/5, and Eisenberg, *Drawing the Line*, 241.

38. J. Smith, *Clay*, 379–381.

39. J. Smith, *Clay*, 382–385, and Eisenberg, *Drawing the Line*, 244–245.

40. Cf. Curry, *Byrnes*, 248–252, and Gimbel, "On Implementation of Potsdam," 246–247, 259–260; Byrnes, *Speaking Frankly*, 187–188.

41. *Department of State Bulletin*, 15 (Sept. 15, 1946), 496–501, and Byrnes, *Speaking Frankly*, 188–192; Eisenberg, *Drawing the Line*, 245–248; Byrnes to Truman, Sept. 2, 1946, PSF, Box 157, Truman Papers.

42. Charles M. Maier, "The Making of 'Pax Americana': Formative Moments of United States Ascendancy," in R. Ahmann et al. (eds.), *The Quest for Stability: Problems of West European Security, 1918–1957* (New York, 1993), cited in Leffler, *Preponderance of Power*, 120.

43. Diary entry for Sept. 10, 1945, J. Blum (ed.), *Price of Vision*, 612–613; Truman cited in entry for Sept. 10, 1946, Davies Diary, Box 22, Davies Papers; on general approval of Byrnes speech, see Ward, *Threat of Peace*, 140–141, and J. Smith, *Clay*, 387; on continued French opposition, Matthews Memorandum, Sept. 24, 1946, *FR 1946*, V, 609–610.

44. Inverchapel to Foreign Office, Sept. 14, 1946, F.O. 371/51610; Eisenberg, *Drawing the Line*, 249–250.

45. Murphy to Byrnes, Oct. 25, 1946, *FR 1946*, V, 631–633.

46. Eisenberg, *Drawing the Line*, 254–255, and J. Smith, *Clay*, 394.

47. Eisenberg, *Drawing the Line*, 256–261; on the Turkish crisis, Wallace-Byrnes dispute, and Russian Report, see below.

48. Resis (ed.), *Molotov Remembers*, 73–74; Orekhov to Acheson, Aug. 7, 1946, *FR 1946*, VII, 823–829.

49. Soviet ambassador quoted in Wilson to Byrnes, Feb. 19, 1946, and Wilson to Byrnes, Mar. 16 and Mar. 23, 1946, *FR 1946*, II, 815–816, 818–820, 820–821; Soviet motives discussed in De Luca, "Soviet-American Politics and the Straits," 521–523; British Joint Intelligence Subcommittee assessment in Mark, " War Scare of 1946," 390–391, 395; Mark adds that after attending a meeting of European Communist leaders in Prague in February, Niko Zacharaidis, head of the Greek Communist Party (KKE), returned in May to tell his comrades that Greece and Turkey were yet to be delivered from "social slavery."

50. Mark, "War Scare of 1946," 398; Wilson to Acheson, Aug. 8, and Durbrow to Byrnes, Aug. 12, 1946, *FR 1946*, VII, 829–830, 836 (on Stalin's earlier assurance, Smith to Byrnes, Mar. 5, 1946, *FR 1946*, VI, 736); on Henderson, Leffler, "Strategy, Diplomacy, and Cold War," 810; on the bases, see for example, Conclusions of a Meeting of the Cabinet, Nov. 1, 1945, CAB 128/3, Halifax to Bevin, Nov. 8, Bevin to Halifax, Nov. 15 and Nov. 27, and Byrnes to Bevin, Dec. 10, 1945, F.O. 800/512, and Conclusions of a Meeting of the Cabinet, Mar. 25, May 3, and May 19, 1946, CAB 128/5; the British worried that U.S. pressure for Icelandic bases would lead to Russian claims on Norway or Denmark.

51. Leffler, "U.S., Turkey, and NATO," 808–809, 811, 813.

52. Schnabel, *History of the JCS*, I, 158–159, Mark, "War Scare of 1946," 398, and Leffler, *Preponderance of Power*, 112–113, 124–125.

53. Acheson quoted in Larson, *Origins of Containment*, 282; on Acheson's new posture,

see Robert L. Beisner, "Patterns of Peril: Dean Acheson Joins the Cold War, 1945–1946," *DH*, 20 (Summer 1996), 343–346.

54. On the White House meeting, Acheson to Byrnes, Aug. 15, 1946, *FR 1946*, VII, 840–842, entry for Aug. 15, 1946, Millis (ed.), *Forrestal Diaries*, 192, Acheson, *Present at the Creation*, 196–197, and Joseph Marion Jones, *The Fifteen Weeks: February 21–June 5, 1947* (New York, 1955), 63–64; Peter Lyon, *Eisenhower: Portrait of a Hero* (Boston, 1974), says that Eisenhower, often cited as the JCS official who asked Truman the question, was not at the meeting; Byrnes, from Paris, "heartily" concurred in the decision, Acheson to Truman, Aug. 16, 1946, *FR 1946*, VII, 843.

55. Acheson to Wilson, Aug. 16 and Aug. 17, and Acheson to Orekhov, Aug. 19, 1946, *FR 1946*, VII, 843–844, 846, 847–848; Patterson to Acheson, Aug. 23, and Joint Chiefs of Staff Memorandum, Aug. 28, 1946, ibid., 856–858.

56. Michael B. Petrovich, "The View from Yugoslavia," in Thomas T. Hammond (ed.), *Witnesses to the Origins of the Cold War* (Seattle and London, 1982), 41–48; Byrnes to Acheson, Aug. 22, Acheson to Byrnes, Aug. 23, Byrnes to Acheson, Aug. 28, and Acheson to Byrnes, Aug. 29, 1946, *FR 1946*, VI, 927–928, 930, 931–933; Acheson, *Present at the Creation*, 195–196; Patterson to Acheson, Sept. 20, 1946, ibid., 955–956; Eisenhower cited in Yergin, *Shattered Peace*, 235.

57. Halsey quoted in Paterson, *Soviet-American Confrontation*, 187; Mark, "War Scare of 1946," 402–403.

58. Bursley to Byrnes, Sept. 26, Sept. 27, and Sept. 30, 1946, *FR 1946*, VII, 860–868; Acheson to Truman and Byrnes to Smith, Oct. 8, and Wilson to Byrnes, Oct. 15, 1946, ibid., 873–874, 874–875, 878–894; Mark, "War Scare of 1946," 409–410.

59. Byrnes-Bevin talk, Kuniholm, *Origins of Cold War in Near East*, 368–369, and Byrnes to Acheson, Oct. 5, 1946, *FR 1946*, VII, 245 n. 15; Division of Near Eastern and African Affairs Memoranda (on Greece and Turkey), Oct. 21, 1946, *FR 1946*, VII, 240–245, 894–897; entry for Sept. 30, 1946, Millis (ed.), *Forrestal Diaries*, 211, and Kuniholm, op. cit., 373–374.

60. Mark, "War Scare of 1946," 408, 412–413; on Maclean and the "Magnificent Five," see Haynes and Klehr, *Venona*, 51–56; the other four spies were H. R. "Kim" Philby, a senior British intelligence officer; Guy Burgess, an intelligence officer and diplomat; John Cairncross, a treasury official who worked in military and intelligence matters; and Anthony Blunt, a Cambridge University don and art expert who recruited potential spies from among his students.

61. Leffler, *Preponderance of Power*, 124; Acheson Memorandum, Aug. 20, 1946, *FR 1946*, VII, 849–850; Mark, "War Scare of 1946," 405–406.

62. Truman to John Garner, Sept. 21, 1946, PSF, Box 187, Truman Papers.

63. Acheson Memorandum, Apr. 12, 1949, *FR 1949*, VI, 1647–1653.

64. Truman Memorandum, Sept. 19, 1946, PSF, Box 333, Truman Papers, and "cat bastard" cited in Yergin, *Shattered Peace*, 246; diary entry for July 24, 1946, J. Blum (ed.), *Price of Vision*, 602–603.

65. Divine, *Second Chance*, 78–81, J. Blum, *Politics and American Culture*, 281–285, and diary entry for Oct. 15, 1945, J. Blum (ed.), *Price of Vision*, 490; diary entry for Oct. 26, 1945, J. Blum (ed.), op. cit., 504; diary entries for May 8 and Oct. 23, 1945, and Mar. 21, 1946, J. Blum (ed.), op. cit., 445, 497, 565–566; entry for Apr. 19, 1946, Millis (ed.), *Forrestal Diaries*, 154–155, and M. Truman, *Truman*, 314; Byrnes thought the Iceland base "the most strategic base on the North Atlantic from either a military or trade viewpoint," diary entry for Apr. 25, 1946, Vandenberg (ed.), *Vandenberg Papers*, 266.

66. Diary entries for Mar. 5, Mar. 13, and Mar. 15, 1946, J. Blum (ed.), *Price of Vision*, 556–561, 562–565; Wallace to Truman, Mar. 14 and Mar. 21, 1946, PSF, Box 187, Truman Papers.

67. Wallace to Truman, July 23, 1946, PSF, Box 156, Truman Papers; this was the letter whose release in September brought Baruch's resignation threat.

68. Elsey Notes, July 24 and July 27, 1946, Box 63, Elsey Papers, Truman to Wallace, Aug. 8, 1946, Box 18, Clifford Papers, and diary entry for Sept. 17, 1946, Ferrell (ed.), *Off the Record*, 94–95.

69. Diary entry for Sept. 12, 1946, J. Blum (ed.), *Price of Vision*, 612–613, and Yergin, *Shattered Peace*, 251; slightly different versions of the speech appear in J. Blum (ed.), *Price of Vision*, 661–669, and Richard J. Walton, *Henry Wallace, Harry Truman, and the Cold War* (New York, 1976), 101–108.

70. Truman Memorandum, Sept. 16, 1946, PSF, Box 333, Truman Papers, cited in Robert Griffith, "Harry S. Truman and the Burden of Modernity," in *Reviews in American History*, 14 (Sept. 1981), 298, diary entry for Sept. 17, 1946, Ferrell (ed.), *Off the Record*, 94–95, Charles G. Ross Memorandum, Sept. 23, 1946, PSF, Box 322, Truman Papers, and Truman, *Year of Decisions*, 557.

71. Ross Memoranda, Sept. 20 and Sept. 21, 1946, PSF, Box 156, Truman Papers, provide a good account of events, especially Truman's views and words; Truman News Conference, Sept. 12, 1946, *PPHST*, II, 428, and Sullivan Memorandum, Sept. 12, 1946, Millis (ed.), *Forrestal Diaries*, 208–209; Clayton to Byrnes, Sept. 14, 1946, Folder 619, Byrnes Papers.

72. Vandenberg Statement in Vandenberg (ed.), *Vandenberg Papers*, 300–301, Truman Statement, Sept. 14, 1946, *PPHST*, II, 426–427, Wallace Statement, Sept. 16, 1946, J. Blum (ed.), *Price of Vision*, 615, 617 (which indicates the State Department was the source of the "leak"), Elsey Memorandum, Sept. 21, 1946, Box 105, Elsey Papers, and Rose Memorandum, Sept. 21, 1946, PSF, Box 322, Truman Papers; on resignations, see Byrnes to Truman and Byrnes to Donald Russell, Sept. 18, 1946, Folder 619, Byrnes Papers, and Hancock Memorandum, Sept. 1946, *FR 1946*, I, 932–935; on Patterson and Forrestal, entry for Sept. 18, 1946, Ayers Diary, Box 25, Ayers Papers, and Donovan, *Conflict and Crisis*, 225; diary entry for Sept. 17, 1946, Ferrell (ed.), *Off the Record*, and Truman to Martha Truman, Sept. 18, 1946, M. Truman, *Truman*, 317.

73. Account of the meeting is in Ross Memorandum, Sept. 20, 1946, PSF, Box 156, Truman Papers, and diary entry for Sept. 18, 1946, J. Blum (ed.), *Price of Vision*, 617–626.

74. Curry, *Byrnes*, 268–271.

75. Truman Memorandum, Sept. 19, 1946, PSF, Box 333, Truman Papers; Truman's letter and Wallace resignation, Ross Memorandum, Sept. 20, 1946, PSF, Box 156, Truman Papers, entry for Sept. 20, 1946, Ayers Diary, Box 25, Ayers Papers, Wallace to Truman, Sept. 20, 1946 (and Oral History recollection for "low level"), J. Blum (ed.), *Price of Vision*, 628–629, and Truman comment in Ross Memorandum, Sept. 20, 1946, PSF, Box 156, Truman Papers; Clark Clifford with Richard Holbrooke, *Counsel to the President: A Memoir* (New York, 1991), 121, says that Clifford's telephone call prompted return of the letter.

76. Elsey Memorandum, Sept. 17, 1946, Box 105, Elsey Papers; at the end of the Wallace matter a tired Truman said he intended to become a "hermit" for a while; but privately he also lambasted Wallace as "a real Commy and a dangerous man" and then said that because of his firing the "crackpots are having conniption fits. I'm glad they are. It convinces me I'm right"; see diary entry for Sept. 21, 1946, Ross Diary, PSF, Box 322, Truman Papers, Truman to Bess Truman, Sept. 20, 1946, Ferrell (ed.), *Dear Bess*, 538–539, and Truman to Mama and Mary, Sept. 21, 1946, Truman *Year of Decisions*, 560; seven months later, when Wallace would criticize Greek-Turkish aid, Truman would write that "he seems to have obtained his ideas of loyalty, both personal and political, from his friends in Moscow . . .," Truman to Congressman John Folger, Apr. 19, 1947, PSF, Box 141, Truman Papers.

77. Diary entries for Feb. 21, and Mar. 15, 1946, Berle (ed.), *Navigating the Rapids*, 569–570, 573.

78. Elsey Notes, July 12, July 17, July 18, 1946, Box 63, Elsey Papers.

79. CMC "first notes" (Russia Project), Box 63, Elsey Papers; Clifford to Leahy [and others], July 18, 1946, Box 63, Elsey Papers; JCS discussion [excerpts], July 23, and JCS Memorandum to Clifford, July 26, Pauley to Truman and Pauley to Clifford, July 24, Forrestal and Nimitz to Truman, July 25, and Patterson to Truman, July 27, 1946, Box 6, Clifford Papers.

80. Acheson to Clifford, Aug. 6, 1946, Box 15, Clifford Papers; Leahy to Clifford [n.d.], Box 63, Elsey Papers.

81. Elsey Notes [n.d.], Box 63, Elsey Papers, and Clifford to Truman, Sept. [24], 1946 and attached memorandum "American Relations with the Soviet Union," Box 15, Clifford Papers; the "Report" is also in Arthur Krock, *Memoirs: Sixty Years on the Firing Line* (New York, 1968), Appendix A, 418–482.

82. Leffler, *Preponderance of Power*, 130–138.

83. Leahy to Clifford, Sept. 21, 1946, Box 15, Clifford Papers.

84. Truman reaction to report in Richard M. Freeland, *The Truman Doctrine and the Origins of McCarthyism: Foreign Policy, Domestic Politics, and Internal Security, 1946–1948* (New York, 1972), 67, and Clifford, *Counsel to the President*, 123–124; on Truman and Peter I's "will," see J. Garry Clifford, "President Truman and Peter the Great's Will," *DH,* 4 (Fall 1980), 374–380, and Orest Subtelny, "'Peter I's Testament': A Reassessment," *Slavic Review,* 33 (Dec. 1974), 663–674.

85. Melvyn P. Leffler, "Commentary on the 'Novikov Telegram,'" *DH,* 15 (Fall 1991), 527–537.

86. See for example, "Commentary on Novikov Telegram," by Melvyn Leffler, ibid., 548–553.

87. Ward, *Threat of Peace,* 129–132, 136; Byrnes' "jury room" cited in Yergin, *Shattered Peace,* 232–233; on Czech issue, Paterson, *Soviet-American Confrontation,* 122–123.

88. Ward, *Threat of Peace,* 147–151; Truman Address, Oct. 23, 1946, *PPHST,* I, 457–463.

89. Byrnes, *Speaking Frankly,* 152–154, Bohlen, *Witness to History,* 244–256, and Bohlen Memoranda, Nov. 25 and Dec. 6, 1946, *FR 1946,* II, 1264–1269, 1437–1441.

90. Walter Lippmann, "A Year of Peacemaking," *Atlantic Monthly,* 30 (Dec. 1946), 36–38, and Yergin, *Shattered Peace,* 259–261; Ward, *Threat of Peace,* 178–179.

91. Byrnes to Truman, Apr. 16, 1946, Folder 618, Byrnes Papers, and Ward, *Threat of Peace,* 169–170; on Marshall's appointment, Donovan, *Conflict and Crisis,* 193.

92. Truman quoted in Daniels, *Man of Independence,* 316; Truman to Byrnes, Jan. 27, and Byrnes to Truman, Jan. 31, 1947, PSF, Box 159, Truman Papers; *Time,* 49 (Jan. 6, 1947), 25–27; see also Messer, *End of an Alliance,* 215–216.

93. Truman longhand notes, cited in McCoy, *Truman Presidency,* 58; draft speech, Oct. 1946 (undelivered), Ferrell (ed.), *Off the Record,* 100–102.

94. On the elections, Donovan, *Conflict and Crisis,* 230–238, and Alonzo L. Hamby, *Beyond the New Deal: Harry S. Truman and American Liberalism* (New York, 1973), 136–138, and *New York Times,* Nov. 7, 1946; on Fulbright, see Randall B. Woods, *Fulbright: A Biography* (Cambridge, 1995), 125–127, and Truman News Conference, Nov. 11, 1946, *PPHST,* II, 479 (Truman's public response was "no comment").

Chapter 8. In Behalf of Europe

1. Truman quoted in J. Jones, *Fifteen Weeks,* 233; entry for Apr. 4, 1952, Ayers Diary, Box 25, Ayers Papers, and Truman, *Years of Trial and Hope,* 106.

2. Diary entry for Jan. 1, 1947, Ferrell (ed.), *Off the Record,* 106–107, and Truman Annual Message . . . on the State of the Union, Jan. 6, 1947, *PPHST,* III, 1–2; Gaddis, *U.S. and Origins of Cold War,* 344–345.

3. Hathaway, *Ambiguous Partnership,* 295–298.

4. Yergin, *Shattered Peace,* 275; Inverchapel to Foreign Office, Jan. 6 and Feb. 8, 1947, F.O. 371/61053, and Balfour to Butler, Jan. 31, 1947, F.O. 371/61045.

5. Mark A. Stoler, *George C. Marshall: Soldier-Statesman of the American Century* (Boston, 1989), 1–48, and Forrest C. Pogue, *George C. Marshall: Organizer of Victory, 1943–1945* (New York, 1973), 1; Truman News Conference, Nov. 20, 1945, *PPHST,* III, 491, and entry for Nov. 28, 1945, Ayers Diary, Box 25, Ayers Papers.

6. Truman News Conference, Jan. 23, 1947; *PPHST,* III, 102; Forrest C. Pogue, *George C. Marshall: Statesman, 1945–1959* (New York, 1987), 145–148, and Yergin, *Shattered Peace,* 262–264; Truman Note, Feb. 18, 1947, Ferrell (ed.), *Off the Record,* 109.

7. Gaddis, *U.S. and Origins of Cold War,* 345, and J. Jones, *Fifteen Weeks,* 90–91.

8. Demetrios Caraley, *The Politics of Military Unification: A Study of Conflict and the Policy Process* (New York, 1966), 1–14.

9. Caraley, *Politics of Military Unification,* 16–20; the five wartime members of the JCS were Admiral Leahy; General Marshall, chief of staff of the Army; Admiral Harold R. Stark, chief of naval operations; Admiral Ernest J. King, chief of the U.S. fleet; and General Henry H. "Hap" Arnold, chief of the Army Air Force.

10. Caraley, *Politics of Military Unification,* 23–38.

11. Entries for June 13 and July 30, 1945, Millis (ed.), *Forrestal Diaries,* 62–63, 88–89, 115; Truman, *Years of Trial and Hope,* 47–48.

12. Caraley, *Politics of Military Unification,* 46–48.

13. Michael J. Hogan, *A Cross of Iron: Harry S. Truman and the Origins of the National Security State, 1945–1954* (Cambridge, 1998), 31–32, and Hoopes and Brinkley, *Driven Patriot,* 319–321; Aide-Mémoire of Forrestal-Truman Conversation, June 13, and entry for July 30, 1945, Millis (ed.), *Forrestal Diaries,* 62–63, 88–89; Forrestal to Eberstadt, June 19, 1945, Millis (ed.), op. cit., 63.

14. Caraley, *Politics of Military Unification,* 40–44, and Hoopes and Brinkley, *Driven Patriot,* 322; Alfred D. Sander, "Truman and the National Security Council, 1945–1947," *JAH,* 59 (Sept. 1972), 369–372, Yergin, *Shattered Peace,* 213–215, and Hogan, *Cross of Iron,* 32–37.

15. Sander, "Truman and NSC," 373–375, Clifford, *Counsel to the President,* 148–149, Hogan, *Cross of Iron,* 49–50, and Truman, *Years of Trial and Hope,* 48–49, and entry for Nov. 21, 1945, Millis (ed.), *Forrestal Diaries,* 115–116.

16. Truman Special Message to the Congress Recommending a Department of National Defense, Dec. 19, 1945, *PPHST,* I, 546–560; Truman, *Years of Trial and Hope,* 48–50.

17. Clifford, *Counsel to the President,* 149, Caraley, *Politics of Military Unification,* 55–56, and Hogan, *Cross of Iron,* 47–52; entries for Mar. 18 and May 13, 1946, Millis (ed.), *Forrestal Diaries,* 148–149, 160–162.

18. Truman Letter to Chairmen of Congressional Committee on Military and Naval Affairs, and Truman Letter to Forrestal and Patterson, June 15, 1946, *PPHST,* II, 303–307; Clifford, *Counsel to the President,* 150–151; Memorandum of MacArthur-Symington Conversation, July 8, 1946, PSF, Box 157, Truman Papers (Stuart Symington was assistant secretary for Air).

19. Hogan, *Cross of Iron,* 53–55, Hoopes and Brinkley, *Driven Patriot,* 341–343, and Sander, "Truman and NSC," 374–378; entries for Jan. 3 and Jan. 16, 1947, Millis (ed.), *Forrestal Diaries,* 228–231; Truman to Patterson and Forrestal, Jan. 16, and Truman to the President of the Senate and the Speaker of the House, Jan. 18, 1947, *PPHST,* III, 99–102.

20. Truman Letter to the President of the Senate and Speaker of the House, Feb. 26,

1947, *PPHST,* III, 153; Yergin, *Shattered Peace,* 264–265, Hoopes and Brinkley, *Driven Patriot,* 346–348, Caraley, *Politics of Military Unification,* 172, and Clifford, *Counsel to the President,* 155–156.

21. Hogan, *Cross of Iron,* 56–57, Sander, "Truman and NSC," 381–388, and Clifford, *Counsel to the President,* 163–167.

22. Truman on the NSC in entry for Sept. 26, 1947, Millis (ed.), *Forrestal Diaries,* 320, and on "Gestapo" in Special Conference with American Society of Newspaper Editors, Apr. 18, 1946, *PPHST,* II, 206, 207.

23. Hogan, *Cross of Iron,* 65–68; Hoopes and Brinkley, *Driven Patriot,* 351, make the shrewd surmise that after Patterson declined the defense secretary position because of lack of finances, Truman opted for Forrestal, who would now have to make the system work rather than battle the new secretary; on the CIA, Clifford, *Counsel to the President,* 170; Caraley, *Politics of Military Unification,* 266–269, says that the National Security Act was "almost exactly" the same as the Eberstadt Report except for the secretary of defense position and that all sides agreed to the bill because they were tired of the fight; this early (1966) study says little about the establishment and implications of the national security agencies.

24. Balfour to Bevin, Feb. 13, 1947, F.O. 371/61045 (Professor Robert H. Ferrell informs me that the State Department soon covered the murals with a curtain).

25. Entry for Apr. 25, 1947, Millis (ed.), *Forrestal Diaries,* 264–265, and Leffler, *Preponderance of Power,* 149; Truman Remarks at Meeting with American Society of Newspaper Editors, Apr. 17, 1947, *PPHST,* III, 207–210.

26. C. M. Woodhouse, *The Struggle for Greece, 1941–1949* (Brooklyn, 1976), 13–65, and Edgar O'Ballance, *The Greek Civil War, 1944–1949* (New York, 1966), 49–65; see also Lawrence S. Wittner, "American Policy toward Greece during World War II," *DH,* 3 (Spring 1979), 129–131, idem, *American Intervention in Greece, 1943–1949* (New York, 1982), 2–3, Howard Jones, *"A New Kind of War": America's Global Strategy and the Truman Doctrine in Greece* (New York, 1989), 3–16, and William H. McNeill, "The View from Greece," in Hammond (ed.), *Witnesses to Cold War,* 102–103.

27. Woodhouse, *Struggle for Greece,* 111–137, and O'Ballance, *Greek Civil War,* 89–112, and Wittner, *American Intervention,* 8–9; Churchill quoted in John O. Iatrides, *Revolt in Athens: The Greek Communist "Second Round," 1944–1945* (Princeton, 1972), 208; the prime minister explicitly conveyed his "no peace without victory" sentiment to Roosevelt; Churchill to Hopkins, Dec. 9, 1944, in Winston Churchill, *The Second World War,* 6 vols. (Boston, 1948–1953), VI: *Triumph and Tragedy,* 297.

28. Woodhouse, *Struggle for Greece,* 163, on responsibility for violence; he also points out (p. 163) that the Varkiza Agreement called for a plebiscite on the monarchy prior to parliamentary elections, but that the U.S. pushed the government to reverse the order, ostensibly to create a calm atmosphere for the plebiscite on the unpopular king; the government dominated all the levers of power in early 1946, however; Wittner, "American Policy toward Greece," *DH,* 3 (1979), 143–148, and idem, *American Intervention in Greece,* 38–43, and McNeill, "View from Greece," in Hammond, *Witnesses to Cold War,* 112–115; on reservations about holding the elections, see Gallman to Byrnes, Feb. 27, and Rankin to State Department, Mar. 2, 1946, *FR 1946,* VII, 115–116, 117.

29. Ole L. Smith, "The Greek Communist Party, 1945–49," in David H. Close (ed.), *The Greek Civil War, 1943–1950: Studies of Polarization* (London and New York, 1993), 135; Wittner, *American Intervention in Greece,* 44–45, and Woodhouse, *Struggle for Greece,* 183–188.

30. Yergin, *Shattered Peace,* 289–291, and Artiom A. Uluniam, "The Soviet Union and 'the Greek Question,' 1946–53," in Gori and Pons (eds.), *Soviet Union and Europe,* 144–145.

31. On Stalin's policy and actions, see Zubok and Pleshakov, *Inside Kremlin's Cold War,*

126–128, who say that Stalin did not want Tito to appear to be a better revolutionary to the Greek Communists, and Uluniam, "Soviet Union and 'Greek Question,'" 145–150; see also Wittner, *American Intervention,* 6–9, 17, 26–27, 32–33, 56–57, and H. Jones, *New Kind of War,* 84–85, 175–176, 253 n. 7.

32. MacVeagh to Stettinius, May 1, 1945, *FR 1945,* VIII, 308–309, and MacVeagh to Byrnes, Jan. 19, 1946, *FR 1946,* VII, 97–99 (MacVeagh was summarizing—and agreeing with—a report written by Captain William H. McNeill, then assistant military attaché at the Athens Embassy, who later became an eminent historian).

33. Paterson, *Soviet-American Confrontation,* 183–185, MacVeagh to Acheson, Aug. 3, Acheson Memorandum to Truman, Aug. 7, and Baxter to Henderson, Aug. 7, 1946, *FR 1946,* VII, 186–188.

34. Bullock, *Bevin,* 243–244, 337–338, Hathaway, *Ambiguous Partnership,* 300–301, and Millis (ed.), *Forrestal Diaries,* 210; see also H. Jones, *New Kind of War,* 27–35.

35. Henderson Memorandum, Oct. 21, and Office of Near Eastern and African Affairs Memorandum, Oct. 21, and Byrnes to MacVeagh, Dec. 19, 1946, *FR 1946,* VII, 240–245, 283 n. 77; Henderson's memo was sent to MacVeagh, who was "elated," and—presumably on instruction—informed Tsaldaris and the king, Lincoln MacVeagh, *Ambassador MacVeagh Reports: Greece, 1933–1947,* ed. John O. Iatrides (Princeton, 1980), 706–708; Byrnes quoted on outposts in Leffler, *Preponderance of Power,* 127.

36. Byrnes Memorandum, Jan. 4, 1947, *FR 1947,* V, 1–2, Acheson, *Present at the Creation,* 199, and Marshall to MacVeagh, Jan. 21, 1947, *FR 1945,* V, 9–11.

37. Porter to Clayton, Feb. 17, 1947, *FR 1947,* V, 17–22.

38. Ethridge to Marshall, Feb. 17, MacVeagh to Marshall, Feb. 20, and Acheson Memorandum to Marshall, Feb. 21, 1947, *FR 1947,* V, 23–25, 28–31; Acheson, *Present at the Creation,* 217.

39. Hathaway, *Ambiguous Partnership,* 293; British Embassy to Department of State (two Aide-Mémoires), Feb. 21, and Henderson Memorandum, Feb. 24, 1947, *FR 1947,* V, 32–37, 43–44; on British policy, Ritchie Ovendale, *The English-Speaking Alliance: Britain, The United States, the Dominions, and the Cold War, 1945–1954* (London, 1985), 53–54.

40. Acheson, *Present at the Creation,* 217–218; H. W. Brands, *Inside the Cold War: Loy Henderson and the Rise of the American Empire 1918–1961* (New York, 1991), 153–156.

41. J. Jones, *Fifteen Weeks,* 133–134; Minutes of the First Meeting of the Special Committee . . . Feb. 24, and Henderson Memorandum to Acheson [undated], *FR 1947,* V, 45–55; there was also U.S. concern that Bevin might succumb to Stalin's recent overtures and left-wing backbench pressure to renegotiate the virtually lapsed wartime Anglo-Soviet treaty directed against Germany to include mutual aid against all nations, including the U.S; but there was not much chance of this, and at the Labor Party conference in May Bevin won a clear victory for his policy of aligning with the U.S.; see Bullock, *Bevin,* 350–351, 368–369, and Wayne Knight, "Labourite Britain: America's 'Sure Friend'? The Anglo-Soviet Treaty Issue, 1947," *DH,* 7 (Fall 1983), 267–282.

42. Acheson to Marshall, Feb. 24, 1947, *FR 1947,* V, 44–45; Marshall quoted in entry for Feb. 24, 1947, Millis (ed.), *Forrestal Diaries,* 245; Minutes of a Meeting of SWNCC, and Marshall Memorandum to Truman, Feb. 26, 1947, *FR 1947,* V, 55–58, and Truman, *Years of Trial and Hope,* 100.

43. Truman, *Years of Trial and Hope,* 103–104, J. Jones, *Fifteen Weeks,* 138–142, and Acheson, *Present at the Creation,* 219; see also Marshall Memorandum to Truman, Feb. 27, 1947, *FR 1947,* V, 60–62, and Pogue, *Statesman,* 164–165; on Henderson and Vandenberg statement, see H. Jones, *New Kind of War,* 260 n. 23, and Eric F. Goldman, *The Crucial Decade—and After: America, 1945–1960* (New York, 1961), 159; the leading conservative Republican, Robert Taft of Ohio, was inadvertently not invited to the meeting but included

thereafter, J. Jones, *Fifteen Weeks,* 138 n. 3; the meeting was officially "secret," and after word inevitably leaked, the participants declined to comment, Inverchapel to Foreign Office, Mar. 3, 1947, F.O. 371/61053.

44. Report on State-War-Navy Coordinating Committee, Feb. 29, 1947, *FR 1947,* V, 66–67; for accounts of drafting the speech, see J. Jones, *Fifteen Weeks,* 149–163, Paterson, *Soviet-American Confrontation,* 196–197, and Acheson, *Present at the Creation,* 220–222; on British and Greek issues, Gallman to Marshall, and Marshall to Embassy in Greece, Feb. 28, 1947, *FR 1947,* V, 68–71.

45. Report by SWNCC Subcommittee on Foreign Policy [Mar. 3], and Russell Memorandum, Mar. 17, 1947, *FR 1947,* V, 76–78, 121–123; J. Jones, *Fifteen Weeks,* 152–153; entry for Mar. 5, 1947, Millis (ed.), *Forrestal Diaries,* 248–249, and diary entry for Mar. 5, 1947, Vandenberg (ed.), *Vandenberg Papers,* 340.

46. Kennan, *Memoirs,* 314–322, and J. Jones, *Fifteen Weeks,* 154–155.

47. Elsey to Clifford, Mar. 8, and Elsey Notation, Mar. 9, 1947, Box 17, Elsey Papers; Bohlen, *Witness,* 261; Truman Address in Mexico City, Mar. 3, and Truman Address on Foreign Economic Policy, Mar. 6, 1947, *PPHST,* III, 164–172; Rundall Minute, and Inverchapel to Foreign Office, Mar. 10, 1947, F.O. 371/61054.

48. Connelly Cabinet Notes, Mar. 7, 1947, Connelly Papers; see also entry for Mar. 7, 1947, Millis (ed.), *Forrestal Diaries,* 250–252, and Larson, *Origins of Containment,* 311.

49. Entry for Mar. 10, 1947, Millis (ed.), *Forrestal Diaries,* 252, Acheson, *Present at the Creation,* 221–222, J. Jones, *Fifteen Weeks,* 155–159, 162–163, 168–170, and Paterson, *Soviet-American Confrontation,* 198 n. 6; Leffler, *Preponderance of Power,* 147.

50. Inverchapel to Foreign Office, Mar. 15, 1947, F.O. 371/61054.

51. Truman Address before a Joint Session of the Senate and the House . . . Mar. 12, 1947, *PPHST,* III, 176–180.

52. H. Jones, *New Kind of War,* 43–46, Inverchapel to Foreign Office, Mar. 15, 1947, F.O. 371/61054, and Acheson, *Present at the Creation,* 233; see Leffler, *Preponderance of Power,* 145–146, which cites a government media poll hailing the speech as a "landmark" akin to the Monroe Doctrine; Truman to Margaret Truman, Mar. 13, 1947, M. Truman, *Truman,* 343, Truman to Bess Truman, Mar. 14, 1947, PPNF, Box 19, Truman Papers, and Truman to Mary Jane Truman, Mar. 28, 1947, Ferrell (ed.), *Off the Record,* 110; Joseph Davies had died in January 1946.

53. On Hoover, Clifford, *Counsel to the President,* 180, 182; on Loyalty Program, Hamby, *Beyond the New Deal,* 170–171, and Donovan, *Conflict and Crisis,* 293–298.

54. David M. Oshinsky, *A Conspiracy So Immense: The World of Joe McCarthy* (New York, 1983), 86–97.

55. On Clark, Hamby, *Man of the People,* 427–428.

56. Inverchapel to Foreign Office, Mar. 29, 1947, F.O. 371/61054; even McCullough, *Truman,* 552–553, concedes the "pernicious influence" of the loyalty program and cites Truman's belated admission that it was "terrible"; interestingly, the senior Army officials in charge of the Venona Project decryption (success came in 1946) denied the president direct knowledge of their work; they informed the White House only of the substance of their information, but not that it came from Soviet cable traffic to and from the U.S.; see Haynes and Klehr, *Venona,* 15.

57. On the administration and alleged Communist opposition to the Truman Doctrine, entries for Mar. 13, Mar. 14, and Mar. 15, 1947, Ayers Diary, Box 25, Ayers Papers, Donald Rigsey Memorandum to Clifford, Mar. [?], 1947, Box 6, Clifford Papers; diary entry for Mar. 24, 1947, Vandenberg (ed.), *Vandenberg Papers,* 342–343; for general discussion of American and European response, see Paterson, *Soviet-American Confrontation,* 201–202, and Wittner, *American Intervention,* 80–89.

58. U.S. Senate, Committee on Foreign Relations, *Legislative Origins of the Truman Doctrine, Hearings Held in Executive Session . . . on S. 938: A Bill to Provide for Assistance to Greece and Turkey* (Washington, 1973), 46, 142, and Francis Case to Truman, May 10, 1947, OF, Box 1278, Truman Papers.

59. Truman to Roosevelt, May 7, 1947, cited in Larson, *Origins of Containment,* 315; Acheson and Forrestal views in U.S. Senate, *Legislative Origins,* 20, 84, 95; MacVeagh and Wilson views in U.S. Senate, op. cit., 46, 47–48.

60. U.S. Senate, *Legislative Origins,* 22, and Acheson, *Present at the Creation,* 225, and J. Jones, *Fifteen Weeks,* 195–196; on Vandenberg amendment, U.S. Senate, op. cit., 146–148, Acheson, op. cit., 223–224, and diary entry for Mar. 5, 1947, Vandenberg (ed.), *Vandenberg Papers,* 341, 344–346.

61. Woodhouse, *Struggle for Greece,* 202; Inverchapel to Foreign Office, Mar. 23, and Apr. 14, 1947, F.O. 371/61054; Paterson, *Soviet-American Confrontation,* 200; Truman Statement, May 22, 1947, *PPHST,* III, 254–255.

62. Wittner, *American Intervention,* 96–97.

63. "Free government" in entry for May 13, 1947, Ayers Diary, Box 25, Ayers Papers; "no attitude" in Truman News Conference, July 10, 1947, *PPHST,* III, 331; Marshall to Embassy in Greece, May 9, 1948, *FR 1948,* IV, 59–60; on U.S. policy in general, Lawrence S. Wittner, "The Truman Doctrine and the Defense of Freedom," *DH,* 4 (Spring 1980), esp. 162–163, 169–170, 174–176, 185–187.

64. Ambassador MacVeagh used the term "rat hole," cited in Wittner, *American Intervention,* 100; on "control" of Greek government, Elsey Notes on Treasury-State Disagreement . . . Mar. 26, 1947, Box 64, Elsey Papers, and Wittner, *American Intervention,* 99–102; Lovett to Griswold, Oct. 17, and Griswold to Lovett, Oct. 24, 1947, *FR 1947,* V, 370–371, 378–380.

65. Lovett quoted in Baxter Memorandum, Aug. 26, 1947, *FR 1947,* V, 314–315 (the Greek rebels began with about 13,000 forces and peaked at about 23,000 in summer 1947, O'Ballance, *Greek Civil War,* 142); Connelly Cabinet Notes, Aug. 8, 1947, Connelly Papers; on troops in 1948, Henderson Memorandum, Dec. 22, 1947, *FR 1947,* V, 458–461, Henderson Memorandum, Feb. 20, Henderson to Rankin, Mar. 25, and Souers Report to National Security Council, May 25, 1948, *FR 1948,* IV, 54, 64–65, 93–95; see also Wittner, *American Intervention,* 235–239, and Robert A. Pollard, *Economic Security and the Origins of the Cold War, 1945–1950* (New York, 1985), 128.

66. On Truman and British troops in 1947 and 1948, British Embassy to Marshall, July 30, 1947, PSF, Box 172, Truman Papers, Connelly Cabinet Notes, Aug. 7, 1947, Connelly Papers, and entries for Aug. 4 and Aug. 8, 1947, Millis (ed.), *Forrestal Diaries,* 301–303; on U.S. aid, Yergin, *Shattered Peace,* 292–293, Paterson, *Soviet-American Confrontation,* 205 n. 122, Pollard, *Economic Security,* 130, and Wittner, *American Intervention in Greece,* 242, 254 (including "dwarfed").

67. Paterson, *Soviet-American Confrontation,* 205; Ethridge quoted in Stephen G. Xydis, *Greece and the Great Powers, 1944–1947: Prelude to the "Truman Doctrine"* (Thessaloniki, 1963), 489; Truman quoted in diary entry for Nov. 4, 1947, C. L. Sulzberger, *A Long Row of Candles: Memoirs and Diaries, 1934–1954* (New York, 1969), 364–365; Marshall Memorandum for Lovett, Oct. 20, 1948, *FR 1948,* IV, 162–164.

68. Churchill cited in Yergin, *Shattered Peace,* 295; Zubok, *Inside Kremlin's Cold War,* 126–128, and Taubman, *Stalin's American Policy,* 151; on Free Democrats, O'Ballance, *Greek Civil War,* 158–159; Mastny, *Cold War and Soviet Insecurity,* 35, says that Stalin allowed the Communists to establish this government, who Russia hoped would gain control of northern Greece; the Cominform, successor to the defunct Communist International, was intended to coordinate foreign policy of member Communist states, Holloway, *Stalin and the Bomb,* 255–257.

69. Djilas, *Conversations with Stalin,* 181–182.

70. Zubok, *Inside Kremlin's Cold War,* 134–135, and Vladimir Dedijer, *The Battle Stalin Lost: Memoirs of Yugoslavia 1948–1953* (New York, 1970), 129–131; see also Leonid Gibianskii, "Soviet-Yugoslav Conflict and the Soviet Bloc," in Gori and Pons (eds.), *Soviet Union and Europe,* 222–249, which says that Yugoslav and Soviet Communists were in close ideological accord until late 1947 and differed mainly over tactics, namely, Tito's claims on Trieste and desires to limit Moscow's dealings with Albania; but the issues cited, as well as the matter of aid to Greece, were major matters and suggest more than tactical differences; in effect, Tito had lofty intentions regarding his ideological and political eadership in the Balkans; on Greek devastation, O'Ballance, *Greek Civil War,* 200–202, Woodhouse, *Struggle for Greece,* 285–286, and Wittner, *American Intervention,* 283.

71. Wittner, *American Intervention,* 263–266; Marshall to Embassy in Greece, Aug. 6, 1948, *FR 1948,* IV, 118–120.

72. Wittner, *American Intervention,* 271–283; H. Jones, *A New Kind of War,* 220–222.

73. Leffler, "U.S., Turkey, and NATO," 816–818, 823–825.

74. Bevin to Truman, Apr. 8, 1949, Bevin Papers, F.O. 800/516; entry for Apr. 14, 1952, Ayers Diary, Box 25, Ayers Papers; Truman, *Years of Trial and Hope,* 106.

75. H. Jones, *A New Kind of War,* 140–151, 162–167; Jones says that the State Department was probably correct in thinking that the rebels began the movement of children to protect them but that the government's emotional reaction led to escalation of the policy on both sides.

76. Jones, *New Kind of War,* passim; Yergin, *Shattered Peace,* 295, raises the issue of a Greek Communist victory; Leffler, *Preponderance of Power,* 125–127, 142–147, is critical of Truman Doctrine hyperbole but notes that policy makers' fears were real; he emphasizes that their strategic and national interest views rested on concern about control of raw materials, bases, and industrial infrastructure; this does not address the question, however, of whether the fears were based on accurate perceptions of reality and, if not, how one can justify such fear-based policy; see also idem, *The Specter of Communism: The United States and the Origins of the Cold War, 1917–1953* (New York, 1994), 25–27.

77. John Lewis Gaddis, "Was the Truman Doctrine a Real Turning Point?" *Foreign Affairs,* 52 (Jan. 1974), 386–402, idem, *U.S. and Origins of Cold War,* 346–352, Hathaway, *Ambiguous Partnership,* 299–303, and Donovan, *Conflict and Crisis,* 280–285.

78. Paterson, *Soviet-American Confrontation,* 193–206, Wittner, *American Intervention,* passim, Yergin, *Shattered Peace,* 286–296, and LaFeber, *America, Russia, and the Cold War,* 52–58; Truman quoted in Glenn D. Paige, *The Korean Decision: June 24–30, 1950* (New York, 1968), 148.

79. See David H. Close, "The Legacy," in Close (ed.), *Greek Civil War,* 214–234, and Wittner, *American Intervention in Greece,* 310–312.

80. J. William Fulbright, "How the Devil Theory Has Bedeviled U.S. Foreign Policies," *The Times,* Jan. 17, 1972, cited in John O. Iatrides, "Greece and the Origins of the Cold War," paper given at "Conference on Greece in the 1940's" (Copenhagen, May 5–8, 1987), 34; McNeill, "View from Greece," in Hammond (ed.), *Witnesses to Cold War,* 121–122; Pollard, *Economic Security,* 130; Wittner, *American Intervention,* 301–307.

81. Truman to Margaret Truman, Mar. 13, 1947, M. Truman, *Truman,* 343, and Truman Remarks to American Society of Newspaper Editors, Apr. 17, 1947, *PPHST,* III, 207–210.

82. Truman Special Conference with Association of Radio News Analysts, May 13, 1947, *PPHST,* III, 238–241.

83. Truman to Bevin, Apr. 12, 1949, Bevin Papers, F.O. 800/516.

Chapter 9. The World Split in Two

1. Truman News Conference, Mar. 11, 1948, *PPHST,* IV, 178; Elsey Notes, Nov. 29, 1947, Box 19, Elsey Papers, cited in Paterson, *Soviet-American Confrontation,* 207; Pollard, *Economic Security,* 131–132.

2. Truman quoted in J. Jones, *Fifteen Weeks,* 233; Truman Special Conference with Editors of Business Magazines and Trade Papers, Apr. 23, 1948, *PPHST,* IV, 231–235.

3. For diverse views of the Marshall Plan, see Joyce Kolko and Gabriel Kolko, *The Limits of Power: The World and United States Foreign Policy, 1945–1954* (New York, 1972), 359–383, 428–476, Scott Jackson, "Prologue to the Marshall Plan: The Origins of the American Commitment for a European Recovery Program," *JAH,* 65 (Mar. 1979), 1043–1068, esp. 1043–1044, Melvyn P. Leffler, "The United States and the Strategic Dimensions of the Marshall Plan," *DH,* 12 (Summer 1988), 277–306, esp. 277–278, Imanuel Wexler, *The Marshall Plan Revisited: The European Recovery Program in Economic Perspective* (Westport, 1983), Michael J. Hogan, *The Marshall Plan: America, Britain, and the Reconstruction of Western Europe, 1947–1952* (Cambridge, 1987), and Alan S. Milward, *The Reconstruction of Western Europe, 1945–1951* (Berkeley, 1984) and idem, "Was the Marshall Plan Necessary?" *DH,* 13 (Spring 1989), 231–253.

4. Yergin, *Shattered Peace,* 305–307, and Eisenberg, *Drawing the Line,* 280–281; Churchill quoted in Feis, *Trust to Terror,* 240.

5. Charles P. Kindleberger Memorandum, July 22, 1948, and Kennan to Acheson, May 23, 1947, *FR 1947,* III, 241–247, 223–230, esp. 229; see also J. Jones, *Fifteen Weeks,* 208–209.

6. Susan M. Hartmann, *Truman and the 80th Congress* (Columbia, 1971), 65–66; Report of the Special "Ad Hoc" Committee of SWNCC, Apr. 21, 1947, *FR 1947,* III, 204–219; Leffler, *Preponderance of Power,* 159–164; Milward, *Reconstruction of Western Europe,* 1–56, argues that the economic crisis of 1947 was not one of economic dislocation but of lack of foreign exchange to pay for imports from the U.S.; Milward says the European governments could have made up for this "dollar gap" by means other then infusion of U.S. dollars, such as changing import priorities from foodstuffs to capital goods; in his view the U.S. did not revive the European economy so much as sustain an investment boom underway.

7. Jackson, "Prologue to Marshall Plan," 1060–1062; Herbert C. Hoover, *An American Epic,* 4 vols. (Chicago, 1959), IV, 246, 253–255.

8. Eisenberg, *Drawing the Line,* 281–287, calls attention to the paper Allen Dulles, former head of the OSS, presented to the Council on Foreign Relations in January 1947, which called for German economic reconstruction even though this meant that "the division of Germany at the Elbe may not wholly disappear for some time"; similarly, in a January speech to the American Publishers Association, John Foster Dulles called for German reconstruction and (Western) European federation.

9. Entry for Mar. 13, 1947, Millis (ed.), *Forrestal Diaries,* 255–256, Harriman to Truman, Mar. 21, and Truman to Harriman, Mar. 22, 1947, PSF, Box 156, Truman Papers, and Acheson to Marshall, Mar. 20, 1947, *FR 1947,* II, 394–395; Jackson, "Prologue to Marshall Plan," 1063–1064; Pauley to Truman, Apr. 15, Truman to Pauley, Apr. 17, and Steelman Memorandum for Truman, undated [Apr. 1947], PSF, Box 12, Truman Papers.

10. R. Murphy, *Diplomat among Warriors,* 305–306, and Marshall to Truman, Mar. 14, 1947, *FR 1947,* II, 251–252; see also Pogue, *Statesman,* 180; on Clay, Eisenberg, *Drawing the Line,* 287–289; Acheson, *Present at the Creation,* 220, and Bullock, *Bevin,* 379.

11. Policy Papers Prepared by the Department of State, *FR 1947,* II, 201–233; Feis, *Trust to Terror,* 208–210, and Eisenberg, *Drawing the Line,* 292–296.

12. Conclusions of a Meeting of the Cabinet, Feb. 27, 1947, CAB 129/19, and Memorandum Marshall-Bevin Conversation, Mar. 26, 1947, *FR 1947,* II, 289–291; Bullock, *Bevin,*

380, 383–384, and Pogue, *Statesman,* 181–187; on Oder–western Neisse, Marshall to Acheson, Apr. 9, 1947, *FR 1947,* II, 320–323.

13. Eisenberg, *Drawing the Line,* 298–299; Feis, *Trust to Terror,* 213–217.

14. Clay Memorandum, Mar. 30, 1947, in Jean Edward Smith (ed.), *The Papers of General Lucius D. Clay: Germany, 1945–1949,* 2 vols. (Bloomington, 1974) I, 328–331; see also Leffler, "Struggle for Germany," 38–39, who says that Clay realized that Stalin did not want to see Germany divided and lose his chance for Ruhr industrial reparations; Stalin also feared a militarized Germany.

15. Marshall to Acheson (for Truman), Mar. 31, Truman to Marshall, Apr. 1, and Marshall to Acheson (for Truman), Apr. 2, 1947, *FR 1947,* II, 298–299, 301–303, 307–309; J. Smith, *Clay,* 419–420; Connelly Cabinet Notes for Apr. 4, 1947, Connelly Papers.

16. Memorandum of Marshall-Stalin Conversation, Apr. 15, 1947, *FR 1947,* II, 337–344.

17. Bohlen, *Witness to History,* 262–263, and Pogue, *Statesman,* 196; R. Murphy, *Diplomat among Warriors,* 307.

18. Trachtenberg, *Constructed Peace,* 58–60; Eisenberg, *Drawing the Line,* 302–303.

19. Adam B. Ulam, *The Rivals: America and Russia since World War II* (New York, 1971), 122–123, and Taubman, *Stalin's American Policy,* 158–159; Bevin believed that Stalin's rejection of a proposed four-power pact was as bad a blunder as having joined with Hitler in the Nazi-Soviet Pact in 1939, Bullock, *Bevin,* 388.

20. Naimark, *Russians in Germany,* 351–352; Loth, "Stalin's Plans for Postwar Germany," 28–29.

21. *New York Times,* Apr. 29, 1947; Kennan, *Memoirs,* I, 325–326, and entry for Apr. 28, 1947, Millis (ed.), *Forrestal Diaries,* 266–268.

22. Report of the Special "Ad Hoc" Committee of the State-War-Navy Coordinating Committee, Apr. 21, 1947, *FR 1947,* III, 204–219; the report was intended as an interim one and was soon outdated by development of the Marshall Plan.

23. Acheson, *Present at the Creation,* 227; Jackson, "Prologue to Marshall Plan," 1057–1058.

24. On opposition to British socialism, entry for May 7, 1947, Millis (ed.), *Forrestal Diaries,* 273; on Bevin telling Marshall of need for dollars for occupation costs, Bevin to Hugh Dalton, Apr. 7 and Apr. 24, 1947, Bevin Papers, CAB 800/14; on policy toward France, JCS Memorandum to SWNCC, May 12, 1947, *FR 1947,* I, 734–750, esp. 741; on the Monnet Plan, William I. Hitchcock, *France Restored: Cold War Diplomacy and the Quest for Leadership in Europe, 1945–1954* (Chapel Hill, 1998), 29–40, 62–71.

25. Hogan, *Marshall Plan,* 39–42.

26. Acheson, *Present at the Creation,* 229; Truman, *Years of Trial and Hope,* 113, and Charles L. Mee, Jr., *The Marshall Plan* (New York, 1984), 95–96.

27. JCS Memorandum, May 12, 1947, *FR 1947,* I, 734–750.

28. Kennan to Acheson, May 16 and May 23, 1947, *FR 1947,* III, 220–230; see also Kennan, *Memoirs,* I, 339–342.

29. Leffler, "Strategic Dimensions of Marshall Plan," 281; Kennan, *Memoirs,* I, 342, for "play it straight"; he also notes that he learned of Marshall's final decision to agree to Soviet participation only upon hearing of his Harvard address; however, Kennan in his own speech at the War College on May 6 insisted that the Russians had obstructed agreement at the CFM because they believed that the U.S. would undergo economic crisis and could not halt Europe's decline because they controlled the needed resources and could name their political price for them; Kennan urged German reconstruction—*"the primary object of our policy"*—without waiting for Soviet accord; on France, see Leffler, op. cit., 281, and Press Release, International Bank for Reconstruction and Development, May 9, 1947, *FR 1947,* III, 708–709.

30. Clayton Memorandum, May 27, 1947, *FR 1947,* III, 230–232.

31. Summary of . . . Problems of . . . Reconstruction of Europe, May 27, 1947, *FR 1947,* III, 234–236; J. Jones, *Fifteen Weeks,* 254–256; Pogue, *Statesman,* 208–210.

32. Bohlen, *Witness to History,* 263–264; Mee, *Marshall Plan,* 100–101, 107, and Pogue, *Statesman,* 210–217; Truman News Conference, June 5, 1947, *PPHST,* III, 265, Inverchapel to Foreign Office, June 5, 1947, F.O. 371/61055, and *New York Times,* June 6, 1947; on Hungary, Matthews to Acheson, Jan. 23, Schofield to Marshall, Feb. 22, and Harriman to Marshall, June 1, 1947, *FR 1947,* IV, 260–261, 271, 301–303.

33. Text of Marshall Speech in Department of State Press Release, June 4, 1947, *FR 1947,* III, 237–239.

34. Bullock, *Bevin,* 405, and Caffery to Marshall, June 18, 1947, *FR 1947,* III, 258.

35. *New York Times,* June 14, 1947, and Cohen Memorandum, undated [June 1947], *FR 1947,* III, 260–261; entry for June 23, 1947, Millis (ed.), *Forrestal Diaries,* 279, and Rundall Minutes, June 13, June 23, and June 27, 1947, F.O. 371/61055.

36. Truman's Commencement Address at Princeton University, June 17, 1947, *PPHST,* III, 281–285, White House Press Release, June 22, 1947, *FR 1947,* III, 264–266, and *New York Times,* June 27, 1947; Hartmann, *Truman and 80th Congress,* 108–110, and Pollard, *Economic Security,* 145–146.

37. Truman Special Conference with Association of Radio News Analysts, May 13, 1947, *PPHST,* III, 248–251; on Soviet statements, Smith to Marshall, June 23 and June 26, 1947, *FR 1947,* III, 266, 294–295; "ray of light" in entry for June 23, 1947, Millis (ed.), *Forrestal Diaries,* 281.

38. Clayton-Bevin talks in Peterson Memoranda, June 24–June 26, 1947, *FR 1947,* III, 268–293.

39. Scott Parrish, "The Marshall Plan and the Division of Europe," in Norman Naimark and Leonid Gibianskii (eds.), *The Establishment of Communist Regimes in Eastern Europe, 1944–1949* (Boulder, 1997), 274–275.

40. Ibid., 277–279.

41. Scott D. Parrish and Mikhail M. Narinsky, "New Evidence on the Soviet Rejection of the Marshall Plan, 1947: Two Reports," CWIHP, Working Paper No. 9 (Mar. 1994), 22–24, 42–44.

42. Ibid., 24; Caffery to Marshall, June 27 and June 28, 1947, *FR 1947,* III, 296–299; see also Parrish, "Marshall Plan and Division of Europe," 283–284.

43. Caffery to Marshall, June 28, June 29, and June 30, 1947, *FR 1947,* III, 299–302.

44. Caffery to Marshall, June 29, July 1, July 2, and July 3, 1947, ibid., 301–303, 304–305, 308–309; Bidault still intended to press French claims on Germany's coal and industry, Hitchcock, *France Restored,* 74–76; on Soviet intelligence and leaving conference, Parrish and Narinsky, "Soviet Rejection of Marshall Plan," 45–47; cf. Mastny, *Cold War and Soviet Insecurity,* 28, who overstates the warning tone of the intelligence report.

45. Balfour to Foreign Office, July 5, 1947, F.O. 371/61055; Truman's "folly of nationalism" in ibid., and *New York Times,* July 5, 1947; Marshall to Caffery (for Bevin and Bidault), July 3, 1947, *FR 1947,* III, 308.

46. Parrish and Narinsky, "Soviet Rejection of Marshall Plan," 48.

47. Anna Di Biagio, "The Marshall Plan and the Founding of the Cominform, June–September 1947," in Naimark and Gibianskii (eds.), *Establishment of Communist Regimes,* 209; Resis (ed.), *Molotov Remembers,* 61–62; see also Parrish and Narinsky, "Soviet Rejection of Marshall Plan," 49–50.

48. Parrish and Narinsky, "Soviet Rejection of Marshall Plan," 50–51; Mastny, *Cold War and Soviet Insecurity,* 29, says that Gottwald really wanted Stalin to take the public onus for refusal to attend but the Soviet leader refused.

49. Parrish and Narinsky, "Soviet Rejection of Marshall Plan," 51; Smith to Marshall,

July 11, 1947, *FR 1947,* III, 327; for further detail on Polish and Czech decisions, see Steinhardt to Marshall and Griffis to Marshall, July 10, 1947, *FR 1947,* III, 318–321; Igor Lukes, "The Czech Road to Communism," in Naimark and Gibianskii (eds.), *Establishment of Communist Regimes,* 251, makes the dubious point that U.S. failure to insist publicly that it was Czechoslovakia's sovereign right to participate in Marshall Plan talks was acquiescence to Stalin's view that whoever liberated a country controlled it, and that this proved fateful to Czechoslovakia in early 1948; Lukes ignores the fact that U.S. policy makers were hostile to Czechoslovakia and indifferent to Prague's involvement.

50. Rundall Minute, July 1, and Balfour to Foreign Office, July 5, 1947, F.O. 371/61055; Inverchapel to Foreign Office, June 22, 1947, F.O. 371/61005; see also Bohlen, *Witness to History,* 264–265, and Mayers, *Kennan,* 140–141.

51. Masaryk quoted in Mee, *Marshall Plan,* 149–150; Hogan, *Marshall Plan,* 1–25, esp. 22.

52. Parrish and Narinsky, "Soviet Rejection of Marshall Plan," 51; see also Parrish, "Marshall Plan and Division of Europe," 286, Leffler, *Preponderance of Power,* 186, Alvin Z. Rubinstein, *Soviet Foreign Policy since World War II, Imperial and Global,* 2nd ed. (Boston, 1972), 59–60, Ulam, *The Rivals,* 128–129, and Taubman, *Stalin's American Policy,* 175–178.

53. Paterson, *Soviet-American Confrontation,* 220–221; on Hungarian elections, Chapin to Marshall, Aug. 24 and Aug. 31, 1947, *FR 1947,* IV, 356–357, 363–364; Vishinsky quoted in Rubinstein, *Soviet Foreign Policy,* 60; Parrish, "Marshall Plan and Division of Europe," 286.

54. Mastny, *Cold War and Soviet Insecurity,* 30–33; on the comparison to the Truman Doctrine, Holloway, *Stalin and the Bomb,* 255–256, who also states that the purpose of the speech was to put pressure on the Western European governments, not effect revolution.

55. On Zhdanov's speech and Stalin's new strategy, Rubinstein, *Soviet Foreign Policy,* 60–63, Parrish and Narinsky, "Soviet Rejection of Marshall Plan," 32–39, Zubok and Pleshakov, *Inside Kremlin's Cold War,* 50–51, Di Biagio, "Marshall Plan and Cominform," 213–216, and Mastny, *Cold War and Soviet Insecurity,* 30–33.

56. *Foreign Affairs,* 25 (July 1947), 566–582; Mayers, *Kennan,* 112–114, and Kennan, *Memoirs,* I, 351–362; Kennan quoted on Truman in Gaddis, *Strategies of Containment,* 54 n.

57. (New York, 1947); see also Mayers, *Kennan,* 114–115.

58. Bohlen Memorandum of Conversation, Aug. 30, and Bohlen Memorandum, Aug. 30, 1947, *FR 1947,* I, 762–765.

59. Feis, *Trust to Terror,* 269–270, Bullock, *Bevin,* 433–434, and Pollard, *Economic Security,* 141–142; Connelly Cabinet Notes, July 18, 1947, Connelly Papers.

60. Harriman to Truman, Aug. 13, and Truman to Harriman, Aug. 14, 1947, PSF, Box 175, Truman Papers; similarly, Kennan said that the French had to choose between "a rise in German production or no European recovery financed by the U.S.," Memo Prepared by the director of the PPS, July 18, 1947, *FR 1947,* III, 332; Hitchcock, *France Restored,* 78–79.

61. Entry for Aug. 15, 1947, Millis (ed.), *Forrestal Diaries,* 304–305; Pollard, *Economic Security,* 140–141, Bullock, *Bevin,* 433–434, and Hitchcock, *France Restored,* 80–82; see also Eisenberg, *Drawing the Line,* 330–333.

62. Hogan, *Marshall Plan,* 61–72, and Lovett to Marshall, Aug. 24, 1947, *FR 1947,* III, 372–376; Jean Monnet was commissioner general of the Plan for Modernization and Reequipment of the French Economy.

63. Marshall to Truman, Aug. 1, 1947, PSF, Box 172, Truman Papers, Connelly Cabinet Notes, Aug. 8, 1947, Connelly Papers, Snyder quoted in entry for Aug. 15, 1947, Millis (ed.), *Forrestal Diaries,* 306–307; Truman to Margaret Truman, Aug. [n.d.], 1947, in

M. Truman, *Truman,* 352; Hogan, *Marshall Plan,* 74, and Caffery to Marshall, Aug. 31, 1947, *FR 1947,* III, 392.

64. Hogan, *Marshall Plan,* 76–82, Lovett to Embassy in France, Aug. 28, Lovett to Truman, Aug. 29, and Kennan Memorandum, Sept. 4, and Marshall to Truman, Sept. 24, 1947, *FR 1947,* 383–391, 397–405, 438–439.

65. Ludlam Minute, Aug. 26, and Inverchapel to Foreign Office, Sept. 26, 1947, F.O. 371/61056.

66. Truman quoted in Yergin, *Shattered Peace,* 328–329; Leahy Memorandum for Truman, "Special Session for Emergency Aid for Europe," undated [Sept. 1947], PSF, Box 119, Truman Papers, and Truman Letter to Committee Chairmen on the Situation in Europe, Oct. 1, 1947, *PPHST,* III, 451; Bevin Memoranda, Sept. 4 and Sept. 8, 1947, Bevin Papers, F.O. 800/514; on Bidault, Mee, *Marshall Plan,* 230–231, 234.

67. Clifford Memoranda, "Pentagon Luncheon," Oct. 2 and Oct. 15, and Elsey Memorandum for Clifford, Oct. 16, 1947, Box 4, Clifford Papers; Connelly Cabinet Notes, Oct. 10, 1947, Connelly Papers; Murphy Memorandum for Truman, Oct. 13, 1947, Box 60, Elsey Papers; see also Sen. Carl Hatch to Truman, Oct. 16, and Congressman Mike Mansfield Memorandum, [Oct.] 1947, Box 4, Clifford Papers; Truman Remarks to National Conference of Editorial Writers, Oct. 17, and Truman News Conference, Oct. 23, 1947, *PPHST,* III, 469–473, 475–476; Truman to Mary Truman, Nov. 15, 1947, in M. Truman, *Truman,* 356.

68. Paterson, *Soviet-American Confrontation,* 221–223, and Pollard, *Economic Security,* 147–148; Michael Wala, "Selling the Marshall Plan at Home: The Committee for the Marshall Plan to Aid European Recovery," *DH,* 10 (Summer 1986), 247–265.

69. Smith to Marshall, Nov. 8, 1947, *FR 1947,* IV, 614–615; Holloway, *Stalin and the Bomb,* 257–258.

70. On U.S. response to Molotov's speech, Gullion to Lovett, Nov. 13, 1947, *FR 1947,* I, 861–863; Policy Planning Staff Report, Nov. 6, 1947, *FR 1947,* I, 770–778; entry for Nov. 7, 1947, Millis (ed.), *Forrestal Diaries,* 341–342; Kennan's later view, *Memoirs,* I, 403, that Marshall never read the report and that it was never brought to Truman's attention is wrong.

71. Connelly Cabinet Notes, Dec. 14, 1947, Connelly Papers; Truman Message to Congress, Nov. 17, 1947, *PPHST,* III, 492–498; Vandenberg (ed.), *Vandenberg Papers,* 380; Hartmann, *Truman and 80th Congress,* 116–120.

72. Marshall quoted in Yergin, *Shattered Peace,* 330–331; Eisenberg, *Drawing the Line,* 353–355; Hitchcock, *France Restored,* 87–89.

73. Eisenberg, *Drawing the Line,* 358–359.

74. Ambassador Smith quoted in J. Smith, *Clay,* 447, who contends that from the time Byrnes was no longer secretary of state, the "essence" of U.S. policy was to divide Germany and make the western zones an anticommunist redoubt; see also Eisenberg, *Drawing the Line,* 358–359.

75. Eisenberg, *Drawing the Line,* 359–360; Marshall quoted in Memorandum of Conversation, Dec. 18, 1947, J. Smith (ed.), *Clay Papers,* I, 513–518; Trachtenberg, *Constructed Peace,* 64–65, uses the Rubicon metaphor; see also Bullock, *Bevin,* 493–496.

76. Connelly Cabinet Notes, Dec. 19, 1947, Connelly Papers; *New York Times,* Dec. 20, 1947.

77. Truman Special Message to Congress on the Marshall Plan, Dec. 19, 1947, *PPHST,* III, 515–529.

78. Truman Annual Budget Message to Congress, Jan. 12, and Truman Press Conference, Jan. 29, 1948, *PPHST,* IV, 20–21, 114–115; Rundall Minutes, Jan. 7, and Child Memorandum, Jan. 14, 1948, F.O. 371/68022.

79. On Marshall, Pogue, *Statesman,* 238–242; on Taft and Wallace, Paterson, *Soviet-*

American Confrontation, 226–227, Hartmann, *Truman and 80th Congress,* 159–161, and Hogan, *Marshall Plan,* 96–97; Vandenberg's role in Vandenberg (ed.), *Vandenberg Papers,* 383–395; Hogan, *Marshall Plan,* 102–109, details ECA structure; see also Pollard, *Economic Security,* 149–151.

80. On the Czech treaty and Benes' alleged self-deception about Stalin's intentions, Mastny, *Russia's Road to Cold War,* 133–142; Paterson, *Soviet-American Confrontation,* 105–108, 121–130, and John A. Armitage, "The View from Czechoslovakia," in Hammond (ed.), *Witnesses to Cold War,* 210–220.

81. Armitage, "View from Czechoslovakia," 221–230; Bruins to Marshall, Jan. 28, and Steinhardt to Marshall, Feb. 26 and Feb. 27, 1948, *FR 1948,* IV, 733–735, 739–742; Mastny, *Cold War and Soviet Insecurity,* 41–42, who says that Zorin told Gottwald that Russian troops were ready to march, but there clearly was no indication at the time that this was the case; see Steinhardt to Marshall, Apr. 30, 1948, *FR 1945,* IV, 747–755, esp. 750; see also Lukes, "Czech Road to Communism," 243, 252–256.

82. Armitage, "View from Czechoslovakia," 221–230; on Apr. 7 Steinhardt, who at first thought that Masaryk had committed suicide, wrote to Harold C. Vedeler, a State Department friend, of his growing belief—especially because Masaryk did not leave a statement—that he had been murdered, *FR 1948,* IV, 743 n. 1; on Finland, Warren to Marshall, Feb. 20 and Feb. 27, 1948, ibid., 761–765.

83. Communiqué . . . of London Conference on Germany, Mar. 6, 1948, *FR 1948,* II, 141–143; on Clay, Eisenberg, *Drawing the Line,* 380–382; Lawrence S. Kaplan, *NATO and the United States: The Enduring Alliance* (Boston, 1988), 17–18; for further detail on these events, see chap. 10.

84. Kennan's warning in Policy Planning Staff Report, Nov. 6, 1947, *FR 1947,* I, 770–771; on Truman, ibid., 771 n. 4; Marshall to Caffery, Feb. 24, 1948, *FR 1948,* I, 736–737; on Prague reports, Steinhardt to Marshall, Mar. 10 and Apr. 30, 1948, *FR 1948,* IV, 743–744, 747–754; on CIA, Review of the World Situation, Mar. 10, 1948, PSF, Box 203, Truman Papers; Bevin Memorandum, Mar. 3, 1948, CAB 129/1625.

85. Truman News Conferences, Mar. 1 and Mar. 10, 1948, *PPHST,* IV, 166, 177–178; Lukes, "Czech Road to Communism," 257, criticizes Marshall's failure to act, as in the cases of Greece and Turkey, but fails to recognize U.S. indifference if not hostility toward the Czech government and that the U.S. was unable to do anything, especially since there was no appeal for help from Prague.

86. "Dirty work" in Lukes, op. cit., 252; Steinhardt to Marshall, Feb. 26, 1948, *FR 1948,* IV, 738–741; on "fifth column" aggression, Hickerson Memorandum, Mar. 8, 1948, *FR 1948,* III, 40–42.

87. Truman to Margaret Truman, Mar. 3, 1948, in M. Truman, *Truman,* 358–360.

88. On Churchill-Clay-Douglas, Roberts Memoranda, Feb. 26 and Feb. 28, 1948, Bevin Papers, F.O. 800/514, and Bevin Memorandum for the Cabinet, "The Threat to Western Civilization," Mar. 3, 1948, CAB 128/25; during discussion of Bevin's paper, he noted: "We should use United States aid to gain time, but our ultimate aim should be to attain a position in which the countries of western Europe could be independent of both the United States and of the Soviet Union," Cabinet minutes, Mar. 5, 1948.

89. Clay to Chamberlin, Mar. 5, 1948, J. Smith (ed.), *Clay Papers,* II, 568–569; see also diary entry for Mar. 5, 1948, Millis (ed.), *Forrestal Diaries,* 387; see also Kennan, *Memoirs,* I, 400, Yergin, *Shattered Peace,* 351; J. Smith, *Clay,* 568–569 says the general should have known better than to send the cable; Eisenberg, *Drawing the Line,* 388, says Clay sought to conjure the Russian menace to derail the effort to internationalize the Ruhr, which he thought violated German sovereignty and would rouse German anger.

90. Elsey Memorandum for Clifford, Mar. 5, 1948, Box 31, Clifford Papers.

91. Clifford Memorandum, Nov. 19, 1947, Box 21, and Clifford Note, Feb. 19, 1947, Box 31, 1947, Clifford Papers; Marshall Memorandum for Truman, Mar. 5, 1948, PSF, Box 154, Truman Papers, and Elsey Notes for Mar. 17 speech, Box 20, Elsey Papers.

92. Truman handwritten note (attached to Marshall Memorandum, Mar. 5, 1948), PSF, Box 154, Truman Papers; Connelly Cabinet Notes, Mar. 12, 1948, Connelly Papers; entry for Mar. 15, 1948, Millis (ed.), *Forrestal Diaries,* 394, and Elsey Notes for Mar. 17 speech, Box 20, Elsey Papers.

93. Truman's remarks in entry for Mar. 16, 1948, Millis (ed.), *Forrestal Diaries,* 394–395, and Truman to Eleanor Roosevelt, Mar. 16, 1948, PSF, Box 132, Truman Papers.

94. Truman Special Message to the Congress on the Threat to the Freedom of Europe, Mar. 17, 1948, *PPHST,* IV, 182–186.

95. Truman St. Patrick's Day Address, Mar. 17, 1948, *PPHST,* IV, 186–190; diary entry for Mar. 17, 1948, Hillman, *Mr. President,* 135; King quoted in Yergin, *Shattered Peace,* 354.

96. Hartmann, *Truman and 80th Congress,* 163–164, Paterson, *Soviet-American Confrontation,* 224–225, and Pogue, *Statesman,* 250–252; Richard Mayne, *The Recovery of Europe, 1945–1973* (Garden City, 1973), 144–145, calculates ECA expenditures.

97. Truman's Special Conference with Editors of Business and Trade Papers, Apr. 23, 1948, *PPHST,* IV, 231–235, esp. 234.

98. Rubinstein, *Soviet Foreign Policy,* 104–106; Mastny, *Cold War and Soviet Insecurity,* 57–58; Pollard, *Economic Security,* 161–164.

99. Djilas, *Conversations with Stalin,* 153.

100. Richard Neustadt, *Presidential Power and the Modern Presidents: The Politics of Leadership from Roosevelt to Reagan* (New York, 1990 ed.), 40–49, Barber, *Presidential Character,* 281–282, and Hartmann, *Truman and 80th Congress,* 108, 121, 165.

101. Hogan, *Marshall Plan,* 430–432, and Pollard, *Economic Security,* 164–166; Charles S. Maier, "The Two Postwar Eras and the Conditions for Stability in Western Europe," *AHR,* 86 (Apr. 1981), 327–367, including comments by Stephen A. Schuker and Charles P. Kindleberger, esp. 341–343 and 357; Milward, *Reconstruction of Western Europe,* 98, and David Reynolds, "The European Response: Primacy of Politics," *Foreign Affairs,* 76 (May/June 1997), 181–182.

102. William C. Foster, "Memorandum on ERP," Aug. 30, 1949, Box 4, Clifford Papers; Pollard, *Economic Security,* 156–161.

103. Conclusions of a Meeting of the Cabinet, May 31, 1948, CAB 128/12; Mee, *Marshall Plan,* 254–255.

104. Conclusions of a Meeting of the Cabinet, Jan. 8, 1948, CAB 128/12, and Hogan, *Marshall Plan,* 88–134; see also Bevin's similar comments to the Cabinet in March 1948 about Europe becoming independent of both the U.S. and USSR as cited in note 88 in this chapter; British official Robert Hall quoted in Lawrence S. Kaplan, *The United States and NATO: The Formative Years* (Lexington, Kentucky, 1984), 131.

105. Ernest H. Van Der Beugel, *From Marshall Aid to Atlantic Partnership: European Integration as a Concern of American Foreign Policy* (Amsterdam, 1966), 166–215, Michael J. Hogan, "American Marshall Planners and the Search for a European Neocapitalism," *AHR,* 90 (Feb. 1988), 44–72, esp. 52–53, and Pollard, *Economic Security,* 166.

106. Hogan, *Marshall Plan,* 380–393.

107. Truman, *Years of Trial and Hope,* 119; A. W. Deporte, *Europe between the Superpowers: The Enduring Balance* (New Haven, 1979), makes the point that partition of Germany resolved the "German problem" and gave a "stable institutional structure to the ad hoc military division of Europe," i.e., since neither the U.S. nor USSR could afford to allow the other to control all of Germany, they divided it to establish a Cold War balance of power.

Chapter 10. Cat on a Sloping Tin Roof

1. Truman to Mary Jane Truman, Nov. 14, 1947, Ferrell (ed.), *Off the Record*, 118–119; [Royall] Memorandum, Jan. 27, 1948, PSF, Box 132, Truman Papers; entry for Oct. 6, 1947, Millis (ed.), *Forrestal Diaries*, 325; Krock, *Memoirs*, 241–243; see also McCullough, *Truman*, 584–586.

2. Clifford Memorandum for the President, Nov. 19, 1947, Box 21, Clifford Papers; for the memorandum's evolution, see Clifford, *Counsel to the President*, 189–194; on Wallace, Truman to George Phillieas, Apr. 9, 1948, PSF, Box 141, Truman Papers.

3. Yergin, *Shattered Peace*, 366.

4. Avi Shlaim, *The United States and the Berlin Blockade 1948–1949* (Berkeley, 1983), 408; Summary of the NSC Meeting, July 22, 1948, PSF, Box 220, Truman Papers; Leffler, *Preponderance of Power*, 220–221.

5. Douglas Memorandum of Marshall-Bidault Conversation, Dec. 17, Murphy Memorandum and Roberts Memorandum of Marshall-Bevin Conversation, Dec. 18, 1948, Box 74, Robert Murphy Papers, Hoover Institution Archives, Stanford, CA; see also Memorandum of Clay-Robertson Conversation, Dec. 16, and Memorandum of Clay-Robertson-Marshall Bevin Conversation, Dec. 18, 1947, in J. Smith (ed.), *Clay Papers*, I, 513, 514–518.

6. Shlaim, *Berlin Blockade*, 110–111.

7. Leffler, *Preponderance of Power*, 210, and Eisenberg, *Drawing the Line*, 364–365; on French, Hitchcock, *France Restored*, 90–91; Cabinet Notes for Jan. 23 and Feb. 13, 1948, Box 2, Connelly Papers, Harriman to Truman, Jan. 23, Marshall to Vandenberg, Feb. 4, and State Department Memorandum (Cabinet Decision on German Reparations), Feb. 16, 1948, PSF, Box 154, Truman Papers.

8. Douglas to Marshall, Mar. 4 (two cables) and Mar. 6, and Communiqué at Recess of London Conference, Mar. 6, 1948, *FR 1948*, II, 126–128, 129–130, 138–139, 142–143; Trachtenberg, *Constructed Peace*, 85.

9. Eisenberg, *Drawing the Line*, 372–379, and Hitchcock, *France Restored*, 95–96.

10. Inverchapel to Foreign Office, Feb. 14, 1948, F.O. 371/68013B; Stalin quoted in Djilas, *Conversations with Stalin*, 153; for Stalin's German strategy, see below.

11. Entry for Mar. 16, 1948, Millis (ed.), *Forrestal Diaries*, 394–395; Kaplan, *NATO and the U.S.*, 20–23; Clay to Draper, Mar. 6, 1948, J. Smith (ed.), *Clay Papers*, II, 571–573; Souers Report (NSC 7), Mar. 30, *FR 1948*, I, Part Two, 545–550.

12. J. Smith, *Clay*, 465; Murphy Memoranda, Feb. 1 and Mar. 3, 1958, *FR 1948*, II, 870–873, 878–879; Eisenberg, *Drawing the Line*, 380–381.

13. Michail Narinskii, "The Soviet Union and the Berlin Crisis," in Gori and Pons (eds.), *Soviet Union and Europe*, 62–63, and Zubok and Pleshakov, *Inside Kremlin's Cold War*, 49–52 (Stalin quoted on p. 50); the latter authors note that Stalin probably feared division of Germany into separate states that might one day be reunified by "a new Bismarck."

14. Wisner Memorandum, Mar. 10, 1948, *FR 1948*, II, 879–880, and 880 n. 2 and n. 3.

15. Shlaim, *Berlin Blockade*, 113; Murphy to Marshall, Mar. 20 and Apr. 1, 1948, *FR 1948*, II, 883–886.

16. Clay-Royall-Bradley, and Clay-Bradley teleconferences, Mar. 31, 1948, J. Smith (ed.), *Clay Papers*, II, 600–607; Clay to Bradley, Mar. 31, 1948, Leahy Diary, Leahy Papers, as cited in Shlaim, *Berlin Blockade*, 122–123; Murphy to Marshall, Apr. 1, 1948, *FR 1948*, II, 886–887.

17. Entry for Mar. 31, 1948, Millis (ed.), *Forrestal Diaries*, 407–408; Clay to Bradley, Apr. 1, 1948, Smith (ed.), *Clay Papers*, II, 607; Murphy to Lovett, Apr. 2, and Murphy to Marshall, Apr. 6, 1948, *FR 1948*, II, 889–891.

18. Shlaim, *Berlin Blockade*, 130–131, Clay to Bradley, Apr. 6 and Apr. 9, and Clay-Bradley teleconference, Apr. 10, 1948, J. Smith (ed.), *Clay Papers*, II, 618–619, 621–625.

19. Murphy to Marshall, Apr. 6, 1948, *FR 1948,* II, 890–891; Shlaim, *Berlin Blockade,* 133–134; Eisenberg, *Drawing the Line,* 394; on SVAG reports, Narinskii, "Soviet Union and Berlin Crisis," 64–65.

20. Shlaim, *Berlin Blockade,* 140–141; Murphy Memorandum of Conversation with Douglas, Clay, and Bevin, May 3, 1948, Box 76, Murphy Papers.

21. For details, see *FR 1948,* III, 85–136; Kaplan, *NATO and the U.S.,* 23; entry for May 11, 1948, Millis (ed.), *Forrestal Diaries,* 434–435.

22. James E. Miller, "Taking Off the Gloves: The United States and the Italian Elections of 1948," *DH,* 7 (Winter 1983), 35–55; Smith to Marshall, Apr. 26, 1948, *FR 1948,* IV, 836–838.

23. Lovett to Smith, Apr. 24, 1948, *FR 1948,* IV, 834–835; on preventive war, entry for Apr. 23, 1948, Millis (ed.), *Forrestal Diaries,* 424–425.

24. Truman remarks to Conference of Editors, Apr. 23, 1948, *PPHST,* IV, 231–235; Smith to Marshall, May 4, 1948, *FR 1948,* IV, 847–850.

25. Smith to Marshall, May 4 and May 10, 1948, *FR 1948,* IV, 847–850, 851–854.

26. Walton, *Henry Wallace,* 217–219; Bullock, *Bevin,* 558–559; entry for May 17, 1948, Ayers Diary, Box 26, Ayers Papers; entry for May 21, 1948, Millis (ed.), *Forrestal Diaries,* 443–445.

27. London Conference Communiqué, June 7, 1948, *FR 1948,* II, 313–316; Truman Comments in Eugene, OR, June 11, and Truman Speech at University of California, Berkeley, June 12, 1948, *PPHST,* IV, 328–340; Elsey to Clifford, June [n.d.], 1948, Box 33, Clifford Papers.

28. Hitchcock, *France Restored,* 96–97; J. Smith, *Clay,* 490–492; Shlaim, *Berlin Blockade,* 157–162; Narinskii, "Soviet Union and Berlin Crisis," in Gori and Pons (eds.), *Soviet Union and Europe,* 66, and Yergin, *Shattered Peace,* 377.

29. J. Smith, *Clay,* 492–492, 495–496; Clay to Draper, June 23, 1948, J. Smith (ed.), *Clay Papers,* II, 693–695; see also Clay to General Charles Gailey, June 13, 1948, ibid., 697, in which Clay states that introduction of the West Mark into Berlin would probably cause the Soviets to try to "force us from Berlin"; Clay also said that if the Soviets had introduced currency reform—and the U.S. had not—he, too, would have closed his border, J. Smith, *Clay,* 491; see also Editor's Note, *FR 1948,* II, 909–910.

30. Shlaim, *Berlin Blockade,* 161–162; Randall B. Woods and Howard Jones, *Dawn of the Cold War: The United States' Quest for Order* (Athens, 1991), 200.

31. Wilfried Loth, *The Division of the World: 1941–1955* (New York, 1988), 202–203, and Kennedy-Pipe, *Stalin's Cold War,* 124–125.

32. William Stivers, "The Incomplete Blockade: Soviet Zone Supply of West Berlin, 1948–1949," *DH,* 21 (Fall 1997), 570–573, 579–583, 593–595; Loth, *Division of the World,* 203, on only means available; Trachtenberg, *Structure of Peace,* 87–91, on air safety and balance of forces; Narinskii, "Soviet Union and Berlin Crisis," 67, on Anglo-U.S. attitude.

33. Harry S. Truman, *Mr. Citizen* (New York, 1960), 261–262; Shlaim, *Berlin Blockade,* 196–197.

34. Douglas to Marshall, June 26, 1948, *FR 1948,* II, 921–926; on territorial exchange, see Shlaim, *Berlin Blockade,* 207–208 n. 27, and Murphy to Marshall, June 23, *FR 1948,* II, 915.

35. Clay to Royall, June 25, 1948, J. Smith (ed.), *Clay Papers,* II, 697–699; Clay quoted in J. Smith, *Clay,* 506–507; Connelly Cabinet Notes, June 25, 1948, Connelly Papers.

36. Clay to Department of Army, June 25, 1948, *FR 1948,* II, 917–918; Shlaim, *Berlin Blockade,* 201–202; Clay to Draper, June 25, and Clay-Royall teleconference, June 25, 1948, J. Smith (ed.), *Clay Papers,* II, 699–704; J. Smith, *Clay,* 498–499.

37. J. Smith, *Clay,* 506; Shlaim, *Berlin Blockade,* 203–206, views the airlift as the most momentous American decision of the crisis because it implied U.S. commitment; R. Murphy,

Diplomat among Warriors, 316; Murphy to Marshall, June 26 (two cables), *FR 1948,* II, 918–921; see also Douglas to Marshall, June 26, 1948, ibid., 923–926.

38. For account of the June 25, 1948, meeting, see Beam Memo, June 28, 1948, *FR 1948,* II, 928–929, and entry for June 25, 1948, Millis (ed.), *Forrestal Diaries,* 451–452; Truman-Stalin and Clay-Zhukov exchanges of 1945 in *FR 1948,* III, 135–137, 353–356; for detailed study of the Berlin access issue, Daniel J. Nelson, *Wartime Origins of the Berlin Dilemma* (Tuscaloosa, 1978).

39. Shlaim, *Berlin Blockade,* 208–211; entry for June 27, 1948, Millis (ed.), *Forrestal Diaries,* 452–454; Marshall to Embassy in London, June 27, 1948, *FR 1948,* II, 926–928.

40. Shlaim, *Berlin Blockade,* 220–224; entry for June 28, 1948, James V. Forrestal Diaries, p. 2340, Seeley G. Mudd Library, Princeton University, Princeton, N.J.; Bullock, *Bevin,* 575–576; on U.S. rights in Berlin, see Humelsine Memorandum (NSC) for Clifford, June 30, 1948, PSF, Box 159, Truman Papers.

41. Eisenberg, *Drawing the Line,* 415–416.

42. Marshall to Embassy in United Kingdom, June 27, 1948, *FR 1948,* II, 926–928.

43. Entry for June 30, 1948, Lilienthal, *Journals,* II: *Atomic Energy Years,* 373–377.

44. On Sokolovsky, Narinskii, "Soviet Union and Cold War," 68; Clay to Royall and Draper, July 3, and Clay to Draper, July 10, 1948, J. Smith (ed.), *Clay Papers,* II, 722–724, 733–735; Shlaim, *Berlin Blockade,* 231–233.

45. Hamby, *Man of the People,* 448–452; Truman's reaction quoted in Bohlen Memorandum, July 14, 1948, *FR 1948,* II, 966–967; on military budget, Truman Statement to Forrestal, May 13, and Truman Memorandum to Forrestal, May 13, 1948, Box 64, Elsey Papers, and Forrestal to Truman, July 10, and Truman Memorandum for Forrestal, July 13, and Truman to Forrestal, July 13, 1948, PSF, Box 156, Truman Papers; diary entry for July 17, 1948, Lilienthal, *Atomic Energy Years,* 385–386, adds Budget Director James Webb's view that Truman was now his own defense secretary; see also Leffler, *Preponderance of Power,* 223–225; Clay to Bradley, July 15, 1948, J. Smith (ed.), *Clay Papers,* II, 739–740.

46. NSC Memorandum for Truman, July 16, 1948, PSF, Box 220, Truman Papers; Shlaim, *Berlin Blockade,* 236–240; Herken, *Winning Weapon,* 241, 260–262; Forrestal cited in entry for June 30, 1948, Lilienthal, *Journals,* II: *Atomic Energy Years,* 377; see also entry for July 15, 1948, Millis (ed.), *Forrestal Diaries,* 457–458.

47. Entries for July 15 and July 21, 1948, Millis (ed.), *Forrestal Diaries,* 458, 460–461, and diary entry for July 21, 1948, Lilienthal, *Journals,* II: *Atomic Energy Years,* 388–392; Truman Statement Reviewing Two Years of Experience with the Atomic Energy Act, July 24, 1948, *PPHST,* IV, 415; on Forrestal's unsubstantiated claim that Truman kept control of the atomic bomb for political reasons, see entry for July 23, 1948, Millis (ed.), *Forrestal Diaries,* 461, and Shlaim, *Berlin Blockade,* 256–257.

48. Entry for July 19, 1948, *Forrestal Diaries,* p. 2369, Mudd Library.

49. Diary entry for July 19, 1948, Ferrell (ed.), *Off the Record,* 145; Ferrell, *Truman,* 258.

50. Clay to Draper, July 19, 1948, J. Smith (ed.), *Clay Papers,* II, 743–746; Shlaim, *Berlin Blockade,* 248–249, 258; entry for July 21, 1948, Millis (ed.), *Forrestal Diaries,* 459–460.

51. Memorandum for the President, July 23, 1948 (Summary of the Discussion of the 16th Meeting of the NSC, July 22, 1948), PSF, Box 220, Truman Papers; there is no evidence to support Clay's later contention in his *Decision in Germany* (Melbourne and London, 1950), 368, that Truman told him after the meeting that he would have approved a convoy but for the opposition of the JCS; see also R. Murphy, *Diplomat among Warriors,* 316–317, who says that he regretted that he did not resign at this time, although this would not have changed government policy.

52. Shlaim, *Berlin Blockade,* 276–278; Truman to Mary Jane Truman, July 26, 1948, M. Truman, *Truman,* 17.

53. Memo on "U.S. Public Opinion on the Berlin Situation," July 29, 1948, PSF, Box 171, Truman Papers, and Eisenberg, *Drawing the Line,* 428; Marshall to Smith, July 26, and Smith to Marshall, July 31 and Aug. 3, 1948, *FR 1948,* II, 985, 996–998, 999–1006; Bohlen, *Witness to History,* 278–281.

54. Smith to Marshall, and Marshall to Smith, Aug. 3, and Bohlen Memorandum, Aug. 4, 1948, *FR 1948,* II, 1006–1007, 1008–1009, 1013–1014; entry for Aug. 10, 1948, Millis (ed.), *Forrestal Diaries,* 170.

55. Shlaim, *Berlin Blockade,* 323–325; on Kennan proposal and State Department view, see Memorandum for Marshall and Lovett ("Policy Questions Concerning a Possible German Settlement"), Aug. 12, and Department of State Policy Statement, Aug. 26, 1948, *FR 1948,* II, 1287–1297 and 1297–1319, and Kennan, *Memoirs,* II, 422–423.

56. Marshall to Smith, Aug. 26, and Smith to Marshall, Aug. 30, 1948, *FR 1948,* II, 1082–1085, 1092–1097.

57. Bohlen "Brief for the President," Sept. 2, 1948, PSF, Box 178, Truman Papers, and Connelly Cabinet Notes, Sept. 3, 1948, Connelly Papers; entries for Sept. 5, Sept. 6, and Sept. 7, 1948, Millis (ed.), *Forrestal Diaries,* 480–484, and Memorandum for the President, Sept. 9, 1948 (Summary of NSC Meeting, Sept. 7, 1948), PSF, Box 220, Truman Papers.

58. Memorandum for the President, Sept. 9, 1948, PSF, Box 220, Truman Papers; entry for Sept. 10, 1948, Millis (ed.), *Forrestal Diaries,* 486; NSC 30, Sept. 10, 1948, "United States Policy on Atomic Policy," *FR 1948,* I, Part Two, 624–628; diary entry for Sept. 13, 1948, Lilienthal, *Journals,* II: *Atomic Energy Years,* 406.

59. Diary entries for Sept. 13, 1948, Ferrell (ed.), *Off the Record,* 148–149, and Millis (ed.), *Forrestal Diaries,* 487.

60. Entry for Sept. 14, 1948, Millis (ed.), *Forrestal Diaries,* 487–488; see Shlaim, *Berlin Blockade,* 340.

61. Entry for Sept. 16, 1948, Millis (ed.), *Forrestal Diaries,* 490; see Shlaim, *Berlin Blockade,* 340–341, who states that Truman decided to postpone the decision because of political concerns.

62. Shlaim, *Berlin Blockade,* 344–356; see also Eisenberg, *Drawing the Line,* 442–443.

63. Shlaim, *Berlin Blockade,* 345–346; on atomic concerns, Dunn to Marshall, Sept. 20, 1948 (Precis of Marshall–de Gasperi Conversation, Sept. 18, 1948), *FR 1948,* III, 883–884; entry for Oct. 6–7, 1948, Ayers Diary, Box 26, Ayers Papers; the speechwriters were David Noyes and Albert Carr; see Hamby, *Man of the People,* 460.

64. Daniels, *Man of Independence,* 28–29; McCullough, *Truman,* 686–687; Tom Connally, *My Name Is Tom Connally* (New York, 1954), 331, and entry for Oct. 5, 1948, Vandenberg (ed.), *Vandenberg Papers,* 457–458; Pogue, *Statesman,* 407, says that Lovett later recalled having sent Marshall a copy of Truman's proposed broadcast and having rushed to the White House to dissuade Truman from his proposal.

65. Divine, *Foreign Policy and U.S. Presidential Elections,* 256–258; Dewey quoted in Joseph C. Goulden, *The Best Years 1945–1950* (New York, 1976), 414; Truman Statement, Oct. 9, 1948, *PPHST,* IV, 724–725; Pogue, *Statesman,* 408, points out that if Truman had lost the election, Marshall's job would have ended anyway; if Truman won, Marshall would have moved aside to allow someone else to start the new term.

66. On Anglo-French concerns, Bohlen Memo, Oct. 8, 1948, *FR 1948,* II, 1214–1216.

67. Truman Addresses in Miami, Chicago, Toledo, Brooklyn, and Independence, Oct. 18, 25, 26, 29, and Nov. 1, 1948, *PPHST,* IV, 815–818, 848–853, 857–861, 925–930, 939–940.

68. Memoranda for the President, Oct. 15 and Oct. 22, 1948 (Summary of Discussions of NSC Meetings, Oct. 15 and Oct. 21, 1948), PSF, Box 220, Truman Papers.

69. Clay comments in J. Smith, *Clay,* 501–502; Clay also praised Truman as a humble and courageous man who rose from being an ordinary senator to a "great President," ibid., 504–505; on Truman's intervention, Shlaim, *Berlin Blockade,* 366.

70. For general election analysis, Irwin Ross, *The Loneliest Campaign: The Truman Victory of 1948* (New York, 1968), 230–254, and McCullough, *Truman,* 709–718; on impact of Berlin crisis, Robert A. Divine, "The Cold War and the Election of 1948," *JAH,* 59 (June 1972), 90–100, esp. 108–109; for quote of Dewey aide (Elliott Bell), see Richard N. Smith, *Thomas E. Dewey and His Times* (New York, 1982), 543; on public opinion, see Eisenberg, *Drawing the Line,* 434–436.

71. Shlaim, *Berlin Blockade,* 366–373, and Eisenberg, *Drawing the Line,* 460–462, 464–467, who points out that U.S. support for the western Berlin elections was intended to promote schism in the city; Policy Planning Staff Report, Nov. 2, 1948, *FR 1948,* II, 1240–1247; Truman News Conference, Nov. 17, 1948, *PPHST,* IV, 944.

72. Hillenkoetter Memorandum for Truman, Dec. 10, 1948, PSF, Box 249, Truman Papers; Summary of NSC Meeting, Dec. 17, 1949, PSF, Box 220, Truman Papers.

73. Shlaim, *Berlin Blockade,* 373–377; Truman, *Years of Trial and Hope,* 130; for Anglo-French concerns, Holmes to Lovett, Jan. 10 and Jan. 12, and Lovett to Embassy in London, Jan. 12, 1948, *FR 1949,* III, 652–656.

74. Stalin Statement in Editorial Notes, *FR 1949,* III, 666–667; Acheson Memorandum of Conversation with President Truman, Jan. 31, 1949, Box 64, Dean G. Acheson Papers, Truman Library; Shlaim, *Berlin Blockade,* 299–303, 380–383; Acheson, *Present at the Creation,* 267–268, and Bohlen, *Witness,* 284–285.

75. Shlaim, *Berlin Blockade,* 382–383; Jessup Memoranda, Feb. 15 and Mar. 15, and Humelsine Memorandum, Mar. 22, 1949, *FR 1949,* III, 694–695, 698–700, 705–708; on currency changeover, Riddleberger to Acheson, and Acheson to Austin, Mar. 17, 1949, op. cit., 692–694; Reuter quoted in J. Smith, *Clay,* 529–530.

76. Kaplan, *NATO and the U.S.,* 29; Truman remark in Summary of NSC Meeting, Jan. 7, 1949, PSF, Box 220, Truman Papers; see also Acheson Memorandum of Conversation with Connally and Vandenberg, Feb. 14, and Acheson Discussions with Truman, Feb. 28 and Mar. 2, 1949, Box 64, Acheson Papers.

77. On Occupation Statute, Thomas A. Schwartz, *America's Germany: John J. McCloy and the Federal Republic of Germany* (Cambridge, 1991), 38–39; Jessup Memoranda, Apr. 11 and Apr. 27, 1949, *FR 1949,* III, 717–720, 730–731; Bevin quoted in Douglas to Acheson, Apr. 25, 1949, ibid., 730–731; Acheson to Embassy in London, Apr. 30, and Bevin to Acheson [n.d.], and Four Power Communiqué, May 5, 1949, *ibid,* 744–746, 749–750, 751; see also Conclusions of a Meeting of the Cabinet, May 2, 1949, CAB 128/15; Shlaim, *Berlin Blockade,* 387–388.

78. Kennan Paper, Mar. 8, 1949, *FR 1949,* III, 96–102, and Kennan, *Memoirs,* II, 442–445; on JCS, Memorandum for the President, May 18, 1948 (Summary of Discussion of NSC Meeting, May 17, 1948), PSF, Box 220, Truman Papers.

79. On Murphy, Eisenberg, *Drawing the Line,* 479–480; on Acheson and East-West merger, Memorandum for the President, May 18, 1949 (Summary of Discussion of NSC Meeting, May 17, 1949), PSF, Box 220, Truman Papers; "hell or high water," quoted in John Lamberton Harper, *American Visions of Europe: Franklin D. Roosevelt, George F. Kennan, and Dean G. Acheson* (Cambridge and New York, 1996), 284; on Acheson and Foreign Relations Committee, Eisenberg, op. cit., 480–481.

80. For CFM deliberations, see *FR 1949,* III, 818–840; for Truman and Acheson interest in breaking the blockade by use of a convoy, see Acheson Memorandum (Meeting with

the President), May 31, Report to the National Security Council (NSC 24/2), June 1, Acheson to Lovett, June 5, Lovett to Acheson, June 6, Lovett Memorandum (Meeting with the President), June 7, Acheson to Lovett, June 11, and Lovett to Acheson, June 12, 1949, *FR 1949*, III, 819–824, 826–831; see also [Murphy], "Comment on JCS Analysis," June 1, Murphy to Acheson, June 9, and Acheson to Murphy, June 16, 1949, Box 36, Murphy Papers.

81. Acheson, *Present at the Creation*, 301, and *New York Times*, June 22, 1949; Ninkovich, *Germany and the United States*, 72–73.

82. Mastny, *Cold War and Soviet Insecurity*, 47–53, 63–67, Narinskii, "Soviet Union and Berlin Crisis," 73–74, and James M. Goldgeier, *Leadership Style and Soviet Foreign Policy: Stalin, Khrushchev, Brezhnev, Gorbachev* (Baltimore, 1994), 34–46; on U.S. concerns about the airlift, Eisenberg, *Drawing the Line*, 427.

83. Shlaim, *Berlin Blockade*, 408.

84. Eisenberg, *Drawing the Line*, 441.

85. Diary entry for July 23, 1949, Lilienthal, *Atomic Energy Years*, 552–553.

86. Eric Morris, *Blockade: Berlin and the Cold War* (New York, 1973), 116, 145; the airlift peaked on May 12, 1949, the last day of the blockade, with more than 1,000 flights and 7,000 tons of supplies.

87. Kennan to James P. Webb, May 26, 1949, PSF, Box 163, Truman Papers.

Chapter 11. "To Make the Whole World Safe for Jews"

1. Henderson Memorandum, Nov. 10, 1945, *FR 1945*, VIII, 10–18, and Truman to Jacob Blaustein, Feb. 12, 1949, PSF, Box 113, Truman Papers.

2. M. Truman, *Truman*, 416, Truman to King Ibn Saud, Oct. 25, 1946, *FR 1946*, VII, 714–717, Walter George to Truman, Oct. 5, and Truman to George, Oct. 8, 1946, PSF, Box 184, Truman Papers; diary entry for July 30, 1946, J. Blum (ed.), *Price of Vision*, 607.

3. Truman to "Mamma and Mary," Sept. 11, 1945, Ferrell (ed.), *Off the Record*, 65–66; Truman to Joseph Ball [unsent], Nov. 24, 1945, PSF, Box 184, Truman Papers; diary entries for July 29 and July 30, 1946, J. Blum (ed.), *Price of Vision*, 605, 607; Truman to Edwin Pauley, Oct. 23, 1946, PSF, Box 184, Truman Papers, Acheson Memorandum, Apr. 25, 1949, Box 64, Acheson Papers, and Truman to Mark Ethridge, Apr. 29, 1949, PSF, Box 184, Truman Papers.

4. John Snetsinger, *Truman, the Jewish Vote, and the Creation of Israel* (Stanford, 1974), emphasizes political expediency; "squalid" politics in entry for Oct. 21, 1948, Millis (ed.), *Forrestal Diaries*, 508; Donovan, *Conflict and Crisis*, 312–331, 369–387, stresses historical circumstances; the most thorough account, Michael J. Cohen, *Truman and Israel* (Berkeley, 1990), explicates Truman's preference for a refugee haven or autonomous Arab-Jewish provinces within a federal political structure; "God's will" gets credence in Steinberg, *Man from Independence*, 308, and McCullough, *Truman*, 620.

5. Truman to Ball [unsent], Nov. 24, 1945, PSF, Box 184, Truman Papers, and Truman to Eddie Jacobson, May 3, 1948, Box 1, Edward Jacobson Papers, Harry S. Truman Library.

6. Howard M. Sachar, *The Emergence of the Middle East, 1914–1924* (New York, 1969), 127, 214–215, 219–220, and M. E. Yapp, *The Near East since the First World War* (London and New York, 1991), 116–117.

7. Yapp, *The Near East*, 118–132, and Michael J. Cohen, *Palestine and the Great Powers, 1945–1948* (Princeton, 1988), 3–8.

8. Churchill speech of May 23, 1939, in Robert Rhodes James (ed.), *Winston Churchill: His Complete Speeches, 1897–1963*, 8 vols. (New York and London, 1974), VI, 6128–6137; the British weighed partition in 1943–1944 but dropped the idea after Jewish terrorists as-

sassinated Lord Moyne, Britain's resident minister in the Middle East, in November 1944, Yapp, *The Near East,* 133–134, and Bullock, *Bevin,* 47; Howard M. Sachar, *A History of the Jews in America* (New York, 1992), 563–567; on Arab League origins, see Lenczowski, *Middle East in World Affairs,* 735–738.

9. On Roosevelt's policies, see David S. Wyman, *Paper Walls: America and the Refugee Crisis, 1938–1941* (Amherst, 1968), and *The Abandonment of the Jews: America and the Holocaust, 1941–1945* (New York, 1984); on FDR and Bermuda, Robert Dallek, *Franklin D. Roosevelt and American Foreign Policy, 1932–1945* (New York, 1965), 446; on FDR in 1944, Sachar, *History of the Jews,* 573–576.

10. Porter and Johnson (eds.), *National Party Platforms,* 403, 413; Sachar, *History of the Jews,* 576–577; William Eddy to Stettinius, Feb. 1, 1945, *FR 1945,* VIII, 87; FDR comment Mar. 1, 1945, *New York Times,* Mar. 2, 1945; on FDR and Ibn Saud visit, Grew to Tuck, Feb. 3, and Eddy Memorandum, Feb. 14, 1945, *FR 1945,* VIII, 1–3, and Sherwood, *Roosevelt and Hopkins,* 871–872.

11. Roosevelt to King Ibn Saud, Apr. 5, and Roosevelt to Abdullah (regent of Iraq), Apr. 12, 1945, *FR 1945,* VIII, 698, 703–704.

12. M. Cohen, *Truman and Israel,* 3–8.

13. R. Miller, *Truman,* 390–391, M. Cohen, *Truman and Israel,* 43–45, and Undated Memorandum, Box 1, Chaim Weizmann Archives, Harry S. Truman Library.

14. R. Miller, *Truman,* 391–393.

15. Wagner to Truman, Apr. 18, 1945, OF, Box 771, Truman Papers, and Sachar, *History of American Jews,* 586–587; Stettinius to Truman, Apr. 18, and Grew to Truman, May 1, 1945, *FR 1945,* VIII, 704–706.

16. Truman to Amir Abdullah of Trans-Jordan, May 17, 1945, *FR 1945,* VIII, 707; Notes for June 1945, Jacobson Notes, Box 2, Jacobson Papers, records that Truman wanted 150,000 Jews admitted to the U.S. but Congress would not do it; Truman to Frank Gannett, July 3, 1945, OF, Box 771, Truman Papers; on Harrison mission, M. Cohen, *Truman and Israel,* 110–111; Wagner to Truman, July 3, and Truman to Wagner, July 6, 1945, OF, Box 771, Truman Papers; Truman to Churchill, July 24, 1945, *FR 1945,* VIII, 716–717.

17. Attlee to Truman, July 31, 1945, *FR 1945,* VIII, 719; for background on Labor position, Yale Memorandum, July 31, 1945, *FR Potsdam,* II, 1402–1406, and Bullock, *Bevin,* 47–48; Truman News Conference, Aug. 16, 1945, *PPHST,* I, 226, 228, and Byrnes to Pinkerton, Aug. 18, 1945, *FR 1945,* VIII, 722.

18. Truman to Attlee, Aug. 31, 1945, *FR 1945,* VIII, 738–739, and Truman to Eisenhower, *PPHST,* I, 355–356.

19. Ovendale, *English-Speaking Alliance,* 91; on Transjordan, Bullock, *Bevin,* 508.

20. Bevin quoted in Bullock, *Bevin,* 113.

21. Bevin to Sir Stafford Cripps, Sept. 20, 1945, F.O. 800/512, Bevin Papers, and Attlee to Truman, Sept. 16, 1945, *FR 1945,* VIII, 740–741; see also Conclusions of a Meeting of the Cabinet, Sept. 11, 1945, CAB 128/3, and Bullock, *Bevin,* 178–183.

22. On Henderson, Clifford, *Counsel to the President,* 5, Brands, *Inside the Cold War,* 165–166, 190–192, and Henderson Memoranda, Sept. 24, Oct. 3, Oct. 9, and Oct. 12, 1945, *FR 1945,* VIII, 727–733, 751–753, 762, 766–769; War Department Memorandum, Sept. 19, 1945, ibid., 742–743; on FDR–Ibn Saud letters, Henderson Memorandum, Oct. 3, Acheson to Byrnes, Oct. 10, and Sands to Byrnes, Oct. 16, and State Department Press Release, Oct. 18, 1945, ibid., 757–758, 763–764, 770, 770–771; see also Memorandum Byrnes-Halifax Conversation, Oct. 19, 1945, ibid., 775–779, in which Byrnes states that FDR was too ill to conduct business when he gave his assurance and that Truman was "embarrassed" to have given his statement so soon after becoming president, and would not have done so if asked at the present time.

23. M. Cohen, *Truman and Israel*, 53–54, M. Truman, *Truman,* 299–300; British reports on Jewish lobbying of the White House include Halifax to Foreign Office, Oct. 6, Oct. 13, Oct. 20, and Oct. 27, 1945, F.O. 371/44541.

24. M. Cohen, *Truman and Israel*, 54–55; on Anglo-American Commission, Memorandum of Byrnes-Halifax Conversation, Oct. 22, and Byrnes to Halifax, Oct. 25, and Halifax to Byrnes, Nov. 9, 1945, *FR 1945,* VIII, 779–783, 785–786, 815–816; see also Bullock, *Bevin,* 178–179, and M. Cohen, op. cit., 122–126.

25. Henderson Memorandum for Acheson, Nov. 13, 1945, *FR 1945,* VIII, 11–18.

26. Truman to Eleanor Roosevelt, Nov. 26, 1945, quoted in M. Cohen, *Truman and Israel,* 125; Truman on House-Senate Resolution in M. Cohen, op. cit., 54–56; Concurrent Resolution in Department of State Memorandum [undated] *FR 1945,* VIII, 841–842 (a concurrent resolution, unlike a joint resolution, does not require presidential approval).

27. Acheson Memorandum, Apr. 25, 1946, *FR 1946,* VII, 585–587; Truman Statement on AAC Report, Apr. 30, 1946, *PPHST,* II, 218–219, and Truman News Conference, May 2, 1946, ibid., 225; Jewish reaction in M. Cohen, *Truman and Israel,* 127–129; Arab reaction in Tuck to Byrnes, May 3, Merriam to Acheson, May 8, and Wadsworth to Byrnes, May 9, 1946, *FR 1946,* VII, 592–594, 597–601; Henderson Memorandum, Apr. 24, 1946, ibid., 587; see also Acheson to Truman, Apr. 26, 1946, Box 775, OF, Truman Papers.

28. Conclusions of Meetings of the Cabinet, Apr. 29, May 1, May 11, and May 13, 1946, CAB 128/5, and Byrnes to Truman, May 9, and Attlee to Truman, May 13, 1946, *FR 1946,* VII, 601–603, 604–605; see also Bullock, *Bevin,* 254–258.

29. On the refugees, M. Cohen, *Truman and Israel,* 109, 117; on Niles, M. Cohen, op. cit., 75–77; Truman to Niles [May 1946], and Niles to Truman, May 7, 1946, PSF, Box 184, Truman Papers, and Hilldring to Acheson, May 3, 1946, *FR 1946,* VII, 591–592.

30. Truman to Attlee, May 16, 1946, *FR 1946,* VII, 608–609, and Truman Statement, June 11, 1946, *PPHST,* II, 297; Truman to Attlee, June 5, and Attlee to Truman, June 10, 1946, *FR 1946,* VII, 617–618, 623–624, and Truman News Conferences, June 6 and June 24, 1946, *PPHST,* II, 287, 302–303; the Jewish Agency offered to pay one-half of resettlement costs for 100,000 refugees for ten years—see Jewish Agency to Truman, June 14, 1946, OF, Box 772, Truman Papers; on July 9 Truman approved instructions for Grady drawn from the top page of a Cabinet Committee Memorandum, which appears in *FR 1946,* VII, 644–645, 644 n. 2; however, the full, but unprinted, memorandum refers to partition, Cabinet Committee, Matters regarding Palestine to Be Considered before the London Conference [July 1946], PSF, Box 172, Truman Papers.

31. Conclusions of Meetings of the Cabinet, June 20, July 1, and July 4, 1946, CAB 128/5, and Conclusions of Meetings of the Cabinet, July 8, July 22, July 23, and July 25, 1946, CAB 128/6; see also Bullock, *Bevin,* 296.

32. White House Statement (Truman), July 2, 1946, *PPHST,* II, 335, Jewish Agency to Truman, July 8, and Truman to Niles, July 10, and Connelly to Jewish Agency, July 18, 1946, OF, Box 772; Truman Statement Condemning . . . Terrorism, July 23, 1946, *PPHST,* II, 354.

33. Report by Chiefs of Staff, July 10, 1946, Cabinet Papers (C.P.) (46) 267 (attached to Conclusions of a Meeting of the Cabinet, July 11, 1946, CAB 129/11); on Bevin, Bullock, *Bevin,* 294–295; for Morrison-Grady Plan, Harriman to Byrnes, July 24, 1946, *FR 1946,* VII, 652–667; for critique of the plan, see Bernard A. Rosenblatt (president, Palestine Foundation Fund) to Edward Flynn, July 29, 1946, PSF, Box 184, Truman Papers.

34. Acheson, *Present at the Creation,* 175–176, and Sachar, *History of American Jews,* 588; for Taft-Wagner statements, see J. Blum (ed.), *Price of Vision,* 605 n. 1, and *New York Times,* July 26, 1946; on Truman-MacDonald, see M. Cohen, *Truman and Israel,* 133; see also diary entry for July 29, 1946, J. Blum (ed.), *Price of Vision,* 605–606, which quotes Truman as saying "I'm not a New Yorker. . . . I am an American."

35. Truman to Martha Truman, July 31, 1946, quoted in M. Truman, *Truman,* 383–384; diary entry for July 31, 1946, J. Blum (ed.), *Price of Vision,* 606, 607; Acheson Memorandum, July 30, and Harriman to Acheson, July 31, 1946, *FR 1946,* VII, 673–674, 675; Truman to Ed Flynn, Aug. 2, 1946, PSF, Box 184, Truman Papers; on Aramco, Daniel Yergin, *The Prize: The Epic Quest for Oil, Money, and Power* (New York, 1991), 410–411.

36. Truman to Attlee, Aug. 7, 1946, *FR 1946,* VII, 676–678; on Arab League, Cecil Lyon to Acheson, Aug. 2, 1946, ibid., 676–677.

37. M. Cohen, *Truman and Israel,* 137–138; Acheson to Harriman, Aug. 12 and Aug. 20, 1946, *FR 1946,* VII, 679–682, 688; Bullock, *Bevin,* 303; Acheson, *Present at the Creation,* 169, adds that he learned from his long relationship with Justices Louis Brandeis and Felix Frankfurter "to understand, but not to share, the mystical emotion of the Jews to return to Palestine and end the Diaspora," and that discussion of Zionism was omitted from his talks with Frankfurter.

38. Truman to Bess Truman, Sept. 15, 1846, Ferrell (ed.), *Dear Bess,* 537; Clayton to Truman, Sept. 12, 1946, *FR 1946,* VII, 693–695; Truman Statement Following Adjournment of Palestine Conference, Oct. 4, 1946, *PPHST,* II, 442–444; for account of Yom Kippur statement, see Eliahu Epstein to Nahum Goldmann, Oct. 4 and Oct. 9, 1946, Box 1, Chaim Weizmann Archives, Truman Library.

39. On "watershed," see M. Cohen, *Truman and Israel,* 145–146; both Acheson, *Present at the Creation,* 176, and Snetsinger, *Truman and Jewish Vote,* 42–43, mistakenly suggest the president called for partition, or a Jewish state; Attlee to Truman, Oct. 4, and Truman to Attlee, Oct. 10, 1946, *FR 1946,* VII, 704–705, 706–708; Ibn Saud to Truman, Oct. 15, 1946, and Truman to Ibn Saud, Oct. 25, and Memorandum of Truman-Amir Faisal Conversation, Dec. 13, 1946, ibid., 708–709, 715–717, 729–731.

40. Truman to Edwin Pauley, Oct. 22, 1946, PSF, Box 184, Truman Papers; Memorandum of Meeting between Mr. Ernest Bevin and President Truman, Dec. 8, 1946, F.O. 800/513, Bevin Papers.

41. Acheson Memorandum, Jan. 21, 1947, *FR 1947,* V, 1008–1011 (in an answer that seems astonishing in retrospect, Acheson said that opposition to partition would be vocal rather than physical); Conclusions of Meetings of the Cabinet, Jan. 15, Feb. 7, and Feb. 14, 1947, CAB 128/9 and CAB 128/11; British Embassy to Department of State, Feb. 7, and Bevin to Marshall, Feb. 7, 1947, *FR 1947,* V, 1033–1037; Bullock, *Bevin,* 365–367.

42. Henderson to Acheson (Summary of Bevin to Marshall), Feb. 17, *FR 1947,* V, 1051–1053, and Conclusions of a Meeting of the Cabinet, Feb. 18, 1947, CAB 128/9; Williams Memorandum, Feb. 25, Department of State to British Embassy, Mar. 28, and Durbrow to Marshall, May 10, 1947, *FR 1947,* V, 1056–1057, 1066–1067, 1081–1082.

43. Conclusions of a Meeting of the Cabinet, Mar. 20, 1947, CAB 128/9, Cadogan to United Nations, Apr. 2, and Marshall to Truman, May 16, 1947, *FR 1947,* V, 1067–1068, 1085–1086; the latter lists the "relatively neutral" UNSCOP nations: Australia, Canada, Czechoslovakia, Guatemala, India, Iran, the Netherlands, Peru, Sweden, Uruguay, and Yugoslavia.

44. Yaacov Ro'i, "Soviet-Israeli Relations, 1945–1947," in Michael Confino and Shimon Shamir (eds.), *The U.S.S.R. and the Middle East* (New York and Jerusalem, 1973), 123–125.

45. Gromyko Statement to General Assembly, May 14, 1947, in *FR 1947,* V, 1083–1084.

46. M. Cohen, *Palestine and Great Powers,* 261–262, and Galia Golan, *Soviet Policies in the Middle East: From World War Two to Gorbachev* (Cambridge, 1990), 34–36.

47. Truman Statement, June 5, 1947, *FR 1947,* V, 1101–1102; Department of State Memorandum, June 4, 1947, ibid., 1096–1101; Macatee to Marshall, July 21, 1947, ibid.,

1128–1131; Bullock, *Bevin,* 446–450, and Lovett Memorandum and Lovett to Douglas, Aug. 22, and Douglas to Marshall, Aug. 26, 1947, ibid., 1138–1141.

48. Truman to Eleanor Roosevelt, Aug. 23, 1947, quoted in M. Truman, *Truman,* 384–385; Connelly Cabinet Notes, Aug. 29, 1947, Box 2, Connelly Papers; M. Cohen, *Truman and Israel,* 92, 152, and Truman Memorandum for Files, Aug. 23, 1947, PSF, Box 184, Truman Papers.

49. M. Cohen, *Truman and Israel,* 149, and Editorial Note, *FR 1947,* V, 1143; Henderson Memorandum, Sept. 9, 1947, *FR 1947,* V, 498–499, and Bullock, *Bevin,* 476; Macatee to Marshall, Sept. 2, and Douglas to Marshall, Sept. 3, 1947, *FR 1947,* V, 1143–1145.

50. Extract from Minutes of Sixth Meeting of U.S. Delegation to the General Assembly, Sept. 15, 1947, *FR 1947,* V, 1147–1151.

51. Marshall Statement to the General Assembly, Sept. 17, and Henderson to Marshall, Sept. 22, 1948, ibid., 1151, 1153–1158.

52. Alling Memorandum, Sept. 23, Hilldring Memorandum, Sept. 24, and Knox Memorandum, Oct. 3, 1947, ibid., 1159–1164, 1173–1174.

53. Brands, *Inside the Cold War,* 182.

54. CIA World Review, Sept. 26, 1947, PSF, Box 184, Truman Papers, and entry for Sept. 26, 1947, Millis (ed.), *Forrestal Diaries,* 320.

55. Entries for July 30, 1945, and Sept. 29, 1947, Millis (ed.), *Forrestal Diaries,* 81, 321–322; M. Cohen, *Truman and Israel,* 136; Jacobson to Truman, Oct. 3, and Truman to Jacobson, Oct. 8, 1947, PSF, Box 184, Truman Papers; see also entry for Oct. 6, 1947, Millis (ed.), *Forrestal Diaries,* 323; Hilldring Memorandum, Oct. 9, 1947, *FR 1947,* V, 1177–1178; *New York Times,* Oct. 12, 1947; on Forrestal's views, see Arnold Rogow, *Victim of Duty: A Study of James Forrestal* (London, 1966), 161–172, who contends that Forrestal's opposition to a Jewish state derived chiefly from his national security concerns, however mistaken, that it would cause the U.S. to become alienated from the Arabs and their oil and open the Middle East to Russian influence; Rogow notes, however, that Forrestal lived most of his life in an anti-Semitic world, that his early family circle was anti-Semitic, that many of his friends and business associates strongly disliked Jews, and that Forrestal himself was indifferent to Holocaust survivors, did not want Jewish emigrants to come to America, and had difficulty accepting Jews as social equals; cf. Hoopes and Brinkley, *Driven Patriot,* 389–391, who insist that Forrestal was motivated exclusively by national interest concerns and was not anti-Semitic or anti-Zionist.

56. Tsarapkin Speech, Oct. 13, 1947, in Yaacov Ro'i (ed.), *From Encroachment to Involvement: A Documentary Study of Soviet Policy in the Middle East, 1945–1973* (New York, 1974), 49–50.

57. Lovett Memorandum, Oct. 15, and Smith to Marshall, Nov. 14, 1947, *FR 1947,* V, 1181–1183, 1263–1264; M. Cohen, *Palestine and Great Powers,* 283–284.

58. Bullock, *Bevin,* 477; on Arab views, Bailey to Marshall, Oct. 15, Wadsworth Memorandum, Oct. 21, and Austin to Marshall, Nov. 11, 1947, *FR 1947,* V, 1184–1185, 1192–1193, 1253–1254; on State Department views, McClintock Memorandum to Lovett, Oct. 20, Henderson to Lovett, Oct. 22, and Marshall to Austin, Nov. 12, 1947, ibid., 1188–1192, 1195–1196, and 1255–1256; on embargo, Henderson to Marshall, Nov. 10, 1947, ibid., 1249; M. Cohen, *Palestine and Great Powers,* 288.

59. Note for Oct. 16, 1947, Jacobson Notes, Box 2, Jacobson Papers; Truman to Claude Pepper, Oct. 20, 1947, Confidential File, Box 59, Truman Papers, and Truman to Elbert Thomas, Nov. 19, 1947, OF, Box 771, Truman Papers; King Ibn Saud to Truman, Oct. 26, and Truman to King Ibn Saud, Nov. 21, 1947, *FR 1947,* V, 1212–1213, 1277–1278.

60. M. Cohen, *Palestine and Great Powers,* 284–288.

61. M. Cohen, *Truman and Israel,* 159–160, McClintock Memoranda (2) for the File,

Nov. 19, and Bohlen Memorandum to Lovett, Nov. 19, 1947, *FR 1947,* V, 1271–1272, 1271 n. 2, 1272 n. 3.

62. Lovett Memoranda (two), Nov. 24, 1947, *FR 1947,* V, 1281–1282 n. 2, 1283–1284, and M. Cohen, *Truman and Israel,* 161; Austin to Marshall, Nov. 25, 1947, *FR 1947,* V, 1287; on Gromyko speech, Ro'i (ed.), *Encroachment to Involvement,* 51.

63. Marshall to Lovett, Nov. 25, Lovett to Embassy in Syria, Nov. 28, and Meminger to Lovett, Nov. 29, and Austin to Marshall, Dec. 1, 1947, *FR 1947,* V, 1288–1291, 1293–1294; entry for Nov. 26, 1947, Millis (ed.), *Forrestal Diaries,* 344–345.

64. M. Cohen, *Truman and Israel,* 164–170, Sachar, *History of American Jews,* 600–602, Notes for Nov. 26 and Nov. 27, 1947, Jacobson Notes, Box 2, Jacobson Papers, and diary entry for Dec. 1, 1947, Forrestal Diary, p. 1956, Forrestal Papers; the two Supreme Court justices were Frank Murphy and Felix Frankfurter, see Millis (ed.), *Forrestal Diaries,* 358; M. Cohen, *Palestine and Great Powers,* 298–299.

65. Note for Nov. 29, 1947, Jacobson Notes, Box 2, Jacobson Papers; Tuck to Marshall, Dec. 3, British Memorandum of Conversation (Bevin-Marshall), Dec. 17, 1947, and Editorial Note, *FR 1947,* V, 1295–1297, 1312–1313; Note for Dec. 8, 1947, Jacobson Notes, Box 2, Jacobson Papers; Truman Memorandum to Lovett, Dec. 11, 1947, *FR 1947,* V, 1309, and Truman to Morgenthau, Dec. 2, and Truman to Weizmann, Dec. 12, 1947, Box 1, Weizmann Archives.

66. Tuck to Marshall, Dec. 3, and MacAttee to Marshall, Dec. 31, 1947, *FR 1947,* V, 1295–1296, 1322–1328; Bullock, *Bevin,* 476–477; Britain's UN ambassador at the time later wrote that he thought Bevin acted quickly on troop withdrawal to "teach the Jews a lesson," Lord Gladwyn [Sir Gladwyn Jebb], *Memoirs,* 204; on Ben-Gurion and fighting, M. Cohen, *Palestine and Great Powers,* 302–303, 309.

67. Forrestal Memorandum for Truman, Jan. 6, 1948, PSF, Box 156, Truman Papers; on oil, Millis (ed.), *Forrestal Diaries,* 358; Rogow, *Forrestal Diaries,* 166, and Hoopes and Brinkley, *Driven Patriot,* 396–397; Childs to Marshall, Dec. 15 and Dec. 22, 1947, *FR 1947,* V, 1340–1341, 1342 n. 2; M. Cohen, *Truman and Israel,* 96, quotes Fraser Wilkins, an official of NEA in 1947–1948 and later its director, as telling him in 1975 that the State Department never received any concrete Arab threat to cut off oil sales and the administration was well aware of Arab dependency on need to export to the U.S.

68. Kennan to Marshall, Jan. 20 (enclosing PPS Report of Jan. 17), 1948, *FR 1948,* V, 545–554; on military planning, see Leffler, *Preponderance of Power,* 238–239; Wadsworth to Henderson, Feb. 4, 1948, and Wadsworth Memorandum to Truman [undated], *FR 1948,* V, 592–599.

69. Rusk to Lovett, Feb. 11, and Butler Memorandum (and PPS Memorandum), Feb. 11, 1948, *FR 1948,* V, 617–625; entries for Feb. 12 and Feb. 18, 1948, Millis (ed.), *Forrestal Diaries,* 370–373, 374–377; NSC Draft Report, Feb. 17, 1948, Box 13, Clifford Papers; Kennan to Marshall and Lovett ("Report by the PPS"), Feb. 24, 1948, *FR 1948,* V, 655–654.

70. Wadsworth Memorandum for Henderson, Feb. 4, 1948, *FR 1948,* V, 592–595; Jacobson to Truman, Feb. 2, and Truman to Jacobson, Feb. 5, 1958, PSF, Box 185, Truman Papers; Connelly to Weizmann, Feb. 10, 1948, Box 1, Weizmann Archives.

71. Entries for Dec. 3, 1947, and Feb. 3, 1948, Millis (ed.), *Forrestal Diaries,* 347–348, 362–364; M. Cohen, *Truman and Israel,* 178–179, and Marshall Memorandum, Feb. 19, 1948, *FR 1948,* V, 633.

72. Entry for Mar. 20, 1948, Ayers Diary, Box 26, Ayers Papers, and Paper Prepared in the State Department [n.d.], and McClintock Memorandum to Lovett, Feb. 19, 1948, *FR 1948,* V, 648–649 n. 1, in which McClintock, who wrote the text, noted that his original draft stated that in the course of preserving peace the UN "might establish conditions" that would

allow UNSCOP to effect partition, but that the department's deletion of this text "knocks the plan for partition in the head"; on British and Soviet challenges to the legal logic of the American plan, M. Cohen, *Palestine and the Great Powers,* 352–353; Policy Planning Staff Report, Feb. 24, 1948, *FR 1948,* V, 655–657.

73. Truman to Marshall, Feb. 22, and Marshall Message to Truman [undated], *FR 1948,* V, 645, 648–649; Austin Statement, Feb. 24, Marshall to Austin, Mar. 5, Marshall to Consulate General at Jerusalem, Mar. 6, and Marshall to Austin, Mar. 8, 1948, ibid., V, 651–654, 679–681, 686–687, 697; Truman's approval of Austin's proposed trusteeship statement was also recalled by Lovett, in Humelsine Memorandum to Marshall, Mar. 22, 1948, ibid., 749–750.

74. Jacobson to Josef Cohn, Apr. 1, 1952 (or "Recollections," i.e., Jacobson's "rambling account" of his interventions with Truman in behalf of the Zionists, notably Weizmann), Box 1, Weizmann Archives, and Truman to Jacobson, Feb. 27, 1948, Box 1, Jacobson Papers; Myers to Truman, Mar. 4, and Truman to Myers, Mar. 6, 1948, PSF, Box 184, Truman Papers; see also Truman to M. J. Slonim, Mar. 6, 1948, OF, Box 774, Truman Papers.

75. Clifford Memoranda, Mar. 6 and Mar. 8, *FR 1948,* V, 687–696; M. Cohen, *Truman and Israel,* 189, notes that Clifford's aide, Max Lowenthal, wrote these (and other) memoranda with material obtained from Eliahu Epstein, the Jewish Agency representative in Washington; Connelly Cabinet Notes, Mar. 12, 1948, Connelly Papers.

76. Jacobson to Cohn ("Recollections"), Apr. 1, 1952, Box 1, Weizmann Archives.

77. M. Cohen, *Truman and Israel,* 187, and Truman, *Years of Trial and Hope,* 161.

78. Marshall to Austin, Mar. 16, Thorp to Embassy in United Kingdom, Mar. 18 (2 cables), and Austin Statement, Mar. 19, 1948, *FR 1948,* V, 728–729, 737–742, 742–743.

79. Entry for Mar. 20, 1948, Ayers Diary, Box 26, Ayers Papers, Clifford interview [Oct. 26, 1949], Box 1, Daniels Papers; Weizmann told Jacobson that he did not believe that Truman knew of Austin's plan and wanted Jacobson to continue to "keep the White House doors open," Jacobson to Cohn ("Recollections"), Apr. 1, 1952, Box 1, Weizmann Archives; M. Cohen, *Truman and Israel,* 191; Marshall Statement, Mar. 20, 1948, in *FR 1948,* V, 748–749; diary entry for Mar. 20, 1948, Ferrell (ed.), *Off the Record,* 127, and Truman to Mary Truman, Mar. 21, 1948, quoted in M. Truman, *Truman,* 389.

80. Murphy Memorandum, Mar. 22, and Marshall Memorandum to Bohlen, Mar. 22, 1948, *FR 1948,* V, 745, 750 n. 3; Truman, *Years of Trial and Hope,* 163, attempts to explain his misjudgment by stating that his Palestine policy was not a commitment to specific dates or circumstances but to the "twin ideals of international obligations and relieving human misery," and that therefore the State Department's trusteeship proposal was "not contrary to my policy"; Marshall told the Senate Foreign Relations Committee in March 1948 that Soviet involvement in partition would threaten ERP, Pogue, *Statesman,* 369.

81. Significantly, David Ben-Gurion, head of the Jewish Agency, stated on Mar. 24, 1948: "It is we who will decide the fate of Palestine," quoted in Sachar, *History of American Jews,* 608.

82. Clifford Memorandum, Mar. 24, 1948, Box 13, Clifford Papers, entries for Mar. 24 and Mar. 25, 1948, Ayers Diary, Box 26, Ayers Papers; Truman News Conference, Mar. 25, 1948, *PPHST,* IV, 191–193, and M. Cohen, *Truman and Israel,* 195–198.

83. Diary entry for Mar. 29, 1948, *Forrestal Diaries, FR 1948,* V, 774; diary entry for Apr. 4, 1948, *Forrestal Diaries,* pp. 2183–2185, and JCS Memorandum for Truman, Apr. 4, 1948, PSF, Box 184, Truman Papers; "preposterous" in Lovett Memorandum, May 3, 1948, *FR 1948,* V, 987 n. 2.

84. Lovett Memorandum, Mar. 26, 1948, *FR 1948,* V, 761–764; M. Cohen, *Palestine and Great Powers,* 364–365, and M. Cohen, *Truman and Israel,* 200–201.

85. M. Cohen, *Truman and Israel,* 203–207, and *FR 1948,* V, 879 n. 2.

86. Shertok (Executive of the Jewish Agency) to Marshall, Apr. 29, Henderson Memorandum, Apr. 29, and Rusk Memorandum, Apr. 30, 1948, *FR 1948*, V, 874–876, 876 n. 3, 877–879.

87. Truman to Jacobson, May 3, 1948, Box 1, Jacobson Papers; Marshall to Embassy in United Kingdom, May 3, Shertok to Rusk, May 4, and Rusk to Lovett, May 4, 1948, *FR 1948*, V, 891–892, 892–896; Pogue, *Statesman,* 370–371, and Marshall Memorandum, May 12, 1948, *FR 1948*, V, 973; Sachar, *History of American Jews,* 610.

88. Henderson Memorandum, May 2, Austin to Marshall, May 3, and John E. Horner Memorandum, May 4, 1948, *FR 1948*, V, 882–886, 886–889, 898–901.

89. Clifford Notes, May 4, 1948, in Editorial Note, *FR 1948*, V, 906, Alfange to Harry Vaughan, May 8, 1948, PSF, Box 184, Truman Papers, Clifford Memorandum, May 9, 1948, Box 13, Clifford Papers; Truman knew and liked Lowenthal, who had been counsel to the Interstate Commerce Commission in the 1930s and also had extensive contacts with Zionists, see M. Cohen, *Truman and Israel,* 77–82, 210–211; Eleanor Roosevelt to Truman, May 11, 1948, PSF, Box 322, Truman Papers.

90. Marshall Memorandum, May 12, 1948, *FR 1948*, V, 972–976; Clifford account in *Counsel to the President,* 5–6, 9–13; see also Elsey undated notes, *FR 1948*, V, 976, and Daniels Notes of Clifford Interview, Oct. 26, 1949, Box 1, Daniels Papers; Marshall to Austin, May 12, 1948, and Editorial Note, *FR 1948*, V, 978–979, 987–988.

91. Clifford Interview, Oct. 26, 1949, Daniels Notes, Box 1, Daniels Papers; *New York Times,* May 14, 1948, and Weizmann to Truman, May 13, and Truman to Weizmann, May 15, 1948, *FR 1948*, V, 982–983, 983 n. 1.

92. Elsey Notes, May 14, and Lovett Memorandum, May 17, 1948, *FR 1948*, V, 989 n. 2, 1005–1006, Clifford interview, Oct. 26, 1949, Daniels Notes, Box 1, Daniels Papers, and Clifford, *Counsel to the President,* 19–20; Epstein to Moshe Shertok, May 14, 1948, Box 1, Weizmann Archives.

93. Clifford, *Counsel to the President,* 21–22, entry for May 14, 1948, Ayers Diary, Box 26, Ayers Papers, and M. Cohen, *Truman and Israel,* 218–219; Truman Statement of Recognition of the State of Israel, May 14, 1948, *PPHST,* IV, 258; Rusk to William Franklin (State Department Historical Office), June 13, 1974, *FR 1948*, V, 993; Rusk's letter indicates that friends of Marshall proposed that he resign, but the secretary said that it would be improper because the president had the constitutional authority to make the decision for recognition.

94. M. Cohen, *Truman and Israel,* 220–221, Rusk (as told to Richard Rusk), *As I Saw It,* 151–152, and Editorial Note and General Assembly Resolution 186, May 14, 1948, *FR 1948*, V, 994–995.

95. Eleanor Roosevelt to Marshall, May 16, and Marshall Memorandum to Lovett, May 17, 1948, *FR 1948*, V, 1015 n. 2, 1007–1008.

96. On British views, M. Cohen, *Palestine and Great Powers,* 364–365, 396.

97. Truman to Eleanor Roosevelt, May 20, 1948, PSF, Box 322, Truman Papers.

98. Lovett Memorandum, May 17, 1948, *FR 1948*, V, 1007; Clifford, *Counsel to the President,* 24.

99. M. Cohen, *Truman and Israel,* 223–224; Weizmann to Truman, May 16 and May 25, 1948, *FR 1948*, V, 1004–1005, 1042–1043; the five Arab states were Egypt, Iraq, Lebanon, Syria, and Transjordan.

100. Henderson to Rusk, May 16, and Rusk to Carter, May 24, and Lovett Memorandum to Truman, May 26, 1948, *FR 1948*, V, 1001–1002, 1037, 1051–1053; Ginsberg to Niles, July 21, 1948, Box 13, Clifford Papers; entry for Sept. 9, 1948, Ayers Diary, Box 26, Ayers Papers, and Memorandum to Marshall [n.d., unsent], Box 13, Clifford Papers; Marshall Memorandum to Truman, Aug. 30, 1948, *FR 1948*, V, 1359–1360.

101. On MacDonald, M. Cohen, *Truman and Israel,* 230–231; on Henderson's firing, entry for Mar. 25, 1948, Ayers Diary, Box 26, Ayers Papers (which notes that White House officials anticipated Henderson's removal from his NEA post soon after the trusteeship episode), M. Cohen, op. cit., 225–226, 229–230, and Brands, *Inside the Cold War,* 190–192; Brands contends that Henderson was not anti-Semitic, although he occasionally "lapsed into stereotypes regarding Jews"; nonetheless, he treated the Zionist cause and Zionists, such as Epstein, with contempt; he went far beyond the call of duty to defeat partition; and he was given to questionable, if not mean-spirited, arguments, such as that the "overwhelming majority" of non-Jewish Americans who knew anything about the Middle East opposed a Jewish—or "theocratic racist state" (see note 51 in this chapter), or that the "thinking peoples of Asia are convinced that the Zionists, with the aid of certain Western countries, have been engaged for years in a slow process of aggression against the Arabs of Palestine," Henderson Memorandum for Marshall, May 25, 1948, *FR 1948,* V, 1044–1045; on Truman and Israel's boundaries, Note for June 6, Jacobson Notes, Box 2, Jacobson Papers; Porter and Johnson (eds.), *National Party Platforms,* 432, 453.

102. On the loan, Jacobson to Weizmann, Aug. 6, 1948, Box 1, Weizmann Archives, Truman Memorandum for Lovett, Aug. 16, 1948, PSF, Box 181, and Weizmann to Truman, Sept. 6, and Truman to Weizmann, Sept. 10, 1948, OF, Box 775, Truman Papers; on the embargo, NEA Memorandum [late May 1948], *FR 1948,* V, 1060–1061, and Leffler, *Preponderance of Power,* 243; the Israelis got many of their weapons, with Russian consent, from Eastern Europe (especially Czechoslovakia) and considerable financial and other assistance from Americans, see Central Intelligence Agency Report, July 27, 1948, *FR 1948,* V, 1240–1248, Leonard Slater, *The Pledge* (New York, 1970), Ro'i, "Soviet Relations with Israel," 128–129, and Golan, *Soviet Policies in Middle East,* 37; Hillenkoetter Memorandum for Truman, July 8, 1948, *FR 1948,* V, 1200.

103. Marshall to Truman, Aug. 31, and Truman approval, Sept. 1, 1948, *FR 1948,* V, 1363, 1363 n. 2; Marshall to MacDonald, Aug. 31 and Sept. 1, 1948, ibid., 1364, 1366–1369.

104. M. Cohen, *Truman and Israel,* 237–238; Marshall Statement in Lovett to Diplomatic and Consular Offices, Sept. 21, 1948, *FR 1948,* V, 1415–1416; Arab and Jewish reactions in Villard Memorandum, Sept. 22, and Kuniholm to Lovett, Sept. 22, and MacDonald to Marshall, Sept. 28, 1948, ibid., 1416–1417, 1428–1429; on American Jewish pressure, Chester Bowles to Clifford, Sept. 23, 1948, Box 13, 1948, Clifford Papers, and M. Cohen, op. cit., 243–244.

105. Notes for Sept. 27 and Sept. 28, 1948, Jacobson Notes, Box 2, Jacobson Papers; Clifford handwritten notes [undated], and Clifford to Murphy, Oct. 1, 1948, Box 13, Clifford Papers; see also Lovett Memorandum, Sept. 29, and McClintock Memorandum, Sept. 30, 1948, *FR 1948,* V, 1430–1431, 1437–1438, and M. Cohen, *Truman and Israel,* 244–247.

106. Lovett to Marshall, Oct. 18, 1948 (original draft of Truman's "request" in Clifford's handwriting, PSF, Box 181, Truman Papers), and Marshall to Lovett, Oct. 21, and Lovett to Marshall, Oct. 22, 1948, *FR 1948,* V, 1489–1490, 1502–1503, 1505.

107. M. Cohen, *Truman and Israel,* 250–254; Lovett to Marshall, Clifford to Truman, and Marshall to Lovett, Oct. 23, 1948, *FR 1948,* V, 1507–1508, 1509, 1511; Truman Statement on Israel, Oct. 24, 1948, *PPHST,* IV, 843–844, and Truman Speech, Oct. 28, 1948, in *New York Times,* Oct. 29, 1948; Notes for Oct. 25 and Oct. 28, 1948, Jacobson Notes, Box 2, Jacobson Papers; Leffler, *Preponderance of Power,* 245, notes that John Foster Dulles, then a member of the UN delegation and Dewey's adviser, could not restrain Dewey from his attack on Truman; it was at this time that Forrestal alleged that America's Palestine policy was made for "squalid political purposes," which he attributed to "David Niles and Clark Clifford," Millis (ed.), *Forrestal Diaries,* 508; for Forrestal's views about Jews, see note 55.

108. Lovett to Truman, Oct. 19, Marshall to Lovett, Oct. 26, Lovett to Marshall, Oct. 27, MacDonald to Lovett, Lovett to Marshall [for Truman], Marshall to Lovett, and Lovett to

Marshall, Oct. 29, 1948, *FR 1948,* V, 1494–1498, 1518–1520, 1523–1524, 1525–1526, 1527, 1527 n. 1, 1528; Lovett's "silly season" comment is in his Oct. 29 cable to Marshall; see also Note for Oct. 28, Jacobson Notes, Box 2, Jacobson Papers, and MacDonald to Clifford, Nov. 26, 1946, Box 14, Clifford Papers, which state that Bevin aimed to "undo" the UN's partition vote by gaining a UN resolution that Israel would have to reject, thus permitting Britain to rearm the Arabs and sustain their war against Israel.

109. Marshall to Lovett, Nov. 1, and UN Security Council Resolution, Nov. 4, 1948, *FR 1948,* V, 1538–1539, 1546–1547; ironically, Truman did not win New York State because Progressive Party candidate Henry Wallace siphoned enough liberal votes to give Dewey the edge there, see McCullough, *Truman,* 708.

110. Military reports in Editorial Notes, *FR 1948,* V, 1541–1542; Weizmann to Truman, and MacDonald to Lovett, Nov. 5, 1948, ibid., 1549–1551, 1553–1554.

111. Lovett Memorandum, Nov. 10, and Douglas to Lovett, Nov. 12, 1948, ibid., 1565–1567, 1570–1572 (under the UN partition plan, Jaffa was to be part of the Jewish state).

112. Marshall Memorandum, Nov. 13, Marshall to Lovett, Nov. 14, and Lovett Memorandum, Nov. 18, 1948, ibid., 1577–1578, 1582–1584; Israel's position in Shertok Statement to UN, Nov. 15, and McClintock to Lovett, Nov. 17, 1948, ibid., 1584 n. 1, 1598–1601; see also M. Cohen, *Truman and Israel,* 262–263.

113. Lovett to U.S. Delegation in Paris, Nov. 22, 1948, *FR 1948,* V, 1621–1623; on establishment of the Palestine Conciliation Commission, U.S. call for recognition of Israel and a negotiated settlement of its borders, and British reaction, see Editorial Notes, ibid., 1617, 1661–1662.

114. Truman to Weizmann, Nov. 29, 1948, Box 1, Weizmann Archives; after a social talk with Truman, Jacobson wrote Weizmann that the president had told him that he had "nothing to worry about" regarding Israel and added that they would soon see "Peace-De Jour [*sic*], Recognition and a Loan," Jacobson to Weizmann, Nov. 29, 1947, Box 1, Weizmann Archives; Lovett Memorandum, Dec. 17, 1948, *FR 1948,* V, 1672–1674; M. Cohen, *Truman and Israel,* 264; see also Burdett to Lovett, Dec. 23 and Dec. 24, 1948, ibid., 1687–1689, 1689 n. 1.

115. Draft Telegrams, Lovett to MacDonald, and Lovett to Embassy in Egypt [undated, unsent], Lovett Memorandum, Dec. 30, and Lovett to MacDonald, Dec. 30, 1948, *FR 1948,* V, 1690–1691, 1701–1703, 1704.

116. MacDonald to Marshall, Jan. 1, and Weizmann to Truman, Jan. 3, 1949, *FR 1949,* VI, 595–595, 600–601; M. Cohen, *Truman and Israel,* 266–267; Bullock, *Bevin,* 650, notes that use of RAF flights was the military's decision, not Bevin's.

117. Lovett to Embassy in London, Jan. 13, 1949, *FR 1949,* VI, 658–659, and M. Cohen, *Truman and Israel,* 270; entry for Jan. 13, 1949, Ayers Diary, Box 26, Ayers Papers.

118. On extension of credit to Israel on Jan. 19, 1949, Editorial Note, *FR 1949,* VI, 680–681; on Truman's rejection of Bevin's "deal," entry for Jan. 22, 1949, Ayers Diary, Box 26, Ayers Papers; M. Cohen, *Truman and Israel,* 273–274.

119. On Israel's elections, postponed since the fall of 1948 owing to the war, MacDonald to Marshall, Jan. 28, 1949, Box 14, Clifford Papers; on de jure recognition, and Truman and Jacobson, Acheson Memorandum, Jan. 27, 1949, Box 64, Acheson Papers, and Note for Jan. 31, 1949, Jacobson Notes, Box 2, Jacobson Papers; Marshall had retired, as planned, at the start of Truman's new administration in mid-January 1949, Pogue, *Statesman,* 413–414.

120. On Israel's entry into the UN, Editorial Note, *FR 1949,* V, 995–996.

121. On Dulles, M. Cohen, *Truman and Israel,* 271.

122. Carter to Connelly (Acheson Memorandum for Truman), Feb. 5, 1949, PSF, Box 181, Truman Papers; on armistices, Nadav Safran, *Israel: The Embattled Ally* (Cambridge and London, 1981), 60.

123. Yapp, *The Near East,* 139, Safran, *Israel,* 60–61; on Truman's view of the territorial settlement, Acheson Memoranda, Apr. 5 and Apr. 25, 1949, Box 64, Acheson Papers, Note for Nov. 25, 1949, Jacobson Notes, Box 2, Jacobson Papers, and Report to the President by the National Security Council on U.S. Policy toward Israel and the Arab States, Oct. 17, 1949, PSF, Box 193, Truman Papers; Truman noted on the NSC report his objection to use of the term "corpus separatum" for Jerusalem, writing "Darn it—why not an 'independent city.' English is *our* language—let us write & speak it."

124. On Arab refugees and Israel's decision not to allow their return, Safran, *Israel,* 62, and Report by the NSC, Oct. 17, 1949, PSF, Box 193, Truman Papers; the refugees' resettlement pattern was about 60 percent to Transjordan, 20 percent to Gaza, and 20 percent to Syria and Lebanon combined; Truman views in Acheson Memorandum, Apr. 25, 1945, Box 64, Acheson Papers, and Truman to Mark Ethridge, Apr. 29, 1949, PSF, Box 184, Truman Papers.

Chapter 12. "Sand in a Rat Hole"

1. Truman, *Years of Trial and Hope,* 61; *Congressional Record,* 90, Part 2, 2299–2300, and entry for July 17, 1946, Ayers Diary, Box 25, Ayers Papers.

2. Office of Far Eastern Affairs Memorandum, Apr. 18, 1945, PSF, Box 73, Truman Papers.

3. "Rottenest" quoted in Gordon H. Chang, *Friends and Enemies: The United States, China, and the Soviet Union, 1948–1971* (Stanford, 1990), 62; "grafters and crooks" in entry for May 11, 1949, Lilienthal, *Journals,* II: *Atomic Energy Years,* 525; "sand in a rat hole" in Connelly Cabinet Notes, Mar. 7, 1947, Connelly Papers; "so-called Commies" and wartime activity in Memorandum, Nov. [15], 1945, Ferrell (ed.), *Off the Record,* 74; Truman on Russia-China, in diary entry for Nov. 27, 1945, J. Blum (ed.), *Price of Vision,* 519–521; Truman on "bandits" and loyalty in Truman to Rep. Hugh De Lacy, Jan. 12, 1946, PSF, Box 173, Truman Papers.

4. Truman Memorandum for Harry Vaughan, Aug. 12, 1950, PSF, Box 113, Truman Papers.

5. O. Edmund Clubb, *Twentieth Century China* (New York, 1964), 36–145; on GMD-Soviet dealings, Ulam, *Stalin,* 274–277.

6. Lloyd E. Eastman, *Seeds of Destruction: Nationalist China in War and Revolution 1937–1949* (Stanford, 1984), 2–3, and Michael Schaller, *The United States and China in the Twentieth Century,* 2nd ed. (New York, 1990), 37–47.

7. Schaller, *U.S. and China,* 58–69.

8. Roosevelt to Morgenthau, Dec. 6, 1934, Edgar B. Nixon (ed.), *Franklin D. Roosevelt and Foreign Affairs, 1933–1937,* 3 vols. (Cambridge, 1969), II, 305–306.

9. Schaller, *U.S. and China,* 70–77.

10. Schaller, *Crusade in China,* 160–185; Mao quoted on p. 185.

11. Ibid., 185–186.

12. Hunt, *Genesis of Communist Foreign Policy,* 74–80, 127–133; Mao quoted in Shu Guang Zhang, "In the Shadow of Mao: Zhou Enlai and New China's Diplomacy," in Gordon A. Craig and Francis L. Loewenheim (eds.), *The Diplomats, 1939–1979* (Princeton, 1994), 340; for analysis of Mao as a proletarian internationalist for whom ideology was primary, see Michael M. Sheng, *Battling Western Imperialism: Mao, Stalin, and the United States* (Princeton, 1997).

13. Hunt, *Genesis of Communist Foreign Policy,* 134–141.

14. Ibid., 141–148.

15. Schaller, *Crusade in China,* 187.

16. Barbara W. Tuchman, *Stilwell and the American Experience in China, 1911–1945* (New York, 1971), 627–642; Schaller, *Crusade in China,* 174–175.

17. Westad, *Cold War and Revolution,* 23, 27.

18. Schaller, *Crusade in China,* 190–200, 204–205; Dallek, *Roosevelt,* 500–501.

19. On reaction to Hurley, Sheng, *Battling Western Imperialism,* 88–89; Mao and Zhou to Wang Ruofei, Dec. 12, 1945, Shu Guang Zhang and Chen Jian (eds.), *Chinese Communist Foreign Policy and the Cold War in Asia: New Documentary Evidence, 1944–1950* (Chicago, 1996), 17–18; Schaller, *Crusade in China,* 204–206; Hurley to Roosevelt, Jan. 14, 1945, *FR 1945,* VII, 172–177.

20. Clemens, *Yalta,* 244–255; Stalin had largely spelled out his terms to Harriman in December 1944 and drew little protest; see Harriman, *Special Envoy,* 306–307.

21. Westad, *Cold War and Revolution,* 17–21, 28–30; for view that FDR held China in contempt, Warren I. Cohen, *America's Response to China: A History of Sino-American Relations,* 3rd ed. (New York, 1990), 143–144; on JCS, Harriman, *Special Envoy,* 399.

22. "Margarine" Communists in Davies to Kennan, August 18, 1945, *FR 1945,* VII, 447–448; on Stalin's China policies, Goncharov et al., *Uncertain Partners,* 8–10, and Westad, *Cold War and Revolution,* 7–10.

23. Schaller, *Crusade in China,* 212–220; Roosevelt to Mao Tse-tung, Mar. 10, 1945, *FR 1945,* VII, 266–267; for assessment of China, Rep. Mike Mansfield to Roosevelt, Jan. 3, 1945, *FR 1945,* VII, 2–20; Sheng, *Battling Western Imperialism,* 95, says the CCP saw FDR's death as leading to a reactionary turn in U.S. policy; of course, the CCP was already unhappy with FDR's policy but regarded him as the best among U.S. policy makers.

24. Kennan [for Hurley] to Stettinius, Apr. 17, and Hurley to Truman, May 20, 1945, *FR 1945,* VII, 107–114, 338–340.

25. Stanton Memorandum, Apr. 19, Kennan to Stettinius, and Stettinius to Hurley, Apr. 23, 1945, *FR 1945,* VII, 338–345, and entry for May 14, 1945, Millis (ed.), *Forrestal Diaries,* 57–58.

26. Grew Memorandum, May 14, and Stimson to Grew, May 21, 1945, *FR 1945,* VII, 101–103, 876–879.

27. Diary entry for May 29, 1945, J. Blum (ed.), *Price of Vision,* 454, and Grew Memoranda, June 9 and June 14, and Grew to Hurley, June 18, 1945, *FR 1945,* VII, 896, 901–903, 907.

28. Diary entry for July 17, 1945, Stimson Diary, Stimson Papers, Truman diary entry, July 17, 1945, Ferrell (ed.), *Off the Record,* 53, and Truman to Bess Truman, July 21, 1945, Ferrell (ed.), *Dear Bess,* 519.

29. Entries for July 20 and July 24, 1945, Brown Diary, Byrnes Papers.

30. Truman diary entry, July 18, 1945, Ferrell (ed.), *Off the Record,* 53–54; Byrnes to Harriman, Aug. 5, and Grew to Hurley, Aug. 6, 1945, *FR 1945,* VII, 955–956, 146.

31. Harriman to Byrnes, Aug. 8, 1945, *FR 1945,* VII, 958–959; entries for Aug. 10, 1945, Stimson Diary, Stimson Papers, and Millis (ed.), *Forrestal Diaries,* 83.

32. General Order #1 [Aug. 15, 1945], *FR 1945,* VII, 530–534; Hurley to Byrnes, Aug. 12, and Harriman to Byrnes, Aug. 14 and Aug. 22, 1945, *FR 1945,* VII, 514–515, 971–973, 978–979.

33. Eastman, *Seeds of Destruction,* 71, 156–157, and Suzanne Pepper, *Civil War in China: The Political Struggle, 1945–1949* (Berkeley, 1978), 7–41.

34. Schaller, *Crusade in China,* 262–263; JCS to Wedemeyer, Aug. 10, and Wedemeyer to Marshall, Aug. 19, 1945, *FR 1945,* VII, 527–528, 531–534.

35. Acheson to Truman, Aug. 12, and Truman to Acheson, Sept. 18, 1945, *FR 1945,* VII, 1027–1028; War Department Memorandum for Truman, Byrnes to Truman, and Elsey Memorandum, Sept. 3, 1945, PSF, Box 173, Truman Papers; Schaller, *Crusade in China,* 271–274.

36. Locke to Truman, Aug. 27, 1945, *FR 1945,* VII, 448–453.

37. Hurley to Byrnes, Aug. 16, 1945, *FR 1945,* VII, 445–446; Westad, *Cold War and Revolution,* 92–93.

38. CCP Central Committee, Instruction, Mar. 15, and CCP Central Committee to CCP Guandong Regional Committee, June 16, 1945, Zhang and Chen (eds.), *Chinese Communist Foreign Policy,* 23, 24–25; Westad, *Cold War and Revolution,* 80.

39. Mao Speech on Aug. 26, 1945, in Zhang and Chen (eds.), *Chinese Communist Foreign Policy,* 32–33; Mao and Zhou quoted Westad, *Cold War and Revolution,* 81; on CCP views on Shandong, see Zhang and Chen (eds.), *Chinese Communist Foreign Policy,* 40–41.

40. Robertson to Byrnes, Oct. 2 and Oct. 9, 1945, *FR 1945,* VII, 470, 473–474; Westad, *Cold War and Revolution,* 106–112; Goncharov et al., *Uncertain Partners,* 11–12.

41. Gallicchio, *Cold War Begins,* 110.

42. Entry for Oct. 19, 1945, "President's Appointments List," Sept.–Dec. 1945, Box 1, Ayers Papers; on Truman and Wedemeyer, Gallicchio, *Cold War Begins,* 112; on Truman's proposed statement, Truman Memorandum, Nov. 1945, Ferrell (ed.), *Off the Record,* 74, diary entry for Nov. 6, 1945, J. Blum (ed.), *Price of Vision,* 506–507, Memorandum for the President, Nov. 11, OF Box 632, and Truman Note, Nov. 15, 1945, PSF, Box 82, Truman Papers, and Westad, *Cold War and Revolution,* 114–115.

43. On Byrnes-Truman, Westad, *Cold War and Revolution,* 116; Rep. Ellis Patterson to Truman, Nov. 14, and Truman to Patterson, Nov. 16, 1945, OF 150, Box 132, Truman Papers; Jiang to Truman, Nov. 14, and Truman to Jiang, Nov. 21, 1945, *FR 45,* VII, 629, 638.

44. Wedemeyer to Marshall, Nov. 5 and Nov. 14, 1945, *FR 1945,* VII, 603–606, 627–628.

45. Minutes of Meeting of Secretaries of State, War, and Navy, Nov. 6, and JCS to Wedemeyer, Nov. 8, 1945, *FR 1945,* VII, 606–607, 610.

46. Westad, *Cold War and Revolution,* 110, 122–127, and Gallicchio, *Cold War Begins,* 118; Minutes of Meeting of Secretaries of State, War, and Navy, Nov. 20, 1945, *FR 1945,* VII, 646–647.

47. Wedemeyer to Eisenhower, Nov. 20 and Nov. 26, 1945, *FR 1945,* VII, 650–660, 679–684.

48. Patterson and Forrestal Memorandum to Byrnes, Nov. 26, 1945, *FR 1945,* VII, 670–678; Gallicchio, *Cold War Begins,* 126, says that Wedemeyer's warnings were seen as proof of need to continue aid to Jiang.

49. Entry for Nov. 19, 1945, Ayers Diary, Box 25, Ayers Papers; Minutes of Meeting of Secretaries of State, War, and Navy, Nov. 27, 1945, *FR 1945,* VII, 684–686.

50. J. Blum (ed.), *Price of Vision,* 519–521.

51. On Marshall appointment, ibid., 522; Vincent Memorandum, Nov. 28, and Marshall to Leahy, Nov. 30, 1945, *FR 1945,* VII, 745–748; Gallicchio, *Cold War Begins,* 131.

52. Marshall Memoranda, Dec. 11 and Dec. 14, and Truman to Marshall, Dec. 15, 1945, *FR 1945,* VII, 767–769, 770–773; Gallicchio, *Cold War Begins,* 132.

53. Truman Statement on "United States Policy toward China," Dec. 15, 1945, *PPHST,* I, 543–545; Memorandum by Soviet Delegation, Foreign Ministers Conversation, and Memorandum Byrnes-Stalin Conversation, Dec. 23, 1945, *FR 1945,* VII, 844–850; Soviet troops departed in April 1946; U.S. forces remained until summer 1947; Moscow Communiqué in Harriman to Acheson, Dec. 27, 1945, *FR 1945,* II, 815–824; I am grateful to Professor Edmund S. Wehrle (emeritus) of the University of Connecticut for pointing to the connection between the Communiqué and Marshall's initial success.

54. Truman to Byrnes, Jan. 5, 1946, PSF, Box 333, Truman Papers; see also chap. 5.

55. Westad, *Cold War and Revolution,* 136–137.

56. On Marshall's early success and the CCP, Stephen I. Levine, *Anvil of Victory: The Communist Revolution in Manchuria* (New York, 1987), 58–62; Marshall to Truman, Dec. 29, 1945, *FR 1945*, VII, 825–826, and Truman to Marshall, Jan. 13, 1946, PSF, Box 183, Truman Papers; on Mao fear of U.S. intervention in China on the British model in Greece, see Sheng, *Battling Western Imperialism*, 85, 99, 104–105.

57. CCP Central Committee Instruction, Feb. 1, 1946, Zhang and Chen (eds.), *Chinese Communist Foreign Policy*, 58-62, Westad, *Cold War and Revolution*, 149, and Bevin Alexander, *Strange Connection: U.S. Intervention in China, 1944–1972* (New York, 1992), 54.

58. Pogue, *Statesman*, 97–106, and Truman quoted in Shepley to Marshall, Mar. 7, 1946, *FR 1946*, IX, 511–512.

59. Notes on Marshall-Zhou Conversation, Dec. 23, 1945, *FR 1945*, VII, 800–803; Westad, *Cold War and Revolution*, 144, 147, 150–151, and Alexander, *Strange Connection*, 50, 54.

60. Westad, *Cold War and Revolution*, 162–164, Alexander, *Strange Connection*, 55, and Marshall to Truman, May 6, 1946, *FR 1946*, IX, 815–818; Levine, *Anvil of Victory*, 78–79, says Stalin withdrew his forces chiefly to forestall a growing world coalition against the Soviets and to blame CCP efforts to gain control in Manchuria for blocking a truce.

61. Pogue, *Statesman*, 113–114, and Marshall to Truman, June 3, 1946, *FR 1946*, IX, 950–973.

62. CCP Central Committee Instruction, Mar. 5, Telegram to Zhou, Apr. 20, and Instruction, May 3, 1946, Zhang and Chen (eds.), *Chinese Communist Foreign Policy*, 62–68; CCP Central Committee to Zhou, May 28, and to Lin Biao, June 25, 1946, ibid., 68–71.

63. Inverchapel to Foreign Office, July 29, 1946, F.O. 371/51607, and Foreign Office Minutes, Aug. 18 and Aug. 29, 1946, F.O. 371/51608; Marshall to Truman, June 17, *FR 1946*, IX, 1099–1101.

64. Entries for July 7, July 8, and July 10, 1946, Millis (ed.), *Forrestal Diaries*, 173–174, 177; entry for July 17, 1946, Ayers Diary, Box 25, Ayers Papers; Pogue, *Statesman*, 113, 118–120.

65. Zhou to Central Committee and Mao, Aug. 10, 1946, Zhang and Chen (eds.), *Chinese Communist Foreign Policy*, 73–75; Truman to Koo (for Jiang), Aug. 10, Marshall to Truman, Aug. 16, and Jiang to Truman, Aug. 28, 1946, *FR 1946*, X, 2–3, 53–54, 91–92; Alexander, *Strange Connection*, 61.

66. Marshall to Truman, Sept. 13, General Zhou Memorandum, Sept. 15, Marshall to Truman, Sept. 23, and Truman to Marshall, Sept. 26, 1946, *FR 1946*, X, 186–187, 189–192, 217–220, 225; Zhou to Central Committee and Mao, Aug. 10, CCP Central Committee to Zhou, Aug. 12 and Sept. 2, and CCP Central Committee Instruction, Sept. 29, 1946, Zhang and Chen (eds.), *Chinese Communist Foreign Policy*, 73–77.

67. Marshall Notes of Meeting with Jiang, Oct. 4, 1946, *FR 1946*, X, 287–289, and Pogue, *Statesman*, 128–129.

68. Marshall Notes of Meeting with Jiang, Dec. 1, 1946, *FR 1946*, X, 575–578.

69. Truman Statement, Dec. 18, 1946, *PPHST*, II, 499–505, and Stuart to Byrnes, Jan. 1, 1947, *FR 1946*, X, 672–677; Marshall to Truman, Dec. 28, 1946, and Marshall Notes on Meeting with Jiang, Jan. 6, 1947, *FR 1946*, X, 661–665, 684–685.

70. Personal Statement by the Special Representative of the President, Jan. 7, 1947, U.S. Department of State, *United States Relations with China, with Special Reference to the Period 1944–1949* (Washington, 1949), 686–689 (hereinafter *China White Paper*); CCP Central Committee to Dong Biwu, Jan. 16, 1947, Zhang and Chen (eds.), *Chinese Communist Foreign Policy*, 77–78.

71. Pauley to Truman, Feb. 14, and Truman to Pauley, Feb. 21, Williams to Truman, Feb. 21, and Truman to Williams, Feb. 25, 1947, PSF, Box 173, Truman Papers; Marshall

Memorandum to Vincent, Feb. 27, 1947, *FR 1947,* VII, 803–804; Connelly Cabinet Notes, Mar. 7, 1947, Connelly Papers.

72. Vincent to Marshall, Jan. 6, Minutes of Meeting of Secretaries of State, War, and Navy, Feb. 12, and Patterson to Marshall, Feb. 26, 1947, *FR 1947,* VII, 6–12, 795–797, 799–802; see also Schnabel, *History of JCS,* II, 442–446.

73. Stuart to Marshall, Mar. 19 and May 16, 1947, *FR 1947,* VII, 71–72, 121–122; Woolridge to Vincent, Apr. 28, Vincent to Woolridge, May 2, Forrestal to Marshall, May 26, and Marshall to Forrestal, June 30, 1947, ibid., 962–963, 967–968; see also Schnabel, *History of JCS,* II, 446–447.

74. Joint Chiefs of Staff Memorandum, June 9, and Vincent Memorandum, June 20, 1947, *FR 1947,* VII, 838–849, 849–850; see also Schnabel, *History of JCS,* II, 447–452.

75. Marshall Memorandum for Truman, July 8, Truman Directive for Wedemeyer, July 9, and State Department Briefing for Wedemeyer Mission, July 14, 1947, *FR 1947,* VII, 639–641, 646–648.

76. Wedemeyer to Marshall, July 29, and Marshall to Wedemeyer, July 30, 1947, *FR 1947,* VII, 682–684; Wedemeyer's Public Remarks in China, and "Report to President Truman," in *China White Paper,* 758–814.

77. Truman-Clifford comments in entry for May 15, 1949, Ayers Diary, Box 25, Ayers Papers; Wedemeyer to Marshall, Sept. 29 and Oct. 3, 1947, *FR 1947,* VII, 778, 781–784, and Pogue, *Statesman,* 273–274.

78. Lewis McCarroll Purifoy, *Harry Truman's China Policy: McCarthyism and the Diplomacy of Hysteria, 1947–1951* (New York, 1976), 54–56; entry for Feb. 12, 1948, Millis (ed.), *Forrestal Diaries,* 371–372, Truman Special Message to Congress, Mar. 16, 1948, *PPHST,* IV, 146; Pogue, *Statesman,* 275–276.

79. Marshall to Stuart, Feb. 9, *FR 1948,* VIII, 13–14, and Department of State Press Release, Mar. 11, 1948, *FR 1948,* VII, 143; Truman News Conference, Mar. 11, 1948, *PPHST,* IV, 179–181, and Sprouse Memorandum, Mar. 15, 1948, *FR 1948,* VII, 151–152; Marshall to Truman, May 14, and Marshall Memorandum, June 11, 1948, *FR 1948,* VIII, 77–79, 90–99.

80. Stuart to Marshall, Aug. 10, and Marshall to Stuart, Aug. 12, 1948, *FR 1948,* VII, 415–416; Souers Note, Aug. 6, and PPS Memorandum, Sept. 7, 1948, *FR 1948,* VIII, 131–135, 146–155.

81. Truman to Jiang, Oct. 16, 1948, *FR 1948,* VII, 180; Purifoy, *Truman's China Policy,* 94–95; Jiang interview, Oct. 31, 1948, in *China White Paper,* 891–893; Alexander, *Strange Connection,* 79–80, and entries for Nov. 22 and Nov. 26, 1948, Millis (ed.), *Forrestal Diaries,* 532–534.

82. Connelly Cabinet Notes, Nov. 28, 1948, Connelly Papers, and entry for May 11, 1949, Lilienthal, *Journals,* II: *Atomic Energy Years,* 525.

83. William Whitney Stueck, Jr., *The Road to Confrontation: American Policy toward China and Korea, 1947–1950* (Chapel Hill, 1981), 510–511, and Ronald McGlothlen, *Controlling the Waves: Dean Acheson and U.S. Foreign Policy in Asia* (New York, 1993), 17–22.

84. Butterworth Memorandum, Jan. 14, and Lapham to Hoffman, Mar. 9, 1949, *FR 1949,* IX, 614, 626–630; Connelly Cabinet Notes, Jan. 19, 1949, Connelly Papers.

85. Diary entry for Feb. 5, 1947, Vandenberg (ed.), *Vandenberg Papers,* 531–532, Acheson Memorandum, Feb. 7, 1949, Box 64, Acheson Papers; Truman to McCormack, Mar. 28, 1949 (first draft), PSF, Box 173, Truman Papers; Acheson to Connally, Mar. 15, 1949, *China White Paper,* 1053; Woodward Memorandum of Conversation, June 22, 1949, *FR 1949,* IX, 708–710.

86. Chen, *China's Road to Korean War,* 9–15; Mao quoted in Hunt, *Genesis of Communist Foreign Policy,* 177.

87. Chen, *China's Road to Korean War,* 9–10, 16–21, and Sheng, *Battling Western Imperialism,* 162–163.

88. Ibid., 15–16, 40–41; Hunt, *Genesis of Communist Foreign Policy,* 174–175, and—on Stalin—Sheng, *Battling Western Imperialism,* 180; on fear of U.S. military intervention, CCP Committee Instruction, Jan. 8, and CCP Central Military Commission Instruction, May 25, 1949, in Zhang and Chen (eds.), *Chinese Communist Foreign Policy,* 93–94, 114–115, and Sheng, op. cit., 64; on diplomatic relations, see CCP Central Committee Instruction, Jan. 19, 1949, in Zhang and Chen, op. cit., 95–99.

89. Chen Jian, "The Sino-Soviet Alliance and China's Entry into the Korean War," CWIHP, Working Paper No. 1 (June 1992), 6–7, and Brian Murray, "Stalin, the Cold War, and the Division of China: A Multiarchival Mystery," CWIHP, Working Paper No. 12 (June 1995), 5–6; Hunt, *Genesis of Communist Foreign Policy,* 179–180, and Goncharov et al., *Uncertain Partners,* 42–43.

90. Sheng, *Battling Western Imperialism,* 168–169; Sheng refers to the Mao-Stalin exchanges as the start of an "equal partnership"; it might be said instead that Stalin's efforts at this time—from Mikoyan's cautious advice to concern about conflict with the U.S. and interest in mediating the civil war—suggests "elder statesman" attempts to constrain a more radical, and potentially rivalrous, leader.

91. On Roshchin's activities, see Murray, "Stalin and Division of China," 6–10; CCP Central Committee to Nanjing Military Commission, Apr. 28, 1949, in Zhang and Chen (eds.), *Chinese Communist Foreign Policy,* 109–110.

92. Nancy Bernkopf Tucker, *Patterns in the Dust: Chinese-American Relations and the Recognition Controversy, 1949–1950* (New York, 1983), 120–126; Truman to McCormack [Mar. 29, 1949], PSF, Box 173, Truman Papers, and Acheson, "Notes for a Meeting with Republican Congressmen," Feb. 24, 1949, Box 64, Acheson Papers; Chang, *Friends and Enemies,* 32; Acheson to Stuart, May 13, 1949, *FR 1949,* IX, 22–23.

93. Souers Notes, Jan. 11, 1949 (NSC 34/1, "U.S. Policy toward China"), and Feb. 4, 1949, *FR 1949,* IX, 474–475, 484–485; Souers Notes, Feb. 28 (NSC 34/2, "U.S. Policy toward China"), and Lay Memorandum to NSC, Mar. 3, 1949, ibid., 491–495.

94. Stuart to Acheson, Mar. 10, and Acheson to Stuart, Apr. 6, 1949, *FR 1949,* VIII, 173–177, 230–231; Clubb to Acheson, June 1 and June 2, and Stuart to Acheson, June 7, 1949, ibid., 357–360, 363–364, 372–373; Webb Memorandum of Conversation with Truman, June 16, and Clubb to Acheson, June 24, 1949, ibid., 388, 397–398.

95. Chen, *China's Road to Korean War,* 52; CCP Central Committee to Nanjing Municipal Committee, May 10, 1949, in Zhang and Chen (eds.), *Chinese Communist Foreign Policy,* 111–112.

96. Stuart to Acheson, June 8 and June 30, 1949, *FR 1949,* VIII, 752–753, 766–767.

97. Stuart to Acheson, June 30, Davies to Kennan, June 30, and Cabot to Acheson, July 1, 1949, ibid., 766–769; on Ward case, Tucker, *Patterns in Dust,* 44, 231 n. 17, and Michael H. Hunt, "Mao Tse-tung and the Issue of Accommodation with the U.S.," in Dorothy Borg and Waldo Heinrichs (eds.), *Uncertain Years: Chinese-American Relations,1947–1950* (New York, 1980), 204, Chen, *China's Road to Korean War,* 33–39, and Sheng, *Battling Western Imperialism,* 172–174, who sees Mao's aim as "squeezing out" Western interests without provoking direct conflict.

98. Acheson to Stuart, July 1, 1949, *FR 1949,* VIII, 769; on Truman, entry for June 27, 1949, Ayers Diary, Box 26, Ayers Papers.

99. On the "lost chance," see Warren I. Cohen, "Conversations with Chinese Friends: Zhou Enlai's Associates on Chinese-American Relations in the 1940s and the Korean War," *DH,* 11 (Summer 1987), 283–289, Zhigong Ho, "'Lost Chance' or 'Inevitable Hostility': Two Contending Interpretations of the Late 1940s Chinese-American Relations," The Society for Historians of American Foreign Relations *Newsletter,* 20 (Sept. 1989), 67–78, and the essays by Chen Jian, John W. Garver, and Odd Arne Westad in "Symposium: Rethinking the Lost Chance in China," *DH,* 21 (Winter 1977), 71–115, which suggest almost no prospect

for serious U.S.-CCP relations; Warren Cohen, in the introduction to the Symposium, states (p. 75) that there was prospect for modest diplomatic and economic relations but that ideology precluded friendly relations; Sheng, *Battling Western Imperialism,* 180–183, views the approach to Stuart as CCP disinformation to preclude U.S. military intervention; he concludes (p. 186) that Mao's regime "was born anti-American and pro-Soviet" but also admits (p. 115) that U.S. aid to the GMD gave the CCP "sufficient reasons to hate the Americans"; on Zhou-Keon contact, Chen, *China's Road to Korean War,* 56, 241–242 n. 82; on CCP and recognition, Chen, *China's Road to Korean War,* 38–42; Christensen, *Useful Adversaries,* 144–147.

100. On Mao's speech, Hunt, "Mao and Accommodation," 211–216, and Hunt, *Genesis of Communist Foreign Policy,* 180–181.

101. On terms for relations with CCP, Christensen, *Useful Adversaries,* 145; British Embassy to United States, Mar. 19, and Acheson Memorandum, June 16, 1949, *FR 1949,* IX, 11–12, 43; Stueck, *Road to Confrontation,* 122–126; on Mao's overtures, General Shen Ming Shu Memorandum, July 10, and Stuart to Acheson, July 14, 1949, *FR 1949,* VIII, 771–779; on Mao and Soviet policy, and emissary to Stuart, Goncharov et al., *Uncertain Partners,* 42–44, 49–55.

102. Acheson Memorandum, July 11, and Acheson to Stuart, July 20, 1949, *FR 1949,* VIII, 780–781, 794; Acheson to Douglas, July 20, 1949, *FR 1949,* IX, 50–52.

103. Tucker, *Patterns in Dust,* 74–75; Clark to Acheson, July 18, 1949, *FR 1949,* IX, 1127; on blockade, Stuart to Acheson, June 24, and Webb Memorandum of Conversation with Truman, Oct. 1, 1949, ibid., 1118–1119, 1141, and Acheson Memorandum of Conversation with Truman, Oct. 10, 1949, Box 64, Acheson Papers; on negative results, Cabot to Acheson, July 7, and Sprouse Memorandum, Aug. 9, 1949, *FR 1949,* IX, 1261–1265.

104. Liu Shaoqi Memorandum to Stalin, July 4, 1949, in Zhang and Chen (eds.), *Chinese Communist Foreign Policy,* 118–122, Hunt, *Genesis of Communist Foreign Policy,* 180–181, and Chen, "Sino-Soviet Alliance," 910, who notes that Liu was not anxious to accept the PRC-USSR East-West division of responsibility for inciting revolutions.

105. Acheson Memorandum for Truman, May 12, and Clifford to Truman, May 17, 1949, *FR 1949,* IX, 1365–1367; Acheson Letter of Transmittal, July 30, 1949, in *China White Paper,* iii–xvii; Truman News Conference, Aug. 11, 1949, *PPHST,* V, 421.

106. On *China White Paper* and "diatribe," Chang, *Friends and Enemies,* 36–41; on bombing, Davies Memorandum, and Sprouse Note, Aug. 24, 1949, *FR 1949,* IX, 536–540 (Sprouse said of Davies' bombing proposal, "Maybe I'm old fashioned, but this has to be read to be believed"); on Mao, Hunt, "Mao and Accommodation," 217–19, and Goncharov et al., *Uncertain Partners,* 73–75.

107. NSC 41 ("Draft Report . . . on United States Policy regarding Trade with China"), Feb. 28, 1949, *FR 1949,* IX, 826–834; Acheson Memorandum, Sept. 13, 1949, ibid., 81–84; Truman Statement, Sept. 23, 1949, *PPHST,* IV, 48.

108. Clubb to Acheson, Oct. 2., 1949, *FR 1949,* IX, 93–94, and *New York Times,* Oct. 3, 1949; Stryker Memorandum, Nov. 2, 1949, *FR 1949,* IX, 156–158; Kirk to Acheson, Oct. 7, and Clubb to Acheson, Oct. 11, 1949, ibid., 106–107, 121–122; Acheson to Certain Diplomatic and Consular Offices, Oct. 13, 1949, *FR 1949,* VIII, 1323; Acheson quoted on PRC in David McLean, "American Nationalism, the China Myth, and the Truman Doctrine: The Question of Accommodation with Beijing in 1949–1950," *DH,* 10 (Winter 1986), 30–31; Acheson Memorandum of Conversation with Truman and Nehru, Oct. 13, 1949, *FR 1949,* IX, 127–128; see also Stueck, *Road to Confrontation,* 131–132.

109. On Ward case, McGlothlen, *Controlling the Waves,* 150–152, and Chen, *China's Road to Korean War,* 59–60; on Truman, Webb Memorandum, Nov. 14, 1949, *FR 1949,* IX, 1008.

110. Acheson Memorandum of Conversation with Truman, Nov. 17, 1949, Box 64, Acheson Papers; Bradley Memorandum, Nov. 18, 1949, *FR 1949*, VIII, 1011–1013, and Acheson Memorandum to Truman, Nov. 21, 1949, ibid., 1015–1016.

111. Ogburn Memorandum, Nov. 2, 1949, *FR 1949*, IX, 160–162, Stueck, *Road to Confrontation*, 131–132, 138–140; on Formosa, McGlothlen, *Controlling the Waves*, 86–106, and Robert J. Donovan, *Tumultuous Years: The Presidency of Harry S. Truman, 1949–1953* (New York, 1982), 86–87; Memorandum Acheson-Franks Conversation, Dec. 8, 1949, *FR 1949*, IX, 442–443, and Souers Memorandum, Dec. 30, 1949 (NSC 42/2, "The Policy of the United States with Respect to Asia"), *FR 1949*, VII, 1215–1220.

112. Truman News Conference, Jan. 5, 1950, *PPHST*, VI, 11–12; entry for Jan. 5, 1950, Ayers Diary, Box 26, Ayers Papers; Acheson, *Present at the Creation*, 351–352; Acheson Memorandum, Jan. 5, 1950, *FR 1950*, VI, 260–263.

113. Acheson quoted in Connelly Cabinet Notes, Dec. 22, 1949, Connelly Papers; Truman believed that the British "had not played squarely with us" on moving toward recognition, Acheson Memorandum, Oct. 16, 1949, *FR 1949*, IX, 32 (formal British recognition came on January 6); Acheson, *Present at the Creation*, 355–357; on Japanese defense, Stueck, *Road to Confrontation*, 147; impact of Acheson speech on Chinese, Edwin W. Martin, *Divided Counsel: The Anglo-American Response to Communist Victory in China* (Lexington, 1986), 111.

114. Webb to Truman, and Acheson to Clubb, Jan. 10, 1950, *FR 1950*, VI, 270–272, 275, and Martin, *Divided Counsel*, 106–113 (the 1901 protocol had been reaffirmed in the 1943 Sino-American treaty in which the U.S. had relinquished extraterritorial privileges in China).

115. Clubb to Acheson, Jan. 20, 1950, *FR 1950*, VI, 286–289; Mao to Liu, Jan. 13 and Jan. 18, 1950, Zhang and Chen (eds.), *Chinese Communist Foreign Policy*, 136, 138; Chen, *China's Road to Korean War*, 60–61.

116. Acheson to Consulate General in Vietnam, Feb. 4, 1950, *FR 1950*, VI, 720–721; Gary Hess, *Vietnam and the United States: Origins and Legacy of War* (Boston, 1990), 38–40; Stueck, *Road to Confrontation*, 146.

117. Stueck, *Road to Confrontation*, 143–145, E. J. Kahn, *The China Hands: American Foreign Service Officers and What Befell Them* (New York, 1975), esp. 212–242, and Harvey Klehr and Ronald Radosh, *The Amerasia Spy Case: Prelude to McCarthyism* (Chapel Hill, 1996), which confirms the "wildness" of McCarthy's charges (pp. 162–165), and that Service's firing in 1951 as a result of Loyalty-Security Review Board hearings had nothing to do with spying or disloyalty; he was "the first victim of the Cold War" (p. 12); see also Hamby, *Man of the People*, 529–532; Truman News Conference, Mar. 30, 1950, *PPHST*, VI, 234–236; Truman also accused the Republicans of seeking a campaign issue.

118. Chen, *China's Road to Korean War*, 80, Goncharov et al., *Uncertain Partners*, 85–86, and Record of Conversation between Comrade I. V. Stalin and Chairman . . . Mao, Dec. 16, 1945, CWIHP, 6–7 (Winter 1995/1996), 5–9; Chen and Goncharov note that Chinese and Russian records of the meeting differ, with the Russian version more explicit about Mao's views.

119. Chen, *China's Road to Korean War*, 80–81; Zhou was both prime minister and foreign minister, and thus the appropriate official to sign a treaty.

120. Terms of treaty in Goncharov et al., *Uncertain Partners*, 260–261; the treaty was to run for thirty years.

121. Text of agreements in ibid., 261–264; according to the Russian Record of Conversation between Comrade I. V. Stalin and Chairman . . . Mao, Jan. 22, 1950, 7–9, the Soviet leader said that Japan's defeat made the Sino-Soviet treaty an "anachronism," and as for Yalta,

"to hell with it"; on Additional Agreement, ibid., 121; on planes, Chen, *China's Road to Korean War,* 84.

122. Goncharov et al., *Uncertain Partners,* 121–123.

123. Hunt, *Genesis of Communist Foreign Policy,* 182, Chen, *China's Road to Korean War,* 90–91, and Goncharov et al., *Uncertain Partners,* 121–129; see also Zhou Speech, Mar. 20, 1950, Zhang and Chen (eds.), *Chinese Communist Foreign Policy,* 143–147.

124. Acheson to Embassy in France, Feb. 11, 1950, *FR 1950,* VI, 308–311; Memorandum Acheson-Truman Conversation, Mar. 9, 1950, Box 65, Acheson Papers; Acheson Speech, "United States Policy toward Asia," Mar. 15, 1950, in *Department of State Bulletin,* 22 (Mar. 29, 1950), 469–470, and McGlothlen, *Controlling the Waves,* 158–159.

125. Sprouse Memorandum, Feb. 16, Hacker Memorandum, Feb. 17, 1950, *FR 1950* VI, 312–314, and Acheson Memorandum, Mar. 27, 1950, Box 65, Acheson Papers.

126. Rusk Memorandum, Apr. 12, 1950, *FR 1950,* VI, 328–329; Truman Address, May 9, 1950, *PPHST,* VI, 333–337.

127. David Mayers, *Cracking the Monolith: U.S. Policy against the Sino-Soviet Alliance, 1949–1955* (Baton Rouge, 1986), 78–79; McGlothlen, *Controlling the Waves,* 117–119.

128. Armstrong Memorandum, May 31, and Rusk Memorandum, May 30, 1950, *FR 1950,* VI, 347–351; Rusk, a former Rhodes Scholar from Georgia, had been a wartime military intelligence officer in the China-Burma-India theater and was currently deputy under secretary of state, a higher position than the one he now took at Acheson's request, Mc-Glothlen, *Controlling the Waves,* 115–116.

129. McGlothlen, *Controlling the Waves,* 125–127.

130. Jessup Memoranda, June 25 and June 26, and Truman Statement, June 27, 1950, *FR 1950,* VII, 157–161, 178–183, 202–203.

131. Goncharov et al., *Uncertain Partners,* 157.

132. Chang, *Friends and Enemies,* 16.

133. Truman to Vandenberg, July 6, 1950, quoted in McLean, "American Nationalism," 40.

Chapter 13. Turning Point

1. Muccio to Acheson, June 25, 1950, *FR 1950,* VII, 125–126 (Korean time was thirteen hours ahead of that of the United States; hence Muccio's cable was dated 10:00 A.M., June 25, 1950).

2. Truman, *Years of Trial and Hope,* 331–333; UN Resolution, June 25, 1950, in *FR 1950,* VII, 155–156; the Soviets may also have been hoping to embroil the PRC with the U.S. in a conflict over Taiwan and possibly Korea; see Peter Lowe, *The Origins of the Korean War* (New York, 1986), 160–161.

3. Christensen, *Useful Adversaries,* 122–127.

4. Truman to Pauley, July 16, 1946, *FR 1946,* VIII, 713–714, and Elsey Note, June 26, 1950, Box 71, Elsey Papers.

5. Truman News Conference, June 29, 1950, *PPHST,* VI, 502–506; "pagan wolves" quoted in Donovan, *Tumultuous Years,* 256.

6. Lowe, *Origins of Korean War,* 1–9.

7. Bruce Cumings, *The Origins of the Korean War,* I: *Liberation and the Emergence of Separate Regimes, 1945–1947* (Princeton, 1981), 104–109; William Whitney Stueck, Jr., *The Korean War: An International History* (Princeton, 1995), 17, notes that an occasional State Department paper (1943) expressed concern that Soviet occupation of Korea would

create "an entirely new strategic situation" there with possible repercussions in China and Japan.

8. Cumings, *Origins of Korean War,* I, 109, and Kathryn Weathersby, "Soviet Aims in Korea and the Origins of the Korean War, 1945–1950: New Evidence from the Soviet Archives," CWIHP, Working Paper No. 8 (Nov. 1993), 5–6; Harriman to Truman, July 3, 1945, *FR 1945,* VII, 912–914, and Stimson Memorandum to Truman, July 16, 1945, *FR 1945: Potsdam,* II, 631.

9. Stueck, *Korean War,* 18; Minutes of Sixth Plenary Conference, July 22, and JCS Minutes, July 24, 1945, *FR 1945: Potsdam,* II, 251–254, 351–352.

10. Pauley to Truman, and Harriman to Truman, Aug. 10, 1945, *FR 1945,* VII, 149, 967; Lowe, *Origins of Korean War,* 14.

11. Rusk Memorandum, July 12, 1950, *FR 1945,* VI, 1039, and Cumings, *Origins of Korean War,* I, 120–123.

12. Stueck, *Korean War,* 19, and Cumings, *Origins of Korean War,* I, 121–122; Weathersby, "Soviet Aims in Korea," 9–11, says that Stalin saw joint administration, with Soviet control in the north, as the means to protect its position in Manchuria by balancing U.S. control in the south (and its Pacific gains) and precluding hostile action from a revived Japan.

13. Lowe, *Origins of Korean War,* 38–39; Dae-Sook Suh, *Kim Il Sung: The North Korean Leader* (New York, 1988), 61, 66–67.

14. Cumings, *Origins of Korean War,* I, 397–418; Suh, *Kim Il Sung,* 3–4, 14–54, 67, 70–73.

15. Truman News Conference, Aug. 16, 1945, *PPHST,* I, 226; on Hodge-Truman comparison, Cumings, *Origins of Korean War,* I, 440; Benninghoff to Byrnes, Sept. 15, 1945, *FR 1945,* VI, 1049–1050; on Hodge's widely quoted reference to Koreans as "same breed of cat" as Japanese, Cumings, op. cit., 138.

16. Charles M. Dobbs, *The Unwanted Symbol: American Foreign Policy, the Cold War, and Korea, 1945–1950* (Kent, 1981), 30–48, and Truman News Conference, Sept. 12, and Truman Statement on the Liberation of Korea, Sept. 18, 1945, *PPHST,* I, 320, 324–325.

17. Lowe, *Origins of Korean War,* 5, and Cumings, *Origins of Korean War,* I, 188–193.

18. Cumings, *Origins of Korean War,* I, 215–216; cf. Dobbs, *Unwanted Symbol,* 63–68.

19. Cumings, *Origins of Korean War,* I, 219–225, 431–432; Harriman, *Special Envoy,* 553.

20. Truman to Byrnes [unsent], Jan. 5, 1946, Ferrell (ed.), *Off the Record,* 79–80; entry for Feb. 25, 1946, Ayers Diary, Box 25, Ayers Papers.

21. Byrnes to Certain Diplomatic Offices, Apr. 11, and SWNCC Memorandum, May 22, 1946, *FR 1946,* VIII, 659, 681–682; Lowe, *Origins of Korean War,* 26–27.

22. Cumings, *Origins of Korean War,* I, 246–256, 405–424, Weathersby, "Soviet Aims in Korea," 16–18, and Suh, *Kim Il Sung,* 89–91.

23. SWNCC Memorandum, May 22, and Pauley to Truman, June 22, 1946, *FR 1946,* VIII, 681–682, 706–709.

24. Truman to Pauley, July 16, 1946, and Draft of Truman Letter to Patterson [n.d.], *FR 1946,* VIII, 713–714, 721–722.

25. Dobbs, *Unwanted Symbol,* 87–91, and Langdon to Marshall, Dec. 27, 1946, *FR 1946,* VIII, 780–782.

26. Memorandum of Special Interdepartmental Committee on Korea, Feb. 25, 1947, *FR 1947,* VI, 608–616, and Schnabel, *History of JCS,* II, 14–15, see also McGlothlen, *Controlling the Waves,* 151–154.

27. Rhee to Truman, Mar. 13, 1947, *FR 1947,* VI, 620, and Acheson Testimony, Mar. 13, 1947, U.S. Senate, *Legislative Origins,* 21–22.

28. Acheson to Patterson, Mar. 28, and Patterson to Acheson, Apr. 4, 1947, *FR 1947,* VI, 621–623, 625–628; Acheson quoted in Dobbs, *Unwanted Symbol,* 96–97; Marshall to Acheson, Apr. 2, 1947, *FR 1947,* VI, 623–624.

29. McGlothlen, *Controlling the Waves,* 58–59, and Lowe, *Origins of Korean War,* 34–35; Lovett to Soviet Embassy, Aug. 26, and Molotov to Marshall, Sept. 4, and Wedemeyer Report excerpt, Sept. 27, 1947, *FR 1947,* VI, 771–774, 779–781, 799–803.

30. Forrestal to Marshall, Sept. 29, 1947, *FR 1947,* VI, 817–818, and Schnabel, *History of JCS,* II, 15–17 (the military believed that any offensive action in Asia would bypass Korea, which could be neutralized through air power); Kennan Memorandum to Butterworth, Sept. 24, and Stevens Memorandum, Sept. 9, 1947, *FR 1947,* VI, 784–785, 814; Butterworth Memorandum to Lovett, Oct. 1, 1947, ibid., 820–821.

31. Austin to Lie, Oct. 17, and Resolution Adopted by the General Assembly, Nov. 14, 1947, *FR 1947,* VI, 832–835, 857–859; Jacobs to Marshall, Oct. 10, 1947, ibid., 848–849; Lovett Memorandum, Jan. 3, and Truman to MacKenzie King (prime minister of Canada), Jan. 5, 1948, *FR 1948,* VI, 1079–1083.

32. Lowe, *Origins of Korean War,* 47; Butterworth Memorandum to Marshall, Mar. 4, and Allison Memorandum, Mar. 5, 1945, *FR 1948,* VI, 1139–1141; Souers Note, Apr. 2, 1948, "NSC 8, Report by the National Security Council on the Position of the United States with Respect to Korea," ibid., 1164–1169 (italics in text in original).

33. Butterworth to Marshall and Lovett, May 11, 1948, *FR 1948,* VI, 1192–1195; White House Statement, Jan. 1, 1949, *PPHST,* V, 1; Lowe, *Origins of Korean War,* 48–52, Goncharov et al., *Uncertain Partners,* 133, and Suh, *Kim Il Sung,* 98–102.

34. Burton I. Kaufman, *The Korean War: Challenge in Crisis, Credibility, and Command* (New York, 1986), 21, and Dobbs, *Unwanted Symbol,* 154–155; Saltzman Memorandum and Lovett Note, Sept. 7, 1948, *FR 1948,* VI, 1292–1298; on withdrawal delay, Lovett to Royall, July 8, 1948, ibid., 1234–1235.

35. Royall Memorandum, Feb. 8, Acheson to Muccio, Apr. 15, Muccio Memorandum, May 2, Muccio to Acheson, May 7 and May 9, and Acheson to Embassy in Korea, May 9, 1949, *FR 1949,* VII, Part 2, 956–958, 992, 1012–1014, 1031–1035; see also Acheson Memorandum, July 11, 1949, Box 64, Acheson Papers.

36. McGlothlen, *Controlling the Waves,* 69–72; Truman Special Message to Congress on Continuation of Economic Assistance to Korea, June 7, 1949, *PPHST,* V, 277–279; on Webb, and the aid bill, Dobbs, *Unwanted Symbol,* 163–168; see also Memorandum for President Truman, July 11, 1949, Box 6, Clifford Papers.

37. Report by the National Security Council to the President, Mar. 22, 1949 (NSC 8/2, "Position of the United States with Respect to Korea"), and Memorandum by the Army Department to the State Department, June 27, 1949, *FR 1949,* VII, Part 2, 969–979, 1046–1056.

38. MacArthur quoted in John W. Spanier, *The Truman-MacArthur Controversy and the Korean War* (New York, 1965), 171; see also Ferrell, *Truman,* 318; Michael Schaller, *Douglas MacArthur: The Far Eastern General* (New York, 1989), 163; NSC 48/1, Dec. 23, and NSC 48/2, Dec. 30, 1949, Thomas H. Etzold and John Lewis Gaddis, *Containment: Documents on American Policy and Strategy, 1945–1950* (New York, 1978), 252–276; Truman to Rhee, Sept. 26, 1949, *FR 1949,* VII, 1084–1085.

39. Acheson, *Present at the Creation,* 355–357, 691, and Bruce Cumings, *The Origins of the Korean War,* II: *The Roaring of the Cataract, 1947–1950* (Princeton, 1990), 420–435; ironically, the main subject of the speech, "Crisis in China—An Estimate of United States Policy," was about Jiang's and the GMD's failings that led to their loss of power; Jessup Memorandum, Jan. 14, 1950, *FR 1950,* VII, 1–7.

40. McGlothlen, *Controlling the Waves,* 74–75.

41. Lowe, *Origins of Korean War,* 64–65, and Cumings, *Origins of Korean War,* II, 485–488, and Stueck, *Korean War,* 40–41; on Korean aid, Bond Memorandum, May 10, 1950, *FR 1950,* VII, 78–83; on Connally, Rusk Memorandum to Webb, May 4, and Rhee Press Conference, May 12, 1950, ibid., 64–66, 85 n. 2; CIA Memorandum, June 19, 1950, ibid., 109–119.

42. On Truman statements, see Annual Message to the Congress, Jan. 4, Address at George Washington Masonic Memorial, Feb. 22, News Conference, Mar. 22, and Address at American Society of Newspaper Editors, Apr. 22, 1950, *PPHST,* VI, 2–11, 172–175, 232–238, 260–264; Herken, *Winning Weapon,* 319–321, and Truman Statement, Jan. 31, 1950, *FR 1950,* I, 141–142.

43. Greg Herken, *Cardinal Choices: Presidential Science Advising from the Atomic Bomb to SDI* (New York, 1992), 35–36, and Holloway, *Stalin and Bomb,* 295, 299.

44. Herken, *Cardinal Choices,* 37–38; Richard Rhodes, *Dark Sun: The Making of the Hydrogen Bomb* (New York, 1995), 372–374; Truman quote in diary entry for Sept. 21, 1950, Lilienthal, *Journals,* II: *Atomic Energy Years,* 571; Truman Statement, Sept. 23, 1949, *PPHST,* V, 216.

45. Herken, *Winning Weapon,* 316, and idem, *Cardinal Choices,* 41.

46. On the Harmon Report, Rosenberg, "American Atomic Strategy," 69–78.

47. Herken, *Cardinal Choices,* 40; on Vandenberg, Rhodes, *Dark Sun,* 387–388.

48. Oppenheimer to Lilienthal, Oct. 30, 1949, *FR 1949,* I, 569–573 for majority report and Rabi-Fermi proposal; see also Herken, *Cardinal Choices,* 40–43.

49. Lilienthal to Truman, Nov. 9, and Truman to NSC, Nov. 19, 1949, *FR 1949,* I, 576–585, 587–588.

50. McMahon to Truman, Nov. 21, Bradley to Johnson, Nov. 23, and Strauss to Truman, Nov. 25, 1949, ibid., 588–599.

51. Rhodes, *Dark Sun,* 405; for Kennan's belief that the U.S. was "traveling down the atomic road too fast" and might wish to weigh a no-use policy on atomic weapons, see Arneson Memorandum, Nov. 2, 1949, *FR 1949,* I, 506–507; for Kennan's proposals, see Report by PPS, Aug. 16, 1949, ibid., 514–516.

52. Acheson, *Present at the Creation,* 348–349.

53. JCS to Johnson, Jan. 13, 1950, *FR 1950,* I, 503–511.

54. Herken, *Winning Weapon,* 317; Acheson Memorandum, Jan. 19, 1950, ibid., 511–512.

55. On Souers, Rhodes, *Dark Sun,* 407 (Truman also told his White House staff on Jan. 21 that he had reached a decision on Super, but he did not reveal it, entry for Jan. 21, 1950, Ayers Diary, Box 26, Ayers Papers); diary entry for Jan. 31, 1950, Lilienthal, *Journals,* II: *Atomic Energy Years,* 623–632.

56. Report by Special NSC Committee to the President, Jan. 31, 1950, *FR 1950,* I, 513–517.

57. Diary entry for Jan. 31, 1950, Lilienthal, *Journals,* II: *Atomic Energy Years,* 632–634; Lilienthal quoted on AEC role in Herken, *Winning Weapon,* 320; Statement by President, Jan. 31, 1950, *PPHST,* VI, 138, and Herken, *Cardinal Choices,* 47; entry for Feb. 4, 1950, Ayers Diary, Box 26, Ayers Papers.

58. Herken, *Cardinal Choices,* 48, and Holloway, *Stalin and the Bomb,* 295, 299, 318.

59. Rabi quoted in Rhodes, *Dark Sun,* 408.

60. Diary entry for Feb. 2, 1950, Lilienthal, *Journals,* II: *Atomic Energy Years,* 634; Ed. Note, *FR 1950,* I, 524, and Haynes and Klehr, *Venona,* 304–307.

61. Johnson to Truman, Feb. 24, and NSC Special Committee Report, Mar. 9, 1950, *FR 1950,* I, 538–539, 541–542; Truman, *Years of Trial and Hope,* 310–311; Herken, *Cardinal Choices,* 50–52, points out that in making his decision, Truman did not consult the

GAC, which could have informed him of the limited value of Fuchs' information on Super and the cost of the "all-out" program to atomic weapons development.

62. Herken, *Cardinal Choices,* 53–54, 58–60, and G. Pascal Zachary, *Endless Frontier: Vannevar Bush, Engineer of the American Century* (New York, 1997), 362–363.

63. Ibid., 61–63, 80, 237 n. 56, and Holloway, *Stalin and the Bomb,* 303.

64. Holloway, *Stalin and the Bomb,* 297–299, 303–315.

65. Ibid., 308, 316–317, and Herken, *Cardinal Choices,* 80–81.

66. On Nitze, Chace, *Acheson,* 273–274.

67. NSC 68 in FR 1950, I, 237–292; Lovett quoted in Chase, *Acheson,* 278–279.

68. Leffler, *Preponderance of Power,* 355–358, stresses that "every program alluded to in NSC 68 either had been or was in process of being launched"; Gaddis Smith, *Morality, Reason, and Power: American Diplomacy in the Carter Years* (New York, 1986), 21–22, emphasizes NSC 68's zero-sum game approach to politics and its substantive similarity to McCarthyism.

69. Gaddis, *Strategies of Containment,* 106, Acheson, *Present at the Creation,* 374, and Chace, *Acheson,* 279; on Johnson, who was finance chairman of Truman's 1948 campaign and may have wanted to cut the budget and run for president in 1952, see Donovan, *Tumultuous Years,* 61–62.

70. Leffler, *Preponderance of Power,* 358–360, and Ernest R. May (ed.), *American Cold War Strategy: Interpreting NSC 68* (Boston, 1993), 14; Truman Special Message to the Congress on Military Aid, *PPHST,* VI, 441–449.

71. Acheson, *Present at the Creation,* 374; Herken, *Winning Weapon,* 329.

72. Lowe, *Origins of Korean War,* 159–160, Kaufman, *Korean War,* 29, and Cumings, *Origins of Korean War,* II, 568–585, who raises questions about ROK provocations and who fired the first shots.

73. Truman Statement on the Violation of the 38th Parallel in Korea, June 26, 1950, *PPHST,* VI, 491–492, and Acheson to Wallace, Aug. 10, 1950, Box 65, Acheson Papers.

74. Cumings, *Origins of Korean War,* I, 245, and idem, *Origins of Korean War,* II, 619–621.

75. Suh, *Kim Il Sung,* 112–121; see also Kathryn Weathersby, "Korea 1949–1950: To Attack or Not to Attack? Kim Il Sung and the Prelude to War," CWIHP, *Bulletin,* 5 (Spring 1995), 1–5.

76. Evegueni Bajanov, "Assessing the Politics of the Korean War, 1949–1951," CWIHP, *Bulletin: The Cold War in Asia,* 6–7 (Winter 1995/1996), 54.

77. Tunkin to Foreign Ministry," Sept. 14, 1950, in Weathersby, "Korea 1949–50," 6–7, and Shen Zhihua, "Sino-Soviet Relations and the Origins of the Korean War: Stalin's Strategic Goals in the Far East," *Journal of Cold War Studies,* 2 (Spring 2000), 48–49.

78. Bajanov, "Assessing Politics of Korean War," 54, 87; Shtykov to Vishinsky, Jan. 19, and Stalin to Shtykov, Jan. 30, 1950, in Weathersby, "Korea 1949–1950," 8–9.

79. Goncharov et al., *Uncertain Partners,* 144–145, and Bajanov, "Assessing Politics of Korean War," 88; on Mao's willingness to receive Kim, see Ignatiev to Vishinsky, Apr. 10, 1950, in Kathryn Weathersby, "New Russian Documents on the Korean War," CWIHP, *Bulletin,* 6–7 (Winter 1995–1996), 36.

80. Goncharov et al., *Uncertain Partners,* 151–152, Weathersby, "Soviet Aims in Korea," 23–26, and Shen "Sino-Soviet Relations," 53–54; Mao had already obtained Stalin's permission to take Taiwan; hence it would have been hard for him to refuse Kim on grounds of fear of U.S. intervention.

81. Shen, "Sino-Soviet Relations," 51–62, and Goncharov et al., *Uncertain Partners,* 152; see also Holloway, *Stalin and the Bomb,* 277–278.

82. Chen, *China's Road to Korean War,* 106–110.

83. Goncharov et al., *Uncertain Partners,* 148, and Chen, *China's Road to Korean War,* 95, 111–112, who says Mao's demobilization of ground forces was intended not only to cut expenses but to permit building of air and naval forces to prepare for long-range confrontation with the U.S.

84. Goncharov et al., *Uncertain Partners,* 152–154, and Chen, *China's Road to Korean War,* 112–113; Bajanov, "Assessing Politics of Korean War," 87, quotes Ambassador Shtykov reporting Mao's view that the U.S. "would not start a world war over such a small territory"; but Shtykov, who wanted the DPRK to attack, may have exaggerated Mao's view; see Shtykov to Vishinsky, May 12, 1950, in Weathersby, "New Documents on Korean War," 37; on Chinese anger, see "Recollection, Shi Zhe," in Zhang and Chen (eds.), *Chinese Communist Foreign Policy,* 153, which quotes Mao as saying on June 28, 1950, of the North Koreans—who sent a field-grade officer to inform about the war—that "they are our close neighbors. When they went to war, they did not consult with us. Now they have encountered troubles, and they come to us."

85. Goncharov et al., *Uncertain Partners,* 147–148, and Lowe, *Origins of Korean War,* 154–159.

86. Donovan, *Tumultuous Years,* 195–196; Truman, *Years of Trial and Hope,* 332–333; McGlothlen, *Controlling the Waves,* 81–82; Elsey Notes, June 26 and June 27, 1950, Box 71, Elsey Papers; Truman to Senator Joseph O'Mahoney, June 28, 1950, PSF, Box 243, Truman Papers.

87. John P. Davies comments, June 25, Office of Intelligence Estimate, June 25, and Dulles Memorandum, June 29, 1950, *FR 1950,* VII, 143, 148–154, 238; British reaction in Minutes of a Meeting of the Cabinet, June 27, 1950, CAB 128/17, and French reaction in Bruce to Acheson, June 26, 1950, *FR 1950,* VII, 175–176; Acheson Memorandum, June 30, 1950, Box 65, Acheson Papers.

88. Acheson to Kirk, June 25, Resolution Adopted by Security Council, June 25, Kirk to Acheson and Acheson to Kirk, June 26, 1950, *FR 1950,* VII, 148, 155–156, 169–170, 177; see also Stueck, *Road to Confrontation,* 192.

89. Lowe, *Origins of Korean War,* 160–161, and Goncharov et al., *Uncertain Partners,* 161–162; Mastny, *Cold War and Soviet Insecurity,* 98–99, says Stalin miscalculated about how fast the Security Council would act.

90. Webb's advice in Ferrell, *Truman,* 322–323; MacArthur Memorandum, June 14, 1950, Annex to Jessup Memorandum, June 25, 1950, *FR 1950,* VII, 161–165; on Truman's increased "hands on" policy, Leffler, *Preponderance of Power,* 363.

91. Jessup Memorandum, June 25, 1950, *FR 1950,* VII, 157–161; Acheson, *Present at the Creation,* 415.

92. Truman Statement, June 26, 1950, *PPHST,* VI, 491–492; Acheson Memorandum and Jessup Memorandum, June 26, 1950, *FR 1950,* VII, 172–173, 178–184.

93. Jessup Memorandum, June 27, *FR 1950,* VII, 200–202; Truman Statement, June 27, 1950, *PPHST,* VI, 492–493; UN Resolution of June 27, 1950, in *FR 1950,* VII, 211; on British request that U.S. omit "centrally-directed communism," Minutes of a Meeting of the Cabinet, June 17, 1950, CAB 128/17; for PRC reaction to U.S. "neutralization" of the Strait as "armed aggression" and declaration of war, see Rosemary Foot, *The Wrong War: American Policy and the Dimensions of the Korean Conflict, 1950–1953* (Ithaca, 1985), 65, and Goncharov et al., *Uncertain Partners,* 157–158.

94. Acheson to Johnson, June 28, 1950, *FR 1950,* VII, 217, and Minutes of a Meeting of the NSC in Cabinet Room, June 28, 1950, Box 65, Acheson Papers.

95. Memorandum of NSC Consultants Meeting and Memorandum of NSC Meeting, June 29, 1950, *FR 1950,* I, 324–326, 327–330; Kirk to Acheson, June 29, 1950, *FR 1950,* VII, 229–230.

96. Truman News Conference, June 29, 1950, *PPHST,* VI, 502–505; for NSC meeting, Truman, *Years of Trial and Hope,* 341–342, and Donovan, *Tumultuous Years,* 211–213; JCS to MacArthur, June 29, 1950, *FR 1950,* VII, 240–241.

97. Truman, *Years of Trial and Hope,* 342.

98. Truman Note, June 30, 1950, PSF, Box 229, Truman Papers.

99. Truman, *Years of Trial and Hope,* 342–343, Donovan, *Tumultuous Years,* 216–217; White House Statement, June 30, 1950, *PPHST,* VI, 523; Acheson, *Present at the Creation,* 413.

100. Donovan, *Tumultuous Years,* 220–222, and Paige, *Korean Decision,* 261–263.

101. Acheson, *Present at the Creation,* 414–415, and Ferrell, *Truman,* 324–325.

102. Jessup Memorandum, July 3, 1950, *FR 1950,* VII, 286–291; Acheson, *Present at the Creation,* 415, and Donovan, *Tumultuous Years,* 224.

103. Elsey Memorandum, July 16, 1951, Box 76, Elsey Papers.

104. Hamby, *Man of the People,* 539; Arthur M. Schlesinger, Jr., *The Imperial Presidency* (Boston, 1973), 635.

105. Truman Statement . . . Designating MacArthur to Lead Allied Military Forces, July 8, 1950, *PPHST,* VI, 520; Truman on MacArthur in entry for June 17, 1945, Ferrell (ed.), *Off the Record,* 46–47, and entry for July 1, 1950, Ayers Diary, Box 26, Ayers Papers; see also Schaller, *MacArthur,* 190–191.

106. Elsey Memorandum, July 19, 1950, Box 72, Truman Papers; Truman Memorandum for MacArthur, July 19, and MacArthur to Truman, July 20, 1950, PSF, Box 129, Truman Papers; Truman Special Message to the Congress, July 19, 1950, *PPHST,* VI, 531–537.

107. Truman Radio and Television Address to the American People, July 19, 1950, *PPHST,* VI, 537–542.

108. Acheson to Paul [Nitze], July 12, 1950 (unfinished), Box 65, Acheson Papers.

Chapter 14. Rollback to Retreat

1. Ferrell (ed.), *Autobiography,* 33; McConaughy Memorandum, Aug. 25, 1950, *FR 1950,* VII, 649–652.

2. Allison and Emmerson Memorandum, and Kennan to Acheson, Aug. 21, 1950, *FR 1950,* VII, 617–638; Bevin Memorandum, Aug. 30, 1950, CAB 129/41.

3. "Man's word," Jessup Memorandum, Dec. 7, 1950, *FR 1950,* VII, 1462; U.S. Delegation Minutes, Dec. 4, 1950, ibid., 1392–1408.

4. Kaufman, *Korean War,* 133–138; Neustadt, *Presidential Power,* 12–13, 18–20; Roger Dingman, "Atomic Diplomacy during the Korean War," *IS,* 13 (Winter 1988/1989), 72–76.

5. Barton J. Bernstein, "The Struggle over the Korean Armistice: Prisoners of Repatriation?" in Bruce Cumings (ed.), *Child of Conflict: The Korean-American Relationship, 1943–1953* (Seattle, 1983), 275–278, 291–296.

6. Entry for Jan. 27, 1952, Truman Diary, PSF, Box 333, Truman Papers.

7. Kaufman, *Korean War,* 66–69; Acheson Notes for Congressional Hearings [n.d.], *FR 1950,* I, 393–395.

8. Stueck, *Korean War,* 48, and Kaufman, *Korean War,* 47–49; Truman quoted in Donovan, *Tumultuous Years,* 256.

9. British Embassy to State Department, July 7, and Acheson to Embassy in London, July 10, 1950 (two cables), *FR 1950,* VII, 329–331, 347–352; see also Bohlen Memorandum, July 7, and Acheson to Embassy in Moscow, July 11, 1950, ibid., 325–327, 359–360; Acheson to Tugwell, Sept. 11, 1950, Box 43, Acheson Papers; Stueck, *Korean War,* 51, and Mastny, *Cold War and Soviet Insecurity,* 99.

10. Acheson, *Present at the Creation,* 422, and Memorandum of a Meeting with the President, Aug. 3, 1950, Box 65, Acheson Papers; Schaller, *MacArthur,* 194–195; on PRC, Chen, *China's Road to Korean War,* 142.

11. Extract of Harriman-MacArthur Conversations, Aug. 6 and Aug. 8, 1950, *FR 1950,* VI, 427–430 (Harriman was an old acquaintance of MacArthur); Acheson, *Present at the Creation,* 422; Acheson Memorandum of a Conversation with the President, Aug. 10, 1950, Box 65, Acheson Papers.

12. Matthews Memorandum, Aug. 14, 1950, *FR 1950,* VII, 573–574; Webb Memoranda, Aug. 15, Aug. 17, Aug. 18, 1950, ibid., 581–582, 593, 599–600; Kennan Memorandum for Webb, Aug. 21, and Acheson to Truman, Sept. 11, 1950, ibid., 612–613, 721–722, 722 n. 1.

13. Stueck, *Korean War,* 68–69, Truman, *Years of Trial and Hope,* 356–357, and Truman to Austin, Aug. 27, 1950, *PPHST,* VI, 599–600; MacArthur Speech in Acheson to Certain Diplomatic Officers, Aug. 26, 1950, *FR 1950,* VI, 451–453; see also Douglas MacArthur, *Reminiscences* (New York, 1964), 342–343.

14. Elsey Memoranda for the Files, Aug. 26 and Oct. 2, 1950, Box 72 and Box 73, Elsey Papers; Battle Memorandum, Aug. 26, and Webb Memorandum, Aug. 27, 1950, *FR 1950,* VI, 453–462; Acheson Memorandum for Webb, Aug. 27, 1950, Box 65, Acheson Papers; Truman, *Years of Trial and Hope,* 356–357.

15. Truman, *Years of Trial and Hope,* 355–356, and *Truman News Conference,* Aug. 31, 1950, *PPHST,* VI, 607–608.

16. Ross Note, Sept. 13, and Elsey Note, Sept. 16, 1950, Box 72, Elsey Papers; Donovan, *Tumultuous Years,* 266–267.

17. Schaller, *MacArthur,* 195–198, Kaufman, *Korean War,* 78–82.

18. Allison to Rusk, July 1, 1950, *FR 1950,* VII, 272.

19. On Dulles and MacArthur, Stueck, *Korean War,* 62; Austin to Acheson, July 19, and Acheson to Embassy in Korea, July 14, 1950, *FR 1950,* VII, 354–355, 387.

20. Lay Memorandum, July 17, PPS Draft Memorandum, July 22, and Allison Memorandum to Nitze, July 24, 1950, *FR 1950,* VII, 411, 449–454, 458–461; Defense Department Draft Memorandum, July 31, Harriman Memoranda MacArthur Conversations, Aug. 6 and Aug. 8, 1950, ibid., 502–510, 543–544; Truman, *Years of Trial and Hope,* 349–353.

21. *New York Times,* Aug. 18 and Aug. 26, 1950 (Matthews offered to resign, Truman said "forget it," but then Truman dismissed him on Sept. 1, 1950, Elsey Memorandum, Oct. 2, 1950, Box 72, Elsey Papers); PPS Draft Memorandum, and Kennan to Acheson, Aug. 21, 1950, *FR 1950,* VII, 615–616, 623–628 (Acheson asked that Kennan's memorandum not be circulated).

22. Foot, *Wrong War,* 69–70; the arrest in July 1950 of Julius and Ethel Rosenberg for atomic spying also put the Democrats on the defensive about lax security.

23. Truman to Householder, Aug. 8, 1950, PSF, Box 113, Truman Papers; McConaughy Memorandum (of NSC meeting), Aug. 25, and Memorandum of Department of Army Teletype Conference, Aug. 30, 1950, *FR 1950,* VII, 649–652, 659–660; Truman News Conference, Aug. 31, and Truman Report to American People, Sept. 1, 1950, *PPHST,* VI, 605–608, 609–614.

24. NSC Draft Memoranda, Aug. 30 and Aug. 31, and Lay Memorandum (NSC 81), Sept. 1, 1950, *FR 1950,* VII, 685–693; NSC Report (NSC 81/1) to the president, Sept. 9, 1950, ibid., 712–721.

25. Bancroft Memorandum, Sept. 23, 1950, *FR 1950,* VII, 759–762, and Stueck, *Korean War,* 92–93; on MacArthur's orders, Webb to UN Mission, Sept. 26, 1950, *FR 1950,* VII, 781–782, Marshall to Truman, Sept. 27, 1950, PSF, Box 243, Truman Papers, and Kaufman, *Korean War,* 103–104.

26. Chace, *Acheson,* 298–299; Acheson to Webb, Sept. 26, Marshall to Truman, Sept. 27, Marshall to MacArthur, Sept. 29, and MacArthur to Marshall, Sept. 30, 1950, *FR 1950,* VII, 785–787, 792–793, 793 n. 2, 826; Schaller, *MacArthur,* 200–201; MacArthur broadcast in *FR 1950,* VII, 796.

27. Stueck, *Korean War,* 93–94; UN Resolution of Oct. 7, 1950, in *FR 1950,* VII, 903–906; Britain's cosponsors were Australia, Brazil, Cuba, the Netherlands, Norway, Pakistan, and the Philippines.

28. Ferrell (ed.), *Autobiography,* 33; Acheson quoted in Connelly Cabinet Notes, Sept. 29, 1950, Box 2, Connelly Papers; "taste of victory" in Leffler, *Preponderance of Power,* 380; see also James I. Matray, "Truman's Plan for Victory: National Self-Determination and the Thirty-Eighth Parallel Decision in Korea," *JAH,* 66 (Sept. 1979), 314–333.

29. Allen S. Whiting, *China Crosses the Yalu: The Decision to Enter the Korean War* (Stanford, 1960), 47–67; Mao quoted in Zhang, *Mao's Military Romanticism,* 63; Goncharov et al., *Uncertain Partners,* 163–167; Stueck, *Korean War,* 69.

30. Truman Report to the American People, Sept. 1, 1950, *PPHST,* VI, 609–614; Acheson quoted in Stueck, *Road to Confrontation,* 230, and Spanier, *Truman-MacArthur Controversy,* 99.

31. Goncharov et al., *Uncertain Partners,* 174–175; Battle Memorandum, and Acheson to Bevin, Sept. 28, 1950, *FR 1950,* VII, 811–812; on Sept. 26 the U.S. informed the UN that inadvertent bombing may have occurred, ibid., 793 n. 1.

32. Chen, *China's Road to Korean War,* 169; Henderson to Acheson, Merchant Memorandum, and Clubb Memorandum to Rusk, Sept. 27, 1950, and Acheson to Webb, Sept. 28, 1950, *FR 1950,* VII, 790–792, 793–796, 797–798.

33. Zhou speech in Wilkinson to Acheson, Oct. 2, 1950, *FR 1950,* VII, 852, 852 n. 1; Henderson to Acheson, Oct. 4, 1950, ibid., 871–873, and Hutchinson to Foreign Office, Oct. 3 and Oct. 4, 1950, F.O. 371/84109 (John Hutchinson was the British chargé d'affaires in Beijing); Zhou Minute of Talk with Panikkar, Oct. 3, 1950, Zhang and Chen (eds.), *Chinese Communist Foreign Policy,* 165–166.

34. Clubb to Merchant, and Allison Memorandum (quoting Acheson), Oct. 4, 1950, *FR 1950,* VII, 864–886, 868–869; Schaller, *MacArthur,* 203, and Truman, *Years of Trial and Hope,* 362; on MacArthur, Editorial Note, and JCS to MacArthur, Oct. 9, 1950, *FR 1950,* VII, 915; Whiting, *China Crosses the Yalu,* 115.

35. Truman to Nellie Noland, Oct. 13, 1950, Ferrell (ed.), *Off the Record,* 195–196; Truman Statement, Oct. 10, 1950, *PPHST,* VI, 665–666, Truman, *Years of Trial and Hope,* 362–363, Schaller, *MacArthur,* 205; on Truman keeping entourage "*very small,*" Murphy Memorandum for Truman, Oct. 9, 1950, Box 72, Elsey Papers (Truman took Bradley, Harriman, Rusk, and roving ambassador Philip Jessup); Acheson, *Present at the Creation,* 456, called the trip (he had not been consulted) "distasteful"; on overflights, Kirk to Acheson, Oct. 10, 1950, *FR 1950,* VII, 917, and Spanier, *Truman-MacArthur Controversy,* 111; the U.S. gave an apology and indemnity, and disciplined the airmen involved.

36. Truman Memorandum, Nov. 25, 1950, Ferrell (ed.), *Off the Record,* 200 (same as Truman Note, Apr. 5, 1951, PSF, Box 243, Truman Papers); Truman, *Years of Trial and Hope,* 364–365.

37. Substance of Statements Made at Wake Island, Oct. 15, 1950, *FR 1950,* VII, 948–960 (Bradley drew the memorandum based on the conferees' notes, with copies to MacArthur); MacArthur's statement that troops other than South Korean would be "pulled back" from PRC-USSR borders was ambiguous, perhaps deliberately so; he did not say whether such forces, notably American, would first be allowed to advance upon those borders, which would have been contrary to his Sept. 27 directive.

38. Truman Address at San Francisco Opera House, Oct. 17, 1950, *PPHST,* VI, 673–

679; Truman to Bowers, Oct. 18, 1950, PSF, Box 172, Truman Papers, and Acheson Memorandum, Oct. 19, 1950, Box 65, Acheson Papers; Truman Press Conference, Oct. 19, 1950, *PPHST,* VI, 679–680, diary entry for Oct. 19, 1959, Ayers Diary, Box 26, Ayers Papers, and *Washington Post,* Oct. 20, 1950.

39. Jessup Memorandum to Acheson, Oct. 9, 1950, *FR 1950,* VII, 915–916; Mansourov, "Stalin, Mao, Kim," 99, 111–112, 114.

40. Goncharov et al., *Uncertain Partners,* 176–179, and Chen, *China's Road to Korean War,* 173–177.

41. Mansourov, "Stalin, Mao, Kim," 101, 106–107 n. 30 (which contains a Russian-version facsimile of Mao's Oct. 2 cable), and Mastny, *Cold War and Soviet Insecurity,* 104.

42. Goncharov et al., *Uncertain Partners,* 180–181; Chen, *China's Road to Korean War,* 181–184, 191; Mao's first choice for military commander was Lin Biao, but he refused, claiming poor health. He also spoke strongly in favor of giving priority to domestic reconstruction.

43. Goncharov et al., *Uncertain Partners,* 182–185.

44. Goncharov et al., *Uncertain Partners,* 193–194; Kaufman, *Korean War,* 93–98; Zubok, *Inside Kremlin's Cold War,* 66–67, says that Stalin was moved by realpolitik: he would press the PRC to intervene to contend with U.S./UN power and hope that the Sino-Soviet pact would deter a major U.S. response.

45. Zhang, *Deterrence and Strategic Culture,* 269–278; Chen, *China's Road to Korean War,* 177–179.

46. Zhang, *Mao's Military Romanticism,* 76–77, 81–82; Chen, *China's Road to Korean War,* 171–181, says that Mao was determined to fight before the U.S. crossed the 38th parallel but concedes that U.S. policy regarding Taiwan and intervention in Korea posed a real threat to PRC security; we also now know Mao declined to fight as late as October 2.

47. Schaller, *MacArthur,* 207; Truman News Conference, Oct. 26, 1950, *PPHST,* VI, 690–691.

48. Clubb Memoranda, Nov. 1 and Nov. 4, 1950, *FR 1950,* VII, 1023–1025, 1038–1041; MacArthur to JCS, Nov. 4, 1950, in Truman, *Years of Trial and Hope,* 373; UN Resolution in *FR 1950,* VII, 1068–1069.

49. Acheson Memoranda of Conversations with Lovett and Rusk, and with Truman, Nov. 6, 1950, *FR 1950,* VII, 1055–1057.

50. Truman, *Years of Trial and Hope,* 377–380; JCS to MacArthur, Nov. 6, and MacArthur to JCS, Nov. 7, 1950, *FR 1950,* VII, 1075–1077; it would be hard to say that Truman made this eleventh-hour decision because of the elections although political considerations always influenced his handling of MacArthur; Republican election gains included twenty House seats and five Senate seats, fewer than in any off-year election since 1934, but widely seen as a defeat for the Democrats and Truman; see Donovan, *Tumultuous Years,* 297, and Stueck, *Korean War,* 116; on hot pursuit, MacArthur cable to JCS on Nov. 7, 1950, in *FR 1950,* VII, 1077 n. 1, and Truman, *Years of Trial and Hope,* 382–383; MacArthur, *Reminiscences,* 370–372, states that the policy of limited hot pursuit was the most indefensible one in U.S. military history and that he wrote, but tore up, his resignation; see Schaller, *MacArthur,* 209, 211.

51. Davies Memorandum, and Clubb Memorandum for Rusk, Nov. 7, 1950, *FR 1950,* VII, 1078–1085, 1087–1093; JCS to MacArthur, Nov. 8, and MacArthur to JCS, Nov. 9, 1950, ibid., 1097–1098, 1107–1110.

52. JCS Memorandum to Marshall, Nov. 9, 1950, *FR 1950,* VII, 1117–1121, and NSC Meeting of Nov. 9, 1950, in Truman, *Years of Trial and Hope,* 378–380; see also NSC Memorandum, Nov. 14, 1950, *FR 1950,* VII, 1150; Sebald Memorandum of Conversation with MacArthur, Nov. 14, 1950, ibid., 1148–1149.

53. *New York Times,* Nov. 16, 1950, and Truman Statement, Nov. 16, 1950, *PPHST,* VII, 711–713; Battle Memorandum and Jessup Memorandum, Nov. 21, and MacArthur to JCS, Nov. 25, 1950, *FR 1950,* VII, 1201–1203, 1204–1208, 1231–1233.

54. MacArthur to JCS, Nov. 28, 1950, *FR 1950,* VII, 1237–1238; Acheson, *Present at the Creation,* 468, chiefly blames the JCS and MacArthur for not modifying policy in November but acknowledges Truman's and his own failure to be more frank about the dangers of PRC intervention.

55. Jessup Memorandum (Notes of the NSC Meeting at the White House), Nov. 28, 1950, *FR 1950,* VII, 1242–1249; Omar N. Bradley and Clay Blair, *A Soldier's Story* (New York, 1983), 598–599.

56. Truman News Conference, and White House Statement, Nov. 30, 1950, *PPSHT,* VI, 724–728, 728 n. 3, and entry for Nov. 30, 1950, Ayers Diary, Box 26, Ayers Papers.

57. Dingman, "Atomic Diplomacy," 55–64; Jessup Memorandum, Nov. 4, and Emmerson Memorandum for Rusk, Nov. 8, 1950, *FR 1950,* VII, 1041–1042, 1098–1100.

58. Dingman, "Atomic Diplomacy," 65–69; Foot, *Wrong War,* 116–117.

59. Jessup Memoranda (including Rusk Notes for Acheson), Dec. 1 and Dec. 3, 1950, *FR 1950,* VII, 1276–1283, 1323–1334; Elsey Notes (of Cabinet Meeting), Dec. 1, 1950, Box 73, Elsey Papers.

60. Diary entry, Dec. 2, 1950, Ferrell (ed.), *Off the Record,* 201–202, Truman, *Years of Trial and Hope,* 391–393; Schaller, *MacArthur,* 217–218, and *U.S. News & World Report,* Dec. 8, 1950 (released Dec. 1, 1950; text in PSF, Box 129, Truman Papers).

61. Matthew B. Ridgway, *The Korean War* (New York, 1967), 61–62, and Acheson, *Present at the Creation,* 476; Truman, *Years of Trial and Hope,* 384; Truman Memorandum, Dec. 5, 1950, Confidential Files, Box 32, Truman Papers, and Neustadt, *Presidential Power,* 12–13, 18–20.

62. Battle Memorandum, Dec. 4, 1950, Box 65, Acheson Papers, and Kennan, *Memoirs,* II, 27–31.

63. U.S. Delegation Minutes, First Meeting, Second Meeting, and Sixth Meeting, Dec. 4, Dec. 5, and Dec. 7, 1950, *FR 1950,* VII, 1361–1374, 1392–1407, 1449–1461; entry for Dec. 5, 1950, Ferrell (ed.), *Off the Record,* 202–203.

64. Jessup Memorandum, Dec. 4, 1950, *FR 1950,* VII, 1375–1377.

65. Jessup Memorandum for the Record, Dec. 7, 1950, ibid., 1462–1465.

66. Communiqué in ibid., 1476–1479; Attlee to Foreign Office, Dec. 10, 1950, Bevin Papers, F.O. 800, and Elsey Notes [Dec. 1950], PSF, Box 164, Truman Papers; see also Connelly Cabinet Notes, Dec. 8, 1950, Box 2, Connelly Papers, for Acheson comment that the "Chinese are being directed by the Russians. It is not a case of the U.S. against China but U.S. and UN against Russia."

67. Collins Report in U.S. Delegation Minutes of Sixth Meeting, *FR 1950,* VII, 1449–1461, and Connelly Cabinet Notes, Dec. 8, 1950, Box 2, Connelly Papers; entry for Dec. 9, 1950, Ferrell (ed.), *Off the Record,* 204, and CIA Report (Prepared by Elsey), Dec. 11, 1950, Box 73, Elsey Papers; Truman Report on National Emergency, Dec. 15, and Proclamation . . . of National Emergency, *PPHST,* VII, 741–747; on congressional debate leading to January 1951 sense-of-the-Senate resolution (passed in mid-April) accepting assignment of four U.S. divisions to NATO in 1951 but calling for the president to seek congressional approval thereafter to send troops abroad, see Donovan, *Tumultuous Years,* 322–324, and James T. Patterson, *Mr. Republican: A Biography of Robert A. Taft* (Boston, 1972), 476–481.

68. Foot, *Wrong War,* 110–112; Acheson, *Present at the Creation,* 513; Zhou Enlai to Acting UN Secretary General, Jan. 17, 1951, *FR 1951,* VII, 91–92; UN Resolution in ibid., 150–151; for discussion, see Connelly Cabinet Notes, Jan. 12, Jan. 15, Jan. 25, and

Jan. 26, 1951, Box 2, Connelly Papers, and Conclusions of a Meeting of the Cabinet, Jan. 23, Jan. 25, Jan. 26, and Jan. 29, 1951, CAB 129/19 (with the British acceding after sanctions were deferred).

69. Rusk Memorandum, Dec. 19, 1950, *FR 1950*, VII, 1570–1576, and Foot, *Wrong War*, 114–115.

70. JCS to MacArthur, Dec. 12, and MacArthur to JCS, Dec. 30, 1950, *FR 1950*, VII, 1625–1626, 1630–1633.

71. JCS to MacArthur, Jan. 9, and MacArthur to JCS, Jan. 10, 1951, *FR 1951*, VII, 41–43, 55–56.

72. Acheson, *Present at the Creation*, 515, Truman, *Years of Trial and Hope*, 435–436, and Jessup Memorandum, Jan. 12, 1951, *FR 1951*, VII, 68–70.

73. Schaller, *MacArthur*, 227–230, and Foot, *Wrong War*, 129–130; Truman News Conferences, Feb. 15 and Mar. 15, 1951, *PPHST*, VII, 155, 188, 190; Truman's proposed statement of Mar. 21, 1951, in *FR 1951*, VII, 263–264.

74. MacArthur Statement of Mar. 24, 1951, in *FR 1951*, VII, 265–266.

75. Truman quoted in Barber, *Presidential Character*, 287–288; Truman, *Years of Trial and Hope*, 445; Truman also naively wrote that he did not think MacArthur "purposefully" sought to challenge civilian control of the military; on deliberations, see BE [Barbara Evans, Acheson's secretary] Memorandum, Mar. 24, and Battle Memorandum, Mar. 26, 1951, Box 66, Acheson Papers; JCS to MacArthur, Mar. 24, 1951, Box 74, Elsey Papers, and Schaller, *MacArthur*, 234.

76. Martin to MacArthur, Mar. 8, and MacArthur to Martin, Mar. 20, 1951, *FR 1951*, VII, 298–299.

77. Diary entry for Apr. 5, 1951, PSF, Box 278, Truman Papers, and entry for Apr. 6, 1951, Ferrell (ed.), *Off the Record*, 210–211; Schaller, *MacArthur*, 232.

78. JCS Memorandum to Marshall, Apr. 6, 1951, *FR 1951*, VII, 309, 309 n. 6; diary entries for Apr. 6, Apr. 9, and Apr. 10, 1951, Roger M. Anders (ed.), *Forging the Atomic Shield: The Office Diary of Gordon E. Dean* (Chapel Hill, 1987), 137–142; Schaller, *MacArthur*, 235–236; Dingman, "Atomic Diplomacy," 72–74, also notes that two weeks later Truman sent a second deployment of B-29s to Guam and a command and control team to Tokyo, let Ridgway undertake aerial reconnaissance of Manchuria and Shandong, and gave him qualified authority for atomic strikes if U.S. forces were attacked from outside of Korea; the B-29s returned to the U.S. in late June 1951.

79. Elsey Memorandum [April 1951], Box 74, Elsey Papers; entries for Apr. 8 and Apr. 9, 1951, Ferrell (ed.), *Off the Record*, 210–211.

80. Donovan, *Tumultuous Years*, 355; Truman Statement and Order on Relieving MacArthur, Apr. 11, 1951, *PPHST*, VII, 221–222, 223–227; M. Miller, *Plain Speaking*, 329, alleges that when Bradley told Truman on Apr. 10 that MacArthur might resign, the president said, "The son-of-a-bitch isn't going to resign on me. I want him fired"; it seems unlikely that Truman, always deferential in the presence of generals, said this to his JCS chair.

81. Truman Speech at Jefferson–Jackson Day Dinner, Apr. 14, 1951, *PPHST*, VII, 227–232.

82. Entry for Apr. 10, 1951, Ferrell (ed.), *Off the Record*, 211; Donovan, *Tumultuous Years*, 359–360; on White House mail and public opinion, Hopkins Memorandum for Truman, May 8, 1951, PSF, Box 129, Truman Papers, and Elsey-Harriman Memorandum, May 17, 1951, Box 75, Elsey Papers.

83. Franks to Foreign Office, Apr. 14, 1951, F.O. 371/90903; entry for Apr. 16, 1951, Ayers Diary, Box 26, Ayers Papers, and Donovan, *Tumultuous Years*, 361; "Welcoming Schedule" [April 1951], Box 74, Elsey Papers.

84. Schaller, *MacArthur*, 243–244, and William Manchester, *American Caesar: Dou-*

glas MacArthur, 1880–1964 (New York, 1979), 788–793; Schaller, op. cit., 250–253, on speaking tour.

85. On administration preparations and "leaks," Hechler Memorandum, Apr. 17, 1951, Box 74, Elsey Papers, and Franks to Foreign Office, May 5, 1951, F.O. 371/90903; on MacArthur, Schaller, *MacArthur,* 246–247.

86. Connelly Cabinet Notes, May 7 and May 14, 1951, Box 2, Connelly Papers; for Truman administration testimony, John Edward Wiltz, "The MacArthur Hearings of 1951: The Secret Testimony," *Military Affairs,* 39 (Dec. 1975), 167–173, and Kaufman, *Korean War,* 167–176; on Ridgway authority, JCS to Ridgway, Apr. 28 and May 1, 1951, *FR 1951,* VII, 386–387, 394–398; Bradley on "wrong war," in Kaufman, op. cit., 173.

87. Notes on Meeting regarding Acheson's Testimony, May 15 and May 18, 1951, Box 63, Acheson Papers; Acheson, *Present at the Creation,* 524–526, and Kaufman, *Korean War,* 174–176.

88. Schaller, *MacArthur,* 249–250; Maverick to HST, June 21, 1950, PSF, Box 128, Truman Papers; entry for June 21, 1951, Ferrell (ed.), *Off the Record,* 213 (Truman added that the facts were too much for "opposition Democrats and Chiang Kai-shek Republicans"); Franks to Foreign Office, May 12 and May 26, 1951, F.O. 371/90904; on Marshall, Austin Memorandum for Hickerson, May 23, 1951, *FR 1951,* VII, 447–448; Rusk speech, May 18, 1951, in *New York Times,* May 19, 1951 (Rusk, *As I Saw It,* 173, alleges that his words were "more taunt than statement," a response to a PRC campaign against the U.S. as "public enemy number one").

89. Elsey Memorandum for Murphy, Apr. 14, 1951, Box 76, Elsey Papers; Acheson, *Present at the Creation,* 532–533, and Stueck, *Korean War,* 205; the State Department also sent an official to Hong Kong to talk with the PRC through intermediaries but gained no result.

90. Kennan to Matthews, May 31 and June 5, and Kennan to Acheson, June 20, 1951, *FR 1951,* VII, 483–487, 507–511, 536–538; Stueck, *Korean War,* 206, 216–222, Zhang, *Mao's Military Romanticism,* 217–222, and Zubok, *Inside Kremlin's Cold War,* 70–72.

91. Entry for June 21, 1951, Ferrell (ed.), *Off the Record,* 212–213; Malik speech of June 23, 1951, in Editorial Note, *FR 1951,* VII, 546–547, and Truman Speech in *PPHST,* VII, 362–363; on PRC, Gifford to Acheson, *FR 1951,* VII, 552–553; Elsey Memorandum ("Chronology"), n.d., Box 76, Elsey Papers, contains Acheson June 26, 1951, statement; Johnson Memorandum (JCS Meeting), June 28, 1951, *FR 1951,* VII, 566–568.

92. Johnson Memorandum, June 29, 1951, *FR 1951,* VII, 586–587, and Stueck, *Korean War,* 209–210; Elsey Memoranda, June 30 and July 2, 1951, Elsey note at end of "Chronology," Box 76, Elsey Papers; Truman Special Message to Congress, July 23, and Report on U.S. Participation in the UN in 1950, July 26, 1950, *PPHST,* VII, 421–424.

93. Ridgway to JCS, July 10, 1951, *FR 1951,* VII, 649–656, and Stueck, *Korean War,* 212–213; Ridgway, *The Korean War,* 182; on U.S. acceptance of the Geneva Convention, which called for return of POWs after hostilities but did not mention how to deal with those who did not wish to be repatriated, *FR 1951,* VII, 793 n. 1, Stueck, *Korean War,* 244, and Bernstein, "Struggle over Korean Armistice," 274–275; the U.S. also rejected a ROK proposal demanding PRC withdrawal and disarmament of the DPRK, Ridgway Memorandum [July 1951], Box 76, Elsey Papers.

94. *New York Times,* July 20, 1951; Memorandum of Lovett-Acheson Conversation, July 23, 1951, Box 67, Acheson Papers; Neustadt Memorandum for Murphy, July 16, and Unsigned Note, July 19, 1951, Box 76, Elsey Papers; Stueck, *Korean War,* 229, 235–237; Kaufman, Korean War, 208–213, 220.

95. Memorandum of State Department–JCS Meeting, Nov. 12, JCS to Ridgway, and Ridgway to JCS, Nov. 13, and JCS to Ridgway, Nov. 14, 1951, *FR 1951,* VII, 1121–1124, 1126, 1128–1130, 1131–1132.

96. Bradley to Marshall [JCS Enclosure], Aug. 8, and Acheson to Marshall, Aug. 27, 1951, ibid., 791–794, 857–859; Ridgway to JCS, Webb Memorandum, and Johnson Note, Oct. 27, 1951, ibid., 1064–1065, 1068–1071, 1073, 1073 n. 3; the stated number of POWs often varied, depending on the lists provided and whether individuals were considered POWs or civilian internees.

97. Ridgway to State Department, Nov. 28, JCS to Truman, Dec. 7, and Truman to JCS, Dec. 8, 1951, ibid., 1197–1198, 1276–1278, 1278 n. 5.

98. Memorandum for the President, Dec. 10, 1951, ibid., 1290–1296.

99. Acheson Memorandum of Conversation with the President, Dec. 17, 1951, Box 66, Acheson Papers; Ridgway to JCS, Dec. 19, and Lay Memorandum (NSC 118/2), Dec. 20, 1951, *FR 1951*, VII, 1381–1382, 1382–1387; Conclusions of a Meeting of the Cabinet, Dec. 1, 1951, CAB 128/23.

100. Stueck, *Korean War,* 251–252; Acheson Memoranda, Jan. 6 and Jan. 9, 1952, Box 66, Acheson Papers.

101. Diary entry for Jan. 27, 1952, PSF, Box 333, Truman Papers.

102. Draft Acheson-Lovett Memorandum, Feb. 4, Acheson Memorandum, and Acheson Memorandum to Truman, Feb. 8, 1952, *FR 1952–1954,* XV, 35–36, 44–45; Bernstein, "Struggle over Korean Armistice," 280–281.

103. Stueck, *Korean War,* 262–263.

104. Acheson Memorandum, Feb. 27, 1952, Box 67, Acheson Papers, and Conclusions of a Meeting of the Cabinet, Apr. 29, 1952, CAB 128/24.

105. Kathryn Weathersby, "Deceiving the Deceivers: Moscow, Beijing, Pyongyang, and Allegations of Bacteriological Weapons Use in Korea," CWIHP, *Bulletin,* 11 (Winter 1998), 178–179; Entry for May 18, 1952, Ferrell (ed.), *Off the Record,* 250–251; Acheson to Truman, Mar. 11, 1952, *FR 1952–1954,* XV, 79–80, and Conclusions of a Meeting of the Cabinet, Apr. 29, 1952, CAB 128/23, which notes use of napalm.

106. Kaufman, *Korean War,* 265–266, Stueck, *Korean War,* 271–272, and Bernstein, "Struggle over Korean Armistice," 283–284; Conclusions of a Meeting of the Cabinet, June 17, 1952, CAB 128/25, refers to apparent willingness of the Communists to settle for 110,000 POWs, including all 20,000 PRC POWs.

107. Ridgway to JCS, Apr. 4, and Memorandum of Substance of State Department–JCS Discussion, Apr. 14, 1952, *FR 1952–1954,* XV, 136–138, 145–154; Stueck, *Korean War,* 269.

108. Truman Statement on General Ridgway's Armistice Proposal, May 7, and Truman Address at West Point Convocation, May 18, 1952, *PPHST,* VIII, 321–322, 350–353; entry for May 18, 1952, Ferrell (ed.), *Off the Record,* 250–251.

109. Kaufman, *Korean War,* 267–268; JCS to Clark, June 5, 1952, *FR 1952–1954,* XV, 308–310.

110. Acheson to Truman, Mar. 21, Evans Memorandum [of Acheson conversation], and Allison Memorandum, May 2, 1952, ibid., 185–186, 187–188, 189; Lightner to State Department, May 30, 1952, ibid., 266–267, 286 n. 2.

111. Truman to Rhee, June 2, Lightner to State Department, June 3, ibid., 285–286, 290–291, and Connelly Cabinet Notes, June 16, 1952, Box 2, Connelly Papers; Editorial Note, *FR 1952–1954,* XV, 376–377, Stueck, *Korean War,* 277–278, and Kaufman, *Korean War,* 273–274.

112. On bombing, Editorial Note, and Bruce to Embassy in Berlin, June 24, 1952, *FR 1952–1954,* XV, 351–353, and Acheson, *Present at the Creation,* 656.

113. Acheson Memorandum of Conversation with Lovett, July 23, 1952, Box 67, Acheson Papers; on atomic jets, Kaufman, *Korean War,* 278–279; on border area attacks, Allison Memorandum, Aug. 26, 1952, *FR 1952–1954,* XV, 458–459; Truman Sixth Annual Report on U.S. Participation in UN, July 3, and Truman Letter to Captain Charles Ewing,

Aug. 20, 1952, *PPHST,* VIII, 464–467, 529; Bernstein, "Struggle over Korean Armistice," 293–294.

114. Memorandum of Substance of JCS Discussion, July 16, and Clark to JCS, July 21, 1952, *FR 1952–1954,* XV, 409–411, 415–418; Acheson to Kennan, July 25, Clark to JCS and Kennan to Acheson, July 30, and JCS to Clark, Aug. 8, 1952, ibid., 422–427, 427–429, 430–435, 451–452.

115. Bruce to Embassy in Soviet Union, Aug. 27, and Allison Memorandum, Sept. 2, 1952, *FR 1952–1954,* XV, 476–472.

116. Murphy to JCS, Sept. 1, Memorandum of JCS Discussion, Sept. 2, and JCS to Clark, Sept. 8, 1952, *FR 1952,* XV, 466–467, 477–478, 499–504; Connelly Cabinet Notes, Sept. 12, 1952, Box 2, Connelly Papers.

117. Lovett Memorandum for the Record, Sept. 15, 1952, *FR 1952–1954,* XV, 512–514.

118. Acheson Memorandum, n.d. [ca. Sept. 16, 1952], "not to leave the secretary's office," Box 67, Acheson Papers; Johnson Memorandum, Sept. 17, 1952, *FR 1952–1954,* XV, 522–525.

119. Lay Memorandum, Sept. 24, and Truman to Clark, Sept. 26, 1952, *FR 1952–1954,* XV, 532–538, 544.

120. Clark to JCS, Sept. 28 and Oct. 8, 1952, ibid., 545–546, 554–557; Truman Address in Oakland, CA, Oct. 4, 1952, *PPHST,* VIII, 708–709.

121. Bruce to Truman, Nov. 13, and Acheson to Truman, Nov. 15, 1952, *FR 1952–1954,* XV, 614–615, 629–633; Acheson, *Present at the Creation,* 700–701.

122. On Eisenhower and Korea, Kaufman, *Korean War,* 287–292; Truman criticism of Eisenhower in Speech in Oakland, CA, Oct. 4, and Statement on Decision to Withdraw U.S. Forces from Korea, Oct. 27, 1952, *PPHST,* VIII, 707–711, 1045–1050; Ferrell, *Truman,* 378–379, and entry for Nov. 15, 1952, Ferrell (ed.), *Off the Record,* 273, in which Truman also worried about what would happen if Eisenhower did not return from Korea; transition meeting in Truman, *Years of Trial and Hope,* 513–521, and *New York Times,* Nov. 20, 1952; Acheson quoted in Stueck, *Korean War,* 299.

123. Kaufman, *Korean War,* 299, and Stueck, *Korean War,* 295, 304–305; Conclusions of a Meeting of the Cabinet, Dec. 4, 1952, CAB 128/25; Acheson to Truman, Nov. 26 [two cables], 1952, *FR 1952–1954,* XV, 683–686.

124. Editorial Note, *FR 1952–1954,* XV, 700–701; Kaufman, *Korean War,* 301–302; President's News Conference, Dec. 11, 1952, *PPHST,* VIII, 1073–1076.

125. Connelly Cabinet Notes, Dec. 5, 1952, Box 2, Connelly Papers; Truman Address to National War College, Dec. 19, 1952, and Annual Message to the Congress, Jan. 7, and President's Farewell Address, Jan. 15, 1953, *PPHST,* VIII, 1090–1096, 1114–1120, 1197–1201.

126. Entry for May 15, 1952, Ferrell (ed.), *Off the Record,* 249–250, and Undelivered Farewell Address, Ferrell (ed.), *Autobiography,* 99–105; Eisenhower's State of the Union Address, Feb. 2, 1953, in *New York Times,* Feb. 3, 1953; Memorandum of NSC Meeting, Feb. 11, 1953, *FR 1952–1954,* XV, 787–789.

127. Zubok, *Inside Kremlin's Cold War,* 157, and Stueck, *Korean War,* 312–313; Memorandum of Eisenhower-Dulles Conversation, and Allison Memorandum, Mar. 20, and Johnson Memorandum, Apr. 20, 1953, *FR 1952–1954,* XV, 824–825, 919–920; Kaufman, *Korean War,* 309; on Eisenhower speech, Emmet John Hughes, *The Ordeal of Power: A Political Memoir of the Eisenhower Years* (New York, 1963), 111–113.

128. See, for example, Memorandum of 131st NSC Meeting, Feb. 11, Memorandum of Special NSC Meeting, Mar. 31, Lay Note to NSC (NSC 147), Apr. 2, Memorandum of 144th NSC Meeting, May 13, and Memorandum of 145th NSC Meeting, May 20, 1953, *FR 1952–*

1954, XV, 769–772, 825–827, 838–856, 1012–1017, 1064–1066; British opposition to greater sanction in Johnson Memorandum, May 4, 1953, ibid., 968–969.

129. Secretary of State to Certain Diplomatic Offices, Apr. 28, and Clark to JCS, Apr. 29, 1953, ibid., 950–954.

130. Clark to JCS, May 11 and May 12, 1953, ibid., 999–1004, 1008–1012; Editorial Note, ibid., 1020.

131. Memorandum of 144th NSC Meeting, May 13, and Acting Secretary to Embassy in Korea, May 15 and May 22, 1953, ibid., 1012–1017, 1086–1090; Memorandum of 145th NSC Meeting, May 20, Dulles Memorandum, May 21, and Clark Memorandum, May 26, 1953, ibid., 1064–1068, 1068–1069, 1106–1110; Clark to JCS, and Briggs (for Clark) to State Department, May 25, 1953, ibid., 1098–1099, 1100–1102; Dingman, "Atomic Diplomacy," 85–86.

132. Acting Secretary to President, May 18, and JCS to Clark, May 22, 1953, *FR 1952–1954*, XV, 1046–1048, 1082–1086.

133. For Communist accord, Editorial Notes, ibid., 1096–1097, 1137–1138, 1151; Bohlen to State Department, May 28, Collins to Clark, May 30, and Dulles to Eisenhower, June 4, 1953, ibid., 1109–1111, 1122–1124, 1138; Stueck, *Korean War*, 325–326.

134. Stueck, *Korean War*, 328–329; see also Chen, *China's Road to Korean War*, 154.

135. "Torpedo" in Briggs to State Department, June 20, *FR 1952–1954*, XV, 1225–1227; Memorandum of 150th NSC Meeting, Young Memorandum, June 18, and Clark to JCS, June 26, 1953, ibid., 1200–1205, 1206–1211, 1276–1277; Kaufman, *Korean War*, 327–329.

136. Memorandum of Eisenhower-Dulles Conversation, June 24, 1953, *FR 1952–1954*, XV, 1264–1265; Robertson on Rhee demands, and as "fanatic," Robertson to JCS, June 26 and July 1, 1953, ibid., 1276–1277, 1291–1292; Robertson to JCS, July 10, 1953, ibid., 1361–1362; Rhee to Eisenhower, Memorandum of Dulles-Eisenhower Telephone Conversation, and Dulles to Rhee, July 24, 1957, ibid., 1428–1432; Clark to Eisenhower, July 27, 1953, ibid., 1442–1443; Kaufman, *Korean War*, 331–332, and Stueck, *Korean War*, 336–337.

137. Editorial Note, *FR 1952–1954*, XV, 1444–1445; Kaufman, *Korean War*, 337–340.

138. Kaufman, *Korean War*, 342; Stueck, *Korean War*, 344, on India.

139. Zhang, *Mao's Military Romanticism*, 249–253, emphasizes PRC leaders' determination to make up for a century of humiliation and reclaim China's status and respect.

140. Foot, *Wrong War*, 246.

141. Paterson, *On Every Front*, 193, Bernstein, "The Truman Administration and Korea," in Michael J. Lacey (ed.), *The Truman Administration* (New York and Cambridge, 1989), 442–444, and Yergin, *Shattered Peace*, 398–404, 408; on Korean devastation, Cumings, *Origins of Korean War*, II, 753–756.

Chapter 15. Double Containment

1. See chap. 10, "Cat on a Sloping Tin Roof"; Acheson quoted in Harper, *Visions*, 284; Kennedy-Pipe, *Stalin's Cold War*, 144–147.

2. Acheson Memorandum, Oct. 17, 1949, Box 64, Acheson Papers; Harper, *Visions*, 290–291; see also Perkins to Acheson, Nov. 7, 1949, Box 63, Acheson Papers, which quotes U.S. high commissioner to West Germany, John J. McCloy, as saying that the USSR intended to make the GDR a "major satellite," and quotes a State Department paper stating that U.S. policy aims to bring "retraction of Soviet troops to behind Soviet borders."

3. Truman to Byrnes, Jan. 5, 1946 [unsent], Ferrell (ed.), *Off the Record,* 79–80; and U.S. Minutes of Truman-Pleven Meeting, Jan. 30, 1951, *FR 1951,* IV, 330–338; see also Jessup Memorandum, Jan. 16, 1951, ibid., 1525–1526; Adenauer quoted in Schwartz, *America's Germany,* 267; Bevin quoted in Conclusions of a Meeting of the Cabinet, May 8, 1950, CAB 128/17.

4. Kaplan, *NATO and the U.S.,* 39–40; Harper, *Visions,* 282–283; Acheson Memorandum, Nov. 17, 1949, Box 64, Acheson Papers.

5. Truman Memorandum to Acheson, June 16, 1950, *FR 1950,* IV, 687–688, and Schwartz, *America's Germany,* 113–114, 122.

6. Ninkovich, *Germany and the United States,* 84–88; Hitchcock, *France Restored,* 140–145.

7. Ninkovich, *Germany and United States,* 88–89, and Hitchcock, *France Restored,* 1146–1147; Truman News Conference, Jan. 4, 1951, *PPHST,* VII, 4.

8. Acheson, *Present at the Creation,* 487.

9. Acheson-Lovett Memorandum for Truman, July 30, 1951, *FR 1951,* III, 849–851.

10. Minutes of Fourth Formal Session, Jan. 19, 1952, *FR 1952,* VI, 846–857; Acheson, *Present at the Creation,* 625–626.

11. The lengthiest work is Rolf Steininger, *The German Question: The Stalin Note of 1952 and the Problem of Reunification,* trans. June T. Hedges, ed. Mark Cioc (New York, 1990); see also Gerhard Wettig, "Stalin and German Reunification: Archival Evidence on Soviet Foreign Policy in Spring 1952," *The Historical Journal,* 37 (1994) 411–419, and Acheson, *Present at the Creation,* 803–806.

12. Acheson to Office of High Commissioner in Bonn, Mar. 22, and Cumming to State Department, Mar. 25, 1952, *FR 1952–1954,* VII, 189–192; "battle of the notes" in Anthony Eden, Earl of Avon, *The Memoirs of Anthony Eden,* vol. 3, *Full Circle* (Boston, 1960), 50–51.

13. Acheson Memoranda, Jan. 24, Jan. 26, Apr. 1, and Apr. 7, 1949, Box 64, Acheson Papers; Bullock, *Bevin,* 668–669, and Eisenberg, *Drawing the Line,* 479–481.

14. Ninkovich, *Germany and the United States,* 70–71; Naimark, *Russians in Germany,* 58–60; see also chap. 10, "Cat on a Sloping Tin Roof."

15. Bullock, *Bevin,* 738–739, Bird, *McCloy,* 326, and Harper, *Visions,* 290–291; Acheson, *Present at the Creation,* 340–342, recounts the trip and unfairly reviles Schumacher for his nationalist policies; Petersberg Agreements in McCloy to Acheson, Nov. 22, 1949, *FR 1949,* III, 343–348.

16. Bullock, *Bevin,* 739, 764; Acheson Memorandum of Conversation with Truman, Nov. 17, 1949, Box 64, Acheson Papers; Schwartz, *America's Germany,* 115, 120.

17. Lawrence S. Kaplan, *A Community of Interests: NATO and the Military Assistance Program, 1948–1951* (Washington, 1980), 77–78; Schwartz, *America's Germany,* 107, 118–119; Johnson Report to NSC, June 8, 1950, *FR 1950,* IV, 686–687.

18. Truman Memorandum to Acheson, June 16, and Acheson to McCloy, June 21, 1950, *FR 1950,* IV, 688–690.

19. Truman Memoranda to Acheson, June 16, 1950, ibid., 688–689; Acheson, *Present at the Creation,* 436.

20. Hitchcock, *France Restored,* 126–129, and Milward, *Reconstruction of Western Europe,* 397–420; McCloy quoted in Schwartz, *America's Germany,* 197; on the Schuman Plan and role of its designer, Jean Monnet, see Schwartz, *America's Germany,* 84–112.

21. Don Cook, *Forging the Alliance: NATO, 1945–1950* (New York, 1989), 238–239; Acheson Report to the NSC (NSC 71/1), July 3, 1950, *FR 1950,* IV, 691–695.

22. McCloy to Acheson, July 14, 1950, *FR 1950,* IV, 696–698, and Schwartz, *America's Germany,* 126–128.

23. Byroade to Acheson, July 23, 1950, *FR 1950*, IV, 699–700; Memorandum for Secretary of Defense, July 13, 1950, *FR 1950*, III, 133–134, and Nitze Memorandum to Acheson, July 20, and Acheson Memoranda, July 21 and July 24, 1950, Box 65, Acheson Papers.

24. Truman July 25 comment quoted in Schwartz, *America's Germany,* 129; Acheson Memorandum, July 31, 1950, Box 65, Acheson Papers.

25. McCloy to Acheson, Aug. 3, and Acheson to McCloy, Aug. 4, *FR 1950*, III, 180–184; on Churchill, Douglas to Acheson (for Truman), Aug. 14, 1950, *FR 1950,* IV, 207–208; Acheson Memoranda, Aug. 3 and Aug. 10, 1950, Box 65, Acheson Papers.

26. Schwartz, *America's Germany,* 133–134, *New York Times,* Aug. 18, 1950, and Acheson Memorandum, Aug. 21, 1950, Box 65, Acheson Papers.

27. Acheson, *Present at the Creation,* 437–440, and Kaplan, *Community of Interests,* 111–112.

28. David S. McLellan, *Dean G. Acheson: The State Department Years* (New York, 1976), 328–330, and Acheson, *Present at the Creation,* 439–440, Kaplan, *Community of Interests,* 113–115; Acheson and Johnson to Truman, Sept. 8, 1950, *FR 1950*, III, 273–284; this letter became the basis of the Sept. 11, 1950, document, NSC 82, "United States Policy regarding the Strengthening of the Defense of Europe and the Nature of Germany's Contribution Thereto," ibid., 273 n. 1.

29. Acheson, *Present at the Creation,* 438, and Acheson to Truman, Sept. 15, 1950, *FR 1950*, III, 1229–1231.

30. Reports of the foreign ministers meeting are in *FR 1950*, III, 1191ff.; U.S. Delegation Minutes of First Meeting, U.S. Minutes of Private Meeting, and U.S. Delegation Minutes of Second Meeting, Sept. 12, 1950, ibid., 1191–1209; Hitchcock, *France Restored,* 140–141.

31. Acheson to Webb [for Truman], Sept. 15, and Acheson to Embassy in France, Sept. 17, 1950, *FR 1950*, III, 314–315, 1229–1231; see also Acheson to Truman, Sept. 14 and Sept. 16, 1950, ibid., 301–302, 313–314, and Conclusions of a Meeting of the Cabinet, Sept. 4 and Sept. 15, 1950, CAB 128/18.

32. U.S. Delegation Minutes, Sept. 19, and Acheson to Webb [for Truman], Truman Memorandum, Sept. 21, and Webb Memorandum, Sept. 25, 1950, *FR 1950*, III, 1242–1244, 1245–1247, 301, 353–354; Conclusions of a Meeting of the Cabinet, Oct. 6 and Oct. 9, 1950, CAB 129/42, CAB 128/18; Bevin stated at these meetings that he had "failed utterly" to persuade the French and that it would be a "tragedy" to lose the chance for U.S. aid and commitment to Europe's defense.

33. Connelly Cabinet Minutes, Sept. 29 and Oct. 27, 1950, Box 2, Connelly Papers, and Acheson, *Present at the Creation,* 457; Ninkovich, *Germany and the United States,* 87–88, Frank Costigliola, *France and the United States: The Cold Alliance since World War II* (New York, 1992), 94, and Hitchcock, *France Restored,* 141–146, who also notes French interest in reaching some agreement with its allies in order to gain Indochina aid.

34. Schwartz, *America's Germany,* 144–147; in October 1950 CDU Minister Gustav Heineman resigned in protest over German rearmament.

35. Truman, *Years of Trial and Hope,* 254–258, and Ambrose, *Eisenhower,* 495–496.

36. Schwartz, *America's Germany,* 151–153; Acheson, *Present at the Creation,* 487; Memorandum of Acheson-Lovett Conversation, Dec. 14, 1950; Donovan, *Tumultuous Years,* 322, says that White House staff sought to have Eisenhower named as NATO commander to eliminate him as a presidential candidate in 1952; Elsey Memorandum, Feb. 7, 1951, Box 58, Elsey Papers, says that Eisenhower's appointment was an "Alphonse and Gaston act": the Europeans indicated desire for him, Truman designated him, and the NATO Council simultaneously appointed him; Eisenhower would report to the president as commander of U.S. forces in Europe but to NATO as supreme commander.

37. Acheson, *Present at the Creation*, 488–450; Truman's News Conference, Dec. 12, 1950, *PPHST*, VI, 761.

38. Donovan, *Tumultuous Years*, 322–323; Patterson, *Mr. Republican*, 474–480.

39. Truman News Conferences, Jan. 4 and Jan. 11, 1951, *PPHST*, 4, 18–19; "hopeless" in Ike diary extract for Nov. 11, 1950, Ambrose, *Eisenhower*, 497; Eisenhower also likened Truman to a man in a stormy lake who knew nothing about swimming, and stated about Truman, "if his wisdom could only equal his good intention"; see also Acheson, *Present at the Creation*, 490–492, and Donovan, *Tumultuous Years*, 323.

40. Truman State of the Union Address, Jan. 8, 1951, *PPHST*, 1951, VII, 6–13; Memorandum of Eisenhower Meeting with the Cabinet, Jan. 31, 1951, Box 73, Elsey Papers; Eisenhower testimony cited in Donovan, *Tumultuous Years*, 323–324.

41. Acheson, *Present at the Creation*, 494–495; Eisenhower to Truman, Feb. 24, 1951, Box 73, Elsey papers; Truman quoted in Donovan, *Tumultuous Years*, 324.

42. Kaplan, *Community of Interests*, 151–153.

43. Kennedy-Pipe, *Stalin's Cold War*, 158–159, and Schwartz, *America's Germany*, 148.

44. Acheson, *Present at the Creation*, 482–493, Battle Memorandum, Nov. 6, and Acheson Memorandum, Nov. 7, 1950, Box 65, Acheson Papers.

45. Schwartz, *America's Germany*, 148–149; Conclusions of a Meeting of the Cabinet, Nov. 15, Dec. 5, and Dec. 12, CAB 128/19 and 128/18; the White House meeting derived from Truman's November 30 assertion that use of the atomic bomb (in Korea) was always under consideration.

46. Acheson Memorandum, Jan. 11, 1951, Box 66, Acheson Papers, Bruce to Acheson, Jan. 23, and U.S. Minutes of Second and Third Meetings, Jan. 30, 1951, *FR 1951*, IV, 298, 316–328, 330–338.

47. Kennedy-Pipe, *Stalin's Cold War*, 158–161.

48. Record of the Western European Ambassadors Conference at Frankfurt, Feb. 5–7, 1951, *FR 1951*, IV, 145–170; Connelly Cabinet Notes, Feb. 9, 1951, Box 2, Connelly Papers.

49. Conclusions of a Meeting of the Cabinet, Apr. 26, 1951, CAB 128/19, and Acheson Memorandum, May 7, 1951, Box 66, Acheson Papers.

50. Acheson, *Present at the Creation*, 554–555, Conclusions of a Meeting of the Cabinet, Apr. 26, June 5, June 14, June 18, and June 21, 1951, CAB 128/19; Charles Bohlen, a participant in the meetings, says that "it was quite obvious that the Western side was not particularly interested in a conference while a war was on in Korea," *Witness*, 297; French election results in Schwartz, *America's Germany*, 226.

51. Acheson to Truman, Jan. 5, 1951, Box 67, Acheson Papers; State Department Memorandum for Truman, Jan. 5, 1951, *FR 1951*, III, 396–400; on Eisenhower, Ambrose, *Eisenhower*, 501–504, Schwartz, *America's Germany*, 150–152, and Elsey Memorandum, Jan. 31, 1951, Box 73, Elsey Papers.

52. Schwartz, *America's Germany*, 210–211.

53. U.S. Minutes of Third Acheson-Schuman Meeting, and Harriman Memorandum, Mar. 30, 1951, *FR 1951*, IV, 377–379; Schwartz, *America's Germany*, 212–213.

54. Schwartz, *America's Germany*, 152–153, 216–224; diary entries for June 11 and July 2, 1951, in Robert H. Ferrell (ed.), *The Eisenhower Diaries* (New York, 1981), 194–195, 196–197.

55. Schwartz, *America's Germany*, 224–225, and Bruce to State Department, July 2, 1951, *FR 1951*, III, 805–812.

56. Acheson Memorandum, July 6, 1951, *FR 1951*, III, 813–819, and Schwartz, *America's Germany*, 229–230.

57. Schwartz, *America's Germany*, 230–231, and Acheson and Lovett Memorandum to Truman (NSC 115, "Definition of the United States Policy on Problems of the Defense of Eu-

rope and the German Contribution"), July 30, 1951, *FR 1951,* III, 849–852.

58. Costigliola, *France and United States,* 91–95; Prime Minister's Memorandum: Germany, Aug. 30, 1951, Acheson to Morison, Aug. 9, and Morison to Acheson, Aug. 18, 1951, CAB 129/47; Schwartz, *America's Germany,* 250–252.

59. Acheson to Truman, Sept. 25, 1951, *FR 1951,* III, 288–289, and Kaplan, *Community of Interests,* 162–166; see also Schwartz, *America's Germany,* 241–242.

60. Schwartz, *America's Germany,* 240, 246–247.

61. Schwartz, *America's Germany,* 244; Truman's opposition to Big Four meeting in Connelly Cabinet Notes, Oct. 19, 1951, Box 2, Connelly Papers, and Kirk Memorandum, Oct. 26, 1951, *FR 1951,* IV, 1665–1667.

62. Acheson to Truman and Webb, Nov. 23, and Acheson to Truman, Nov. 30, 1951, *FR 1951,* III, 1609–1611, 1730–1732; Connelly Cabinet Notes, Dec. [?], 1951, Box 2, Connelly Papers.

63. Acheson Memorandum of Dinner on *Williamsburg,* Jan. 8, 1952, *FR 1952,* VI, 730–739.

64. U.S. Delegation Minutes, First and Fourth Truman-Churchill Meetings, Jan. 7 and Jan. 8, and U.S. Delegation Minutes of Truman-Churchill Meeting, Jan. 18, 1952, *FR 1952,* VI, 746–755, 794–802, 846–857.

65. Acheson Memorandum of Dinner on *Williamsburg,* Jan. 8, 1952, *FR 1952,* VI, 730–739, and Battle Memorandum, Jan. 9, 1952, Box 66, Acheson Papers.

66. Costigliola, *France and United States,* 92–93; Schwartz, *America's Germany,* 254, McLellan, *Acheson,* 361.

67. Acheson Memorandum, Feb. 4, 1952, Box 66, Acheson Papers; McLellan, *Acheson,* 363, Schwartz, *America's Germany,* 253–254, and Hitchcock, *France Restored,* 166–167.

68. Schwartz, *America's Germany,* 255–260; Acheson, *Present at the Creation,* 625–627.

69. Kaplan, *Community of Interests,* 167.

70. Soviet Foreign Ministry to U.S. Embassy, Mar. 10, 1952, *FR 1952–1954,* VII, 169–172.

71. Stalin's views on a rebuilt Germany in J. V. Stalin, "Economic Problems of Socialism in the U.S.S.R.," in Bruce Franklin (ed.), *The Essential Stalin* (Garden City, 1972), 469–473; see also Schwartz, *America's Germany,* 263–264; Gromyko quoted in Wettig, "Stalin and German Reunification," 417; on analysis of Stalin's Note, see Steininger, *German Question,* passim, who argues that the note was serious but that Acheson and the U.S. were bent on integration and paid only lip service to unification, while Adenauer—the chief bar to negotiations, in Steininger's view—sought to align the FRG with the West as a means to "liberate" all of Europe from Soviet control; Wettig, "Stalin and German Reunification," 411–419, views Stalin's Note as a grossly misconceived effort to help West German Communists rouse the public against Adenauer's government; Ruud Van Dijk, "The 1952 Stalin Note Debate: Myth or Missed Opportunity for German Unification?" CWIHP, Working Paper No. 14 (May 1996), usefully reviews new documents and literature and argues that Stalin's Note was a "last, desperate attempt" (p. 17) to prevent FRG membership in the EDC and to create political disarray among the Western powers; see also Kennedy-Pipe, *Stalin's Cold War,* 161–163, who says that Stalin's Note reflected Soviet "ambivalence" about Germany: desire to control the East but recognition that four-power accord offered a say in all of Germany that would limit the threat of a rebuilt Germany on Soviet borders; the Soviets could not decide whether U.S. forces in the West meant that the FRG would be "contained" or brought into an anti-Soviet atomic alliance.

72. Acheson to Truman, Mar. 11, 1952, Box 66, Acheson Papers; "golden apple" in Acheson, *Present at the Creation,* 632.

73. Gifford to Acheson, Mar. 11, and Acheson to London Embassy, July 14, 1952, *FR 1952–1954,* VII, 172–173, 176–177.

74. Steininger, *German Question,* 22–28, and Kirkland to Foreign Office, Mar. 17, in Steininger, op. cit., 141–142, and Hay [acting U.S. high commissioner for Germany] to State Department, Mar. 17, 1952, *FR 1952–1954,* VII, 182–183; Kaiser quoted in Schwartz, *America's Germany,* 267.

75. McCloy to Acheson, Mar. 12, Bonsal to Acheson, Mar. 15, and Minutes of a Meeting of U.S., U.K., French, and German Representatives, Mar. 20, 1952, in Steininger, *German Question,* 125–127, 139–140, 143–145; Bonsal [for McCloy] to State Department, Mar. 17, 1952, *FR 1952–1954,* VII, 180–181.

76. Kennan, *Memoirs,* II, 105–108.

77. Ibid., 108–109.

78. Acheson to Embassy in London, Mar. 14 and Mar. 17, 1952, *FR 1952–1954,* VII, 173–175, 183–184; Steininger, *German Question,* 49–54; Schwartz, *America's Germany,* 265.

79. Editorial Note, and Acheson to U.S. High Commissioner for Germany, Mar. 22, and Cumming to Department of State, Mar. 25, 1952, *FR 1952–1954,* VII, 188–191.

80. Acheson to Embassy in United Kingdom, Mar. 25, 1952, ibid., 192–193, and Ferguson Memorandum, Mar. 27, 1952, in Steininger, *German Question,* 146–150; McLellan, *Acheson,* 371.

81. Minutes of a Conversation with Stalin, Molotov, Malenkov, Pieck, Ulbricht, and Grotewohl, Apr. 7, 1952, Soviet Foreign Ministry Archives, CWIHP, *Bulletin* (Fall 1994), 48; see also Van Dijk, "1952 Stalin Note Debate," 24.

82. Soviet Ministry of Foreign Affairs to U.S. Embassy, Apr. 9, Acheson to U.S. High Commissioner at Bonn, Apr. 12, and Acheson to Embassy in United Kingdom, Apr. 30, and Acheson Memorandum, May 1, 1952, *FR 1952–1954,* VII, 199–202, 203–206, 220–223, 237 n. 1.

83. Gifford to State Department, May 3, 1952, ibid., VII, 225–226, and McCloy to Acheson, May 3, 1952, in Steininger, *German Question,* 157–158.

84. Acheson Memorandum, May 9, U.S. Embassy to the Soviet Ministry for Foreign Affairs, May 13, and Soviet Ministry for Foreign Affairs to U.S. Embassy, May 24, 1952, *FR 1952–1954,* VII, 237–238, 242–247, and 247–252.

85. Eden quoted in Acheson to Embassy in United Kingdom, June 10, 1952, *FR 1952–1954,* VII, 263–264, and Eden, *Full Circle,* 50; "feeble" in Acheson to Embassy in France, June 19, and Kennan to State Department, May 25, 1952, *FR 1952–1954,* VII, 271–273, 252–253; on sealing off the GDR and creating a full-fledged satellite, see Mastny, *Cold War and Soviet Insecurity,* 138–140.

86. Acheson Memorandum, June 22, 1952, Box 67, Acheson Papers; Acheson, *Present at the Creation,* 642.

87. Acheson, *Present at the Creation,* 640, Schwartz, *America's Germany,* 369–370; Conclusions of a Meeting of the Cabinet, May 7, 1952, CAB 128/24.

88. Schwartz, *America's Germany,* 271–276, Bird, *McCloy,* 382–385; Convention on Relations between the Three Powers and the Federal Republic of Germany, May 26, 1952, *FR 1952–1954,* VII, 112–118.

89. Acheson, *Present at the Creation,* 694–696; Schwartz, *America's Germany,* 276.

90. Bird, *McCloy,* 384–385, and Harper, *Visions,* 319; McLellan, *Acheson,* 319, records French president Vincent Auriol's tirade to Acheson that the threat to Europe was Germany not Russia; on Truman success, Schwartz, *America's Germany,* 276–277, and Leffler, *Preponderance of Power,* 460; Truman Special Message to the Senate Transmitting a Conven-

tion on Relations with Germany and Related Documents, June 2, 1952, *PPHST,* VIII, 395–398; Acheson, *Present at the Creation,* 650.

91. Acheson to Embassy in United Kingdom, June 10, 1952, *FR 1952–1954,* VII, 263–264; Jessup Memorandum, June 12, 1952, Box 67, Acheson Papers; McCloy to State Department, June 25, 1952, *FR 1952–1954,* VII, 273–275.

92. Acheson to State Department, June 28, 1952, *FR 1952–1954,* VII, 275–276.

93. U.S. Embassy to the Soviet Foreign Ministry, July 10, and Soviet Foreign Ministry to the U.S. Embassy, Aug. 23, 1952, ibid., 288–291, 292–297.

94. Bruce to Embassy in France, Aug. 25, and U.S. Embassy to the Soviet Foreign Ministry, Sept. 23, 1952, ibid., 298–299, 324–327.

95. Henry Kissinger, *Diplomacy* (New York, 1994), 494–500 (Kissinger does not think that the West can be criticized for not negotiating over Germany in 1952); see also Ruud Van Dijk, "The Stalin-Note: Last Chance for Unification?" paper presented at conference on "The Soviet Union, Germany, and the Cold War, 1945–1962: New Evidence from the Archives," Essen, Germany (June 1994), 8–9.

96. Mastny, *Cold War and Soviet Insecurity,* 138–140, and Gaddis, *We Now Know,* 128–129, dismiss Stalin's proposal and insist that he wanted only to dominate all of Germany; but surely Stalin knew from the West's powerful hold on West Germany by 1952 that this was unlikely to happen; nor was he so naive to try to gain control through negotiation; more likely, he was willing to weigh a neutralized Germany, as the French surmised, that would not "be entirely on the side of the west in east-west questions."

97. Bird, *McCloy,* 381, Schwartz, *America's Germany,* 300.

98. Leffler, *Preponderance of Power,* 463; Kennan, *Memoirs,* II, 161.

99. Schwartz, *America's Germany,* 280–282, Gaddis, *We Now Know,* 132–133; Eisenhower Speech in *Public Papers of the Presidents: Dwight D. Eisenhower,* 8 vols. (Washington, D.C., 1960–1961), I: *1953,* 179–188; Christian F. Ostermann, "The United States, the East German Uprising of 1953, and the Limits of Rollback," CWIHP, Working Paper No. 11 (Dec. 1994), 12–13, cites Dulles as insisting that "this was not the time for us to be soft"; that if "we keep our pressures on, psychological and otherwise, we may either force a collapse of the Kremlin regime or else transform the Soviet orbit from a union of satellites dedicated to aggression into a coalition for defense only."

100. Memorandum of Discussion of 150th Meeting of National Security Council, June 18, 1953, *FR 1952–1954,* VII, 1587–1590; Ostermann, "U.S. and East German Uprising," 2, 4–7, 17–18, 42–43; Ostermann explains the revolts as resulting from the volatile mix of the GDR's year-old, extremely unpopular "crash socialization program" and the recent Moscow-directed, more liberal "New Course," which did not end the higher productivity norms imposed on workers, who began protests in East Berlin that spread across the country and almost toppled the government.

101. Schwartz, *America's Germany,* 284–286, and James G. Hershberg, "'Explosion in the Offing': German Rearmament and American Diplomacy, 1953–1955," *DH,* 16 (Fall 1992), 532–533.

102. Townsend Hoopes, *The Devil and John Foster Dulles* (Boston, 1973), 193–197, and Schwartz, *America's Germany,* 286; Dulles to Adenauer, Nov. 20, 1953, *FR 1952–1954,* VII, 1477–1478; Costigliola, *France and United States,* 98.

103. Schwartz, *America's Germany,* 287–289; Hershberg, "Explosion in the Offing," 544–545, and Gaddis, *We Now Know,* 133–134.

104. Schwartz, *America's Germany,* 289–290; Costigliola, *France and United States,* 98–100.

105. Costigliola, *France and United States,* 101–104; Schwartz, *America's Germany,*

292–294; Lawrence S. Kaplan, "NATO and the Warsaw Pact: The Past," in Robert W. Clawson and Lawrence S. Kaplan (eds.), *NATO and the Warsaw Pact: Political Purpose and Military Means* (Wilmington, 1982), 67–74.

106. Truman Address at National War College, Dec. 19, 1952, *PPHST,* VIII, 1090–1096.

Chapter 16. Conclusion

1. Paterson, *On Every Front,* 18–20.

2. Ibid., 8–12; the total number of European lives lost has been estimated at 55 million; China lost about 10 million people, Japan about 2.5 million, and the Vietnamese about 1 million.

3. "Overreach" adapted from diary entry for July 16, 1945, Ferrell (ed.), *Off the Record,* 52.

4. Diary entry for July 5, 1948, Lilienthal, *Journals,* II: *Atomic Energy Years,* 378–379.

Bibliography

Personal Papers

Acheson, Dean, Harry S. Truman Library (HSTL), Independence, Mo.
Anderson, Clinton, HSTL
Ayers, Eben A., HSTL
Bevin, Ernest, Public Record Office (PRO), Kew Gardens, London
Butler, Nevile, PRO
Byrnes, James F., Robert M. Cooper Library, Clemson University, Clemson, S.C.
Clayton, Will L., HSTL
Clifford, Clark M., HSTL
Connelly, Matthew J., HSTL
Daniels, Jonathan, HSTL
Davies, Joseph E., Manuscript Division, Library of Congress, Washington, D.C.
Dennison, Robert L., HSTL
Elsey, George M., HSTL
Finletter, Thomas K., HSTL
Forrestal, James V., Seeley G. Mudd Library, Princeton University, Princeton, N.J.
Grady, Henry F., HSTL
Grew, Joseph C., Houghton Library, Harvard University, Cambridge, Mass.
Hoffman, Paul G., HSTL
Jacobson, Edward, HSTL
Kennan, George, Seeley G. Mudd Library, Princeton University, Princeton, N.J.
Kindleberger, Charles P., HSTL
Locke, Edwin A., HSTL
Matthews, Francis P., HSTL
Murphy, Robert, Hoover Institution Archives, Stanford, Calif.
Porter, Paul A., HSTL
Ross, Charles G., HSTL
Smith, Harold, HSTL
Stimson, Henry L., Sterling Library, Yale University, New Haven, Conn.

Taylor, Myron C., HSTL
Truman, Harry S. (Papers pertaining to family, business, and personal affairs; Papers as Presiding Judge of the Jackson County Court; Papers as U.S. Senator and Vice President; Papers as President of the United States: Map Room File, National Security Council Files, President's Secretary's Files, and White House Central Files; Post-Presidential Papers), HSTL
Webb, James E., HSTL
Weizmann, Chaim, Weizmann Archives, HSTL

Oral History Interviews

Elsey, George, HSTL
Ethridge, Mark, HSTL
Locke, Edwin A., HSTL
Murphy, Charles, HSTL
Ringwalt, Arthur, HSTL
Sprouse, Philip D., HSTL
Vaughan, Harry, HSTL

Government Records, Unpublished and Published

Ministry of Foreign Affairs of the U.S.S.R. *Stalin's Correspondence with Roosevelt and Truman, 1941–1945*. New York: Capricorn Books, 1965.
Public Papers of the Presidents of the United States: Dwight D. Eisenhower. 8 vols. Washington, D.C.: Government Printing Office (GPO), 1960–1961.
Public Papers of the Presidents of the United States: Harry S. Truman. 8 vols. Washington, D.C.: GPO, 1961–1966.
Records of the British Cabinet Office, PRO.
Records of the British Foreign Office, PRO.
Rosenman, Samuel I., comp. *The Public Papers and Addresses of Franklin D. Roosevelt.* 13 vols. New York: Random House; Macmillan; Harper and Bros., 1938–1950.
U.S. Department of State. *The Conference of Berlin (The Potsdam Conference), 1945.* 2 vols. Washington, D.C.: GPO, 1960.
———. *Foreign Relations of United States, Diplomatic Papers, 1945.* 9 vols. Washington, D.C.: GPO, 1967–1969.
———. *FR 1946.* 11 vols. Washington, D.C.: GPO, 1969–1972.
———. *FR 1947.* 8 vols. Washington, D.C.: GPO, 1971–1977.
———. *FR 1948.* 9 vols. Washington, D.C.: GPO, 1972–1976.
———. *FR 1949.* 9 vols. Washington, D.C.: GPO, 1974–1978.
———. *FR 1950.* 7 vols. Washington, D.C.: GPO, 1977–1980.
———. *FR 1951.* 7 vols. Washington, D.C.: GPO, 1977–1985.
———. *FR 1952–1954.* 26 vols. Washington: GPO, 1979–1989.
———. *United States Relations with China, with Special Reference to the Period 1944–1949.* Washington, D.C.: GPO, 1949.
U.S. Senate, Committee on Foreign Relations. *Legislative Origins of the Truman Doctrine, Hearings Held in Executive Session . . . on S. 938: A Bill to Provide Assistance to Greece and Turkey.* Washington, D.C.: GPO, 1973.

———. *The Vandenberg Resolution and the North Atlantic Treaty, Hearings Held in Executive Session . . . on S. Res. 239, Reaffirming the Policy of the United States to Achieve International Peace and Security through the United Nations.* Washington, D.C.: GPO, 1973.

Books

Acheson, Dean. *Present at the Creation: My Years in the State Department.* New York: Norton, 1969.

Alexander, Bevin. *Strange Connection: U.S. Intervention in China, 1944–1972.* New York: Greenwood Press, 1992.

Alperovitz, Gar. *Atomic Diplomacy: Hiroshima and Potsdam and the Use of the Atomic Bomb and the American Confrontation with Soviet Power.* Rev. ed. New York: Penguin, 1985.

———. *The Decision to Use the Atomic Bomb and the Architecture of an American Myth.* New York: Knopf, 1995.

Ambrose, Stephen E. *Eisenhower and Berlin, 1945: The Decision to Halt at the Elbe.* New York: Norton, 1967.

———. *Eisenhower: Soldier, General, and President-Elect, 1890–1952.* New York: Simon and Schuster, 1983.

Anders, Roger M., ed. *Forging the Atomic Shield: Excerpts from the Office Diary of Gordon E. Dean.* Chapel Hill: University of North Carolina Press, 1987.

Andrew, Christopher, and Vasili Mitrokhin. *The Sword and the Shield: The Mitrokhin Archive and the Secret History of the KGB.* New York: Basic Books, 1999.

Barber, James David. *The Presidential Character: Predicting Presidential Performance in the White House.* Englewood Cliffs, N.J.: Prentice Hall, 1972.

Barkley, Alben W. *That Reminds Me.* Garden City, N.Y.: Doubleday, 1954.

Beitzell, Robert. *The Uneasy Alliance: America, Britain, and Russia, 1941–1943.* New York: Knopf, 1968.

Berle, Beatrice Bishop, and Travis Beal Jacobs, eds. *Navigating the Rapids, 1918–1971: From the Papers of Adolf A. Berle.* New York: Harcourt Brace Jovanovich, 1971.

Bill, James A. *The Eagle and the Lion: The Tragedy of American-Iranian Relations.* New Haven, Conn.: Yale University Press, 1988.

Bird, Kai. *The Chairman: John J. McCloy, the Making of the American Establishment.* New York: Simon and Schuster, 1992.

Birkenhead, The Earl of. *Halifax: The Life of Lord Halifax.* Boston: Houghton Mifflin, 1966.

Blum, John Morton. *From the Morgenthau Diaries: Years of War, 1941–1945.* Boston: Houghton Mifflin, 1967.

———. *V Was for Victory: Politics and American Culture during World War II.* New York: Harcourt Brace Jovanovich, 1976.

———, ed. *The Price of Vision: The Diary of Henry A. Wallace, 1942–1946.* Boston: Houghton Mifflin, 1973.

Blum, Robert M. *Drawing the Line: The Origin of American Containment Policy in East Asia.* New York: Norton, 1982.

Bohlen, Charles E. *Witness to History, 1929–1969.* New York: Norton, 1973.

Borden, Morton. *America's Eleven Greatest Presidents.* 2nd ed. New York: Rand McNally, 1971.

Borg, Dorothy, and Waldo Heinrichs, eds. *Uncertain Years: Chinese-American Relations, 1947–1950.* New York: Columbia University Press, 1980.

Bradley, Omar N., and Clay Blair. *A Soldier's Story.* New York: Simon and Schuster, 1983.

Brands, H. W. *Inside the Cold War: Loy Henderson and the Rise of the American Empire, 1918–1961.* New York: Oxford University Press, 1991.

Buhite, Russell D. *Soviet-American Relations in Asia, 1945–1954.* Norman: University of Oklahoma Press, 1981.

Bullock, Allan. *Ernest Bevin: Foreign Secretary, 1945–1951.* New York: Oxford University Press, 1983.

Bundy, McGeorge. *Danger and Survival: Choices about the Bomb in the First Fifty Years.* New York: Vintage Books, 1988.

Burns, James MacGregor. *Roosevelt: The Lion and the Fox, 1882–1940.* New York: Harcourt Brace, 1956.

———. *Roosevelt: The Soldier of Freedom.* New York: Harcourt Brace Jovanovich, 1970.

Butcher, Harry C. *My Three Years with Eisenhower: The Personal Diary of Captain Harry C. Butcher, 1942–1945.* New York: Simon and Schuster, 1946.

Byrnes, James F. *All in One Lifetime.* New York: Harper, 1958.

———. *Speaking Frankly.* New York: Harper, 1947.

Campbell, Thomas M. *Masquerade Peace: America's UN Policy, 1944–1945.* Tallahassee: Florida State University Press, 1973.

Campbell, Thomas M., and George C. Herring, eds. *The Diaries of Edward R. Stettinius, Jr., 1943–1946.* New York: New Viewpoints, 1975.

Caraley, Demetrios. *The Politics of Military Unification: A Study of Conflict and the Policy Process.* New York: Columbia University Press, 1966.

Chace, James. *Acheson: The Secretary of State Who Created the American World.* New York: Simon and Schuster, 1998.

Chang, Gordon H. *Friends and Enemies: The United States, China, and the Soviet Union, 1948–1971.* Stanford: Stanford University Press, 1990.

Charmley, John. *Churchill's Grand Alliance: The Anglo-American Special Relationship, 1940–1957.* New York: Harcourt Brace, 1995.

Chen, Jian. *China's Road to the Korean War: The Making of the Sino-American Confrontation.* New York: Columbia University Press, 1994.

Christensen, Thomas J. *Useful Adversaries: Grand Strategy, Domestic Mobilization, and Sino-American Conflict, 1947–1958.* Princeton, N.J.: Princeton University Press, 1996.

Churchill, Winston S. *The Second World War.* 6 vols. Boston: Houghton Mifflin, 1948–1953.

Clawson, Robert W., and Lawrence S. Kaplan, eds. *NATO and the Warsaw Pact: Political Purpose and Military Means.* Wilmington, Del.: Scholarly Resources, 1982.

Clay, Lucius D. *Decision in Germany.* Melbourne and London: W. Heinemann, 1950.

Clemens, Diane Shaver. *Yalta.* New York: Oxford University Press, 1970.

Clifford, Clark, with Richard Holbrooke. *Counsel to the President: A Memoir.* New York: Anchor Books, 1991.

Close, David H., ed. *The Greek Civil War, 1943–1950: Studies of Polarization.* London and New York: Routledge, 1993.

Clubb, O. Edmund. *Twentieth Century China.* New York: Columbia University Press, 1964.

Cochran, Bert. *Harry Truman and the Crisis Presidency.* New York: Funk and Wagnalls, 1973.

Cohen, Michael J. *Palestine and the Great Powers, 1945–1948.* Princeton, N.J.: Princeton University Press, 1988.

———. *Truman and Israel.* Berkeley: University of California Press, 1990.

Cohen, Warren I. *America's Response to China: A History of Sino-American Relations.* 3rd. ed. New York: Columbia University Press, 1990.

Condit, Kenneth W. *The History of the Joint Chiefs of Staff.* Vol. II: *The Joint Chiefs of Staff and National Policy, 1947–1949.* Wilmington, Del.: Glazier, 1979.

Connally, Tom. *My Name Is Tom Connally.* New York: Crowell, 1954.

Cook, Don. *Forging the Alliance: NATO, 1945–1950.* New York: Twayne, 1989.

Costigliola, Frank. *France and the United States: The Cold Alliance since World War II.* New York: Twayne, 1992.

Craig, Gordon A., and Francis L. Loewenheim, eds. *The Diplomats, 1939–1979.* Princeton, N.J.: Princeton University Press, 1994.

Cumings, Bruce. *Korea's Place in the Sun: A Modern History.* New York: Norton, 1997.

———. *The Origins of the Korean War.* Vol. I: *Liberation and the Emergence of Separate Regimes, 1945–1947.* Princeton, N.J.: Princeton University Press, 1981.

———. *The Origins of the Korean War.* Vol. II: *The Roaring of the Cataract, 1947–1950.* Princeton, N.J.: Princeton University Press, 1990.

———, ed. *Child of Conflict: The Korean-American Relationship, 1943–1953.* Seattle: University of Washington Press, 1983.

Curry, George W. *James F. Byrnes.* Vol. 14 in *The American Secretaries of State and Their Diplomacy.* New York: Cooper Square, 1965.

Dallek, Robert. *Franklin D. Roosevelt and American Foreign Policy, 1932–1945.* New York: Oxford University Press, 1979.

Daniels, Jonathan. *Man of Independence.* Philadelphia: Lippincott, 1950.

Davies, Joseph E. *Mission to Moscow.* New York: Simon and Schuster, 1941.

Davis, Lynn Ethridge. *The Cold War Begins: Soviet-American Conflict over Eastern Europe.* Princeton, N.J.: Princeton University Press, 1974.

Dedijer, Vladimir. *The Battle Stalin Lost: Memoirs of Yugoslavia 1948–1953.* New York: Viking, 1970.

DePorte, A. W. *Europe between the Superpowers: The Enduring Balance.* New Haven, Conn.: Yale University Press, 1979.

DeSantis, Hugh. *The Diplomacy of Silence: The American Foreign Service, the Soviet Union, and the Cold War, 1933–1947.* Chicago: University of Chicago Press, 1980.

Dilks, David, ed. *The Diaries of Sir Alexander Cadogan, 1938–1945.* New York: G. P. Putnam's, 1972.

Divine, Robert A. *Foreign Policy and U.S. Presidential Elections, 1940–1948.* New York: New Viewpoints, 1974.

———. *Roosevelt and World War II.* Baltimore: Johns Hopkins University Press, 1969.

———. *Second Chance: The Triumph of Internationalism in America during World War II.* New York: Atheneum, 1967.

Dixon, Pierson. *Double Diploma: The Life of Sir Pierson Dixon.* London: Hutchinson, 1968.

Djilas, Milovan. *Conversations with Stalin.* Translated by Michael B. Petrovich. New York: Harcourt Brace and World, 1962.

Dobbs, Charles M. *The Unwanted Symbol: American Foreign Policy, the Cold War, and Korea, 1945–1950.* Kent, Ohio: Kent State University Press, 1981.

Dobney, Frederick J. *Selected Papers of Will Clayton.* Baltimore: Johns Hopkins University Press, 1971.

Donovan, Robert J. *Conflict and Crisis: The Presidency of Harry S. Truman, 1945–1948.* New York: Norton, 1977.

———. *Tumultuous Years: The Presidency of Harry S. Truman, 1949–1953.* New York: Norton, 1982.

Dorsett, Lyle W. *The Pendergast Machine.* New York: Oxford University Press, 1968.

Driberg, Tom. *The Mystery of Moral Rearmament: A Study of Frank Buchman and His Movement.* New York: Knopf, 1965.

Drury, Allen. *A Senate Journal, 1943–1945.* Garden City, N.Y.: Doubleday, 1963.

Eastman, Lloyd E. *Seeds of Destruction: Nationalist China in War and Revolution 1937–1949.* Stanford: Stanford University Press, 1984.

Eden, Anthony, Earl of Avon. *The Memoirs of Anthony Eden, Earl of Avon.* Vol. 2: *The Reckoning.* Boston: Houghton Mifflin, 1965.

———. *The Memoirs of Anthony Eden.* Vol. 3: *Full Circle.* Boston: Houghton Mifflin, 1960.

Edmonds, Robin. *The Big Three: Churchill, Roosevelt, and Stalin in Peace and War.* New York: Norton, 1991.

Eisenberg, Carolyn Woods. *Drawing the Line: The American Decision to Divide Germany, 1944–1949.* Cambridge: Cambridge University Press, 1996.

Etzold, Thomas H., and John Lewis Gaddis, eds. *Containment: Documents on American Policy and Strategy, 1945–1950.* New York: Columbia University Press, 1978.

Feis, Herbert. *From Trust to Terror: The Onset of the Cold War, 1945–1950.* New York: Norton, 1970.

Ferrell, Robert H. *Harry S. Truman: A Life.* Columbia: University of Missouri Press, 1994.

———. *Harry S. Truman and the Modern American Presidency.* Boston: Little, Brown, 1983.

———, ed. *The Autobiography of Harry S. Truman.* Boulder: Colorado Associated University Press, 1980.

———, ed. *Dear Bess: The Letters from Harry to Bess Truman, 1910–1959.* New York: Norton, 1983.

———, ed. *The Eisenhower Diaries.* New York: Norton, 1981.

———, ed. *Off the Record: The Private Papers of Harry S. Truman.* New York: Penguin, 1980.

Fleming, Donald, and Bernard Bailyn, eds. *The Intellectual Migration: Europe and America, 1930–1960.* Cambridge, Mass.: Harvard University Press, 1969.

Foot, Rosemary. *The Wrong War: American Policy and the Dimensions of the Korean Conflict, 1950–1953.* Ithaca, N.Y.: Cornell University Press, 1985.

Franklin, Bruce, ed. *The Essential Stalin.* Garden City, N.Y.: Doubleday, 1972.

Freeland, Richard M. *The Truman Doctrine and the Origins of McCarthyism: Foreign Policy, Domestic Politics, and Internal Security, 1946–1948.* New York: Knopf, 1972.

Gaddis, John Lewis. *The Long Road: Inquiries into the History of the Cold War.* New York: Oxford University Press, 1987.

———. *Russia, the Soviet Union, and the United States: An Interpretive History.* 2nd ed. New York: McGraw-Hill, 1990.

———. *Strategies of Containment: A Critical Appraisal of Postwar American National Security Policy.* New York: Oxford University Press, 1982.

———. *The United States and the Origins of the Cold War, 1941–1947.* New York: Columbia University Press, 1972.

———. *We Now Know: Rethinking Cold War History.* New York: Oxford University Press, 1997.

Gallicchio, Marc S. *The Cold War Begins in Asia: American East Asian Policy and the Fall of the Japanese Empire.* New York: Columbia University Press, 1988.

Garber, Marjorie, and Rebecca L. Walkowitz, eds. *The Rosenberg Case, McCarthyism, and Fifties America.* New York: Routledge, 1995.

Gardner, Lloyd C. *Architects of Illusions: Men and Ideas in American Foreign Policy, 1941–1949.* Chicago: Quadrangle, 1970.

Gimbel, John. *The American Occupation of Germany: Politics and the Military, 1945–1949.* Stanford: Stanford University Press, 1968.

———. *The Origins of the Marshall Plan.* Stanford: Stanford University Press, 1976.

Gladwyn, Lord. *The Memoirs of Lord Gladwyn.* New York: Weybright and Talley, 1972.

Golan, Galia. *Soviet Policies in the Middle East: From World War Two to Gorbachev.* Cambridge: Cambridge University Press, 1990.

Goldgeier, James M. *Leadership Style and Soviet Foreign Policy: Stalin, Khrushchev, Brezhnev, Gorbachev.* Baltimore: Johns Hopkins University Press, 1994.

Goncharov, Sergei, John W. Lewis, and Xue Litai. *Uncertain Partners: Stalin, Mao, and the Korean War.* Stanford: Stanford University Press, 1993.

Gori, Francesca, and Silvia Pons, eds. *The Soviet Union and Europe in the Cold War, 1943–53.* New York: St Martin's, 1996.

Gosnell, Harold F. *Truman's Crises: A Political Biography of Harry S. Truman.* Westport, Conn.: Greenwood Press, 1980.

Goulden, Joseph C. *The Best Years 1945–1950.* New York: Atheneum, 1976.

Green, David. *The Containment of Latin America: A History of the Myths and Realities of the Good Neighbor Policy.* Chicago: Quadrangle, 1971.

Gromyko, Andrei. *Memoirs.* Translated by Harold Shukman. New York: Doubleday, 1989.

Hamby, Alonzo L. *Beyond the New Deal: Harry S. Truman and American Liberalism.* New York: Oxford University Press, 1973.

———. *Man of the People: A Life of Harry S. Truman.* New York: Oxford University Press, 1995.

Hammond, Thomas T., ed. *Witnesses to the Origins of the Cold War.* Seattle and London: University of Washington Press, 1982.

Hanhimaki, Jussi M. *Containing Coexistence: America, Russia, and the "Finnish Solution," 1945–1956.* Kent, Ohio: Kent State University Press, 1997.

Harbutt, Fraser. *The Iron Curtain: Churchill, America, and the Origins of the Cold War.* New York: Oxford University Press, 1986.

Harper, John Lamberton. *American Visions of Europe: Franklin D. Roosevelt, George F. Kennan, and Dean G. Acheson.* Cambridge and New York: Cambridge University Press, 1994.

Harriman, W. Averell, and Elie Abel. *Special Envoy to Churchill and Stalin, 1941–1946.* New York: Random House, 1975.

Hartmann, Susan M. *Truman and the 80th Congress.* Columbia: University of Missouri Press, 1971.

Hathaway, Robert M. *Ambiguous Partnership: Britain and America, 1944–1947.* New York: Columbia University Press, 1981.

Haynes, John Earl, and Harvey Klehr. *Venona: Decoding Soviet Espionage in America.* New Haven, Conn.: Yale University Press, 1999.

Herken, Gregg. *Cardinal Choices: Presidential Science Advising from the Atomic Bomb to SDI.* New York: Oxford University Press, 1992.

———. *The Winning Weapon: The Atomic Bomb and the Cold War, 1945–1950.* New York: Columbia University Press, 1981.

Herring, George C., Jr. *Aid to Russia, 1941–1946: Strategy, Diplomacy, and the Origins of the Cold War.* New York: Columbia University Press, 1973.

Hess, Gary. *The United States' Emergence as a Southeast Asian Power, 1945–1950.* New York: Columbia University Press, 1987.

———. *Vietnam and the United States: Origins and Legacy of War.* Boston: Twayne, 1990.

Hewlett, Richard G., and Oscar E. Anderson, Jr. *A History of the United States Atomic Energy Commission*. Vol. I: *The New World, 1939–1946*. University Park: Pennsylvania State University Press, 1962.

Hewlett, Richard G., and Francis Duncan. *A History of the United States Atomic Energy Commission*. Vol. II: *Atomic Shield, 1947–1952*. University Park: Pennsylvania State University Press, 1969.

Hillman, William, ed. *Mr. President: The First Publication from the Personal Diaries, Private Letters, Papers, and Revealing Interviews of Harry S. Truman, Thirty-second President of the United States*. New York: Farrar, Straus, and Young, 1952.

Hitchcock, William I. *France Restored: Cold War Diplomacy and the Quest for Leadership in Europe, 1945–1954*. Chapel Hill: University of North Carolina Press, 1998.

Hixson, Walter L. *George F. Kennan: Cold War Iconoclast*. New York: Columbia University Press, 1989.

Hogan, Michael J. *A Cross of Iron: Harry S. Truman and the Origins of the National Security State, 1945–1954*. Cambridge: Cambridge University Press, 1998.

———. *The Marshall Plan: America, Britain, and the Reconstruction of Western Europe, 1947–1952*. Cambridge: Cambridge University Press, 1987.

Holloway, David. *Stalin and the Bomb: The Soviet Union and Atomic Energy, 1939–1956*. New Haven, Conn.: Yale University Press, 1994.

Hoopes, Townsend. *The Devil and John Foster Dulles*. Boston: Little, Brown, 1973.

Hoopes, Townsend, and Douglas Brinkley. *Driven Patriot: The Life and Times of James Forrestal*. New York: Knopf, 1992.

Hoover, Herbert C. *An American Epic*. 4 vols. Chicago: Henry Regnery, 1959.

Hughes, Emmet John. *The Ordeal of Power: A Political Memoir of the Eisenhower Years*. New York: Atheneum, 1963.

Hull, Cordell. *The Memoirs of Cordell Hull*. 2 vols. New York: Macmillan, 1948.

Hunt, Michael H. *The Genesis of Chinese Communist Foreign Policy*. New York: Columbia University Press, 1996.

Iatrides, John O. *Revolt in Athens: The Greek Communist "Second Round," 1944–1945*. Princeton, N.J.: Princeton University Press, 1972.

Ickes, Harold L. *The Secret Diary of Harold L. Ickes*. 3 vols. New York: Simon and Schuster, 1953–1955.

Iriye, Akira. *Power and Culture: The Japanese-American War, 1941–1945*. Cambridge, Mass.: Harvard University Press, 1981.

Isaacson, Walter, and Evan Thomas. *The Wise Men: Six Friends and the World They Made*. New York: Simon and Schuster, 1986.

James, Robert Rhodes, ed. *Winston S. Churchill: His Complete Speeches, 1897–1963*. New York and London: Chelsea House, 1974.

Jenkins, Roy. *Truman*. New York: Harper and Row, 1986.

Jones, Howard. *"A New Kind of War": American Global Strategy and the Truman Doctrine in Greece*. New York: Oxford University Press, 1989.

Jones, Joseph Marion. *The Fifteen Weeks: February 21–June 5, 1947*. New York: Harcourt Brace and World, 1955.

Kahn, E. J. *The China Hands: American Foreign Service Officers and What Befell Them*. New York: Penguin, 1975.

Kaplan, Lawrence S. *A Community of Interests: NATO and the Military Assistance Program, 1948–1951*. Washington, D.C.: Office of the Secretary of Defense, 1980.

———. *NATO and the United States: The Enduring Alliance*. Boston: Twayne, 1988.

———. *The United States and NATO: The Formative Years*. Lexington: University of Kentucky Press, 1984.

Karski, Jan. *The Great Powers and Poland, 1919–1945: From Versailles to Yalta.* Lanham, Md.: University Press of America, 1985.

Kaufman, Burton I. *The Korean War: Challenge in Crisis, Credibility, and Command.* New York: Knopf, 1986.

Kennan, George F. *Memoirs, 1925–1963.* 2 vols. Boston: Little, Brown, 1967–1972.

Kennedy-Pipe, Carolyn. *Stalin's Cold War: Soviet Strategies in Europe, 1943–1956.* Manchester, England: Manchester University Press, 1996.

Kersten, Krystyna. *The Establishment of Communist Rule in Poland, 1943–1948.* Translated by John Micgiel and Michael H. Bernhard. Berkeley: University of California Press, 1991.

Kimball, Warren F. *Forged in War: Roosevelt, Churchill, and the Second World War.* New York: William Morrow, 1997.

———, ed. *Churchill and Roosevelt: The Complete Correspondence.* 3 vols. Princeton, N.J.: Princeton University Press, 1984.

Klehr, Harvey, and Ronald Radosh. *The Amerasia Spy Case: Prelude to McCarthyism.* Chapel Hill: University of North Carolina Press, 1996.

Knebel, Fletcher, and Charles W. Bailey II. *No High Ground.* New York: Knopf, 1960.

Kolko, Joyce, and Gabriel Kolko. *The Limits of Power: The World and United States Foreign Policy, 1945–1954.* New York: Harper and Row, 1972.

Krock, Arthur. *Memoirs: Sixty Years on the Firing Line.* New York: Funk and Wagnalls, 1968.

Kucklick, Bruce. *American Policy and the Division of Germany: The Clash with Russia over Reparations.* Ithaca, N.Y.: Cornell University Press, 1972.

Kuniholm, Bruce Robellet. *The Origins of the Cold War in the Near East: Great Power Conflict and Diplomacy in Iran, Turkey, and Greece.* Princeton, N.J.: Princeton University Press, 1980.

Lacey, Michael J., ed. *The Truman Administration.* New York and Cambridge: Woodrow Wilson Center for Scholars and Cambridge University Press, 1989.

LaFeber, Walter. *America, Russia, and the Cold War, 1945–1992.* 7th ed. New York: Norton, 1993.

———. *The Clash: A History of U.S.-Japan Relations.* New York: Norton, 1997.

Larson, Deborah Welch. *Origins of Containment: A Psychological Explanation.* Princeton, N.J.: Princeton University Press, 1985.

Leahy, William D. *I Was There.* New York: Whittlesey House, 1950.

Lederer, Ivo J., and Wayne S. Vucinich, eds. *The Soviet Union in the Middle East: The Post World War II Era.* Stanford: The Hoover Institution, 1974.

Leffler, Melvyn P. *A Preponderance of Power: National Security, the Truman Administration, and the Cold War.* Stanford: Stanford University Press, 1992.

———. *The Specter of Communism: The United States and the Origins of the Cold War, 1917–1953.* New York: Hill and Wang, 1994.

Lenczowski, George. *The Middle East in World Affairs.* 4th ed. Ithaca, N.Y.: Cornell University Press, 1980.

Levine, Stephen I. *Anvil of Victory: The Communist Revolution in Manchuria.* New York: Columbia University Press, 1987.

Lilienthal, David E. *The Journals of David E. Lilienthal.* 6 vols. New York: Harper and Row, 1964–1976.

Lippmann, Walter. *The Cold War: A Study in U.S. Foreign Policy.* New York: Harper, 1947.

Loth, Wilfried. *The Division of the World, 1941–1955.* New York: St. Martin's, 1988.

Lowe, Peter. *The Origins of the Korean War.* New York: Longman, 1986.

Lyon, Peter. *Eisenhower: Portrait of a Hero.* Boston: Little, Brown, 1974.

MacArthur, Douglas. *Reminiscences.* New York: McGraw-Hill, 1964.

MacVeagh, Lincoln. *Ambassador MacVeagh Reports: Greece, 1933–1947.* Edited by John O. Iatrides. Princeton, N.J.: Princeton University Press, 1980.

Maddox, Robert J. *From War to Cold War: The Education of Harry S. Truman.* Boulder, Colo.: Westview Press, 1988.

Manchester, William. *American Caesar: Douglas MacArthur, 1880–1964.* New York: Dell, 1979.

Martin, Edwin M. *Divided Counsel: The Anglo-American Response to Communist Victory in China.* Lexington: University of Kentucky Press, 1986.

Mastny, Vojtech J. *The Cold War and Soviet Insecurity: The Stalin Years.* New York: Oxford University Press, 1996.

———. *Russia's Road to the Cold War: Diplomacy, Warfare, and the Politics of Communism, 1941–1945.* New York: Columbia University Press, 1979.

May, Ernest R. *"Lessons" of the Past: Use and Misuse of History in American Foreign Policy.* New York: Oxford University Press, 1973.

———. *The Truman Administration and China, 1945–1949.* New York: Lippincott, 1975.

———, ed. *American Cold War Strategy: Interpreting NSC 68.* Boston: Bedford/St. Martin's, 1993.

Mayers, David. *The Ambassadors and America's Soviet Policy.* New York: Oxford University Press, 1995.

———. *Cracking the Monolith: U.S. Policy against the Sino-Soviet Alliance, 1949–1955.* Baton Rouge and London: Louisiana State University Press, 1986.

———. *George Kennan and the Dilemmas of US Foreign Policy.* New York: Oxford University Press, 1988.

Mayne, Richard. *The Recovery of Europe, 1945–1973.* Garden City, N.Y.: Doubleday, 1973.

McCoy, Donald R. *The Presidency of Harry S. Truman, 1945–1953.* Lawrence: University Press of Kansas, 1984.

McCullough, David. *Truman.* New York: Simon and Schuster, 1992.

McGlothlen, Ronald. *Controlling the Waves: Dean Acheson and U.S. Foreign Policy in Asia.* New York: Norton, 1993.

McLellan, David S. *Dean G. Acheson: The State Department Years.* New York: Dodd, Mead, 1976.

Mee, Charles L., Jr. *The Marshall Plan.* New York: Simon and Schuster, 1984.

———. *Meeting at Potsdam.* New York: Evans, 1975.

Messer, Robert L. *The End of an Alliance: James F. Byrnes, Roosevelt, Truman, and the Origins of the Cold War.* Chapel Hill: University of North Carolina Press, 1982.

Miller, Merle. *Plain Speaking: An Oral Biography of Harry S. Truman.* New York: Berkeley Medallion, 1973.

Miller, Richard Lawrence. *Truman: The Rise to Power.* New York: McGraw-Hill, 1986.

Millis, Walter, ed. *The Forrestal Diaries.* New York: Viking Press, 1951.

Milward, Alan S. *The Reconstruction of Western Europe, 1945–1951.* Berkeley: University of California Press, 1984.

Miner, Stephen Merritt. *Between Churchill and Stalin: The Soviet Union, Great Britain, and the Origins of the Grand Alliance.* Chapel Hill: University of North Carolina Press, 1988.

Moran, Lord Charles. *Churchill: Taken from the Diaries of Lord Moran.* Boston: Houghton Mifflin, 1966.

Morris, Eric. *Blockade: Berlin and the Cold War.* New York: Stein and Day, 1973.

Murphy, John F. *The Pinnacle: The Contemporary American Presidency.* Philadelphia: Lippincott, 1974.

Murphy, Robert. *Diplomat among Warriors.* New York: Doubleday, 1964.

Naimark, Norman M. *The Russians in Germany: A History of the Soviet Zone of Occupation, 1945–1949*. Cambridge, Mass.: Harvard University Press, 1995.

Naimark, Norman M., and Leonid Gibianskii, eds. *The Establishment of Communist Regimes in Eastern Europe, 1944–1949*. Boulder, Colo.: Westview Press, 1997.

Nelson, Daniel J. *Wartime Origins of the Berlin Dilemma*. Tuscaloosa: University of Alabama Press, 1978.

Neustadt, Richard E. *Presidential Power and the Modern Presidents: The Politics of Leadership from Roosevelt to Reagan*. New York: Free Press, 1990 ed.

Neustadt, Richard E., and Ernest R. May. *Thinking in Time: The Use of History for Decision-Makers*. New York: Free Press, 1986.

Ninkovich, Frank A. *Germany and the United States: The Transformation of the German Question since 1945*. Boston: Twayne, 1988.

Nixon, Edgar B., ed. *Franklin D. Roosevelt and Foreign Affairs, 1933–1937*. 3 vols. Cambridge, Mass.: Harvard University Press, 1969.

O'Ballance, Edgar. *The Greek Civil War, 1944–1949*. New York: Praeger, 1966.

O'Connor, Raymond G. *Diplomacy for Victory: FDR and Unconditional Surrender*. New York: Norton, 1971.

Offner, Arnold A., and Theodore A. Wilson, eds. *Victory in Europe 1945: From World War to Cold War*. Lawrence: University Press of Kansas, 2000.

Oshinsky, David M. *A Conspiracy So Immense: The World of Joe McCarthy*. New York: The Free Press, 1983.

Ovendale, Ritchie. *The English-Speaking Alliance: Britain, the United States, the Dominions, and the Cold War, 1945–1954*. London: George Allen and Unwin, 1985.

Overy, Richard. *Russia's War: Blood upon the Snow*. New York: TV Books, 1997.

Paige, Glenn D. *The Korean Decision: June 24–30, 1950*. New York: Free Press, 1968.

Paterson, Thomas G. *Meeting the Communist Threat: Truman to Reagan*. New York: Oxford University Press, 1988.

———. *On Every Front: The Making and Unmaking of the Cold War*. Rev. ed. New York: Oxford University Press, 1992.

———. *Soviet-American Confrontation: Postwar Reconstruction and the Origins of the Cold War*. Baltimore: Johns Hopkins University Press, 1973.

Patterson, James T. *Mr. Republican: A Biography of Robert A. Taft*. Boston: Houghton Mifflin, 1972.

Pemberton, William E. *Harry S. Truman: Fair Dealer and Cold Warrior*. Boston: Twayne, 1989.

Pepper, Suzanne. *Civil War in China: The Political Struggle, 1945–1949*. Berkeley: University of California Press, 1978.

Peterson, Edward H. *The American Occupation of Germany: Retreat to Victory*. Detroit: Wayne State University Press, 1978.

Pogue, Forrest C. *George C. Marshall: Organizer of Victory, 1943–1945*. New York: Viking, 1973.

———. *George C. Marshall: Statesman, 1945–1959*. New York: Viking, 1987.

Pollard, Robert A. *Economic Security and the Origins of the Cold War, 1945–1950*. New York: Columbia University Press, 1985.

Porter, Kirk H., and Donald Bruce Johnson, eds. *National Party Platforms, 1840–1960*. 2nd ed. Urbana: University of Illinois Press, 1961.

Purifoy, Lewis McCarroll. *Harry Truman's China Policy: McCarthyism and the Diplomacy of Hysteria, 1947–1951*. New York: New Viewpoints, 1976.

Resis, Albert. *Stalin, the Politburo, and the Origins of the Cold War, 1945–1946*. Pittsburgh: University of Pittsburgh Press, 1988.

————, ed. *Molotov Remembers: Inside Kremlin Politics, Conversations with Felix Chuev.* Chicago: Ivan R. Dee, 1993.

Rhodes, Richard. *Dark Sun: The Making of the Hydrogen Bomb.* New York: Simon and Schuster, 1995.

————. *The Making of the Atomic Bomb.* New York: Simon and Schuster, 1986.

Riddle, Donald. *The Truman Committee.* New Brunswick, N.J.: Rutgers University Press, 1963.

Ridgway, Matthew B. *The Korean War.* New York: DaCapo, 1967.

Robertson, David. *Sly and Able: A Political Biography of James F. Byrnes.* New York: Norton, 1994.

Rogow, Arnold. *Victim of Duty: A Study of James Forrestal.* London: Hart-Davis, 1966.

Ro'i, Yaacov, ed. *From Encroachment to Involvement: A Documentary Study of Soviet Policy in the Middle East, 1945–1973.* New York: Israel Universities Press, 1974.

————. *The Limits to Power: Soviet Policy in the Middle East.* New York: St. Martin's, 1979.

Roosevelt, Elliott, ed. *F.D.R.: His Personal Letters, 1928–1945.* New York: Duell, Sloan and Pearce, 1950.

Rose, Lisle A. *Dubious Victory: The United States and the End of World War II.* Kent, Ohio: Kent State University Press, 1973.

Ross, Irwin. *The Loneliest Campaign: The Truman Victory of 1948.* New York: Signet, 1968.

Rubinstein, Alvin Z. *Soviet Foreign Policy since World War II: Imperial and Global.* 2nd ed. Boston: Little, Brown, 1972.

Rusk, Dean, as told to Richard Rusk. *As I Saw It.* New York: Penguin, 1990.

Sachar, Howard M. *The Emergence of the Middle East, 1914–1924.* New York: Knopf, 1969.

————. *A History of the Jews in America.* New York: Simon and Schuster, 1992.

Safran, Nadav. *Israel: The Embattled Ally.* Cambridge, Mass., and London: The Belknap Press of Harvard University Press, 1981.

Schaller, Michael. *The American Occupation of Japan: The Origins of the Cold War in Asia.* New York: Oxford University Press, 1985.

————. *Douglas MacArthur: The Far Eastern General.* New York: Oxford University Press, 1989.

————. *The United States and China in the Twentieth Century.* 2nd ed. New York: Oxford University Press, 1990.

————. *The U.S. Crusade in China, 1938–1945.* New York: Columbia University Press, 1979.

Schechter, Jerrold, with Vyacheslav V. Luchkov, trans. and eds. *Khrushchev Remembers: The Glasnost Tapes.* Boston: Little, Brown, 1990.

Schlesinger, Arthur M., Jr. *The Imperial Presidency.* Boston: Houghton Mifflin, 1973.

Schnabel, James F. *The History of the Joint Chiefs of Staff.* Vol. I: *The Joint Chiefs of Staff and National Policy, 1945–1947.* Wilmington, Del.: Glazier, 1979.

Schnabel, James F., and Robert J. Watson. *The History of the Joint Chiefs of Staff.* Vol. III: *The Joint Chiefs of Staff and National Policy, The Korean War.* Wilmington, Del.: Glazier, 1979.

Schwartz, Thomas A. *America's Germany: John J. McCloy and the Federal Republic of Germany.* Cambridge, Mass.: Harvard University Press, 1991.

Sheng, Michael. *Battling Western Imperialism: Mao, Stalin, and the United States.* Princeton, N.J.: Princeton University Press, 1997.

Sherwin, Martin J. *A World Destroyed: Hiroshima and the Origins of the Arms Race.* Rev. ed. New York: Vintage, 1987.

Sherwood, Robert E. *Roosevelt and Hopkins: An Intimate History.* New York: Harper, 1948.

Shlaim, Avi. *The United States and the Berlin Blockade 1948–1949*. Berkeley: University of California Press, 1983.

Sigal, Leon V. *Fighting to a Finish: The Politics of War Termination in the United States and Japan, 1945*. Ithaca, N.Y.: Cornell University Press, 1988.

Skates, John Roy. *The Invasion of Japan: Alternative to the Bomb*. Columbia: University of South Carolina Press, 1994.

Slater, Leonard. *The Pledge*. New York: Simon and Schuster, 1970.

Smith, Bradley F., and Elena Agarossi. *Operation Sunrise: The Secret Surrender*. New York: Basic Books, 1979.

Smith, Gaddis. *Morality, Reason, and Power: American Diplomacy in the Carter Years*. New York: Hill and Wang, 1986.

Smith, Jean Edward. *Lucius D. Clay: An American Life*. New York: Henry Holt, 1990.

———, ed. *The Papers of General Lucius D. Clay: Germany, 1945–1949*. 2 vols. Bloomington: Indiana University Press, 1974.

Smith, Richard N. *Thomas E. Dewey and His Times*. New York: Simon and Schuster, 1982.

Smith, Walter Bedell. *My Three Years in Moscow*. Philadelphia: Lippincott, 1950.

Snetsinger, John. *Truman, the Jewish Vote, and the Creation of Israel*. Stanford: Hoover Institution Press, 1974.

Spanier, John W. *The Truman-MacArthur Controversy and the Korean War*. Rev. ed. New York: Norton, 1965.

Steinberg, Alfred. *The Man From Missouri: The Life and Times of Harry S. Truman*. New York: Putnam, 1962.

Steininger, Rolf. *The German Question: The Stalin Note of 1952 and the Problem of Reunification*. Translated by June T. Hedges. Edited by Mark Cioc. New York: Columbia University Press, 1990.

Stephanson, Anders. *Kennan and the Art of Foreign Policy*. Cambridge, Mass.: Harvard University Press, 1989.

Stimson, Henry L., and McGeorge Bundy. *On Active Service in Peace and War*. New York: Harper, 1947.

Stoler, Mark A. *George C. Marshall: Soldier-Statesman of the American Century*. Boston: Twayne, 1989.

Stueck, William Whitney, Jr. *The Korean War: An International History*. Princeton, N.J.: Princeton University Press, 1995.

———. *The Road to Confrontation: American Policy toward China and Korea, 1947–1950*. Chapel Hill: University of North Carolina Press, 1981.

Suh, Dae-Sook. *Kim Il Sung: The North Korean Leader*. New York: Columbia University Press, 1988.

Sulzberger, C. L. *A Long Row of Candles: Memoirs and Diaries, 1934–1954*. New York: Macmillan, 1969.

Talbott, Strobe, trans. *Khrushchev Remembers*. London: Andre Deutsch, 1971.

Taubman, William. *Stalin's American Policy: From Entente to Detente to Cold War*. New York: Norton, 1982.

Trachtenberg, Marc. *A Constructed Peace: The Making of the European Settlement, 1945–1963*. Princeton, N.J.: Princeton University Press, 1999.

Truman, Harry S. *Memoirs*. 2 vols. Garden City, N.Y.: Doubleday, 1955–1956.

———. *Mr. Citizen*. New York: Bernard Geis, 1960.

Truman, Margaret. *Bess W. Truman*. New York: Jove Books, 1986.

———. *Truman*. New York: Morrow, 1973.

Tuchman, Barbara W. *Stilwell and the American Experience in China, 1911–1945*. New York: Macmillan, 1971.

Tucker, Nancy Bernkopf. *Patterns in the Dust: Chinese-American Relations and the Recognition Controversy, 1949–1950.* New York: Columbia University Press, 1983.

Ulam, Adam B. *The Rivals: America and Russia since World War II.* New York: Viking, 1971.

———. *Stalin: The Man and His Era.* Boston: Beacon Press, 1973.

Vandenberg, Arthur, Jr., ed. *The Private Papers of Senator Vandenberg.* Boston: Houghton Mifflin, 1952.

Van Der Beugel, Ernest H. *From Marshall Aid to Atlantic Partnership: European Integration as a Concern of American Foreign Policy.* Amsterdam: Elsevier, 1966.

Volkogonov, Dmitri. *Stalin: Triumph and Tragedy.* Edited and translated by Harold Shukman. Rocklin, Calif.: Prima Publishing, 1996.

Walker, J. Samuel. *Prompt and Utter Destruction: Truman and the Use of the Atomic Bombs against Japan.* Chapel Hill: University of North Carolina Press, 1997.

Wall, Irwin. *The United States and the Making of Postwar France, 1945–1954.* Cambridge, Mass.: Harvard University Press, 1991.

Walton, Richard J. *Henry Wallace, Harry Truman, and the Cold War.* New York: Viking, 1976.

Ward, Patricia Dawson. *The Threat of Peace: James F. Byrnes and the Council of Foreign Ministers, 1945–1946.* Kent, Ohio: Kent State University Press, 1979.

Weill, Martin. *A Pretty Good Club: The Founding Fathers of the U.S. Foreign Service.* New York: Norton, 1978.

Weinberg, Gerhard. *A World at Arms: A Global History of World War II.* Cambridge: Cambridge University Press, 1994.

Weinstein, Allen, and Alexander Vassiliev. *The Haunted Wood: Soviet Espionage in America—The Stalin Era.* New York: Random House, 1999.

Westad, Odd Arne. *Cold War and Revolution: Soviet-American Rivalry and the Origins of the Chinese Civil War, 1944–1946.* New York: Columbia University Press, 1993.

Wexler, Imanuel. *The Marshall Plan Revisited: The European Recovery Program in Economic Perspective.* Westport, Conn.: Greenwood, 1983.

Whiting, Allen S. *China Crosses the Yalu: The Decision to Enter the Korean War.* Stanford: Stanford University Press, 1960.

Wittner, Lawrence S. *American Intervention in Greece, 1943–1949.* New York: Columbia University Press, 1982.

Woodhouse, C. M. *The Struggle for Greece, 1941–1949.* Brooklyn: Beekman/Esanu, 1976.

Woods, Randall B. *Fulbright: A Biography.* Cambridge: Cambridge University Press, 1995.

Woods, Randall B., and Howard Jones. *Dawn of the Cold War: The United States' Quest for World Order.* Athens: University of Georgia Press, 1991.

Wyman, David S. *The Abandonment of the Jews: America and the Holocaust, 1941–1945.* New York: Pantheon, 1984.

———. *Paper Walls: America and the Refugee Crisis, 1938–1941.* Amherst: University of Massachusetts Press, 1968.

Xydis, Stephen G. *Greece and the Great Powers, 1944–1947: Prelude to the "Truman Doctrine."* Thessaloniki, Greece: Institute for Balkan Studies, 1963.

Yapp, M. E. *The Near East since the First World War.* London and New York: Longman, 1991.

Yergin, Daniel. *The Prize: The Epic Quest for Oil, Money, and Power.* New York: Simon and Schuster, 1991.

———. *Shattered Peace: The Origins of the Cold War and the National Security State.* Boston: Houghton Mifflin, 1977.

Zachary, G. Pascal. *Endless Frontier: Vannevar Bush, Engineer of the American Century.* New York: Free Press, 1997.

Zhang, Shu Guang. *Deterrence and Strategic Culture: Chinese-American Confrontations, 1949–1958.* Ithaca, N.Y.: Cornell University Press, 1992.

———. *Mao's Military Romanticism: China and the Korean War, 1950–1953.* Lawrence: University Press of Kansas, 1995.

Zhang, Shu Guang, and Jian Chen, eds. *Chinese Communist Foreign Policy and the Cold War in Asia: New Documentary Evidence, 1944–1950.* Chicago: Imprint Publications, 1996.

Zhukov, Georgi. *The Memoirs of Georgi Zhukov.* New York: Delacorte Press, 1971.

Zubok, Vladislav, and Constantine Pleshakov. *Inside the Kremlin's Cold War: From Stalin to Khrushchev.* Cambridge, Mass.: Harvard University Press, 1996.

Articles

Abbreviations

AHR: *American Historical Review*
CWIHP: Cold War International History Project, Woodrow Wilson Center, Washington, D.C.
DH: *Diplomatic History*
IS: *International Security*
JAH: *Journal of American History*
PHR: *Pacific Historical Review*
PSQ: *Political Science Quarterly*

Adler, Les K., and Thomas G. Paterson. "Red Fascism: The Merger of Nazi Germany and Soviet Russia in the American Image of Totalitarianism, 1930s–1950s." *AHR,* 75 (Apr. 1970).

Armitage, John A. "The View from Czechoslovakia." In *Witnesses to the Origins of the Cold War,* edited by Thomas T. Hammond. Seattle and London: University of Washington Press, 1982.

Asada, Sadao. "The Shock of the Atomic Bomb and Japan's Decision to Surrender—A Reconsideration." *PHR,* 67 (1998).

Bajanov, Evegueni. "Assessing the Politics of the Korean War, 1949–1951." CWIHP, *Bulletin: The Cold War in Asia,* 6–7 (Winter 1995/1996).

Beisner, Robert L. "Patterns of Peril: Dean Acheson Joins the Cold War, 1945–1946." *DH,* 20 (Summer 1996).

Bernstein, Barton J. "Eclipsed by Hiroshima and Nagasaki: Early Thinking about Tactical Nuclear Weapons." *IS,* 65 (Spring 1991).

———. "The Perils and Politics of Surrender: Ending the War with Japan and Avoiding the Third Atomic Bomb." *PHR,* 46 (Feb. 1977).

———. "Seizing the Contested Terrain of Early Nuclear History: Stimson, Conant, and Their Allies Explain the Decision to Use the Atomic Bomb." *DH,* 17 (Winter 1993).

———. "The Struggle over the Korean Armistice: Prisoners of Repatriation?" In *Child of Conflict: The Korean-American Relationship, 1943–1953,* edited by Bruce Cumings. Seattle: University of Washington Press, 1983.

———. "The Truman Administration and Korea." In *The Truman Administration,* edited by Michael J. Lacey. New York and Cambridge: The Woodrow Wilson Center and Cambridge University Press, 1989.

———. "Understanding the Atomic Bomb and the Japanese Surrender: Missed Opportunities, Little-Known Near Disasters, and Modern Memory." *DH,* 19 (Spring 1995).

Bix, Herbert. "Japan's Delayed Surrender: A Reinterpretation." *DH,* 19 (Spring 1995).

Byrnes, James F. "Byrnes Answers Truman." *Colliers,* Apr. 26, 1952.

Chen, Jian. "The Sino-Soviet Alliance and China's Entry into the Korean War." CWIHP, Working Paper No. 1 (June 1992).

Christensen, Thomas J. "Threats, Assurances, and the Last Chance for Peace: The Lessons of Mao's Korean War Telegrams." *IS,* 17 (Summer 1992).

Cienciala, Anna M. "The View from Poland." In *Victory in Europe, 1945: From World War to Cold War,* edited by Arnold A. Offner and Theodore A. Wilson. Lawrence: University Press of Kansas, 2000.

Clifford, J. Garry. "President Truman and Peter the Great's Will." *DH,* 4 (Fall 1980).

Close, David H. "The Legacy." In *The Greek Civil War, 1943–1950,* edited by David H. Close. London and New York: Routledge, 1993.

Cohen, Warren I. "Conversations with Chinese Friends: Zhou En-Lai's Associates on Chinese-American Relations in the 1940s and the Korean War." *DH,* 11 (Summer 1987).

Crenshaw, James T. "The 1940 Senatorial Campaign in Missouri." Part II, *Whistle Stop* (Harry S. Truman Library Institute Newsletter), 3, 1980.

Dallin, David. "Stalin and the Prospects for Post-War Germany." In *The Soviet Union and Europe in the Cold War, 1943–53,* edited by Francesca Gori and Silvia Pons. New York: St. Martin's, 1996.

De Luca, Arthur R. "Soviet-American Politics and the Turkish Straits." *PSQ,* 92 (Fall 1977).

DeSantis, Hugh. "American Career Diplomats in the Balkans." *PSQ,* 94 (Fall 1979).

Di Biagio, Anna. "The Marshall Plan and the Founding of the Cominform, June–September 1947." In *The Establishment of Communist Regimes in Eastern Europe, 1944–1949,* edited by Norman Naimark and Leonid Gibianskii. Boulder, Colo.: Westview Press, 1997.

Dinardo, Richard S. "Glimpse of an Old World Order?: Reconsidering the Trieste Crisis of 1945." *DH,* 21 (Summer 1997).

Dingman, Roger. "Atomic Diplomacy during the Korean War." *IS,* 13 (Winter 1988/1989).

Divine, Robert A. "The Cold War and the Election of 1948." *JAH,* 59 (June 1972).

Fulbright, J. William. "How the Devil Theory Has Bedeviled U.S. Foreign Policies." *The Times,* Jan. 17, 1972.

Gaddis, John Lewis. "The Tragedy of Cold War History." *DH,* 17 (Winter 1993).

———. "Was the Truman Doctrine a Real Turning Point?" *Foreign Affairs,* 52 (Jan. 1974).

Gerber, Larry G. "The Baruch Plan and the Origins of the Cold War." *DH,* 6 (Winter 1982).

Gibianskii, Leonid. "Soviet-Yugoslav Conflict and the Soviet Bloc." In *The Soviet Union and Europe in the Cold War, 1943–53,* edited by Francesca Gori and Silvia Pons. New York: St. Martin's, 1996.

Gimbel, John. "On Implementation of the Potsdam Agreement: An Essay on U.S. Postwar Policy." *PSQ,* 87 (June 1972).

Gormly, James L. "The Washington Declaration and the 'Poor Relations': Anglo-American Atomic Diplomacy, 1945–1946." *DH,* 8 (Spring 1984).

Griffith, Robert. "Harry S. Truman and the Burden of Modernity." *Reviews in American History,* 14 (Sept. 1981).

Herring, George C., Jr. "The United States and British Bankruptcy, 1944–1945." *PSQ,* 86 (June 1971).

Hershberg, James G. "'Explosion in the Offing': German Rearmament and American Diplomacy, 1953–1955." *DH,* 16 (Fall 1992).

High, Stanley. "Senator Truman Saves a Billion." *The American Mercury,* 57 (Sept. 1943).

Ho, Zhigong, "'Lost Chance' or 'Inevitable Hostility': Two Contending Interpretations of the Late 1940s Chinese-American Relations," The Society for Historians of American Foreign Relations Newsletter, 20 (Sept. 1989).

Hogan, Michael J. "American Marshall Planners and the Search for a European Neocapitalism." *AHR*, 90 (Feb. 1988).

Hunt, Michael H. "Beijing and the Korean Crisis, June 1950–June 1951," *PSQ*, 107 (Fall 1992).

———. "Mao Tse-tung and the Issue of Accommodation with the U.S." In *Uncertain Years: Chinese-American Relations, 1947–1950*, edited by Dorothy Borg and Waldo Heinrichs. New York: Columbia University Press, 1980.

Jackson, Scott. "Prologue to the Marshall Plan: The Origins of the American Commitment for a European Recovery Program." *JAH*, 65 (Mar. 1979).

Kaplan, Lawrence S. "NATO and the Warsaw Pact: The Past." In *NATO and the Warsaw Pact: Political Purpose and Military Means*, edited by Robert W. Clawson and Lawrence S. Kaplan. Wilmington, Del.: Scholarly Resources, 1982.

Kennan, George F. "X". "The Sources of Soviet Conduct." *Foreign Affairs*, 25 (July 1947).

Kirkendall, Richard S. "Truman and the Cold War." In *Studies in Mediaevalia and Americana: Essays in Honor of William Lyle Davis, S.J.*, edited by Gerald G. Steckler and Leo Donald Davis. Spokane, Wash.: Gonzaga University Press, 1973.

Knight, Jonathan. "America's International Guarantees for the Straits: Prelude to the Truman Doctrine." *Middle Eastern Studies*, 13 (May 1997).

Knight, Wayne. "Labourite Britain: America's 'Sure Friend'? The Anglo-Soviet Treaty Issue, 1947." *DH*, 7 (Fall 1983).

Leffler, Melvyn P. "The American Conception of National Security and the Beginnings of the Cold War." *AHR*, 89 (Apr. 1984).

———. "The Cold War: What Do 'We Now Know'?" *AHR*, 104 (Apr. 1999).

———. "Commentary on 'The Novikov Telegram.'" *DH*, 15 (Fall 1991).

———. "Inside Enemy Archives: The Cold War Reopened." *Foreign Affairs*, 75 (July/Aug. 1996).

———. "Strategy, Diplomacy, and the Cold War: The United States, Turkey, and NATO, 1945–1954." *JAH*, 71 (Mar. 1985).

———. "The Struggle for Germany and the Origins of the Cold War." German Historical Institute Occasional Paper No. 16. Washington, D.C.: German Historical Institute, 1996.

———. "The United States and the Strategic Dimensions of the Marshall Plan." *DH*, 12 (Summer 1988).

Lippmann, Walter. "A Year of Peacemaking." *Atlantic Monthly*, 30 (Dec. 1946).

Loth, Wilfried. "Stalin's Plans for Postwar Germany." In *The Soviet Union and Europe in the Cold War, 1943–53*, edited by Francesca Gori and Silvia Pons. New York: St. Martin's, 1996.

Lukes, Igor. "The Czech Road to Communism." In *The Establishment of Communist Regimes in Eastern Europe, 1944–1949*, edited by Norman Naimark and Leonid Gibianskii. Boulder, Colo.: Westview Press, 1997.

MacDonald, Douglas J. "Communist Bloc Expansion in the Early Cold War: Challenging Realism, Refuting Revisionism." *IS*, 20 (Winter 1995/1996).

Maier, Charles M. "The Making of 'Pax Americana': Formative Moments of United States Ascendancy." In *The Quest for Stability: Problems of West European Security, 1918–1957*, edited by R. Ahmann, A. M. Birke, and M. Howard. New York: Oxford University Press, 1993.

———. "The Two Postwar Eras and the Conditions for Stability in Western Europe." *AHR*, 86 (Apr. 1981).

Mansourov, Alexandre Y. "Stalin, Mao, Kim, and China's Decision to Enter the Korean War, September 16–October 15, 1950: New Evidence from the Russian Archives." CWIHP, *Bulletin: The Cold War in Asia,* 6–7 (Winter 1995/1996).

Mark, Eduard. "American Policy toward Eastern Europe." *JAH,* 68 (Sept. 1981).

———. "The War Scare of 1946 and Its Consequences." *DH,* 21 (Spring 1997).

Matray, James I. "Truman's Plan for Victory: National Self-Determination and the Thirty Eighth Parallel Decision in Korea." *JAH,* 66 (Sept. 1979).

McFarland, Stephen L. "A Peripheral View of the Origins of the Cold War: The Crises in Iran, 1941–1947." *DH,* 4 (Fall 1970).

McLean, David. "American Nationalism, the China Myth, and the Truman Doctrine: The Question of Accommodation with Beijing in 1949–1950." *DH,* 10 (Winter 1986).

McNeill, William H. "The View from Greece." In *Witnesses to the Origins of the Cold War,* edited by Thomas T. Hammond. Seattle and London: University of Washington Press, 1982.

Messer, Robert L. "Paths Not Taken: The United States Department of State and Alternatives to Containment, 1945–1946." *DH,* 1 (Fall 1977).

Miles, Rufus E., Jr. "Hiroshima: The Strange Myth of a Half Million Lives Saved." *IS,* 10 (Fall 1985).

Miller, James E. "Taking Off the Gloves: The United States and the Italian Elections of 1948." *DH,* 7 (Winter 1983).

Milward, Alan S. "Was the Marshall Plan Necessary?" *DH,* 13 (Spring 1989).

Miscamble, Wilson D. "Anthony Eden and the Truman-Molotov Conversations, April 1945." *DH,* 2 (Spring 1978).

———. "The Evolution of an Internationalist: Harry S. Truman and American Foreign Policy." *The Australian Journal of Politics and History,* 23 (Aug. 1977).

———. "Harry S. Truman, the Berlin Blockade, and the 1948 Election." *Presidential Studies Quarterly,* 8 (Summer 1980).

Murray, Brian. "Stalin, the Cold War, and the Division of China: A Multiarchival Mystery." CWIHP, Working Paper No. 12 (June 1995).

Naimark, Norman. "'To Know Everything and to Report Everything Worth Knowing': Building the East German Police State, 1945–1949." CWIHP, Working Paper No. 10 (Aug. 1994).

Narinskii, Michail. "The Soviet Union and the Berlin Crisis." In *The Soviet Union and Europe in the Cold War, 1943–53,* edited by Francesca Gori and Silvia Pons. New York: St. Martin's, 1996.

Offner, Arnold A. "'Another Such Victory': President Truman, American Foreign Policy, and the Cold War." *DH,* 23 (June 1999).

———. "Research on German-American Relations: A Critical View." In *America and the Germans: A 300-Year History,* edited by Frank Trommler and Joseph McVeigh. 2 vols. Philadelphia: University of Pennsylvania Press, 1985.

———. "Uncommon Ground: Anglo-American–Soviet Diplomacy, 1941–1942." *Soviet Union/Union Sovietique,* 18 (1991).

Ostermann, Christian F. "The United States, the East German Uprising of 1953, and the Limits of Rollback." CWIHP, Working Paper No. 11 (Dec. 1994).

Pape, Robert A. "Why Japan Surrendered." *IS,* 18 (Fall 1993).

Parrish, Scott D. "The Marshall Plan and the Division of Europe." In *The Establishment of Communist Regimes in Eastern Europe, 1944–1949,* edited by Norman Naimark and Leonid Gibianskii. Boulder, Colo.: Westview Press, 1997.

Parrish, Scott D., and Mikhail M. Narinsky. "New Evidence on the Soviet Rejection of the Marshall Plan, 1947: Two Reports." CWIHP, Working Paper No. 9 (Mar. 1994).

Paterson, Thomas G. "Consent: American Public Opinion, Congress, and the Cold War Mentality." In Thomas G. Paterson, *On Every Front: The Making and Unmaking of the Cold War.* Rev. ed. New York: Oxford University Press, 1992.

———. "Harry S. Truman, American Power, and the Soviet Threat." In Thomas G. Paterson, *Meeting the Communist Threat: Truman to Reagan.* New York: Oxford University Press, 1988.

———. "Toughness: Truman's Style of Diplomacy." In Thomas G. Paterson, *On Every Front: The Making and Unmaking of the Cold War.* Rev. ed. New York: Oxford University Press, 1992.

Pechatnov, Vladimir O. "'The Allies Are Pressing on You to Break Your Will . . .': Foreign Policy Correspondence between Stalin and Molotov and Other Politburo Members, September 1945–December 1946." CWIHP, Working Paper No. 26 (Sept. 1999).

———. "The Big Three after World War II: New Documents on Soviet Thinking about Post War Relations with the United States and Britain." CWIHP, Working Paper No. 13 (July 1995).

Petrovich, Michael B. "The View from Yugoslavia." In *Witnesses to the Origins of the Cold War,* edited by Thomas T. Hammond. Seattle and London: University of Washington Press, 1982.

Phillips, Hugh. "Mission to America: Maksim M. Litvinov in the United States, 1941–1943." *DH,* 12 (Summer 1988).

Resis, Albert: "The Churchill-Stalin 'Percentages' Agreement on the Balkans, Moscow, October 1944." *AHR,* 83 (Apr. 1978).

Reynolds, David. "The European Response: Primacy of Politics." *Foreign Affairs,* 76 (May/June 1997).

Ro'i, Yaacov. "Soviet-Israeli Relations, 1945–1947." In *The U.S.S.R. and the Middle East,* edited by Michael Confino and Simon Shamir. New York and Jerusalem: John Wiley, 1973.

Rosenberg, David Alan. "American Atomic Strategy and the Hydrogen Bomb Decision." *JAH,* 66 (June 1979).

Ryan, Henry B. "A New Look at Churchill's 'Iron Curtain' Speech." *The Historical Journal,* 22 (1979).

Sander, Alfred D. "Truman and the National Security Council, 1945–1947." *JAH,* 59 (Sept. 1972).

Scheid, F. "Stalin's Reluctant Bid for Iranian Azerbaijan, 1941–1946: A View from the Azerbaijani Archives." Draft Paper for Conference, "Stalin and the Cold War, 1945–1953," Yale University, September 1999.

Schlesinger, Arthur M. "Our Presidents: A Rating by 75 Historians." *New York Times Magazine,* July 2, 1962.

Schmidtlein, Gene. "Pursuing the Gleam: Truman's First Senatorial Election." *Whistle Stop* (Harry S. Truman Library Institute Newsletter), 6 (Fall 1978).

Shen, Zhihua. "Sino-Soviet Relations and the Origins of the Korean War: Stalin's Strategic Goals in the Far East." *Journal of Cold War Studies,* 2 (Spring 2000).

Smith, Ole L. "The Greek Communist Party, 1945–49." In *The Greek Civil War, 1943–1950,* edited by David H. Close. London and New York: Routledge, 1993.

Stalin, J. V. "Economic Problems of Socialism in the U.S.S.R." In *The Essential Stalin,* edited by Bruce Franklin. Garden City, N.Y.: Doubleday, 1972.

Stimson, Henry L. "The Decision to Use the Atomic Bomb." *Harper's Magazine,* 194 (Feb. 1947).

Stivers, William. "The Incomplete Blockade: Soviet Zone Supply of West Berlin, 1948–1949." *DH,* 21 (Fall 1997).

Subtelny, Orest. "'Peter I's Testament': A Reassessment." *Slavic Review,* 33 (Dec. 1974).

Symposium. "Rethinking the Lost Chance in China." *DH,* 21 (Winter 1997).

Symposium. "Soviet Archives: Recent Revelations and Cold War Historiography." *DH,* 21 (Spring 1997).

Szilard, Leo. "Reminiscences." In *The Intellectual Migration: Europe and America, 1930–1960,* edited by Donald Fleming and Bernard Bailyn. Cambridge, Mass.: Harvard University Press, 1969.

Theoharris, Athan. "Roosevelt and Truman on Yalta: The Origins of the Cold War." *PSQ,* 87 (June 1972).

Tillapaugh, J. "Closed Hemisphere and Open World?: The Disputes over Regional Security at the UN Conference, 1945." *DH,* 2 (Winter 1978).

Tozer, Warren W. "Last Bridge to China: The Shanghai Power Company, the Truman Administration, and the Chinese Communists." *DH,* 1 (Winter 1977).

Uluniam, Artiom A. "The Soviet Union and 'the Greek Question,' 1946–53." In *The Soviet Union and Europe, 1943–53,* edited by Francesca Gori and Silvia Pons. New York: St. Martin's, 1996.

Van Dijk, Ruud. "The 1952 Stalin Note Debate: Myth or Missed Opportunity for German Unification?" CWIHP, Working Paper No. 14 (May 1996).

———. "The Stalin-Note: Last Chance for Unification?" Paper presented at conference on "The Soviet Union, Germany, and the Cold War, 1945–1962: New Evidence from the Eastern Archives," Essen, Germany, June 1994.

Wala, Michael. "Selling the Marshall Plan at Home: The Committee for the Marshall Plan to Aid European Recovery." *DH,* 10 (Summer 1986).

Warner, Geoffrey. "From 'Ally' to Enemy: Britain's Relations with the Soviet Union, 1941–1948." In *The Soviet Union and Europe in the Cold War, 1943–53,* edited by Francesca Gori and Silvia Pons. New York: St. Martin's, 1996.

Weathersby, Kathryn. "Deceiving the Deceivers: Moscow, Beijing, Pyongyang, and Allegations of Bacteriological Weapons Use in Korea." CWIHP, *Bulletin,* 11 (Winter 1998).

———. "Korea, 1949–1950: To Attack or Not to Attack? Kim Il Sung and the Prelude to War." CWIHP, *Bulletin,* 5 (Spring 1995).

———. "New Findings on the Korean War." CWIHP, *Bulletin,* 3 (Fall 1993).

———. "New Russian Documents on the Korean War." CWIHP, *Bulletin,* 6–7 (Winter 1995/1996).

———. "Soviet Aims in Korea and the Origins of the Korean War, 1945–1950: New Evidence from the Russian Archives." CWIHP, Working Paper No. 8 (Nov. 1993).

Wettig, Gerhard. "Stalin and German Reunification: Archival Evidence on Soviet Foreign Policy in Spring 1952." *The Historical Journal,* 37 (1994).

Wiltz, John Edward. "The MacArthur Hearings of 1951: The Secret Testimony." *Military Affairs,* 39 (Dec. 1975).

Wittner, Lawrence S. "American Policy toward Greece during World War II." *DH,* 3 (Spring 1979).

———. "The Truman Doctrine and the Defense of Freedom." *DH,* 4 (Spring 1980).

Yegorova, Natalia I. "The 'Iran Crisis' of 1945–1946: A View from the Russian Archives." CWIHP, Working Paper No. 15 (May 1996).

Zhang, Shu Guang. "In the Shadow of Mao: Zhou Enlai and New China's Diplomacy." In *The Diplomats, 1939–1979,* edited by Gordon A. Craig and Francis L. Loewenheim. Princeton, N.J.: Princeton University Press, 1994.

Index

AAC. *See* Anglo-American Commission of Enquiry (AAC) on Palestine

Abdullah, King, 296, 300

ACCs. *See* Allied Control Commissions (ACCs)

Acheson, Dean G.: and Anglo-American alliance, 137; and atomic power, 106–7, 117, 123, 144–46, 150–52, 174, 459; and Baruch, 147; and Berlin blockade, 268–69; and Bonn agreements, 448–49, 450; and China, 114, 329, 330, 332–33, 336–40, 342–45, 357, 374, 399, 465, 466; and Committee for Marshall Plan Aid to Europe, 232; and Communism versus democracy, 199–200; and Economic Cooperation Administration (ECA), 235; and Ethridge Report, 498n.66; and European defense, 425, 431, 434, 435, 438, 439, 441, 442, 449, 463; family background and education of, 329; and Germany, 158, 269, 270, 424–34, 436, 437, 439, 441–44, 446–50, 452, 462, 562n.15, 565n.71, 566n.90; and Greece, 196, 197–202, 205–6; and hydrogen (Super) bomb, 360–62, 365; and Iranian crisis, 140; and Japanese surrender, 72; and Korea, 354, 356, 357, 379, 412; and Korean War,

347, 367, 372–77, 380, 383, 384, 388–90, 395–99, 401, 405–6, 409, 413, 556n.54; and Korean War armistice talks, 407, 408, 410, 411, 414–16; and Kurile Islands, 126; and MacArthur, 385–86, 404; and MacArthur's firing, 402–3, 405–6; and Marshall, 186; and Marshall Plan, 220, 221, 222; and military spending, 383; and Moscow Conference (1945) and Byrnes, 121, 122; and NATO, 430, 431, 432, 434, 441, 442; and NSC 68 report, 366, 367, 425; and Pacific defense perimeter, 357, 369, 379; and Palestine, 281–84, 531n.41; as secretary of state, 268, 329–30; and Soviet-American relations, 179; and Stalin Note, 444, 446–48, 452; and Taiwan, 342–43, 373–75, 385, 399; and Truman Doctrine, 216, 329; Truman's relationship with, 3, 329–30; and Turkey, 169–70, 172–73, 198, 204; and Wake Island meeting between MacArthur and Truman, 391, 392; and Yugoslavia, 171

Act of Chapultepec, 37, 38, 39

ADA. *See* Atomic Development Authority (ADA)

Aden, 278

Fleet in Taiwan Strait, 343–44, 374, 380, 467. *See also* China; Chinese Communist Party (CCP)

Marines, 190, 191, 316, 317, 319, 320, 326, 464

Mark, Eduard, 172, 506n.49

Marshall, George C.: and Allied invasion of Japan, 66–67; appointment of, as defense secretary, 386, 432; appointment of, as secretary of state, 183, 186–87, 324; as army chief of staff in World War II, 186; and atomic bomb, 60, 63, 64, 77, 259, 263–64, 398, 486n.49; and Berlin blockade, 257, 259–63, 272, 273; and budget for 1948, 187; and casualty estimates, 492n.79; and China, xi, 115, 186, 320–29, 334, 344, 394, 406, 464; and Communism versus democracy, 199, 200; and Czech crisis, 521n.85; and Czechoslovakia, 237; and European Army, 439; and European defense, 435; family background and education of, 186; and Germany, 216–18, 220, 234, 238–39, 246–48, 251, 462; and Greece, 196, 197–99, 205–8; and Israel, 300–303, 305; and Japanese invasion, 60; and Japanese surrender, 63; as Joint Chiefs of Staff (JCS) member, 510n.9; and Kennan's world summary report, 233, 520n.70; and Korea, 349, 354, 355; and Korean War, 388, 396–98, 405; and London Program for western Germany, 248; and MacArthur's firing, 402–3, 404; and Marshall Plan, 185, 213–14, 220–44; and military unification, 187–88; and Moscow meeting of Council of Foreign Ministers (CFM) in 1947, 216–20; and National Security Act (1947), 191; and Navy Department, 191; and Palestine, 286, 288, 290–92, 294–99; and Pleven Plan, 433; resignation of, as secretary of state, 265, 526n.65, 535n.93; on S-1 Committee, 486n.41; and Soviet-American relations, 32, 63, 64, 220; and Soviet entry into Pacific war, 75–76; Stalin on, 321; and Truman Doctrine, 206, 216, 461; Truman's relationship with, 3, 186–87, 320; and Vinson

mission to Stalin, 264, 265; in World War I, 186

Marshall Islands, 148, 149

Marshall Plan: amount of aid, 231, 232, 233, 235, 240, 243, 461; assessment of, 185, 213–14, 240–44; and Brussels Treaty, 237; and Conference on European Economic Cooperation (CEEC), 230–31; and Congress, 223, 227, 231–33, 235–36, 238, 240; and Eastern Europe, 221–27, 241, 461; end of, 243–44; and European economic crisis of 1947, 214–15, 516n.6; and Germany, 225, 226, 230, 234, 237–39, 241, 246–48, 253, 255, 424, 461; and increase in Europe's GNP, 242; and Joint Chiefs of Staff (JCS), 221; and national security, 220, 221; origins of, 220–21; purposes of, 221–23, 243, 461; and Soviet Union, 221–29, 232–33, 461, 517n.29, 518n.48; speech on, 222–23; and Truman, 223–24, 226, 231–32, 235, 238–42, 244; and Truman Doctrine, 185, 213, 228, 519n.54

Martin, Joseph, Jr., 185, 198, 328, 402, 404

Marx, Karl, x

Marxist-Leninist ideology, 26, 27, 128, 133, 179, 181, 232

Masaryk, Jan, 168, 227, 236, 239, 521n.82

Mastny, Vojtech J., 451, 478n.16, 514n.68, 518n.48, 521n.81, 567n.96

Matthews, Francis, 387, 553n.21

Maximos, Dimitrios, 196–97

May, Alan Nunn, 126

May, Andrew, 145

May 14 Movement, 310

McCarran, Pat, 330

McCarthy, Joseph R., 203, 340, 365, 387, 404, 423, 470, 545n.117, 550n.68

McClellan, George, 403

McClintock, Robert M., 533–34n.72

McCloy, John: and atomic bombs used on Japan, 67, 487n.56; and atomic diplomacy with Soviet Union, 102; and atomic energy, 144; and Bonn agreements, 448–49; and China, 319; and European Army, 439; and European Coal and Steel Community, 429; and European Defense Community (EDC), 448–49; and Germany, 158, 445,